Is it in Force?
1994

CW01072735

Is it in Force?
1994

A Guide to the commencement
of statutes passed since
1st January 1969

Editor
Robin Mitchell, LLB

Assistant Editors
Andrea Naylor, BA   Euan Callum, LLB
Susan Ng, BA

London
Butterworths
1994

UNITED KINGDOM	Butterworth & Co (Publishers) Ltd, 88 Kingsway, **London** WC2B 6AB, and 4 Hill Street, **Edinburgh**, EH2 3JZ
AUSTRALIA	Butterworths Pty Ltd, **Sydney, Melbourne, Brisbane, Adelaide, Perth, Canberra** and **Hobart**
CANADA	Butterworths (Canada) Ltd, **Toronto** and **Vancouver**
IRELAND	Butterworth (Ireland) Ltd, **Dublin**
MALAYSIA	Malayan Law Journal Sdn Bhd, **Kuala Lumpur**
NEW ZEALAND	Butterworths of New Zealand Ltd, **Wellington** and **Auckland**
PUERTO RICO	Equity de Puerto Rico, Inc, **Hato Rey**
SINGAPORE	Butterworths Asia, **Singapore**
USA	Butterworth Legal Publishers, **St Paul**, Minnesota; **Seattle**, Washington; **Boston**, Massachusetts; **Austin**, Texas; Equity Publishing, **Orford**, New Hampshire; D and S Publishers, **Clearwater**, Florida

ISBN 0 406 025673
      0 406 025797 (Scottish edition)

Typeset by Phoenix Photosetting, Chatham
Printed by Mackays of Chatham PLC, Chatham, Kent

Preface

Is it in Force? contains the information you need to establish the exact commencement dates of Acts of general application in England, Wales and Scotland and General Synod Measures passed between 1 January 1969 and 31 December 1993.

1 What's in *Is it in Force?*

The short title and chapter number of every Act is given, and unless an Act is of limited or local application only, or has been repealed, the following details are provided:

    (a) the date on which the Act received the royal assent;

    (b) a list of provisions which deal with the commencement of an Act or any part of an Act (including any commencement orders which have been made);

    (c) in limited circumstances (see para 2 below), information on whether the commencement of provisions has been superseded by their repeal/substitution etc;

    (d) any date or dates which have been appointed for the provisions of the Act to come into force;

    (e) an indication where any provision is not in force.

2 How to use *Is it in Force?*

Acts passed during each calendar year are arranged alphabetically, and the years are dealt with in chronological order.

Each Act is dealt with according to its commencement provisions. Thus, an Act is treated as a single unit if the whole Act was brought into force on one date. An Act will only be treated on a section by section or subsection by subsection basis where the complexity of its commencement provisions demands this. It therefore follows that, whereas the repeal of a whole Act will always be noted, *partial* repeals, substitutions etc of many Acts (which are not otherwise broken down into parts) will not.

It should also be noted that saving and transitional provisions, non-textual amendments (eg extensions or applications) and textual amendments *within* sections, subsections etc, are not in general noted to any Act in this book. **For information about repeals, amendments, savings etc, reference should be made to the volumes of Halsbury's Statutes, and to the Cumulative Supplement and the Noter-up to that work.**

Where a provision of an Act applying both to England and Wales and to Scotland is brought into force on the same date by different provisions, it is noted thus:

    11 Apr 1983 (SI 1982/1857; SI 1983/24)

Where such a provision is brought into force on different dates, it is noted thus:

    1 Jul 1978 (EW) (SI 1977/2164); 1 Sep 1978 (S) (1978/816)

Where a provision of an Act which applies both to England and Wales and to Scotland is repealed, substituted etc in relation to one jurisdiction only, it is noted thus:

    30 Dec 1986 (EW) (SI 1986/2145); repealed (S)

3 Finance Acts

Finance Acts are not dealt with in detail, as the dates from which their provisions take effect are usually stated clearly and unambiguously in the text of the Act, and charging provisions will normally state for which year or years of assessment they are to have effect.

The following information may be of use to readers when considering the effect of taxing provisions in Finance Acts which are expressed to have effect from a date prior to that on which the Act received royal assent:

  (a) Income tax and corporation tax are annual taxes which have to be reimposed by Parliament for each year of assessment (Income and Corporation Taxes Act 1988, ss 1, 6).
  (b) Under the rules of procedure of the House of Commons a ways and means resolution is a necessary preliminary to the imposition, increase or extension of income tax (but not for its alleviation).
  (c) From 1993, the Chancellor of the Exchequer will normally open his budget in November or December (usually on a Tuesday) and at the conclusion of his speech move a set of ways and means resolutions which embody his proposals.
  (d) The Provisional Collection of Taxes Act 1968, s 1, makes provision, subject to certain conditions, for statutory effect to be given to those resolutions in so far as they relate to income tax for a period ending on 5 May in the next calendar year (or at the end of 4 months after the date on which the resolution takes effect if the resolution is passed other than in November or December).
  (e) If statutory effect is lost, or expires without an Act coming into operation to renew or vary the tax, or the provisions in the resolution are modified by the Act renewing or varying the tax, any money paid or overpaid must be repaid or made good (Provisional Collection of Taxes Act 1968, s 1(6), (7)).
  (f) It may be desirable that some motions should have immediate effect without waiting for the conclusion of the Budget debate. The House of Commons may therefore resolve that *provisional* statutory effect shall be given to one or more motions which, if passed, would be resolutions to which statutory effect could be given under s 1 of the 1968 Act. Upon the House so resolving, the motions have statutory effect immediately, subject to that motion or a similar motion being agreed to by a confirmatory resolution of the House within the next 10 sitting days; the provisions of s 1 then apply. If not confirmed, the motion is of no effect and any money paid or overpaid must be repaid or made good; there is similar adjustment if the confirmatory resolution differs from the original motion (Provisional Collection of Taxes Act 1968, s 5). Motions regarding corporation tax and advance corporation tax (ACT) may also be given provisional statutory effect under s 5 of the 1968 Act.

4 General principles governing commencement of statutes

  (a) 'Commencement' means the time when the Act comes into force (Interpretation Act 1978, s 5, Sch 1).
  (b) Where no provision is made for the coming into force of an Act, it comes into force at the beginning of the day on which it receives the Royal Assent (Interpretation Act 1978, s 4(b)).

(c) Where provision is made for an Act to come into force on a particular day, it comes into force at the beginning of that day (Interpretation Act 1978, s 4(a)).

(d) Where an Act does not come into force immediately on its passing, and it confers power to make subordinate legislation, or to make appointments, give notices, prescribe forms or do any other thing for the purposes of the Act, then, unless the contrary intention appears, the power may be exercised, and any instrument made under it may be made so as to come into force, at any time after the passing of the Act so far as may be necessary or expedient for the purpose of (1) bringing the Act or any provision of the Act into force, or (2) giving full effect to the Act or any such provision at or after the time when it comes into force (Interpretation Act 1978, s 13).

(e) There is a general presumption that an enactment is not intended to have retrospective effect. Parliament undoubtedly has power to enact with retrospective effect, so the general presumption applies only unless the contrary is clearly stated (44 Halsbury's Laws (4th Edn) 922).

Updating

Is it in Force? is an annual publication. Each subsequent edition incorporates the most recent year's statutes and in addition deals with new commencement orders, repeals and amendments affecting material already published.

Interim updating is provided for subscribers to Halsbury's Statutes Fourth Edition as part of their Service in the form of looseleaf pages filed following the guide card 'Is it in Force?' in the Noter-up Service binder.

Queries on the content or scope of this work should be directed to the Managing Editor, Halsbury's Statutes, at 88 Kingsway, London, WC2B 6AB.
Document Exchange (DX) number 1023.

BUTTERWORTH LAW PUBLISHERS LTD

This book includes the effect of commencement orders published up to 24 January 1994.

Contents

1969

Administration of Justice Act 1969 (c 58)

RA: 22 Oct 1969

Commencement provisions: s 36(5); Adminstration of Justice Act 1969 (Commencement No 1) Order 1969, SI 1969/1607; Administration of Justice Act 1969 (Commencement No 2) Order 1970, SI 1970/672

s 1–11	Repealed
12–16	1 Jan 1970 (SI 1969/1607)
17–19	Repealed
20–22	1 Jan 1970 (SI 1969/1607)
23	Repealed
24	1 Dec 1969 (SI 1969/1607)
25–29	Repealed
30	1 Jan 1970 (SI 1969/1607)
31–33	Repealed
34–36	1 Dec 1969 (SI 1969/1607)
Sch 1	1 Dec 1969 (except so far as relates to Settled Land Act 1925; Solicitors Act 1957; County Courts Act 1959; Northern Ireland Act 1962) (SI 1969/1607)
	26 May 1970 (otherwise, except as noted below) (SI 1970/672)
	Repealed (entries relating to Solicitors Act 1957; Northern Ireland Act 1962)
2	Repealed

Age of Majority (Scotland) Act 1969 (c 39)

RA: 25 Jul 1969

Commencement provisions: s 2(3); Age of Majority (Scotland) Act 1969 (Commencement) Order 1969, SI 1969/1243

1 Jan 1970 (SI 1969/1243)

Agriculture (Spring Traps) (Scotland) Act 1969 (c 26)

Whole Act repealed

Air Corporations Act 1969 (c 43)

RA: 25 Jul 1969

25 Jul 1969 (RA)

Appropriation Act 1969 (c 31)

Whole Act repealed

Architects Registration (Amendment) Act 1969 (c 42)

RA: 25 Jul 1969

25 Jul 1969 (RA)

Army Reserve Act 1969 (c 23)

Whole Act repealed

Auctions (Bidding Agreements) Act 1969 (c 56)

RA: 22 Oct 1969

Commencement provisions: s 5(2)

22 Nov 1969 (s 5(2))

Betting, Gaming and Lotteries (Amendment) Act 1969 (c 17)

RA: 16 May 1969

16 May 1969 (RA)

Children and Young Persons Act 1969 (c 54)

RA: 22 Oct 1969

Commencement provisions: s 73(2); Children and Young Persons Act 1969
(Commencement No 1) Order 1969, SI 1969/1552; Children and Young Persons
Act 1969 (Commencement No 2) Order 1969, SI 1969/1565; Children and Young
Persons Act 1969 (Commencement No 3) Order 1970, SI 1970/1498, as amended
by SI 1970/1883; Children and Young Persons Act 1969 (Commencement No 4)
Order 1971, SI 1971/588

s 1–4	Repealed
5(1)–(7)	Repealed
(8)	1 Jan 1971 (SI 1970/1498)
(9)	1 Jan 1971 (so far as relates to the definition 'the appropriate local authority') (SI 1970/1498) *Not in force* (otherwise)
6	Repealed
7	1 Jan 1971 (SI 1970/1498)
7A, 8	Repealed
9–11	1 Jan 1971 (SI 1970/1498)
11A	Repealed
12, 12A	Substituted for s 12 together with ss 12B–12D by Criminal Justice Act 1988, s 128(1), Sch 10, Pt I (qv)

Children and Young Persons Act 1969 (c 54)—*cont*

s 12AA	Inserted by Children Act 1989, s 108(4), Sch 12, para 23 (qv)
12B–12D	Substituted for s 12 together with ss 12, 12A by Criminal Justice Act 1988, s 128(1), Sch 10, Pt I (qv)
13, 14	1 Jan 1971 (SI 1970/1498)
14A	Repealed
15	Substituted by Criminal Justice Act 1991, s 66, Sch 7 (qv)
16	1 Jan 1971 (SI 1970/1498)
16A	Inserted by Criminal Justice Act 1988, s 128(4), Sch 10, Pt IV (qv)
17, 18	1 Jan 1971 (SI 1970/1498)
19	Substituted by Criminal Justice Act 1982, s 21(1) (qv)
20–22	Repealed
23	Substituted by Criminal Justice Act 1991, s 60(1) (qv)
24	Repealed
25, 26	1 Jan 1971 (SI 1970/1498)
27, 28	Repealed
29	Substituted by Police and Criminal Evidence Act 1984, s 119(1), Sch 6, Pt I, para 19(b) (qv)
30	1 Jan 1971 (SI 1970/1498)
31	Repealed
32	1 Jan 1971 (SI 1970/1498)
32A–32C, 33	Repealed
34	1 Jan 1971 (SI 1970/1498)
35–45	Repealed
46(1)	1 Dec 1969 (SI 1969/1565)
(2)	See Sch 3 below
47–51	Repealed
52	1 Jan 1970 (SI 1969/1565)
53–64A	Repealed
65–67	1 Dec 1969 (SI 1969/1565)
68	Repealed
69, 70	16 Nov 1969 (SI 1969/1552)
71	1 Dec 1969 (SI 1969/1565)
72	See Schs 4, 5, 6, 7 below
73	16 Nov 1969 (SI 1969/1552)
Sch 1, 2	Repealed
3, para 1–4	1 Dec 1969 (SI 1969/1565)
5–8	1 Jan 1971 (SI 1970/1498)
9, 10	1 Dec 1969 (SI 1969/1565)
4, para 1	1 Jan 1971 (SI 1970/1498)
1A	Inserted by Administration of Justice Act 1970, s 51(2), (3) (qv)
2–4	Repealed
5(1)	*Not in force*
(2)	Repealed
6	Repealed
7–9	1 Jan 1971 (SI 1970/1498)
10	Repealed
11, 12	1 Jan 1971 (SI 1970/1498)
13	Repealed
14	1 Dec 1969 (SI 1969/1565)
15	1 Jan 1971 (SI 1970/1498)
16	Repealed

Children and Young Persons Act 1969 (c 54)—*cont*

Sch 4, para 17, 18	1 Jan 1971 (SI 1970/1498)
19–24	Repealed
5, para 1, 2	Repealed
3	1 Jan 1971 (SI 1970/1498)
4	1 Dec 1969 (SI 1969/1565)
5	Repealed
6, 7	1 Jan 1971 (SI 1970/1498)
8–10	Repealed
11	*Not in force*
12	1 Jan 1971 (SI 1970/1498)
13–23	Repealed
24	1 Jan 1971 (SI 1970/1498)
25, 26	Repealed
27, 28	Spent
29–45	Repealed
46	1 Jan 1971 (SI 1970/1498)
47, 48	Repealed
49	1 Jan 1971 (SI 1970/1498)
50–52	Repealed
53	1 Jan 1971 (SI 1970/1498)
54	Repealed
55	*Not in force*
56	Repealed
57–62	1 Jan 1971 (SI 1970/1498)
63	16 Nov 1969 (SI 1969/1552)
64(1)	16 Nov 1969 (SI 1969/1552)
(2)	1 Jan 1971 (SI 1970/1498)
65(1)	1 Jan 1971 (SI 1970/1498)
(2)	1 Dec 1969 (SI 1969/1565)
66	1 Dec 1969 (SI 1969/1565)
67, 68	Repealed
69	16 Nov 1969 (SI 1969/1552)
70–72	1 Jan 1971 (SI 1970/1498)
73	Repealed
74	1 Jan 1971 (SI 1970/1498)
75, 76	16 Nov 1969 (SI 1969/1552)
77	1 Jan 1971 (SI 1970/1498)
78	Repealed
79–81	1 Jan 1971 (SI 1970/1498)
82	Repealed
83	1 Jan 1971 (SI 1970/1498)
6	16 Nov 1969 (in part) (SI 1969/1552)
	1 Dec 1969 (in part) (SI 1969/1565)
	1 Jan 1970 (in part) (SI 1969/1565)
	1 Jan 1971 (in part) (SI 1970/1498)
	15 Apr 1971 (in part) (SI 1971/588)
	Not in force (repeals of or in Children and Young Persons Act 1933, ss 55 (except repeals in sub-ss (2), (4) thereof), 56(1), 58, 59(1), 77(2), (2A), 79(1)–(3), (5), 80, 81(1), (3), 103, 104, 106(3)–(5), 107(1) (definitions 'approved school' and 'managers'), Sch 4, paras 1–3, 14; Superannuation (Miscellaneous Provisions) Act 1948, s 14; Children Act 1948, ss 49(1), 59(2); Criminal Justice Act 1948, ss 49(1)–(4), (6), 77, 80(1) (definitions 'approved school' and 'remand home'), Sch 9 (so far as relates to Children and

Children and Young Persons Act 1969 (c 54)—*cont*

Sch 6–*cont*	Young Persons Act 1933, ss 58, 77); Magistrates' Courts Act 1952, s 32; Criminal Justice Act 1961, ss 1, 4, 7(2), 8(1), 10(2), 18, 19; London Government Act 1963, s 47; Children and Young Persons Act 1963, Sch 3, para 15)
7	Repealed

Clergy Pensions (Amendment) Measure 1969 (No 1)

Whole Measure repealed

Consolidated Fund Act 1969 (c 3)

Whole Act repealed

Consolidated Fund (No 2) Act 1969 (c 9)

Whole Act repealed

Customs Duties (Dumping and Subsidies) Act 1969 (c 16)

RA: 24 Apr 1969

Commencement provisions: s 19(3)

1 May 1969 (s 19(3))

Customs (Import Deposits) Act 1969 (c 64)

Whole Act repealed

Decimal Currency Act 1969 (c 19)

RA: 16 May 1969

Commencement provisions: s 19(2)

s 1	Repealed
2–12	16 May 1969 (RA)
13	Expired 15 Feb 1971
14, 15	Repealed
16–19	16 May 1969 (RA)
Sch 1, 2	16 May 1969 (RA)
3	Repealed
4	16 May 1969 (RA)

Development of Tourism Act 1969 (c 51)

RA: 25 Jul 1969

Commencement provisions: s 21(2)

25 Aug 1969 (s 21(2))

Divorce Reform Act 1969 (c 55)

Whole Act repealed

Education (Scotland) Act 1969 (c 49)

Whole Act repealed

Electricity (Scotland) Act 1969 (c 1)

Whole Act repealed

Employers' Liability (Compulsory Insurance) Act 1969 (c 57)

RA: 22 Oct 1969

Commencement provisions: s 7(3); Employers' Liability (Compulsory Insurance) Act 1969 (Commencement) Order 1971, SI 1971/1116

1 Jan 1972 (SI 1971/1116)

Employers' Liability (Defective Equipment) Act 1969 (c 37)

RA: 25 Jul 1969

Commencement provisions: s 2(2)

25 Oct 1969 (s 2(2))

Expiring Laws Act 1969 (c 61)

Whole Act repealed

Family Law Reform Act 1969 (c 46)

RA: 25 Jul 1969

Commencement provisions: s 28(3); Family Law Reform Act 1969 (Commencement No 1) Order 1969, SI 1969/1140; Family Law Reform Act 1969 (Commencement No 2) Order 1971, SI 1971/1857

s 1–3	1 Jan 1970 (SI 1969/1140)
4–7	Repealed
8–12	1 Jan 1970 (SI 1969/1140)
13–18	Repealed
19	1 Jan 1970 (SI 1969/1140)
20–25	1 Mar 1972 (SI 1971/1857)
26	1 Jan 1970 (SI 1969/1140)

Family Law Reform Act 1969 (c 46)—*cont*

s 27	Repealed
28	1 Jan 1970 (SI 1969/1140)
Sch 1–3	1 Jan 1970 (SI 1969/1140)

Finance Act 1969 (c 32)

RA: 25 Jul 1969

See the note concerning Finance Acts at the front of this book

---

Foreign Compensation Act 1969 (c 20)

RA: 16 May 1969

16 May 1969 (RA)

Genocide Act 1969 (c 12)

RA: 27 Mar 1969

27 Mar 1969 (RA)

Horserace Betting Levy Act 1969 (c 14)

RA: 27 Mar 1969

27 Mar 1969 (RA)

Housing Act 1969 (c 33)

RA: 25 Jul 1969

Commencement provisions: s 91(4)

Whole Act repealed except ss 82, 91(1), (5), (6), Sch 10 which came into force on 25 Jul 1969 (s 91(4))

Housing (Scotland) Act 1969 (c 34)

Whole Act repealed

Immigration Appeals Act 1969 (c 21)

Whole Act repealed

Iron and Steel Act 1969 (c 45)

Whole Act repealed

Late Night Refreshment Houses Act 1969 (c 53)

RA: 22 Oct 1969

Commencement provisions: s 15(2)

1 Jan 1970 (s 15(2))

Whole Act repealed (as far as it relates to London borough councils), by London
  Local Authorities Act 1990, s 20, as from days to be fixed by individual borough
  councils in accordance with s 3

Law of Property Act 1969 (c 59)

RA: 22 Oct 1969

Commencement provisions: s 31(2)

1 Jan 1970 (s 31(2)), except s 28(6), which came into force on 22 Oct 1969 (RA)

Licensing (Scotland) Act 1969 (c 13)

Whole Act repealed

Local Government Grants (Social Need) Act 1969 (c 2)

RA: 30 Jan 1969

30 Jan 1969 (RA)

Note

Grants under s 1 of the Act are authorised for the year 1968–69 or any later year

Medical Act 1969 (c 40)

Whole Act repealed

Mines and Quarries (Tips) Act 1969 (c 10)

RA: 27 Mar 1969

Commencement provisions: s 38(3); Mines and Quarries (Tips) Act 1969
  (Commencement No 1) Order 1969, SI 1969/804; Mines and Quarries (Tips) Act
  1969 (Commencement No 2) Order 1969, SI 1969/805; Mines and Quarries
  (Tips) Act 1969 (Commencement No 3) Order 1969, SI 1969/870

s 1–7	30 Jun 1969 (SI 1969/804
8, 9	Repealed
10	30 Jun 1969 (SI 1969/804)
11–27	30 Jun 1969 (SI 1969/805; SI 1969/870)
28	Substituted by High Court and County Courts Jurisdiction Order 1991, SI 1991/724, art 2(8), Schedule, as from 1 Jul 1991
29–36	30 Jun 1969 (SI 1969/805; SI 1969/870)
37, 38	27 Mar 1969 (RA)
Sch 1	30 Jun 1969 (SI 1969/804)
2–4	30 Jun 1969 (SI 1969/805; SI 1969/870)

National Insurance Act 1969 (c 44)

Whole Act repealed

National Insurance &c Act 1969 (c 4)

Whole Act repealed

National Mod (Scotland) Act 1969 (c 41)

Whole Act repealed

National Theatre Act 1969 (c 11)

Whole Act repealed

New Towns Act 1969 (c 5)

Whole Act repealed

Nuclear Installations Act 1969 (c 18)

RA: 16 May 1969

16 May 1969 (RA)

Nurses Act 1969 (c 47)

Whole Act repealed

Overseas Resources Development Act 1969 (c 36)

Whole Act repealed

Pensions (Increase) Act 1969 (c 7)

Whole Act repealed

Police Act 1969 (c 63)

RA: 11 Dec 1969

Commencement provisions: s 7(2); Police Act 1969 (Commencement No 1) Order 1969,
SI 1969/1775; Police Act 1969 (Commencement No 2) Order 1970, SI 1970/1028;
Police Act 1969 (Commencement No 3) Order 1971, SI 1971/408

s 1(1)–(3)	13 Mar 1971 (SI 1971/408)
(4)	Repealed
2	17 Dec 1969 (SI 1969/1775)
3	*Not in force*
4, 5	Repealed
6, 7	17 Dec 1969 (SI 1969/1775)

Ponies Act 1969 (c 28)

Whole Act repealed

Post Office Act 1969 (c 48)

RA: 25 Jul 1969

25 Jul 1969 (RA; but note that by Post Office Act 1969 (Appointed Day) Order 1969, SI 1969/1066, made under s 1(1) (repealed), the day appointed for the abolition of the office of master of the Post Office was 1 Oct 1969)

Public Health (Recurring Nuisances) Act 1969 (c 25)

Whole Act repealed

Redundancy Rebates Act 1969 (c 8)

Whole Act repealed

Redundant Churches and other Religious Buildings Act 1969 (c 22)

RA: 16 May 1969

16 May 1969 (RA)

Rent (Control of Increases) Act 1969 (c 62)

Whole Act repealed

Representation of the People Act 1969 (c 15)

Whole Act repealed

Sharing of Church Buildings Act 1969 (c 38)

RA: 25 Jul 1969

25 Jul 1969 (RA)

Shipbuilding Industry Act 1969 (c 6)

Whole Act repealed

Statute Law (Repeals) Act 1969 (c 52)

RA: 22 Oct 1969

Commencement provisions: s 7(2)

1 Jan 1970 (s 7(2))

Synodical Government Measure 1969 (No 2)

RA: 25 Jul 1969

25 Jul 1969 (RA); but note that the Church Assembly was renamed and reconstituted
  as the General Synod as from 4 Nov 1970 (see *London Gazette*, 16 Jun 1970)

Tanzania Act 1969 (c 29)

RA: 25 Jun 1969

s 1, 2	25 Jun 1969 (RA)
3	26 Apr 1964 (retrospective; s 3(3))
4–8	25 Jun 1969 (RA)

Tattooing of Minors Act 1969 (c 24)

RA: 16 May 1969

Commencement provisions: s 4(2)

16 Jun 1969 (s 4(2))

Town and Country Planning (Scotland) Act 1969 (c 30)

RA: 25 Jun 1969

Commencement provisions: s 104; Town and Country Planning (Scotland) Act 1969
  (Commencement No 1) Order 1969, SI 1969/1569; Town and Country Planning
  (Scotland) Act 1969 (Commencement No 3) Order 1970, SI 1970/1034

s 1–31	Repealed
32	8 Dec 1969 (SI 1969/1569)
33–97	Repealed
98	8 Dec 1969 (SI 1969/1569)
99–102	Repealed
103	8 Dec 1969 (SI 1969/1569)
104–107	Repealed
108	8 Dec 1969 (SI 1969/1569)
Sch 1–11	Repealed

Transport (London) Act 1969 (c 35)

Whole Act repealed

Transport (London) Amendment Act 1969 (c 60)

Whole Act repealed

Trustee Savings Banks Act 1969 (c 50)

Whole Act repealed

Ulster Defence Regiment Act 1969 (c 65)

Whole Act repealed

Vehicle and Driving Licences Act 1969 (c 27)

RA: 25 Jun 1969

Commencement provisions: s 38(2); Vehicle and Driving Licences Act 1969
(Commencement No 1) Order 1969, SI 1969/866; Vehicle and Driving Licences
Act 1969 (Commencement No 2) Order 1969, SI 1969/913; Vehicle and Driving
Licences Act 1969 (Commencement No 3) Order 1969, SI 1969/1579; Vehicle and
Driving Licences Act 1969 (Commencement No 4) Order 1969, SI 1969/1637;
Vehicle and Driving Licences Act 1969 (Commencement No 5) Order 1970,
SI 1970/169; Vehicle and Driving Licences Act 1969 (Commencement No 6) Order
1970, SI 1970/757; Vehicle and Driving Licences Act 1969 (Commencement No 7)
Order 1971, SI 1971/244; Vehicle and Driving Licences Act 1969 (Commencement
No 8) Order 1971, SI 1971/376; Vehicle and Driving Licences Act 1969
(Commencement No 9) Order 1971, SI 1971/1477

s 1	Repealed
2(1), (2)	Repealed
(3)	19 Nov 1969 (SI 1969/1579)
(4)–(8)	Repealed
3–15	Repealed
16(1)	Repealed
(2)	See Sch 2 below
(3)–(7)	Repealed
17–33	Repealed
34	30 Jun 1969 (SI 1969/866)
35–37	Repealed
38	30 Jun 1969 (SI 1969/866)
Sch 1	Repealed
2, para 8, 11	1 Feb 1970 (SI 1969/1637)
remainder	Repealed
3	Repealed

1970

Administration of Justice Act 1970 (c 31)

RA: 29 May 1970

Commencement provisions: s 54(4); Administration of Justice Act 1970
(Commencement No 1) Order 1970, SI 1970/886; Administration of Justice Act
1970 (Commencement No 2) Order 1970, SI 1970/1207; Administration of Justice
Act 1970 (Commencement No 3) Order 1970, SI 1970/1962; Administration of
Justice Act 1970 (Commencement No 4) Order 1971, SI 1971/834; Administration
of Justice Act 1970 (Commencement No 5) Order 1971, SI 1971/1244

s 1	1 Oct 1971 (SI 1971/1244)
2, 3	Repealed
4	1 Oct 1971 (SI 1971/1244)
5–9	Repealed
10	1 Jul 1970 (SI 1970/886)
11	2 Aug 1971 (SI 1971/834)
12–26	Repealed
27(1), (2)	Repealed
(3)	2 Aug 1971 (SI 1971/834)
28	1 Sep 1970 (definition 'maintenance order' for purposes of s 48) (SI 1970/1207)
	2 Aug 1971 (remainder) (SI 1971/834)
29(1)–(4)	Repealed
(5)	2 Aug 1971 (SI 1971/834)
30	Repealed
31–35	2 Aug 1971 (SI 1971/834)
36	1 Feb 1971 (SI 1970/1962)
37, 38	Repealed
38A	Inserted by Consumer Credit Act 1974, s 192, Sch 4, Pt 1, para 30 (qv)
39	1 Feb 1971 (SI 1970/1962)
40	1 Jul 1970 (SI 1970/886)
41	2 Aug 1971 (SI 1971/834)
42, 43	Repealed
44	1 Jul 1970 (SI 1970/886)
45–47	Repealed
48	1 Sep 1970 (SI 1970/1207)
49–50	Repealed
51(1)	Repealed
(2), (3)	1 Jan 1971 (SI 1970/1962)
52	1 Jul 1970 (SI 1970/886)
53	Repealed
54(1), (2)	1 Jul 1970 (SI 1970/886)
(3)	See Sch 11 below
(4), (5)	1 Jul 1970 (SI 1970/886)
(6)	1 Feb 1971 (SI 1970/1462)
Sch 1	Repealed

Administration of Justice Act 1970 (c 31)—*cont*

Sch 2, 3	1 Oct 1971 (SI 1971/1244)
4	2 Aug 1971 (SI 1971/834)
5–7	Repealed
8, 9	2 Aug 1971 (SI 1971/834)
10	Repealed
11	1 Jul 1970 (repeals of or in Guardianship of Infants Act 1886, ss 5, 11; Supreme Court of Judicature (Consolidation) Act 1925, s 63; Patents Act 1949; Registered Designs Act 1949; Administration of Justice Act 1964; Criminal Appeal Act 1966; Criminal Appeal Act 1968, s 45(2)) (SI 1970/886)
	1 Sep 1970 (repeals of or in Maintenance Orders Act 1958, s 4(3); Maintenance Orders Act 1968) (SI 1970/1207)
	2 Aug 1971 (repeals of or in Forfeiture Act 1870; Bankruptcy Act 1914; Children and Young Persons Act 1933; Summary Jurisdiction (Appeals) Act 1933; Criminal Justice Act 1948; Costs in Criminal Cases Act 1952; Magistrates' Courts Act 1952; Maintenance Orders Act 1958 (except s 4(3), repealed as noted above); County Courts Act 1959; Matrimonial Causes Act 1965; Ministry of Social Security Act 1966; Criminal Justice Act 1967; Criminal Appeal Act 1968, Sch 5; Family Law Reform Act 1969; Children and Young Persons Act 1969) (SI 1971/834)
	1 Oct 1971 (repeals of or in Administration of Estates Act 1925; Supreme Court of Judicature (Consolidation) Act 1925, ss 5(1), 58, 225) (SI 1971/1244)

Agriculture Act 1970 (c 40)

RA: 29 May 1970

Commencement provisions: ss 24(1), 29(6), 31(3), 32(8), 35(1), 65(1), 87(1), 108(3), Sch 5; Agriculture Act 1970 (Commencement No 1) Order 1970, SI 1970/1045; Agriculture Act 1970 (Commencement No 2) Order 1970, SI 1970/1048; Agriculture Act 1970 (Commencement No 3) Order 1970, SI 1970/1098; Agriculture Act 1970 (Commencement No 4) Order 1970, SI 1970/1755; Agriculture Act 1970 (Commencement No 5) Order 1973, SI 1973/1520; Hill Farming (Appointed Day for Repeal) Order 1986, SI 1986/707

s 1–27	Repealed
28	29 May 1970 (RA)
29	29 May 1970 (RA; note that Farm Capital Grant (Repeal of Enactments) Order 1970, SI 1970/1867, made under s 29(6), appointed 1 Jan 1971 for the purposes of that subsection; note also that Farm Capital Grant (Repeal of Enactments) (Savings) Order 1970, SI 1970/1758, made under s 29(7), continued the enactments specified in Sch 5, Pt I, and instruments made thereunder, in force for 4 years after 1 Jan 1971 for certain purposes)

Agriculture Act 1970 (c 40)—*cont*

s 30	29 May 1970 (RA)
31	Repealed
32	1 Jan 1971 (s 32(8) and Farm Capital Grant (Repeal of Enactments) Order 1970, SI 1970/1867, made under s 29(6))
33, 34	29 May 1970 (RA)
35, 36	Repealed
37–56	1 Aug 1970 (SI 1970/1048)
57	Repealed
58–65	1 Aug 1970 (SI 1970/1048)
66–73	1 Jan 1974 (SI 1973/1520)
73A	Inserted by Agriculture Act 1970 Amendment Regulations 1982, SI 1982/980, art 7
74	1 Jan 1974 (SI 1973/1520)
74A	Inserted by European Communities Act 1972, s 4, Sch 4, para 6 (qv)
75–87	1 Jan 1974 (SI 1973/1520)
88–91	Repealed
92	29 May 1970 (RA)
93	Repealed
94	29 May 1970 (RA)
95–97	Repealed
98	29 May 1970 (RA)
99–101	Repealed
102	29 May 1970 (RA)
103–105	Repealed
106	29 May 1970 (RA)
107	Repealed
108(1), (2)	29 May 1970 (RA)
(3)	31 Jul 1970 (SI 1970/1045; SI 1970/1098)
(4), (5)	29 May 1970 (RA)
109	Repealed
110, 111	29 May 1970 (RA)
112	Repealed
113	29 May 1970 (RA)
Sch 1	Repealed
2	29 May 1970 (RA)
3, 4	1 Aug 1970 (SI 1970/1048)
5	Repealed

Appropriation Act 1970 (c 25)

Whole Act repealed

Appropriation (No 2) Act 1970 (c 48)

Whole Act repealed

Building (Scotland) Act 1970 (c 38)

RA: 29 May 1970

Commencement provisions: s 8(3); Building (Scotland) Act 1970 (Commencement) Order 1971, SI 1971/744

s 1	29 Jun 1970 (s 8(3))
2	15 Jun 1971 (SI 1971/744)
3	29 Jun 1970 (s 8(3))
4	15 Jun 1971 (SI 1971/744)
5	29 Jun 1970 (s 8(3))
6	See Schs 1, 2 below
7, 8	29 Jun 1970 (s 8(3))
Sch 1, Pt I, para 1 (a), (b)	15 Jun 1971 (SI 1971/744)
(c)	29 Jun 1970 (s 8(3))
2–4	15 Jun 1971 (SI 1971/744)
5	Repealed
6	29 Jun 1970 (s 8(3))
7 (a)	15 Jun 1971 (SI 1971/744)
(b)	29 Jun 1970 (s 8(3))
8	15 Jun 1971 (SI 1971/744)
9	29 Jun 1970 (s 8(3))
Pt II, para 1, 2	29 Jun 1970 (s 8(3))
3, 4	Repealed
5	29 Jun 1970 (s 8(3))
6	15 Jun 1971 (SI 1971/744)
7	29 Jun 1970 (s 8(3))
2	29 Jun 1970 (except so far as relates to Building (Scotland) Act 1959, s 10, Sch 5) (s 8(3))
	15 Jun 1971 (otherwise) (SI 1971/744)

Chronically Sick and Disabled Persons Act 1970 (c 44)

RA: 29 May 1970

Commencement provisions: s 29(4); Chronically Sick and Disabled Persons Act 1970 (Commencement No 1) Order 1971, SI 1971/698; Chronically Sick and Disabled Persons Act 1970 (Commencement No 2) Order 1971, SI 1971/1491

s 1	1 Oct 1971 (SI 1971/698)
2	29 Aug 1970 (s 29(4)(c))
3	Substituted by Housing (Consequential Provisions) Act 1985, s 4, Sch 2, para 20 (qv)
4–6	29 Nov 1970 (s 29(4)(b))
7	Substituted by Disabled Persons Act 1981, s 5 (qv)
8	29 Nov 1970 (s 29(4)(b))
8A	Inserted by Chronically Sick and Disabled Persons (Amendment) Act 1976, s 2 (qv)
8B	Inserted by Disabled Persons Act 1981, s 7 (qv)
9	29 Aug 1970 (s 29(4)(c))
10	29 Aug 1970 (s 29(4)(c)); repealed (S)
11	Repealed
12–18	29 Aug 1970 (s 29(4)(c))
19	Repealed
20	29 Aug 1970 (s 29(4)(c))
21	1 Dec 1971 (SI 1971/1491)
22–24	29 Aug 1970 (s 29(4)(c))
25–27	Repealed

Chronically Sick and Disabled Persons Act 1970 (c 44)—*cont*

s 28	29 Aug 1970 (s 29(4)(c))
28A	Inserted by Children Act 1989, s 108(5), Sch 13, para 27 (qv)
29	29 Aug 1970 (s 29(4)(c))

Church Commissioners Measure 1970 (No 3)

RA: 17 Dec 1970

17 Dec 1970 (RA)

Collegiate Churches (Capital Endowments) Measure 1970 (No 1)

RA: 24 Mar 1970

24 Mar 1970 (RA)

Conservation of Seals Act 1970 (c 30)

RA: 29 May 1970

Commencement provisions: s 17(4)

29 Aug 1970 (s 17(4))

Consolidated Fund Act 1970 (c 1)

Whole Act repealed

Consolidated Fund (No 2) Act 1970 (c 12)

Whole Act repealed

Contingencies Fund Act 1970 (c 56)

RA: 17 Dec 1970

Commencement provisions: s 3(2)

17 Jan 1971 (s 3(2))

Conveyancing and Feudal Reform (Scotland) Act 1970 (c 35)

RA: 29 May 1970

Commencement provisions: s 54(2); Conveyancing and Feudal Reform (Scotland) Act 1970 (Commencement) Order 1971, SI 1971/199

s 1–6	1 Mar 1971 (SI 1971/199)
7	29 Nov 1970 (s 54(2))
8	Repealed
9–49	29 Nov 1970 (s 54(2))
50	29 May 1970 (s 54(2))

Conveyancing and Feudal Reform (Scotland) Act 1970 (c 35)—*cont*

s 51–53	29 May 1970 (so far as relate to s 50) (s 54(2))
	29 Nov 1970 (so far as relate to the remainder of the Act, except ss 1–6) (s 54(2))
	1 Mar 1971 (so far as relate to ss 1–6) (SI 1971/199)
54	29 May 1970 (s 54(2))
Sch 1	1 Mar 1971 (SI 1971/199)
2–9	29 Nov 1970 (s 54(2))
10, Pt I	29 Nov 1970 (s 54(2))
II	See s 52 above
11, Pt I, II	29 Nov 1970 (s 54(2))
III	See s 52 above

Education (Handicapped Children) Act 1970 (c 52)

RA: 23 Jul 1970

23 Jul 1970 (RA; but note that this Act mainly took effect from 1 Apr 1971, the day appointed by Education (Handicapped Children) Act 1970 (Appointed Day) Order 1971, SI 1971/187, made under s 1(1))

Education (School Milk) Act 1970 (c 14)

Whole Act repealed

Equal Pay Act 1970 (c 41)

RA: 29 May 1970

Commencement provisions: s 9

29 Dec 1975 (s 9(1))

Expiring Laws Continuance Act 1970 (c 58)

Whole Act repealed

Export Guarantees and Payments Act 1970 (c 15)

Whole Act repealed

Family Income Supplements Act 1970 (c 55)

Whole Act repealed

Fiji Independence Act 1970 (c 50)

RA: 23 Jul 1970

Appointed Day: 10 Oct 1970

Films Act 1970 (c 26)

Whole Act repealed

Finance Act 1970 (c 24)

RA: 29 May 1970

See the note about Finance Acts at the front of this book

Fishing Vessels (Safety Provisions) Act 1970 (c 27)

RA: 29 May 1970

Commencement provisions: s 11(4); Fishing Vessels (Safety Provisions) Act 1970 (Commencement) Order 1975, SI 1975/337

30 Apr 1975 (SI 1975/337)

Food and Drugs (Milk) Act 1970 (c 3)

RA: 29 Jan 1970

29 Jan 1970 (RA); *whole Act repealed (EW)*

Game Act 1970 (c 13)

RA: 26 Mar 1970

Commencement provisions: s 2(1)

2 Feb 1971 (s 2(1))

General Rate Act 1970 (c 19)

Whole Act repealed

Guyana Republic Act 1970 (c 18)

RA: 15 May 1970

15 May 1970 (RA; but note that has retrospective effect as Guyana became a republic on 23 Feb 1970)

Harbours (Amendment) Act 1970 (c 53)

Whole Act repealed

Housing (Amendment) (Scotland) Act 1970 (c 5)

Whole Act repealed

Income and Corporation Taxes Act 1970 (c 10)

Whole Act repealed

Income and Corporation Taxes (No 2) Act 1970 (c 54)

Whole Act repealed

Indecent Advertisements (Amendment) Act 1970 (c 47)

Whole Act repealed

Industrial Development (Ships) Act 1970 (c 2)

Whole Act repealed

Insolvency Services (Accounting and Investment) Act 1970 (c 8)

Whole Act repealed

International Monetary Fund Act 1970 (c 49)

Whole Act repealed

Law Reform (Miscellaneous Provisions) Act 1970 (c 33)

RA: 29 May 1970

Commencement provisions: s 7(3)

1 Jan 1971 (s 7(3))

Local Authorities (Goods and Services) Act 1970 (c 39)

RA: 29 May 1970

29 May 1970 (RA)

Local Authority Social Services Act 1970 (c 42)

RA: 29 May 1970

Commencement provisions: s 15(4); Local Authority Social Services Act 1970
(Commencement No 1) Order 1970, SI 1970/1143; Local Authority Social Services
Act 1970 (Commencement No 2) Order 1970, SI 1970/1813; Local Authority Social
Services Act 1970 (Commencement No 3) Order 1971, SI 1971/1221

s 1	1 Sep 1970 (SI 1970/1143)
2	1 Jan 1971 (ss 2, 4, 5, 7(1), Sch 1, Sch 2, paras 1, 10, 12, Sch 3 (part) brought into force in relation to all local authorities except those noted below) (SI 1970/1813)
	1 Apr 1971 (Hertfordshire) (SI 1970/1813)
	26 May 1971 (Manchester) (SI 1970/1813)
3	Substituted by Local Government, Planning and Land Act 1980, s 183(1) (qv)
3A	Inserted by Local Government, Planning and Land Act 1980, s 183(2) (qv)
4, 5	See note to s 2 above

Local Authority Social Services Act 1970 (c 42)—*cont*

s 6	1 Jan 1971 (s 6, Sch 3 (part) brought into force in relation to all local authorities except those noted below) (SI 1970/1813)
	1 Apr 1971 (Hertfordshire) (SI 1970/1813)
	26 May 1971 (Manchester) (SI 1970/1813)
	1 Oct 1971 (Lancashire) (SI 1970/1813)
7(1)	See note to s 2 above
(2), (3)	Repealed
7A–7E	Inserted by National Health Service and Community Care Act 1990, s 50 (qv)
8	Repealed
9	1 Sep 1970 (SI 1970/1143)
10, 11	Repealed
12, 13	1 Sep 1970 (SI 1970/1143)
14(1), (2)	See Schs 2, 3 below
(3), (4)	1 Sep 1970 (SI 1970/1143)
15	1 Sep 1970 (SI 1970/1143)
Sch 1	See note to s 2 above
2, para 1	See note to s 2 above
2–7	Repealed
8	1 Sep 1970 (SI 1970/1143)
9	Repealed
10	See note to s 2 above
11	Repealed
12	See note to s 2 above
3	1 Sep 1970 (repeals of or in Local Government Act 1958; London Government Act 1963; Health Services and Public Health Act 1968) (SI 1970/1143)
	See notes to s 6 (repeal of Children Act 1948, s 41) (SI 1970/1813)
	See notes to s 2 above (all remaining repeals) (SI 1970/1813)

Local Employment Act 1970 (c 7)

RA: 26 Feb 1970

Commencement provisions: s 9(3)

5 Mar 1970 (s 9(3)); but note that no substantive provisions of this Act remain unrepealed

Local Government (Footpaths and Open Spaces) (Scotland) Act 1970 (c 28)

RA: 29 May 1970

29 May 1970 (RA)

Marriage (Registrar General's Licence) Act 1970 (c 34)

RA: 29 May 1970

Commencement provisions: s 20(3)

1 Jan 1971 (s 20(3))

Matrimonial Proceedings and Property Act 1970 (c 45)

RA: 29 May 1970

Commencement provisions: s 43(2)

Whole Act repealed except ss 30(2), 37, 39, 43(1), (3), which came into force as follows:

s 30	1 Jan 1971 (s 43(2) (repealed))
37, 39, 43	1 Aug 1970 (s 43(2) (repealed))

Merchant Shipping Act 1970 (c 36)

RA: 29 May 1970

Commencement provisions: s 101(4); Merchant Shipping Act 1970 (Commencement No 1) Order 1972, SI 1972/1977; Merchant Shipping Act 1970 (Commencement No 2) Order 1974, SI 1974/1194; Merchant Shipping Act 1970 (Commencement No 3) Order 1974, SI 1974/1908; Merchant Shipping Act 1970 (Commencement No 4) Order 1975, SI 1975/2156; Merchant Shipping Act 1970 (Commencement No 5) Order 1978, SI 1978/797; Merchant Shipping Act 1970 (Commencement No 6) Order 1979, SI 1979/809; Merchant Shipping Act 1970 (Commencement No 7) Order 1981, SI 1981/1186; Merchant Shipping Act 1970 (Commencement No 8) Order 1982, SI 1982/840; Merchant Shipping Act 1970 (Commencement No 9) Order 1982, SI 1982/1617; Merchant Shipping Act 1970 (Commencement No 10) Order 1986, SI 1986/2066

s 1–5	1 Jan 1973 (SI 1972/1977)
6	*Not in force*; repealed by Merchant Shipping (Registration, etc) Act 1993, s 8(4), Sch 5, Pt II, as from 1 May 1994 (qv)
7–14	1 Jan 1973 (SI 1972/1977)
15	1 Aug 1979 (SI 1979/809)
16–18	1 Jan 1973 (SI 1972/1977)
19	1 Aug 1979 (SI 1979/809); repealed by Merchant Shipping (Registration, etc) Act 1993, s 8(3), (4), Sch 4, para 8, Sch 5, Pt II, as from 1 May 1994 (qv)
20	19 Dec 1975 (SI 1975/2156)
21	Repealed
22	1 Jan 1973 (SI 1972/1977)
23, 24	Repealed
25, 26	1 Jan 1973 (SI 1972/1977)
27	Substituted by Merchant Shipping Act 1988, s 32 (qv)
28	1 Jan 1973 (SI 1972/1977)
29	Repealed
30	1 Jan 1973 (SI 1972/1977)
31	Repealed
32, 33	1 Jan 1973 (SI 1972/1977)
34–38	Repealed
39–42	1 Jan 1973 (SI 1972/1977)
43–47	19 Dec 1975 (SI 1975/2156)
48	1 Jan 1973 (SI 1972/1977)
49	19 Dec 1975 (SI 1975/2156)
50	1 Sep 1981 (SI 1981/1186)
51	*Not in force*
52–54	1 Jan 1983 (SI 1982/1617)
55	Repealed

Merchant Shipping Act 1970 (c 36)—*cont*

s 56	1 Jul 1983 (SI 1982/1617)
57	1 Jan 1983 (so far as applies to an inquiry under ss 52, 54) (SI 1982/1617)
	1 Jul 1983 (otherwise) (SI 1982/1617)
58	1 Dec 1982 (SI 1982/1617)
59	1 Jan 1983 (so far as applies to an inquiry under ss 52, 54) (SI 1982/1617)
	1 Jul 1983 (otherwise) (SI 1982/1617)
60	1 Sep 1981 (SI 1981/1186)
61–64	1 Jan 1973 (SI 1972/1977)
65, 66	Repealed
67–72	1 Jan 1973 (SI 1972/1977)
73	1 Jan 1973 (SI 1972/1977); prospectively repealed by Merchant Shipping Act 1988, s 57(5), Sch 7 (qv)
74, 75	1 Jan 1973 (SI 1972/1977)
75A	Inserted by Merchant Shipping Act 1988, s 48, Sch 5 (qv)
76–83	1 Jan 1973 (SI 1972/1977)
84	1 Jan 1973 (SI 1972/1977); repealed by Merchant Shipping (Registration, etc) Act 1993, s 8(4), Sch 5, Pt II, as from 1 May 1994 (qv)
85, 86	18 Nov 1974 (SI 1974/1908)
87	*Not in force*; repealed by Merchant Shipping (Registration, etc) Act 1993, s 8(3), (4), Sch 4, para 8, Sch 5, Pt II, as from 1 May 1994 (qv)
88	1 Jan 1973 (SI 1972/1977)
89	1 Jan 1973 (SI 1972/1977); prospectively repealed by Merchant Shipping Act 1988, ss 48, 57(5), Schs 5, 7 (qv)
90	1 Jan 1973 (SI 1972/1977); repealed by Merchant Shipping (Registration, etc) Act 1993, s 8(4), Sch 5, Pt II, as from 1 May 1994 (qv)
91	16 Jul 1982 (SI 1982/840)
92–94	1 Jan 1973 (SI 1972/1977); repealed by Merchant Shipping (Registration, etc) Act 1993, s 8(4), Sch 5, Pt II, as from 1 May 1994 (qv)
95(1)	1 Jan 1973 (SI 1972/1977)
(2)	1 Aug 1979 (SI 1979/809)
(3)	*Not in force*
(4), (5)	1 Jan 1973 (SI 1972/1977)
(6)	Substituted by Merchant Shipping Act 1988, s 57(4), Sch 6 (qv); repealed by Merchant Shipping (Registration, etc) Act 1993, s 8(4), Sch 5, Pt II, as from 1 May 1994 (qv)
96–99	1 Jan 1973 (SI 1972/1977)
100	See Schs 3–5 below
101	1 Jan 1973 (SI 1972/1977)
Sch 1	18 Nov 1974 (SI 1974/1908)
2, Pt I, para 1	1 Jan 1973 (SI 1972/1977)
2	Repealed
3–5	*Not in force*
II	1 Jan 1973 (SI 1972/1977)
3, para 1	Repealed
2–4	1 Jan 1973 (SI 1972/1977)
5–7	1 Sep 1981 (SI 1981/1186)
8	Repealed

Merchant Shipping Act 1970 (c 36)—*cont*

Sch 3, para 9	1 Jan 1973 (SI 1972/1977)
10	18 Nov 1974 (SI 1974/1908)
11–13	1 Jan 1973 (SI 1972/1977)
14	6 Apr 1974 (SI 1972/1977)
4, para 1–4	1 Jan 1973 (SI 1972/1977)
5–7	*Not in force*
8	1 Jan 1983 (so far as applies to an inquiry) (SI 1982/ 1617)
	1 Jul 1983 (otherwise) (SI 1982/1617)
9	1 Sep 1981 (SI 1981/1186)
10	*Not in force*
5	1 Jan 1973 (so far as relates to the following repeals:

    (i) Merchant Shipping Act 1894, in Pt I, s 85(3), the words 'in the ship's official log book, and also', in Pt II, ss 105–109, 113–125, 127–156, 159–199, 201–206, 211–255, 257–266, in Pt III, ss 268–270, 271(3), 289–355, 356, para (a), 357, 358, 359(2), 360(1), (2), 361, 362, in s 363, the words 'or emigrant ship', ss 364, 365 in Pt IV, in s 370 in the definition of 'fishing boat', the words from 'but' to 'profit', ss 376–384, 387, 388, 391–412, Pt V, ss 423, 425, 426, 436(3), in s 458(1), the words from 'and in every' to 'on board any ship', in s 463, the words 'or apprentice' wherever they occur, in Pt VI, s 477, in s 487(3) the words from 'by the local marine board' to 'board', and s 491, in Pt VIII, s 507, in Pt XIII, s 690, in Pt XIV, in s 714 the words 'local marine boards and', s 725, in s 745(1)(b), the words 'savings bank or', and Schs 7 and 8

    (ii) Merchant Shipping Act 1906, ss 9, 12, 14, in s 16(1) the words 'whether cabin or steerage passengers', ss 17–20, 23–26, 28–43, in s 44, in para (a) of sub-s (1), the words 'in the case of a foreign-going ship' and the words from 'before whom the offender is discharged' to 'at which the crew are discharged', in para (b) of sub-s (1), the words 'by whose sanction he is discharged' and in para (b) of sub-s (2), the words from 'before whom the crew is discharged' to 'the port at which the crew is discharged', ss 45–48, 57, 59–63, 65, 74, 82(1) and Sch 1

    (iii) Merchant Shipping (Seamen's Allotment) Act 1911

    (iv) Fees (Increase) Act 1923, s 2(1)(c)

    (v) Merchant Shipping Acts (Amendment) Act 1923

    (vi) Illegal Trawling (Scotland) Act 1934, in s 6 the words 'mercantile marine office'

    (vii) Merchant Shipping (Superannuation Contributions) Act 1937

    (viii) Sea Fish Industry Act 1938, Pt IV

    (ix) Emergency Laws (Transitional Provisions) Act 1946, in Sch 2, the entry relating to the Merchant Shipping Act 1894

Merchant Shipping Act 1970 (c 36)—*cont*
Sch 5—*cont*

(x) Emergency Laws (Miscellaneous Provisions) Act 1947, s 2(2)

(xi) Merchant Shipping Act 1948, s 7

(xii) Consular Conventions Act 1949, s 5(1)

(xiii) Merchant Shipping (Safety Conventions) Act 1949, ss 2(3), 18(5), 19(1)(d), 22(6), (7)

(xiv) Merchant Shipping Act 1950, s 2 and Sch 2

(xv) Births and Deaths Registration Act 1953, s 13(3)

(xvi) Emergency Laws (Miscellaneous Provisions) Act 1953, s 4

(xvii) Contracts of Employment Act 1963, s 6(2)(b)

(xviii) Contracts of Employment and Redundancy Payments Act (Northern Ireland) 1965, s 6(1)(b)

(xix) Administration of Estates (Small Payments) Act 1965, in Sch 1, Pt I, the entry relating to the Merchant Shipping Act 1894

(xx) Ministry of Social Security Act 1966, ss 37, 38(c) and the word 'and' preceding that paragraph, Sch 5 and Sch 6, paras 1, 2

(xxi) Supplementary Benefits &c. Act (Northern Ireland) 1966, s 41 and Sch 4

(xxii) Births and Deaths Registration Act (Northern Ireland) 1967, s 28(5)

(xxiii) Merchant Shipping (Load Lines) Act 1967, in s 10(1), para (b) and the word 'and' immediately preceding that paragraph, and in sub-s (2), para (a)

(xxiv) Children and Young Persons Act (Northern Ireland) 1968, Sch 7, paras 1, 2

(xxv) Post Office Act 1969, in Sch 6, Pt III the entry relating to the Merchant Shipping Act 1894, s 141) (SI 1972/1977)

6 Apr 1974 (repeal of Income and Corporation Taxes Act 1970, s 414(1)(c) and the word 'or' before it, and the definition of 'seamen's savings bank' in s 414(7)) (SI 1972/1977)

1 Oct 1974 (repeal of Merchant Shipping Act 1894, s 200) (SI 1974/1194)

18 Nov 1974 (repeal in Merchant Shipping (Safety Convention) Act 1949, s 5(2)) (SI 1974/1908)

1 Jul 1979 (repeals of Merchant Shipping Act 1948, ss 1–4; Merchant Shipping Act 1950, s 1, Sch 1; Merchant Shipping Act 1952) (SI 1978/797)

1 Aug 1979 (repeals of Merchant Shipping Act 1894, ss 157, 158; Merchant Shipping (International Labour Conventions) Act 1925, s 1, Sch 1, Pt I) (SI 1979/809)

1 Sep 1981 (so far as relates to the following repeals:

(i) Merchant Shipping Act 1894, in Pt II, ss 92, 93, 96–104, 209, except so far as those sections apply in relation to:

Merchant Shipping Act 1970 (c 36)—*cont*
Sch 5—*cont*

(a) fishing vessels by virtue of s 414 of that Act; or

(b) British ships registered outside the United Kingdom

(ii) Merchant Shipping Act 1906, in Pt III, s 27 and in Pt V, ss 56 and 64, except to the extent that ss 27 and 56 apply in relation to British ships registered outside the United Kingdom

(iii) Merchant Shipping (Certificates) Act 1914

(iv) Merchant Shipping Act 1948, ss 6, 8–12

(v) Merchant Shipping Act 1950, s 6

(vi) Merchant Shipping Act 1967, the whole Act except so far as s 92(2) of the 1894 Act, as amended, applies in relation to British ships registered outside the United Kingdom) (SI 1981/1186)

16 Jul 1982 (repeal of Merchant Shipping Act 1894, ss 92, 93, 96–104, 209—all so far as apply in relation to British ships registered in the Channel Islands or the Isle of Man) (SI 1982/840)

1 Jan 1983 (so far as relates to the following repeals except in relation to fishing vessels:

(i) Merchant Shipping Act 1894, in Pt VI, ss 470 (so far as applies in relation to an inquiry), 471, 472, 473, 474 (so far as ss 473, 474 apply in relation to a certificate cancelled or suspended under s 470 (so far as now repealed)), 475 and 479 (so far as ss 475, 479 apply in relation to an inquiry into the conduct of a master, mate or engineer under Pt VI of the Act of 1894)

(ii) Merchant Shipping Act 1906, in Pt V, ss 66 (so far as applies in relation to an inquiry under Part VI of the Merchant Shipping Act 1894), 67 and 68

(iii) Merchant Shipping Act 1950, s 3) (SI 1982/1617)

1 Jul 1983 (so far as relates to the following repeals except in relation to fishing vessels:

(i) Merchant Shipping Act 1894, in Pt VI, ss 464–467, 470 (so far as s 470 applies in relation to a formal investigation) 473, 474 (so far as ss 473, 474 apply in relation to a certificate cancelled or suspended under s 470 so far as it related to formal investigations) 475, s 479 (so far as ss 475, 479 apply in relation to a formal investigation into the conduct of a master, mate or engineer under Pt VI of the Act of 1894) and 476

(ii) the Merchant Shipping Act 1906, in Pt V, s 66 (so far as applies in relation to a formal investigation under Pt VI of the Merchant Shipping Act 1894)) (SI 1982/1617)

Merchant Shipping Act 1970 (c 36)—*cont*

Sch 5—*cont* 1 Jan 1987 (repeal of Merchant Shipping Act 1894,
ss 369, 385, 386, 390, 413, 415–417) (SI 1986/2066)
1 Sep 1987 (repeals of or in Merchant Shipping Act
1894, ss 92, 93, 96–104 so far as they apply to fishing
vessels by virtue of s 414 of the 1894 Act, s 209 so far
as applies to fishing vessels, s 370 (definitions of
'second hand' and 'voyage'), 371, 414, ss 464–468,
470–476, 479 so far as unrepealed; Merchant
Shipping Act 1906, ss 66–68 so far as unrepealed,
81) (SI 1986/2066)
Not in force (remaining repeals or purposes)

National Health Service Contributions Act 1970 (c 16)

Whole Act repealed

National Insurance (Old persons' and widows' pensions and attendance allowance) Act 1970 (c 51)

Whole Act repealed

New Forest Act 1970 (c 21)

Local application only

Parish Councils and Burial Authorities (Miscellaneous Provisions) Act 1970 (c 29)

RA: 29 May 1970

29 May 1970 (RA)

Proceedings Against Estates Act 1970 (c 17)

Whole Act repealed

Radiological Protection Act 1970 (c 46)

RA: 29 May 1970

Commencement provisions: s 7(2); Radiological Protection Act 1970
(Commencement) Order 1970, SI 1970/1330

1 Oct 1970 (SI 1970/1330)

Republic of The Gambia Act 1970 (c 37)

RA: 29 May 1970

29 May 1970 (RA; note that by s 1(3), s 1 was deemed to have effect from 24 April
1970, the day The Gambia became a republic)

Riding Establishments Act 1970 (c 32)

RA: 29 May 1970

Commencement provisions: s 8(3)

1 Jan 1971 (s 8(3))

Road Traffic (Disqualification) Act 1970 (c 23)

Whole Act repealed

Roads (Scotland) Act 1970 (c 20)

Whole Act repealed

Rural Water Supplies and Sewerage (Scotland) Act 1970 (c 6)

RA: 26 Feb 1970

26 Feb 1970 (RA)

Sea Fish Industry Act 1970 (c 11)

RA: 12 Mar 1970

Commencement provisions: s 62(2)

Whole Act repealed except ss 14, 42, 62 which came into force on 12 May 1970 (s 62(2))

Sharing of Church Buildings Measure 1970 (No 2)

RA: 24 Mar 1970

24 Mar 1970 (RA)

Taxes Management Act 1970 (c 9)

RA: 12 Mar 1970

Commencement provisions: s 119(1)

6 Apr 1970 (s 119(1))

Tonga Act 1970 (c 22)

RA: 15 May 1970

Independence Day: 4 Jun 1970

Town and Country Planning Regulations (London) (Indemnity) Act 1970 (c 57)

Whole Act repealed

Trees Act 1970 (c 43)

RA: 29 May 1970

29 May 1970 (RA)

Valuation for Rating (Scotland) Act 1970 (c 4)

RA: 26 Feb 1970

26 Feb 1970 (RA)

1971

Administration of Estates Act 1971 (c 25)

RA: 12 May 1971

Commencement provisions: s 14(2)

s 1–7	1 Jan 1972 (s 14(2))
8	Repealed
9–12	1 Jan 1972 (s 14(2))
13	Repealed
14	12 May 1971 (s 14(2))
Sch 1, 2	1 Jan 1972 (s 14(2))

Air Corporations Acts 1971 (c 5)

Whole Act repealed

Anguilla Act 1971 (c 63)

Whole Act repealed

Animals Act 1971 (c 22)

RA: 12 May 1971

Commencement provisions: s 13(3)

1 Oct 1971 (s 13(3))

Appropriation Act 1971 (c 67)

Whole Act repealed

Armed Forces Act 1971 (c 33)

RA: 27 May 1971

Commencement provisions: s 78(3); Armed Forces Act 1971 (Commencement) Order 1972, SI 1972/359

s 1	Repealed
2–77	1 Jul 1972 (SI 1972/359)
78	27 May 1971 (RA)
Sch 1–4	1 Jul 1972 (SI 1972/359)

Atomic Energy Authority Act 1971 (c 11)

RA: 16 Mar 1971

16 Mar 1971 (RA)

Attachment of Earnings Act 1971 (c 32)

RA: 12 May 1971

Commencement provisions: s 29(4)★; Administration of Justice Act 1970
(Commencement No 4) Order 1971, SI 1971/834 (made under Administration of
Justice Act 1970, s 54)

2 Aug 1971 (SI 1971/834)

★ s 29(4) provides that this Act is to come into force on the day appointed under
Administration of Justice Act 1970, s 54, for the coming into force of Pt II of that
Act

Banking and Financial Dealings Act 1971 (c 80)

RA: 16 Dec 1971

Commencement provisions: s 3(3)

s 1, 2	16 Dec 1971 (RA)
3	16 Jan 1972 (s 3(3))
4, 5	16 Dec 1971 (RA)
Sch 1, 2	16 Dec 1971 (RA)

Betting, Gaming and Lotteries (Amendment) Act 1971 (c 26)

Whole Act repealed

Carriage of Goods by Sea Act 1971 (c 19)

RA: 8 Apr 1971

Commencement provisions: s 6(5); Carriage of Goods by Sea Act 1971
(Commencement) Order 1977, SI 1977/981

23 Jun 1977 (SI 1977/981)

Civil Aviation Act 1971 (c 75)

Whole Act repealed

Civil Aviation (Declaratory Provisions) Act 1971 (c 6)

Whole Act repealed

Coal Industry Act 1971 (c 16)

RA: 30 Mar 1971

30 Mar 1971 (RA)

Coinage Act 1971 (c 24)

RA: 12 May 1971

Commencement provisions: s 14(2)

1 Sep 1971 (s 14(2))

Consolidated Fund Act 1971 (c 1)

Whole Act repealed

Consolidated Fund (No 2) Act 1971 (c 14)

Whole Act repealed

Consolidated Fund (No 3) Act 1971 (c 79)

Whole Act repealed

Consumer Protection Act 1971 (c 15)

Whole Act repealed

Copyright (Amendment) Act 1971 (c 4)

Whole Act repealed

Courts Act 1971 (c 23)

RA: 12 May 1971

Commencement provisions: s 59(2); Courts Act 1971 (Commencement) Order 1971, SI 1971/1151

s 1–15	Repealed
16–22	1 Jan 1972 (SI 1971/1151)
23	Repealed
24	Substituted by Supreme Court Act 1981, s 146 (qv)
25, 26	Repealed
27–30	1 Jan 1972 (SI 1971/1151)
31–40	Repealed
41–44	1 Jan 1972 (SI 1971/1151)
45–50	Repealed
51, 52	1 Jan 1972 (SI 1971/1151)
53	Spent
54, 55	1 Jan 1972 (SI 1971/1151)

Courts Act 1971 (c 23)—*cont*
s 56(1)–(3)	1 Jan 1972 (SI 1972/1151)
(4)	See Sch 11 below
57	1 Jan 1972 (SI 1971/1151)
58	Repealed
59	1 Oct 1971 (SI 1971/1151)
Sch 1	Repealed
2, 3	1 Jan 1972 (SI 1971/1151)
4	Repealed
5–10	1 Jan 1972 (SI 1971/1151)
11, Pt I	1 Oct 1971 (repeal of County Courts Act 1959, s 96(3)) (SI 1971/1151)
	1 Jan 1972 (remainder) (SI 1971/1151)
II, III	1 Jan 1972 (SI 1971/1151)
IV	1 Oct 1971 (repeal of Magistrates' Courts Act 1952, s 1(4); Criminal Appeal Act 1966, s 1(3)) (SI 1971/1151)
	1 Jan 1972 (remainder) (SI 1971/1151)

Criminal Damage Act 1971 (c 48)

RA: 14 Jul 1971

Commencement provisions: s 12(1)

14 Oct 1971 (s 12(1))

Dangerous Litter Act 1971 (c 35)

Whole Act repealed

Diplomatic and other Privileges Act 1971 (c 64)

RA: 27 Jul 1971

Commencement provisions: s 4(2); Commonwealth Countries and Republic of Ireland (Immunities and Privileges) Order 1971, SI 1971/1237★

s 1	27 Jul 1971 (RA)
2	Repealed
3	27 Jul 1971 (RA)
4(1)	27 Jul 1971 (RA)
(2)	1 Sep 1971 (SI 1971/1237)★
Schedule	27 Jul 1971 (RA)

★ SI 1971/1237 was made under Consular Relations Act 1968, s 12, as inserted by the Schedule to this Act

---

Education (Milk) Act 1971 (c 74)

Whole Act repealed

Education (Scotland) Act 1971 (c 42)

Whole Act repealed

Finance Act 1971 (c 68)

RA: 5 Aug 1971

See the note concerning Finance Acts at the front of this book

---

Fire Precautions Act 1971 (c 40)

RA: 27 May 1971

Commencement provisions: s 44(3); Fire Precautions Act 1971 (Commencement No 1) Order 1972, SI 1972/236; Fire Precautions Act 1971 (Commencement No 2) Order 1976, SI 1976/2006

s 1, 2	20 Mar 1972 (SI 1972/236)
3, 4	*Not in force*
5	20 Mar 1972 (SI 1972/236)
5A, 5B	Inserted by Fire Safety and Safety of Places of Sport Act 1987, s 1(4) (qv)
6–8	20 Mar 1972 (SI 1972/236)
8A	Inserted by Fire Safety and Safety of Places of Sport Act 1987, s 2(1) (qv)
8B	Inserted by Fire Safety and Safety of Places of Sport Act 1987, s 3 (qv)
9	20 Mar 1972 (SI 1972/236)
9A	Inserted by Health and Safety at Work etc Act 1974, s 78 (qv); substituted by Fire Safety and Safety of Places of Sport Act 1987, s 5 (qv)
9B, 9C	Inserted by Fire Safety and Safety of Places of Sport Act 1987, s 6 (qv)
9D–9F	Inserted by Fire Safety and Safety of Places of Sport Act 1987, s 7(1) (qv)
10	Substituted by Fire Safety and Safety of Places of Sport Act 1987, s 9(1) (qv)
10A, 10B	Inserted by Fire Safety and Safety of Places of Sport Act 1987, s 9(2) (qv)
11	Repealed
12(1)	1 Jan 1977 (SI 1976/2006)
(2)	*Not in force*
(3)–(8)	1 Jan 1977 (SI 1976/2006)
(9)	*Not in force*
(10)	1 Jan 1977 (SI 1976/2006)
(11)	*Not in force*
(12)	Repealed
13, 14	20 Mar 1972 (SI 1972/236)
15	Repealed
16(1)(a)	20 Mar 1972 (SI 1972/236)
(b)	*Not in force*

Fire Precautions Act 1971 (c 40)—*cont*

s 16(2)(a)	20 Mar 1972 (SI 1972/236)
(b)	*Not in force*
(3)	20 Mar 1972 (SI 1972/236)
17, 18	20 Mar 1972 (SI 1972/236)
19(1), (2)	20 Mar 1972 (SI 1972/236)
(3)(a),(b)	20 Mar 1972 (SI 1972/236)
(c)	*Not in force*
(d)	20 Mar 1972 (SI 1972/236)
(4)–(6)	20 Mar 1972 (SI 1972/236)
20–27	20 Mar 1972 (SI 1972/236)
27A	Inserted by Fire Safety and Safety of Places of Sport Act 1987, s 12(1) (qv)
28	1 Jan 1977 (SI 1976/2006)
28A	Inserted by Fire Safety and Safety of Places of Sport Act 1987, s 16(1), (2), Sch 1 (qv)
29–33	20 Mar 1972 (SI 1972/236)
34	*Not in force*
35	20 Mar 1972 (SI 1972/236)
36	*Not in force*
37–39	20 Mar 1972 (SI 1972/236)
40	20 Mar 1972 (except so far as relates to ss 3, 4, 12) (SI 1972/236)
	1 Jan 1977 (otherwise, except so far as relates to ss 3, 4, 12(2), (9)) (SI 1976/2006)
	Not in force (so far as relates to ss 3, 4, 12(2), (9))
41	20 Mar 1972 (SI 1972/236)
42	Repealed
43, 44	20 Mar 1972 (SI 1972/236)
Sch 1 Pt I, II	Repealed
III	*Not in force*
IV	Inserted by Housing (Financial Provisions) (Scotland) Act 1972, Sch 9, para 31(4) (qv)
2	Inserted by Fire Safety and Safety of Places of Sport Act 1987, s 16(2), Sch 1 (qv)

Friendly Societies Act 1971 (c 66)

RA: 27 Jul 1971

Commencement provisions: s 15(6); Friendly Societies Act 1971 (Commencement) Order 1971, SI 1971/1899

Whole Act repealed except ss 11(5), 15(4), (5), which came into force as follows:

11, 14, 31 Dec 1971 (SI 1971/1899)

Guardianship of Minors Act 1971 (c 3)

Whole Act repealed

Highways Act 1971 (c 41)

Whole Act repealed

Hijacking Act 1971 (c 70)

Whole Act repealed

Hospital Endowments (Scotland) Act 1971 (c 8)

Whole Act repealed

Housing Act 1971 (c 76)

Whole Act repealed

Hydrocarbon Oil (Customs and Excise) Act 1971 (c 12)

Whole Act repealed

Immigration Act 1971 (c 77)

RA: 28 Oct 1971

Commencement provisions: ss 34(1), 35(1)–(3); Immigration Act 1971
(Commencement) Order 1972, SI 1972/1514

s 1	1 Jan 1973 (SI 1972/1514)
2	Substituted by British Nationality Act 1981, s 39(2) (qv)
3–24	1 Jan 1973 (SI 1972/1514)
25(1)	28 Nov 1971 (s 35(2))
(2)	1 Jan 1973 (SI 1972/1514)
(3)–(8)	28 Nov 1971 (s 35(2))
26, 27	1 Jan 1973 (SI 1972/1514)
28(1), (2)	28 Oct 1971 (so far as relates to Commonwealth Immigrants Act 1962, s 4A) (s 35(3))
	28 Nov 1971 (so far as relates to s 25(1) of this Act) (s 35(2))
	1 Jan 1973 (otherwise) (SI 1972/1514)
(3), (4)	1 Jan 1973 (SI 1972/1514)
29	28 Oct 1971 (RA)
30	Repealed
31–37	28 Oct 1971 (RA)
Sch 1	Repealed
2–5	1 Jan 1973 (SI 1972/1514)
6	28 Oct 1971 (s 34(1))

Industrial Relations Act 1971 (c 72)

Whole Act repealed

Industry Act 1971 (c 17)

Whole Act repealed

Interest on Damages (Scotland) Act 1971 (c 31)

RA: 12 May 1971

12 May 1971 (RA)

Investment and Building Grants Act 1971 (c 51)

Whole Act repealed

Land Commission (Dissolution) Act 1971 (c 18)

RA: 8 Apr 1971

Commencement provisions: s 1(2); Land Commission (Dissolution) (Appointed Day)
    Order 1971, SI 1971/670

s 1–7	8 Apr 1971 (RA)
Sch 1, Pt I, II	8 Apr 1971 (RA)
III	1 May 1971 (SI 1971/670)
2	8 Apr 1971 (RA)
3, Pt I	8 Apr 1971 (RA)
II	1 May 1971 (SI 1971/670)

Land Registration and Land Charges Act 1971 (c 54)

RA: 27 Jul 1971

Commencement provisions: s 15(5); Land Registration and Land Charges Act 1971
    (Commencement No 1) Order 1971, SI 1971/1489

s 1, 2	1 Oct 1971 (SI 1971/1489)
3, 4	27 Jul 1971 (s 15(5))
5–11	Repealed
12, 13	27 Jul 1971 (s 15(5))
14(1)	27 Jul 1971 (s 15(5))
(2)(a)	27 Jul 1971 (s 15(5))
(b)	See Sch 2, Pt II below
15	27 Jul 1971 (s 15(5))
Sch 1	Repealed
2, Pt I	27 Jul 1971 (s 15(5))
II	1 Oct 1971 (except provisions specified below) (SI 1971/1489)
	2 Oct 1972 (so far as relates to Land Registration Act 1925, s 85(5)) (SI 1971/1489)
	Not in force (so far as it relates to Land Charges Act 1925, ss 16, 17(4) repealed))

Law Reform (Jurisdiction in Delict) (Scotland) Act 1971 (c 55)

Whole Act repealed

Law Reform (Miscellaneous Provisions) Act 1971 (c 43)

RA: 1 Jul 1971

Commencement provisions: s 6(2)

Whole Act repealed (subject to a saving in the case of s 5(2)) except s 6 which came into force on 1 Aug 1971 (s 6(2))

Licensing (Abolition of State Management) Act 1971 (c 65)

Whole Act repealed

Local Authorities (Qualification of Members) Act 1971 (c 7)

Whole Act repealed

Medicines Act 1971 (c 69)

RA: 5 Aug 1971

5 Aug 1971 (RA)

Merchant Shipping (Oil Pollution) Act 1971 (c 59)

RA: 27 Jul 1971

Commencement provisions: s 21(3); Merchant Shipping (Oil Pollution) Act 1971 (Commencement) Order 1971, SI 1971/1423; Merchant Shipping (Oil Pollution) Act 1971 (Commencement No 2) Order 1975, SI 1975/867

s 1(1)	9 Sep 1971 (SI 1971/1423)
(2)	19 Jun 1975 (SI 1975/867)
(3)–(5)	9 Sep 1971 (SI 1971/1423)
2, 3	9 Sep 1971 (SI 1971/1423)
4–8	19 Jun 1975 (SI 1975/867)
8A	Repealed
9	9 Sep 1971 (SI 1971/1423)
10–12	19 Jun 1975 (SI 1975/867)
13(1)	9 Sep 1971 (SI 1971/1423)
(2)	19 Jun 1975 (SI 1975/867)
(3)	19 Jun 1975 (SI 1975/867)
14(1)	9 Sep 1971 (SI 1971/1423)
(2), (3)	19 Jun 1975 (SI 1975/867)
15–17	9 Sep 1971 (SI 1971/1423)
18	Repealed by Merchant Shipping (Registration, etc) Act 1993, s 8(4), Sch 5, Pt II, as from 1 May 1994 (qv)
19	19 Jun 1975 (SI 1975/867)
20	9 Sep 1971 (SI 1971/1423)
21	9 Sep 1971 (SI 1971/1423)

Mineral Workings Act 1971 (c 71)

Whole Act repealed

Mineral Workings (Offshore Installations) Act 1971 (c 61)

RA: 27 Jul 1971

Commencement provisions: s 14(2); Mineral Workings (Offshore Installations) Act 1971 (Commencement) Order 1972, SI 1972/644

s 1	Substituted by Oil and Gas (Enterprise) Act 1982, s 24 (qv)
2	Repealed
3	1 May 1972 (SI 1972/644)
4, 5	31 Aug 1972 (SI 1972/644)
6	Repealed
7	1 May 1972 (SI 1972/644)
8	Repealed
9	1 May 1972 (SI 1972/644)
10	Repealed
11–14	1 May 1972 (SI 1972/644)
Schedule	Repealed

Mines Management Act 1971 (c 20)

Whole Act Repealed

Misuse of Drugs Act 1971 (c 38)

RA: 27 May 1971

Commencement provisions: s 40(3); Misuse of Drugs Act 1971 (Commencement No 1) Order 1971, SI 1971/2120; Misuse of Drugs Act 1971 (Commencement No 2) Order 1973, SI 1973/795

s 1	1 Feb 1972 (SI 1971/2120)
2–9	1 Jul 1973 (SI 1973/795)
9A	Inserted by Drug Trafficking Offences Act 1986, s 34 (qv)
10–23	1 Jul 1973 (SI 1973/795)
24	1 Jul 1973 (SI 1973/795); repealed (EW)
25	1 Jul 1973 (SI 1973/795)
26	Repealed
27–31	1 Jul 1973 (SI 1973/795)
32	1 Feb 1972 (SI 1971/2120)
33, 34	Repealed
35	1 Feb 1972 (SI 1971/2120)
36	1 Jul 1973 (SI 1973/795)
37, 38	1 Feb 1972 (SI 1971/2120)
39	1 Jul 1973 (SI 1973/795)
40	1 Feb 1972 (SI 1971/2120)
Sch 1	1 Feb 1972 (SI 1971/2120)
2–5	1 Jul 1973 (SI 1973/795)

Motor Vehicles (Passenger Insurance) Act 1971 (c 36)

Whole Act repealed

Mr Speaker King's Retirement Act 1971 (c 13)

Limited application only

National Insurance Act 1971 (c 50)

Whole Act repealed

National Savings Bank Act 1971 (c 29)

RA: 12 May 1971

Commencement provisions: s 29(2)

12 Jun 1971 (s 29(2))

New Towns Act 1971 (c 81)

Whole Act repealed

Nullity of Marriage Act 1971 (c 44)

Whole Act repealed

Oil in Navigable Waters Act 1971 (c 21)

Whole Act repealed

Pensions (Increase) Act 1971 (c 56)

RA: 27 Jul 1971

27 Jul 1971 (RA)

Pool Competitions Act 1971 (c 57)

Whole Act expired

Powers of Attorney Act 1971 (c 27)

RA: 12 May 1971

Commencement provisions: s 11(4)

1 Oct 1971 (s 11(4))

Prevention of Oil Pollution Act 1971 (c 60)

RA: 27 Jul 1971

Commencement provisions: s 34(2); Prevention of Oil Pollution Act 1971 (Commencement) Order 1973, SI 1973/203

1 Mar 1973 (SI 1973/203)

Rating Act 1971 (c 39)

RA: 27 May 1971

Whole Act repealed in relation to financial years beginning in or after 1990, by the Local Government Finance Act 1988, s 149, Sch 13, Pt I (qv)

27 May 1971 (RA)

Recognition of Divorces and Legal Separations Act 1971 (c 53)

Whole Act repealed

Redemption of Standard Securities (Scotland) Act 1971 (c 45)

RA: 1 Jul 1971

1 Jul 1971 (RA)

Rent (Scotland) Act 1971 (c 28)

RA: 12 May 1971

Whole Act repealed except Sch 18, Pt II, which came into force on 12 Aug 1971 (s 136(2) (repealed))

Rolls-Royce (Purchase) Act 1971 (c 9)

Whole Act repealed

Rural Water Supplies and Sewerage Act 1971 (c 49)

Whole Act repealed

Sheriff Courts (Scotland) Act 1971 (c 58)

RA: 27 Jul 1971

Commencement provisions: s 47(2); Sheriff Courts (Scotland) Act 1971 (Commencement No 1) Order 1971, SI 1971/1582; Sheriff Courts (Scotland) Act 1971 (Commencement No 2) Order 1973, SI 1973/276; Sheriff Courts (Scotland) Act 1971 (Commencement No 3) Order 1976, SI 1976/236

s 1–20	1 Nov 1971 (SI 1971/1582)
21	Repealed

Sheriff Courts (Scotland) Act 1971 (c 58)—*cont*

s 22	1 Nov 1971 (SI 1971/1582)
23–30	1 Apr 1973 (SI 1973/276)
31	1 Sept 1976 (SI 1976/236)
32–34	1 Nov 1971 (SI 1971/1582)
35, 36	1 Sept 1976 (SI 1976/236)
36A, 36B	Inserted by Law Reform (Miscellaneous Provisions) (Scotland) Act 1985, s 18(2) (qv)
37, 38	1 Sept 1976 (SI 1976/236)
39, 40	Repealed
41, 42	1 Sept 1976 (SI 1976/236)
43	1 Nov 1971 (SI 1971/1582)
44(1), (2)	1 Nov 1971 (SI 1971/1582)
(3)	1 Apr 1973 (SI 1973/276)
45–47	1 Nov 1971 (SI 1971/1582)
Sch 1, para 1	1 Nov 1971 (SI 1971/1582)
2, 3	1 Sept 1976 (SI 1976/236)
4	Repealed
2, Pt I	1 Nov 1971 (repeals of or in Sheriffs of Edinburgh and Lanark Act 1822; Sheriff Courts (Scotland) Act 1907, ss 12, 13, 15, 16, 18, 19, 21, 25, 26; Sheriff Courts and Legal Officers (Scotland) Act 1927, s 14; Administration of Justice (Scotland) Act 1933, ss 31(2)–(5), 32, 34, 35; Sheriff Courts (Scotland) Act 1939; Administration of Justice (Scotland) Act 1948, s 4) (SI 1971/1582) 1 April 1973 (otherwise) (SI 1973/276)
Pt II	1 Sept 1976 (SI 1976/236)

Shipbuilding Industry Act 1971 (c 46)

Whole Act repealed

Social Security Act 1971 (c 73)

Whole Act repealed

Statute Law (Repeals) Act 1971 (c 52)

RA: 27 Jul 1971

27 Jul 1971 (RA)

Teaching Council (Scotland) Act 1971 (c 2)

RA: 17 Feb 1971

Commencement provisions: s 5(2); Social Work (Scotland) Act 1968 (Commencement No 5) Order 1971, SI 1971/184

17 Feb 1971 (s 5(2)), except Schedule, para 2, which came into force on 15 Apr 1971 (SI 1971/184 (made under Social Work (Scotland) Act 1968, s 98))

Town and Country Planning Act 1971 (c 78)

Whole Act repealed

Tribunals and Inquiries Act 1971 (c 62)

Whole Act repealed

Unsolicited Goods and Services Act 1971 (c 30)

RA: 12 May 1971

Commencement provisions: s 7(2)

12 Aug 1971 (s 7(2))

Vehicles (Excise) Act 1971 (c 10)

RA: 16 Mar 1971

Commencement provisions: s 40(2); Vehicle and Driving Licences (Transfer of Functions) (Appointed Date) Order 1971, SI 1971/377

s 1–18	1 Apr 1971 (SI 1971/377)
18A	Inserted by Finance Act 1982, s 7(1) (qv)
18B	Prospectively inserted by Finance Act 1991, s 9(2) (qv)
19–26	1 Apr 1971 (SI 1971/377)
26A	Inserted by Finance Act 1989, s 14(1) (qv)
27, 28	1 Apr 1971 (SI 1971/377)
28A	Inserted by Finance Act 1991, s 10, Sch 3, para 13 (qv)
29–38	1 Apr 1971 (SI 1971/377)
39(1)	1 Apr 1971 (SI 1971/377)
(2), (3)	16 Mar 1971 (RA)
(4)–(6)	1 Apr 1971 (SI 1971/377)
40	16 Mar 1971 (RA)
Sch 1–3	1 Apr 1971 (SI 1971/377)
4	Substituted by Finance Act 1982, s 5(4), Sch 5, Pt A (qv)
4A	Inserted by Finance Act 1988, s 4(7), Sch 2, Pt II, para 5 (qv)
5	1 Apr 1971 (SI 1971/377)
6	Repealed
7, 8	1 Apr 1971 (SI 1971/377)

Water Resources Act 1971 (c 34)

Whole Act repealed (For savings, see Water Act 1989, s 190(2), (3), Sch 26, Pt VII, para 41, Sch 27, Pt I)

Welsh National Opera Company Act 1971 (c 37)

RA: 27 May 1971

27 May 1971 (RA)

Wild Creatures and Forest Laws Act 1971 (c 47)

RA: 1 Jul 1971

1 Jul 1971 (RA)

1972

Administration of Justice (Scotland) Act 1972 (c 59)

RA: 9 Aug 1972

Commencement provisions: s 5(3); Administration of Justice (Scotland) Act 1972 (Commencement) Order 1973, SI 1973/339

s 1	2 Apr 1973 (SI 1973/339)
2	Repealed
3	2 Apr 1973 (SI 1973/339)
4, 5	9 Aug 1972 (RA)

Admission to Holy Communion Measure 1972 (No 1)

RA: 10 Feb 1972

10 Feb 1972 (RA)

Affiliation Proceedings (Amendment) Act 1972 (c 49)

Whole Act repealed

Agriculture (Miscellaneous Provisions) Act 1972 (c 62)

RA: 9 Aug 1972

Commencement provisions: s 27(2), (3); Agriculture (Miscellaneous Provisions) Act 1972 (Commencement) Order 1972, SI 1972/1260

s 1–3	Repealed
4	9 Aug 1972 (RA)
5–7	Repealed
8–12	9 Aug 1972 (RA)
13	Repealed
14	9 Aug 1972 (RA)
15	Repealed
16, 17	9 Aug 1972 (RA)
18	15 Aug 1972 (SI 1972/1260); repealed (EW)
19–25	9 Aug 1972 (RA)
26(1), (2)	9 Aug 1972 (RA)
(3)	See Sch 6 below
(4)	9 Aug 1972 (RA)
27	9 Aug 1972 (RA)
Sch 1–3	Repealed
4, 5	9 Aug 1972 (RA)
6	9 Aug 1972 (except repeals of or in Agriculture Act 1947, ss 77, 78) (RA)

Agriculture (Miscellaneous Provisions) Act 1972 (c 62)—*cont*
Sch 6—*cont*   15 Aug 1972 (exception noted above) (SI 1972/1260)
                                     1 Jan 1974 (repeals of or in Slaughterhouses Act
                                         1954; Food and Drugs Act 1955, ss 65, 70(1),
                                         75–78; Slaughterhouses Act 1958; London
                                         Government Act 1963, s 54(2)) (s 27(2))

Airports Authority Act 1972 (c 8)

Whole Act repealed

Appropriation Act 1972 (c 56)

Whole Act repealed

Benefices Measure 1972 (No 3)

RA: 10 Feb 1972

10 Feb 1972 (RA)

Betting and Gaming Duties Act 1972 (c 25)

Whole Act repealed

British Library Act 1972 (c 54)

RA: 27 Jul 1972

27 Jul 1972 (RA)

Carriage by Railway Act 1972 (c 33)

Whole Act repealed

Children Act 1972 (c 44)

RA: 27 Jul 1972

27 Jul 1972 (RA)

Chronically Sick and Disabled Persons (Scotland) Act 1972 (c 51)

RA: 27 Jul 1972

27 Jul 1972 (RA)

Civil Evidence Act 1972 (c 30)

RA: 12 Jun 1972

Commencement provisions: s 6(3); Civil Evidence Act 1972 (Commencement No 1) Order 1974, SI 1974/280; Civil Evidence Act 1972 (Commencement No 2) Order 1974, SI 1974/1137

s 1	1 Jun 1974 (for purpose of proceedings other than in bankruptcy in the Supreme Court; proceedings before tribunals to which strict rules of evidence apply; arbitrations and references (other than references under County Courts Act 1959, s 92 (now County Courts Act 1984, s 64)) to which strict rules of evidence apply; applications and appeals arising from the above) (SI 1974/280)
	1 Sep 1974 (proceedings, other than in bankruptcy, in county courts) (SI 1974/1137)
	Not in force (otherwise)
2, 3	1 Jan 1973 (s 6(3))
4(1)	1 Jan 1973 (s 6(3))
(2)–(5)	See note to s 1 above
5, 6	1 Jan 1973 (s 6(3))

Civil List Act 1972 (c 7)

RA: 24 Feb 1972

Commencement provisions: s 8(5), (6)

s 1–3	Effective as respects payments for 1972 onwards (s 8(5))
4(1)	1 Apr 1972 (s 8(6))
(2)	24 Feb 1972 (RA)
5–7	24 Feb 1972 (RA)
8(1)–(3)	24 Feb 1972 (RA)
(4)	See Schedule below
(5), (6)	24 Feb 1972 (RA)
Schedule	24 Feb 1972 (except repeal of Civil List Act 1952, s 13(1)) (RA)
	1 Apr 1972 (exception noted above) (s 8(6))

Clergy Pensions (Amendment) Measure 1972 (No 5)

RA: 9 Aug 1972

9 Aug 1972 (RA)

Companies (Floating Charges and Receivers) (Scotland) Act 1972 (c 67)

Whole Act repealed

Consolidated Fund Act 1972 (c 13)

Whole Act repealed

Consolidated Fund (No 2) Act 1972 (c 23)

Whole Act repealed

Consolidated Fund (No 3) Act 1972 (c 78)

Whole Act repealed

Contracts of Employment Act 1972 (c 53)

Whole Act repealed

Counter-Inflation (Temporary Provisions) Act 1972 (c 74)

Whole Act repealed

Criminal Justice Act 1972 (c 71)

RA: 26 Oct 1972

Commencement provisions: s 66(6); Criminal Justice Act 1972 (Commencement No 1) Order 1972, SI 1972/1763; Criminal Justice Act 1972 (Commencement No 2) Order 1973, SI 1973/272; Criminal Justice Act 1972 (Commencement No 3) Order 1973, SI 1973/1472; Criminal Justice Act 1972 (Commencement No 4) Order 1973, SI 1973/1995; Criminal Justice Act 1972 (Commencement No 5) Order 1976, SI 1976/299

s 1–5	Repealed
6	1 Jan 1973 (SI 1972/1763)
7–23	Repealed
24(1), (2)	Repealed
(3)	1 Apr 1973 (SI 1973/272)
(4)	1 Apr 1973 (SI 1973/272) (EW); substituted (S) by Criminal Procedure (Scotland) Act 1975, Sch 9, para 48 (qv)
25–27	Repealed
28, 29	1 Jan 1973 (SI 1972/1763)
30	Repealed
31	1 Jan 1973 (SI 1972/1763)
32	Repealed
33	1 Jan 1973 (SI 1972/1763)
34	1 Apr 1976 (SI 1976/299)
35	Repealed
36	1 Oct 1973 (SI 1973/1472)
37–45	Repealed
46	1 Jan 1973 (SI 1972/1763)
47	Repealed
48	1 Jan 1973 (SI 1972/1763)
49	*Not in force*
50	Repealed
51	1 Jan 1973 (SI 1972/1763)
52–57	Repealed
58–60	1 Jan 1973 (SI 1972/1763)
61, 62	Repealed
63(1)	Repealed
(2)	1 Jan 1973 (SI 1972/1763)
(3)	Repealed

Criminal Justice Act 1972 (c 71)—*cont*
 s 64   See Schs 5, 6 below
 65, 66   1 Jan 1973 (SI 1972/1763)

Sch 1–4   Repealed
  5   1 Jan 1973 (amendments in Petty Sessions (Ireland)
           Act 1851; Incitement to Disaffection Act 1934;
           Dogs Amendment Act 1938; Prevention of Fraud
           (Investment) Act 1958; Criminal Justice Act 1967,
           ss 18(7), 67(1); Theft Act 1968; Children and
           Young Persons Act 1969, s 7(8); Immigration Act
           1971) (SI 1972/1763)
           1 Mar 1973 (amendment in Criminal Justice Act 1967,
           s 60(2)) (SI 1973/272)
           1 Apr 1973 (amendment in Road Traffic Act 1972,
           s 105(2)) (SI 1973/272)
           Repealed (otherwise)
  6   1 Jan 1973 (repeals of or in Forfeiture Act 1870;
           Summary Jurisdiction (Scotland) Act 1908;
           Protection of Animals Act 1911; Criminal Justice
           Act 1948; Costs in Criminal Cases Act 1952; Prison
           Act 1952; Magistrates' Courts Act 1952; First
           Offenders Act 1958; Criminal Justice Act 1961;
           Criminal Justice (Scotland) Act 1963;
           Administration of Justice Act 1964, s 22, Sch 3,
           para 19; Criminal Law Act 1967; Criminal Justice
           Act 1967, ss 39, 54; Firearms Act 1968; Theft Act
           1968; Children and Young Persons Act 1969;
           Administration of Justice Act 1970; Courts Act
           1971; Criminal Damage Act 1971) (SI 1972/1763)
           1 Mar 1973 (repeal in Criminal Justice Act 1967,
           s 60(2)) (SI 1973/272)
           1 Apr 1973 (repeals in Pt II so far as not already in
           force) (SI 1973/272)
           30 Mar 1974 (repeals in Pt I, except repeal of Aliens
           Restriction (Amendment) Act 1919, s 8) (SI 1973/
           1472)
           Not in force (otherwise; but note that many of the Acts
           in which repeals are made by this Act have been
           consolidated or otherwise superseded and those
           repeals will therefore never be brought into force)

Deaconesses and Lay Ministry Measure 1972 (No 4)

RA: 9 Aug 1972

9 Aug 1972 (RA)

Defective Premises Act 1972 (c 35)

RA: 29 Jun 1972

Commencement provisions: s 7(2)

1 Jan 1974 (s 7(2))

Deposit of Poisonous Waste Act 1972 (c 21)

Whole Act repealed

Electricity Act 1972 (c 17)

Whole Act repealed

Employment Medical Advisory Service Act 1972 (c 28)

RA: 22 May 1972

Commencement provisions: s 9(2); Employment Medical Advisory Service Act 1972 (Commencement) Order 1973, SI 1973/28

1 Feb 1973 (SI 1973/28)

European Communities Act 1972 (c 68)

RA: 17 Oct 1972

Commencement provisions: See Sch 3 below

This Act largely came into force on receiving Royal Assent on 17 Oct 1972 but for most purposes it did not have practical effect until 1 Jan 1973 (the date the UK joined the European Communities). The repeals effected by Sch 3 have effect or are to have effect from dates appointed or to be appointed as follows:

Sch 3, Pt I	1 Jan 1974 (repeal of Import Duties Act 1958, ss 5(2), (3), (6), 9(4), (5) (words from 'and' onwards)) (Import Duties Act 1958 (Repeals) (Appointed Day) Order 1973, SI 1973/2176) 1 Sep 1976 (repeals of Import Duties Act 1958, ss 5(5), 7(1)(c), 16(3), Schs 2, 6; European Free Trade Association Act 1960; Finance Act 1965, s 2 (except sub-s (5)); Finance Act 1966, ss 1(6), 9) (Customs Duties (Repeals) (Appointed Day) Order 1976, SI 1976/1304) 1 Jan 1978 (repeals of Import Duties Act 1958, ss 1–3, 11, 12 (except part of sub-s (4)), Sch 1, Sch 4, para 1; Finance Act 1971, s 1(1)–(3)) (Customs Duties (Repeals) (Appointed Day) Order 1977, SI 1977/2028, as amended by SI 1987/2106)
II	1 Feb 1973 (repeals of Sugar Act 1956, ss 3(2)(b), 4(2), (3), 17(1) (from the beginning to words 'this section'), (3)–(5), 18(3), (4), 21, 22, 24–32, 33(2) (words 'except' to 'subsection'), (3), (5), Sch 4; South Africa Act 1962, Sch 2, para 5; Finance Act 1968, s 58) (Sugar Act 1956 (Repeals) (Appointed Day) (No 1) Order 1973, SI 1973/135) 1 Jul 1973 (repeals of Sugar Act 1956, ss 7–16, 20(6), 33(1) (words 'regulations or'), (2) (words 'Every instrument containing any such regulations, and,'), 34 (words 'or the Commissioners'), 35(2) (definitions of 'Commissioners,' 'composite sugar products', 'distribution payments', 'distribution repayments', 'manufacture', 'refiner', 'surcharge',

European Communities Act 1972 (c 68)—*cont*

Sch 3, Pt II—*cont*
'surcharge repayment'), (4)–(6), 36(2); Finance Act
1962, s 3(6) (words from 'the Sugar Act 1956'
onwards), Sch 5, Pt II; Finance Act 1964, s 22;
Finance Act 1966, s 52) (Sugar Act 1956 (Repeals)
(Appointed Day) (No 2) Order 1973, SI 1973/1019)

1 Aug 1975 (repeals of Sugar Act 1956, s 17(2), (6),
(7), Sch 3, paras 2, 3; Agriculture Act 1957, ss 4,
36(2) (words 'and to sugar beet'); Agriculture
(Miscellaneous Provisions) Act 1963, s 25) (Sugar
Act 1956 (Repeals) (Appointed Day) (No 3) Order
1975, SI 1975/1164)

5 May 1976 (repeals of Sugar Act 1956, ss 3(1) (words
from 'including' onwards), 19, 20(1)–(5), (7), (8),
35(2) (definitions of 'the Consolidated Fund' and
'refined sugar'), Sch 3, para 4) (Sugar Act 1956
(Repeals) (Appointed Day) (No 4) Order 1976,
SI 1976/548)

1 Dec 1976 (repeals of Sugar Act 1956, ss 5, 23(5),
35(2) (definition of 'the Minister'); National Loans
Act 1968, Sch 1, the entry for the Sugar Act 1956)
(Sugar Act 1956 (Repeals) (Appointed Day) (No 5)
Order 1976, SI 1976/2016)

1 Sep 1981 (repeal of Sugar Act 1956, s 23(1)–(3), but
without prejudice to the modification made by
s 23(2) in the articles of the British Sugar
Corporation) (Sugar Act 1956 (Repeals)
(Appointed Day) (No 6) Order 1981, SI 1981/1192)
Not in force (otherwise)

III
1 Sep 1978 (repeals of Plant Varieties and Seeds Act
1964, s 32; Trade Descriptions Act 1968, s 2(4)(a))
(Plant Varieties and Seeds Act 1964 (Repeals)
(Appointed Day) Order 1978, SI 1978/1003)

16 Aug 1982 (all repeals in 1964 Act save s 32
mentioned above; repeal of Agriculture
(Miscellaneous Provisions) Act 1968, Sch 7) (Plant
Varieties and Seeds Act 1964 (Repeals) (Appointed
Day) Order 1982, SI 1982/1048)

IV
17 Oct 1972 (RA)

Field Monuments Act 1972 (c 43)

Whole Act repealed

Finance Act 1972 (c 41)

Budget Day: 21 Mar 1972

RA: 27 Jul 1972

See the note concerning Finance Acts at the front of this book

---

Gas Act 1972 (c 60)

Whole Act repealed except s 46(1) in relation to its operation as applied by the Gas
Act 1965, s 22 (Gas Act 1986, s 67(3), (4), Sch 8, para 15, Sch 9, Pt I)

Harbours Development (Scotland) Act 1972 (c 64)

RA: 9 Aug 1972

9 Aug 1972 (RA)

Harbours (Loans) Act 1972 (c 16)

RA: 23 Mar 1972

23 Mar 1972 (RA)

Harbours, Piers and Ferries (Scotland) Act 1972 (c 29)

RA: 12 Jun 1972

12 Jun 1972 (RA)

Horserace Totalisator and Betting Levy Boards Act 1972 (c 69)

RA: 17 Oct 1972

Commencement provisions: s 3(3)

s 1, 2	17 Oct 1972 (RA)
3	*Not in force*
4–8	17 Oct 1972 (RA)

Housing Finance Act 1972 (c 47)

Whole Act repealed

Housing (Financial Provisions) (Scotland) Act 1972 (c 46)

RA: 27 Jul 1972

Commencement provisions: s 81(3); Housing (Financial Provisions) (Scotland) Act 1972 (Commencement) Order 1972, SI 1972/1130

Whole Act repealed except ss 69, 78, 81 and Sch 9, para 31, which came into force as follows:

s 69, 78, 81	3 Aug 1972 (SI 1972/1130)
Sch 9, para 31	27 Aug 1972 (s 81(3))

Industry Act 1972 (c 63)

RA: 9 Aug 1972

9 Aug 1972 (RA)

Iron and Steel Act 1972 (c 12)

Whole Act repealed

Island of Rockall Act 1972 (c 2)

RA: 10 Feb 1972

10 Feb 1972 (RA)

Land Charges Act 1972 (c 61)

RA: 9 Aug 1972

Commencement provisions: s 19(2); Land Charges Act 1972 (Commencement) Order 1972, SI 1972/2058

29 Jan 1973 (SI 1972/2058)

Legal Advice and Assistance Act 1972 (c 50)

Whole Act repealed

Local Employment Act 1972 (c 5)

RA: 10 Feb 1972

Commencement provisions: s 23(2)

10 Mar 1972 (s 23(2))

Local Government Act 1972 (c 70)

RA: 26 Oct 1972

Commencement provisions: ss 1(1), 20(1), 273; Local Government Act 1972 (Commencement No 1) (England) Order 1973, SI 1973/373; Local Government Act 1972 (Commencement No 2) (Wales) Order 1973, SI 1973/375

This Act largely came into force on receiving Royal Assent, and the whole Act was effective from 1 Apr 1974. The details of its commencement (whereby for administrative reasons slightly earlier dates were prescribed for the coming into force of certain provisions) are of only historical interest; consequently the section by section commencement dates are omitted here

---

Maintenance Orders (Reciprocal Enforcement) Act 1972 (c 18)

RA: 23 Mar 1972

Commencement provisions: s 49(2); Maintenance Orders (Reciprocal Enforcement) Act 1972 (Commencement No 1) Order 1974, SI 1974/517; Maintenance Orders (Reciprocal Enforcement) Act 1972 (Commencement No 2) Order 1975, SI 1975/377

s 1–21	1 Apr 1974 (SI 1974/517)
22(1)	1 Apr 1974 (SI 1974/517)
(2)	*Not in force*
23, 24	1 Apr 1974 (SI 1974/517)
25, 26	12 Apr 1975 (SI 1975/377)
27A–27C, 28	Substituted together with ss 28A–28C for original ss 27, 28, 28A by Maintenance Orders (Reciprocal Enforcement) Act 1992, s 1(2), Sch 1, Pt II (qv)

Maintenance Orders (Reciprocal Enforcement) Act 1972 (c 18)—*cont*

s 28A	Inserted (EW) by Domestic Proceedings and Magistrates' Courts Act 1978 (qv); substituted as noted to ss 27A–27C, 28 above
28B, 28C	Substituted as noted to ss 27A–27C, 28 above
29	12 Apr 1975 (SI 1975/377); substituted by Maintenance Orders (Northern Ireland Consequential Amendments) Order 1990, SI 1990/564, art 4(3)
29A	Inserted (EW) by Domestic Proceedings and Magistrates' Courts Act 1978, s 59 (qv); substituted by Maintenance Orders (Northern Ireland Consequential Amendments) Order 1990, SI 1990/564, art 4(4)
30–34	12 Apr 1975 (SI 1975/377)
34A	Inserted by Maintenance Enforcement Act 1991, s 10, Sch 1, para 19(2) (qv)
35, 35A	Substituted for s 35 by Maintenance Orders (Reciprocal Enforcement) Act 1992, s 1(2), Sch 1, Pt II, para 16 (qv)
36–38	12 Apr 1975 (SI 1975/377)
38A	Inserted by Maintenance Orders (Reciprocal Enforcement) Act 1992, s 1(2), Sch 1, Pt II, para 17 (qv)
39	12 Apr 1975 (SI 1975/377)
40	1 Apr 1974 (SI 1974/517)
41	Repealed
42, 43	1 Apr 1974 (SI 1974/517)
43A	Inserted (S) by Domestic Proceedings and Magistrates' Courts Act 1978, s 61 (qv)
44–49	1 Apr 1974 (SI 1974/517)
Schedule	1 Apr 1974 (SI 1974/517)

Matrimonial Proceedings (Polygamous Marriages) Act 1972 (c 38)

RA: 29 Jun 1972

29 Jun 1972 (RA)

Mineral Exploration and Investment Grants Act 1972 (c 9)

RA: 24 Feb 1972

24 Feb 1972 (RA)

Ministerial and other Salaries Act 1972 (c 3)

Whole Act repealed

Museums and Galleries Admission Charges Act 1972 (c 73)

RA: 26 Oct 1972

26 Oct 1972 (RA)

Note

Charges are not currently levied in pursuance of this Act

National Debt Act 1972 (c 65)

RA: 9 Aug 1972

9 Aug 1972 (RA)

National Health Service (Family Planning) Amendment Act 1972 (c 72)

Whole Act repealed

National Health Service (Scotland) Act 1972 (c 58)

RA: 9 Aug 1972

Commencement provisions: s 65(1) (repealed); National Health Service (Scotland) Act 1972 (Commencement No 1) Order 1972, SI 1972/1256; National Health Service (Scotland) Act 1972 (Commencement No 2) Order 1973, SI 1973/372; National Health Service (Scotland) Act 1972 (Commencement No 4) Order 1974, SI 1974/145

s 1–23	Repealed
24(1)	Repealed
(2)	1 Apr 1974 (SI 1974/145)
(3)	Repealed
25	Repealed
26, 27	1 Apr 1974 (SI 1974/145)
28	21 Aug 1972 (SI 1972/1256)
29–31	Repealed
32–36	1 Apr 1974 (SI 1974/145)
37–51	Repealed
52	1 Mar 1973 (SI 1973/372)
53	1 Apr 1974 (SI 1974/145)
54–60	Repealed
61(1)–(3)	1 Mar 1973 (SI 1973/372)
(4), (5)	Repealed
62, 63	Repealed
64(1)	See Sch 6 below
(2)	Repealed
65	Repealed
Sch 1–3	Repealed
4	1 Apr 1974 (SI 1974/145)
5	Repealed
6, para 37–77, 82, 83(a), 84–93, 94(b), 95–97, 101, 102, 104, 119–122, 126, 127, 129, 135(a)–(c), 136(b), 138–140, 150, 154–156★	1 Apr 1974 (SI 1974/145)
156A★	Inserted by National Health Service Reorganisation Act 1973, s 57(1), Sch 4 (repealed)
Remainder	Repealed
7	Repealed

★ These paragraphs of Sch 6, although repealed, are saved by National Health Service (Scotland) Act 1978, s 109, Sch 15, para 10 (qv)

National Insurance Act 1972 (c 57)

Whole Act repealed

National Insurance (Amendment) Act 1972 (c 36)

Whole Act repealed

National Insurance Regulations (Validation) Act 1972 (c 4)

Whole Act repealed

Northern Ireland Act 1972 (c 10)

Whole Act repealed

Northern Ireland (Border Poll) Act 1972 (c 77)

Whole Act repealed

Northern Ireland (Financial Provisions) Act 1972 (c 76)

Whole Act repealed

Northern Ireland (Temporary Provisions) Act 1972 (c 22)

RA: 30 Mar 1972

30 Mar 1972 (RA; note that s 1 expired on 1 Jan 1974, the commencement date for the Northern Ireland Constitution Act 1973, Pt II)

Overseas Investment and Export Guarantees Act 1972 (c 40)

Whole Act repealed

Parliamentary and other Pensions Act 1972 (c 48)

RA: 27 Jul 1972

27 Jul 1972 (RA)

Pensioners and Family Income Supplement Payments Act 1972 (c 75)

Whole Act repealed

Pensioners' Payments and National Insurance Contributions Act 1972 (c 80)

Whole Act repealed

Performers' Protection Act 1972 (c 32)

Whole Act repealed

Poisons Act 1972 (c 66)

RA: 9 Aug 1972

Commencement provisions: s 13(1); Medicines Act 1968 (Commencement No 7) Order
1977, SI 1977/2128

1 Feb 1978 (SI 1977/2128)

Police Act 1972 (c 39)

RA: 29 Jun 1972

29 Jun 1972 (RA)

Post Office (Borrowing) Act 1972 (c 79)

Whole Act repealed

Repair of Benefice Buildings Measure 1972 (No 2)

RA: 10 Feb 1972

This Measure came into force in different dioceses on different dates, as shown below,
in accordance with orders of the Church Commissioners (and is in force for every
diocese):

Bath and Wells	1 Jan 1973
Birmingham	1 Jan 1974
Blackburn	1 Jan 1974
Bradford	1 Apr 1973
Bristol	1 Jan 1973
Canterbury	1 Jul 1973
Carlisle	1 Jan 1974
Chelmsford	1 Jan 1974
Chester	1 Jan 1974
Chichester	1 Jan 1974
Coventry	1 Apr 1973
Derby	1 Jan 1974
Durham	1 Jan 1974
Ely	1 Jan 1973
Exeter	1 Jan 1973
Gloucester	1 Jan 1974
Guildford	1 Jan 1974
Hereford	1 Apr 1973
Leicester	1 Apr 1974
Lichfield	1 Apr 1974
Lincoln	1 Jan 1974
Liverpool	1 Jan 1973
London	1 Jan 1974
Manchester	1 Jan 1974
Newcastle	1 Jan 1973
Norwich	1 Jan 1974
Oxford	1 Jan 1974
Peterborough	1 Apr 1974
Portsmouth	1 Jan 1974
Ripon	1 Jan 1974
Rochester	1 Jan 1973
St Albans	1 Jan 1973

Repair of Benefice Buildings Measure 1972 (No 2)—*cont*

St Edmundsbury and Ipswich	1 Jan 1974
Salisbury	1 Apr 1973
Sheffield	1 Jan 1974
Southwark	1 Jan 1974
Southwell	1 Jan 1974
Truro	1 Jan 1973
Wakefield	1 Jan 1974
Winchester	1 Apr 1973
Worcester	1 Jan 1974
York	1 Jan 1974

Road Traffic Act 1972 (c 20)

Whole Act repealed

Road Traffic (Foreign Vehicles) Act 1972 (c 27)

RA: 11 May 1972

Commencement provisions: s 8(2); Road Traffic (Foreign Vehicles) Act 1972
    Commencement Order 1972, SI 1972/1018

31 Jul 1972 (SI 1972/1018)

Salmon and Freshwater Fisheries Act 1972 (c 37)

Whole Act repealed

Sierra Leone Republic Act 1972 (c 1)

RA: 10 Feb 1972

10 Feb 1972 (RA; but as Sierra Leone became a Republic before this date, this Act is
    deemed to have come into force on 19 Apr 1971 (s 1(4)))

Social Work (Scotland) Act 1972 (c 24)

Whole Act repealed

Sound Broadcasting Act 1972 (c 31)

Whole Act repealed

Sri Lanka Republic Act 1972 (c 55)

RA: 27 Jul 1972

27 Jul 1972 (RA; but as Ceylon became a Republic before this date, this Act is deemed
    to have come into force on 22 May 1972 (s 1(6)))

Summer Time Act 1972 (c 6)

RA: 10 Feb 1972

Commencement provisions: s 6(2)

10 Mar 1972 (s 6(2))

Sunday Cinema Act 1972 (c 19)

Whole Act repealed

Sunday Theatre Act 1972 (c 26)

RA: 11 Apr 1972

Commencement provisions: s 6(3)

11 May 1972 (s 6(3))

Superannuation Act 1972 (c 11)

RA: 1 Mar 1972

Commencement provisions: s 30(4); Superannuation Act 1972 (Commencement No 1)
    Order 1972, SI 1972/325; Superannuation Act 1972 (Commencement No 2) Order
    1972, SI 1972/384*

25 Mar 1972 (SI 1972/325)

* Provisions brought into force by SI 1972/384 are all now repealed

---

Town and Country Planning (Amendment) Act 1972 (c 42)

RA: 27 Jul 1972

Commencement provisions: s 12(2) (repealed)*

27 Jul 1972 (RA)

Whole Act repealed (EW)

* Provisions brought into force by s 12(2) are all now repealed

---

Town and Country Planning (Scotland) Act 1972 (c 52)

RA: 27 Jul 1972

Commencement provisions: ss 18, 279, 280; Town and Country Planning (Scotland)
    Act 1972 (Commencement No 1) (Orkney Islands Area) Order 1975, SI 1975/
    379; Town and Country Planning (Scotland) Act 1972 (Commencement No 2)
    Order 1975, SI 1975/380; Town and Country Planning (Scotland) Act 1972
    (Commencement No 3) Order 1975, SI 1975/1203; Town and Country Planning
    (Scotland) Act 1972 (Commencement No 4) Order 1976, SI 1976/464

The Act mainly came into force on 27 Aug 1972 (s 280(1)), except for s 280, Sch 23
    (so far as it relates to the repeal of Pt I of the Control of Office and Industrial
    Development Act 1965), any provisions conferring power to make regulations
    or orders or conferring power to revoke or vary any regulations or orders and
    any provisions relating to the exercise of such powers, and other provisions now
    repealed (together with other provisions insofar as they related to the repealed
    provisions), which came into force on 27 Jul 1972 (s 280(2)). Provision was made

Town and Country Planning (Scotland) Act 1972 (c 52)—*cont*
in s 18 for Pt II (dealing with development plans), with certain exceptions, to
come into force on days appointed by the Secretary of State, with different days
appointed for the commencement of the same provisions in different areas; see
SI 1975/379, appointing 1 April 1975 for the Orkney Islands Area and SI 1975/
380 appointing 16 May 1975 for the remainder of Scotland. In addition, ss 58(5),
59(1)–(3) came into force on 17 Jul 1975 by virtue of SI 1975/1203 and Sch 7
came into force on 1 Apr 1976 by virtue of SI 1976/464

Trade Descriptions Act 1972 (c 34)

Whole Act repealed

**Trading Representations (Disabled Persons) Amendment Act 1972
(c 45)**

RA: 27 Jul 1972

Commencement provisions: s 3(2)

1 Jan 1973 (s 3(2))

Transport (Grants) Act 1972 (c 15)

RA: 23 Mar 1972

23 Mar 1972 (RA)

Transport Holding Company Act 1972 (c 14)

RA: 23 Mar 1972

23 Mar 1972 (RA)

1973

Administration of Justice Act 1973 (c 15)

RA: 18 Apr 1973

Commencement provisions: s 20

s 1	1 Apr 1974 (s 20(1)(a))
2–4	Repealed
5	Substituted by Justices of the Peace Act 1979, s 71 (qv)
6	18 Apr 1973 (RA)
7	Repealed
8	18 May 1973 (s 20(1)(b))
9	18 Apr 1973 (RA)
10, 11	Repealed
12	18 Apr 1973 (RA)
13	Repealed
14	18 Apr 1973 (RA)
15–17	Repealed
18	18 May 1973 (s 20(1)(b))
19, 20	Repealed
21	18 Apr 1973 (RA)
Sch 1	1 Apr 1974 (s 20(1))
2	18 Apr 1973 (RA)
3–5	Repealed

Appropriation Act 1973 (c 40)

Whole Act repealed

Atomic Energy Authority (Weapons Group) Act 1973 (c 4)

RA: 6 Mar 1973

6 Mar 1973 (RA; but note that ss 1–5 had no effect until 1 Apr 1973, the day appointed
for the purposes of s 1(1) by Atomic Energy Authority (Weapons Group) Act 1973
(Appointed Day) Order 1973, SI 1973/463)

Badgers Act 1973 (c 57)

Whole Act repealed

Bahamas Independence Act 1973 (c 27)

RA: 14 Jun 1973

Appointed day: 10 Jul 1973

Bangladesh Act 1973 (c 49)

RA: 25 Jul 1973

25 Jul 1973 (RA; but note that Bangladesh was recognised as an independent sovereign state on 4 Feb 1972, and most provisions of this Act are deemed to have had effect from that date)

Breeding of Dogs Act 1973 (c 60)

RA: 25 Oct 1973

Commencement provisions: s 7

1 Apr 1974 (s 7(3))

Channel Tunnel (Initial Finance) Act 1973 (c 66)

RA: 13 Nov 1973

13 Nov 1973 (RA)

Coal Industry Act 1973 (c 8)

RA: 22 Mar 1973

Commencement provisions: s 14(3)

22 Mar 1973 (RA; except for s 2(1) (repealed), and the provisions in Sch 2 which relate to the Coal Industry Acts 1965, 1967 and 1971, which came into force on 1 Apr 1973 (s 14(3))

Concorde Aircraft Act 1973 (c 7)

Whole Act repealed

Consolidated Fund Act 1973 (c 1)

Whole Act repealed

Consolidated Fund (No 2) Act 1973 (c 10)

Whole Act repealed

Costs in Criminal Cases Act 1973 (c 14)

Whole Act repealed

Counter-Inflation Act 1973 (c 9)

RA: 22 Mar 1973

The provisions of this Act were not intended to have permanent effect and are now
repealed; note that the repeal of ss 17(6), (8), (9), 18(4), (5), 19, 20(4), (5)(i), (iii),
23(2), Sch 4, para 4 (except sub-para (2)(b)) takes effect from 1 Jan 2011
(Competition Act 1980, s 33(4), Sch 2)

Dentists (Amendment) Act 1973 (c 31)

Whole Act repealed

Domicile and Matrimonial Proceedings Act 1973 (c 45)

RA: 25 Jul 1973

Commencement provisions: s 17(5)

1 Jan 1974 (s 17(5))

Education Act 1973 (c 16)

RA: 18 Apr 1973

Commencement provisions: s 1(5); Education Act 1973 (Commencement) Order 1973,
SI 1973/1661

s 1(1)(a)	1 Feb 1974 (SI 1973/1661)
(b)	18 Apr 1973 (RA); prospectively repealed by Education Act 1993, s 307(1), (3), Sch 19, para 51, Sch 21, Pt I (qv)
(2)–(5)	18 Apr 1973 (RA)
2, 3	18 Apr 1973 (RA)
4	Repealed
5	18 Apr 1973 (RA)
Sch 1	18 Apr 1973 (RA)
2, Pt I, II	18 Apr 1973 (RA)
III	1 Feb 1974 (SI 1973/1661)

Education (Scotland) Act 1973 (c 59)

Whole Act repealed

Education (Work Experience) Act 1973 (c 23)

RA: 23 May 1973

23 May 1973 (RA); *whole Act repealed (S)*

Employment Agencies Act 1973 (c 35)

RA: 18 Jul 1973

Commencement provisions: s 14(4); Employment Agencies Act 1973
(Commmencement) Order 1976, SI 1976/709

Employment Agencies Act 1973 (c 35)—*cont*

s 1	30 Jun 1976 (purposes of s 1(3)) (SI 1976/709)
	1 Nov 1976 (all other purposes) (SI 1976/709)
2	1 Jul 1976 (SI 1976/709)
3	Substituted for original ss 3, 4 by Employment Protection Act 1975, s 114, Sch 13, para 4 (qv)
4	See note to s 3
5–7	1 Jul 1976 (SI 1976/709)
8	Repealed
9–13	1 Jul 1976 (SI 1976/709)
14	18 Jul 1973 (RA)
Schedule	1 Jul 1976 (SI 1976/709)

Employment and Training Act 1973 (c 50)

RA: 25 Jul 1973

Commencement provisions: s 15(2); Employment and Training Act 1973 (Commencement No 1) Order 1973, SI 1973/2063; Employment and Training Act 1973 (Commencement No 2) Order 1974, SI 1974/398; Employment and Training Act 1973 (Commencement No 3) Order 1974, SI 1974/1463; Employment and Training Act 1973 (Commencement No 4) Order 1975, SI 1975/689

Note that references to the Employment Service Agency and the Training Services Agency are repealed and accordingly no note is made of commencement dates relating to those Agencies

s 1	Repealed
2	Substituted by Employment Act 1988, s 25(1) (qv)
3	Repealed
4, 5	1 Jan 1974 (SI 1973/2063)
6, 7	Repealed
(8, 9, 10	Substituted as from 1 Apr 1994 (ES) and 1 Apr 1995 (W) by Trade Union Reform and Employment Rights Act 1993, s 45 (qv); exception s 10(7) took effect from 30 Nov 1993)
8	1 Apr 1974 (SI 1974/398); repealed (S); substituted as noted above
9(1), (2)	1 Apr 1974 (SI 1974/398); repealed (S); substituted as noted above
(3), (4)	*Not in force*; repealed (S); substituted as noted above
(5)	Repealed; substituted as noted above
(6)	1 Apr 1974 (SI 1974/398); repealed (S); substituted as noted above
10	1 Apr 1974 (SI 1974/398); repealed (S); substituted as noted above
10A	Inserted as from 1 Apr 1994 (ES) and 1 Apr 1995 (W) by Trade Union Reform and Employment Rights Act 1993, s 46 (qv)
11	1 Jan 1974 (SI 1973/2063)
12(1)	1 Jan 1974 (SI 1973/2063)
(1A)	Inserted by Employment Act 1988, s 25(2), Sch 2, para 2 (qv)
(2)	Substituted by Social Security Act 1988, s 16, Sch 4, para 2 (qv)
(3)	Repealed
(4)	1 Jan 1974 (SI 1973/2063)
(5)	Repealed

Employment and Training Act 1973 (c 50)—*cont*

s 12(6)	1 Jan 1974 (SI 1973/2063)
13	1 Jan 1974 (SI 1973/2063)
14	See Schs 3, 4 below
15	1 Jan 1974 (SI 1973/2063)
Sch 1, 2	Repealed
3, para 1	1 Apr 1974 (SI 1974/398)
2	1 Oct 1974 (SI 1974/463)
3, 4	1 Jan 1974 (SI 1973/2063)
5, 6	Repealed
7(1)	1 Oct 1974 (SI 1974/463)
(2)	1 Apr 1974 (SI 1974/398)
(3)	1 Jan 1974 (SI 1973/2063)
8	1 Apr 1974 (SI 1974/398)
9, 10	Repealed
11(1)	1 Apr 1974 (SI 1974/398)
(2)	1 Jan 1974 (SI 1973/2063)
12–15	Repealed
4	1 Jan 1974 (repeals of or in Employment and Training Act 1948, ss 4, 20(2); Industrial Training Act 1964, ss 3(1), 6, 11, 13, Schedule, para 6(2); Chronically Sick and Disabled Persons Act 1970, s 13(2)) (SI 1973/2063)
	1 Apr 1974 (repeal of Industrial Training Act 1964, ss 2(1)(f) (so far as relates to arrangements made by local education authorities in England and Wales), 5, 17) (SI 1973/2063)
	1 Apr 1974 (repeals of or in Unemployment Insurance Act 1935, s 80; Employment and Training Act 1948, ss 3, 8–13, 14(2), 15 and Sch 1; Agriculture (Miscellaneous Provisions) Act 1949, s 8(5); London Government Act 1963, s 34; National Insurance (Industrial Injuries) Act 1965, s 72; Agriculture Act 1970, s 104; Local Government Act 1972, s 209) (SI 1974/398)
	1 Oct 1974 (repeals of or in Disabled Persons (Employment) Act 1944, ss 2–4, 16 (in part); Employment and Training Act 1948, s 2(5), (8); National Insurance (Industrial Injuries) Act 1965, s 25(2)(c); Local Employment Act 1972, s 6) (SI 1974/1463)
	16 May 1975 (repeal of Industrial Training Act 1964, s 2(1)(f) (so far as unrepealed)) (SI 1973/2063)
	16 May 1975 (repeals of or in Employment and Training Act 1948 (so far as unrepealed); Criminal Justice Act 1967, in Sch 3, the entry relating to Employment and Training Act 1948; Employment Medical Advisory Service Act 1972, s 5(2)) (SI 1975/689)

Employment of Children Act 1973 (c 24)

RA: 23 May 1973

Commencement provisions: s 3(4)

Not in force

Fair Trading Act 1973 (c 41)

RA: 25 Jul 1973

Commencement provisions: s 140(3); Fair Trading Act 1973 (Commencement No 1)
   Order 1973, SI 1973/1545; Fair Trading Act 1973 (Commencement No 2) Order
   1973, SI 1973/1652

s 1–28	1 Nov 1973 (SI 1973/1652)
29–32	14 Sep 1973 (SI 1973/1545)
33(1)	1 Nov 1973 (SI 1973/1652)
(2)(a), (b)	1 Nov 1973 (SI 1973/1652)
(c), (d)	14 Sep 1973 (SI 1973/1545)
34–42	1 Nov 1973 (SI 1973/1652)
43	Repealed
44–66	1 Nov 1973 (SI 1973/1652)
66A	Inserted by Companies Act 1989, s 150(1) (qv)
67–75	1 Nov 1973 (SI 1973/1652)
75A–75F	Inserted by Companies Act 1989, s 146 (qv)
75G–75K	Inserted by Companies Act 1989, s 147 (qv)
76–93	1 Nov 1973 (SI 1973/1652)
93A	Inserted by Companies Act 1989, s 148 (qv)
93B	Inserted by Companies Act 1989, s 151 (qv)
94	1 Nov 1973 (SI 1973/1652)
95–117	Repealed
118–123	14 Sep 1973 (SI 1973/1545)
124, 125	1 Nov 1973 (SI 1973/1652)
126	Repealed
127	1 Nov 1973 (SI 1973/1652)
128	Repealed
129	14 Sep 1973 (SI 1973/1545)
130, 131	1 Nov 1973 (SI 1973/1652)
132	14 Sep 1973 (SI 1973/1545)
133	1 Nov 1973 (SI 1973/1652)
134	14 Sep 1973 (SI 1973/1545)
135(1)	1 Nov 1973 (SI 1973/1652)
(2)(a), (b)	14 Sep 1973 (SI 1973/1545)
(c), (d)	1 Nov 1973 (SI 1973/1652)
(3)	Repealed
136	Repealed
137	14 Sep 1973 (SI 1973/1545)
138, 139	1 Nov 1973 (SI 1973/1652)
140	14 Sep 1973 (SI 1973/1545)
Sch 1–9	1 Nov 1973 (SI 1973/1652)
10	Repealed
11–13	1 Nov 1973 (SI 1973/1652)

Finance Act 1973 (c 51)

Budget Day: 6 Mar 1973

RA: 25 Jul 1973

See the note concerning Finance Acts at the front of this book

Fire Precautions (Loans) Act 1973 (c 11)

RA: 29 Mar 1973

29 Mar 1973 (RA)

Fuel and Electricity (Control) Act 1973 (c 67)

Whole Act repealed (note, however, that the Act remains partly in force in Northern Ireland, and remains in force in its application to the Channel Islands and the Isle of Man so long as it extends there by Order in Council)

Furnished Lettings (Rent Allowances) Act 1973 (c 6)

Whole Act repealed

Gaming (Amendment) Act 1973 (c 12)

RA: 18 Apr 1973

18 Apr 1973 (RA)

Government Trading Funds Act 1973 (c 63)

RA: 25 Oct 1973

25 Oct 1973 (RA)

Guardianship Act 1973 (c 29)

RA: 5 Jul 1973

Commencement provisions: s 15(3); Guardianship Act 1973 (Commencement No 1) Order 1974, SI 1974/695; Guardianship Act 1973 (Commencement No 2) Order 1974, SI 1974/836

8 May 1974 (SI 1974/695, SI 1974/836)

Whole Act repealed (EW)

Hallmarking Act 1973 (c 43)

RA: 25 Jul 1973

Commencement provisions: s 24(2)

s 1–12	1 Jan 1975 (s 24(2))
13	1 Jan 1974 (s 24(2))
14–24	1 Jan 1975 (s 24(2))
Sch 1–3	1 Jan 1975 (s 24(2))
4	1 Jan 1974 (s 24(2))
5–7	1 Jan 1975 (s 24(2))

Heavy Commercial Vehicles (Controls and Regulations) Act 1973 (c 44)

Whole Act repealed

Housing (Amendment) Act 1973 (c 5)

Whole Act repealed

Independent Broadcasting Authority Act 1973 (c 19)

Whole Act repealed (except as extended to the Isle of Man)

Insurance Companies Amendment Act 1973 (c 58)

RA: 25 Jul 1973

Commencement provisions: s 57(3)–(8)★

s 1–49	Repealed
50, 51	25 Jul 1973 (RA)
52–56	Repealed
57(1)	25 Jul 1973 (RA)
(2)–(8)	Repealed
Sch 1–5	Repealed

★ Provisions brought into force by s 57(3)–(8) are all repealed

---

International Cocoa Agreement Act 1973 (c 46)

RA: 25 Jul 1973

Commencement provisions: s 2(2); International Cocoa Agreement Act 1973 (Commencement) Order 1973, SI 1973/1617

1 Oct 1973 (SI 1973/1617)

International Sugar Organisation Act 1973 (c 68)

RA: 19 Dec 1973

19 Dec 1973 (RA)

Land Compensation Act 1973 (c 26)

RA: 23 May 1973

Commencement provisions: s 89(2)

s 1–12	23 Jun 1973 (s 89(2))
12A	Inserted by Leasehold Reform, Housing and Urban Development Act 1993, s 187(1), Sch 21, para 5 (qv)
13	23 Jun 1973 (s 89(2))
14	Repealed
15–19	23 Jun 1973 (s 89(2))
20	23 May 1973 (RA)

Land Compensation Act 1973 (c 26)—*cont*

s 20A	Inserted by Planning and Compensation Act 1991, s 70, Sch 15, para 5 (qv)
21–25	Repealed
26–29	23 May 1973 (RA)
29A	Inserted by Planning and Compensation Act 1991, s 69 (qv)
30	Substituted by Planning and Compensation Act 1991, s 68(3), (9) (qv)
31	Repealed
32–48	23 May 1973 (RA)
49	Repealed
50–52	23 May 1973 (RA)
52A	Inserted by Planning and Compensation Act 1991, s 63(2) (qv)
53–59	23 May 1973 (qv)
60	Repealed
61	23 May 1973 (RA)
62	Repealed
63	23 May 1973 (RA)
64–83	Repealed
84–89	23 May 1973 (RA)
Sch 1, 2	Repealed
3	23 May 1973 (RA)

Land Compensation (Scotland) Act 1973 (c 56)

RA: 25 Jul 1973

25 Jul 1973 (RA)

Law Reform (Diligence) (Scotland) Act 1973 (c 22)

Whole Act repealed

Local Government (Scotland) Act 1973 (c 65)

RA: 25 Oct 1973

Commencement provisions: s 238(2); Local Government (Scotland) Act 1973 (Commencement No 1) Order 1973, SI 1973/1886; Local Government (Scotland) Act 1973 (Commencement No 2) Order 1973, SI 1973/2181

s 1, 2	20 Dec 1973 (SI 1973/2181)
3(1)–(5)	20 Dec 1973 (SI 1973/2181)
(6)	16 May 1975 (SI 1973/2181)
(7)	20 Dec 1973 (SI 1973/2181)
3A	Inserted by Local Government, Planning and Land Act 1980, s 27(1) (qv)
4, 5	20 Dec 1973 (SI 1973/2181)
6–10	Repealed
11(1)	12 Nov 1973 (SI 1973/1886)
(2)	Repealed
(3)	See Sch 3 below
(4)	Repealed

Local Government (Scotland) Act 1973 (c 65)—*cont*

s 12–33	20 Dec 1973 (SI 1973/2181)
33A	Inserted by Local Government and Housing Act 1989, s 30(1) (qv)
34–43	20 Dec 1973 (SI 1973/2181)
44–45A	Repealed
46–49	16 May 1975 (SI 1973/2181)
49A	Repealed
50	16 May 1975 (SI 1973/2181)
50A–50K	Inserted by Local Government (Access to Information) Act 1985, s 2(1) (qv)
51–53	20 Dec 1973 (SI 1973/2181)
54	Repealed
55	20 Dec 1973 (SI 1973/2181)
56(1)	20 Dec 1973 (SI 1973/2181)
(2)	Substituted by Local Government and Planning (Scotland) Act 1982, s 32 (qv)
(3)–(5)	20 Dec 1973 (SI 1973/2181)
(6)	Substituted by Local Government Finance Act 1992, s 117(1), Sch 13, para 36 (subject to transitional provisions) (qv)
(7)	20 Dec 1973 (SI 1973/2181)
(8)–(10)	16 May 1975 (SI 1973/2181)
(11)–(13)	Repealed
(14), (15)	20 Dec 1973 (SI 1973/2181)
57–63	20 Dec 1973 (SI 1973/2181)
64(1)–(3)	20 Dec 1973 (SI 1973/2181)
(4), (5)	16 May 1975 (SI 1973/2181)
(6), (7)	20 Dec 1973 (SI 1973/2181)
65–68	20 Dec 1973 (SI 1973/2181)
69	16 May 1975 (SI 1973/2181)
70–74	20 Dec 1973 (SI 1973/2181)
74A	Repealed
75	16 May 1975 (SI 1973/2181)
76, 77	20 Dec 1973 (SI 1973/2181)
78	16 May 1975 (SI 1973/2181)
79–81	20 Dec 1973 (SI 1973/2181)
82, 83	16 May 1975 (SI 1973/2181)
84	20 Dec 1973 (SI 1973/2181)
85	16 May 1975 (SI 1973/2181)
86–89	20 Dec 1973 (SI 1973/2181)
90	16 May 1975 (SI 1973/2181)
90A	Inserted by Local Government and Planning (Scotland) Act 1982, s 11(2) (qv)
91	Repealed
92	16 May 1975 (SI 1973/2181)
93–96	20 Dec 1973 (SI 1973/2181)
97(1), (2)	20 Dec 1973 (SI 1973/2181)
(2A), (2B)	Inserted by National Health Service and Community Care Act 1990, s 36, Sch 7 (qv)
(3), (4)	20 Dec 1973 (SI 1973/2181)
(4A)–(4D)	Inserted by National Health Service and Community Care Act 1990, s 36, Sch 7 (qv)
(5), (6)	20 Dec 1973 (SI 1973/2181)
(6A)	Inserted by National Health Service and Community Care Act 1990, s 36, Sch 7 (qv)
97A, 97B	Inserted by Local Government Act 1988, s 35 (qv)

Local Government (Scotland) Act 1973 (c 65)—*cont*

s 98–104	20 Dec 1973 (SI 1973/2181)
104A	Inserted by National Health Service and Community Care Act 1990, s 36, Sch 7, para 11 (qv)
105, 106	20 Dec 1973 (SI 1973/2181)
107–108C	Repealed
109	16 May 1975 (SI 1973/2181)
110	20 Dec 1973 (SI 1973/2181); prospectively substituted by Local Government and Housing Act 1989, s 141(3) (qv); prospectively repealed by Local Government Finance Act 1992, s 117, Sch 13, para 38, Sch 14 (qv)
110A	Repealed, subject to transitional provisions, by Local Government Finance Act 1992, s 117, Sch13, para 38, Sch 14 (qv)
111	20 Dec 1973 (SI 1973/2181)
112–115	Repealed
116	20 Dec 1973 (SI 1973/2181)
117	Repealed
118	16 May 1975 (SI 1973/2181)
119	Repealed
120	20 Dec 1973 (SI 1973/2181); repealed as from 1 Apr 1994 by Abolition of Domestic Rates etc (Scotland) Act 1987, s 34, Sch 6 (qv)
121	Repealed
122	See Sch 9 below
123, 124	16 May 1975 (SI 1973/2181)
125	Repealed
126–128	16 May 1975 (SI 1973/2181)
129	Repealed
130–134	16 May 1975 (SI 1973/2181)
135A	Inserted by Natural Heritage (Scotland) Act 1991, s 27(1), Sch 10, para 6 (qv)
135(1)	16 May 1975 (SI 1973/2181)
(2)–(7)	20 Dec 1973 (SI 1973/2181)
(8)–(10)	16 May 1975 (SI 1973/2181)
136	16 May 1975 (SI 1973/2181); prospectively repealed by Control of Pollution Act 1974, s 109(2), Sch 4 (qv)
137, 138	16 May 1975 (SI 1973/2181)
139	Repealed
140–145	16 May 1975 (SI 1973/2181)
146(1)–(6)	16 May 1975 (SI 1973/2181)
(7)	20 Dec 1973 (SI 1973/2181)
(8)	16 May 1975 (SI 1973/2181)
(9)	20 Dec 1973 (SI 1973/2181)
(10)	16 May 1975 (SI 1973/2181)
147(1)	16 May 1975 (SI 1973/2181)
(2)	20 Dec 1973 (SI 1973/2181)
(3)	Repealed
(4)–(6)	20 Dec 1973 (SI 1973/2181)
(7), (8)	16 May 1975 (SI 1973/2181)
148(1)	16 May 1975 (SI 1973/2181)
(2)–(7)	Repealed
(8)	See Sch 17 below
(9)	Repealed
149	Repealed

Local Government (Scotland) Act 1973 (c 65)—*cont*

s 150(1), (2)	16 May 1975 (SI 1973/2181)
(3)	20 Dec 1973 (SI 1973/2181)
(4)	16 May 1975 (SI 1973/2181)
(5)	Repealed
151, 152	Repealed
153, 154	16 May 1975 (SI 1973/2181)
154A, 154B	Inserted by Local Government and Planning (Scotland) Act 1982, s 7 (qv)
155–157	16 May 1975 (SI 1973/2181)
158	Repealed
159	16 May 1975 (SI 1973/2181)
160	Repealed
161	16 May 1975 (SI 1973/2181)
162	Repealed
163	16 May 1975 (SI 1973/2181)
164	Repealed
165	20 Dec 1973 (SI 1973/2181)
166	16 May 1975 (SI 1973/2181)
167	Repealed
168–170	16 May 1975 (SI 1973/2181)
170A, 170B	Inserted by Electricity Act 1989, s 102, Sch 13 (qv)
171	16 May 1975 (SI 1973/2181)
172(1)	16 May 1975 (SI 1973/2181)
(2)	20 Dec 1973 (SI 1973/2181)
(3), (4)	16 May 1975 (SI 1973/2181)
173, 174	16 May 1975 (SI 1973/2181)
175	20 Dec 1973 (SI 1973/2181)
176, 177	16 May 1975 (SI 1973/2181)
178	Repealed
179	Substituted by Local Government and Planning (Scotland) Act 1982, s 69(2), Sch 3, para 24 (qv)
180	Repealed
181–184	16 May 1975 (SI 1973/2181)
185, 186	Repealed
187–189	16 May 1975 (SI 1973/2181)
190–197	20 Dec 1973 (SI 1973/2181)
198–202	16 May 1975 (SI 1973/2181)
202A–202C	Inserted by Civic Government (Scotland) Act 1982, ss 110(3), 137(2) (qv)
203, 204	16 May 1975 (SI 1973/2181)
205	Repealed
206, 207	16 May 1975 (SI 1973/2181)
208	20 Dec 1973 (SI 1973/2181)
209, 210	16 May 1975 (SI 1973/2181)
210A	Inserted by Housing and Planning Act 1986, s 53, Sch 11, Pt II, para 39(4) (qv)
211–213	16 May 1975 (SI 1973/2181)
214	See Sch 27 below
215–217	20 Dec 1973 (SI 1973/2181)
218–221	Repealed
222, 223	20 Dec 1973 (SI 1973/2181)
224	12 Nov 1973 (SI 1973/1886)
225(1)–(7)	20 Dec 1973 (SI 1973/2181)
(8)	16 May 1975 (SI 1973/2181)
(9), (10)	20 Dec 1973 (SI 1973/2181)
226	20 Dec 1973 (SI 1973/2181)
227–229	16 May 1975 (SI 1973/2181)

Local Government (Scotland) Act 1973 (c 65)—*cont*

s 230–232	20 Dec 1973 (SI 1973/2181)
233	12 Nov 1973 (SI 1973/1886)
234–236	20 Dec 1973 (SI 1973/2181)
237(1)	See Sch 29 below
237(2)	20 Dec 1973 (SI 1973/2181)
238	20 Dec 1973 (SI 1973/2181)
Sch 1	20 Dec 1973 (SI 1973/2181)
2	12 Nov 1973 (SI 1973/1886)
3, para 1	16 May 1975 (SI 1973/2181)
2–18	Repealed
19	16 May 1975 (SI 1973/2181)
20–23	Repealed
4–7	20 Dec 1973 (SI 1973/2181)
7A	Inserted by Local Government (Access to Information) Act 1985, s 1(2), Sch 1, Pt II (qv)
8	20 Dec 1973 (SI 1973/2181)
9, para 1, 2	16 May 1975 (SI 1973/2181)
3–5	Repealed
6, 7	16 May 1975 (SI 1973/2181)
8	Repealed
9–12	16 May 1975 (SI 1973/2181)
13–15	Repealed
16–43	16 May 1975 (SI 1973/2181)
44	20 Dec 1973 (in relation to regional and islands councils) (SI 1973/2181) 16 May 1975 (otherwise) (SI 1973/2181)
45, 46	Repealed
47–53	16 May 1975 (SI 1973/2181)
54	20 Dec 1973 (in relation to any financial year commencing on or after 16 May 1975) (SI 1973/2181) 16 May 1975 (otherwise) (SI 1973/2181)
55–57	16 May 1975 (SI 1973/2181)
58	20 Dec 1973 (in relation to any financial year commencing on or after 16 May 1975) (SI 1973/2181) 16 May 1975 (otherwise) (SI 1973/2181)
59–61	16 May 1975 (SI 1973/2181)
62(a)	16 May 1974 (SI 1973/2181)
(b)	16 May 1975 (SI 1973/2181)
63	16 May 1975 (SI 1973/2181)
64	Repealed
65	20 Dec 1973 (SI 1973/2181)
66–72	20 Dec 1973 (in relation to any financial year commencing on or after 16 May 1975) (SI 1973/2181) 16 May 1975 (otherwise) (SI 1973/2181)
73, 74	Repealed
10	16 May 1975 (SI 1973/2181)
11	Repealed
12–16	16 May 1975 (SI 1973/2181)
17, para 1, 2	16 May 1975 (SI 1973/2181)
3–63	Repealed
64	16 May 1975 (SI 1973/2181); prospectively repealed by Water Act 1983, s 11(3), Sch 5, Pt I (qv)
18–23	16 May 1975 (SI 1973/2181)
24, para 1–24	Repealed

Local Government (Scotland) Act 1973 (c 65)—*cont*

Sch 24, para 25–27	16 May 1975 (SI 1973/2181)
28, 29	Repealed
30–32	16 May 1975 (SI 1973/2181)
33	Repealed
34	16 May 1975 (SI 1973/2181)
35	Repealed
36–45	16 May 1975 (SI 1973/2181)
46	Repealed
47	16 May 1975 (SI 1973/2181)
25, 26	16 May 1975 (SI 1973/2181)
27, para 1–5	16 May 1975 (SI 1973/2181)
6, 7	Repealed
8–14	16 May 1975 (SI 1973/2181)
15	Repealed
16–49	16 May 1975 (SI 1973/2181)
50	Repealed
51–77	16 May 1975 (SI 1973/2181)
78	Repealed
79–89	16 May 1975 (SI 1973/2181)
90	Repealed
91–96	16 May 1975 (SI 1973/2181)
97, 98	Repealed
99, 100	16 May 1975 (SI 1973/2181)
101	Repealed
102–113	16 May 1975 (SI 1973/2181)
114, 115	Repealed
116–127	16 May 1975 (SI 1973/2181)
128	Repealed
129–131	16 May 1975 (SI 1973/2181)
132	Repealed
133–139	16 May 1975 (SI 1973/2181)
140	Repealed
141–143	16 May 1975 (SI 1973/2181)
144	Repealed
145–148	16 May 1975 (SI 1973/2181)
149, 150	Repealed
151, 152	16 May 1975 (SI 1973/2181)
153	Repealed
154, 155	16 May 1975 (SI 1973/2181)
156, 157	Repealed
158–161	16 May 1975 (SI 1973/2181)
162, 163	Repealed
164	16 May 1975 (SI 1973/2181)
165	Repealed
166, 167	16 May 1975 (SI 1973/2181)
168–170	Repealed
171–186	16 May 1975 (SI 1973/2181)
187	20 Dec 1973 (SI 1973/2181)
188–190	Repealed
191–196	16 May 1975 (SI 1973/2181)
197	Repealed
198–200	16 May 1975 (SI 1973/2181)
201	Repealed
202–206	16 May 1975 (SI 1973/2181)
207	Repealed
208–211	16 May 1975 (SI 1973/2181)
28	Repealed

Local Government (Scotland) Act 1973 (c 65)—*cont*

Sch 29	20 Dec 1973 (repeals of or in Representation of the People Act 1949, s 55(6); Valuation and Rating (Scotland) Act 1956, s 1 (in relation to regional and islands councils); Local Government (Scotland) Act 1966, s 2(2)(b)) (SI 1973/2181)
	1 Apr 1974 (repeals of or in Representation of the People Act 1949, s 173(3), (8), Sch 3; Representation of the People Act 1969, ss 12(2), 13(5), 14, Schs 1, 2) (SI 1973/2181)
	16 May 1974 (repeals of Rating Act 1966, ss 5–8; Rate Rebate Act 1973) (SI 1973/2181)
	16 May 1975 (otherwise) (SI 1973/2181)

London Cab Act 1973 (c 20)

RA: 23 May 1973

23 May 1973 (RA)

Maplin Development Act 1973 (c 64)

Whole Act repealed

Matrimonial Causes Act 1973 (c 18)

RA: 23 May 1973

Commencement provisions: s 55(2); Matrimonial Causes Act 1973 (Commencement) Order 1973, SI 1973/1972

1 Jan 1974 (SI 1973/1972)

National Health Service Reorganisation Act 1973 (c 32)

RA: 5 Jul 1973

Commencement provisions: ss 55(1), 58(2), (3); National Health Service Reorganisation Act 1973 (Appointed Day) Order 1973, SI 1973/1956; National Health Service Reorganisation Act 1973 (Commencement No 1) (Scotland) Order 1973, SI 1973/1185; National Health Service Reorganisation Act 1973 (Commencement No 2) Order 1973, SI 1973/1523; Isles of Scilly (National Health Service) Order 1973, SI 1973/1935; National Health Service Reorganisation Act 1973 (Commencement No 3) Order 1974, SI 1974/188; National Health Service Reorganisation Act 1973 (Commencement No 4) Order 1974, SI 1974/1191

Whole Act repealed (S), subject to saving for certain amendments in Sch 4

s 1	5 Jul 1973 (s 58(2))
2–13	Repealed
14	5 Jul 1973 (s 58(2); but note that appointed day for purposes of s 14 is 1 Apr 1974 (SI 1973/1956))
15	5 Jul 1973 (s 58(2); but note that appointed day for purposes of s 15(2) is 1 Apr 1974: SI 1973/1956)

National Health Service Reorganisation Act 1973 (c 32)—*cont*

s 16–20	5 Jul 1973 (s 58(2); but note that appointed day for purposes of ss 16(1), (2), (4), 17(1), 18(1)–(3) is 1 Apr 1974 (SI 1973/1956))
21, 22	Repealed
23–26	5 Jul 1973 (s 58(2); but note that appointed day for purposes of ss 24, 25(1)–(3) is 1 Apr 1974 (SI 1973/1956))
27	1 Apr 1974 (SI 1974/188; but note that 1 Apr is also appointed day for purposes of s 27(1) (SI 1973/1956))
28	Repealed
29, 30	5 Jul 1973 (s 58(2); but note that appointed day for purposes of s 29(1) is 1 Apr 1974 (SI 1973/1956))
31–43	Repealed
44	5 Jul 1973 (s 58(2))
45–48	Repealed
49	5 Jul 1973 (s 58(2))
50–53	Repealed
54–56	5 Jul 1973 (s 58(2))
57	Repealed
58	5 Jul 1973 (s 58(2))
Sch 1	Repealed
2	5 Jul 1973 (s 58(2))
3	Repealed
4	Repealed, subject to saving for certain amendments in Sch 4
5	5 Jul 1973 (entry relating to National Health Service Act 1946, s 36(3)(c)) (s 58(2))
	5 Jul 1973 (entries relating to National Health Service (Scotland) Act 1947; National Health Service (Scotland) Act 1972) (SI 1973/1185)
	1 Apr 1975 (entries relating to National Health Service Act 1946, ss 7(5)(a), (b), (7), 52(2)) (SI 1973/1185)
	1 Apr 1976 (entry relating to National Health Service 1946, s 56) (SI 1974/188)
	1 Apr 1974 (otherwise, except entries relating to Ministry of Social Security Act 1966) (SI 1974/188)
	1 Nov 1974 (entries relating to Ministry of Social Security Act 1966, subject to transitional provisions) (SI 1974/1191)

National Insurance and Supplementary Benefit Act 1973 (c 42)

Whole Act repealed

National Theatre and Museum of London Act 1973 (c 2)

Whole Act repealed

Nature Conservancy Council Act 1973 (c 54)

RA: 25 Jul 1973

Commencement provisions: s 1(7) (repealed); Nature Conservancy Council (Appointed Day) Order 1973, SI 1973/1721

Nature Conservancy Council Act 1973 (c 54)—*cont*
Whole Act repealed except ss 1(3), (9), 5, Sch 1, Sch 2 which came into force on 25
Jul 1973 (RA; but note that this Act for the most part took effect from 1 Nov
1973, the day appointed by SI 1973/1721 on and after which the Council was to
discharge its functions under the Act)

Northern Ireland Assembly Act 1973 (c 17)

RA: 3 May 1973

3 May 1973 (RA; but note that the Assembly had no legislative powers until 11 Jan
1974, when the Northern Ireland Constitution Act 1973, Pt II, came into force)

Northern Ireland Constitution Act 1973 (c 36)

RA: 18 Jul 1973

Commencement provisions: ss 2, 41(1), 43(5), (6); Northern Ireland Constitution Act
1973 (Commencement No 1) Order 1973, SI 1973/1418; Northern Ireland
Constitution (Devolution) Order 1973, SI 1973/2162

s 1–3	18 Jul 1973 (s 43(5))
4–16	1 Jan 1974 (SI 1973/2162)
17–23	1 Sep 1973 (SI 1973/1418)
24–43	18 Jul 1973 (s 43(5))
Sch 1–3	18 Jul 1973 (s 43(5))
4	1 Jan 1974 (SI 1973/2162)
5	18 Jul 1973 (s 43(5))
6, Pt I	18 Jul 1973 (s 41(1)(a))
II	1 Jan 1974 (s 41(1)(b); SI 1973/2162)

Northern Ireland Constitution (Amendment) Act 1973 (c 69)

RA: 19 Dec 1973

19 Dec 1973 (RA)

Northern Ireland (Emergency Provisions) Act 1973 (c 53)

RA: 25 Jul 1973

Commencement provisions: s 30(1)–(3)

8 Aug 1973 (s 30(1))

Overseas Pensions Act 1973 (c 21)

RA: 23 May 1973

23 May 1973 (RA)

Pakistan Act 1973 (c 48)

Whole Act repealed

Pensioners' Payments and National Insurance Act 1973 (c 61)

RA: 25 Oct 1973

Commencement provisions: s 8(1); Pensioners' Payments and National Insurance Act 1973 (Commencement) Order 1973, SI 1973/1969

25 Oct 1973 (RA; note that the only provision brought into force by SI 1973/1969 is repealed)

Whole Act repealed partly prospectively (s 7 and the Schedule), by Social Security Act 1986, s 86(2), Sch 11 (qv)

Powers of Criminal Courts Act 1973 (c 62)

RA: 25 Oct 1973

Commencement provisions: s 60(2); Powers of Criminal Courts Act 1973 (Commencement No 1) Order 1974, SI 1974/941

1 Jul 1974 (SI 1974/941), except s 6(3)(b), (6)(b), (10) (repealed)

Prescription and Limitation (Scotland) Act 1973 (c 52)

RA: 25 Jul 1973

Commencement provisions: s 25(2)

s 1–8	25 Jul 1976 (s 25(2))
8A	Inserted by Prescription and Limitation (Scotland) Act 1984, s 1 (qv)
9–16	25 Jul 1976 (s 25(2))
16A	Inserted by Consumer Protection Act 1987, Sch 1 (qv)
17–19	Substituted by ss 17, 18 by Prescription and Limitation (Scotland) Act 1984, ss 2, 5(1) (qv)
18A	Inserted by Law Reform (Miscellaneous Provisions) (Scotland) Act 1985, s 12(2) (qv)
19A	Inserted by Law Reform (Miscellaneous Provisions) (Scotland) Act 1980, s 23(a) (qv)
20, 21	Repealed
22	Substituted by Prescription and Limitation (Scotland) Act 1984, s 3 (qv)
23	Repealed
23A	Inserted by Prescription and Limitation (Scotland) Act 1984, ss 4, 5(2) (qv)
24, 25	25 Jul 1973 (s 25(2))
Sch 1–3	25 Jul 1976 (s 25(2))
4, Pt I	25 Jul 1976 (s 25(2))
II	25 Jul 1973 (s 25(2))
5, Pt I	25 Jul 1976 (s 25(2))
II	25 Jul 1973 (s 25(2))

Protection of Aircraft Act 1973 (c 47)

Whole Act repealed

Protection of Wrecks Act 1973 (c 33)

RA: 18 Jul 1973

18 Jul 1973 (RA)

Rate Rebate Act 1973 (c 28)

Whole Act repealed

Sea Fish Industry Act 1973 (c 3)

Whole Act repealed

Sea Fisheries (Shellfish) Act 1973 (c 30)

RA: 5 Jul 1973

Commencement provisions: s 2(2)

1 May 1974 (s 2(2))

Social Security Act 1973 (c 38)

RA: 18 Jul 1973

Commencement provisions: s 101(2); Social Security Act 1973 (Commencement) Order 1973, SI 1973/1249; Social Security Act 1973 (Commencement No 2) Order 1973, SI 1973/1433; Social Security Act 1973 (Commencement No 3) Order 1974, SI 1974/164; Social Security Act 1973 (Commencement No 4) Order 1974, SI 1974/823; Social Security Act 1973 (Commencement No 5) Order 1975, SI 1975/124

s 1–50	Repealed
51 (whole section)	5 Sep 1973 (for purposes of issue, cancellation, variation or surrender before, but with effect from dates not earlier than, 6 Apr 1975, of recognition certificates and for connected purposes) (SI 1973/1433)
(s 51(1), (2)	Repealed
(3)	6 Apr 1975 (otherwise) (SI 1973/1433, as amended by SI 1974/823); prospectively repealed by Pension Schemes Act 1993, s 188(1), Sch 5, Pt I (qv)
(4)	Repealed
(5)	6 Apr 1975 (otherwise) (SI 1973/1433, as amended by SI 1974/823); prospectively repealed by Pension Schemes Act 1993, s 188(1), Sch 5, Pt I (qv)
(6)–(9)	Repealed
(10)	6 Apr 1975 (otherwise) (SI 1973/1433, as amended by SI 1974/823); prospectively repealed by Pension Schemes Act 1993, s 188(1), Sch 5, Pt I (qv))
	Not in force (otherwise)
52	5 Sep 1973 (SI 1973/1433)
53–57	Repealed

Social Security Act 1973 (c 38)—*cont*

s 58(1) (except para (c)), (2)	5 Sep 1973 (for purpose of issue, cancellation, variation or surrender before, but with effect from dates not earlier than, 6 Apr 1975, of recognition certificates and for connected purposes) (SI 1973/1433, as amended by SI 1974/823)
	6 Apr 1975 (otherwise) (SI 1973/1433, as amended by SI 1974/823); prospectively repealed by Pension Schemes Act 1993, s 188(1), Sch 5, Pt I (qv)
(2A), (2B)	Inserted by Social Security Act 1989, s 24, Sch 6, para 2 (qv); prospectively repealed by Pension Schemes Act 1993, s 188(1), Sch 5, Pt I (qv)
(3)–(5)	Repealed
59(1)	5 Sep 1973 (for purpose of issue, cancellation, variation or surrender before, but with effect from dates not earlier than, 6 Apr 1975, of recognition certificates and for connected purposes) (SI 1973/1433, as amended by SI 1974/823)
	6 Apr 1975 (otherwise) (SI 1973/1433, as amended by SI 1974/823)
(2)–(9)	Repealed
60–62	Repealed
63	5 Sep 1973 (for purpose of enabling steps to be taken to ensure that on and after 6 Apr 1975 schemes conform with the preservation requirements and for connected purposes) (SI 1973/1433)
	6 Apr 1975 (otherwise) (SI 1973/1433); prospectively repealed by Pension Schemes Act 1993, s 188(1), Sch 5, Pt I (qv)
64, 65	5 Sep 1973 (SI 1973/1433); prospectively repealed by Pension Schemes Act 1993, s 188(1), Sch 5, Pt I (qv)
66(1), (2)	5 Sep 1973 (SI 1973/1433); prospectively repealed by Pension Schemes Act 1993, s 188(1), Sch 5, Pt I (qv)
(3)	Repealed
(4), (5)	5 Sep 1973 (SI 1973/1433); prospectively repealed by Pension Schemes Act 1993, s 188(1), Sch 5, Pt I (qv)
(6)	Repealed
(6A)	Substituted together with s 6 for original s 6 by Social Security Act 1981, s 8, Sch 2, para 1 (qv); prospectively repealed by Pension Schemes Act 1993, s 188(1), Sch 5, Pt I (qv)
(7), (8)	5 Sep 1973 (SI 1973/1433); prospectively repealed by Pension Schemes Act 1993, s 188(1), Sch 5, Pt I (qv)
(9)	Repealed
(10)	Inserted by Social Security Pensions Act 1975, s 65(1), Sch 4, para 26 (qv); substituted by Social Security Act 1986, s 86(1), Sch 10, Pt I, para 4 (qv); prospectively repealed by Pension Schemes Act 1993, s 188(1), Sch 5, Pt I (qv)
67	5 Sep 1973 (SI 1973/1433); prospectively repealed by Pension Schemes Act 1993, s 188(1), Sch 5, Pt I (qv)

Social Security Act 1973 (c 38)—*cont*

s 68	18 Jan 1974 (SI 1973/1433); prospectively repealed by Pension Schemes Act 1993, s 188(1), Sch 5, Pt I (qv)
69(1)–(6)	5 Sep 1973 (SI 1973/1433); prospectively repealed by Pension Schemes Act 1993, s 188(1), Sch 5, Pt I (qv)
(7)	*Not in force*
(8)	5 Sep 1973 (SI 1973/1433)
70	Repealed
71, 72	5 Sep 1973 (SI 1973/1433); prospectively repealed by Pension Schemes Act 1993, s 188(1), Sch 5, Pt I (qv)
73–85	Repealed
86	5 Sep 1973 (in relation to Occupational Pensions Board) (SI 1973/1433, 1974/164, both as amended by SI 1974/823) *Not in force* (in relation to Reserve Pensions Board); prospectively repealed by Pension Schemes Act 1993, s 188(1), Sch 5, Pt I (qv)
87, 88	Repealed
89(1)	6 Apr 1975 (SI 1974/164, as amended by SI 1974/823); prospectively repealed by Pension Schemes Act 1993, s 188(1), Sch 5, Pt I (qv)
(2)	5 Sep 1973 (SI 1974/1433, as amended by SI 1974/823); prospectively repealed by Pension Schemes Act 1993, s 188(1), Sch 5, Pt I (qv)
(2A)	Inserted by Social Security Pensions Act 1975, s 65(1), Sch 4, para 31 (qv); prospectively repealed by Pension Schemes Act 1993, s 188(1), Sch 5, Pt I (qv)
(3)	5 Sep 1973 (in relation to s 89(2)) (SI 1973/1433, as amended by SI 1974/823) 6 Apr 1975 (otherwise) (SI 1974/164, as amended by SI 1974/823); prospectively repealed by Pension Schemes Act 1993, s 188(1), Sch 5, Pt I (qv)
(4)	Repealed
90–94	Repealed
95(1)	19 Jul 1973 (SI 1973/1249) (in relation to s 96) 28 Feb 1974 (otherwise) (SI 1974/164)
(2)	Repealed
(3)	28 Feb 1974 (SI 1974/164)
(4), (5)	Repealed
96, 97	19 Jul 1973 (SI 1973/1249)
98	5 Sep 1973 (SI 1973/1433)
99	19 Jul 1973 (SI 1973/1249)
100	See Schs 26, 27, 28 below
101	19 Jul 1973 (SI 1973/1249)
Sch 1–15	Repealed
16	5 Sep 1973 (for purpose of issue, cancellation, variation or surrender before, but with effect from dates not earlier than, 6 Apr 1975, of recognition certificates and for connected purposes) (SI 1973/1433, as amended by SI 1974/823) 6 Apr 1975 (otherwise) (SI 1974/164); prospectively repealed by Pension Schemes Act 1993, s 188(1), Sch 5, Pt I (qv)

Social Security Act 1973 (c 38)—*cont*

Sch 17		5 Sep 1973 (SI 1973/1433); prospectively repealed by Pension Schemes Act 1993, s 188(1), Sch 5, Pt I (qv)
	18–26	Repealed
	27, para 6, 10, 15 17, 19	6 Apr 1975 (SI 1974/164)
	24, 64	6 Apr 1975 (except the words 'or premiums' and 'or premium') (SI 1974/164)
		Not in force (exception noted above)
	72	6 Apr 1975 (SI 1974/164)
	78	6 Apr 1975 (except the words 'or premiums' and 'or premium') (SI 1974/164)
		Not in force (exception noted above)
	80	6 Apr 1975 (except the words 'or premiums in sub-paras (a), (b)) (SI 1974/164)
		Not in force (exception noted above)
	85, 88 107, 110, 118– 121, 167, 175	*Not in force*
	remainder	Repealed or spent
28		28 Feb 1974/1 Apr 1974/1 Apr 1975/1 Apr 1976 (as provided by SI 1974/164) (entries relating to National Insurance Act 1965, ss 83(1)(c), (2)–(6), 84, 86, 87, 104(3), Sch 10; National Insurance (Industrial Injuries) Act 1965, ss 59(2)–(4), 60; National Insurance Act (Northern Ireland) 1966, ss 81(1)(c), (2)–(6), 82, 84; National Insurance (Industrial Injuries) Act (Northern Ireland) 1966, ss 57(2)–(4), 58) (SI 1974/164)
		6 Apr 1975 (remaining entries, except those specified below) (SI 1974/164)
		Not in force (entries relating to Superannuation and other Trust Funds (Validation) Act 1927, ss 1–8, 10, 11(2) from 'but save as aforesaid' onwards; Superannuation and other Trust Funds (Validation) Act (Northern Ireland) 1928)
		Repealed (entries relating to National Insurance Act 1967, s 4(4); National Insurance Act (Northern Ireland) 1967, s 5(4))

Statute Law (Repeals) Act 1973 (c 39)

RA: 18 Jul 1973

18 Jul 1973 (RA)

Statute Law Revision (Northern Ireland) Act 1973 (c 55)

RA: 25 Jul 1973

25 Jul 1973 (RA)

Succession (Scotland) Act 1973 (c 25)

RA: 23 May 1973

23 May 1973 (RA)

Supply of Goods (Implied Terms) Act 1973 (c 13)

RA: 18 Apr 1973

Commencement provisions: s 18(3)

s 1–7	Repealed
8–12	Substituted by Consumer Credit Act 1974, s 192(3)(a), Sch 4, para 35 (qv)
13	Repealed
14, 15	Substituted by Consumer Credit Act 1974, s 192(3)(a), Sch 4, para 36 (qv)
16–18	18 May 1973 (s 18(3))

Ulster Defence Regiment Act (c 34)

Whole Act repealed

Water Act 1973 (c 37)

RA: 18 Jul 1973

Commencement provisions: s 39(1)

s 1–33	Repealed (for savings in respect of ss 1–3, 5, 7–13, 14(1)–(3), (5), (8), 15–17, 20–22, 24, 24A, 26(1), 27–31, 32A, 33, see Water Act 1989, s 190(2), Sch 26)
34, 35	18 Jul 1973 (RA); prospectively (in part) repealed by Water Act 1989, s 190(3), Sch 27, Pt II (qv)
36(1), (2)	18 Jul 1973 (RA; prospectively repealed by Water Act 1989, s 190(3), Sch 27, Pt II (qv)
(3)	Repealed (for savings see Water Act 1989, s 190(2), Sch 26)
37–39	Repealed (for savings see Water Act 1989, s 190(2), Sch 26)
40(1)	18 Jul 1973 (RA)
(2)	See Sch 8 below
(3)	See Sch 9 below
(4), (5)	18 Jul 1973 (RA)
(6)	Repealed
Sch 1–5	Repealed (for savings in respect of Schs 1, 2, Sch 3, Pts I, III, Schs 4, 4A, see Water Act 1989, s 190(2), Sch 26)
6, Pt I	Repealed
Pt II	18 Jul 1973 (RA); prospectively repealed by Water Act 1989, s 190(3), Sch 27, Pt II (qv)
7	Repealed
8	1 Apr 1974 (s 39(1))
9	1 Apr 1974 (s 39(1))

1974

Appropriation Act 1974 (c 2)
Whole Act repealed

Appropriation (No 2) Act 1974 (c 31)
Whole Act repealed

Biological Weapons Act 1974 (c 6)
RA: 8 Feb 1974

8 Feb 1974 (RA)

Carriage of Passengers by Road Act 1974 (c 35)
RA: 31 Jul 1974

Commencement provisions: s 14(5)

s 1–6	*Not in force*
7–14	31 Jul 1974 (RA)
Sch	*Not in force*

Charlwood and Horley Act 1974 (c 11)
RA: 8 Feb 1974

8 Feb 1974 (RA)

Church of England (Worship and Doctrine) Measure 1974 (No 3)
RA: 12 Dec 1974

Commencement provisions: s 7(2); Instrument of the Archbishops of 22 Jul 1975

1 Sep 1975 (Instrument of the Archbishops of 22 Jul 1975)

Consolidated Fund Act 1974 (c 1)
Whole Act repealed

Consolidated Fund (No 2) Act 1974 (c 12)
Whole Act repealed

Consolidated Fund (No 3) Act 1974 (c 15)
Whole Act repealed

Consolidated Fund (No 4) Act 1974 (c 57)

Whole Act repealed

Consumer Credit Act 1974 (c 39)

RA: 31 Jul 1974

Commencement provisions: s 192(2), (4); Consumer Credit Act 1974 (Commencement No 1) Order 1975, SI 1975/2123; Consumer Credit Act 1974 (Commencement No 2) Order 1977, SI 1977/325; Consumer Credit Act 1974 (Commencement No 3) Order 1977, SI 1977/802; Consumer Credit Act 1974 (Commencement No 4) Order 1977, SI 1977/2163; Consumer Credit Act 1974 (Commencement No 5) Order 1979, SI 1979/1685; Consumer Credit Act 1974 (Commencement No 6) Order 1980, SI 1980/50; Consumer Credit Act 1974 (Commencement No 7) Order 1981, SI 1981/280; Consumer Credit Act 1974 (Commencement No 8) Order 1983, SI 1983/1551; Consumer Credit Act 1974 (Commencement No 9) Order 1984, SI 1984/436; Consumer Credit Act 1974 (Commencement No 10) Order 1989, SI 1989/1128

With the exception of the provisions specified below, this Act came into force on 31 Jul 1974 (RA).

The orders mentioned here amend Sch 3 to the Act and appoint days as shown in the following table:—

Sch 3 para	Subject matter	Appointed day	Order
Sch 3, para 1	Consumer credit and consumer hire agreements made on and after the appointed day to be regulated agreements	1 Apr 1977	SI 1977/325
3	S 19(3)	19 May 1985	SI 1983/1551
5	S 21 not to apply to any description of business before the day appointed in relation to that description of business	1 Oct 1977 in the case of all consumer credit and consumer hire businesses except those consumer credit businesses carried on by individuals in the course of which only regulated consumer credit agreements for credit not exceeding £30 are made	SI 1977/325 (substituted by Consumer Credit Act 1974 (Commencement No 10) Order 1989, SI 1989/1128, art 3, Schedule)
		31 Jul 1989 in the case of any consumer credit business which is carried on by an individual and in the course of which only regulated consumer credit agreements for fixed-sum credit or running-account credit not exceeding £30 are made (provision amended but retaining 1977 references)	SI 1989/1128

Consumer Credit Act 1974 (c 39)—*cont*

Sch 3 para	Subject matter	Appointed day	Order
Sch 3, para 6	Ss 35, 36	2 Feb 1976	SI 1975/2123
7	S 40 not to apply to a regulated agreement made in the course of any business before the day specified or referred to in para 5(1) in relation to the description of business in question	See entry to para 5	SI 1977/325 (substituted by art 3, Sch 1 thereof)
8	Pt IV of the Act not to apply to any advertisement published before the day appointed for the purposes of this paragraph	6 Oct 1980	SI 1980/50
9	S 49	1 Oct 1977	SI 1977/802
10	S 50	1 Jul 1977	SI 1977/802
11	S 51	1 Jul 1977	SI 1977/802
12	S 56 to apply to regulated agreements where negotiations begin after the appointed day	16 May 1977	SI 1977/325
13	Ss 57–59, 61–65, 67–73	19 May 1985	SI 1983/1551
14	S 66	19 May 1985	SI 1983/1551
15	S 75 in relation to regulated agreements made on or after the appointed day	1 Jul 1977	SI 1977/802
16–18	Ss 76–81	19 May 1985	SI 1983/1551
19	S 82	1 Apr 1977	SI 1977/325
20–38	Ss 83–111	19 May 1985	SI 1983/1551
39	Ss 114–122 in respect of articles taken in pawn under a regulated consumer credit agreement only	19 May 1985	SI 1983/1551
40	Ss 123, 125	19 May 1985	SI 1984/436
41	S 126	19 May 1985	SI 1983/1551
42	Ss 137–140	16 May 1977	SI 1977/325
43	Pt IX (ss 127–136, 141–144)	19 May 1985	SI 1983/1551
44	S 21	3 Aug 1976	SI 1975/2123
		3 Aug 1976	SI 1977/325
		1 Jul 1978	SI 1977/2163
45	S 148(1)	3 Aug 1976	SI 1975/2123
		3 Aug 1976	SI 1977/325
		1 Jul 1978	SI 1977/2163
46	S 149	1 Jul 1978	SI 1977/2163
47	S 151(1), (2) not to apply to any advertisement published before the day appointed for the purposes of this paragraph	6 Oct 1980	SI 1980/50
48	Ss 157, 158 to apply to requests for information received on and after the appointed day	16 May 1977	SI 1977/325

The amendments made by the following paragraphs of Sch 4 take effect on the days appointed as shown below:—

Sch 4 para	Subject matter	Appointed day	Order
Sch 4, para 1	Amendment of Bills of Sale Act (1878) Amendment Act 1882	19 May 1985	SI 1983/1551
2	Amendment of Factors Act 1889	19 May 1985	SI 1983/1551
3, 4	Repealed		
5	Amendment of Law of Distress Amendment Act 1908 (except in relation to consumer hire agreements)	19 May 1985	SI 1983/1551

Consumer Credit Act 1974 (c 39)—*cont*

Sch 4 para	Subject matter	Appointed day	Order
Sch 4, para 6	Repealed		
7, 8	Amendment of Compensation (Defence) Act 1939	19 May 1985	SI 1983/1551
9	Amendment of Liability for War Damage (Miscellaneous Provisions) Act 1939	19 May 1985	SI 1983/1551
10	Repealed		
11	Amendment of Rag Flock and Other Filling Materials Act 1951	19 May 1985	SI 1983/1551
12–14	Amendment of Reserve and Auxiliary Forces (Protection of Civil Interests) Act 1951	19 May 1985	SI 1983/1551
15, 16	Repealed		
17	Spent		
18–21	Repealed		
22	Amendment of Hire-Purchase Act 1964	19 May 1985	SI 1983/1551
23	Amendment of Emergency Laws (Re-enactments and Repeals) Act 1964	19 May 1985	SI 1983/1551
24–26	Amendment of Trading Stamps Act 1964	6 Oct 1980	SI 1980/50
27	Repealed		
28	Amendment of Trade Descriptions Act 1968	1 Apr 1977	SI 1977/325
29	Repealed		
30, 31	Amendment of Administration of Justice Act 1970	19 May 1985	SI 1983/1551
32	Amendment of Vehicles (Excise) Act 1971	19 May 1985	SI 1983/1551
33	Repealed		
34	Spent		
35, 36	Amendment of Supply of Goods (Implied Terms) Act 1973	19 May 1985	SI 1983/1551
37	Amendment of Fair Trading Act 1973	19 May 1985	SI 1983/1551
38	Repealed		
39	Amendment of Bills of Sale (Ireland) Act (1879) Amendment Act 1883	19 May 1985	SI 1983/1551
40	Amendment of Liability for War Damage (Miscellaneous Provisions) Act (Northern Ireland) 1939	19 May 1985	SI 1983/1551
41, 42	Repealed		
43–45	Amendment of Trading Stamps Act (Northern Ireland) 1965	6 Oct 1980	SI 1980/50
46, 47	Repealed		
48	Repealed		
49	Amendment of Hire-Purchase Act (Northern Ireland) 1966	19 May 1985	SI 1983/1551
50	Repealed		
51	Amendment of miscellaneous transferred excise duties Act (Northern Ireland) 1972	1 Oct 1977	SI 1977/325

Consumer Credit Act 1974 (c 39)—*cont*

The following repeals take effect on the days appointed and to the extent shown below:—

UNITED KINGDOM (Sch 5, Pt I)

Short title	Extent of repeal	Agreements in relation to which repeal not to have effect	Day appointed for coming into operation	Order
Statutory Declarations Act 1835	S 12		19 May 1985	SI 1983/1551
Metropolitan Police Act 1839	S 50		19 May 1985	SI 1983/1551
Police Courts (Metropolis) Act 1839	In s 27 the words 'pawned, pledged' and the words 'or of any person who shall have advanced money upon the credit of such goods'. In s 28 the words 'pawned, pledged or' (in each place)		19 May 1985	SI 1983/1551
Pawnbrokers Act 1872	The whole Act, so far as unrepealed	Pledges taken in pawn before 19 May 1985	19 May 1985	SI 1983/1551
	S 13		6 Oct 1980	SI 1980/50
	Ss 37, 44 and Sch 6		1 Aug 1977	SI 1977/325
	In s 52, the words 'or by the refusal of a certificate for a licence'		1 Aug 1977	SI 1977/325
Commissioners for Oaths Act 1891	In s 1, the words 'or the Pawnbrokers Act 1872'		19 May 1985	SI 1983/1551
Betting and Loans (Infants) Act 1892	Ss 2–4		1 Jul 1977	SI 1977/802
	S 6, except as far as it extends to Northern Ireland		1 Jul 1977	SI 1977/802
	In s 7, the definitions of 'indictment' and 'summary conviction'		1 Jul 1977	SI 1977/802
Burgh Police (Scotland) Act 1892	In s 453, the words 'and all offences committed against the provisions of the Pawnbrokers Act 1872'		19 May 1985	SI 1983/1551
Local Government Act 1894	S 27(1)(b)		1 Aug 1977	SI 1977/325
Police (Property) Act 1897	In s 1(1), the words 'or section thirty-four of the Pawnbrokers Act 1872'		19 May 1985	SI 1983/1551
Moneylenders Act 1900	The whole Act, so far as unrepealed	Agreements made with, or any loan made by or security taken by, a moneylender before 19 May 1985	19 May 1985	SI 1983/1551

Consumer Credit Act 1974 (c 39)—*cont*

Short title	Extent of repeal	Agreements in relation to which repeal not to have effect	Day appointed for coming into operation	Order
Money-lenders Act 1900—*cont*	S 1	Agreements made before 16 May 1977 which are not personal credit agreements	16 May 1977	SI 1977/325
	S 4		6 Oct 1980	SI 1980/50
	S 5		1 Jul 1977	SI 1977/802
Law of Distress Amendment Act 1908	In s 4(1) the words 'bill of sale, hire purchase agreement or'		19 May 1985	SI 1983/1551
Money-lenders Act 1927	The whole Act, so far as unrepealed	Agreements made with, or any loan made by or security taken by a money-lender before 19 May 1985 (except s 8)	19 May 1985	SI 1983/1551
	Ss 1–3, 4(1) and in s 4(2), the words 'the provisions of the last fore-going section and of'		1 Aug 1977	SI 1977/325
	S 4(2)	Moneylending transactions made before 27 Jan 1980	27 Jan 1980	SI 1979/1685
	S 4(3)		6 Oct 1980	SI 1980/50
	S 5(1), (2), (4), (5), (6)	Moneylending transactions made before 27 Jan 1980	27 Jan 1980	SI 1979/1685
	S 5(3)	Moneylending transactions made before 1 Oct 1977	1 Oct 1977	SI 1977/802
	Ss 6–8		27 Jan 1980	SI 1979/1685
	S 9	Moneylending transactions made before 27 Jan 1980	27 Jan 1980	SI 1979/1685
	S 10	Agreements made before 16 May 1977 which are not personal credit agreements	16 May 1977	SI 1977/325
	Ss 11–14		27 Jan 1980	SI 1979/1685
	In s 13(2), the words 'Without prejudice to the powers of a court under section one of the Moneylenders Act, 1900'	In the case of the said words in s 13(2), agreements made before 16 May 1977 which are not personal credit agreements	16 May 1977	SI 1977/325
	In s 14(1)(a), the words ', and the rate of interest charged shall not exceed the rate of twenty per cent. per annum'.		30 Mar 1981	SI 1981/280
	S 15(2)		27 Jan 1980	SI 1979/1685
	S 16		27 Jan 1980	SI 1979/1685
	S 18(a), (b), (c)		1 Aug 1977	SI 1977/325

Consumer Credit Act 1974 (c 39)—*cont*

Short title	Extent of repeal	Agreements in relation to which repeal not to have effect	Day appointed for coming into operation	Order
Children and Young Persons Act 1933	S 8		19 May 1985	SI 1983/1551
Children and Young Persons (Scotland) Act 1937	S 19		19 May 1985	SI 1983/1551
Compensation (Defence) Act 1939	In s 18(1) the words from 'the expression "hire purchase agreement"' to 'omitted'		19 May 1985	SI 1983/1551
Liability for War Damage (Miscellaneous Provisions) Act 1939	Ss 4, 6(b)		19 May 1985	SI 1983/1551
Law Reform (Miscellaneous Provisions) (Scotland) Act 1940	In s 4(2), paras (b), (c)		19 May 1985	SI 1983/1551
Limitation (Enemies and War Prisoners) Act 1945	In s 2, the words 'subsection (1) of section thirteen of the Moneylenders Act 1927'; in s 4, the words 'subsection (1) of section thirteen of the Moneylenders Act 1927'		19 May 1985	SI 1983/1551
Companies Act 1948	S 201(2)(c)		1 Aug 1977	SI 1977/325
Finance Act 1949	In s 15, sub-ss (1)–(3), (6)–(8A)		1 Aug 1977	SI 1977/325
Customs and Excise Act 1952	In s 313(1) the words 'or section 15 of the Finance Act 1949'		1 Aug 1977	SI 1977/325
Pawnbrokers Act 1960	The whole Act	Pledges taken in pawn before 19 May 1985	19 May 1985	SI 1983/1551
Finance Act 1961	S 11(1) from 'or section 15 of the Finance Act 1949' onwards		1 Aug 1977	SI 1977/325
Administration of Justice Act 1964	S 9(3)(b)		1 Aug 1977	SI 1977/325
Hire-Purchase Act 1964	The whole Act, except Pt III and s 37		19 May 1985	SI 1983/1551
Emergency Laws (Re-enactments and Repeals) Act 1964	S 1(4)		19 May 1985	SI 1983/1551

Consumer Credit Act 1974 (c 39)—*cont*

Short title	Extent of repeal	Agreements in relation to which repeal not to have effect	Day appointed for coming into operation	Order
Trading Stamps Act 1964	In s 10(1) the definition of 'purchase'		6 Oct 1980	SI 1980/50
Hire-Purchase Act 1965	The whole Act	Hire-purchase agreements, conditional sale agreements and credit-sale agreements or guarantees and indemnities relating to such agreements provided by a guarantor, before 19 May 1985, unless the agreement would have been a regulated agreement if made on that day	19 May 1985	SI 1983/1551
Hire-Purchase (Scotland) Act 1965	The whole Act	Hire-purchase agreements, conditional sale agreements and credit-sale agreements or guarantees and indemnities relating to such agreements provided by a guarantor, before 19 May 1985, unless the agreement would have been a regulated agreement if made on that day	19 May 1985	SI 1983/1551
Local Government Act 1966	In Sch 3, Pt II, the entries relating to s 37 of the Pawnbrokers Act 1872 and s 1(1) of the Moneylenders Act 1927		1 Aug 1977	SI 1977/325
Local Government (Scotland) Act 1966	In Sch 4, Pt II, the entries relating to s 37 of the Pawnbrokers Act 1872 and s 1(1) of the Moneylenders Act 1927		1 Aug 1977	SI 1977/325
Advertisements (Hire-Purchase) Act 1967	The whole Act		6 Oct 1980	SI 1980/50
Companies Act 1967	Ss 123–125		19 May 1985	SI 1983/1551
Theft Act 1968	In Sch 2, Pt III, the entry relating to the Pawnbrokers Act 1872		1 Aug 1977	SI 1977/325

Consumer Credit Act 1974 (c 39)—*cont*

Short title	Extent of repeal	Agreements in relation to which repeal not to have effect	Day appointed for coming into operation	Order
Decimal Currency Act 1969	In Sch 2, para 2		19 May 1985	SI 1983/1551
Post Office Act 1969	In Sch 4, para 31		19 May 1985	SI 1983/1551
Courts Act 1971	In Sch 9, Pt I, the entry relating to the Pawnbrokers Act 1872		19 May 1985	SI 1983/1551
	In Sch 9, Pt I, the entry relating to the Moneylenders Act 1927		1 Aug 1977	SI 1977/325
Local Government Act 1972	S 213(1)(a), (b), (3)		1 Aug 1977	SI 1977/325
Local Government (Scotland) Act 1973	In Sch 27, para 96		1 Aug 1977	SI 1977/325
	In Sch 29, the entry relating to the Finance Act 1949		1 Aug 1977	SI 1977/325

NORTHERN IRELAND (Sch 5, Pt II)

Short title	Extent of repeal	Agreements in relation to which repeal not to have effect	Day appointed for coming into operation	Order
Charitable Pawn Offices (Ireland) Act 1842	The whole Act		1 Oct 1977	SI 1977/325
Moneylenders Act (Northern Ireland) 1933	The whole Act, so far as unrepealed	Agreements made with, or any loan made by or security taken by, a moneylender before 19 May 1985 (except s 8)	19 May 1985	SI 1983/1551
	Ss 1–3, 4(1)		1 Aug 1977	SI 1977/325
	In s 4(2) the words 'the provisions of sub-s (1) of this section and of' and, in paragraph (a) the words 'followed by the words "licensed moneylender"'		1 Aug 1977	SI 1977/325
	S 4(2)	Moneylending transactions made before 27 Jan 1980	27 Jan 1980	SI 1979/1685
	S 4(3)		6 Oct 1980	SI 1980/50
	S 5(1), (2), (4)–(6)	Moneylending transactions made before 27 Jan 1980	27 Jan 1980	SI 1979/1685

Consumer Credit Act 1974 (c 39)—*cont*

Short title	Extent of repeal	Agreements in relation to which repeal not to have effect	Day appointed for coming into operation	Order
Moneylenders Act (Northern Ireland) 1933 —*cont*	S 5(3)	Moneylending transactions made before 1 Oct 1977	1 Oct 1977	SI 1977/802
	Ss 6–8		27 Jan 1980	SI 1979/1685
	S 9	Moneylending transactions made before 27 Jan 1980	27 Jan 1980	SI 1979/1685
	Ss 10, 11	Agreements made before 16 May 1977 which are not personal credit agreements	16 May 1977	SI 1977/325
	Ss 12–16		27 Jan 1980	SI 1979/1685
	In s 13(2), the words 'Without prejudice to the powers of a court under section one of the Moneylenders Act 1900'	In the case of the said words in s 13(2), agreements made before 16 May 1977 which are not personal credit agreements	16 May 1977	SI 1977/375
	In s 4(1)(a), the words ', and the rate of interest charged shall not exceed the rate of twenty per cent per annum'.		30 Mar 1981	SI 1981/280
	Sch 1		27 Jan 1980	SI 1979/1685
Liability for War Damage (Miscellaneous Provisions) Act (Northern Ireland) 1939	In s 5(1) the definition of 'hire-purchase agreement'		19 May 1985	SI 1983/1551
Agriculture Act (Northern Ireland) 1949	S 7(2)		19 May 1985	SI 1983/1551
Pawnbrokers Act (Northern Ireland) 1954	The whole Act, so far as unrepealed	Pledges taken in pawn before 19 May 1985	19 May 1985	SI 1983/1551
	Ss 5–9		1 Aug 1977	SI 1977/325
	S 11		6 Oct 1980	SI 1980/50
Betting and Lotteries Act (Northern Ireland) 1957	S 3(1)(j)		1 Aug 1977	SI 1977/325
Companies Act (Northern Ireland) 1960	S 192(3)(c)		1 Aug 1977	SI 1977/325
Trading Stamps Act (Northern Ireland) 1965	In s 9 the definition of 'purchase'		6 Oct 1980	SI 1980/50

Consumer Credit Act 1974 (c 39)—*cont*

Short title	Extent of repeal	Agreements in relation to which repeal not to have effect	Day appointed for coming into operation	Order
Hire-Purchase Act (Northern Ireland) 1966	The whole Act so far as unrepealed, except Pt VI and s 68	Hire-purchase agreements, conditional sale agreements and credit-sale agreements or guarantees and indemnities relating to such agreements provided by a guarantor, before 19 May 1985, unless the agreement would have been a regulated agreement if made on that day	19 May 1985	SI 1983/1551
Increase of Fines Act (Northern Ireland) 1967	Pt V and Sch 4		6 Oct 1980	SI 1980/50
	In Pt I of the Schedule the entries relating to ss 4(2), (3), 5(5) of the Moneylenders Act (Northern Ireland) 1933		6 Oct 1980	SI 1980/50
	In Pt I of the Schedule the entry relating to s 16(1) of the Moneylenders Act (Northern Ireland) 1933		19 May 1985	SI 1983/1551
Criminal Justice (Miscellaneous Provisions) Act (Northern Ireland) 1968	In Sch 2 the entry relating to s 5(5) of the Moneylenders Act (Northern Ireland) 1933		6 Oct 1980	SI 1980/50
	In Sch 2 the entry relating to s 16(1) of the Moneylenders Act (Northern Ireland) 1933		19 May 1985	SI 1983/1551
Theft Act (Northern Ireland) 1969	In Sch 2, the entry relating to the Pawnbrokers Act (Northern Ireland) 1954		1 Aug 1977	SI 1977/325
Industrial and Provident Societies Act (Northern Ireland) 1969	S 96		19 May 1985	SI 1983/1551
Moneylenders (Amendment) (Northern Ireland) 1969	The whole Act	Agreements made with, or any loan made by or security taken by, a moneylender before 19 May 1985	19 May 1985	SI 1983/1551

Consumer Credit Act 1974 (c 39)—*cont*

Short title	Extent of repeal	Agreements in relation to which repeal not to have effect	Day appointed for coming into operation	Order
Judgments (Enforcement) Act (Northern Ireland) 1969	In Sch 4 the amendments of the Hire Purchase Act (Northern Ireland) 1966		19 May 1985	SI 1983/1551
Licensing Act (Northern Ireland) 1971	S 2(5)(b)		1 Aug 1977	SI 1977/325
Miscellaneous Transferred Duties Act (Northern Ireland) 1972	Pt VI		1 Oct 1977	SI 1977/325
	Pt VII		1 Aug 1977	SI 1977/325
	In Sch 4 the entry relating to the Pawnbrokers Act (Northern Ireland) 1954		1 Aug 1977	SI 1977/325

Contingencies Fund Act 1974 (c 18)

RA: 23 May 1974

23 May 1974 (RA)

Control of Pollution Act 1974 (c 40)

RA: 31 Jul 1974

Commencement provisions: s 109(2); Control of Pollution Act 1974 (Commencement No 1) Order 1974, SI 1974/2039; Control of Pollution Act 1974 (Commencement No 2) Order 1974, SI 1974/2169; Control of Pollution Act 1974 (Commencement No 3) Order 1975, SI 1975/230; Control of Pollution Act 1974 (Commencement No 4) Order 1975, SI 1975/2118; Control of Pollution Act 1974 (Commencement No 5) Order 1976, SI 1976/731; Control of Pollution Act 1974 (Commencement No 6) Order 1976, SI 1976/956; Control of Pollution Act 1974 (Commencement No 7) Order 1976, SI 1976/1080; Control of Pollution Act 1974 (Commencement No 8) Order 1977, SI 1977/336; Control of Pollution Act 1974 (Commencement No 9) Order 1977, SI 1977/476; Control of Pollution Act 1974 (Commencement No 10) Order 1977, SI 1977/1587; Control of Pollution Act 1974 (Commencement No 11) Order 1977, SI 1977/2164; Control of Pollution Act 1974 (Commencement No 12) Order 1978, SI 1978/816; Control of Pollution Act 1974 (Commencement No 13) Order 1978, SI 1978/954; Control of Pollution Act 1974 (Commencement No 14) Order 1981, SI 1981/196; Control of Pollution Act 1974 (Commencement No 15) (Scotland) Order 1982, SI 1982/624; Control of Pollution Act 1974 (Commencement No 15 (renumbered 16 by Order No 17 below)) Order 1983, SI 1983/1175; Control of Pollution Act 1974 (Commencement No 17) Order 1984, SI 1984/853; Control of Pollution Act 1974 (Commencement No 18) Order 1985, SI 1985/70; Control of Pollution Act 1974 (Commencement No 19) Order 1988, SI 1988/818; Control of Pollution Act 1974 (Commencement No 20) (Scotland) Order 1991, SI 1991/1173

s 1   *Not in force*; prospectively repealed by
                                 Environmental Protection Act 1990, s 162,
                                 Sch 16, Pt II (qv)

Control of Pollution Act 1974 (c 40)—*cont*

s 2	Repealed
3–11	14 Jun 1976 (EW) (SI 1976/731); 1 Jan 1978 (S) (SI 1977/1587); prospectively repealed by Environmental Protection Act 1990, s 162, Sch 16, Pt II (qv)
12(1)–(4)	6 Jun 1988 (EW) (SI 1988/818); *not in force* (S); prospectively (in part) repealed by Environmental Protection Act 1990, s 162, Sch 16, Pt II (qv)★
(5)	1 Jan 1976 (so far as defines 'privy' for the purpose of s 30(4)) (SI 1975/2118); prospectively (in part) repealed by Environmental Protection Act 1990, s 162, Sch 16, Pt II (qv)★
	1 Apr 1977 (EW) (as respects inner London boroughs) (SI 1977/336); prospectively (in part) repealed by Environmental Protection Act 1990, s 162, Sch 16, Pt II (qv)★
	6 Jun 1988 (EW) (otherwise) (SI 1988/818); prospectively (in part) repealed by Environmental Protection Act 1990, s 162, Sch 16, Pt II (qv)★
	Repealed (S)
(6)	1 Jan 1976 (EW) (in its application to s 21) (SI 1975/2118); prospectively (in part) repealed by Environmental Protection Act 1990, s 162, Sch 16, Pt II (qv)★
	6 Jun 1988 (EW) (otherwise) (SI 1988/818); prospectively (in part) repealed by Environmental Protection Act 1990, s 162, Sch 16, Pt II (qv)★
	Repealed (S)
(7)	1 Jan 1976 (EW) (in its application to ss 21, 26) (SI 1975/2118); prospectively (in part) repealed by Environmental Protection Act 1990, s 162, Sch 16, Pt II (qv)★
	6 Jun 1988 (EW) (otherwise) (SI 1988/818); prospectively (in part) repealed by Environmental Protection Act 1990, s 162, Sch 16, Pt II (qv)★
	Repealed (S)
(8), (9)	6 Jun 1988 (EW) (SI 1988/818); repealed (S); prospectively (in part) repealed (EW) by Environmental Protection Act 1990, s 162, Sch 16, Pt II (qv)★
(10)	*Not in force*; prospectively (in part) repealed by Environmental Protection Act 1990, s 162, Sch 16, Pt II (qv)★
(11)	6 Jun 1988 (EW) (SI 1988/818); prospectively (in part) repealed by Environmental Protection Act 1990, s 162, Sch 16, Pt II (qv); repealed (S)★
13(1), (1A)	Substituted for original sub-s (1) by Local Government, Planning and Land Act 1980, s 1(2), Sch 2 (qv); prospectively repealed by Environment Protection Act 1990, s 162, Sch 16, Pt II (qv); repealed (S)★
(2)	6 Jun 1988 (EW) (SI 1988/818); prospectively repealed by Environmental Protection Act 1990, s 162, Sch 16, Pt II (qv); repealed (S)★
(3)	1 Aug 1978 (EW) (in relation to appeals under sub-s (6) against a notice under sub-s (5)) (SI 1978/954); prospectively (in part) repealed by

Control of Pollution Act 1974 (c 40)—*cont*

s 13(3)–*cont*	Environmental Protection Act 1990, s 162, Sch 16, Pt II (qv)★
	6 Jun 1988 (EW) (otherwise) (SI 1988/818); prospectively (in part) repealed by the Environmental Protection Act 1990, s 162, Sch 16, Pt II (qv)★
	Repealed (S)
(4)	6 Jun 1988 (EW) (SI 1988/818); prospectively (in part) repealed by Environmental Protection Act 1990, s 162, Sch 16, Pt II (qv); repealed (S)★
(5), (5A)	Substituted for original sub-s (5) by Local Government, Planning and Land Act 1980, s 1(2), Sch 2, para 10(3) (qv); prospectively (in part) repealed by Environmental Protection Act 1990, s 162, Sch 16, Pt II (qv)★
(6)	1 Aug 1978 (EW) (SI 1978/954); prospectively (in part) repealed by Environmental Protection Act 1990, s 162, Sch 16, Pt II (qv); repealed (S)★
(7), (7A)	Substituted for original sub-s (7) by Local Government, Planning and Land Act 1980, s 1(2), Sch 2, para 10(5) (qv); prospectively (in part) repealed by Environmental Protection Act 1990, s 162, Sch 16, Pt II (qv)★
(8)	1 Aug 1978 (EW) (so far as relates to sub-ss (3), (5)–(7)) (SI 1978/954); prospectively (in part) repealed by Environmental Protection Act 1990, s 162, Sch 16, Pt II (qv)★
	6 Jun 1988 (EW) (otherwise) (SI 1988/818); prospectively (in part) repealed by Environmental Protection Act 1990, s 162, Sch 16, Pt II (qv)★
	Repealed (S)
14(1)–(5)	6 Jun 1988 (SI 1988/818); prospectively (in part) repealed by Environmental Protection Act 1990, s 162, Sch 16, Pt II (qv)★
(6)	6 Jun 1988 (SI 1988/818); prospectively repealed by Environmental Protection Act 1990, s 162, Sch 16, Pt II (qv)★
(7), (8)	6 Jun 1988 (SI 1988/818); prospectively (in part) repealed by Environmental Protection Act 1990, s 162, Sch 16, Pt II (qv)★
(9), (10)	1 Apr 1977 (in relation to inner London boroughs) (SI 1977/336); prospectively (in part) repealed by Environmental Protection Act 1990, s 162, Sch 16, Pt II (qv)★
	6 Jun 1988 (otherwise) (SI 1988/818); prospectively (in part) repealed by Environmental Protection Act 1990, s 162, Sch 16, Pt II (qv)★
(11)	Substituted by Water Act 1989, s 190(1), Sch 25, para 48(5)(c) (qv); prospectively (in part) repealed by Environmental Protection Act 1990, s 162, Sch 16, Pt II (qv)★
(12)	6 Jun 1988 (SI 1988/818); prospectively repealed by Environmental Protection Act 1990, s 162, Sch 16, Pt II (qv)
15	Repealed
16	14 Jun 1976 (EW) (SI 1976/731); 1 Jan 1978 (S) (SI 1977/1587); prospectively repealed by

Control of Pollution Act 1974 (c 40)—*cont*

s 16–*cont*	Environmental Protection Act 1990, s 162, Sch 16, Pt II (qv)
17	1 Jan 1976 (EW) (SI 1975/2118); 18 Jul 1976 (S) (except s 17(3)(a)) (SI 1976/1080); 1 Jan 1978 (S) (s 17(3)(a)) (SI 1977/1587); prospectively repealed by Environmental Protection Act 1990, s 162, Sch 16, Pt II (qv)
18(1), (2)	14 Jun 1976 (EW) (SI 1976/731); 1 Jan 1978 (S) (SI 1977/1587); prospectively repealed by Environmental Protection Act 1990, s 162, Sch 16, Pt II (qv)
(3)	6 Jun 1988 (EW) (SI 1988/818); *not in force* (S); prospectively repealed by Environmental Protection Act 1990, s 162, Sch 16, Pt II (qv)
19	1 Jan 1976 (EW) (SI 1975/2118); *not in force* (S); prospectively repealed by Environmental Protection Act 1990, s 162, Sch 16, Pt II (qv)
20	1 Jan 1976 (EW) (SI 1975/2118); 1 Jan 1978 (S) (SI 1977/1587); prospectively repealed by Environmental Protection Act 1990, s 162, Sch 16, Pt II (qv)
21	1 Jan 1976 (EW) (SI 1975/2118); *not in force* (S); prospectively repealed by Environmental Protection Act 1990, s 162, Sch 16, Pt II (qv)
22(1), (2)	Repealed
(3), (4)	14 Jun 1976 (EW) (SI 1976/731); repealed (S)
(5)	Repealed
23	14 Jun 1976 (EW) (SI 1976/731); repealed (S)
24(1)–(3)	*Not in force*; prospectively repealed by Litter Act 1983, s 12(3), Sch 2 (qv)
(4)	Repealed
25	1 Jan 1976 (SI 1975/2118)
26	Repealed
27(1)(a)	1 Jan 1976 (EW) (SI 1975/2118); 18 Jul 1976 (S) (SI 1976/1080); prospectively repealed by Environmental Protection Act 1990, s 162, Sch 16, Pt II (qv)
(b)	6 Jun 1988 (EW) (SI 1988/818); *not in force* (S); prospectively repealed by Environmental Protection Act 1990, s 162, Sch 16, Pt II (qv)
(2)	1 Jan 1976 (EW) (SI 1975/2118); 18 Jul 1976 (S) (SI 1976/1080); prospectively repealed by Environmental Protection Act 1990, s 162, Sch 16, Pt II (qv)
28	1 Jan 1976 (EW) (so far as applies to ss 12(6), 21(4), 26) (SI 1975/2118); prospectively repealed by Environmental Protection Act 1990, s 162, Sch 16, Pt II (qv)
	6 Jun 1988 (EW) (otherwise, except so far as applies to s 15(2)) (SI 1988/818); prospectively repealed by Environmental Protection Act 1990, s 162, Sch 16, Pt II (qv)
	Not in force (S); prospectively repealed by Environmental Protection Act 1990, s 162, Sch 16, Pt II (qv)

Control of Pollution Act 1974 (c 40)—*cont*

s 29, 30	1 Jan 1976 (SI 1975/2118); prospectively repealed by Environmental Protection Act 1990, s 162, Sch 16, Pt II (qv)
30A–30E	Substituted (S) together with ss 31, 31A–31D, 32, 34–42, for former ss 31–42 by Water Act 1989, s 168, Sch 23, para 4 (qv)
31	Repealed (EW); see note to ss 30A–30E above (S)
31A–31D	See note to ss 30A–30E above
32	Repealed (EW); see note to ss 30A–30E above (S)
33	Repealed (EW); prospectively substituted (S) by Water Act 1989, s 168, Sch 23, para 4 (qv)
34–42	Repealed (EW); see note to ss 30A–30E above (S)
43–45	Repealed
46	Repealed (EW); substituted (S) by Water Act 1989, s 168, Sch 23, para 5 (qv)
47, 48	Repealed (EW); prospectively substituted (S) by Water Act 1989, s 168, Sch 23, para 5 (qv)
49–51	Repealed (EW); substituted (S) by Water Act 1989, s 168, Sch 23, para 5 (qv)
52	Repealed
53	Substituted by Water Act 1989, s 168, Sch 23, para 6 (qv)
54, 55	Repealed (EW); substituted (S) by Water Act 1989, s 168, Sch 23, para 6 (qv)
55A	Inserted (S) by National Heritage (Scotland) Act 1991, s 27(1), Sch 10, para 7(1), (3) (qv)
56	Repealed (EW); substituted (S) by Water Act 1989, s 168, Sch 23, para 6 (qv)
57(a)	Repealed
(b)	1 Jan 1976 (EW) (SI 1975/2118); 1 Aug 1982 (S) (SI 1982/624)
58	Repealed
58A, 58B	Inserted (S) by Noise and Statutory Nuisance Act 1993, s 6(1), Sch 1, para 3 (qv)
59	Repealed
59A	Inserted (S) by Noise and Statutory Nuisance Act 1993, s 6(1), Sch 1, para 5 (qv)
60, 61	1 Jan 1976 (EW) (SI 1975/2118); 1 Aug 1982 (S) (SI 1982/624)
62	1 Jan 1976 (EW) (SI 1975/2118); 18 Jul 1976 (S) (SI 1976/1080)
63–67	1 Jan 1976 (EW) (SI 1975/2118); 1 Aug 1982 (S) (SI 1982/624)
68	1 Jan 1976 (EW) (SI 1975/2118); 18 Jul 1976 (S) (SI 1976/1080)
69	1 Jan 1976 (EW) (SI 1975/2118); 18 Jul 1976 (S) (except so far as applies or refers to 'a noise reduction notice' or to s 65) (SI 1976/1080); 1 Aug 1982 (S) (so far as so applying or referring) (SI 1982/624)
70	1 Jan 1976 (EW) (SI 1975/2118); 18 Jul 1976 (S) (SI 1976/1080)
71	1 Jan 1976 (EW) (SI 1975/2118)
(1)	18 Jul 1976 (S) (SI 1976/1080)
(2)	1 Aug 1982 (S) (SI 1982/624)
(3)	18 Jul 1976 (S) (SI 1976/1080)
72	1 Jan 1976 (EW) (SI 1975/2118); 18 Jul 1976 (S) (SI 1976/1080)

Control of Pollution Act 1974 (c 40)—*cont*

s 73	1 Jan 1976 (EW) (SI 1975/2118); 18 Jul 1976 (S) (except definitions of 'noise abatement order', 'noise abatement zone' 'noise level register' and 'noise reduction notice') (SI 1976/1080); 1 Aug 1982 (S) (remainder) (SI 1982/624)
74	1 Jan 1976 (EW) (SI 1975/2118); 18 Jul 1976 (S) (SI 1976/1080)
75–84	Repealed
85	1 Jan 1976 (EW) (SI 1975/2118); 18 Jul 1976 (S) (SI 1976/1080)
86	Repealed
87	1 Jan 1976 (EW) (SI 1975/2118); 18 Jul 1976 (S) (SI 1976/1080)
88	14 Jun 1976 (EW) (SI 1976/731); 1 Jan 1978 (S) (SI 1977/1587)
89–93	1 Jan 1976 (EW) (SI 1975/2118); 18 Jul 1976 (S) (SI 1976/1080)
94	1 Jan 1976 (EW) (SI 1975/2118); 18 Jul 1976 (S) (except s 94(2)(a)(ii)) (SI 1976/1080); 31 Jan 1985 (S) (s 94(2)(a)(ii)) (SI 1985/70)
95	Substituted by Water Act 1989, s 190(1), Sch 25, para 48(10) (qv)
96	1 Jan 1976 (EW) (SI 1975/2118); 18 Jul 1976 (S) (SI 1976/1080)
97	1 Jan 1976 (SI 1975/2118)
98	1 Jan 1976 (EW) (SI 1975/2118); 18 Jul 1976 (S) (SI 1976/1080)
99	1 Jan 1976 (SI 1975/2118)
100	Repealed
101, 102	1 Jan 1976 (SI 1975/2118)
103	Repealed
104, 105	12 Dec 1974 (SI 1974/2039)
106	1 Jan 1976 (SI 1975/2118)
107	12 Dec 1974 (SI 1974/2039)
108	See Schs 3, 4 below
109	12 Dec 1974 (SI 1974/2039)
Sch 1	Substituted by Local Government, Planning and Land Act 1980, Sch 2, para 18 (qv)
1A	Inserted (S) by Water Act 1989, s 168, Sch 23, para 8 (qv)
2	1 Jan 1976 (SI 1975/2118)
3, para 1, 2	1 Jan 1975 (SI 1974/2169)
3, 4	Spent
5, 6	Repealed
7	*Not in force*
8–10	Repealed
11, 12	31 Jan 1985 (SI 1985/70)
13–15	4 Jul 1984 (SI 1984/853)
16	Repealed
17	4 Jul 1984 (SI 1984/853)
18	14 Jun 1976 (SI 1976/731)
19–22	Repealed
23, 24	31 Jan 1985 (SI 1985/70)
25	Repealed
26	1 Jan 1976 (EW) (SI 1975/2118); 18 Jul 1976 (S) (SI 1976/1080)

Control of Pollution Act 1974 (c 40)—*cont*

Sch 3, para 27–31   Repealed
4   1 Jan 1975 (repeals in Alkali and Works Regulation
                                     Act 1906) (SI 1974/2169)
                                   3 Mar 1975 (repeal in Local Government (Scotland)
                                     Act 1973, s 135(3)) (SI 1975/230)
                                   1 Jan 1976 (repeals of or in Clean Air Act 1956, s 16(1),
                                     proviso, para i; Criminal Justice Act 1967, entries
                                     relating to Clean Air Act 1956, s 27(1), (2);
                                     Administration of Justice (Appeals) Act 1934; Public
                                     Health (Drainage of Trade Premises) Act 1937,
                                     ss 2(4), 3(2), 7(1) proviso, 11, definition of 'interested
                                     body' in s 14(1); Rivers (Prevention of Pollution) Act
                                     1951, s 4; Clean Air Act 1956, s 25(a), (b), the words
                                     'manufacturing process or' in s 26, the amendments
                                     of the Alkali Act 1936, ss 3, 8, 18 in Sch 2; Noise
                                     Abatement Act 1960; Public Health Act 1961,
                                     ss 55(4), 57(3); London Government Act 1963,
                                     s 40(4)(g), Sch 11, Pt I, para 32; Criminal Justice Act
                                     1967, entries relating to Public Health Act 1936,
                                     ss 94(2), 95(1)) (SI 1975/2118)
                                   14 Jun 1976 (repeals of or in Public Health Act 1875;
                                     Trunk Roads Act 1936; Highways Act 1959;
                                     London Government Act 1963, Sch 11, Pt I, so far
                                     as it repeals para 14(1)(c)) (SI 1976/731)
                                   18 Jul 1976 (repeals of or in Clean Air Act 1956, Sch 2;
                                     Noise Abatement Act 1960; Criminal Justice Act
                                     1967, entry relating to Public Health (Scotland) Act
                                     1897, s 22) (S) (SI 1976/1080)
                                   20 Jul 1976 (repeals of or in Public Health (Drainage of
                                     Trade Premises) Act 1937; Public Health Act 1961,
                                     ss 55(1)–(3), (5)–(9), 56, 57(1), (2), (4)–(8), 58,
                                     63(5)) (SI 1976/956)
                                   1 Apr 1977 (as respects inner London boroughs,
                                     repeals of or in Public Health Act 1936, s 72(1)(b),
                                     (2) (in relation to cleansing of earthclosets, privys,
                                     ashpits or cesspools); London Government Act
                                     1963, Sch 11, Pt I, para 14(1), to the extent that the
                                     Public Health Act 1936, s 72(1)(b), (2) relate to the
                                     cleansing of the above items) (SI 1977/336)
                                   1 Apr 1977 (repeal of Public Health Act 1936, s 77)
                                     (SI 1977/476))
                                   16 Mar 1981 (repeal of Deposit of Poisonous Waste
                                     Act 1972) (SI 1981/196)
                                   31 Jan 1985 (repeals of or in Salmon Fisheries
                                     (Scotland) Act 1862; Sea Fisheries Regulation
                                     (Scotland) Act 1895; Public Health Act 1936,
                                     s 259(2); Rivers (Prevention of Pollution) Act 1951,
                                     except ss 5(1)(c), (6), (7), 11(1) (so far as defines
                                     'stream'), (6), 12(1), (3); Rivers (Prevention of
                                     Pollution) (Scotland) Act 1951, except (in addition
                                     to provisions saved in col 3 of Sch 4) ss 18(6),
                                     25(1)(c), (4), 26(2), (4), (7)–(9) and certain
                                     definitions in s 35(1); Clean Rivers (Estuaries and
                                     Tidal Waters) Act 1960; Rivers (Prevention of
                                     Pollution) Act 1961; Water Resources Act 1963,
                                     except s 79; Rivers (Prevention of Pollution)
                                     (Scotland) Act 1965; Water Act 1973) (SI 1985/70)

Control of Pollution Act 1974 (c 40)—*cont*

Sch 4—*cont*   6 Jun 1988 (repeals of or in Public Health Act 1936,
                                         ss 72(1)–(5), 73–76; London Government Act 1963,
                                         Sch 11, Pt I, paras 14, 16, 32; Local Government
                                         Act 1972, Sch 14, paras 5–8) (SI 1988/818)
                                     31 May 1991 (repeals of or in Rivers (Prevention of
                                         Pollution) (Scotland) Act 1951, ss 25(1)(c), (4),
                                         26(2), (7)–(9)) (S) (SI 1991/1173)
                                     Not in force (remainder)

*Ss 12, 13, 14(1)–(5), (7)–(11) repealed except so far as relate to industrial waste in
  England and Wales

Dumping at Sea Act 1974 (c 20)

Whole Act repealed

Ecclesiastical Jurisdiction (Amendment) Measure 1974 (No 2)

RA: 9 Jul 1974

9 Jul 1974 (RA)

**Education (Mentally Handicapped Children) (Scotland) Act 1974
(c 27)**

RA: 17 Jul 1974

17 Jul 1974 (RA; but note that the Act largely took effect from 16 May 1975, the
  day appointed by Education (Mentally Handicapped Children) (Scotland) Act
  1974 (Commencement) Order 1975, SI 1975/307)

Finance Act 1974 (c 30)

Budget day: 26 Mar 1974

RA: 31 Jul 1974

See the note concerning Finance Acts at the front of this book

---

Friendly Societies Act 1974 (c 46)

RA: 31 Jul 1974

Commencement provisions: s 117(2); Friendly Societies Act 1974 (Commencement)
  Order 1975, SI 1975/204

s 1–7	1 Apr 1975 (SI 1975/204)
8	Repealed
9–14	1 Apr 1975 (SI 1975/204)
15	See note to s 15A below
15A	Substituted (subject to savings) for original s 15 by Friendly Societies Act 1992, s 95, Sch 16, paras 1, 6(1) (qv)
16	1 Apr 1975 (SI 1975/204)
17	Repealed (subject to savings)
18–23	1 Apr 1975 (SI 1975/204)
23A	Inserted by Friendly Societies Act 1992, s 95, Sch 16, paras 1, 8 (qv)

Friendly Societies Act 1974 (c 46)—*cont*

s 24	1 Apr 1975 (SI 1975/204); prospectively substituted by Friendly Societies Act 1992, s 95, Sch 16, paras 1, 9 (qv)
25	1 Apr 1975 (SI 1975/204)
26	Substituted by Friendly Societies Act 1992, s 95, Sch 16, paras 1, 10 (qv)
27, 28	Repealed
29–45	1 Apr 1975 (SI 1975/204); prospectively repealed in relation to registered friendly societies and registered branches of such societies by Friendly Societies Act 1992, s 95, Sch 16, paras 1, 12 (qv)
46–57	1 Apr 1975 (SI 1975/204)
57A	Prospectively inserted by Friendly Societies Act 1992, s 95, Sch 16, paras 1, 21 (qv)
58–63	1 Apr 1975 (SI 1975/204)
63A	Inserted by Friendly Societies Act 1992, s 95, Sch 16, paras 1, 22 (qv)
64	Repealed
65	1 Apr 1975 (SI 1975/204)
65A, 65B	Inserted by Friendly Societies Act 1992, s 95, Sch 16, paras 1, 23 (qv)
66–69	1 Apr 1975 (SI 1975/204)
70–74	1 Apr 1975 (SI 1975/204); prospectively repealed by Friendly Societies Act 1992, ss 95, 120(2), Sch 16, paras 1, 24, Sch 22, Pt I (qv)
75	Repealed (subject to savings)
76	1 Apr 1975 (SI 1975/204)
77	Repealed
78–83	1 Apr 1975 (SI 1975/204)
84	1 Apr 1975 (SI 1975/204); prospectively repealed in relation to registered friendly societies by Friendly Societies Act 1992, s 95, Sch 16, paras 1, 31 (qv)
84A	Inserted (sub-s (8) prospectively) by Friendly Societies Act 1992, s 95, Sch 16, para 32 (qv)
85, 86	1 Apr 1975 (SI 1975/204)
87	1 Apr 1975 (SI 1975/204); prospectively substituted by Friendly Societies Act 1992, s 95, Sch 16, paras 1, 34 (qv)
88, 89	Repealed
90	1 Apr 1975 (SI 1975/204); repealed in relation to registered friendly societies by Friendly Societies Act 1992, s 95, Sch 16, paras 1, 36 (qv)
91–94	1 Apr 1975 (SI 1975/204)
95	1 Apr 1975 (SI 1975/204); repealed in relation to registered friendly societies by Friendly Societies Act 1992, s 95, Sch 16, paras 1, 39 (qv)
95A	Inserted by Friendly Societies Act 1992, s 95, Sch 16, paras 1, 39 (qv)
96–105	1 Apr 1975 (SI 1975/204)
106	Repealed
107, 108	1 Apr 1975 (SI 1975/204)
109	31 Jul 1974 (so far as relates to regulations under s 115 (s 117(2))
	1 Apr 1975 (otherwise) (SI 1975/204)
110, 111	1 Apr 1975 (SI 1975/204)
112, 113	31 Jul 1974 (s 117(2))

Friendly Societies Act 1974 (c 46)—*cont*

s 114	1 Apr 1975 (SI 1975/204)
115	31 Jul 1974 (s 117(2)); prospectively repealed by Friendly Societies Act 1992, ss 95, 120(2), Sch 16, paras 1, 49, Sch 22, Pt I (qv)
116	1 Apr 1975 (SI 1975/204)
117	31 Jul 1974 (s 117(2))
Sch 1	Repealed (subject to savings)
2	1 Apr 1975 (SI 1975/204)
3	Repealed
4	1 Apr 1975 (SI 1975/204)
5	Repealed
6	1 Apr 1975 (SI 1975/204); prospectively repealed by Friendly Societies Act 1992, s 120(2), Sch 22, Pt I (qv)
6A	Inserted by Friendly Societies Act 1992, s 95, Sch 16, paras 1, 52 (qv)
7	1 Apr 1975 (SI 1975/204)
8	Repealed
9–11	1 Apr 1975 (SI 1975/204)

Health and Safety at Work etc. Act 1974 (c 37)

RA: 31 Jul 1974

Commencement provisions: s 85(2); Health and Safety at Work etc. Act 1974 (Commencement No 1) Order 1974, SI 1974/1439; Health and Safety at Work etc. Act 1974 (Commencement No 2) Order 1975, SI 1975/344; Health and Safety at Work etc. Act 1974 (Commencement No 3) Order 1975, SI 1975/1364; Health and Safety at Work etc. Act 1974 (Commencement No 4) Order 1977, SI 1977/294; Health and Safety at Work etc Act 1974 (Commencement No 5) Order 1980, SI 1980/208; Health and Safety at Work etc. Act 1974 (Commencement No 6) Order 1980, SI 1980/269

s 1	1 Oct 1974 (SI 1974/1439)
2–4	1 Apr 1975 (SI 1974/1439)
5	1 Apr 1975 (SI 1974/1439); prospectively repealed by Environmental Protection Act 1990, s 162, Sch 16, Pt I (qv)
6–9	1 Apr 1975 (SI 1974/1439)
10(1)	1 Oct 1974 (in relation to the Commission) (SI 1974/1439)
	1 Jan 1975 (in relation to the Executive) (SI 1974/1439)
(2)–(4)	1 Oct 1974 (SI 1974/1439)
(5)	1 Jan 1975 (SI 1974/1439)
(6), (7)	1 Oct 1974 (in relation to the Commission) (SI 1974/1439)
	1 Jan 1975 (in relation to the Executive) (SI 1974/1439)
(8)	Inserted by Employment Protection Act 1975, s 116, Sch 15, para 3 (qv)
11(1)–(3)	1 Oct 1974 (in relation to the Commission) (SI 1974/1439)
	1 Jan 1975 (in relation to the Executive) (SI 1974/1439)
(4), (5)	1 Jan 1975

Health and Safety at Work etc. Act 1974 (c 37)—*cont*

s 11(6)	1 Oct 1974 (in relation to the Commission) (SI 1974/1439)
	1 Jan 1975 (in relation to the Executive) (SI 1974/1439)
12, 13	1 Oct 1974 (SI 1974/1439)
14	1 Jan 1975 (SI 1974/1439)
15, 16	1 Oct 1974 (SI 1974/1439)
17–25	1 Jan 1975 (SI 1974/1439)
25A	Inserted by Consumer Protection Act 1987, s 36, Sch 3, para 3 (qv)
26, 27	1 Jan 1975 (SI 1974/1439)
27A	Inserted by Consumer Protection Act 1987, s 36, Sch 3, para 4 (qv)
28	1 Jan 1975 (SI 1974/1439)
29–32	Repealed
33(1)(a), (b)	1 Apr 1975 (SI 1974/1439)
(c)–(o)	1 Jan 1975 (SI 1974/1439)
(1A)	Inserted by Offshore Safety Act 1992, s 4(2) (qv)
(2)	1 Jan 1975 (SI 1974/1439)
(2A)	Inserted by Offshore Safety Act 1992, s 4(3) (qv)
(3), (4)	1 Jan 1975 (SI 1974/1439)
(5)	Repealed
(6)	1 Jan 1975 (SI 1974/1439)
34–42	1 Jan 1975 (SI 1974/1439)
43	1 Oct 1974 (in relation to payments to the Commission) (SI 1974/1439)
	1 Jan 1975 (otherwise) (SI 1974/1439)
44–46	1 Jan 1975 (SI 1974/1439)
47	1 Jan 1975 (except in relation to ss 2–8) (SI 1974/1439)
	1 Apr 1975 (exception noted above) (SI 1974/1439)
48	1 Jan 1975 (except in relation to ss 2–9) (SI 1974/1439)
	1 Apr 1975 (exception noted above) (SI 1974/1439)
49	1 Jan 1975 (SI 1974/1439)
50–52	1 Oct 1974 (SI 1974/1439)
53	1 Oct 1974, 1 Jan 1975 (in relation to other provisions in force on those dates) (SI 1974/1439)
	1 Apr 1975 (otherwise) (SI 1974/1439)
54–60	1 Jan 1975 (SI 1974/1439)
61–74	Repealed
75	See Sch 7 below
76	Repealed
77(1)	1 Oct 1974 (SI 1974/1439)
(2)	1 Jan 1975 (SI 1974/1439)
78	1 Apr 1974 (SI 1974/1439)
79	Repealed
80–82	1 Oct 1974 (SI 1974/1439)
83	Repealed
84, 85	1 Oct 1974 (SI 1974/1439)
Sch 1	1 Oct 1974 (SI 1974/1439)
2, para 1–9	1 Oct 1974 (SI 1974/1439)
10–12	1 Jan 1975 (SI 1974/1439)
13–19	1 Oct 1974 (SI 1974/1439)
20	1 Jan 1975 (SI 1974/1439)
3	1 Oct 1974 (SI 1974/1439)
4–6	Repealed

Health and Safety at Work etc. Act 1974 (c 37)—*cont*

Sch 7, para 1		27 Mar 1975 (SI 1975/344)
	2(a), (b)	27 Mar 1975 (SI 1975/344)
	(c)	*Not in force*
	3	*Not in force*
	4–6	27 Mar 1975 (SI 1975/344)
	7	17 Mar 1980 (SI 1980/269)
	8, 9	*Not in force*
8		1 Apr 1975 (SI 1974/1439)
9, 10		Repealed

Horticulture (Special Payments) Act 1974 (c 5)

RA: 8 Feb 1974

8 Feb 1974 (RA)

Housing Act 1974 (c 44)

RA: 31 Jul 1974

Commencement provisions: ss 18(6), 118(5), 131(3); Housing Act 1974 (Commencement No 1) Order 1974, SI 1974/1406; Housing Act 1974 (Commencement No 2) Order 1974, SI 1974/1562; Housing Act 1974 (Commencement No 3) Order 1974, SI 1974/1791; Housing Act 1974 (Commencement No 4) Order 1975, SI 1975/374; Housing Act 1974 (Commencement No 5) Order 1975, SI 1975/1113; Housing Act 1974 (Commencement No 6) Order 1979, SI 1979/1214

s 1–17		Repealed
18		Repealed (EW)
	(1)	Repealed (S)
	(2)–(6)	2 Dec 1974 (SI 1974/1791)
19–117		Repealed
118		31 Jul 1974 (s 118(5))
119–128		Repealed
129		20 Aug 1974 (SI 1974/1406); repealed (EW)
130		See Schs 13–15 below
131		20 Aug 1974 (SI 1974/1406)
Sch 1, 2		Repealed
3, Pt I, II		Repealed
	III	2 Dec 1974 (SI 1974/1791); repealed (EW)
4–7		Repealed
8		31 Jul 1974 (s 118(5))
9–12		Repealed
13, para 1–37		Repealed
	38–45	20 Aug 1974 (SI 1974/1406)
	46	*Not in force*
14, 15		Repealed

Housing (Scotland) Act 1974 (c 45)

Whole Act repealed

Independent Broadcasting Authority Act 1974 (c 16)

Whole Act repealed

Independent Broadcasting Authority (No 2) Act 1974 (c 42)

Whole Act repealed

Insurance Companies Act 1974 (c 49)

Whole Act repealed

Juries Act 1974 (c 23)

RA: 9 Jul 1974

Commencement provisions: s 23(3)

9 Aug 1974 (s 23(3))

Land Tenure Reform (Scotland) Act 1974 (c 38)

RA: 31 Jul 1974

Commencement provisions: s 24(2)

1 Sep 1974 (s 24(2))

Legal Aid Act 1974 (c 4)

Whole Act repealed

Local Government Act 1974 (c 7)

RA: 8 Feb 1974

Commencement provisions: s 43(2), (3); Local Government Act 1974 (Commencement No 1) Order 1974, SI 1974/335; Local Government Act 1974 (Commencement No 2) Order 1977, SI 1977/943; Local Government Act 1974 (Commencement No 3) Order 1978, SI 1978/1583

s 1(1)–(7)	8 Feb 1974 (RA)
(8)	Repealed
2–4	8 Feb 1974 (RA)
5(1)	8 Feb 1974 (RA)
(2)	Repealed
(3), (4)	8 Feb 1974 (RA)
6–10	8 Feb 1974 (RA)
11–22	Repealed
23	8 Feb 1974 (RA)
23A	Inserted by Local Government and Housing Act 1989, s 25(2) (qv)
24	Repealed
25–31	8 Feb 1974 (RA)
31A	Inserted by Local Government and Housing Act 1989, s 28(1) (qv)
32–34	8 Feb 1974 (RA)
35	1 Apr 1974 (SI 1974/335)
36	8 Feb 1974 (RA)
37, 38	Repealed
39	8 Feb 1974 (RA)
40	Repealed
41	8 Feb 1974 (RA)

Local Government Act 1974 (c 7)—*cont*

s 42	4 Mar 1974 (SI 1974/335; see also Schs 7, 8 below)
43	8 Feb 1974 (RA)
Sch 1, Pt I	Repealed
II, III	8 Feb 1974 (RA)
2	8 Feb (RA)
3	Repealed
4, 5	8 Feb 1974 (RA)
6, para 1, 2	1 Apr 1974 (SI 1974/335)
3	Repealed
4	1 Apr 1974 (SI 1974/335)
5	Repealed
6	1 Apr 1974 (SI 1974/335)
7	Repealed
8	1 Apr 1974 (SI 1974/335)
9	Repealed
10	1 Apr 1974 (SI 1974/335)
11, 12	Repealed
13, 14	1 Apr 1974 (SI 1974/335)
15	Repealed
16–19	1 Apr 1974 (SI 1974/335)
20, 21	Repealed
22	1 Apr 1974 (SI 1974/335)
23	Repealed
24	1 Apr 1974 (SI 1974/335)
25	Repealed and spent
26	1 Apr 1974 (SI 1974/335)
7, para 1–13	Repealed
14, 15	1 Apr 1974 (SI 1974/335)
8	1 Apr 1974 (except as below) (SI 1974/335)
	1 Oct 1974 (repeals in Weights and Measures Act 1963) (SI 1974/335)
	1 Apr 1975 (repeals of or in Local Government Act 1966, s 27(2); Road Traffic Regulation Act 1967, ss 72(6)(a), 84B(8)(a); Transport Act 1968, s 34(2), (3); Transport (London) Act 1969, ss 7(5), (6), 29(1)(a); Highways Act 1971; Town and Country Planning Act 1971, s 212(1)) (SI 1974/335)
	1 Jun 1977 (repeals of or in National Parks and Access to the Countryside Act 1949, s 98; Local Government Act 1966, ss 1–5, 10, Sch 1; General Rate Act 1967, s 49, Sch 9; Transport Act 1968, ss 13(7), 138(6); Transport (London) Act 1969, s 3(1); Housing Finance Act 1972; Local Government Act 1972, s 203(5), Sch 24, para 12; Rate Rebate Act 1973) (SI 1977/943)
	1 Apr 1979 (repeals of or in National Parks and Access to the Countryside Act 1949, s 97; Rating Act 1966, ss 9, 12(a); Local Government Act 1966, s 8; Countryside Act 1968, ss 33–36) (SI 1978/1583)

Lord Chancellor (Tenure of Office and Discharge of Ecclesiastical Functions) Act 1974 (c 25)

RA: 9 Jul 1974

9 Jul 1974 (RA)

Lord High Commissioner (Church of Scotland) Act 1974 (c 19)

RA: 27 Jun 1974

27 Jun 1974 (RA)

Merchant Shipping Act 1974 (c 43)

RA: 31 Jul 1974

Commencement provisions: s 24(2); Merchant Shipping Act 1974 (Commencement No 1) Order 1974, SI 1974/1792; Merchant Shipping Act 1974 (Commencement No 2) Order 1975, SI 1975/866; Merchant Shipping Act 1974 (Commencement No 3) Order 1978, SI 1978/1466; Merchant Shipping Act 1974 (Commencement No 4) Order 1979, SI 1979/808

s 1	16 Oct 1978 (SI 1978/1466)
2	16 Oct 1978 (SI 1978/1466)
3	1 Nov 1974 (SI 1974/1792)
4	16 Oct 1978 (SI 1978/1466)
5	16 Oct 1978 (SI 1978/1466); prospectively repealed by Merchant Shipping Act 1988, ss 34, 57(5), Sch 4, Pt II, para 18, Sch 7 (qv)
6–8	16 Oct 1978 (SI 1978/1466)
8A	Prospectively inserted by Merchant Shipping Act 1988, s 34, Sch 4, Pt II, para 22 (qv)
9–13	Repealed
14, 15	1 Aug 1979 (SI 1979/808)
16–19	1 Nov 1974 (SI 1974/1792)
20	Repealed by Merchant Shipping (Registration, etc) Act 1993, s 8(4), Sch 5, Pt II, as from 1 May 1994 (qv)
21	1 Nov 1974 (SI 1974/1792)
22	Repealed by Merchant Shipping (Registration, etc) Act 1993, s 8(4), Sch 5, Pt II, as from 1 May 1994 (qv)
23	1 Nov 1974 (SI 1974/1792)
24(1)–(3)	1 Nov 1974 (SI 1974/1792)
(4)	Repealed
(5)	1 Nov 1974 (SI 1974/1792)
Sch 1	16 Oct 1978 (SI 1978/1466); prospectively substituted by Merchant Shipping Act 1988, s 34, Sch 4, Pt II, para 24 (qv)
2, 3	Repealed
4	1 Aug 1979 (SI 1979/808)
5	1 Nov 1974 (SI 1974/1792)

Mines (Working Facilities and Support) Act 1974 (c 36)

RA: 31 Jul 1974

31 Jul 1974 (RA)

Ministers of the Crown Act 1974 (c 21)

Whole Act repealed

National Insurance Act 1974 (c 14)

RA: 13 May 1974

Commencement provisions: s 8(4), Sch 5 (repealed); National Insurance Act 1974 (Commencement) Order 1974, SI 1974/841

s 1–5	Repealed
6(1)–(3)	Repealed
(4)	13 Jun 1974 (SI 1974/841); prospectively repealed by Pension Schemes Act 1993, s 188(1), Sch 5, Pt I (qv)
(5)	Spent (on repeal of Sch 4)
7	Repealed
8(1)	13 May 1974 (Sch 5, para 1(1) (repealed))
(2)–(5)	Repealed
(6)	17 May 1974 (SI 1974/841)
Sch 1–6	Repealed

National Theatre Act 1974 (c 55)

RA: 29 Nov 1974

29 Nov 1974 (RA)

Northern Ireland Act 1974 (c 28)

RA: 17 Jul 1974

17 Jul 1974 (RA)

Northern Ireland (Young Persons) Act 1974 (c 33)

Whole Act repealed

Pakistan Act 1974 (c 34)

Whole Act repealed

Parks Regulation (Amendment) Act 1974 (c 29)

RA: 17 Jul 1974

17 Jul 1974 (RA)

Pensioners' Payments Act 1974 (c 54)

Whole Act repealed

Pensions (Increase) Act 1974 (c 9)

RA: 8 Feb 1974

8 Feb 1974 (RA)

Policing of Airports Act 1974 (c 41)

Whole Act repealed

Prevention of Terrorism (Temporary Provisions) Act 1974 (c 56)

Whole Act repealed

Prices Act 1974 (c 24)

RA: 9 Jul 1974

9 Jul 1974 (RA)

Rabies Act 1974 (c 17)

Whole Act repealed

Railways Act 1974 (c 48)

RA: 31 Jul 1974

Commencement provisions: s 10(4)

s 1	1 Jan 1975 (s 10(4))
2	Repealed
3(1)–(3A)	Substituted for original sub-ss (1)–(3) by London Regional Transport Act 1984, s 37(1), (2) (qv); prospectively repealed by Railways Act 1993, ss 136(13), 152, Sch 14 (qv)
(4)	Substituted by Transport (Finance) Act 1982, s 2 (qv); prospectively repealed by Railways Act 1993, ss 136(13), 152, Sch 14 (qv)
(5)	31 Jul 1974 (RA)
(5A), (5B)	Inserted by British Railways Board (Finance) Act 1991, s 2(2) (qv); prospectively repealed by Railways Act 1993, ss 136(13), 152, Sch 14 (qv)
(6)	31 Jul 1974 (RA); prospectively repealed by Railways Act 1993, ss 136(13), 152, Sch 14 (qv)
(7)	1 Jan 1975 (s 10(4)); prospectively repealed by Railways Act 1993, ss 136(152), Sch 14 (qv)
4	31 Jul 1974 (RA)
5–7	Repealed
8	31 Jul 1974 (RA); prospectively repealed by Railways Act 1993, ss 139(8), 152, Sch 14 (qv)
9	31 Jul 1974 (RA); prospectively repealed by Railways Act 1993, s 152, Sch 12, para 9, Sch 14 (qv)
10	31 Jul 1974 (RA)

Rehabilitation of Offenders Act 1974 (c 53)

RA: 31 Jul 1974

Commencement provisions: s 11(2)

1 Jul 1975 (s 11(2))

Rent Act 1974 (c 51)

RA: 31 Jul 1974

Commencement provisions: s 17(5)

14 Aug 1974 (s 17(5))

Whole Act repealed (S)

Representation of the People Act 1974 (c 10)

Whole Act repealed

Representation of the People (No 2) Act 1974 (c 13)

Whole Act repealed

Road Traffic Act 1974 (c 50)

RA: 31 Jul 1974

Commencement provisions: s 24(4); Road Traffic Act 1974 (Commencement No 1) Order 1974, SI 1974/2075; Road Traffic Act 1974 (Commencement No 2) (Section 20: Northern Ireland) Order 1975, SI 1975/264; Road Traffic Act 1974 (Commencement No 3) Order 1975, SI 1975/489; Road Traffic Act 1974 (Commencement No 4) Order 1975, SI 1975/756; Road Traffic Act 1974 (Commencement No 5) Order 1975, SI 1975/1154; Road Traffic Act 1974 (Commencement No 6) Order 1975, SI 1975/1479; Road Traffic Act 1974 (Commencement No 7) Order 1975, SI 1975/1653; Road Traffic Act 1974 (Commencement No 1) (Scotland) Order 1979, SI 1979/85; Road Traffic Act 1984 (Commencement No 8) Order 1984, SI 1984/811

s 1–15	Repealed
16	1 Jan 1975 (SI 1974/2075)
17	Repealed
18	1 Jan 1975 (SI 1974/2075)
19–22	Repealed
23	1 Jan 1975 (SI 1974/2075)
24(1)	1 Jan 1975 (SI 1974/2075)
(2)	See Sch 6 below
(3)	See Sch 7 below
(4), (5)	1 Jan 1975 (SI 1974/2075)
Sch 1–3	Repealed
4	1 Jan 1975 (SI 1974/2075)
5	Repealed
6, para 1–9	Repealed

Road Traffic Act 1974 (c 50)—*cont*
Sch 6, para 10, 11   1 Jan 1975 (SI 1974/2075)
            12–24   Repealed
            7   1 Jan 1975 (repeals of or in Road Traffic Act 1960,
                              s 133(4); Road Traffic Act 1962, Schs 1, 4; Road
                              Traffic Regulation Act 1967, ss 9(10), 31(3), 42(4),
                              85(1); Criminal Justice Act 1967, Sch 3; Road
                              Traffic Act 1972, ss 47, 48(3), 50, 51, 53(2),
                              62(2)(c), 64, 88(5) (without affecting regulations
                              made under it), 162(1)(iii), 188; Road Traffic
                              (Foreign Vehicles) Act 1972, ss 5, 7(7)) (SI 1974/
                              2075)
                           1 Apr 1975 (repeals of or in Road Traffic Act 1972,
                              s 65, Sch 4, Pt I) (SI 1975/489)
                           1 Sep 1975 (repeal of Road Traffic Regulation Act
                              1967, s 80(10), 24(3) thereof so far as relates to
                              s 80(10)) (SI 1975/1154)
                           1 Jan 1976 (repeal of Road Traffic Act 1972,
                              ss 104(1)–(3), (6)(a), 105(2)) (SI 1975/1479)
                           1 Aug 1984 (repeals of or in Road Traffic Act 1972,
                              ss 68–80, 81(1), 82) (SI 1984/811)
                           Not in force (otherwise)

Slaughterhouses Act 1974 (c 3)

RA: 8 Feb 1974

Commencement provisions: s 48(3)

1 Apr 1974 (s 48(3))

Social Security Amendment Act 1974 (c 58)

Whole Act repealed

Solicitors Act 1974 (c 47)

RA: 31 Jul 1974

Commencement provisions: s 90(2); Solicitors Act 1974 (Commencement) Order
   1975, SI 1975/534

1 May 1975 (SI 1975/534)

Solicitors (Amendment) Act 1974 (c 26)

Whole Act repealed

Statute Law (Repeals) Act 1974 (c 22)

RA: 27 Jun 1974

27 Jun 1974 (RA)

Statutory Corporations (Financial Provisions) Act 1974 (c 8)

RA: 8 Feb 1974

8 Feb 1974 (RA)

Synodical Government (Amendment) Measure 1974 (No 1)

RA: 9 Jul 1974

9 Jul 1974 (RA)

Town and Country Amenities Act 1974 (c 32)

RA: 31 Jul 1974

Commencement provisions: s 13(3), (4); Town and Country Amenities Act 1974
   (Commencement) Order 1975, SI 1975/147; Town and Country Amenities Act
   1974 (Commencement) (Scotland) Order 1975, SI 1975/1202

s 1–4	31 Aug 1974 (s 13(3))
5	Repealed
6, 7	31 Aug 1974 (s 13(3))
8	Repealed
9	17 Jul 1975 (SI 1975/1202)
10	Repealed
11–13	31 Aug 1974 (s 13(3))
Schedule	31 Aug 1974 (s 13(3))

Trade Union and Labour Relations Act 1974 (c 52)

Whole Act repealed

1975

Air Travel Reserve Fund Act 1975 (c 36)

RA: 22 May 1975

22 May 1975 (RA)

Airports Authority Act 1975 (c 78)

Whole Act repealed

Appropriation Act 1975 (c 44)

Whole Act repealed

Arbitration Act 1975 (c 3)

RA: 25 Feb 1975

Commencement provisions: s 8; Arbitration Act 1975 (Commencement) Order 1975, SI 1975/1662

23 Dec 1975 (SI 1975/1662)

Biological Standards Act 1975 (c 4)

RA: 25 Feb 1975

Commencement provisions: s 9; Biological Standards Act 1975 (Commencement) Order 1976, SI 1976/885

1 Jul 1976 (SI 1976/885)

British Leyland Act 1975 (c 43)

RA: 3 Jul 1975

3 Jul 1975 (RA)

Child Benefit Act 1975 (c 61)

Whole Act repealed

Children Act 1975 (c 72)

Whole Act repealed

Church Commissioners (Miscellaneous Provisions) Measure 1975 (No 1)

RA: 1 Aug 1975

1 Aug 1975 (RA)

Cinematograph Films Act 1975 (c 73)

Whole Act repealed

Civil List Act 1975 (c 82)

RA: 19 Dec 1975

19 Dec 1975 (RA)

Coal Industry Act 1975 (c 56)

RA: 1 Aug 1975

Commencement provisions: s 8(2)

1 Sep 1975 (s 8(2))

Community Land Act 1975 (c 77)

Whole Act repealed

Conservation of Wild Creatures and Wild Plants Act 1975 (c 48)

Whole Act repealed

Consolidated Fund Act 1975 (c 1)

Whole Act repealed

Consolidated Fund (No 2) Act 1975 (c 12)

Whole Act repealed

Consolidated Fund (No 3) Act 1975 (c 79)

Whole Act repealed

Criminal Jurisdiction Act 1975 (c 59)

RA: 7 Aug 1975

Commencement provisions: s 14(2), (3); Criminal Jurisdiction Act 1975
(Commencement No 1) Order 1975, SI 1975/1347; Criminal Jurisdiction Act 1975
(Commencement No 2) Order 1976, SI 1976/813

s 1	1 Jun 1976 (SI 1976/813)
2	21 Aug 1975 (SI 1975/1347) (only as respects an act done in Northern Ireland)
	1 Jun 1976 (otherwise) (SI 1976/813)
3	1 Jun 1976 (SI 1976/813)
4	21 Aug 1975 (so far as relates to Sch 2, paras 2(2), (3)) (SI 1975/1347)
	1 Jun 1976 (otherwise) (SI 1976/813)
5–7	1 Jun 1976 (SI 1976/813)
8	Repealed
9–11	1 Jun 1976 (SI 1976/813)
12	7 Aug 1975 (s 14(2)); repealed (EW)
13	7 Aug 1975 (s 14(2))
14	7 Aug 1975 (except as noted below) (s 14(2))
	1 Jun 1976 (so far as s 14(5) relates to Sch 6, Pts III, IV) (SI 1976/813)
Sch 1	1 Jun 1976 (SI 1976/813)
2, para 1, 2(1)	Repealed
2(2), (3)	21 Aug 1975 (SI 1975/1347)
3	Repealed
3, 4	1 Jun 1976 (SI 1976/813)
5	7 Aug 1975 (s 14(2))
6, Pt I, II	7 Aug 1975 (s 14(2))
III, IV	1 Jun 1976 (SI 1976/813)

Criminal Procedure (Scotland) Act 1975 (c 21)

RA: 8 May 1975

Commencement provisions: s 464(2)–(4); Criminal Procedure (Scotland) Act 1975
(Commencement No 1) Order 1991, SI 1991/2883

16 May 1975 (s 464(2)), except ss 23, 329, which came into force on 6 Jan 1992
(SI 1991/2883), and ss 214, 423, which are *not in force*

Diseases of Animals Act 1975 (c 40)

Whole Act repealed

District Courts (Scotland) Act 1975 (c 20)

RA: 27 Mar 1975

Commencement provisions: s 27(2)

s 1	16 May 1975 (s 27(2))
1A	Inserted by Law Reform (Miscellaneous Provisions) (Scotland) Act 1985, s 33 (qv)

District Courts (Scotland) Act 1975 (c 20)—*cont*

s 2–7	16 May 1975 (s 27(2))
8	27 Mar 1975 (RA)
9	16 May 1975 (s 27(2))
10, 11	27 Mar 1975 (RA)
12, 13	16 May 1975 (s 27(2))
13A	Inserted by Statute Law (Repeals) Act 1989, s 1(2), Sch 2, Pt 1 (qv)
14	27 Mar 1975 (RA)
15	16 May 1975 (s 27(2))
16, 17	27 Mar 1975 (RA)
18	16 May 1975 (s 27(2))
19	Repealed
20	27 Mar 1975 (RA)
21, 22	Repealed
23	27 Mar 1975 (RA)
24, 25	16 May 1975 (s 27(2))
26, 27	27 Mar 1975 (RA)
Sch 1, 2	16 May 1975 (s 27(2))

Ecclesiastical Offices (Age Limit) Measure 1975 (No 2)

RA: 1 Aug 1975

Commencement provisions: s 7(4)

1 Jan 1976 (day appointed by Archbishops of Canterbury and York under s 7(4))

Education Act 1975 (c 2)

RA: 25 Feb 1975

Commencement provisions: s 5(4), (5)

Whole Act prospectively repealed by Education Act 1993, s 307(3), Sch 21, Pt II (qv)

s 1, 2	Repealed
3	25 Feb 1975 (RA)
4	See Schedule below
5	25 Feb 1975 (RA)
Sch Pt I	1 Sep 1975 (s 5(4))
II	25 Feb 1975 (RA; but repeals do not affect contributions or grants in respect of expenditure on work begun before 6 Nov 1974; see s 5(5))

Employment Protection Act 1975 (c 71)

RA: 12 Nov 1975

Commencement provisions: s 129(3); Employment Protection Act 1975 (Commencement No 1) Order 1975, SI 1975/1938; Employment Protection Act 1975 (Commencement No 2) Order 1976, SI 1976/144; Employment Protection Act 1975 (Commencement No 3) Order 1976, SI 1976/321*; Employment Protection Act 1975 (Commencement No 4) Order 1976, SI 1976/530 (as amended by SI 1976/1379, SI 1977/82); Employment Protection Act 1975 (Commencement No 6) Order 1976, SI 1976/1996; Employment Protection Act

Employment Protection Act 1975 (c 71)—*cont*
1975 (Commencement No 7) Order 1977, SI 1977/433★; Employment
Protection Act 1975 (Commencement No 8) Order 1977, SI 1977/936;
Employment Protection Act 1975 (Commencement No 9) Order 1977, SI 1977/
2075★

s 1–96	Repealed
97	1 Jan 1976 (SI 1975/1938)
98–110	Repealed
111	1 Feb 1977 (SI 1976/1996)
112, 113	Repealed
114, 115	1 Jan 1976 (SI 1975/1938)
116	1 Jan 1976 (so far as relates to Sch 15, paras 2, 3, 9) (SI 1975/1938)
	1 Mar 1976 (otherwise) (SI 1975/1938)
117–123	Repealed
124	1 Jan 1976 (SI 1975/1938)
125(1)	See Sch 16 below
(2)	See Sch 17 below
(3)	See Sch 18 below
126–128	Repealed
129	1 Jan 1976 (SI 1975/1938)
Sch 1–8	Repealed
9, 10	1 Jan 1976 (SI 1975/1938)
11, 12	Repealed
13, 14	1 Jan 1976 (SI 1975/1938)
15, para 1	1 Mar 1976 (SI 1975/1938)
2, 3	1 Jan 1976 (SI 1975/1938)
4–8	1 Mar 1976 (SI 1975/1938)
9	1 Jan 1976 (SI 1975/1938)
10–21	1 Mar 1976 (SI 1975/1938)
16, Pt I–III	Repealed
IV, para 1–5	Repealed
6	1 Jan 1976 (SI 1975/1938)
7–17	Repealed
18(1)	1 Jun 1976 (so far as relates to para 13(6) (10), (11)) (SI 1975/1938)
	1 Jan 1976 (otherwise) (SI 1976/530)
(2)	1 Jan 1976 (SI 1976/530)
(3)	1 Jan 1976 (so far as relates to para 13(6), (10), (11)) (SI 1975/1938)
	1 Jan 1976 (otherwise) (SI 1976/530)
17, para 12, 14, 15, 18, 19	1 Jan 1976 (SI 1975/1938)
Remainder	Repealed
18	1 Jan 1976 (so far as it relates to Conciliation Act 1896; Agricultural Wages (Scotland) Act 1949; Public Records Act 1958; Wages Councils Act 1959; Equal Pay Act 1970; Superannuation Act 1972; Employment Agencies Act 1973; Employment and Training Act 1973; Health and Safety at Work etc Act 1974, s 2(5); Trade Union and Labour Relations Act 1974, s 8(10), Sch 1, para 26(1), Sch 3, para 9(4), (6), (7); House of Commons Disqualification Act 1975, Sch 1, Pt III; Northern Ireland Assembly Disqualification Act

Employment Protection Act 1975 (c 71)—*cont*
   s 18—*cont*
                    1975, Sch 1, Pt III; Sex Discrimination Act 1975)
                    (SI 1975/1938)
                    1 Feb 1976 (so far as relates to Trade Union Act
                    1913; Industrial Courts Act 1919; Road Haulage
                    Wages Act 1938; National Health Service
                    (Amendment) Act 1949; Trade Union
                    (Amalgamations, etc) Act 1964; Remuneration of
                    Teachers Act 1965; Remuneration of Teachers
                    (Scotland) Act 1967; Transport Act 1968;
                    Consumer Credit Act 1974; Trade Union and
                    Labour Relations Act 1974, ss 8(1), (8), 30(1),
                    Sch 3, paras 2(6), 3, 10(4), (6), 15; House of
                    Commons Disqualification Act 1975, Sch 1, Pt II;
                    Northern Ireland Assembly Disqualification Act
                    1975, Sch 1, Pt II) (SI 1975/1938)
                    1 Mar 1976 (remaining repeals in Health and Safety
                    at Work etc Act 1974) (SI 1975/1938)
                    1 Jun 1976 (so far as relates to Education (Scotland)
                    Act 1962; Redundancy Payments Act 1965; Social
                    Security Act 1973; remaining provisions relating to
                    Trade Union and Labour Relations Act 1974,
                    except Sch 1, para 9(1)(a)) (SI 1976/530)
                    1 Jan 1977 (so far as relates to Terms and Conditions of
                    Employment Act 1959) (SI 1976/1996)
                    1 Feb 1977 (otherwise) (SI 1976/1996)

   ★ Provisions brought into force by these orders are now all repealed or spent

---

Evidence (Proceedings in other Jurisdictions) Act 1975 (c 34)

RA: 22 May 1975

Commencement provisions: s 10(2); Evidence (Proceedings in other Jurisdictions) Act
  1975 (Commencement) Order 1976, SI 1976/429

4 May 1976 (SI 1976/429)

Export Guarantees Act 1975 (c 38)

Whole Act repealed

Export Guarantees Amendment Act 1975 (c 19)

Whole Act repealed

Farriers (Registration) Act 1975 (c 35)

RA: 22 May 1975

Commencement provisions: s 19(2), (3); Farriers (Registration) Act 1975
  (Commencement No 1) Order 1975, SI 1975/2018; Farriers (Registration) Act 1975
  (Commencement No 2) Order 1978, SI 1978/1928; Farriers (Registration) Act 1975
  (Commencement No 3) Order 1981, SI 1981/767

Farriers (Registration) Act 1975 (c 35)—*cont*

s 1–6	1 Jan 1976 (SI 1975/2018)
7	Substituted by Farriers (Registration) (Amendment) Act 1977, s 1(1), Schedule (qv)
8–15	1 Jan 1976 (SI 1975/2018)
15A	Inserted by Farriers (Registration) (Amendment) Act 1977, ss 1(1), 2(3), Schedule (qv)
16	1 Jun 1979 (EW) (SI 1978/1928); 1 Nov 1981 (S, except in Highland Region, Western Isles Islands Area, Orkney Islands Area, Shetland Islands Area and all other islands) (SI 1981/767)
	Not in force (exceptions noted above)
17–19	1 Jan 1976 (SI 1975/2018)
Sch 1–3	1 Jan 1976 (SI 1975/2018)

Finance Act 1975 (c 7)

RA: 13 Mar 1975

See the note concerning Finance Acts at the front of this book

---

Finance (No 2) Act 1975 (c 45)

Budget Day: 15 Apr 1975

RA: 1 Aug 1975

See the note concerning Finance Acts at the front of this book

---

General Rate Act 1975 (c 5)

Whole Act repealed

Guard Dogs Act 1975 (c 50)

RA: 1 Aug 1975

Commencement provisions: s 8(2); Guard Dogs Act 1975 (Commencement No 1) Order 1975, SI 1975/1767

s 1	1 Feb 1976 (SI 1975/1767)
2–4	*Not in force*
5	1 Feb 1976 (SI 1975/1767; but note *not in force* in relation to ss 2–4, 6)
6	*Not in force*
7, 8	1 Feb 1976 (SI 1975/1767)

Hearing Aid Council (Extension) Act 1975 (c 39)

RA: 3 Jul 1975

Commencement provisions: s 2(2); Hearing Aid Council (Extension) Act 1975 (Commencement) Order 1975, SI 1975/1882

29 Dec 1975 (SI 1975/1882)

House of Commons Disqualification Act 1975 (c 24)

RA: 8 May 1975

8 May 1975 (RA)

Housing Finance (Special Provisions) Act 1975 (c 67)

Whole Act repealed

Housing Rents and Subsidies Act 1975 (c 6)

Whole Act repealed

Housing Rents and Subsidies (Scotland) Act 1975 (c 28)

RA: 8 May 1975

Commencement provisions: s 17(4) (repealed)

Whole Act repealed except Sch 3, paras 9, 10, which came into force on 16 May 1975
(s 17(4))

Industrial and Provident Societies Act 1975 (c 41)

RA: 3 Jul 1975

Commencement provisions: s 3(4)

3 Aug 1975 (s 3(4))

**Industrial Injuries and Diseases (Northern Ireland Old Cases) Act 1975
(c 17)**

Applies to Northern Ireland only

Industrial Injuries and Diseases (Old Cases) Act 1975 (c 16)

Whole Act repealed

Industry Act 1975 (c 68)

RA: 12 Nov 1975

Commencement provisions: s 39(6), (7); Industry Act 1975 (Commencement) Order
1975, SI 1975/1881

20 Nov 1975 (SI 1975/1881)

Inheritance (Provision for Family and Dependants) Act 1975 (c 63)

RA: 12 Nov 1975

Commencement provisions: s 27(3)

1 Apr 1976 (s 27(3); note that Act only applies to persons dying on or after this date)

International Road Haulage Permits Act 1975 (c 46)

RA: 1 Aug 1975

Commencement provisions: s 5(2)

1 Sep 1975 (s 5(2))

Iron and Steel Act 1975 (c 64)

Whole Act repealed

Limitation Act 1975 (c 54)

Whole Act repealed

Litigants in Person (Costs and Expenses) Act 1975 (c 47)

RA: 1 Aug 1975

Commencement provisions: s 2(2); Litigants in Person (Costs and Expenses) Act 1975
(Commencement) Order 1976, SI 1976/364; Litigants in Person (Costs and
Expenses) Act 1975 (Commencement) (Scotland) Order 1976, SI 1976/1432;
Litigants in Person (Costs and Expenses) Act 1975 (Commencement) (Northern
Ireland) Order 1977, SI 1977/509; Litigants in Person (Costs and Expenses) Act
1975 (Commencement No 2) (Scotland) Order 1980, SI 1980/1152; Litigants in
Person (Costs and Expenses) Act 1975 (Commencement No 2) Order 1980,
SI 1980/1158

1 Apr 1976 (as respects civil proceedings in a county court, the Supreme Court and
    the Lands Tribunal) (EW) (SI 1976/364)
1 Oct 1976 (as respects civil proceedings in the sheriff court, the Scottish Land
    Court, the Court of Session, the House of Lords on appeal from the Court of
    Session and the Lands Tribunal for Scotland) (S) (SI 1976/1432)
1 May 1977 (as respects civil proceedings in a county court, the Supreme Court
    and the Lands Tribunal) (NI) (SI 1977/509)
1 Sep 1980 (remainder) (EW) (SI 1980/1158)
            (remainder) (S) (SI 1980/1152)

Local Government (Scotland) Act 1975 (c 30)

RA: 8 May 1975

Commencement provisions: s 39(2); Local Government (Scotland) Act 1975
(Commencement) Order 1975, SI 1975/824; Local Government (Scotland) Act
1975 (Commencement No 2) Order 1975, SI 1975/1055

s 1	16 May 1975 (SI 1975/824)
2(1)(a)–(c)	16 Sep 1975 (SI 1975/824)
(d)	1 Apr 1976 (SI 1975/824)
(e)	16 Sep 1975 (SI 1975/824)
(ee)	Inserted by Rating and Valuation (Amendment) (Scotland) Act 1984, s 21, Sch 2, para 13(2) (qv)
(f), (g)	16 Sep 1975 (SI 1975/824)

Local Government (Scotland) Act 1975 (c 30)—*cont*

s 2(1)(gg), (ggg)	Inserted by SI 1991/646–649, 914–917, 940, 941, 943–950, 1992/864, 865, 1782–1796, in different terms, and for different purposes, as from 1 Apr 1990 (SI 1991/646–649, 916), as from 1 Apr 1991 (SI 1991/914, 915, 917, 940, 941, 953–950), as from 1 Apr 1992 (SI 1992/864, 865) and as from 17 Jul 1992 (SI 1992/1782–1796)
(h)	16 Sep 1975 (SI 1975/824)
(2)(a), (b)	16 Sept 1975 (SI 1975/824)
(c)	1 Apr 1976 (SI 1975/824)
(cc)	Inserted by Rating and Valuation (Amendment) (Scotland) Act 1984, s 21, Sch 2, para 14 (qv)
(d)	16 Sep 1975 (SI 1975/824)
(3)	16 Sep 1975 (SI 1975/824)
(4)	Repealed
3	16 Sep 1975 (SI 1975/824)
4	15 Aug 1975 (SI 1975/824)
5	1 Apr 1976 (SI 1975/824)
6	Substituted by Local Government (Scotland) Act 1978, s 1 (qv)
7	16 May 1975 (SI 1975/824)
7A	Inserted by Local Government Finance Act 1992, s 110(1) (qv)
7B	Prospectively substituted for s 7A by Local Government Finance Act 1992, s 110(2) (qv)
8	1 Apr 1976 (SI 1975/824)
9	16 May 1975 (SI 1975/824)
9A	Inserted by Local Government Finance Act 1988, s 137, Sch 12, Pt II, para 13 (qv); substituted by Local Government Finance Act 1992, s 110(4) (qv)
10, 11	16 May 1975 (SI 1975/824)
12	See Sch 2 below
13–19	16 May 1975 (SI 1975/824)
20	Repealed
21–29	16 May 1975 (SI 1975/824)
29A	Inserted by Local Government and Housing Act 1989, s 29(1) (qv)
30–37	16 May 1975 (SI 1975/824)
38(1)	See Sch 6 below
(2)	See Sch 7 below
39	8 May 1975 (RA)
Sch 1	Repealed
2, para 1	16 May 1975 (SI 1975/824)
2	16 May 1975 (as respects rate support grants for the year 1976–77 and any subsequent year) (SI 1975/824)
3	(the new s 4(1)–(3), (6), (7)) 16 May 1975 (as respects rate support grants for the year 1975–76 and any subsequent year) (SI 1975/824)
	(the new s 4(4), (5)) 16 May 1975 (as respects rate support grants for the year 1976–77 and any subsequent year) (SI 1975/824)
4	16 May 1975 (as respects rate support grants for the year 1976–77 and any subsequent year) (SI 1975/824)

Local Government (Scotland) Act 1975 (c 30)—*cont*

Sch 2, para 5	16 May 1975 (as respects rate support grants for the year 1975–76 and any subsequent year) (SI 1975/824)
6, 7	16 May 1975 (as respects rate support grants for the year 1976–77 and any subsequent year) (SI 1975/824)
3–5	16 May 1975 (SI 1975/824)
6, Pt I, para 1	1 Apr 1976 (SI 1975/824)
2	16 May 1975 (SI 1975/824)
Pt II, para 1	16 May 1975 (SI 1975/824)
2, 3	1 Apr 1976 (SI 1975/824)
4–6	16 May 1975 (SI 1975/824)
7	1 Apr 1976 (SI 1975/824)
8	16 May 1975 (SI 1975/824)
9	1 Apr 1976 (SI 1975/824)
10	Repealed
11–13	16 May 1975 (SI 1975/824)
14	1 Apr 1976 (SI 1975/824)
15, 16	Repealed
17, 18	1 Apr 1976 (SI 1975/824)
19–21	16 May 1975 (SI 1975/824)
22	Repealed
23	16 May 1975 (SI 1975/824)
24	16 May 1975 (as respects rate support grants for the year 1976–77 and any subsequent year) (SI 1975/824)
25–31	16 May 1975 (SI 1975/824)
32	16 Sep 1975 (SI 1975/824)
33–36	16 May 1975 (SI 1975/824)
37	1 Apr 1976 (SI 1975/824)
38	16 May 1975 (SI 1975/824)
39	Repealed
40–42	16 May 1975 (SI 1975/824)
43	Repealed
44, 45	16 May 1975 (SI 1975/824)
46	16 May 1975 (SI 1975/824); prospectively repealed by Local Government and Housing Act 1989, s 194, Sch 12, Pt II (qv)
47–62	16 May 1975 (SI 1975/824)
7	16 May 1975 (except entries noted below) (SI 1975/824)
	16 May 1975 (as respects rate support grants for the year 1976–77 and any subsequent year (repeals of or in Local Government (Financial Provisions) (Scotland) Act 1963 ss 3, 9(4); Local Government (Scotland) Act 1966, s 13; Local Government (Scotland) Act 1973, Sch 9, para 54(b))) (SI 1975/824)
	21 Jun 1975 (repeal of Local Government (Scotland) Act 1947, s 231) (SI 1975/1055)
	15 Aug 1975 (repeal of Valuation and Rating (Scotland) Act 1956, s 5) (SI 1975/824)
	16 Sep 1975 (repeals of or in Lands Valuation (Scotland) Act 1854, ss 1, 5; Valuation and Rating (Scotland) Act 1956, ss 9(1), (2), (4), (7), 13(2), Sch 2; Local Government (Financial Provisions) (Scotland) Act 1962, s 9, Sch 2, para 4) (SI 1975/824)

Local Government (Scotland) Act 1975 (c 30)—*cont*

Sch 7—*cont*   1 Apr 1976 (repeals of or in Lands Valuation
                            (Scotland) Act 1854, ss 23, 24, 27; Valuation of
                            Lands (Scotland) Acts Amendment Act 1894;
                            Local Government (Scotland) Act 1947, s 232;
                            Local Government Act 1948; Rating and
                            Valuation (Scotland) Act 1952; Valuation and
                            Rating (Scotland) Act 1956, ss 9(6), 10; Local
                            Government (Financial Provisions) (Scotland) Act
                            1963, s 21; Local Government (Development and
                            Finance) (Scotland) Act 1964, s 12; Rating Act
                            1966; Local Government (Scotland) Act 1966,
                            Sch 2; Local Government (Scotland) Act 1973,
                            Sch 9, para 57) (SI 1975/824)
                            1 Apr 1977 (repeal of Lands Valuation (Scotland)
                            Act 1854, s 9) (SI 1975/824)
                            1 Apr 1978 (repeals of or in Lands Valuation
                            (Scotland) Act 1854, s 42; Registration
                            Amendment (Scotland) Act 1885; Local
                            Government (Financial Provisions) (Scotland) Act
                            1963, s 13(1), (2)(b), (e), (3), (4), (6), (7), (8))
                            (SI 1975/824)

Local Land Charges Act 1975 (c 76)

RA: 12 Nov 1975

Commencement provisions: s 20(3); Local Land Charges Act 1975 (Commencement)
    Order 1977, SI 1977/984

1 Aug 1977 (SI 1977/984)

Lotteries Act 1975 (c 58)

RA: 7 Aug 1975

Commencement provisions: s 20(6) (repealed); Lotteries Act 1975 (Commencement
    No 1) Order 1975, SI 1975/1413

Whole Act repealed except s 20(1), (3), Sch 4, para 6 which came into force on 5 Sep
    1975 (SI 1975/1413)

Malta Republic Act 1975 (c 31)

RA: 8 May 1975

Independence Day: 13 Dec 1974

Mental Health (Amendment) Act 1975 (c 29)

Whole Act repealed

Ministerial and other Salaries Act 1975 (c 27)

RA: 8 May 1975

8 May 1975 (RA)

Ministers of the Crown Act 1975 (c 26)

RA: 8 May 1975

8 May 1975 (RA)

Mobile Homes Act 1975 (c 49)

RA: 1 Aug 1975

Commencement provisions: s 10(2)

1 Oct 1975 (s 10(2))

Moneylenders (Crown Agents) Act 1971 (c 81)

Whole Act repealed

New Towns Act 1975 (c 42)

RA: 3 Jul 1975

Whole Act repealed except for s 2(3) (S), which came into force on 3 Jul 1975 (RA)

Northern Ireland Assembly Disqualification Act 1975 (c 25)

RA: 8 May 1975

8 May 1975 (RA)

Northern Ireland (Emergency Provisions) (Amendment) Act 1975 (c 62)

RA: 7 Aug 1975

Commencement provisions: s 21(1)

21 Aug 1975 (s 21(1))

Northern Ireland (Loans) Act 1975 (c 83)

RA: 19 Dec 1975

19 Dec 1975 (RA)

Nursing Homes Act 1975 (c 37)

Whole Act repealed

OECD Support Fund Act 1975 (c 80)

RA: 19 Dec 1975

19 Dec 1975 (RA)

Offshore Petroleum Development (Scotland) Act 1975 (c 8)

RA: 13 Mar 1975

13 Mar 1975 (RA)

Oil Taxation Act 1975 (c 22)

RA: 8 May 1975

8 May 1975 (RA)

Petroleum and Submarine Pipelines Act 1975 (c 74)

RA: 12 Nov 1975

Commencement provisions: s 49(2); Petroleum and Submarine Pipe-lines Act 1975
   (Commencement) Order 1975, SI 1975/2120

1 Jan 1976 (SI 1975/2120)

Policyholders Protection Act 1975 (c 75)

RA: 12 Nov 1975

12 Nov 1975 (RA)

Prices Act 1975 (c 32)

RA: 8 May 1975

8 May 1975 (RA)

Public Service Vehicles (Arrest of Offenders) Act 1975 (c 53)

RA: 1 Aug 1975

1 Aug 1975 (RA) although note s 1, in part, *not in force* in pursuance of s 2(3);
   whole Act prospectively repealed by Transport and Works Act 1992, s 68(1),
   Sch 4, Pt I (qv)

Recess Elections Act 1975 (c 66)

RA: 12 Nov 1975

Commencement provisions: s 5(7)

12 Dec 1975 (s 5(7))

Referendum Act 1975 (c 33)

Whole Act repealed

Remuneration, Charges and Grants Act 1975 (c 57)

Whole Act repealed

Reservoirs Act 1975 (c 23)

RA: 8 May 1975

Commencement provisions: s 29; Reservoirs Act 1975 (Commencement No 1) Order 1983, SI 1983/1666; Reservoirs Act 1975 (Commencement No 2) Order 1985, SI 1985/176; Reservoirs Act 1975 (Commencement No 3) Order 1986, SI 1986/466; Reservoirs Act 1975 (Commencement No 4) Order 1986, SI 1986/2202

s 1	30 Nov 1983 (SI 1983/1666)
2, 3	1 Apr 1985 (SI 1985/176)★
4, 5	30 Nov 1983 (SI 1983/1666)
6–10	1 Apr 1986 (SI 1986/466)★★
11	1 Apr 1985 (SI 1985/176)★
12–14	1 Apr 1986 (SI 1986/466)★★
15(1)–(3)	1 Apr 1986 (SI 1986/466)★★
(4)	1 Apr 1985 (so far as applied by s 16(5)) (SI 1985/176)★
	1 Apr 1986 (otherwise) (SI 1986/466)★★
(5)	1 Apr 1986 (SI 1986/466)★★
16	1 Apr 1985 (SI 1985/176)★
17(1)(a)	1 Apr 1985 (SI 1985/176)★
(b)–(d)	1 Apr 1986 (SI 1986/466)★★
(e)	1 Apr 1985 (SI 1985/176)★
(2)	1 Apr 1985 (SI 1985/176)★
(3)	1 Apr 1986 (SI 1986/466)★★
(4)–(9)	1 Apr 1985 (SI 1985/176)★
18	1 Apr 1985 (SI 1985/176)★
19, 20	1 Apr 1986 (SI 1986/466)★★
21(1)–(4)	1 Apr 1986 (SI 1986/466)★★
(5), (6)	1 Apr 1985 (so far as relate to the provision of information to persons appointed under s 16(3)) (SI 1985/176)★
	1 Apr 1986 (otherwise) (SI 1986/466)★★
22	1 Apr 1985 (so far as relates to provisions brought into force by SI 1983/1666 or 1985/176) (SI 1985/176)★
	1 Apr 1986 (otherwise) (SI 1986/466)★★
23	1 Apr 1986 (SI 1986/466)★★
24	1 Apr 1985 (SI 1985/176)★
25–28	1 Apr 1986 (SI 1986/466)★★
29, 30	30 Nov 1983 (SI 1983/1666)
Sch 1	30 Nov 1983 (SI 1983/1666)
2	1 Apr 1986 (SI 1986/466)★★

★ Brought into force in the areas of Metropolitan Counties or Greater London on 1 Apr 1986 (SI 1986/466)

★★ Brought into force in the areas of Metropolitan Counties or Greater London on 1 Apr 1987 (SI 1986/2202)

Safety of Sports Grounds Act 1975 (c 52)

RA: 1 Aug 1975

Commencement provisions: s 19(6); Safety of Sports Grounds Act 1975 (Commencement) Order 1975, SI 1975/1375

1 Sep 1975 (SI 1975/1375)

Salmon and Freshwater Fisheries Act 1975 (c 51)

RA: 1 Aug 1975

Commencement provisions: s 43(4)

1 Aug 1975 (s 43(4))

Scottish Development Agency Act 1975 (c 69)

RA: 12 Nov 1975

Commencement provisions: ss 8(6), 15(5), 28(2); Scottish Development Agency Act 1975
(Commencement) Order 1975, SI 1975/1898

Whole Act repealed (by Enterprise and New Towns (Scotland) Act 1990, s 38(2),
Sch 5), except ss 1, 20, 28, Sch 1, paras 1–6, 11–14, 16, 17

Sex Discrimination Act 1975 (c 65)

RA: 12 Nov 1975

Commencement provisions: s 83(2), (4), (5); Sex Discrimination Act 1975
(Commencement) Order 1975, SI 1975/1845 (amended by SI 1975/2112)

s 1–5	12 Nov 1975 (RA)
6, 7	29 Dec 1975 (SI 1975/1845)
8(1)–(5)	29 Dec 1975 (SI 1975/1845)
(6)	See Sch 1 below
9–13	29 Dec 1975 (SI 1975/1845)
14	Substituted by Employment Act 1989, s 7(1) (qv)
15–21	29 Dec 1975 (SI 1975/1845)
22	29 Dec 1975 (SI 1975/1845; note however that this section and s 25, so far as relate to admission of pupils to educational establishments for certain purposes, do not apply to offers of, or applications for, admission on date before 1 Sep 1976)
22A	Inserted (EW) by Further and Higher Education Act 1992, s 93(1), Sch 8, Pt II, paras 75, 77 (qv)
23	29 Dec 1975 (SI 1975/1845)
23A	Inserted (EW) by Further and Higher Education Act 1992, s 93(1), Sch 8, Pt II, paras 75, 78 (qv)
23B	Inserted (S) (prospectively in part) by Further and Higher Education (Scotland) Act 1992, s 62(2), Sch 9, para 4(1), (3) (qv)
23C	Prospectively inserted (EW) by Education Act 1993, s 307(1), Sch 19, para 57 (qv)
24	29 Dec 1975 (SI 1975/1845)
25	29 Dec 1975 (SI 1975/1845; see note to s 22 above)
26–35	29 Dec 1975 (SI 1975/1845)
35A	Inserted by Courts and Legal Services Act 1990, s 64(1) (qv)
35B	Inserted by Courts and Legal Services Act 1990, s 65(2) (qv)
36, 37	29 Dec 1975 (SI 1975/1845)

Sex Discrimination Act 1975 (c 65)—*cont*

s 38	29 Dec 1975 (SI 1975/1845 as amended by SI 1975/2112; but note not unlawful to publish or cause to be published printed advertisement before 1 Apr 1976 if printed or made up for publication before 15 Dec 1975)
39–50	29 Dec 1975 (SI 1975/1845)
51	Substituted by Employment Act 1989, s 3(3) (qv)
51A	Inserted by Employment Act 1989, s 3(3) (qv)
52	29 Dec 1975 (SI 1975/1845)
52A	Inserted by Employment Act 1989, s 3(4) (qv)
53	12 Nov 1975 (SI 1975/1845)
54, 55	29 Dec 1975 (SI 1975/1845)
56	1 Jan 1976 (SI 1975/1845)
56A	Inserted by Race Relations Act 1976, s 79(4), Sch 4, para 1 (qv)
57–61	29 Dec 1975 (SI 1975/1845)
62	Substituted by Race Relations Act 1976, s 79(4), Sch 4, para 3 (qv)
63–76	29 Dec 1975 (SI 1975/1845)
77–85	12 Nov 1975 (RA)
85A	Inserted by Trade Union and Labour Relations (Consolidation) Act 1992, s 300(2), Sch 2, para 6 (qv)
85B	Inserted by Trade Union Reform and Employment Rights Act 1993, s 49(1), Sch 7, para 9 (qv)
86, 87	12 Nov 1975 (RA)
Sch 1	29 Dec 1975 (SI 1975/1845; but note so far as Schedule amends Equal Pay Act 1970, s 6, and as regards that Act as set out in Pt II of this Schedule, it came into force on 6 April 1978 (SI 1975/1845). In interim period SI 1975/1845 provided for substituted para 3 of this Schedule for the purposes of s 8(6) of this Act)
2, 3	29 Dec 1975 (SI 1975/1845)
4	12 Nov 1975 (RA)
5, 6	29 Dec 1975 (SI 1975/1845)

Social Security Act 1975 (c 14)

Whole Act repealed

Social Security Benefits Act 1975 (c 11)

RA: 13 Mar 1975

Commencement provisions: s 14(5), Sch 5; Social Security Benefits Act 1975 (Commencement) (No 1) Order 1975, SI 1975/400; Social Security Benefits (1975 Act) (Commencement No 1) (Northern Ireland) Order 1975, SR (NI) 1975/60; Social Security Benefits Act 1975 (Commencement) (No 2) Order 1975, SI 1975/1336; Social Security Benefits (1975 Act) (Commencement No 2) (Northern Ireland) Order 1975, SR (NI) 1975/243

s 1–11	Repealed
12	24 Mar 1975 (SI 1975/400)
13	24 Mar 1975 (SR (NI) 1975/60)
14(1), (2)	24 Mar 1975 (SI 1975/400, SR (NI) 1975/60)
(3)	Repealed

Social Security Benefits Act 1975 (c 11)—*cont*

s 14(4), (5)	24 Mar 1975 (SI 1975/400, SR (NI) 1975/60)
(6)	See Sch 6 below

Sch 1–3	Repealed
4, 5	24 Mar 1975 (SI 1975/400, SR (NI) 1975/60)
6, Pt I	SI 1975/400 brought following repeals into force on dates as indicated:

    (a) provisions of the National Insurance (Industrial Injuries) Act 1965—

      (i) ss 19(3)(d), 21(4)(part) .... 6 Apr 1975

      (ii) Sch 5, para 1 (parts).............. 7 Apr 1975

    (b) Supplementary Benefit Act 1966, Sch 2, para 2(2) .... 7 Apr 1975

    (c) provisions of the Family Allowances and National Insurance Act 1968.................... 8 Apr 1975

    (d) provision of the National Insurance Act 1969.................... 6 Apr 1975

    (e) provision of the National Insurance Act 1971.................... 6 Apr 1975

    (f) provisions of the Social Security Act 1973—

      (i) ss 9(3)(parts), 24(8)(part), 25(11)(part), 39, Sch 11, Sch 13, paras 4, 9(part) .... 24 Mar 1975

      (ii) s 14(6)(c)(part)................... 16 May 1975

      (iii) s 32(4)(a)(parts).................. 7 Apr 1975

      (iv) Sch 28, Pt I, so much as relates to the National Insurance Act 1967, s 4(4) .... 6 Apr 1975

    (g) provisions of the National Insurance Act 1974—

      (i) ss 1(1), 7(a), Sch 1 .... 6 Apr 1975

      (ii) s 3(1), (2), Sch 3 in the case of—

        (aa) injury benefit (including increase for dependants) ..... 10 Apr 1975

        (bb) disablement benefit (including increases of disablement pension), increase of unemployability supplement under s 13A, maximum under s 29(1)(a) of aggregate of weekly benefits payable for successive accidents and maximum disablement gratuity under s 12(3) .... 9 Apr 1975

        (cc) widow's pension under s 19, widower's pension under s 20 and allowances in respect of children of deceased's family under s 21.. 7 Apr 1975

        (dd) benefit under the Industrial Injuries and Diseases (Old Cases) Act 1967................ 9 Apr 1975

Social Security Benefits Act 1975 (c 11)—*cont*

Sch 6, Pt I—*cont*

        (iii) s 5, Sch 4, para 22 ....24 Mar 1975

SR (NI) 1975/60 brought following repeals into force in Northern Ireland on the dates indicated:

Provisions of the Social Security Act 1973—

    (i) ss 9(3)(parts), 24(8)(part), 25(11)(part), Sch 13, paras 4, 9 (parts) ......24 Mar 1975

    (ii) s 14(6)(c)(part) ....6 May 1975

    (iii) s 32(4)(a)(parts) ....7 Apr 1975

    (iv) Sch 28, Pt II, so much as relates to the National Insurance Act (Northern Ireland) 1967, s 5(4) ....6 Apr 1975

SI 1975/1336 brought following repeals into force on 17 Nov 1975:

    (i) Supplementary Benefit Act 1966, Sch 2, para 23(1)

    (ii) Family Income Supplements Act 1970, s 13(3)

    (iii) Social Security Act 1973, Sch 27, para 70(d), (e)

    (iv) National Insurance and Supplementary Benefit Act 1973, Sch 4, para 8

    (v) National Insurance Act 1974, Sch 4, para 14

SR (NI) 1975/243 brought following repeals into force in Northern Ireland on 17 Nov 1975:

    (i) Social Security Act 1973, Sch 7, para 161(d), (e)

    (ii) National Insurance and Supplementary Benefit Act 1973, Sch 4, para 8

    (iii) National Insurance Act 1974, Sch 4, para 56

Pt II

SR (NI) 1975/60 brought following repeals into force in Northern Ireland on the dates indicated:

  (a) provisions of the National Insurance (Industrial Injuries) Act (Northern Ireland) 1966—

    (i) ss 19(3)(d), 21(4)(part) ....6 Apr 1975

    (ii) Sch 5, para 1(parts) ....7 Apr 1975

  (b) Supplementary Benefits &c (Northern Ireland) 1966, Sch 2, para 2(2) ....7 Apr 1975

  (c) provisions of the Family Allowances and National Insurance (No 2) Act (Northern Ireland) 1968 ....8 Apr 1975

  (d) provision of the National Insurance &c (No 2) Act (Northern Ireland) 1969 ....6 Apr 1975

  (e) provision of the Social Services (Parity) Order (Northern Ireland) 1971 ....6 Apr 1975

  (f) provisions of the National Insurance Measure (Northern Ireland) 1974—

    (i) s 1(1), Sch 1 ....6 Apr 1975

    (ii) s 3(1), (2) and Sch 3 in the case of—

      (aa) injury benefit (including increases for dependants) ....10 Apr 1975

      (bb) disablement benefit (including increases of disablement pension), increases of

Social Security Benefits Act 1975 (c 11)—*cont*

Sch 6, Pt II—*cont*

> unemployability
> supplement under s 13A,
> maximum under s 29(1)(a)
> of aggregate of weekly
> benefits payable for
> successive accidents and
> maximum disablement
> gratuity under s 12(4) .... 9 Apr 1975
>
> (cc) widow's pension under
> s 19, widower's pension
> under s 20 and allowances
> in respect of children of
> deceased's family under
> s 21 .... 7 Apr 1975
>
> (dd) benefit under the
> Workmen's Compensation
> (Supplementation) Act
> (Northern Ireland) 1966 ..... 9 Apr 1975
>
> (iii) Sch 4, para 2(b) so far as it
> relates to the Social Security
> Act 1973, Sch 13, para 5(2) ..... 16 May 1975

SR (NI) 1975/243 brought following repeals into force
in Northern Ireland on 17 Nov 1975:

> (i) Supplementary Benefits Act (Northern
> Ireland) 1966, Sch 2, para 23(1)
>
> (ii) Family Income Supplements Act (Northern
> Ireland) 1971, s 13(3)

Social Security (Consequential Provisions) Act 1975 (c 18)

Whole Act repealed

Social Security (Northern Ireland) Act 1975 (c 15)

Applies to Northern Ireland only

Social Security Pensions Act 1975 (c 60)

RA: 7 Aug 1975

Commencement provisions: s 67(1), (2), (3); Social Security Pensions Act 1975
    (Commencement No 1) Order 1975, SI 1975/1318; Social Security Pensions Act 1975
    (Commencement No 2) Order 1975, SI 1975/1572; Social Security Pensions Act 1975
    (Commencement No 3) Order 1975, SI 1975/1689; Social Security Pensions Act 1975
    (Commencement No 4) Order 1975, SI 1975/2079; Social Security Pensions Act 1975
    (Commencement No 5) Order 1976, SI 1976/141; Social Security Pensions Act 1975
    (Commencement No 6) Order 1976, SI 1976/1173; Social Security Pensions Act 1975
    (Commencement No 7) Order 1976, SI 1976/2129; Social Security Pensions Act 1975
    (Commencement No 8) Order 1977, SI 1977/778; Social Security Pensions Act 1975
    (Commencement No 9) Order 1977, SI 1977/1403; Social Security Pensions Act 1975
    (Commencement No 10) Order 1977, SI 1977/1617; Social Security Pensions Act 1975
    (Commencement No 11) Order 1977, SI 1977/2028; Social Security Pensions Act 1975
    (Commencement No 12) Order 1978, SI 1978/367; Social Security Pensions Act 1975
    (Commencement No 13) Order 1979, SI 1979/171; Social Security Pensions Act 1975

Social Security Pensions Act 1975 (c 60)—*cont*
(Commencement No 14) Order 1979, SI 1979/367 (revoked); Social Security Pensions
Act 1975 (Commencement No 15) Order 1979, SI 1979/394; Social Security Pensions
Act 1975 (Commencement No 16) Order 1979, SI 1979/1030

s 1–25	Repealed
(26–58B	prospectively repealed by Pension Schemes Act 1993, s 188(1), Sch 5, Pt I (qv))
26	21 Nov 1975 (for purpose of issue, cancellation, variation or surrender before, but with effect from dates not earlier than, 6 Apr 1978, of contracted-out certificates and for purposes connected therewith) (SI 1975/1689)
	6 Apr 1978 (otherwise) (SI 1975/1689)
27, 28	6 Apr 1978 (SI 1975/1689)
29	6 Apr 1979 (SI 1975/1689)
29A–29C	Inserted by Social Security (Consequential Provisions) Act 1992, s 4, Sch 2, para 24 (qv)
30(1)–(3)	21 Nov 1975 (for purposes noted to s 26 above) (SI 1975/1689)
	6 Apr 1978 (otherwise) (SI 1975/1689)
(4)	21 Nov 1975 (SI 1975/1689)
(5)	Repealed
31	21 Nov 1975 (SI 1975/1689)
32, 33	21 Nov 1975 (for purposes noted to s 26 above) (SI 1975/1689)
	6 Apr 1978 (otherwise) (SI 1975/1689)
34	Repealed
35, 36	21 Nov 1975 (for purposes noted to s 26 above) (SI 1975/1689)
	6 Apr 1978 (otherwise) (SI 1975/1689)
37	Repealed
37A	Inserted by Social Security Act 1986, s 9(7) (qv)
38–41	21 Nov 1975 (for purposes noted to s 26 above) (SI 1975/1689)
	6 Apr 1978 (otherwise) (SI 1975/1689)
41A–41E	Inserted by Health and Social Security Act 1984, s 20, Sch 6 (qv)
42–44	6 Apr 1978 (SI 1976/141)
44ZA	Inserted by Social Security Act 1986, s 6, Sch 2, para 7 (qv)
44A	Inserted by Social Security Act 1985, s 2, Sch 1, Pt I, para 1 (qv)
45	6 Apr 1978 (SI 1976/141)
46	Repealed
47	6 Apr 1978 (SI 1976/141)
48, 49	6 Apr 1978 (SI 1975/1689)
50, 51	21 Nov 1975 (SI 1975/1689)
51A	Inserted by Social Security and Housing Benefits Act 1982, s 40 (qv)
52	21 Nov 1975 (SI 1975/1689)
52A–52D	Inserted by Social Security Act 1985, s 2, Sch 1, Pt I, para 2 (qv)
53–55	21 Nov 1975 (for purpose of enabling steps to be taken before 6 Apr 1978 to secure compliance of occupational pension scheme with equal access requirements and connected purposes) (SI 1975/1689)
	6 Apr 1978 (otherwise) (SI 1975/1689)

Social Security Pensions Act 1975 (c 60)—*cont*

s (53–55	Prospectively repealed by Social Security Act 1989, ss 23, 31(2), Sch 5, Pt I, para 11(a), Sch 9 (qv))
56(1)–(4)	21 Nov 1975 (as noted to ss 53–55 above) (SI 1975/1689)
	6 Apr 1978 (otherwise) (SI 1975/1689)
(5)	21 Nov 1975 (SI 1975/1689)
(56	Prospectively repealed by Social Security Act 1989, ss 23, 31(2), Sch 5, Pt I, para 11(a), Sch 9 (qv))
56A	Inserted by Social Security Act 1985, s 3, Sch 2 (in part prospectively) (qv)
56B–56D	Repealed
56E	Inserted by Social Security Act 1985, s 3, Sch 2 (in part prospectively) (qv)
56F–56K	Repealed
56L	Inserted by Social Security Act 1985, s 3, Sch 2 (in part prospectively) (qv)
56M, 56N	Repealed
56P	Inserted by Social Security Act 1986, s 11 (qv)
57	21 Nov 1975 (SI 1975/1689)
57A–57D	Inserted by Social Security Act 1990, s 14, Sch 4, paras 1, 3, 11 (qv)
58	See Sch 3 below
58A	Inserted by Social Security Act 1990, s 11(1) (qv)
58B	Prospectively inserted by Social Security Act 1990, s 14, Sch 4, para 2 (qv)
59	6 Apr 1979 (SI 1975/1689)
59A	Inserted by Social Security Act 1979, s 11(4) (qv)
(59B–60B	prospectively repealed by Pension Schemes Act 1993, s 188(1), Sch 5, Pt I (qv))
59B–59J	Inserted by Social Security Act 1990, s 12(1), Sch 3 (qv)
59K	Inserted by Social Security Act 1990, s 13(1) (qv)
60	21 Nov 1975 (SI 1975/1689)
60ZA	Inserted by Social Security Act 1990, s 14, Sch 4, para 12 (qv)
60ZB–60ZF	Inserted by Social Security (Consequential Provisions) Act 1992, s 4, Sch 2, para 36 (qv)
60A	Inserted by Social Security Act 1979, s 18 (qv)
60B	Inserted by Social Security Act 1988, s 9, Sch 2, para 2 (qv)
61	7 Aug 1975 (SI 1975/1318)
61A	Inserted by Social Security (Consequential Provisions) Act 1992, s 4, Sch 2, para 37 (qv); prospectively repealed by Pension Schemes Act 1993, s 188(1), Sch 5, Pt I (qv)
61B	Inserted by Social Security (Consequential Provisions) Act 1992, s 4, Sch 2, para 37 (qv)
62–64	7 Aug 1975 (SI 1975/1318)
65(1)	See Sch 4 below
(2)	7 Aug 1975 (SI 1975/1318)
(3)	See Sch 5 below
(4)	Repealed
(5)	7 Aug 1975 (SI 1975/1318)
66	7 Aug 1975 (SI 1975/1318); prospectively repealed by Pension Schemes Act 1993, s 188(1), Sch 5, Pt I (qv)
67, 68	7 Aug 1975 (SI 1975/1318)

Social Security Pensions Act 1975 (c 60)—*cont*

Sch 1	Repealed
1A	Inserted by Social Security Act 1985, s 2, Sch 1, Pt II, para 3 (qv); prospectively repealed by Pension Schemes Act 1993, s 188(1), Sch 5, Pt I (qv)
2	21 Nov 1975 (SI 1975/1689); prospectively repealed by Pension Schemes Act 1993, s 188(1), Sch 5, Pt I (qv)
(3	prospectively repealed by Pension Schemes Act 1993, s 188(1), Sch 5, Pt I (qv)
3, para 1, 2	6 Apr 1978 (SI 1975/1689)
3	6 Apr 1978 (SI 1976/141)
4	6 Apr 1978 (SI 1975/1689)
3A	Inserted by Social Security Act 1990, s 11(2), Sch 2 (qv)
4, para 1–3	Repealed
4	6 Apr 1979 (SI 1975/1689)
5–9	Repealed
10	6 Apr 1979 (SI 1975/1689)
11, 12	Repealed
13	7 Aug 1975 (SI 1975/1318)
14	Repealed
15	6 Apr 1978 (SI 1975/1689)
16	7 Aug 1975 (SI 1975/1318)
17	Repealed
18, 19	6 Apr 1979 (SI 1975/1689)
20	Repealed
21	Spent
22	Repealed
23–28	21 Nov 1975 (SI 1975/1689); prospectively repealed by Pension Schemes Act 1993, s 188(1), Sch 5, Pt I (qv)
29, 30	7 Aug 1975 (SI 1975/1318)
31–33	21 Nov 1975 (SI 1975/1689); prospectively repealed by Pension Schemes Act 1993, s 188(1), Sch 5, Pt I (qv)
34	Spent
35–64	Repealed
65	Spent
66–70	Repealed
71	Repealed and spent
5	7 Aug 1975 (repeals of or in Public Records Act 1958; Income and Corporation Taxes Act 1970; Attachment of Earnings Act 1971; Social Security Act 1973, Pt III, ss 85, 86, 89(4), 98, Schs 18–20; Social Security Act 1975, ss 27(6), 133(6), Sch 20; Social Security (Consequential Provisions) Act 1975, Sch 2, paras 53–59, 63, 64(a), Sch 3; House of Commons Disqualification Act 1975) (SI 1975/1318)
	21 Nov 1975 (repeals of or in Contracts of Employment Act 1972; Social Security Act 1973, ss 1, 23, 51–62, 88, 89(3), 91, 92, 99, Schs 15, 22, 23; National Insurance Act 1974; Social Security (Consequential Provisions) Act 1975, Sch 2, paras 51, 62, 64(b), 65) (SI 1975/1689)
	6 Apr 1977 (repeals of or in Social Security Act 1975, ss 4, 5, 7(2)(c), 130, 167) (SI 1975/1689)
	6 Apr 1978 (repeals of or in Social Security Act 1973,

Social Security Pensions Act 1975 (c 60)—*cont*

Sch 5—*cont*   s 93, Sch 24; Social Security Act 1975, ss 6, 7(2)(a),
                                        (b), (3), 8, 9, 120; Social Security (Consequential
                                        Provisions) Act 1975, Sch 2, paras 1(b), 2(b), 7(a))
                                        (SI 1975/1689)
                                      6 Apr 1979 (repeals of or in Pensions (Increase) Act
                                        1971; Superannuation Act 1972; Parliamentary and
                                        other Pensions Act 1972; Pensions (Increase) Act
                                        1974; Social Security Act 1975, ss 28, 29, Schs 4, 7;
                                        Social Security (Consequential Provisions) Act 1975,
                                        Sch 2, para 47) (SI 1975/1689)
                                      Repealed (otherwise)

Statute Law (Repeals) Act 1975 (c 10)

RA: 13 Mar 1975

13 Mar 1975 (RA)

Statutory Corporations (Financial Provisions) Act 1975 (c 55)

RA: 1 Aug 1975

1 Aug 1975 (RA)

Supply Powers Act 1975 (c 9)

RA: 13 Mar 1975

Commencement provisions: s 9(2)

13 Apr 1975 (s 9(2))

Unsolicited Goods and Services (Amendment) Act 1975 (c 13)

RA: 20 Mar 1975

Commencement provisions: s 4(2), (3); Unsolicited Goods and Services (Amendment) Act
    1975 (Commencement No 1) Order 1975, SI 1975/731

    s 1*   20 Mar 1975 (s 4(2))
      2(1)   *Not in force*
      (2)   30 May 1975 (SI 1975/731)
      3, 4   20 Mar 1975 (s 4(2))

* Note that any regulations made by virtue of s 1 of this Act (inserts the Unsolicited
Goods and Services Act 1971, s 3A) shall not come into force before the commencement
of s 2 of this Act

Welsh Development Agency Act 1975 (c 70)

RA: 12 Nov 1975

Commencement provisions: s 29(2); Welsh Development Agency Act 1975
    (Commencement) Order 1975, SI 1975/2028

    s 1, 2   1 Jan 1976 (SI 1975/2028)

Welsh Development Agency Act 1975 (c 70)—*cont*

s 3	Repealed
4–11	1 Jan 1976 (SI 1975/2028)
12	Repealed
13–15	1 Jan 1976 (SI 1975/2028)
16	Substituted by Derelict Land Act 1982, s 2(1) (qv)
17–28	1 Jan 1976 (SI 1975/2028)
29	12 Nov 1975 (RA)
Sch 1–3	1 Jan 1976 (SI 1975/2028)

1976

Adoption Act 1976 (c 36)

RA: 22 Jul 1976

Commencement provisions: s 74(2); Children Act 1975 and the Adoption Act 1976
(Commencement) Order 1983, SI 1983/1946; Children Act 1975 and the Adoption
Act 1976 (Commencement No 2) Order 1987, SI 1987/1242

s 1–9	1 Jan 1988 (SI 1987/1242)
10	Repealed
11–20	1 Jan 1988 (SI 1987/1242)
21	Substituted by Children Act 1989, s 88, Sch 10, para 9 (qv)
22, 23	1 Jan 1988 (EW) (SI 1987/1242); repealed (S)
24, 25	1 Jan 1988 (SI 1987/1242)
26	Repealed
27–33	1 Jan 1988 (SI 1987/1242)
34	Repealed
35–39	1 Jan 1988 (SI 1987/1242)
40	Repealed
41–51	1 Jan 1988 (SI 1987/1242)
51A	Inserted by Children Act 1989, s 88, Sch 10, para 21 (qv)
52–57	1 Jan 1988 (SI 1987/1242)
57A	Inserted by Children Act 1989, s 88, Sch 10, para 25 (qv)
58	1 Jan 1988 (SI 1987/1242)
58A	27 May 1984 (inserted by Health and Social Services and Social Security Adjudications Act 1983, s 9, Sch 2, para 35 (qv); note that SI 1983/1946 brought the section into force as noted here, but that the insertion was actually made as from the 15 Aug 1983; see the Health and Social Services and Social Security Adjudications Act 1983 (Commencement No 1) Order 1983, SI 1983/974)
59–65	1 Jan 1988 (SI 1987/1242)
65A	Inserted by Children Act 1989, s 88, Sch 10, para 29 (qv)
66–72	1 Jan 1988 (SI 1987/1242)
73(1)	1 Jan 1988 (SI 1987/1242)
(2)	See Sch 3 below
(3)	See Sch 4 below
74	27 May 1984 (SI 1983/1946)
Sch 1, 2	1 Jan 1988 (SI 1987/1242)
3, para 1–8	Repealed or superseded
9, 10	1 Jan 1988 (SI 1987/1242)
11–14	Repealed or superseded
15	1 Jan 1988 (SI 1987/1242)

Adoption Act 1976 (c 36)—*cont*

Sch 3, para 16	Repealed
17	1 Jan 1988 (SI 1987/1242)
18–22	Repealed or superseded
23, 24	1 Jan 1988 (SI 1987/1242)
25–44	Repealed
4	15 Aug 1983 (repeal of Adoption Act 1958, s 33; see HASSASSAA 1983, s 9, Sch 2, para 1 and SI 1983/974, noted to s 58A above)
	1 Jan 1988 (otherwise except repeal of Children Act 1975, Sch 3, paras 6, 26, 63) (SI 1987/1242)
	Not in force (exception noted above)

Agriculture (Miscellaneous Provisions) Act 1976 (c 55)

RA: 15 Nov 1976

Commencement provisions: s 27(2), (3); Agriculture (Miscellaneous Provisions) Act 1976 (Commencement No 1) Order 1977, SI 1977/39; Agriculture (Miscellaneous Provisions) Act 1976 (Commencement No 2) Order 1978, SI 1978/402

s 1	15 Nov 1976 (RA)
2	Repealed
3	1 Feb 1977 (SI 1977/39)
4, 5	15 Nov 1976 (RA)
6	15 Nov 1976 (RA); repealed (EW)
7	15 Nov 1976 (RA)
8–12	Repealed
13, 14	7 Apr 1978 (SI 1978/402); repealed (S)
15	15 Nov 1976 (RA)
16–24	Repealed
25–27	15 Nov 1976 (RA)
Sch 1	1 Feb 1977 (SI 1977/39)
2	15 Nov 1976 (RA); repealed (EW)
3	15 Nov 1976 (RA)
3A	Repealed
4, Pt I	15 Nov 1976 (RA)
II	15 Nov 1976 (except repeals in Agriculture Act 1967) (RA)
	1 Feb 1977 (exception noted above) (SI 1977/39)

Appropriation Act 1976 (c 43)

Whole Act repealed

Armed Forces Act 1976 (c 52)

RA: 26 Oct 1976

Commencement provisions: s 22(7)–(9); Armed Forces Act 1976 (Commencement) Order 1977, SI 1977/897

s 1	Repealed
2–9	1 Jul 1977 (SI 1977/897)

Armed Forces Act 1976 (c 52)—*cont*

s 10	26 Oct 1976 (s 22(7))
11–16	1 Jul 1977 (SI 1977/897)
17(1)	26 Oct 1976 (s 22(7))
(2)	1 Jul 1977 (SI 1977/897)
18, 19	1 Jul 1977 (SI 1977/897)
20(a)	26 Oct 1976 (s 22(7))
(b)	1 Jul 1977 (SI 1977/897)
21	26 Oct 1976 (s 22(7))
22(1)–(4)	26 Oct 1976 (s 22(7))
(5)	See Sch 9 below
(6)	See Sch 10 below
(7)–(9)	26 Oct 1976 (s 22(7))
Sch 1–8	1 Jul 1977 (SI 1977/897)
9, para 1	1 Jul 1977 (SI 1977/897)
2	Repealed
3	1 Jul 1977 (SI 1977/897)
4	26 Oct 1976 (s 22(7))
5–8	1 Jul 1977 (SI 1977/897)
9	Repealed
10	1 Jul 1977 (SI 1977/897)
11	26 Oct 1976 (s 22(7))
12	Repealed
13–18	1 Jul 1977 (SI 1977/897)
19	Repealed
20(1)	1 Jul 1977 (SI 1977/897)
(2)	26 Oct 1976 (s 22(7))
(3)	1 Jul 1977 (SI 1977/897)
(4), (5)	26 Oct 1976 (s 22(7))
21, 22	1 Jul 1977 (SI 1977/897)
10	26 Oct 1976 (repeals of or in Naval Knights of Windsor (Dissolution) Act 1892; Armed Forces Act 1971, s 1; House of Commons Disqualification Act 1975, s 10(4); Northern Ireland Assembly Disqualification Act 1975, s 5(3)) (s 22(7)) 1 Jul 1977 (otherwise) (SI 1977/897)

Atomic Energy Authority (Special Constables) Act 1976 (c 23)

RA: 10 Jun 1976

10 Jun 1976 (RA)

Bail Act 1976 (c 63)

RA: 15 Nov 1976

Commencement provisions: s 13(2); Bail Act 1976 (Commencement) Order 1978, SI 1978/132

s 1–9	17 Apr 1978 (SI 1978/132)
10, 11	Repealed
12	17 Apr 1978 (SI 1978/132)
13	15 Nov 1976 (RA)
Sch 1–4	17 Apr 1978 (SI 1978/132)

Cathedrals Measure 1976 (No 1)

RA: 25 Mar 1976

25 Mar 1976 (RA)

Chronically Sick and Disabled Persons (Amendment) Act 1976 (c 49)

RA: 26 Oct 1976

26 Oct 1976 (RA)

Church of England (Miscellaneous Provisions) Measure 1976 (No 3)

RA: 15 Nov 1976

Commencement provisions: s 8(3)

15 Dec 1976 (s 8(3))

Companies Act 1976 (c 69)

Whole Act repealed

Congenital Disabilities (Civil Liability) Act 1976 (c 28)

RA: 22 Jul 1976

22 Jul 1976 (RA)

Consolidated Fund Act 1976 (c 2)

Whole Act repealed

Consolidated Fund (No 2) Act 1976 (c 84)

Whole Act repealed

Crofting Reform (Scotland) Act 1976 (c 21)

RA: 10 Jun 1976

10 Jun 1976 (RA)

Damages (Scotland) Act 1976 (c 13)

RA: 13 Apr 1976

Commencement provisions: s 12(3)

13 May 1976 (s 12(3))

Dangerous Wild Animals Act 1976 (c 38)

RA: 22 Jul 1976

Commencement provisions: s 10(2)

22 Oct 1976 (s 10(2))

Development Land Tax Act 1976 (c 24)

Whole Act repealed

Development of Rural Wales Act 1976 (c 75)

RA: 22 Nov 1976

Commencement provisions: s 35(2); Development of Rural Wales (Commencement No 1) Order 1976, SI 1976/2038; Development of Rural Wales (Commencement No 2) Order 1977, SI 1977/116

s 1	1 Jan 1977 (SI 1976/2038)
2	1 Apr 1977 (SI 1977/116)
3(1)	1 Apr 1977 (SI 1977/116)
(2)(a)	11 Feb 1977 (SI 1977/116)
(b)	1 Apr 1977 (SI 1977/116)
(3), (4)	11 Feb 1977 (SI 1977/116)
(5)–(8)	1 Apr 1977 (SI 1977/116)
4–6	1 Apr 1977 (SI 1977/116)
7	Repealed
8–10	1 Apr 1977 (SI 1977/116)
11	1 Jan 1977 (SI 1976/2038)
12, 13	1 Apr 1977 (SI 1977/116)
13A	Inserted (EW) by New Towns and Urban Development Corporations Act 1985, s 11, Sch 2, para 1 (qv)
14(1)(a)	1 Jan 1977 (SI 1976/2038)
(b)	1 Apr 1977 (SI 1977/116)
(2)–(6)	1 Apr 1977 (SI 1977/116)
15–17	1 Apr 1977 (SI 1977/116)
18	1 Apr 1977 (SI 1977/116); prospectively repealed by Housing Act 1980, s 152(3), Sch 26 (qv)
19, 20	Repealed
21, 22	1 Apr 1977 (SI 1977/116)
23(1)–(3)	1 Jan 1977 (SI 1976/2038)
(4)	1 Apr 1977 (SI 1977/116)
24	11 Feb 1977 (SI 1977/116)
25–28	1 Apr 1977 (SI 1977/116)
29(1), (2)	1 Jan 1977 (SI 1976/2038)
(3)	11 Feb 1977 (SI 1977/116)
(4)–(6)	1 Apr 1977 (SI 1977/116)
30	1 Apr 1977 (SI 1977/116)
31	Repealed by Finance Act 1985, s 98(6), Sch 27, Pt X, in relation to a disposal (as defined in s 93(1) of that Act) taking place on or after 19 Mar 1985
	1 Apr 1977 (SI 1977/116) (so far as unrepealed)
32–34	1 Apr 1977 (SI 1977/116)
35	22 Nov 1976 (RA)

Development of Rural Wales Act 1976 (c 75)—*cont*

Sch 1	1 Jan 1977 (SI 1976/2038)
2, para 1, 2	1 Apr 1977 (SI 1977/116)
3–5	11 Feb 1977 (SI 1977/116)
6	1 Apr 1977 (SI 1977/116)
3, para 1(1)	1 Apr 1977 (SI 1977/116)
(2)	11 Feb 1977 (SI 1977/116)
(3)–(6)	1 Apr 1977 (SI 1977/116)
2–38	1 Apr 1977 (SI 1977/116)
39	Substituted by Telecommunications Act 1984, s 109(1), Sch 4, para 67(4) (qv)
40–50	1 Apr 1977 (SI 1977/116)
51, 52	Repealed
53–56	1 Apr 1977 (SI 1977/116)
4, Pt I	Repealed
II	1 Apr 1977 (SI 1977/116)
5, Pt I	1 Apr 1977 (SI 1977/116); prospectively repealed by Housing Act 1980, s 152, Sch 26 (qv)
II	1 Apr 1977 (SI 1977/116)
III	Repealed
6, para 1	11 Feb 1977 (SI 1977/116)
2	1 Apr 1977 (SI 1977/116)
3–5	11 Feb 1977 (SI 1977/116)
6	1 Apr 1977 (SI 1977/116)
7	1 Apr 1977 (SI 1977/116)

Divorce (Scotland) Act 1976 (c 39)

RA: 22 Jul 1976

Commencement provisions: s 14(2)

1 Jan 1977 (s 14(2)), except s 8 (repealed)

Dock Work Regulation Act 1976 (c 79)

Whole Act repealed

Domestic Violence and Matrimonial Proceedings Act 1976 (c 50)

RA: 26 Oct 1976

Commencement provisions: s 5(2); Domestic Violence and Matrimonial Proceedings Act 1976 (Commencement) Order 1977, SI 1977/559

1 Jun 1977 (SI 1977/559)

Drought Act 1976 (c 44)

Whole Act repealed (For savings see Water Act 1989, s 190(2), Sch 26, Pt IV, para 34)

Ecclesiastical Judges and Legal Officers Measure 1976 (No 2)

RA: 25 Mar 1976

Commencement provisions: s 9(2)

25 Apr 1976 (s 9(2))

Education Act 1976 (c 81)

RA: 22 Nov 1976

Whole Act repealed except ss 6, 11, 12, which came into force on 22 Nov 1976 (RA)

Education (School-leaving Dates) Act 1976 (c 5)

Whole Act repealed

Education (Scotland) Act 1976 (c 20)

Whole Act repealed

Electricity (Financial Provisions) (Scotland) Act 1976 (c 61)

Whole Act repealed

Endangered Species (Import and Export) Act 1976 (c 72)

RA: 22 Nov 1976

Commencement provisions: s 13(3)

3 Feb 1977 (s 13(3))

Endowments and Glebe Measure 1976 (No 4)

RA: 22 Nov 1976

Commencement provisions: s 49(2); Order of the Church Commissioners dated 11 Aug 1977

s 1–8	1 Apr 1978 (order dated 11 Aug 1977)
9	22 Nov 1976 (s 49(2))
10–15	1 Apr 1978 (order dated 11 Aug 1977)
16	22 Nov 1976 (s 49(2))
17, 18	1 Apr 1978 (order dated 11 Aug 1977)
19(1)	1 Apr 1978 (order dated 11 Aug 1977)
(2)–(4)	22 Nov 1976 (s 49(2))
20–30	1 Apr 1978 (order dated 11 Aug 1977)
31, 32	22 Nov 1976 (s 49(2))
33	1 Apr 1978 (order dated 11 Aug 1977)
34	22 Nov 1976 (s 49(2))
35–42	1 Apr 1978 (order dated 11 Aug 1977)
43, 44	Repealed
45–49	1 Apr 1978 (order dated 11 Aug 1977)
Sch 1–8	1 Apr 1978 (order dated 11 Aug 1977)

Energy Act 1976 (c 76)

RA: 22 Nov 1976

Commencement provisions: s 23(2); Energy Act 1976 (Commencement No 1) Order 1976,
SI 1976/1964; Energy Act 1976 (Commencement No 2) Order 1976, SI 1976/2127;
Energy Act 1976 (Commencement No 3) Order 1977, SI 1977/652

s 1–6	30 Nov 1976 (SI 1976/1964)
7, 8	Repealed
9	Substituted for original ss 9–11 by Oil and Gas (Enterprise) Act 1982, s 37, Sch 3, para 37 (qv)
(10, 11	See s 9 above)
12	1 May 1977 (SI 1977/652)
13	Repealed
14, 15	1 Jan 1977 (SI 1976/2127)
16	Repealed
17–21	30 Nov 1976 (so far as relate to ss 1–6, 13, Sch 1 or provisions made under them) (SI 1976/1964)
	1 Jan 1977 (so far as relate to ss 7, 14–16 or provisions made under them or to obligations specified in Sch 3) (SI 1976/2127)
	1 May 1977 (otherwise) (SI 1977/652)
22	See Sch 4 below
23	30 Nov 1976 (SI 1976/1964)
Sch 1	30 Nov 1976 (SI 1976/1964)
2, 3	As ss 17–21 above
4	30 Nov 1976 (repeal of Fuel and Electricity (Control) Act 1973) (SI 1976/1964)
	1 May 1977 (otherwise) (SI 1977/652)

Explosives (Age of Purchase etc) Act 1976 (c 26)

RA: 22 Jul 1976

Commencement provisions: s 2(3)

22 Aug 1976 (s 2(3))

Fatal Accidents Act 1976 (c 30)

RA: 22 Jul 1976

Commencement provisions: s 7(2)

1 Sep 1976 (s 7(2); note the Act does not apply to any cause of action arising on a
death before that date)

Fatal Accidents and Sudden Deaths Inquiry (Scotland) Act 1976 (c 14)

RA: 13 Apr 1976

Commencement provisions: s 10(5); Fatal Accidents and Sudden Deaths Inquiry
(Scotland) Act 1976 Commencement Order 1977, SI 1977/190

1 Mar 1977 (SI 1977/190)

Fair Employment (Northern Ireland) Act 1976 (c 25)

Applies to Northern Ireland only

Finance Act 1976 (c 40)

Budget day: 6 Apr 1976

RA: 29 Jul 1976

See the note concerning Finance Acts at the front of this book

Fishery Limits Act 1976 (c 86)

RA: 22 Dec 1976

Commencement provisions: s 12(2)

1 Jan 1977 (s 12(2))

Food and Drugs (Control of Food Premises) Act 1976 (c 37)

Whole Act repealed

Freshwater and Salmon Fisheries (Scotland) Act 1976 (c 22)

RA: 10 Jun 1976

10 Jun 1976 (RA)

Health Services Act 1976 (c 83)

Whole Act repealed

Housing (Amendment) (Scotland) Act 1976 (c 11)

Whole Act repealed

Industry (Amendment) Act 1976 (c 73)

Whole Act repealed

Industrial Common Ownership Act 1976 (c 78)

RA: 22 Nov 1976

22 Nov 1976 (RA)

Insolvency Act 1976 (c 60)

RA: 15 Nov 1976

Commencement provisions: s 14(5); Insolvency Act 1976 (Commencement No 1) Order
1976, SI 1976/1960; Insolvency Act 1976 (Commencement No 2) Order 1977,

Insolvency Act 1976 (c 60)—*cont*
SI 1977/363; Insolvency Act 1976 (Commencement No 3) Order 1977, SI 1977/1375;
Insolvency Act 1976 (Commencement No 4) Order 1978, SI 1978/139

s 1–11	Repealed
12	1 Mar 1978 (SI 1978/139)
13	20 Dec 1976 (SI 1976/1960)
14	See Sch 3 below
Sch 1	Repealed
2	1 Apr 1977 (SI 1977/363)
3	1 Oct 1977 (repeals of Bankruptcy Act 1914, s 92(3); Companies Act 1948, s 249(3)) (SI 1977/1375) 1 Mar 1978 (otherwise) (SI 1978/139)

International Carriage of Perishable Foodstuffs Act 1976 (c 58)

RA: 15 Nov 1976

Commencement provisions: s 21(2); International Carriage of Perishable Foodstuffs Act 1976 (Commencement) Order 1979, SI 1979/413

1 Oct 1979 (SI 1979/413)

Iron and Steel (Amendment) Act 1976 (c 41)

Whole Act repealed

Land Drainage Act 1976 (c 70)

RA: 15 Nov 1976

Commencement provisions: s 118(2)

Whole Act repealed except ss 105, 118, Sch 5, which came into force on 17 Jan 1977 (s 118(2))

Land Drainage (Amendment) Act 1976 (c 17)

Whole Act repealed

Legitimacy Act 1976 (c 31)

RA: 22 Jul 1976

Commencement provisions: s 12(2)

22 Aug 1976 (s 12(2))

Licensing (Amendment) Act 1976 (c 18)

RA: 27 May 1976

27 May 1976 (RA)

Licensing (Scotland) Act 1976 (c 66)

RA: 15 Nov 1976

Commencement provisions: s 141(2); Licensing (Scotland) Act 1976 (Commencement
No 1) Order 1976, SI 1976/2068; Licensing (Scotland) Act 1976 (Commencement
No 2) Order 1977, SI 1977/212; Licensing (Scotland) Act 1976 (Commencement
No 3) Order 1977, SI 1977/718

s 1, 2	1 Mar 1977 (SI 1977/212)
3–7	1 Jul 1977 (SI 1977/718)
8	1 Mar 1977 (SI 1977/212)
9–16	1 Jul 1977 (SI 1977/718)
16A	Inserted by Law Reform (Miscellaneous Provisions) (Scotland) Act 1990, s 53(1) (qv)
17–21	1 Jul 1977 (SI 1977/718)
22	Repealed
23–46	1 Jul 1977 (SI 1977/718)
47–53	Repealed
54(1)	13 Dec 1976 (SI 1976/2068)
(2)	1 Jul 1977 (SI 1977/718)
(3)–(5)	13 Dec 1976 (SI 1976/2068)
55	1 Jul 1977 (SI 1977/718)
56–59	13 Dec 1976 (SI 1976/2068)
60	1 Mar 1977 (SI 1977/212)
61	Repealed
62	1 Jul 1977 (SI 1977/718)
63	1 May 1977 (SI 1977/718)
64–66	1 Jul 1977 (SI 1977/718)
67	13 Dec 1976 (SI 1976/2068)
68–90	1 Jul 1977 (SI 1977/718)
90A	Inserted by Law Reform (Miscellaneous Provisions) (Scotland) Act 1990, s 52 (qv)
91–93	1 Jul 1977 (SI 1977/718)
94	Repealed
95–97	1 Jul 1977 (SI 1977/718)
97A	Inserted by Law Reform (Miscellaneous Provisions) (Scotland) Act 1990, s 54(1) (qv)
98–118	1 Jul 1977 (SI 1977/718)
119	1 May 1977 (SI 1977/718)
120–130	1 Jul 1977 (SI 1977/718)
131, 132	Repealed
133(1)–(3)	1 Jul 1977 (SI 1977/718)
(4)	1 Oct 1977 (SI 1977/718)
134, 135	1 Jul 1977 (SI 1977/718)
136(1)	1 Jul 1977 (SI 1977/718)
(2)	See Sch 8 below
137, 138	1 Jul 1977 (SI 1977/718)
139	13 Dec 1976 (so far as necessary for purposes of SI 1976/2068) (SI 1976/2068)
	1 Mar 1977 (so far as necessary for purposes of SI 1977/212) (SI 1977/212)
	1 Jul 1977 (otherwise) (SI 1977/718)
140(1)	Repealed
(2)	13 Dec 1976 (SI 1976/2068)
(3)	Repealed
(4)–(8)	13 Dec 1976 (SI 1976/2068)

Licensing (Scotland) Act 1976 (c 66)—*cont*

s 141	15 Nov 1976 (s 141(2))
Sch 1, 2	1 Jul 1977 (SI 1977/718)
3	Repealed
4	1 Jul 1977 (SI 1977/718)
5	13 Dec 1976 (entries relating to ss 54(1)(a), (b), 57(7), (8), 58(7), (8), 59(7)) (SI 1976/2068)
	1 Mar 1977 (entry relating to s 2) (SI 1977/212)
	1 May 1977 (entry relating to s 119) (SI 1977/718)
	1 Jul 1977 (otherwise) (SI 1977/718)
6, 7	1 Jul 1977 (SI 1977/718)
8	13 Dec 1976 (repeals of Licensing (Scotland) Act 1959, ss 121, 126; Licensing (Scotland) Act 1962, ss 3(3), 4–8) (SI 1976/2068)
	1 Mar 1977 (repeal of Licensing (Scotland) Act 1959, s 29) (SI 1977/212)
	1 May 1977 (repeal of Licensing (Scotland) Act 1959, s 130; Licensing (Scotland) Act 1962, s 20) (SI 1977/718)
	1 Jul 1977 (otherwise, except repeals noted below) (SI 1977/718)
	1 Oct 1977 (repeals of Betting, Gaming and Lotteries Act 1963, Sch 1, para 24(2); Gaming Act 1968, Sch 2, paras 33(2), (3), 34(2)) (SI 1977/718)

Local Government (Miscellaneous Provisions) Act 1976 (c 57)

RA: 15 Nov 1976

Commencement provisions: ss 45, 83(2); Local Government (Miscellaneous Provisions) Act 1976 (Commencement) Order 1977, SI 1977/68

s 1–6	Repealed
7	14 Feb 1977 (SI 1977/68)
8–10	Repealed
11–27	14 Feb 1977 (SI 1977/68)
28	Repealed (except in relation to any body which is not mentioned in Local Government and Housing Act 1989, s 39(1)(a)–(j), and has not been prescribed by regulations under s 39(3) of the 1989 Act)
29–33	14 Feb 1977 (SI 1977/68)
34	Repealed
35, 36	14 Feb 1977 (SI 1977/68)
37	Repealed
38–42	14 Feb 1977 (SI 1977/68)
43	Repealed
44	14 Feb 1977 (SI 1977/68)
45–80	Came into force for different areas on different dates in accordance with resolutions of district councils (see s 45)
81–83	14 Feb 1977 (SI 1977/68)
Sch 1, 2	14 Feb 1977 (SI 1977/68)

Lotteries and Amusements Act 1976 (c 32)

RA: 22 Jul 1976

Commencement provisions: s 25(9)

1 May 1977 (s 25(9))

Maplin Development Authority (Dissolution) Act 1976 (c 51)

Whole Act repealed

Motor-Cycle Crash-Helmets (Religious Exemption) Act 1976 (c 62)

Whole Act repealed

National Coal Board (Finance) Act 1976 (c 1)

RA: 4 Mar 1976

4 Mar 1976 (RA)

National Health Service (Vocational Training) Act 1976 (c 59)

Whole Act repealed

National Insurance Surcharge Act 1976 (c 85)

Whole Act repealed

New Towns (Amendment) Act 1976 (c 68)

Whole Act repealed

Parliamentary and Other Pensions and Salaries Act 1976 (c 48)

RA: 12 Oct 1976

12 Oct 1976, but certain provisions were retrospective in effect (see, in particular s 6 which has effect as from 1 Jan 1975 (s 6(5)); the other provisions with retrospective effect have been repealed)

Police Act 1976 (c 46)

RA: 6 Aug 1976

Commencement provisions: s 13(1); Police Act 1976 (Commencement No 1) Order 1976, SI 1976/1998; Police Act 1976 (Commencement No 2) Order 1977, SI 1977/576

Police Act 1976 (c 46)—*cont*

s 1(1)–(4)	Repealed
(5)	8 Dec 1976 (SI 1976/1998)
2–13	Repealed
14(1)	8 Dec 1976 (SI 1976/1998)
(2)	Repealed
Schedule	8 Dec 1976 (SI 1976/1998)

Police Pensions Act 1976 (c 35)

RA: 22 Jul 1976

22 Jul 1976 (RA)

Post Office (Banking Services) Act 1976 (c 10)

RA: 25 Mar 1976

25 Mar 1976 (RA)

Prevention of Terrorism (Temporary Provisions) Act 1976 (c 8)

Whole Act repealed

Protection of Birds (Amendment) Act 1976 (c 42)

Whole Act repealed

Race Relations Act 1976 (c 74)

RA: 22 Nov 1976

Commencement provisions: s 79(2); Race Relations Act 1976 (Commencement No 1) Order 1977, SI 1977/680; Race Relations Act 1976 (Commencement No 2) Order 1977, SI 1977/840

s 1–12	13 Jun 1977 (SI 1977/840)
13	Substituted by Employment Act 1989, s 7(2) (qv)
14–17	13 Jun 1977 (SI 1977/840)
17A	Inserted (EW) by Further and Higher Education Act 1992, s 93(1), Sch 8, Pt II, paras 84, 86 (qv)
18	13 Jun 1977 (SI 1977/840)
18A	Inserted (EW) by Further and Higher Education Act 1992, s 93(1), Sch 8, Pt II, paras 84, 87 (qv)
18B	Inserted (S) (in part prospectively) by Further and Higher Education (Scotland) Act 1992, s 62(2), Sch 9, para 5(1), (3) (qv)
18C	Inserted (EW) by Education Act 1993, s 307(1), Sch 19, para 65 (qv)
19	13 Jun 1977 (SI 1977/840)
19A	Inserted by Housing and Planning Act 1986, s 55 (qv)
20–26	13 Jun 1977 (SI 1977/840)
26A, 26B	Inserted by Courts and Legal Services Act 1990, s 64(2), 65(2) respectively (qv)
27–69	13 Jun 1977 (SI 1977/840)
70	Repealed

Race Relations Act 1976 (c 74)—*cont*

s 71, 72	13 Jun 1977 (SI 1977/840)
73–75	28 Apr 1977 (SI 1977/680)
75A, 75B	Inserted by Trade Union and Labour Relations (Consolidation) Act 1992, s 300(2), Sch 2, paras 7, 10 (qv)
76	13 Jun 1977 (SI 1977/840)
77, 78	28 Apr 1977 (SI 1977/680)
79(1)	28 Apr 1977 (SI 1977/680)
(2)	22 Nov 1976 (RA)
(3)–(5)	28 Apr 1977 (SI 1977/840)
(6)	Repealed
(7)	22 Nov 1976 (RA)
80	28 Apr 1977 (SI 1977/680)
Sch 1	13 Jun 1977 (SI 1977/840)
2	28 Apr 1977 (SI 1977/680)
3	Repealed
4	28 Apr 1977 (SI 1977/680)

Note

S 43(1)–(4), Sch 1 of this Act came into force on 28 Apr 1977 (SI 1977/680) for the purposes of bringing into existence the Commission for Racial Equality and enabling it to make preparatory arrangements for the exercise of its powers

---

Rating (Caravan Sites) Act 1976 (c 15)

RA: 13 Apr 1976

13 Apr 1976 (RA; but mainly effective for rate periods beginning after Mar 1976, see s 1(9))

Rating (Charity Shops) Act 1976 (c 45)

RA: 6 Aug 1976

6 Aug 1976 (RA)

Rent (Agriculture) Act 1976 (c 80)

RA: 22 Nov 1976

Commencement provisions: s 1(5), (6); Rent (Agriculture) Act 1976 (Commencement No 1) Order 1976, SI 1976/2124; Rent (Agriculture) Act 1976 (Commencement No 2) Order 1977, SI 1977/1268

1 Jan 1977 (SI 1976/2124; but note that in relation to forestry workers the Act came into force on 1 Oct 1976, by virtue of s 1(5)(b), Sch 3, Pt II, SI 1977/1268)

Representation of the People (Armed Forces) Act 1976 (c 29)

Whole Act repealed

Resale Prices Act 1976 (c 53)

RA: 26 Oct 1976

Commencement provisions: s 30(3); Resale Prices Act 1976 (Commencement) Order 1976, SI 1976/1876

15 Dec 1976 (SI 1976/1876)

Retirement of Teachers (Scotland) Act 1976 (c 65)

Whole Act repealed

Restrictive Practices Court Act 1976 (c 33)

RA: 22 Jul 1976

Commencement provisions: s 12(3); Restrictive Practices Court Act 1976 (Commencement) Order 1976, SI 1976/1896

15 Dec 1976 (SI 1976/1896)

Restrictive Trade Practices Act 1976 (c 34)

RA: 22 Jul 1976

Commencement provisions: s 45(3); Restrictive Trade Practices Act 1976 (Commencement) Order 1976, SI 1976/1877

15 Dec 1976 (SI 1976/1877)

Road Traffic (Drivers' Ages and Hours of Work) Act 1976 (c 3)

RA: 25 Mar 1976

Commencement provisions: s 4(2)–(4); Road Traffic (Drivers' Ages and Hours of Work) Act 1976 (Commencement No 1) Order 1976, SI 1976/471; Road Traffic (Drivers' Ages and Hours of Work) Act 1976 (Commencement No 2) Order 1978, SI 1978/6

s 1	Repealed
2	4 Jan 1978 (SI 1978/6)
3	25 Mar 1976 (s 4(2))
4	25 Mar 1976 (s 4(2))
Sch 1, 2	Repealed
3, Pt I	25 Mar 1976 (s 4(2))
II	4 Jan 1978 (SI 1978/6)

Sexual Offences (Amendment) Act 1976 (c 82)

RA: 22 Nov 1976

Commencement provisions: s 7(4); Sexual Offences (Amendment) Act 1976 (Commencement) Order 1978, SI 1978/485

s 1–4	22 Dec 1976 (s 7(4))
5(1)(a)	22 Dec 1976 (s 7(4))

Sexual Offences (Amendment) Act 1976 (c 82)—*cont*

s 5(1)(b)	22 Apr 1978 (SI 1978/485)
(c)–(e)	22 Dec 1976 (s 7(4))
(2)–(6)	22 Dec 1976 (s 7(4))
6	Repealed
7	22 Dec 1976 (s 7(4))

Sexual Offences (Scotland) Act 1976 (c 67)

RA: 15 Nov 1976

Commencement provisions: s 22(2)

15 Dec 1976 (s 22(2))

Seychelles Act 1976 (c 19)

RA: 27 May 1976

Appointed day: 29 Jun 1976

Solicitors (Scotland) Act 1976 (c 6)

Whole Act repealed

Statute Law (Repeals) Act 1976 (c 16)

RA: 27 May 1976

27 May 1976 (RA)

Statute Law Revision (Northern Ireland) Act 1976 (c 12)

RA: 13 Apr 1976

13 Apr 1976 (RA)

Stock Exchange (Completion of Bargains) Act 1976 (c 47)

RA: 12 Oct 1976

Commencement provisions: s 7(4); Stock Exchange (Completion of Bargains) Act 1976 (Commencement Order) 1979, SI 1979/55

12 Feb 1979 (SI 1979/55)

Supplementary Benefit (Amendment) Act 1976 (c 56)

Whole Act repealed

Supplementary Benefits Act 1976 (c 71)

RA: 15 Nov 1976

Commencement provisions: s 36(3)

Whole Act repealed except ss 30, 35, 36, Schs 5–8 which came into force on 15 Nov 1976
  (s 36(3); note that repeals of provisions of Sch 8, Pt II did not come into force until those
  provisions had themselves come into force)

Theatres Trust Act 1976 (c 27)

RA: 22 Jul 1976

Commencement provisions: s 6(2); Theatres Trust Act (Appointed Day) Order 1976,
  SI 1976/2236

21 Jan 1977 (SI 1976/2236)

Note

The Act was extended to Scotland by the Theatres Trust (Scotland) Act 1978,
  s 1(1) (qv) and came into force there on the passing of that Act

---

Trade Union and Labour Relations (Amendment) Act 1976 (c 7)

Whole Act repealed

Trinidad and Tobago Republic Act 1976 (c 54)

RA: 26 Oct 1976

Appointed day: 26 Oct 1976 (Trinidad and Tobago Republic Appointed Day Order
  1976, SI 1976/1914)

Trustee Savings Banks Act 1976 (c 4)

Whole Act repealed

Note that the repeal of this Act is subject to transitional provisions and savings
  contained in Trustee Savings Banks Act 1981, s 55(2), Sch 7

Valuation and Rating (Exempted Classes) (Scotland) Act 1976 (c 64)

RA: 15 Nov 1976

15 Nov 1976 (RA)

Water Charges Act 1976 (c 9)

Whole Act repealed

Weights and Measures &c Act 1976 (c 77)

RA: 22 Nov 1976

Commencement provisions: s 15(2)

Whole Act repealed, except ss 12–14, 15(1)–(3) and Sch 6, which came into force on 22
Dec 1976 (s 15(2))

1977

Administration of Justice Act 1977 (c 38)

RA: 29 Jul 1977

Commencement provisions: s 32(5)–(7); Administration of Justice Act 1977 (Commencement No 1) Order 1977, SI 1977/1405; Administration of Justice Act 1977 (Commencement No 2) Order 1977, SI 1977/ 1490; Administration of Justice Act 1977 (Commencement No 3) Order 1977, SI 1977/1589; Administration of Justice Act 1977 (Commencement No 4) Order 1977, SI 1977/2202; Administration of Justice Act 1977 (Commencement No 5) Order 1978, SI 1978/810; Administration of Justice Act 1977 (Commencement No 6) Order 1979, SI 1979/972; Administration of Justice Act 1977 (Commencement No 7) Order 1980, SI 1980/1981

s 1	Spent (EW); repealed (S)
2	29 Aug 1977 (s 32(5))
3	See Sch 3 below
4, 5	29 Aug 1977 (s 32(5))
6	Repealed
7	29 Aug 1977 (s 32(5))
8–10	Repealed
11	29 Aug 1977 (s 32(5)); prospectively repealed by Administration of Justice Act 1982, s 75, Sch 9, Pt I (qv); (this section amends provisions of the Administration of Justice Act 1965 which are repealed and is therefore spent)
12	Spent
13–16	Repealed
17(1)	Repealed
(2)	29 Aug 1977 (s 32(5))
18	Repealed
19(1)	Repealed
(2)	Spent
(3), (4)	Repealed
(5)	3 Jul 1978 (SI 1978/810)
20, 21	Repealed
22	29 Aug 1977 (s 32(5))
23	17 Oct 1977 (SI 1977/1589)
24	29 Aug 1977 (s 32(5))
25	Repealed
26	29 Aug 1977 (s 32(5))
27	Repealed
28	15 Sep 1977 (SI 1977/1490)
29, 30	29 Aug 1977 (s 32(5))
31, 32	29 Jul 1977 (RA)
Sch 1	Repealed
2	29 Aug 1977 (s 32(5))

Administration of Justice Act 1977 (c 38)—*cont*

Sch 3, para 1–10	1 Jan 1981 (SI 1980/1981)
11, 12	1 Sept 1977 (SI 1977/1405)
4	17 Oct 1977 (SI 1977/1589)
5, Pt I–IV	29 Aug 1977 (s 32(5))
V	17 Oct 1977 (SI 1977/1589)
VI	29 Jul 1977 (s 32(6))

Agricultural Holdings (Notices to Quit) Act 1977 (c 12)

Whole Act repealed

Aircraft and Shipbuilding Industries Act 1977 (c 3)

RA: 17 Mar 1977

17 Mar 1977 (RA)

Note

Under ss 19, 56, vesting date for aircraft industry was 29 Apr 1977 (under Aircraft and Shipbuilding Industries (Aircraft Industry Vesting Date) Order 1977, SI 1977/539) and for shipbuilding industry was 1 Jul 1977 (under Aircraft and Shipbuilding Industries (Shipbuilding Industry Vesting Date) Order 1977, SI 1977/540)

Appropriation Act 1977 (c 35)

Whole Act repealed

British Airways Board Act 1977 (c 13)

Whole Act repealed

Coal Industry Act 1977 (c 39)

RA: 29 Jul 1977

Commencement provisions: s 16(2)

29 Aug 1977 (s 16(2))

Consolidated Fund Act 1977 (c 1)

Whole Act repealed

Consolidated Fund (No 2) Act 1977 (c 52)

Whole Act repealed

Control of Food Premises (Scotland) Act 1977 (c 28)

Whole Act repealed

Control of Office Development Act 1977 (c 40)

Whole Act repealed

Covent Garden Market (Financial Provisions) Act 1977 (c 2)

Limited application only

Criminal Law Act 1977 (c 45)

RA: 29 Jul 1977

Commencement provisions: s 65(7); Criminal Law Act 1977 (Commencement No 1) Order 1977, SI 1977/1365; Criminal Law Act 1977 (Commencement No 2) Order 1977, SI 1977/1426; Criminal Law Act 1977 (Commencement No 3) Order 1977, SI 1977/1682; Criminal Law Act 1977 (Commencement No 4) (Scotland) Order 1977, SI 1977/1744; Criminal Law Act 1977 (Commencement No 5) Order 1978, SI 1978/712; Criminal Law Act 1977 (Commencement No 6) (Scotland) Order 1978, SI 1978/900; Criminal Law Act 1977 (Commencement No 7) Order 1980, SI 1980/487; Criminal Law Act 1977 (Commencement No 8) (Scotland) Order 1980, SI 1980/587; Criminal Law Act 1977 (Commencement No 9) Order 1980, SI 1980/1632; Criminal Law Act 1977 (Commencement No 10) (Scotland) Order 1980, SI 1980/1701; Criminal Law Act 1977 (Commencement No 11) Order 1982, SI 1982/243; Criminal Law Act 1977 (Commencement No 12) Order 1985, SI 1985/ 579

s 1	1 Dec 1977 (SI 1977/1682)
1A	Prospectively inserted by Criminal Justice Act 1993, s 5(1) (qv)
2–4	1 December 1977 (SI 1977/1682)
5(1)–(9)	1 Dec 1977 (SI 1977/1682)
(10)(a)	1 Dec 1977 (SI 1977/1682)
(b)	8 Sep 1977 (SI 1977/1365)
(11)	Repealed
6–10	1 Dec 1977 (SI 1977/1682)
11	Repealed
12, 13	1 Dec 1977 (SI 1977/1682)
14	Repealed
15(1)	17 Jul 1978 (SI 1978/712)
(2), (3)	Repealed
(4)	17 Jul 1978 (SI 1978/712; SI 1978/900)
(5)	17 Jul 1978 (SI 1978/712)
16–27	Repealed
28	17 Jul 1978 (SI 1978/712)
29	Repealed
30(1), (2)	17 Jul 1978 (SI 1978/712)
(3)	17 Jul 1978 (SI 1978/712; SI 1978/900)
(4)	Repealed
31(1)	8 Sep 1977 (SI 1977/1365)
(2)–(6)	17 Jul 1978 (SI 1978/712)
(7)	Repealed
(8), (9)	17 Jul 1978 (SI 1978/712)
(10)	17 Jul 1978 (SI 1978/712; SI 1978/900)
(11)	17 Jul 1978 (SI 1978/712)
32(1)	17 Jul 1978 (SI 1978/712)

Criminal Law Act 1977 (c 45)—*cont*

s 32(2)	Repealed
(3)	17 Jul 1978 (SI 1978/712; SI 1978/900)
33	8 Sep 1977 (SI 1977/1365)
34, 35	Repealed
36, 37	17 Jul 1978 (SI 1978/712)
38	12 May 1980 (SI 1980/487; SI 1980/587)
38A	Inserted by Criminal Justice (Scotland) Act 1980, s 51 (qv)
38B	Inserted by Criminal Justice Act 1982, s 52 (qv)
39	12 May 1980 (SI 1980/487; SI 1980/587)
40	1 Dec 1980 (SI 1980/1632; SI 1980/1701)
41–43	Repealed
44	1 Dec 1977 (SI 1977/1682)
45	Repealed
46	17 Jul 1978 (SI 1978/712)
47	Repealed
48	20 May 1985 (SI 1985/579)
49	1 Dec 1977 (SI 1977/1682)
50	Repealed
51, 52	8 Sep 1977 (SI 1977/1365)
53	1 Dec 1977 (SI 1977/1682)
54	8 Sep 1977 (SI 1977/1365)
55, 56	Repealed
57	8 Sep 1977 (SI 1977/1365)
58	17 Jul 1978 (SI 1978/712)
59–62	Repealed
63(1)	8 Sep 1977 (SI 1977/1365)
(2)	8 Sep 1977 (so far as relates to ss 33, 51, 52, 55, 65, Schs 12 (part), 13 (part), 14) (SI 1977/1365)
	1 Dec 1977 (so far as relates to s 50, Schs 12 (part), 13 (part)) (SI 1977/1744)
	17 Jul 1978 (so far as relates to ss 15(2)–(4), 30(3), 31(10), 32(3), Schs 9, para 3(3), 12 (part), 13 (part)) (SI 1978/900)
	12 May 1980 (so far as relates to ss 38, 39, Sch 13 (part)) (SI 1980/587)
	1 Dec 1980 (so far as relates to s 40, Schs 7, 12 (part), 13 (part)) (SI 1980/1701)
64	17 Jul 1978 (SI 1978/712)
65	8 Sep 1977 (SI 1977/1365)
Sch 1	17 Jul 1978 (SI 1978/712)
2–4	Repealed
5	17 Jul 1978 (SI 1978/712)
6	8 Sep 1977 (SI 1977/1365)
7, para 1	Repealed
2	1 Dec 1980 (SI 1980/1701)
3	1 Dec 1980 (SI 1980/1632)
8	Repealed
9 (except para 3(3))	29 Mar 1982 (SI 1982/243)
para 3(3)	17 Jul 1978 (SI 1978/900)
10	Repealed
11, para 1, 2	17 Jul 1978 (SI 1978/900)
3	Repealed
4	1 Dec 1977 (SI 1977/1744)
5	8 Sep 1977 (so far as relates to Criminal Procedure (Scotland) Act 1975, s 289C(1)) (SI 1977/1365)

Criminal Law Act 1977 (c 45)—*cont*

Sch 11, para 5—*cont*	1 Dec 1977 (so far as relates to the definition of 'the prescribed sum' in Criminal Procedure (Scotland) Act 1975, s 289B(6)) (SI 1977/1744)
	17 Jul 1978 (remainder) (SI 1978/900)
6	Repealed
7	17 Jul 1978 (SI 1978/900)
8	1 Dec 1980 (SI 1980/1701)
9	1 Dec 1977 (SI 1977/1744)
10–13	Repealed
12	8 Sep 1977 (so far as relates to Offences Against the Person Act 1861; Explosive Substances Act 1883; Sexual Offences Act 1956, Sch 2, Pt II, paras 14, 15; Housing (Scotland) Act 1966; Children and Young Persons Act 1969, s 13(3); Powers of Criminal Courts Act 1973, ss 15(2), 17(3); Adoption Act 1976; Bail Act 1976, ss 3(8), 5) (SI 1977/1365)
	1 Dec 1977 (so far as relates to Metropolitan Police Courts Act 1839; Public Stores Act 1875; Obscene Publications Act 1959; Criminal Justice Act 1961; Criminal Justice Act 1967, ss 60, 91; Theft Act 1968; Finance Act 1972; Criminal Justice Act 1972; Administration of Justice Act 1973; Powers of Criminal Courts Act 1973, ss 1, 2(5); Legal Aid Act 1974 (repealed); Juries Act 1974; Bail Act 1976, s 7(4)) (EW) (SI 1977/1682)
	1 Dec 1977 (so far as relates to Public Stores Act 1875; Prison Act 1952 (in its application for persons for the time being in Scotland); Criminal Justice Act 1961, ss 26, 28, 29, 39(1); Criminal Justice Act 1967, s 60; Road Traffic Act 1972, s 179) (S) (SI 1977/1744)
	1 Jan 1978 (so far as relates to Coroners Act 1887; Births and Deaths Registration Act 1953; Bail Act 1976, s 2(2)) (SI 1977/1682)
	17 Jul 1978 (so far as relates to Night Poaching Act 1828; Accessories and Abettors Act 1861; Sexual Offences Act 1956, Sch 2, Pt II, paras 17, 18; Criminal Law Act 1967; Firearms Act 1968; Children and Young Persons Act 1969, ss 15, 16; Powers of Criminal Courts Act 1973, s 9(1); Health and Safety at Work etc Act 1974; Rehabilitation of Offenders Act 1974) (EW) (SI 1978/712)
	17 Jul 1978 (so far as relates to Night Poaching Act 1828; Health and Safety at Work etc Act 1974; Rehabilitation of Offenders Act 1974) (S) (SI 1978/900)
	Repealed or spent (remainder)
Sch 13	8 Sep 1977 (repeals of or in Criminal Justice Act 1848, s 19(3); Criminal Justice Act 1967, Sch 3, Pt I; Children and Young Persons Act 1969, s 13(3); Powers of Criminal Courts Act 1973, Sch 3, para 9; Bail Act 1976, Sch 2, para 38) (SI 1977/1365)
	8 Sep 1977 (repeals of or in Exchange Control Act 1947, Sch 5, Pt II, para 3(1); Customs and Excise Act 1952, s 285(1); Magistrates' Courts Act 1952, Sch 3, para 3; Land Commission Act 1967, s 82(5); Criminal Justice Act 1967, s 93) (SI 1977/1426)

Criminal Law Act 1977 (c 45)—*cont*

Sch 13—*cont*

1 Dec 1977 (repeals of or in Forcible Entry Act 1381;
Statutes concerning forcible entries and riots
confirmed; Forcible Entry Acts, 1429, 1588, 1623;
Metropolitan Police Courts Act 1839, s 24;
Offences against the Person Act 1861, s 4; Public
Stores Act 1875, ss 7, 9, 10; Conspiracy and
Protection of Property Act 1875, s 3; Justices of the
Peace Act 1949, s 43(3); Obscene Publications Act
1959, s 1(3); Criminal Justice Act 1961, ss 26(6),
28(2); Licensing Act 1964, s 30(5); Road Traffic
Regulation Act 1967, ss 43(2), 80(5), (11); Criminal
Justice Act 1967, ss 60(6)(a), (8)(d), 91(5); Transport
Act 1968, s 131(2); Road Traffic Act 1972, Sch 4,
Pt I; Criminal Justice Act 1972, s 34(1); Powers of
Criminal Courts Act 1973, ss 2(8)(a), 49(1)–(3),
50(1)–(3), 51, 57(1), Sch 1, para 3(2)(b), Sch 3,
paras 11, 12, 18(1)(b); Road Traffic Act 1974, Sch 5,
Pts II, III) (SI 1977/1682; SI 1977/1744)

1 Jan 1978 (repeals of or in Prosecution of Offences
Act 1879, s 5; Coroners Act 1887, ss 4(2), (3), 5, 9,
10, 16, 18(4), (5), 20; City of London Fire Inquests
Act 1888; Interpretation Act 1889, s 27; Indictments
Act 1915, s 8(3); Coroners (Amendment) Act 1926,
ss 13(2)(a), (d), 25; Suicide Act 1961, Sch 1;
Criminal Justice Act 1967, s 22(4); Administration
of Justice Act 1970, Sch 9, Pt I, para 4; Courts Act
1971, s 57(2); and Bail Act 1976, ss 2(2), 10, Sch 2,
paras 4, 37(4)) (SI 1977/1682)

17 Jul 1978 (repeals of or in Night Poaching Act 1828,
ss 4, 11; Truck Act 1831, s 10; Conspiracy and
Protection of Property Act 1875, ss 5, 7, 9, 19(1),
(2); Cruelty to Animals Act 1876, ss 15, 17;
Newspaper Libel and Registration Act 1881, s 5;
Truck Amendment Act 1887, s 13(1), (3);
Witnesses (Public Inquiries) Protection Act 1892,
ss 3, 6, para 2; Criminal Justice Act 1925, s 28(3);
Water Act 1945, Sch 3, s 71(1); Exchange Control
Act 1947, Sch 5, Pt II, para 2(3); Children Act 1948,
s 29(5); Customs and Excise Act 1952, s 283(2)(a);
Magistrates' Courts Act 1952, ss 18, 19, 24, 25, 32,
104, 125, 127(2), Sch 1, Sch 2, para 8; Protection of
Animals (Amendment) Act 1954, s 3; Sexual
Offences Act 1956, Sch 2, Pt II, Sch 3; Police, Fire
and Probation Officers Remuneration Act 1956;
Magistrates' Courts Act 1957, s 1(1)(a); Prevention
of Fraud (Investments) Act 1958, s 13(2); Obscene
Publications Act 1959, s 2(2), (3); Films Act 1960,
s 45(3); Criminal Justice Act 1961, ss 8(1), 11(2);
Criminal Justice Administration Act 1962, ss 12(3),
13, Sch 3, Sch 4, Pt II; Penalties for Drunkenness
Act 1962, s 1(2)(a), (b); Public Order Act 1963,
s 1(1); Building Control Act 1966, s 1(8); Industrial
Development Act 1966, s 8(10); Veterinary
Surgeons Act 1966, ss 19(2), 20(6); Finance Act
1967, Sch 7, para 4; Criminal Law Act 1967, ss 4(5),
5(4); Sexual Offences Act 1967, ss 4(2), 5(2),
7(2)(b), 9; Road Traffic Regulation Act 1967, s 91;

Criminal Law Act 1977 (c 45)—*cont*

Sch 13—*cont* Criminal Justice Act 1967, ss 27, 35, 43, 92(8),
106(2)(f), Sch 3, Pt II; Firearms Act 1968, s 57(4);
Theft Act 1968, s 29(2), Sch 2, Pt III; Transport Act
1968, Sch 8, para 8; Decimal Currency Act 1969,
Sch 2, para 21; Development of Tourism Act 1969,
Sch 2, para 3(2), (4); Children and Young Persons
Act 1969, ss 3(1)(b), (6), 6(1), (2), 12(2)(a),
(3)(b)–(e), 15(1), 34(5), Sch 5, para 56; Auctions
(Bidding Agreements) Act 1969, s 1(2), (4);
Administration of Justice Act 1970, s 51(1); Courts
Act 1971, Sch 8, paras 15(1), 16, 20, 34(1); Misuse
of Drugs Act 1971, s 26(4); Road Traffic Act 1972,
Sch 5, Pt IV, para 3; Gas Act 1972, s 43(2)(b);
Industry Act 1972, Sch 1, para 4(2), (5); Criminal
Justice Act 1972, s 47; Costs in Criminal Cases Act
1973, s 20(3); Hallmarking Act 1973, Sch 3,
para 2(2), (5); Powers of Criminal Courts Act 1973,
s 30(1), (2); Control of Pollution Act 1974, s 87(3);
Housing Act 1974, Sch 13, para 2; Road Traffic Act
1974, Sch 5, Pt IV, para 4(1)–(3), (4)(a); Trade
Union and Labour Relations Act 1974, s 29(7);
District Courts (Scotland) Act 1975, ss 3(3), 27(1),
Sch 1, para 26; Criminal Procedure (Scotland) Act
1975, s 403(4); Protection of Birds (Amendment)
Act 1976) (SI 1978/712; SI 1978/900)

12 May 1980 (repeals of or in Magistrates' Courts Act
1952, s 102(3); Criminal Procedure (Scotland) Act
1975, ss 17, 325, 463(1)(a), (b)) (SI 1980/487;
SI 1980/587)

1 Dec 1980 (repeals of or in Criminal Justice
(Scotland) Act 1963, ss 26, 53(1), Sch 3, Pt II;
Criminal Justice Act 1967, s 106(2)(f), Sch 6, paras
14–16, 21; Administration of Justice Act 1970,
s 41(6)(a); Courts Act 1971, s 59(5)(e), Sch 8,
paras 34(3), 48(a); Powers of Criminal Courts Act
1973, ss 33, 58(a), Sch 5, paras 6, 8; Criminal
Procedure (Scotland) Act 1975, ss 403(1), (5),
463(1); District Courts (Scotland) Act 1975, Sch 1,
para 26) (SI 1980/1632; SI 1980/1701)

29 Mar 1982 (repeals of or in Criminal Procedure
(Scotland) Act 1975, Sch 9, paras 15, 35) (SI 1982/
243)

14 8 Sep 1977 (SI 1977/1365)

Farriers (Registration) (Amendment) Act 1977 (c 31)

RA: 22 Jul 1977

Commencement provisions: s 2(2), (3)

s 1, 2	22 Oct 1977 (s 2(2))
Schedule, para 1–4	22 Oct 1977 (s 2(2))
5	22 Jan 1978 (s 2(3))
6, 7	22 Oct 1977 (s 2(2))

Finance Act 1977 (c 36)

Budget Day: 29 Mar 1977

RA: 29 Jul 1977

See the note concerning Finance Acts at the front of this book

Finance (Income Tax Reliefs) Act 1977 (c 53)

Whole Act repealed

General Rate (Public Utilities) Act 1977 (c 11)

RA: 30 Mar 1977

30 Mar 1977 (RA)

Whole Act repealed, with savings, by Local Government Finance (Repeals, Savings and Consequential Amendments) Order 1990, SI 1990/776, art 3, Sch 1

Housing (Homeless Persons) Act 1977 (c 48)

Whole Act repealed

Incumbents (Vacation of Benefices) Measure 1977 (No 1)

RA: 30 Jun 1977

Commencement provisions: s 21(3)

s 1	30 Dec 1977 (s 21(3)) (as originally enacted); prospectively renumbered as s 1A and new s 1 prospectively inserted by Incumbents (Vacation of Benefices) (Amendment) Measure 1993 (No 1), s 1 (qv)
1A	Prospectively renumbered as noted above
2–4	30 Dec 1977 (s 21(3))
5	30 Dec 1977 (s 21(3)); prospectively substituted by Incumbents (Vacation of Benefices) (Amendment) Measure 1993 (No 1), s 14(1), Sch 3, para 3 (qv)
6, 7	30 Dec 1977 (s 21(3))
7A	Prospectively inserted by Incumbents (Vacation of Benefices) (Amendment) Measure 1993 (No 1), s 5 (qv)
8, 9	30 Dec 1988 (s 21(3)
9A	Prospectively inserted by Incumbents (Vacation of Benefices) (Amendment) Measure 1993 (No 1), s 6 (qv)
10–12	30 Dec 1977 (s 21(3))
13	30 Dec 1977 (s 21(3)); prospectively substituted by Incumbents (Vacation of Benefices) (Amendment) Measure 1993 (No 1), s 8 (qv)
14	30 Dec 1977 (s 21(3))
15	Repealed
16, 17	30 Dec 1977 (s 21(3))

Incumbents (Vacation of Benefices) Measure 1977 (No 1)—*cont*

s 18	30 Dec 1977 (s 21(3)); prospectively substituted by Incumbents (Variation of Benefices) (Amendment) Measure 1993 (No 1), s 9 (qv)
19	30 Dec 1997 (s 21(3))
19A	Prospectively inserted by Incumbents (Vacation of Benefices (Amendment) Measure 1993 (No 1), s 10 (qv)
20, 21	30 Dec 1977 (s 21(3))
(Schedule	prospectively renumbered as Sch 1 and prospectively substituted by Incumbents (Vacation of Benefices) (Amendment) Measure 1993 (No 1), s 12, Sch 1 (qv); original Schedule came into force as follows:)
Schedule, para 1	30 Dec 1977 (s 21(3))
2(1), (2)	30 Jun 1977 (s 21(3))
(3)	30 Dec 1977 (s 21(3))
3–18	30 Dec 1977 (s 21(3))
Sch 2	Prospectively inserted by Incumbents (Vacation of Benefices) (Amendment) Measure 1993 (No 1), s 12, Sch 1 (qv)

Insurance Brokers (Registration) Act 1977 (c 46)

RA: 29 Jul 1977

Commencement provisions: s 30(3), (4); Insurance Brokers (Registration) Act 1977 (Commencement No 1) Order 1977, SI 1977/1782; Insurance Brokers (Registration) Act 1977 (Commencement No 2) Order 1978, SI 1978/1393; Insurance Brokers (Registration) Act 1977 (Commencement No 3) Order 1980, SI 1980/1824

s 1	1 Dec 1977 (SI 1977/1782)
2–5	20 Oct 1978 (SI 1978/1393)
6–8	1 Dec 1977 (SI 1977/1782)
9	20 Oct 1978 (SI 1978/1393)
10–12	1 Dec 1977 (SI 1977/1782)
13–18	20 Oct 1978 (SI 1978/1393)
19(1)–(3)	20 Oct 1978 (SI 1978/1393)
(4)–(6)	1 Dec 1977 (SI 1977/1782)
20	20 Oct 1978 (SI 1978/1393)
21	1 Dec 1977 (SI 1977/1782)
22–24	1 Dec 1981 (SI 1980/1824)
25–30	1 Dec 1977 (SI 1977/1782)
Schedule	1 Dec 1977 (SI 1977/1782)

International Finance, Trade and Aid Act 1977 (c 6)

Whole Act repealed

Job Release Act 1977 (c 8)

RA: 30 Mar 1977

30 Mar 1977 (RA)

Job Release Act 1977 (c 8)—*cont*
Note: s 1(4) of the Act stated that it would have effect for a period of eighteen
months from Royal Assent unless further extended by order made by the Secretary
of State; the last such order extended the Act to 29 Sep 1988 (SI 1987/1339)

Licensing (Amendment) Act 1977 (c 26)

RA: 22 Jul 1977

Commencement provisions: s 2(2)

22 Aug 1977 (s 2(2))

Local Authorities (Restoration of Works Powers) Act 1977 (c 47)

RA: 29 Jul 1977

29 Jul 1977 (RA)

Marriage (Scotland) Act 1977 (c 15)

RA: 26 May 1977

Commencement provisions: s 29(2)

s 1–23	1 Jan 1978 (s 29(2))
23A	Inserted (retrospectively) by Law Reform (Miscellaneous Provisions) (Scotland) Act 1980, s 22(1)(d) (qv)
24–28	1 Jan 1978 (s 29(2))
29	26 May 1977 (RA)
Sch 1–3	1 Jan 1978 (s 29(2))

Merchant Shipping (Safety Convention) Act 1977 (c 24)

RA: 22 Jul 1977

Commencement provisions: s 4(1); Merchant Shipping (Safety Convention) Act 1977
(Commencement) Order 1980, SI 1980/528

25 May 1980 (SI 1980/528)

Whole Act repealed by Merchant Shipping (Registration, etc) Act 1993, s 8(4), Sch
5, Pt II, as from 1 May 1994 (qv)

Minibus Act 1977 (c 25)

Whole Act repealed

National Health Service Act 1977 (c 49)

RA: 29 Jul 1977

Commencement provisions: s 130(5)

29 Aug 1977 (s 130(5))

New Towns Act 1977 (c 23)

Whole Act repealed

New Towns (Scotland) Act 1977 (c 16)

RA: 26 May 1977

26 May 1977 (RA)

Northern Ireland (Emergency Provisions) (Amendment) Act 1977 (c 34)

Whole Act repealed

Nuclear Industry (Finance) Act 1977 (c 7)

RA: 30 Mar 1977

30 Mar 1977 (RA)

Passenger Vehicles (Experimental Areas) Act 1977 (c 21)

Whole Act repealed

Patents Act 1977 (c 37)

RA: 29 Jul 1977

Commencement provisions: s 132(5); Patents Act 1977 (Commencement No 1) Order 1977, SI 1977/2090; Patents Act 1977 (Commencement No 2) Order 1978, SI 1978/586; Patents (Amendment) Rules 1987, SI 1987/288, r 4 (made for the purposes of ss 77(9), 78(8))

s 1–28	1 Jun 1978 (SI 1978/586)
28A	Inserted by Copyright, Designs and Patents Act 1988, s 295, Sch 5, para 7 (qv)
29–31	1 Jun 1978 (SI 1978/586)
32	Substituted by Patents, Designs and Marks Act 1986, s 1, Sch 1, para 4 (qv)
33, 34	1 Jun 1978 (SI 1978/586)
35	Repealed
36–50	1 Jun 1978 (SI 1978/586)
51	Substituted by Copyright, Designs and Patents Act 1988, s 295, Sch 5, para 14 (qv)
52	1 Jun 1978 (SI 1978/586)
53(1)	*Not in force*

Patents Act 1977 (c 37)—*cont*

s 53(2)–(5)	1 Jun 1978 (SI 1978/586)
54–57	1 Jun 1978 (SI 1978/586)
57A	Inserted by Copyright, Designs and Patents Act 1988, s 295, Sch 5, para 16(1) (qv)
58, 59	1 Jun 1978 (SI 1978/586)
60(1)–(3)	1 Jun 1978 (SI 1978/586)
(4)	*Not in force*
(5)–(7)	1 Jun 1978 (SI 1978/586)
61–63	1 Jun 1978 (SI 1978/586)
64	Substituted by Copyright, Designs and Patents Act 1988, s 295, Sch 5, para 17 (qv)
65–75	1 Jun 1978 (SI 1978/586)
76	Substituted by Copyright, Designs and Patents Act 1988, s 295, Sch 5, para 17 (qv)
77(1), (2)	1 Jun 1978 (SI 1978/586)
(3)	Substituted by Copyright, Designs and Patents Act 1988, s 295, Sch 5, para 21 (1), (2) (qv)
(4), (4A)	Substituted for original sub-s (4) by Copyright, Designs and Patents Act 1988, s 295, Sch 5, para 21(1), (3) (qv)
(5)	1 Jun 1978 (SI 1978/586)
(6)	1 Sep 1987 (SI 1987/288)
(7)	29 Jul 1977 (RA)
(8)	1 Jun 1978 (SI 1978/586)
(9)	29 Jul 1977 (RA)
78(1)–(4)	1 Jun 1978 (SI 1978/586)
(5), (5A)	Substituted for original sub-s (5) by Copyright, Designs and Patents Act 1988, s 295, Sch 5, para 22 (qv)
(6)	1 Jun 1978 (SI 1978/586)
(7)	1 Sep 1987 (SI 1987/288)
(8)	29 Jul 1977 (RA)
79–83	1 Jun 1978 (SI 1978/586)
84, 85	Repealed
86, 87	*Not in force*
88	Repealed
89–89B	Substituted for original s 89 by Copyright, Designs and Patents Act 1988, s 295, Sch 5, para 25 (qv)
90–95	1 Jun 1978 (SI 1978/586)
96	Repealed
97–99	1 Jun 1978 (SI 1978/586)
99A, 99B	Inserted by Copyright, Designs and Patents Act 1988, s 295, Sch 5, para 26 (qv)
100, 101	1 Jun 1978 (SI 1978/586)
102, 102A	Substituted for original s 102 by Copyright, Designs and Patents Act 1988, s 295, Sch 5, para 27 (qv)
103	1 Jun 1978 (SI 1978/586)
104	Repealed
105–113	1 Jun 1978 (SI 1978/586)
114, 115	Repealed
116–125	1 Jun 1978 (SI 1978/586)
125A	Inserted by Copyright, Designs and Patents Act 1988, s 295, Sch 5, para 30 (qv)
126	1 Jun 1978 (SI 1978/586)
127(1)–(4)	1 Jun 1978 (SI 1978/586)
(5)	See Sch 3 below
(6), (7)	1 Jun 1978 (SI 1978/586)

Patents Act 1977 (c 37)—*cont*

s 128, 129	1 Jun 1978 (SI 1978/586)
130	31 Dec 1977 (SI 1977/2090)
131	1 Jun 1978 (SI 1978/586)
132(1)–(4)	1 Jun 1978 (SI 1978/586)
(5)	29 Jul 1977 (RA)
(6)	1 Jun 1978 (SI 1978/586)
(7)	See Sch 6 below
Sch 1, 2	1 Jun 1978 (SI 1978/586)
3	29 Jul 1977 (repeal of Patents Act 1949, s 41) (RA)
	1 Jun 1978 (otherwise) (SI 1978/586)
4, 5	1 Jun 1978 (SI 1978/586)
6	29 Jul 1977 (repeal of Patents Act 1949, s 41) (RA)
	31 Dec 1977 (repeal of Patents Act 1949, s 88) (SI 1977/2090)
	1 Jun 1978 (otherwise) (SI 1978/586)

Pensioners Payments Act 1977 (c 51)

Whole Act repealed

Presumption of Death (Scotland) Act 1977 (c 27)

RA: 22 Jul 1977

Commencement provisions: s 20(2); Presumption of Death (Scotland) Act 1977 (Commencement) Order 1978, SI 1978/159

s 1–19	1 Mar 1978 (SI 1978/159)
20	22 Jul 1977 (RA)
Sch 1, 2	1 Mar 1978 (SI 1978/159)

Price Commission Act 1977 (c 33)

RA: 22 Jul 1977

Commencement provisions: s 24(2) (repealed)

Whole Act repealed, except ss 16, 17, by the Competition Act 1980, s 33(4), Sch 2 (the repeal of s 15(4) and Sch 2, para 4(b), (d) being as from 1 Jan 2011). S 17 repealed by Statute Law (Repeals) Act 1989, s 1(1), Sch 1, Pt II. S 16 came into force on 1 Aug 1977 (s 24(2))

Post Office Act 1977 (c 44)

Whole Act repealed

Protection from Eviction Act 1977 (c 43)

RA: 29 Jul 1977

Commencement provisions: s 13(2)

29 Aug 1977 (s 13(2))

Redundancy Rebates Act 1977 (c 22)

Whole Act repealed

Rent Act 1977 (c 42)

RA: 29 Jul 1977

Commencement provisions: s 156(2)

29 Aug 1977 (s 156(2))

Rent (Agriculture) Amendment Act 1977 (c 17)

RA: 26 May 1977

Commencement provisions: s 2(2)

9 Jun 1977 (s 2(2))

Rentcharges Act 1977 (c 30)

RA: 22 Jul 1977

Commencement provisions: s 18(2); Rentcharges Act 1977 (Commencement) Order 1978, SI 1978/15

s 1–3	22 Aug 1977 (s 18(2))
4–11	1 Feb 1978 (SI 1978/15)
12–15	22 Aug 1977 (s 18(2))
16	1 Feb 1978 (SI 1978/15)
17(1)	22 Aug 1977 (in relation to Sch 1, para 2) (s 18(2))
	1 Feb 1978 (otherwise) (SI 1978/15)
(2)	See Sch 2 below
(3)	22 Aug 1977 (s 18(2))
(4), (5)	1 Feb 1978 (SI 1978/15)
(6)	22 Aug 1977 (s 18(2))
18	22 Aug 1977 (s 18(2))
Sch 1, para 1	1 Feb 1978 (SI 1978/15)
2	22 Aug 1977 (s 18(2))
3, 4	1 Feb 1978 (SI 1978/15)
2	1 Feb 1978 (repeal of Inclosure Act 1854, s 10; Law of Property Act 1925, s 191) (SI 1978/15)
	22 Aug 1977 (otherwise) (s 18(2))

Representation of the People Act 1977 (c 9)

Whole Act repealed

Restrictive Trade Practices Act 1977 (c 19)

RA: 30 Jun 1977

30 Jun 1977 (RA)

Returning Officers (Scotland) Act 1977 (c 14)

Whole Act repealed

Roe Deer (Close Seasons) Act 1977 (c 4)

Whole Act repealed

Social Security (Miscellaneous Provisions) Act 1977 (c 5)

RA: 30 Mar 1977

Commencement provisions: s 25(2), (3), (4); Social Security (Miscellaneous Provisions) Act 1977 (Commencement No 1) Order 1977, SI 1977/617; Social Security (Miscellaneous Provisions) Act 1977 (Commencement No 2) Order 1977, SI 1977/618

s 1, 2	Repealed
3	25 Apr 1977 (SI 1977/618)
4–11	Repealed
12	25 Apr 1977 (SI 1977/618)
13	Repealed
14	Repealed or spent
15–20	Repealed
21	6 Apr 1978 (SI 1977/618); prospectively repealed by Pension Schemes Act 1993, s 188, Sch 5, Pt I (qv)
22(1)–(6)	Repealed
(7), (8)	25 Apr 1977 (SI 1977/618); prospectively repealed by Pension Schemes Act 1993, s 188, Sch 5, Pt I (qv)
(9)–(12)	Repealed
(13)	6 Apr 1978 (SI 1977/618); prospectively repealed by Pension Schemes Act 1993, s 188, Sch 5, Pt I (qv)
(14)	25 Apr 1977 (SI 1977/618); prospectively repealed by Pension Schemes Act 1993, s 188, Sch 5, Pt I (qv)
(15), (16)	Repealed
(17)	Spent
23	25 Apr 1977 (SI 1977/618)
24(1)	30 Mar 1977 (RA)
(2)	Repealed
(3)	30 Mar 1977 (RA)
(4)	Repealed
(5)	30 Mar 1977 (RA)
(6)	See Sch 2 below
25	30 Mar 1977 (RA)
Sch 1	Repealed
2	30 Mar 1977 (repeals of or in Social Security Act 1975, ss 30(2), 45(4), 66(5), 124(1)(d)) (RA)
	6 Apr 1977 (repeals of or in Employment Protection Act 1975, s 113; Supplementary Benefits Act 1976, Sch 7, para 41) (SI 1977/617)
	25 Apr 1977 (repeals of or in Tribunals and Inquiries Act 1971; Social Security Act 1975, s 1(5)(pt), 129(3); Social Security (NI) Act 1975; Social Security Pensions Act 1975; Employment

Social Security (Miscellaneous Provisions) Act 1977 (c 5)—*cont*
Sch 2—*contd*   Protection Act 1975, s 40(3); Supplementary
                                       Benefits Act 1976, s 29) (SI 1977/618)
                                       27 Jun 1977 (repeals of or in Social Security Act
                                         1975, Sch 20(pt)) (SI 1977/618)
                                       1 Jul 1977 (repeals of or in Industrial Injuries and
                                         Diseases (Old Cases) Act 1975) (SI 1977/618)

Statute Law (Repeals) Act 1977 (c 18)

RA: 16 Jun 1977

16 Jun 1977 (RA)

Torts (Interference with Goods) Act 1977 (c 32)

RA: 22 Jul 1977

Commencement provisions: s 17(2); Torts (Interference with Goods) Act 1977
    (Commencement No 1) Order 1977, SI 1977/1910; Torts (Interference with
    Goods) Act 1977 (Commencement No 2) Order 1978, SI 1978/627; Torts
    (Interference with Goods) Act 1977 (Commencement No 3) Order 1980,
    SI 1980/2024★

s 1–11	1 Jun 1978 (SI 1978/627)
12–16	1 Jan 1978 (SI 1977/1910)
17(1), (2)	1 Jan 1978 (SI 1977/1910)
(3)	1 Jun 1978 (SI 1978/627)
Sch 1	1 Jan 1978 (SI 1977/1910)
2	1 Jun 1978 (SI 1978/627)

★ Note that Torts (Interference with Goods) Act 1977 (Commencement No 3) Order
1980, SI 1980/2024, brought this Act into force, so far as not already in force by virtue
of SI 1977/1910, in Northern Ireland on 1 Jan 1981 (SI 1978/627 applied to England
and Wales only)

Town and Country Planning (Amendment) Act 1977 (c 29)

Whole Act repealed

Town and Country Planning (Scotland) Act 1977 (c 10)

RA: 30 Mar 1977

30 Mar 1977 (RA)

Transport (Financial Provisions) Act 1977 (c 20)

RA: 30 Jun 1977

30 Jun 1977 (RA)

Whole Act prospectively repealed by Railways Act 1993, s 152, Sch 14 (qv)

Unfair Contract Terms Act 1977 (c 50)

RA: 26 Oct 1977

Commencement provisions: s 31(1)

1 Feb 1978 (s 31(1); note that does not apply to contracts before this date but applies to
  liability for loss or damage suffered on or after that date (s 31(2)))

Water Charges Equalisation Act 1977 (c 41)

Whole Act repealed

1978

Adoption (Scotland) Act 1978 (c 28)

RA: 20 Jul 1978

Commencement provisions: s 67(2); Adoption (Scotland) Act 1978 Commencement
Order 1984, SI 1984/1050

s 1, 2	1 Feb 1985 (SI 1984/1050)
3–9	1 Sep 1984 (SI 1984/1050)
10	Repealed
11–20	1 Sep 1984 (subject to transitional provisions) (SI 1984/1050)
21	Substituted by Children Act 1989, s 88, Sch 10, para 37 (qv)
22–39	1 Sep 1984 (subject to transitional provisions) (SI 1984/1050)
40	Repealed
41–67	1 Sep 1984 (subject to transitional provisions) (SI 1984/1050)
Sch 1–4	1 Sep 1984 (SI 1984/1050)

Appropriation Act 1978 (c 57)

Whole Act repealed

Chronically Sick and Disabled Persons (Northern Ireland) Act 1978 (c 53)

Applies to Northern Ireland only

Church of England (Miscellaneous Provisions) Measure 1978 (No 3)

RA: 30 Jun 1978

Commencement provisions: s 13(4)

30 Jul 1978 (s 13(4))

Civil Aviation Act 1978 (c 8)

RA: 23 Mar 1978

Commencement provisions: s 16(2); Civil Aviation Act 1978 (Commencement) Order
1978, SI 1978/486

s 1–12	Repealed

Civil Aviation Act 1978 (c 8)—*cont*

s 13(1)	23 Mar 1978 (SI 1978/486)
(2)	As originally enacted repealed; new sub-s (2) inserted by Civil Aviation Act 1982, s 109(2), Sch 15, para 20(2) (qv)
(3)	23 Mar 1978 (SI 1978/486)
14(1)(a)	1 May 1978 (SI 1978/486)
(b)	Repealed
(2)	1 May 1978 (SI 1978/486)
(3)	Repealed
15(1)	Repealed
(2)	1 May 1978 (SI 1978/486)
16(1), (2)	23 Mar 1978 (SI 1978/486)
(3), (4)	Repealed
(5)(a)	23 Mar 1978 (SI 1978/486)
(b)	Repealed
(6)	23 Mar 1978 (SI 1978/486)
Sch 1, para 1–3	Repealed
4	1 May 1978 (SI 1978/486)
5–11	Repealed
2	1 May 1978 (SI 1978/486)

Civil Liability (Contribution) Act 1978 (c 47)

RA: 31 Jul 1978

Commencement provisions: s 10(2)

1 Jan 1979 (s 10(2))

Commonwealth Development Corporation Act 1978 (c 2)

RA: 23 Mar 1978

Commencement provisions: s 19(2)

23 Apr 1978 (s 19(2))

Community Service by Offenders (Scotland) Act 1978 (c 49)

RA: 31 Jul 1978

Commencement provisions: s 15(2); Community Service by Offenders (Scotland) Act 1978 (Commencement No 1) Order 1978, SI 1978/1944; Community Service by Offenders (Scotland) Act 1978 (Commencement No 2) Order 1980, SI 1980/268

s 1–5	1 Feb 1979 (SI 1978/1944)
6	1 Apr 1980 (SI 1980/268)
6A, 6B	Inserted by Criminal Justice Act 1982, s 68, Sch 13, Pt II, para 6 (qv)
7–14	1 Feb 1979 (SI 1978/1944)
15(1)–(4)	1 Feb 1979 (SI 1978/1944)
(5)	1 Apr 1980 (SI 1980/268)
Sch 1	Repealed
2	1 Feb 1979 (SI 1978/1944)

Consolidated Fund Act 1978 (c 7)

Whole Act repealed

Consolidated Fund (No 2) Act 1978 (c 59)

Whole Act repealed

Consumer Safety Act 1978 (c 38)

Whole Act repealed

Co-operative Development Agency Act 1978 (c 21)

Whole Act repealed

Dioceses Measure 1978 (No 1)

RA: 2 Feb 1978

Commencement provisions: s 25(2)

2 May 1978 (s 25(2))

Dividends Act 1978 (c 54)

Whole Act repealed

Domestic Proceedings and Magistrates' Courts Act 1978 (c 22)

RA: 30 Jun 1978

Commencement provisions: s 89(3); Domestic Proceedings and Magistrates' Courts Act 1978 (Commencement No 1) Order 1978, SI 1978/997; Domestic Proceedings and Magistrates' Courts Act 1978 (Commencement No 2) Order 1978, SI 1978/1489; Domestic Proceedings and Magistrates' Courts Act 1978 (Commencement No 1) (Scotland) Order 1978, SI 1978/1490; Domestic Proceedings and Magistrates' Courts Act 1978 (Commencement No 3) Order 1979, SI 1979/731; Domestic Proceedings and Magistrates' Courts Act 1978 (Commencement No 4) Order 1980, SI 1980/1478; Domestic Proceedings and Magistrates' Courts Act 1978 (Commencement No 2) (Scotland) Order 1980, SI 1980/2036; Children Act 1975 and the Domestic Proceedings and Magistrates' Courts Act 1978 (Commencement) Order 1985, SI 1985/779

s 1, 2	1 Feb 1981 (SI 1980/1478)
3	Substituted by Matrimoninal and Family Proceedings Act 1984, s 9 (qv)
4, 5	1 Feb 1981 (SI 1980/1478)
6	Substituted by Matrimonial and Family Proceedings Act 1984, s 10 (qv)
7	1 Feb 1981 (SI 1980/1478)
8	Substituted by Children Act 1989, s 108(5), Sch 13, para 36 (qv)
9–15	Repealed
16–18	1 Nov 1979 (SI 1979/731)

Domestic Proceedings and Magistrates' Courts Act 1978 (c 22)—*cont*

s 19, 20	1 Feb 1981 (SI 1980/1478)
20ZA	Inserted by Maintenance Enforcement Act 1991, s 5 (qv)
20A	Inserted by Family Law Reform Act 1987, s 33(1), Sch 2, para 69 (qv); substituted by Children Act 1989, s 108(5), Sch 15, para 39(1) (qv)
21	Repealed
22, 23	1 Feb 1981 (SI 1980/1478)
24	Repealed
25–27	1 Feb 1981 (SI 1980/1478)
28	1 Nov 1979 (SI 1979/731)
29(1), (2)	1 Nov 1979 (SI 1979/731)
(3)	1 Feb 1981 (SI 1980/1478)
(4)	Repealed
(5)	1 Nov 1979 (SI 1979/731)
30	1 Nov 1979 (SI 1979/731)
31, 32	1 Feb 1981 (SI 1980/1478)
33, 34	Repealed
35	1 Feb 1981 (SI 1980/1478)
36–53	Repealed
54	1 Feb 1981 (SI 1980/1478)
55	23 Oct 1978 (SI 1978/1490)
56	1 Feb 1981 (SI 1980/1478)
57, 58	Repealed
59, 60	1 Feb 1981 (SI 1980/1478)
61	23 Oct 1978 (SI 1978/1490)
62, 63	1 Feb 1981 (SI 1980/1478)
64–72	Repealed
73	20 Nov 1978 (SI 1978/1489)
74	20 Nov 1978 (EW) (SI 1978/1489); repealed (S)
75–86	Repealed
87	23 Oct 1978 (S) (SI 1978/1490)
	20 Nov 1978 (EW) (SI 1978/1489)
88(1)–(4)	1 Nov 1979 (SI 1979/731)
(5)	18 Jul 1978 (SI 1978/997)
89(1)	18 Jul 1978 (SI 1978/997)
(2)(a)	23 Oct 1978 (S) (so far as brings Sch 2, paras 17, 18 into force) (SI 1978/1490)
	29 Nov 1978 (EW) (SI 1978/1489)
	1 Feb 1981 (S) (otherwise) (SI 1980/2036)
(b)	18 Jul 1978 (SI 1978/997)
(3)–(6)	18 Jul 1978 (SI 1978/997)
90	18 Jul 1978 (SI 1978/997)
Sch 1	18 Jul 1978 (SI 1978/997)
2, para 1, 2	1 Feb 1981 (SI 1980/1478)
3–5	Repealed
6	1 Feb 1981 (SI 1980/1478)
7	Spent
8	Repealed
9	1 Feb 1981 (SI 1980/1478)
10, 11	Spent
12	1 Nov 1979 (SI 1979/731)
13, 14	1 Feb 1981 (SI 1980/1478)
15	Repealed
16	Spent

Domestic Proceedings and Magistrates' Courts Act 1978 (c 22)—*cont*

Sch 2, para 17–20		Repealed or spent
	21–25	Repealed
	26	1 Feb 1981 (SI 1980/1478)
	27	Repealed
	28	1 Feb 1981 (SI 1980/1478)
	29–31	Repealed
	32, 33	1 Feb 1981 (SI 1980/1478)
	34, 35	1 Feb 1981 (SI 1980/1478); prospectively repealed by Maintenance Orders (Reciprocal Enforcement) Act 1992, s 2(2), Sch 3 (qv)
	36	Repealed
	37	1 Feb 1981 (SI 1980/1478)
	38, 39	1 Nov 1979 (SI 1979/731)
	40	Spent
	41–50	Repealed
	51	20 Nov 1978 (SI 1978/1489)
	52	Repealed
	53	20 Nov 1978 (SI 1978/1489)
	54	Spent
3		18 Jul 1978 (repeal in Administration of Justice Act 1964, s 2) (SI 1978/997)

20 Nov 1978 (repeals of or in Adoption (Hague Convention) Act (Northern Ireland) 1969, s 7(2); Children Act 1975, Sch 3, para 26; Adoption Act 1976, Sch 1, para 6) (SI 1978/1489)

1 Nov 1979 (repeals of or in National Assistance Act 1948, s 43(7); Magistrates' Courts Act 1952, ss 57(4), 60(1), (2)(a), 61, 62, 121(2); Matrimonial Proceedings (Magistrates' Courts) Act 1960, s 8(3); Criminal Justice Act 1961, Sch 4; Maintenance Orders (Reciprocal Enforcement) Act 1972, s 17(1)–(3), Schedule, para 1; Affiliation Proceedings (Amendment) Act 1972, s 3(1), (2); Children Act 1975, s 21(3), Sch 3, para 12; Adoption Act 1976, s 64(c), Sch 3, para 4; Supplementary Benefits Act 1976, s 18(7), Sch 7) (SI 1979/731)

1 Feb 1981 (repeals of or in Maintenance Orders Act 1950, s 2(3); Magistrates' Courts Act 1952, s 59; Affiliation Proceedings Act 1957, s 7(1)–(3); Matrimonial Proceedings (Magistrates' Courts) Act 1960 except s 8(3) (repealed as above); Administration of Justice Act 1964, Sch 3, para 27; Matrimonial Causes Act 1965, s 42; Criminal Justice Act 1967, Sch 3 (entry relating to Matrimonial Proceedings (Magistrates' Courts) Act 1960); Family Law Reform Act 1969, s 5(2); Local Authority Social Services Act 1970, Sch 1 (entry relating to Matrimonial Proceedings (Magistrates' Courts) Act 1960); Matrimonial Proceedings and Property Act 1970, ss 30(1), 31–33; Guardianship of Minors Act 1971, ss 9(3), 14(4); Misuse of Drugs Act 1971, s 34; Maintenance Orders (Reciprocal Enforcement) Act 1972, s 27(3); Local Government Act 1972, Sch 23, para 10; Matrimonial Causes Act 1973, s 27(8); Guardianship Act 1973, ss 2(5), 3(2), 8, Sch 2,

Domestic Proceedings and Magistrates' Courts Act 1978 (c 22)—*cont*

Sch 3—*cont*   para 1(2); Legal Aid Act 1974, Sch 1, para 3(a);
                                          Children Act 1975, ss 17(1), 91; Adoption Act 1976,
                                          s 26(1)) (SI 1980/1478)

Education (Northern Ireland) Act 1978 (c 13)

Applies to Northern Ireland only

Employment (Continental Shelf) Act 1978 (c 46)

RA: 31 Jul 1978

31 Jul 1978 (RA)

Whole Act prospectively repealed by Oil and Gas (Enterprise) Act 1982, s 37, Sch 4
(qv)

Employment Protection (Consolidation) Act 1978 (c 44)

RA: 31 Jul 1978

Commencement provisions: s 160(2)

s 1–6	Substituted (subject to savings) for ss 1, 2, 2A, 4, 5, 5A, 6 by Trade Union Reform and Employment Rights Act 1993, ss 26, 50, Sch 4, Sch 9, para 3 (qv) (original s 3 repealed by Employment Act 1982, s 21(3), Sch 4 (qv); s 2A originally inserted by Employment Act 1989, s 13(1), (3) (qv); s 5A originally inserted by Employment Act 1982, s 20, Sch 2, para 8(4) (qv))
7	Repealed
8–22	1 Nov 1978 (s 160(2))
22A–22C	Inserted by Trade Union Reform and Employment Rights Act 1993, s 28, Sch 5, para 1 (qv)
23–28	Repealed
29–31	1 Nov 1978 (s 160(2))
31A	Inserted by Employment Act 1980, s 13 (qv)
32	Substituted by Trade Union and Labour Relations (Consolidation) Act 1992, s 300(2), Sch 2, para 13 (qv)
(Pt III (ss 33–48)	prospectively substituted by new Pt III (ss 33–37, 37A, 38, 38A, 39–47) by Trade Union Reform and Employment Rights Act 1993, ss 23, 25, Schs 2, 3 (qv)
33	1 Nov 1978 (s 160(2))
34–44	Repealed
45–56	1 Nov 1978 (s 160(2))
56A	Inserted by Employment Act 1980, s 12 (qv)
57	1 Nov 1978 (s 160(2))
57A	Inserted by Trade Union Reform and Employment Rights Act 1993, s 28, Sch 5, para 3 (qv)
58, 58A	Repealed
59	1 Nov 1978 (s 160(2))

Employment Protection (Consolidation) Act 1978 (c 44)—*cont*

s 60	1 Nov 1978 (s 160(2)); prospectively substituted by Trade Union Reform and Employment Rights Act 1993, s 24(1) (qv)
60A	Inserted by Trade Union Reform and Employment Rights Act 1993, s 29(1) (qv)
61	1 Nov 1978 (s 160(2))
62, 62A	Repealed
63, 64	1 Nov 1978 (s 160(2))
64A	Repealed
65–71	1 Nov 1978 (s 160(2))
72	Substituted by Trade Union and Labour Relations (Consolidation) Act 1992, s 300(2), Sch 2, para 16 (qv)
72A	Repealed
73–75	1 Nov 1978 (s 160(2))
75A	Inserted by Trade Union Reform and Employment Rights Act 1993, s 28, Sch 5, para 9 (qv) (original s 75A inserted by Employment Act 1982, s 5(3) (qv) and repealed by Trade Union and Labour Relations (Consolidation) Act 1992, s 300(1), Sch 17 (qv)
76	1 Nov 1978 (s 160(2))
76A	Repealed
77, 77A, 78, 78A, 79	Inserted by Trade Union Reform and Employment Rights Act 1993, s 28, Sch 5, para 10 (qv) (original ss 77, 78, 79 repealed by Trade Union and Labour Relations (Consolidated) Act 1992, s 300(1), Sch 17 (qv)
80–93	1 Nov 1978 (s 160(2))
94, 95	Repealed
96	1 Nov 1978 (s 160(2))
97	Repealed
98–102	1 Nov 1978 (s 160(2))
103–105	Repealed
106, 107	1 Nov 1978 (s 160(2))
108	Substituted as from 16 Jan 1990 by Employment Act 1989, s 29(3), Sch 6, para 22 (qv)
109	Repealed
110–112	1 Nov 1978 (s 160(2))
113	Repealed
114–120	1 Nov 1978 (s 160(2))
121	1 Nov 1978 (s 160(2)); repealed (EW)
122–136	1 Nov 1978 (s 160(2))
136A	Inserted by Trade Union Reform and Employment Rights Act 1993, s 42 (qv)
137, 138	1 Nov 1978 (s 160(2))
138A	Prospectively inserted by Trade Union Reform and Employment Rights Act 1993, s 31(2) (qv)
139(1)	1 Nov 1978 (s 160(2))
(2)–(9)	1 Jan 1979 (s 160(2))
139A	Inserted by Trade Union Reform and Employment Rights Act 1993, s 49(1), Sch 11 (qv)
140–142	1 Nov 1978 (s 160(2))
143	Repealed
144	1 Nov 1978 (s 160(2))
145	Repealed
146	1 Nov 1978 (s 160(2))

Employment Protection (Consolidation) Act 1978 (c 44)—*cont*

s 146A	Inserted as from 30 Nov 1993 by Trade Union Reform and Employment Rights Act 1993, s 49(1), Sch 7, para 5 (qv) (except insofar as relating to s 60 of this Act)
	Not in force (exception noted above)
147	Repealed
148–150	1 Nov 1978 (s 160(2))
151	Substituted by Employment Act 1982, s 20, Sch 2, para 7(1) (qv)
152–160	1 Nov 1978 (s 160(2))
Sch 1–4	1 Nov 1978 (s 160(2))
5	Repealed
6	Repealed
7–16	1 Nov 1978 (s 160(2))
17	1 Nov 1978 (except repeals in Employment Protection Act 1975, s 122)
	1 Jan 1979 (exception noted above) (s 160(2))

Employment Subsidies Act 1978 (c 6)

Whole Act lapsed in accordance with terms of s 3(4)

European Parliamentary Elections Act 1978 (c 10)

RA: 5 May 1980

5 May 1980 (RA)

Export Guarantees and Overseas Investment Act 1978 (c 18)

Whole Act repealed

Finance Act 1978 (c 42)

Budget Day: 11 Apr 1978

RA: 31 Jul 1978

See the note about Finance Acts at the front of this book

Gun Barrel Proof Act 1978 (c 9)

RA: 5 May 1978

Commencement provisions: s 9(3); Gun Barrel Proof Act 1978 (Commencement No 1) Order 1978, SI 1978/1587; Gun Barrel Proof Act 1978 (Commencement No 2) Order 1980, SI 1980/640

s 1	5 Jun 1980 (SI 1980/640)
2–7	1 Dec 1978 (SI 1978/1587)

Gun Barrel Proof Act 1978 (c 9)—*cont*

s 8(1)	1 Dec 1978 (so far as relates to Sch 3) (SI 1978/1587)
	5 Jun 1980 (otherwise) (SI 1980/640)
(2)	1 Dec 1978 (SI 1978/1587)
(3)	5 Jun 1980 (SI 1980/640)
9	1 Dec 1978 (SI 1978/1587)
Sch 1, 2	5 Jun 1980 (SI 1980/640)
3, para 1(a)	5 Jun 1980 (SI 1980/640)
(b)	1 Dec 1978 (except definition of 'convention proof mark') (SI 1978/1587)
	5 Jun 1980 (exception noted above) (SI 1980/640)
2–9	1 Dec 1978 (SI 1978/1587)
10(1)	1 Dec 1978 (SI 1978/1587)
(2)	1 Jun 1980 (SI 1980/640)
11–14	1 Dec 1978 (SI 1978/1587)
15(1), (2)	1 Dec 1978 (SI 1978/1587)
(3)	1 Jun 1980 (SI 1980/640)
16	1 Dec 1980 (except words 'or which is or at any time was a convention proof mark'), (SI 1978/1587)
	1 Jun 1980 (exception noted above) (SI 1980/640)
17–20	1 Dec 1978 (SI 1978/1587)
4	1 Dec 1978 (SI 1978/1587)

Homes Insulation Act 1978 (c 48)

Whole Act repealed

Home Purchase Assistance and Housing Corporation Guarantee Act 1978 (c 27)

Whole Act repealed

House of Commons (Administration) Act 1978 (c 36)

RA: 20 Jul 1978

Commencement provisions: s 5(5)

s 1	20 Jul 1978 (RA)
2	1 Jan 1979 (s 5(5))
3–5	20 Jul 1978 (RA)
Sch 1	20 Jul 1978 (RA)
2, para 1, 2	20 Jul 1978 (RA)
3	1 Jan 1979 (s 5(5))
4, 5	Repealed
3	1 Jan 1979 (s 5(5))

Housing (Financial Provisions) (Scotland) Act 1978 (c 14)

RA: 25 May 1978

Commencement provisions: s 19(2), (3) (repealed)

Whole Act repealed, except for Sch 2, paras 12–14, 39, which came into force on 25 Jun 1978 (s 19(2))

Import of Live Fish (Scotland) Act 1978 (c 35)

RA: 20 Jul 1978

20 Jul 1978 (RA)

Independent Broadcasting Authority Act 1978 (c 43)

Whole Act repealed

Industrial and Provident Societies Act 1978 (c 34)

RA: 20 Jul 1978

Commencement provisions: s 3(3)

20 Aug 1978 (s 3(3))

Inner Urban Areas Act 1978 (c 50)

RA: 31 Jul 1978

31 Jul 1978 (RA)

Internationally Protected Persons Act 1978 (c 17)

RA: 30 Jun 1978

Commencement provisions: s 5(5); Internationally Protected Persons Act 1978
    (Commencement) Order 1979, SI 1979/455

24 May 1979 (SI 1979/455)

Interpretation Act 1978 (c 30)

RA: 20 Jul 1978

Commencement provisions: s 26

1 Jan 1979 (s 26)

Iron and Steel (Amendment) Act 1978 (c 41)

Whole Act repealed

Judicature (Northern Ireland) Act 1978 (c 23)

RA: 30 Jun 1978

Commencement provisions: s 123(2); Judicature (Northern Ireland) Act 1978
    (Commencement No 1) Order 1978, SI 1978/1101; Judicature (Northern Ireland)
    Act 1978 (Commencement No 2) Order 1978, SI 1978/1829; Judicature (Northern
    Ireland) Act 1978 (Commencement No 3) Order 1979, SI 1979/124; Judicature
    (Northern Ireland) Act 1978 (Commencement No 4) Order 1979, SI 1979/422

Judicature (Northern Ireland) Act 1978 (c 23)—*cont*

s 1–27	18 Apr 1979 (SI 1979/422)
28	Repealed
29–33	18 Apr 1979 (SI 1979/422)
33A	Inserted by Administration of Justice Act 1982, s 69(1), Sch 7 (qv)
34–38	18 Apr 1979 (SI 1979/422)
39, 40	Repealed
41–51	18 Apr 1979 (SI 1979/422)
52, 53	21 Aug 1978 (SI 1978/1101)
54–56	2 Jan 1979 (SI 1978/1829) (Note that s 54(2)–(4), (6), 55(3), 56(1)–(3) came into force on 21 Aug 1978 so far as apply to the Crown Court Rules Committee and Crown Court Rules (SI 1978/1101))
57–72	18 Apr 1979 (SI 1979/422)
73	Substituted by the Supreme Court (Departments and Officers) (Northern Ireland) Order 1982, SR 1982/300, art 5(1)
74	18 Apr 1979 (SI 1979/422)
75	Substituted by SR 1982/300, art 4 (see s 73 above)
76–82	18 Apr 1979 (SI 1979/422)
83	Repealed
84–94	18 Apr 1979 (SI 1979/422)
94A	Inserted by Administration of Justice Act 1982, s 70, Sch 8 (qv)
95, 96	Repealed
97, 98	18 Apr 1979 (SI 1979/422)
99	21 Aug 1978 (SI 1978/1101)
100	18 Apr 1979 (SI 1979/422)
101	Repealed
102–106	18 Apr 1979 (SI 1979/422)
107	21 Aug 1978 (SI 1978/1101)
108–115	18 Apr 1979 (SI 1979/422)
116	21 Aug 1978 (SI 1978/1101)
117	18 Apr 1979 (SI 1979/422)
117A	Inserted by Administration of Justice Act 1982, s 70, Sch 8 (qv)
118–121	21 Aug 1978 (SI 1978/1101)
122	See Schs 5–7 below
123	21 Aug 1978 (SI 1978/1101)
Sch 1–4	18 Apr 1979 (SI 1979/422)
5, Pt I, para 1, 2	18 Apr 1979 (SI 1979/422)
3, 4	2 Jan 1979 (SI 1978/1829)
Pt II	21 Aug 1978 (amendments to Bills of Sale (Ireland) Act 1879; Deeds of Arrangement Act 1887; Deeds of Arrangement Amendment Act 1890) (SI 1978/1101)
	2 Jan 1979 (amendments to Probates and Letters of Administration Act (Ireland) 1857; Juries Act (Ireland) 1871, s 18; Bankruptcy (Ireland) Amendment Act 1872, ss 57, 124; Bills of Sale (Ireland) Act 1879, s 4; Land Law (Ireland) Act 1887; Foreign Judgments (Reciprocal Enforcement) Act 1933; Trade Marks Act 1938; Exchange Control Act 1947; Representation of the People Act 1949, s 163; Arbitration Act 1950; Arbitration (International Investment Disputes)

Judicature (Northern Ireland) Act 1978 (c 23)—*cont*

Sch 5, Pt II—*cont*
Act 1966; Criminal Appeal (Northern Ireland) Act 1968, ss 49, 50 (definition 'rules of court'); Administration of Justice Act 1969, ss 20(5), 21(4); Social Security (Northern Ireland) Act 1975) (SI 1978/1829)
18 Apr 1979 (all other amendments to Acts of UK Parliament) (SI 1979/422)
21 Aug 1978, 2 Jan 1979, 21 Feb 1979, 18 Apr 1979 and 1 Sep 1979 (Acts of Irish Parliament and Parliament of Northern Ireland; Orders in Council)

6
18 Apr 1979 (SI 1979/422); except para 3, and para 10 so far as it relates to para 3, which came into force on 2 Jan 1979 (SI 1978/1829); and except para 7 and, para 10 so far as it relates to para 7, which came into force on 21 Aug 1978 (SI 1978/1101)

7, Pt I
21 Aug 1978 (repeal of Supreme Court of Judicature Act (Ireland) 1877) (SI 1978/1101)
2 Jan 1979 (repeals of or in Law of Property Amendment Act 1860, s 10; Settled Estates Act 1877, s 42; Bills of Sale (Ireland) Act 1879, s 21; Conveyancing Act 1881, ss 48(5), 72(5); Deeds of Arrangement Act 1887, s 18; Deeds of Arrangement Amendment Act 1890, s 3; Administration of Justice Act 1920, ss 11, 12(2); Representation of the People Act 1949, s 160; Arbitration Act 1950, s 42(4); Administration of Justice Act 1960, s 9(2); Northern Ireland Act 1962, ss 7–9, Sch 1; Criminal Appeal (Northern Ireland) Act 1968, s 49) (SI 1978/1829)
18 Apr 1979 (all other repeals to Acts of UK Parliament) (SI 1979/422)

II, III
21 Aug 1978, 2 Jan 1979 and 18 Apr 1979 (Acts of Irish Parliament and Parliament of Northern Ireland; Orders in Council)

Local Government Act 1978 (c 39)

RA: 20 Jul 1978

20 Jul 1978 (RA)

Local Government (Scotland) Act 1978 (c 4)

RA: 23 Mar 1978

Commencement provisions: s 8(3)

23 Mar 1978 (RA), except Schedule, para 2, (repealed)

Medical Act 1978 (c 12)

Whole Act repealed

National Health Service (Scotland) Act 1978 (c 29)

RA: 20 Jul 1978

Commencement provisions: s 110(4)

1 Jan 1979 (s 110(4))

Northern Ireland (Emergency Provisions) Act 1978 (c 5)

Whole Act repealed

Nuclear Safeguards and Electricity (Finance) Act 1978 (c 25)

RA: 30 Jun 1978

30 Jun 1978 (RA)

Oaths Act 1978 (c 19)

RA: 30 Jun 1978

Commencement provisions: s 8(5)

1 Aug 1978 (s 8(5))

Parliamentary Pensions Act 1978 (c 56)

Whole Act repealed

Parochial Registers and Rewards Measure 1978 (No 2)

RA: 2 Feb 1978

Commencement provisions: s 27(2)

1 Jan 1979 (day appointed by the Archbishops of Canterbury and York under
  s 27(2))

Participation Agreements Act 1978 (c 1)

RA: 23 Feb 1978

23 Feb 1978 (RA)

Pensioners Payments Act 1978 (c 58)

Whole Act repealed

Protection of Children Act 1978 (c 37)

RA: 20 Jul 1978

Commencement provisions: s 9(3)

s 1–7	20 Aug 1978 (s 9(3))
8, 9	20 Jul 1978 (s 9(3))

Rating (Disabled Persons) Act 1978 (c 40)

RA: 20 Jul 1978

Commencement provisions: s 9(4)

1 Apr 1979 (s 9(4))

Whole Act repealed (EW) except s 9, Sch 2 (by Local Government Finance (Repeals, Savings and Consequential Amendments) Order 1990, SI 1990/776, art 3(1), Sch 1, as from 1 Apr 1990)

Refuse Disposal Amenity Act 1978 (c 3)

RA: 23 Mar 1978

Commencement provisions: s 13(2)

23 Apr 1978 (s 13(2))

Representation of the People Act 1978 (c 32)

Whole Act repealed

Scotland Act 1978 (c 51)

Whole Act repealed

Shipbuilding (Redundancy Payments) Act 1978 (c 11)

RA: 5 May 1978

5 May 1978 (RA)

Whole Act prospectively repealed by Statute Law (Repeals) Act 1993, s 1(1), Sch 1, Pt IX (qv)

Solomon Islands Act 1978 (c 15)

RA: 25 May 1978

Independence Day: 7 Jul 1978

State Immunity Act 1978 (c 33)

RA: 20 Jul 1978

Commencement provisions: s 23(5); State Immunity Act 1978 (Commencement) Order 1978, SI 1978/1572

22 Nov 1978 (SI 1978/1572; note that Pts I, II of this Act do not apply to proceedings in respect of matters that occurred before 22 Nov 1978 (s 23(3), (4)))

Statute Law (Repeals) Act 1978 (c 45)

RA: 31 Jul 1978

31 Jul 1978 (RA)

Suppression of Terrorism Act 1978 (c 26)

RA: 30 Jun 1978

Commencement provisions: s 9(3); Suppression of Terrorism Act 1978 (Commencement) Order 1978, SI 1978/1063

21 Aug 1978 (SI 1978/1063)

Theatres Trust (Scotland) Act 1978 (c 24)

RA: 30 Jun 1978

30 Jun 1978 (RA)

Theft Act 1978 (c 31)

RA: 20 Jul 1978

Commencement provisions: s 7(2)

20 Oct 1978 (s 7(2))

Transport Act 1978 (c 55)

RA: 2 Aug 1978

Commencement provisions: s 24(1); Transport Act 1978 (Commencement No 1) Order 1978, SI 1978/1150; Transport Act 1978 (Commencement No 2) Order 1978, SI 1978/1187; Transport Act 1978 (Commencement No 3) Order 1978, SI 1978/1289

s 1–8	Repealed
9	1 Nov 1978 (SI 1978/1187)
10	1 Sep 1978 (SI 1978/1187)
11, 12	Repealed
13	1 Sep 1978 (SI 1978/1187)
14	Repealed
15	4 Aug 1978 (SI 1978/1150)
16	1 Sep 1978 (SI 1978/1187); prospectively repealed by Railways Act 1993, s 152(3), Sch 14 (qv)

Transport Act 1978 (c 55)—*cont*

s 17	Repealed
18	4 Aug 1978 (SI 1978/1150)
19, 20	Repealed
21	4 Aug 1978 (SI 1978/1150)
22	Spent
23	4 Aug 1978 (SI 1978/1150)
24(1)–(3)	4 Aug 1978 (SI 1978/1150)
(4)	See Sch 4 below
Sch 1, 2	Repealed
3	1 Nov 1978 (SI 1978/1187)
4	1 Sep 1978 (repeals except in Transport Act 1968, Sch 2, para 3, Road Traffic Act 1972, s 57(7)) (SI 1978/1187)
	4 Aug 1978 (repeal in Transport Act 1968, Sch 2, para 3) (SI 1978/1150)
	1 Nov 1978 (repeal in Road Traffic Act 1972, s 57(7)) (SI 1978/1187)

Trustee Savings Banks Act 1978 (c 16)

Whole Act repealed

Tuvalu Act 1978 (c 20)

RA: 30 Jun 1978

Independence Day: 1 Oct 1978

Wales Act 1978 (c 52)

Whole Act repealed

1979

Administration of Justice (Emergency Provisions) (Scotland) Act 1979 (c 19)

Whole Act repealed

Agricultural Statistics Act 1979 (c 13)

RA: 4 Apr 1979

Commencement provisions: s 8(2)

22 Apr 1979 (s 8(2))

Alcoholic Liquor Duties Act 1979 (c 4)

RA: 22 Feb 1979

Commencement provisions: s 93(2)

1 Apr 1979 (s 93(2))

Ancient Monuments and Archaeological Areas Act 1979 (c 46)

RA: 4 Apr 1979

Commencement provisions: s 65(2); Ancient Monuments and Archaeological Areas Act 1979 (Commencement No 1) Order 1979, SI 1979/786; Ancient Monuments and Archaeological Areas Act 1979 (Commencement No 2) Order 1981, SI 1981/1300; Ancient Monuments and Archaeological Areas Act 1979 (Commencement No 3) Order 1981, SI 1981/1466; Ancient Monuments and Archaeological Areas Act 1979 (Commencement No 4) Order 1982, SI 1982/362

s 1	9 Oct 1981 (EW) (SI 1981/1300)
	30 Nov 1971 (S) (SI 1981/1466)
1A	Inserted by National Heritage Act 1983, s 33, Sch 4, para 26 (qv)
2–6	9 Oct 1981 (EW) (SI 1981/1300)
	30 Nov 1981 (S) (SI 1981/1466)
6A	Inserted by National Heritage Act 1983, s 33, Sch 4, para 32 (qv)
7–32	9 Oct 1981 (EW) (SI 1981/1300)
	30 Nov 1981 (S) (SI 1981/1466)
33–41	14 Apr 1982 (EW) (SI 1982/362); *not in force* (S)
42–47	9 Oct 1981 (except so far as relate to Pt II) (EW) (SI 1981/1300)
	30 Nov 1981 (S) (SI 1981/1466)

Ancient Monuments and Archaeological Areas Act 1979 (c 46)—*cont*

s 42–47—*cont*	14 Apr 1982 (so far as relate to Pt II) (EW) (SI 1982/362)
48, 49	16 Jul 1979 (EW) (SI 1979/786)
	30 Nov 1981 (S) (SI 1981/1466)
50–52	9 Oct 1981 (except so far as relate to Pt II) (EW) (SI 1981/1300)
	30 Nov 1981 (S) (SI 1981/1466)
	14 Apr 1982 (so far as relate to Pt II) (EW) (SI 1982/362)
52A	Inserted (EW) by Norfolk and Suffolk Broads Act 1988, s 2(5), Sch 3, Pt I, para 30(1) (qv)
53–62	9 Oct 1981 (except so far as relate to Pt II) (EW) (SI 1981/1300)
	30 Nov 1981 (S) (SI 1981/1466)
	14 Apr 1982 (so far as relate to Pt II) (EW) (SI 1982/362)
63	Repealed
64	9 Oct 1981 (except so far as relates to Pt II) (EW) (SI 1981/1300)
	30 Nov 1981 (S) (SI 1981/1466)
	14 Apr 1982 (so far as relates to Pt II) (EW) (SI 1982/362)
65	4 Apr 1979 (RA)
Sch 1	9 Oct 1981 (EW) (SI 1981/1300)
	30 Nov 1981 (S) (SI 1981/1466)
2	14 Apr 1982 (EW) (SI 1982/362); *not in force* (S)
3–5	9 Oct 1981 (EW) (except so far as relate to Pt II) (SI 1981/1300)
	30 Nov 1981 (S) (SI 1981/1466)
	14 Apr 1982 (EW) (so far as relate to Pt II) (SI 1982/362)

Appropriation Act 1979 (c 24)

Whole Act repealed

Appropriation (No 2) Act 1979 (c 51)

Whole Act repealed

Arbitration Act 1979 (c 42)

RA: 4 Apr 1979

Commencement provisions: s 8(2); Arbitration Act 1979 (Commencement) Order 1979, SI 1979/750

1 Aug 1979 (except in relation to arbitrations commenced before that date; if all the parties to a reference to arbitration which commenced before that date agree in writing that the Act should apply to that arbitration, the Act applies from 1 Aug 1979 or the date of the agreement, whichever is the later) (SI 1979/750)

Banking Act 1979 (c 37)

RA: 4 Apr 1979

Commencement provisions: s 52(3), (4); Banking Act 1979 (Commencement No 1) Order 1979, SI 1979/938; Banking Act 1979 (Commencement No 2) Order 1982, SI 1982/188; Banking Act 1979 (Commencement No 3) Order 1985, SI 1985/797

s 1–37	Repealed
38	1 Oct 1979 (SI 1979/938)
39–46	Repealed
47	1 Oct 1979 (SI 1979/938)
48–50	Repealed
51(1)	19 Feb 1982 (so far as relates to the provisions of Sch 6 coming into force on that date) (SI 1982/188)
	1 Jul 1985 (so far as relates to the provisions of Sch 6 coming into force on that date) (SI 1985/797)
(2)	Spent
52	1 Oct 1979 (SI 1979/938)
Sch 1–5	Repealed
6, para 1–3	19 Feb 1982 (SI 1982/188)
4–8	Repealed
9	1 Jul 1985 (SI 1985/797)
10	Spent
11, 12	Repealed
13–15	19 Feb 1982 (SI 1982/188)
16–18	Repealed
19	19 Feb 1982 (SI 1982/188)
7	Repealed

Capital Gains Tax Act 1979 (c 14)

Whole Act repealed

Carriage by Air and Road Act 1979 (c 28)

RA: 4 Apr 1979

Commencement provisions: ss 2(2), 7(2); Carriage by Air and Road Act 1979 (Commencement No 1) Order 1980, SI 1980/1966

s 1	*Not in force*
2	4 Apr 1979 (does not apply to loss which occurred before that date) (s 2(2))
3(1), (2)	*Not in force*
(3)	28 Dec 1980 (SI 1980/1966)
(4)	*Not in force*
4(1)	*Not in force*
(2)	28 Dec 1980 (SI 1980/1966)
(3)	*Not in force*
(4)	28 Dec 1980 (so far as relates to amendment of Carriage of Goods by Road Act 1965 by s 4(2)) (SI 1980/1966)
	Not in force (otherwise)
5	28 Dec 1980 (so far as relates to amendment of Carriage of Goods by Road Act 1965 by s 4(2)) (SI 1980/1966)
	Not in force (otherwise)
6(1)(a)	*Not in force*

Carriage by Air and Road Act 1979 (c 28)—*cont*
  s 6(1)(b)   28 Dec 1980 (SI 1980/1966)
      (c)   *Not in force*
   (2)–(4)   *Not in force*
  7   4 Apr 1979 (RA)

Sch 1, 2   *Not in force*

Charging Orders Act 1979 (c 53)

RA: 14 Nov 1979

Commencement provisions: s 8(2); Charging Orders Act 1979 (Commencement) Order 1980, SI 1980/627

3 Jun 1980 (SI 1980/627)

Confirmation to Small Estates (Scotland) Act 1979 (c 22)

RA: 29 Mar 1979

Commencement provisions: s 3(2); Confirmation to Small Estates (Scotland) Act 1979 (Commencement) Order 1980, SI 1980/734

  s 1, 2   1 Jul 1980 (SI 1980/734)
  3   29 Mar 1979 (RA)

Schedule   1 Jul 1980 (SI 1980/734)

Consolidated Fund Act 1979 (c 20)

Whole Act repealed

Consolidated Fund (No 2) Act 1979 (c 56)

Whole Act repealed

Credit Unions Act 1979 (c 34)

RA: 4 Apr 1979

Commencement provisions: s 33(2); Credit Unions Act 1979 (Commencement No 1) Order 1979, SI 1979/936; Credit Unions Act 1979 (Commencement No 2) Order 1980, SI 1980/481

  s 1, 2   20 Aug 1979 (SI 1979/936)
  3(1)   20 Aug 1979 (SI 1979/936)
   (2), (3)   *Not in force*
   (4)   20 Aug 1979 (SI 1979/936)
  4–14   20 Aug 1979 (SI 1979/936)
  15   1 Oct 1980 (SI 1980/481)
  16–24   20 Aug 1979 (SI 1979/936)

Credit Unions Act 1979 (c 34)—*cont*

s 25	Repealed
26–31	20 Aug 1979 (SI 1979/936)
32, 33	4 Apr 1979 (s 33(2))
Sch 1, 2	20 Aug 1979 (SI 1979/936)
3	Repealed

Criminal Evidence Act 1979 (c 16)

RA: 22 Mar 1979

Commencement provisions: s 2(2)

22 Apr 1979 (s 2(2))

Crown Agents Act 1979 (c 43)

RA: 4 Apr 1979

4 Apr 1979 (RA; but note that most of the provisions of the Act became effective from 1 Jan 1980, the day appointed by the Crown Agents Act 1979 (Appointed Day) Order 1979, SI 1979/1672, made under s 1(1))

Customs and Excise Duties (General Reliefs) Act 1979 (c 3)

RA: 22 Feb 1979

Commencement provisions: ss 20(2), 59(7), 62(2)

1 Apr 1979 (s 20(2))

Customs and Excise Management Act 1979 (c 2)

RA: 22 Feb 1979

Commencement provisions: ss 59(7), 62(2), 178(3)

1 Apr 1979 (s 178(3)) except ss 59, 62(2) which are *not in force*

Education Act 1979 (c 49)

RA: 26 Jul 1979

26 Jul 1979 (RA)

Electricity (Scotland) Act 1979 (c 11)

RA: 22 Mar 1979

Commencement provisions: s 47(4)

Whole Act repealed, except s 1, Sch 1, paras 2–6, which came into force on 22 Apr 1979 (s 47(4))

Estate Agents Act 1979 (c 38)

RA: 4 Apr 1979

Commencement provisions: s 36(2); Estate Agents Act 1979 (Commencement No 1)
   Order 1981, SI 1981/1517

s 1–15	3 May 1982 (SI 1981/1517)
16, 17	*Not in force*
18	3 May 1982 (SI 1981/1517)
19	*Not in force*
20, 21	3 May 1982 (SI 1981/1517)
22	*Not in force*
23–34	3 May 1982 (SI 1981/1517)
35	Repealed
36	3 May 1982 (SI 1981/1517)
Sch 1, 2	3 May 1982 (SI 1981/1517)

European Parliament (Pay and Pensions) Act 1979 (c 50)

RA: 26 Jul 1979

26 Jul 1979 (RA)

European Communities (Greek Accession) Act 1979 (c 57)

RA: 20 Dec 1979

20 Dec 1979 (RA; but note that the accession of Greece to the European Communities
   did not take effect until 1 Jan 1981)

Exchange Equalisation Account Act 1979 (c 30)

RA: 4 Apr 1979

Commencement provisions: s 5(3)

5 May 1979 (s 5(3))

Excise Duties (Surcharges or Rebates) Act 1979 (c 8)

RA: 22 Feb 1979

Commencement provisions: s 5(2)

1 Apr 1979 (s 5(2))

Films Act 1979 (c 9)

Whole Act repealed

Finance Act 1979 (c 25)

Whole Act repealed

Finance (No 2) Act 1979 (c 47)

Budget Day: 12 Jun 1979

RA: 26 Jul 1979

See the note concerning Finance Acts at the front of this book

---

Forestry Act 1979 (c 21)

RA: 29 Mar 1979

Commencement provisions: s 3(3)

30 May 1979 (s 3(3))

House of Commons (Redistribution of Seats) Act 1979 (c 15)

Whole Act repealed

Hydrocarbon Oil Duties Act 1979 (c 5)

RA: 22 Feb 1979

Commencement provisions: s 29(2)

1 Apr 1979 (s 29(2))

Independent Broadcasting Authority Act 1979 (c 35)

Whole Act repealed

Industry Act 1979 (c 32)

RA: 4 Apr 1979

4 Apr 1979 (RA)

International Monetary Fund Act 1979 (c 29)

RA: 4 Apr 1979

Commencement provisions: s 7(2)

5 May 1979 (s 7(2))

Isle of Man Act 1979 (c 58)

RA: 20 Dec 1979

Commencement provisions: s 14(6), (7)

s 1–5	1 Apr 1980 (s 14(6))
6, 7	20 Dec 1979 (subject to the proviso that no Order in Council and no provision by virtue of s 6(5) or 7(5) be made by or under an Act of Tynwald so as to come into force before 1 Apr 1980) (s 14(7))
8, 9	1 Apr 1980 (s 14(6))
10	20 Dec 1979 (s 14(7))
11	20 Dec 1979 (subject to the proviso that no Order in Council be made under this section so as to come into force before 1 Apr 1980) (s 14(7))
12–14	1 Apr 1980 (s 14(6))
Sch 1, 2	1 Apr 1980 (s 14(6))

Justices of the Peace Act 1979 (c 55)

RA: 6 Dec 1979

Commencement provisions: s 72(2)

6 Mar 1980 (s 72(2))

Kiribati Act 1979 (c 27)

RA: 19 Jun 1979

Independence Day: 12 Jul 1979

Land Registration (Scotland) Act 1979 (c 33)

RA: 4 Apr 1979

Commencement provisions: s 30(2); Land Registration (Scotland) Act 1979 (Commencement No 1) Order 1980, SI 1980/1412; Land Registration (Scotland) Act 1979 (Commencement No 2) Order 1982, SI 1982/520; Land Registration (Scotland) Act 1979 (Commencement No 3) Order 1983, SI 1983/745; Land Registration (Scotland) Act 1979 (Commencement No 4) Order 1985, SI 1985/501; Land Registration (Scotland) Act 1979 (Commencement No 5) Order 1992, SI 1992/815; Land Registration (Scotland) Act 1979 (Commencement No 6) Order 1992, SI 1992/2060

s 1	4 Apr 1979 (s 30(2))
2(1), (2)	6 Apr 1981 (in the area, for the purpose of registration of writs, of the County of Renfrew) (SI 1980/1412)
	4 Oct 1982 (in the area, for the purpose of registration of writs, of the County of Dunbarton) (SI 1982/520)
	3 Jan 1984 (in the area, for the purpose of registration of writs, of the County of Lanark) (SI 1983/745)

Land Registration (Scotland) Act 1979 (c 33)—*cont*

s 2(1), (2)—*cont*	30 Sep 1985 (in the area, for the purpose of registration of writs, of the Barony and Regality of Glasgow) (SI 1985/501)
	1 Oct 1992 (in the area, for the purpose of registration of writs, of the County of Clackmannan) (SI 1992/815)
	1 Apr 1993 (in the area, for the purpose of registration of writs, of the County of Stirling) (SI 1992/2060)
	Not in force (otherwise)
(3)–(6)	6 Apr 1981 (SI 1980/1412)
3(1), (2)	6 Apr 1981 (SI 1980/1412)
(3)	6 Apr 1981 (in the area, for the purpose of registration of writs, of the County of Renfrew) (SI 1980/1412)
	4 Oct 1982 (in the area for the purpose of registration of writs, of the County of Dunbarton) (SI 1982/520)
	3 Jan 1984 (in the area, for the purpose of registration of writs, of the County of Lanark) (SI 1983/745)
	30 Sep 1985 (in the area, for the purpose of registration of writs, of the Barony and Regality of Glasgow) (SI 1985/501)
	1 Oct 1992 (in the area, for the purpose of registration of writs, of the County of Clackmannan) (SI 1992/815)
	1 Apr 1993 (in the area, for the purpose of registration of writs, of the County of Stirling) (SI 1992/2060)
	Not in force (otherwise)
(4)–(7)	6 Apr 1981 (SI 1980/1412)
4–15	6 Apr 1981 (SI 1980/1412)
16–22	4 Apr 1979 (s 30(2))
22A	Inserted by Law Reform (Miscellaneous Provisions) Act 1985, s 2 (qv)
23	4 Apr 1979 (s 30(2))
24–29	4 Apr 1979 (so far as relate to ss 1, 16–23, 30) (s 30(2))
	6 Apr 1981 (otherwise) (SI 1980/1412)
30	4 Apr 1979 (s 30(2))
Sch 1	4 Apr 1979 (s 30(2))
2–4	4 Apr 1979 (so far as relate to ss 1, 16–23, 30) (s 30(2))
	6 Apr 1981 (otherwise) (SI 1980/1412)

Leasehold Reform Act 1979 (c 44)

RA: 4 Apr 1979

4 Apr 1979 (RA)

Legal Aid Act 1979 (c 26)

Whole Act repealed

Matches and Mechanical Lighters Duties Act 1979 (c 6)

Whole Act repealed

Merchant Shipping Act 1979 (c 39)

RA: 4 Apr 1979

Commencement provisions: s 52(2); Merchant Shipping Act 1979 (Commencement No 1) Order 1979, SI 1979/807; Merchant Shipping Act 1979 (Commencement No 2) Order 1979, SI 1979/1578; Merchant Shipping Act 1979 (Commencement No 3) Order 1980, SI 1980/354; Merchant Shipping Act 1979 (Commencement No 4) Order 1980, SI 1980/923; Carriage of Passengers and their Luggage by Sea (Interim Provisions) Order 1980, SI 1980/1092; Merchant Shipping Act 1979 (Commencement No 5) Order 1981, SI 1981/405; Merchant Shipping Act 1979 (Commencement No 6) Order 1982, SI 1982/1616; Merchant Shipping Act 1979 (Commencement No 7) Order 1983, SI 1983/440; Merchant Shipping Act 1979 (Commencement No 8) Order 1983, SI 1983/1312; Merchant Shipping Act 1979 (Commencement No 9) Order 1985, SI 1985/1827; Merchant Shipping Act 1979 (Commencement No 10) Order 1986, SI 1986/1052; Merchant Shipping Act 1979 (Commencement No 11) Order 1987, SI 1987/635; Merchant Shipping Act 1979 (Commencement No 12) Order 1987, SI 1987/719; Merchant Shipping Act 1979 (Commencement No 13) Order 1989, SI 1989/1881

s 1–13	Repealed
14(1), (2)	30 April 1987 (SI 1987/635)
(3)	10 Nov 1989 (SI 1989/1881)
(4), (5)	30 April 1987 (SI 1987/635)
(6)	30 April 1987 (except in its application to s 14(3)) (SI 1987/635)
	10 Nov 1989 (in its application to s 14(3)) (SI 1989/ 1881)
(7)	30 April 1987 (SI 1987/635)
15(1)	17 Dec 1979 (SI 1979/1578)
(2)	17 Dec 1979 (from 'and any' to the end) (SI 1979/1578)
	30 April 1987 (otherwise) (SI 1987/635)
(3)	*Not in force*
16	1 Aug 1979 (SI 1979/807)
17, 18	1 Dec 1986 (SI 1986/1052)
19(1)	1 Dec 1986 (SI 1986/1052)
(2), (3)	17 Dec 1979 (SI 1979/1578); repealed by Merchant Shipping (Registration, etc) Act 1993, s 8(4), Sch 5, Pt II, as from 1 May 1994 (qv)
(4)	1 Dec 1986 (SI 1986/1052)
20–22	1 Aug 1979 (SI 1979/807)
23(1)–(6)	*Not in force*
(7)	31 Dec 1985 (SI 1985/1827)
24, 25	*Not in force*
26	1 Aug 1979 (SI 1979/807)
27, 28	1 Oct 1979 (SI 1979/807)
29, 30	1 Jan 1980 (SI 1979/807)
31	Repealed
32(1)	1 Aug 1979 (SI 1979/807)
(2), (3)	Repealed
33, 34	1 Aug 1979 (SI 1979/807)
35(1)	1 Aug 1979 (except so far as applies to fishing vessels) (SI 1979/807)
	Not in force (exception noted above)

Merchant Shipping Act 1979 (c 39)—*cont*

s 35(2)	30 Apr 1987 (except so far as applies to fishing vessels) (SI 1987/719)
	10 Nov 1989 (exception noted above) (SI 1989/1881)
36(1)	1 Aug 1979 (SI 1979/807)
(2)	1 Apr 1980 (SI 1980/354)
(3)	1 Aug 1979 (SI 1979/807)
37(1)–(3)	1 Aug 1979 (SI 1979/807)
(4)	Repealed
(5)	1 Aug 1979 (SI 1979/807)
(6)	*Not in force*
(7), (8)	1 Aug 1979 (SI 1979/807)
38(1)	8 Apr 1981 (SI 1981/405); prospectively repealed by Merchant Shipping Act 1988, s 57(5), Sch 7 (qv)
(2)	8 Apr 1981 (SI 1981/405)
(3)	8 Apr 1981 (SI 1981/405); prospectively repealed by Merchant Shipping Act 1988, s 57(5), Sch 7 (qv)
(4)	*Not in force*; paras (a), (b), (d)–(g) prospectively repealed by Merchant Shipping Act 1988, s 57(5), Sch 7 (qv) and Merchant Shipping Act 1974, s 4(13), as inserted by para (4)(c), prospectively repealed by 1988 Act, ss 34, 57(5), Sch 4, Pt II, para 17(4), Sch 7 (qv)
(5)	17 Dec 1979 (SI 1979/1578)
(6)	8 Apr 1981 (SI 1981/405)
39–41	1 Aug 1979 (SI 1979/807)
42, 43	1 Jan 1980 (SI 1979/807)
44	Repealed
45	1 Jan 1980 (SI 1979/807)
46	1 Oct 1979 (except in sub-s (1) the words and figures '23(6)' and 'or 44(1)') (SI 1979/807)
	4 Jul 1980 (otherwise) (SI 1980/923); repealed by Merchant Shipping (Registration, etc) Act 1993, s 8(4), Sch 5, Pt II, as from 1 May 1994 (qv)
(47	Repealed by Merchant Shipping (Registration, etc) Act 1993, s 8(4), Sch 5, Pt II, as from 1 May 1994 (qv))
47(1)	1 Aug 1979 (by SI 1979/1578 this subsection was also purportedly brought into force on 17 Dec 1979) (SI 1979/807)
(2)	1 Aug 1979 (so far as relates to ss 21, 22, 26, 32(1), 35(1) (except so far as it applies to fishing vessels), 37(2), (3), (5), (7), (8), 39, 41, 49, 50(1), (2), (4) (so far as it relates to those provisions of Sch 7, Pt II, which came into force on 1 Aug 1979), 52) (SI 1979/807)
	1 Oct 1979 (so far as relates to ss 27, 28, 46, 50(4) so far as the latter relates to those provisions of Sch 7, Pt II which came into force on 1 Oct 1979) (SI 1979/807)
	1 Jan 1980 (so far as relates to ss 45, 50(4) so far as the latter relates to those provisions of Sch 7, Pt II which came into force on 1 Jan 1980) (SI 1979/804)
	17 Dec 1979 (so far as relates to ss 48–52 and Sch 7, Pt I) (SI 1979/1578)
	14 Sep 1983 (remainder) (SI 1983/1312)

Merchant Shipping Act 1979 (c 39)—*cont*

s 47(3)	1 Aug 1979 (SI 1979/807; but note that by SI 1979/ 1578 this subsection was also purportedly brought into force on 17 Dec 1979)
48, 49	1 Aug 1979 (SI 1979/807)
50(1), (2)	1 Aug 1979 (SI 1979/807)
(3)	4 Jul 1980 (SI 1980/923)
(4)	See Sch 7 below
51(1)	1 Aug 1979 (SI 1979/807)
(2)	1 Jan 1983 (so far as relates to s 38(2)) (SI 1982/1616) *Not in force* (otherwise)
(3)	1 Aug 1979 (SI 1979/807)
52	1 Aug 1979 (SI 1979/807)
Sch 1, 2	Repealed
3, Pt I	1 Jan 1981 (for some purposes, with modifications) (SI 1980/1092) 30 April 1987 (otherwise) (SI 1987/635)
II	30 April 1987 (SI 1987/635)
III	10 Nov 1989 (SI 1989/1881)
4, 5	1 Dec 1986 (SI 1986/1052)
6	1 Jan 1980 (SI 1979/807)
7, Pt I	1 Dec 1986 (SI 1986/1052)
II	1 Aug 1979 (repeals of or in Merchant Shipping Act 1894, ss 637, 638, 640, 641, 670–72, 675, 677; Merchant Shipping (Mercantile Marine Fund) Act 1898, ss 2(1), (2), 7, Sch 3, para II; Pilotage Act 1913, ss 1, 2, 6, 7(4), 8, 9, 17(1)(i), 22, 30, 35, 39, 48, 56, 58, 59; Merchant Shipping (Load Lines) Act 1967, s 27; Merchant Shipping Act 1970, s 15) (SI 1979/807) 1 Oct 1979 (repeals of or in Merchant Shipping Act 1894, ss 420, 431, 729, 730; Merchant Shipping Act 1964; Merchant Shipping (Load Lines) Act 1967, ss 11, 17, 24; Fishing Vessels (Safety Provisions) Act 1970; Prevention of Oil Pollution Act 1971) (SI 1979/807) 1 Jan 1980 (repeals of or in Merchant Shipping Act 1894, ss 73, 360, 446, 724; Merchant Shipping Act 1906; Merchant Shipping (Safety Convention) Act 1949; Merchant Shipping (Load Lines) Act 1967, s 4, Sch 1; Merchant Shipping Act 1970, s 6, Schs 2, 5; Merchant Shipping Act 1974, s 19(2); Criminal Procedure (Scotland) Act 1975; Criminal Law Act 1977) (SI 1979/807) 1 Apr 1980 (repeal of or in Merchant Shipping (Mercantile Marine Fund) Act 1898, s 5, Sch 2) (SI 1980/354) 4 Jul 1980 (repeals of or in Pilotage Act 1913, ss 11, 14, 24; Aliens Restriction (Amendment) Act 1919) (SI 1980/923) 1 Sep 1980 (repeals of or in Pilotage Act 1913, ss 7(5), (6), 17(1)(f), (h), 34, Sch 1) (SI 1980/923) 8 Apr 1981 (repeals in Merchant Shipping (Oil Pollution) Act 1971) (SI 1981/405) 3 May 1983 (repeals in Merchant Shipping Act 1965) (SI 1983/440)

Merchant Shipping Act 1979 (c 39)—*cont*
Sch 7, Pt II—*cont*   31 Dec 1985 (repeals of or in Merchant Shipping Act
                                    1970, ss 34–38, 95(1)(a)) (1985/1827)

Nurses, Midwives and Health Visitors Act 1979 (c 36)

RA: 4 Apr 1979

Commencement provisions: s 24(2); Nurses, Midwives and Health Visitors Act 1979
(Commencement No 1) Order 1980, SI 1980/893; Nurses, Midwives and Health
Visitors Act 1979 (Commencement No 2) Order 1982, SI 1982/963; Nurses,
Midwives and Health Visitors Act 1979 (Commencement No 3) Order 1982,
SI 1982/1565; Nurses, Midwives and Health Visitors Act 1979 (Commencement
No 4) Order 1983, SI 1983/668

s 1	1 Nov 1980 (SI 1980/893)
2	1 Jul 1983 (SI 1983/668)
3(1)	1 Nov 1980 (so far as relates to the Finance Committee and s 3(2)) (SI 1980/893)
	1 Dec 1982 (otherwise) (SI 1982/1565)
(2)	1 Nov 1980 (SI 1980/893)
(3)	1 Dec 1982 (SI 1982/1565)
(4)(a)	1 Nov 1980 (so far as relates to the Finance Committee and s 3(2)) (SI 1980/893)
	1 Dec 1982 (otherwise) (SI 1982/1565)
(b)	1 Dec 1982 (SI 1982/1565)
4	1 Jul 1983 (SI 1983/668)
5	15 Sep 1980 (SI 1980/893)
6	1 Jul 1983 (SI 1983/668)
7–9	Repealed
10, 11	1 Jul 1983 (SI 1983/668)
11A	Inserted by Nursing and Midwifery Qualifications (EEC Recognition) Order 1983, SI 1983/884, art 4
12	1 Jul 1983 (SI 1983/668)
12A	Inserted by Nurses, Midwives and Health Visitors Act 1992, s 9 (qv)
13–17	1 Jul 1983 (SI 1983/668)
18	Repealed
19(1), (2)	1 Jul 1983 (SI 1983/668)
(3)(a)	Repealed
(b), (c)	1 Jul 1983 (SI 1983/668)
(d)	Added by Nurses, Midwives and Health Visitors Act 1992, s 13(2)(b) (qv)
(4)	Repealed
(5)	15 Sep 1980 (so far as relates to National Boards) (SI 1980/893)
	1 Nov 1980 (otherwise) (SI 1980/893)
20	15 Sep 1980 (so far as relates to National Boards) (SI 1980/893)
	1 Nov 1980 (otherwise) (SI 1980/893)
21(1)	1 Jul 1983 (SI 1983/668)
(2)	4 Apr 1979 (s 24(2))
(3)	1 Jul 1983 (SI 1983/668)
(4)	Repealed
22	1 Jul 1983 (SI 1983/668)

Nurses, Midwives and Health Visitors Act 1979 (c 36)—*cont*

s 22A, 22B	Inserted by Nursing and Midwifery Qualifications (EEC Recognition) Order 1983, SI 1983/884
23(1)–(3)	15 Sep 1980 (SI 1980/893)
(4), (5)	1 Jul 1983 (SI 1983/668)
24	4 Apr 1979 (s 24(2))
Sch 1	Substituted by Nurses, Midwives and Health Visitors Act 1992, s 1(2), Sch 1 (qv))
2, Pt I	Repealed
II, para 2–4	Repealed
5	15 Sep 1980 (SI 1980/893)
6	Repealed
7	15 Sep 1983 (SI 1980/893); prospectively repealed by Nurses, Midwives and Health Visitors Act 1992, s 16(2), Sch 3 (qv)
8	Repealed
3	1 Jul 1983 (SI 1983/668)
4	Repealed
5	1 Jul 1983 (SI 1983/668)
6	15 Sep 1980 (SI 1980/893)
7, 8	1 Jul 1983 (SI 1983/668)

Pensioners' Payments and Social Security Act 1979 (c 48)

Whole Act repealed

Pneumoconiosis etc (Workers' Compensation) Act 1979 (c 41)

RA: 4 Apr 1979

Commencement provisions: s 10(3)

4 Jul 1979 (s 10(3))

Price Commission (Amendment) Act 1979 (c 1)

Whole Act repealed

Prosecution of Offences Act 1979 (c 31)

Whole Act repealed

Public Health Laboratory Service Act 1979 (c 23)

RA: 29 Mar 1979

29 Mar 1979 (RA)

Public Lending Right Act 1979 (c 10)

RA: 22 Mar 1979

Commencement provisions: s 5(3); Public Lending Right Act 1979 (Commencement) Order 1980, SI 1980/83

1 Mar 1980 (SI 1980/83)

Representation of the People Act 1979 (c 40)

Whole Act repealed

Sale of Goods Act 1979 (c 54)

RA: 6 Dec 1979

Commencement provisions: s 64(2)

1 Jan 1980 (s 64(2))

Shipbuilding Act 1979 (c 59)

RA: 20 Dec 1979

20 Dec 1979 (RA)

Social Security Act 1979 (c 18)

RA: 22 Mar 1979

Commencement provisions: s 21(2), (3); Social Security Act 1979 (Commencement No 1) Order 1979, SI 1979/369; Social Security Act 1979 (Commencement No 2) Order 1979, SI 1979/1031; Social Security Act 1986, s 72

s 1	22 Mar 1979 (RA)
2–10	Repealed
11	6 Apr 1979 (s 21(3))
12–15	Repealed
16	22 Mar 1979 (RA); repealed (EW)
17	Repealed
18	22 Mar 1979 (RA); prospectively repealed by Pension Schemes Act 1993, s 188(2), Sch 5, Pt I (qv)
19	Repealed
20, 21	22 Mar 1979 (RA)
Sch 1, 2	Repealed
3, para 1–2	Repealed
3	22 Mar 1979 (RA); prospectively repealed by Pension Schemes Act 1993, s 188(2), Sch 5, Pt I (qv)
4–11	Repealed
12	Spent
13	22 Mar 1979 (RA)
14–16	Repealed
17	Spent
18	6 Apr 1979 (s 21(3)); prospectively repealed by Pension Schemes Act 1993, s 188(2), Sch 5, Pt I (qv)
19	Spent
20	6 Apr 1979 (s 21(3))
21	22 Mar 1979 (RA)
22	6 Apr 1979 (s 21(3))
23–29	Repealed
30	Repealed or spent
31, 32	Repealed

Southern Rhodesia Act 1979 (c 52)

RA: 14 Nov 1979

Appointed Day: 18 Apr 1980

Tobacco Products Duty Act 1979 (c 7)

RA: 22 Feb 1979

Commencement provisions: s 12(2)

1 Apr 1979 (s 12(2))

Vaccine Damage Payments Act 1979 (c 17)

RA: 22 Feb 1979

22 Feb 1979 (RA)

Wages Councils Act 1979 (c 12)

Whole Act repealed

Weights and Measures Act 1979 (c 45)

Whole Act repealed

Zimbabwe Act 1979 (c 60)

RA: 20 Dec 1979

Independence Day: 18 Apr 1980

1980

Anguilla Act 1980 (c 67)

RA: 16 Dec 1980

16 Dec 1980 (RA; but note the Anguilla (Appointed Day) Order 1980, SI 1980/1953, appointing 19 Dec 1980 for the purposes of s 1(1))

Appropriation Act 1980 (c 54)

Whole Act repealed

Bail etc (Scotland) Act 1980 (c 4)

RA: 31 Jan 1980

Commencement provisions: s 13(2); Bail etc (Scotland) Act 1980 (Commencement) Order 1980, SI 1980/315

s 1–12	31 Mar 1980 (SI 1980/315)
13	31 Jan 1980 (RA)
Sch 1, 2	31 Mar 1980 (SI 1980/315)

Bees Act 1980 (c 12)

RA: 20 Mar 1980

Commencement provisions: s 5(2); Bees Act 1980 (Commencement) Order 1980, SI 1980/791

10 Jun 1980 (SI 1980/791)

Betting, Gaming and Lotteries (Amendment) Act 1980 (c 18)

Whole Act repealed

British Aerospace Act 1980 (c 26)

RA: 1 May 1980

1 May 1980 (RA; but note Act largely took effect on 1 Jan 1981, the day appointed under s 14(1))

Broadcasting Act 1980 (c 64)

Whole Act repealed

Child Care Act 1980 (c 5)

Whole Act repealed

Civil Aviation Act 1980 (c 60)

RA: 13 Nov 1980

Commencement provisions: ss 10(1), 12 (repealed); Civil Aviation Act 1980
(Commencement) Order 1981, SI 1981/671; Civil Aviation Act 1980 (Appointed
Day) Order 1983, SI 1983/1940

s 1	13 Nov 1980 (RA), but not effective until 1 Apr 1984, the day appointed under s 10(1) by SI 1983/1940
2	Spent
3–10	13 Nov 1980 (RA), but not effective until 1 Apr 1984, the day appointed under s 10(1) by SI 1983/1940
11–19	Repealed
20	13 Nov 1980 (RA)
21–26	Repealed
27	13 Nov 1980 (RA)
28	See Sch 3 below
29–31	13 Nov 1980 (RA)
Sch 1, 2	13 Nov 1980 (RA)
3	13 Nov 1980 (except repeal of Civil Aviation Act 1971, s 24(2)) (RA)
	22 May 1981 (exception noted above) (SI 1981/671)

Coal Industry Act 1980 (c 50)

RA: 8 Aug 1980

8 Aug 1980 (RA)

Companies Act 1980 (c 22)

Whole Act repealed

Competition Act 1980 (c 21)

RA: 3 Apr 1980

Commencement provisions: s 33(5); Competition Act 1980 (Commencement No 1)
Order 1980, SI 1980/497; Competition Act 1980 (Commencement No 2) Order
1980, SI 1980/978

s 1	Repealed

Competition Act 1980 (c 21)—*cont*

s 2	12 Aug 1980 (SI 1980/978)
3(1)–(6)	12 Aug 1980 (SI 1980/978)
(7), (8)	1 May 1980 (as applied by s 13(7)) (SI 1980/497)
	12 Aug 1980 (otherwise) (SI 1980/978)
(9), (10)	12 Aug 1980 (SI 1980/978)
4–10	12 Aug 1980 (SI 1980/978)
11(1), (2)	4 Apr 1980 (SI 1980/497)
(3)(a)	4 Apr 1980 (SI 1980/497)
(aa)	Inserted by Railways Act 1993, s 152(1), Sch 12, para 12(1)(qv)
(b)	Substituted by Transport Act 1985, s 114(1) (qv)
(bb)	Inserted by London Regional Transport Act 1984, s 71(3)(a), Sch 6, para 15 (qv)
(c)	Substituted by Water Act 1989, s 190(1), Sch 25, para 59(1) (qv)
(d), (e)	4 Apr 1980 (SI 1980/497)
(f)	4 Apr 1980 (except so far as relates to s 11(3)(b)) (SI 1980/497)
	12 Aug 1980 (exception noted above) (SI 1980/978)
(4), (5)	12 Aug 1980 (SI 1980/978)
(6)–(11)	4 Apr 1980 (SI 1980/497)
12, 13	1 May 1980 (SI 1980/497)
14	Repealed
15(1)	1 May 1980 (SI 1980/497)
(2)(a), (b)	12 Aug 1980 (SI 1980/978)
(c)	4 Apr 1980 (for purposes of s 11) (SI 1980/497)
	12 Aug 1980 (otherwise) (SI 1980/978)
(3), (4)	12 Aug 1980 (SI 1980/978)
(5)	4 Apr 1980 (for purposes of s 11) (SI 1980/497)
	12 Aug (otherwise) (SI 1980/978)
16	4 Apr 1980 (for purposes of reports under s 11) (SI 1980/497)
	12 Aug 1980 (otherwise) (SI 1980/978)
17(1)–(5)	4 Apr 1980 (for purposes of reports under s 11) (SI 1980/497)
(1), (3)–(5)	1 May 1980 (for purposes of reports under s 13) (SI 1980/497)
(6)	1 May 1980 (for purposes of reports under s 12) (SI 1980/497)
(1)–(6)	12 Aug 1980 (otherwise) (SI 1980/978)
18	1 May 1980 (SI 1980/497)
19	4 Apr 1980 (SI 1980/497)
20–22	1 May 1980 (SI 1980/497)
23	4 Apr 1980 (SI 1980/497)
24–30	1 May 1980 (SI 1980/497)
31(1)	4 Apr 1980 (SI 1980/497)
(2)	12 Aug 1980 (SI 1980/978)
(3)	1 May 1980 (for purposes of s 12) (SI 1980/497)
	12 Aug 1980 (otherwise) (SI 1980/978)
(4)	1 May 1980 (SI 1980/497)
32	4 Apr 1980 (SI 1980/497)
33(1), (2)	4 Apr 1980 (SI 1980/497)
(3)	1 May 1980 (SI 1980/497)
(4)	See Sch 2 below
(5)–(8)	4 Apr 1980 (SI 1980/497)
Sch 1	Repealed

Competition Act 1980 (c 21)—*cont*
Sch 2   4 Apr 1980 (except as noted below) (SI 1980/457)
                                   1 Jan 2011 (repeals of Counter-Inflation Act 1973,
                                       ss 17(6), (8), (9), 18(4), (5), 19, 20(4), (5)(i), (iii),
                                       (7), 23(2), Sch 4, para 4 (except sub-para 2(b));
                                       Price Commission Act 1977, s 15(4), Sch 2,
                                       para 4(b), (d)) (SI 1980/497)

**Concessionary Travel for Handicapped Persons (Scotland) Act 1980
(c 29)**

RA: 23 May 1980

23 May 1980 (RA)

Consolidated Fund Act 1980 (c 14)

Whole Act repealed

Consolidated Fund (No 2) Act 1980 (c 68)

Whole Act repealed

Consular Fees Act 1980 (c 23)

RA: 1 May 1980

1 May 1980 (RA)

Coroners Act 1980 (c 38)

Whole Act repealed

Criminal Appeal (Northern Ireland) Act 1980 (c 47)

RA: 1 Aug 1980

Commencement provisions: s 52(2)

1 Sep 1980 (s 52(2))

Criminal Justice (Scotland) Act 1980 (c 62)

RA: 13 Mar 1980

Commencement provisions: s 84(2); Criminal Justice (Scotland) Act 1980
   (Commencement No 1) Order 1981, SI 1981/50; Criminal Justice (Scotland) Act
   1980 (Commencement No 2) Order 1981, SI 1981/444; Criminal Justice (Scotland)
   Act 1980 (Commencement No 3) Order 1981, SI 1981/766; Criminal Justice
   (Scotland) Act 1980 (Commencement No 4) Order 1981, SI 1981/1751; Criminal
   Justice (Scotland) Act 1980 (Commencement No 5) Order 1983, SI 1983/1580

   s 1   1 Feb 1981 (SI 1981/50)

Criminal Justice (Scotland) Act 1980 (c 62)—*cont*

s 2, 3	1 Jun 1981 (SI 1981/766)
3A–3D	Inserted by Law Reform (Miscellaneous Provisions) (Scotland) Act 1985, s 35 (qv)
4	1 Feb 1981 (SI 1981/50)
5	1 Jun 1981 (SI 1981/766)
6	1 Jan 1982 (SI 1981/1751)
7	1 Feb 1981 (SI 1981/50)
8	Repealed
9	1 Feb 1981 (SI 1981/50)
10	1 Apr 1981 (SI 1981/444)
11	1 Feb 1981 (SI 1981/50)
12, 13	1 Jan 1982 (SI 1981/1751)
14, 15	1 Feb 1981 (SI 1981/50)
16	1 Jan 1982 (SI 1981/1751)
17–30	1 Feb 1981 (SI 1981/50)
31	Repealed
32	1 Feb 1981 (SI 1981/50)
32A	Inserted by Prisoners and Criminal Proceedings (Scotland) Act 1993, s 32 (qv)
33–35	1 Apr 1981 (SI 1981/444)
36	1 Jan 1982 (SI 1981/1751)
37–42	1 Feb 1981 (SI 1981/50)
43	1 Apr 1981 (SI 1981/444)
44	Repealed
45	15 Nov 1983 (SI 1983/1580)
46–50	1 Feb 1981 (SI 1981/50)
51	1 Jun 1981 (SI 1981/766)
52–54	1 Feb 1981 (SI 1981/50)
55	Repealed
56, 57	1 Feb 1981 (SI 1981/50)
58–67	1 Apr 1981 (SI 1981/444)
68–70	1 Feb 1981 (SI 1981/50)
70A	Inserted by Public Order Act 1986, Sch 1 (qv)
71, 72	1 Feb 1981 (SI 1981/50)
72A	Inserted by Public Order Act 1986, Sch 1 (qv)
73–82	1 Feb 1981 (SI 1981/50)
83	See Schs 6–8 below
84(1)–(4)	1 Feb 1981 (SI 1981/50)
(5)	1 Feb 1981 (for purposes of extending to England and Wales ss 22, 84(1)–(5), Sch 6, paras 2, 8, Sch 7, paras 8, 9, 11(a), 24(c), 58, 79, Sch 8 (so far as repeals Criminal Procedure (Scotland) Act 1978, s 365)) (SI 1981/50)
	1 Apr 1981 (for purposes of extending to England and Wales s 66, Sch 6, para 9) (SI 1981/444)
	1 Jun 1981 (for purposes of extending to England and Wales s 51, Sch 6, para 10) (SI 1981/766)
	15 Nov 1983 (for purposes of extending to England and Wales Sch 7, paras 6(a), 10, 24(a), (b)(i), (ii), (d)(i), (ii), Sch 8 (so far as repeals Criminal Justice Act 1961, s 32(2)(b) and words in ss 32(2)(f), 38(3)(a))) (SI 1983/1580)
(6)	1 Feb 1981 (for purposes of extending to Northern Ireland ss 22, 84(1)–(4), (6), Sch 6, paras 2, 8, Sch 7, paras 8, 9, 11(a), 77) (SI 1981/50)
	1 Apr 1981 (for purposes of extending to Northern Ireland s 66, Sch 6, para 9) (SI 1981/444)

Criminal Justice (Scotland) Act 1980 (c 62)—*cont*

s 84(6)—*cont*	1 Jun 1981 (for purposes of extending to Northern Ireland s 51, Sch 6, para 10) (SI 1981/766)
	15 Nov 1983 (for purposes of extending to Northern Ireland Sch 7, paras 6(a), 10, Sch 8 (so far as repeals Criminal Justice Act 1961, s 32(2)(b) and words in ss 32(2)(f), 38(3)(a))) (SI 1983/1580)
(7)	15 Nov 1983 (for purposes of extending to Channel Islands and Isle of Man s 84(1)–(4), (7), Sch 7, paras 6(a), 10(a), Sch 8 (so far as repeals the Criminal Justice Act 1961, s 32(2)(b))) (SI 1983/1580)
Sch 1	1 Feb 1981 (SI 1981/50)
2, 3	1 Apr 1981 (SI 1981/444)
4	1 Jan 1982 (SI 1981/1751)
5	Repealed
6, para 1–8	1 Feb 1981 (SI 1981/50)
9	1 Apr 1981 (SI 1981/444)
10	1 Jun 1981 (SI 1981/766)
7, para 1–7	Repealed
8, 9	1 Feb 1981 (SI 1981/50)
10	15 Nov 1983 (SI 1983/1580)
11(a)	1 Feb 1981 (SI 1981/50)
(b)	Spent
12	Repealed
13	1 Feb 1981 (SI 1981/50)
14, 15	Repealed
16	1 Feb 1981 (SI 1981/50)
17–20	Repealed
21	1 Feb 1981 (SI 1981/50)
22	1 Feb 1981 (SI 1981/50); prospectively repealed by Transport Act 1981, s 40(4), Sch 12, Pt III (qv)
23	Repealed
24(a)	1 Apr 1981 (SI 1981/444)
(b)(i)	1 Apr 1981 (SI 1981/444)
(ii)	15 Nov 1983 (SI 1983/1580)
(c)	1 Feb 1981 (SI 1981/50)
(d)(i)	15 Nov 1983 (SI 1983/1580)
(ii)	1 Apr 1981 (SI 1981/444)
25	1 Jun 1981 (SI 1981/766)
26–30	1 Feb 1981 (SI 1981/50)
31	1 Jan 1982 (SI 1981/1751)
32	1 Apr 1981 (SI 1981/444)
33–37	1 Feb 1981 (SI 1981/50)
38	15 Nov 1983 (SI 1983/1580)
39	1 Feb 1981 (SI 1981/50)
40	15 Nov 1983 (SI 1983/1580)
41–45	1 Apr 1981 (SI 1981/444)
46	15 Nov 1983 (SI 1983/1580)
47–49	1 Feb 1981 (SI 1981/50)
50	Repealed
51	1 Feb 1981 (SI 1981/50)
52	1 Jun 1981 (SI 1981/766)
53–59	1 Feb 1981 (SI 1981/50)
60	15 Nov 1983 (SI 1983/1580)

Criminal Justice (Scotland) Act 1980 (c 62)—*cont*

Sch 7, para 61–66	1 Feb 1981 (SI 1981/50)
67, 68	15 Nov 1983 (SI 1983/1580)
69	1 Feb 1981 (SI 1981/50)
70	15 Nov 1983 (SI 1983/1580)
71, 72	1 Feb 1981 (SI 1981/50)
73, 74	15 Nov 1983 (SI 1983/1580)
75	1 Feb 1981 (SI 1981/50)
76	Substituted by Law Reform (Miscellaneous Provisions) (Scotland) Act 1990, s 74, Sch 8, para 30 (qv)
77	1 Feb 1981 (SI 1981/50)
78	1 Jan 1982 (SI 1981/1751)
79	1 Feb 1981 (SI 1981/50)
8	1 Feb 1981 (repeals of or in Treason Act 1708, s 7; Treason Act 1800; Conspiracy and Protection of Property Act 1875, s 11; Burgh Police (Scotland) Act 1892, s 382; Children and Young Persons Act 1933, s 26(5); Treason Act 1945; Criminal Justice (Scotland) Act 1949, ss 21, 75(3)(e); Prisons (Scotland) Act 1952, ss 7(4), 19, 31(4), 35(5)(a); Road Traffic Act 1960, s 246; Penalties for Drunkenness Act 1962, s 1(2)(a), (b); Road Traffic Regulation Act 1967, s 93; Criminal Justice Act 1961, s 70(1); Firearms Act 1968, Sch 6, Pt II, para 1; Road Traffic Act 1972, Sch 4, Pt IV, para 3; Social Security Act 1975, s 147(6); Criminal Procedure (Scotland) Act 1975, ss 141, 191(1), 193(2), 195, 197–202, 228, 285, 289D(3)(c), 296(5), 310, 314(3), 337(e), 346, 365, 392(1), 399(1), 405, 410, 411(2), 417, 434(3), 460(5), (6), Schs 4, 7B, para 1; Child Benefit Act 1975, s 11(8); Licensing (Scotland) Act 1976, s 128(2); Sexual Offences (Scotland) Act 1976, ss 7, 16; Supplementary Benefits Act 1976, s 26(5); Criminal Law Act 1977, Sch 11, paras 11–13; Customs and Excise Management Act 1979, s 149(2)) (SI 1981/50)
	1 Apr 1981 (repeals of or in Railways Clauses Consolidation (Scotland) Act 1845, s 144; Protection of Animals (Scotland) Act 1912, s 4; Criminal Justice Act 1967, s 60(6), (8); Immigration Act 1971, s 6(5); Criminal Procedure (Scotland) Act 1975, ss 229, 232, 234(1), (3), 236, 240, 245(3), 247, 253(2), 257, 263(1), 265(3), 272, 274(1), 277, 444(6), 445, 447(2), 448(9), 454(2), Sch 9, para 40) (SI 1981/444)
	1 Jan 1982 (repeals of or in Criminal Procedure (Scotland) Act 1887, Schs F, G; Criminal Procedure (Scotland) Act 1975, ss 68(3), 74(3), 105–107, 120–122) (SI 1981/1751)
	15 Nov 1983 (repeals of or in Prisons (Scotland) Act 1952, ss 32, 33, 37(2); Criminal Justice Act 1961, ss 32(2)(b), (f), 38(3)(a); Criminal Justice (Scotland) Act 1963, ss 2, 4, 5, 9(1), (2), 11, 50(1); Rehabilitation of Offenders Act 1975, s 5(2); Criminal Procedure (Scotland) Act 1975, ss 204, 208–11, 218, 414, 416, 418–420) (SI 1983/1580)

Criminal Justice (Scotland) Act 1980 (c 62)—*cont*
Remainder   Repealed or spent

Deaconesses and Lay Workers (Pensions) Measure 1980 (No 1)

RA: 20 Mar 1980

20 Mar 1980 (RA)

Deer Act 1980 (c 49)

Whole Act repealed

Diocese in Europe Measure 1980 (No 2)

RA: 30 Jun 1980

Commencement provisions: s 7(2)

2 Jul 1980 (s 7(2) (following establishment of Diocese in Europe))

Education Act 1980 (c 20)

RA: 3 Apr 1980

Commencement provisions: s 37(2); Education Act 1980 (Commencement No 1) Order
  1980, SI 1980/489; Education Act 1980 (Commencement No 2) Order 1980,
  SI 1980/959; Education Act 1980 (Commencement No 3) Order 1981, SI 1981/789;
  Education Act 1980 (Commencement No 4) Order 1981, SI 1981/1064

s 1	5 May 1980 (SI 1980/489)
2–4	Repealed
5	1 Jul 1981 (SI 1981/789)
6–9	1 Oct 1980 (SI 1980/959)
10, 11	Repealed
12(1)(a)–(d)	1 Aug 1980 (SI 1980/489)
(e)	5 May 1980 (SI 1980/489)
(1A), (1B)	Prospectively inserted by Education Act 1993, s 229(1) (qv)
(2)	5 May 1980 (SI 1980/489)
(2A)	Inserted by Education Reform Act 1988, s 31(4) (qv)
(3)	5 May 1980 (SI 1980/489)
(4)	1 Aug 1980 (SI 1980/489)
(5)–(9)	5 May 1980 (SI 1980/489)
13	1 Aug 1980 (SI 1980/489)
14(1), (2)	5 May 1980 (SI 1980/489)
(3)	1 Aug 1980 (SI 1980/489)
(4)	5 May 1980 (SI 1980/489); prospectively repealed by Education Act 1993, s 307(1), (3), Sch 19, para 77(b), Sch 21, Pt II (qv)
15	Repealed
16(1)	5 May 1980 (SI 1980/489)
(1A)	Inserted by Education Act 1993, s 307(1), Sch 19, para 78 (qv)
(2), (3)	1 Aug 1980 (SI 1980/489)

Education Act 1980 (c 20)—*cont*

s 16(3A), (3B)	Inserted by Education Reform Act 1988, s 237(1), Sch 2, Pt III, para 81 (qv)
(4), (5)	1 Aug 1980 (SI 1980/489)
(6), (7)	5 May 1980 (SI 1980/489)
17, 18	1 Oct 1980 (SI 1980/959)
19	5 May 1980 (SI 1980/489)
20	5 May 1980 (SI 1980/489); repealed (S)
21	5 May 1980 (SI 1980/489)
22	14 April 1980 (SI 1980/489)
23	Repealed
24	1 May 1980 (SI 1980/489)
25	Repealed
26	5 May 1980 (SI 1980/489)
27	Repealed
28–30	5 May 1980 (SI 1980/489)
31, 32	Repealed
33(1)	Repealed
(2)	5 May 1980 (SI 1980/489); repealed (S)
(3)	1 Sep 1981 (SI 1981/1064)
34	1 Oct 1980 (SI 1980/959)
35	14 Apr 1980 (SI 1980/489); repealed (S)
36	14 Apr 1980 (SI 1980/489)
37	14 Apr 1980 (SI 1980/489); repealed (S)
38(1)–(3)	14 Apr 1980 (SI 1980/489)
(4)	1 Oct 1980 (SI 1980/959)
(5)	1 Aug 1980 (SI 1980/489)
(5A)	Inserted by Education Reform Act 1988, s 31(6) (qv)
(6)	See Sch 7 below
(7)	14 Apr 1980 (SI 1980/489)
	Whole section repealed (S)
Sch 1	5 May 1980 (SI 1980/489)
2	1 Oct 1980 (SI 1980/959)
3	1 Aug 1980 (SI 1980/489)
4	1 Oct 1980 (SI 1980/959)
5	5 May 1980 (SI 1980/489)
6	Repealed
7	14 Apr 1980 (repeals of or in Education Act 1944, s 49; Education (Scotland) Act 1962, ss 53, 55; Education (Milk) Act 1971; Education (Scotland) Act 1976, s 3; Education Act 1976, s 9) (SI 1980/489)
	5 May 1980 (repeals of or in Education Act 1944, ss 8(2)(b), 9(1), 11, 12, 31(1), 32, 53(1), 61(2), 66, 82–84, 90, 97, 100(1), 114, Sch 1, Pt I, para 3, Sch 3, para 3; Education (Miscellaneous Provisions) Act 1953, s 6(1); Local Government Act 1958, Sch 8, para 16(2); London Government Act 1963, ss 31(1)–(3), 33; Local Government Act 1966, s 14; Education Act 1973, s 4; Education Act 1975, ss 1, 2, 5(4); Education Act 1976, ss 5, 7, 8) (SI 1980/489)
	1 Aug 1980 (repeals of or in Education Act 1944, s 13; Education Act 1946, Sch 2, Pt II; Education (Miscellaneous Provisions) Act 1948, ss 6, 7; Education (Miscellaneous Provisions) Act 1953 ss 7, 9, 16, Sch 1; London Government Act 1963, s 31(9); Education Act 1968, ss 1(2), 3, 5, Sch 1,

Education Act 1980 (c 20)—*cont*

Sch 7—*cont*　　　　　　　　para 7, Sch 3, Pt A; Education Act 1976, s 4)
　　　　　　　　　　　　　(SI 1980/489)
　　　　　　　　　　　　　1 Aug 1981 (repeals of Education Act 1944, s 21(2),
　　　　　　　　　　　　　　Sch 4) (SI 1981/789)
　　　　　　　　　　　　　1 Sep 1981 (repeal of Sex Discrimination Act 1975,
　　　　　　　　　　　　　　Sch 2, para 2) (SI 1981/1064)

Education (Scotland) Act 1980 (c 44)

RA: 1 Aug 1980

Commencement provisions: s 137(2)–(4); Education (Scotland) Act 1980
　(Commencement) Order 1980, SI 1980/1287

s 1(1), (2)	1 Sep 1980 (s 137(2))
(2A)	Inserted by Further and Higher Education (Scotland) Act 1992, s (qv)
(3)	1 Sep 1980 (except so far as relates to compulsory further education and junior colleges) (s 137(2), (3))
	Not in force (exception noted above)
(4), (5)	1 Sep 1980 (s 137(2))
2–4	1 Sep 1980 (s 137(2))
5	Repealed
6–9	1 Sep 1980 (s 137(2))
10, 11	1 Sep 1980 (except so far as relates to junior colleges) (s 137(2), (3))
	Not in force (exception noted above)
12–14	1 Sep 1980 (s 137(2))
14ZA	Inserted by Further and Higher Education (Scotland) Act 1992, s 62, Sch 9, para 7(1), (2) (qv)
14A	Inserted by Education (Scotland) Act 1981, s 12 (qv)
15–19	1 Sep 1980 (s 137(2))
19A	Inserted by Education (Amendment) (Scotland) Act 1984, s 1 (qv)
20–22	1 Sep 1980 (s 137(2))
22A–22D	Inserted by Education (Scotland) Act 1981, s 6 (qv)
23(1)–(4)	1 Sep 1980 (except so far as relates to junior colleges) (s 137(2), (3))
	Not in force (exception noted above)
(5)–(7)	Repealed
24–28	1 Sep 1980 (s 137(2))
28A–28H	Inserted by Education (Scotland) Act 1981, s 1(1) (qv)
28I–28K	Prospectively inserted by Education (Schools) Act 1992, s 17 (qv)
29	Repealed
30–44	1 Sep 1980 (s 137(2))
45–48	Repealed
48A	Inserted by Education (No 2) Act 1986, s 48 (qv)
49	1 Sep 1980 (s 137(2))
50(1)(a), (b)	1 Sep 1980 (except so far as relates to junior colleges) (s 137(2), (3))
	Not in force (exception noted above)
(c)	*Not in force*

Education (Scotland) Act 1980 (c 44)—*cont*

s 50(2)	1 Sep 1980 (except so far as relates to junior colleges) (s 137(2), (3))
	Not in force (exception noted above)
(3), (4)	Inserted by Education (Scotland) Act 1981, s 2(2)(b) (qv)
51	1 Sep 1980 (s 137(2))
52	1 Sep 1980 (except so far as relates to junior colleges) (s 137(2), (3))
	Not in force (exception noted above)
53–56	1 Sep 1980 (s 137(2))
57, 58	1 Sep 1980 (except so far as relates to junior colleges) (s 137(2), (3))
	Not in force (exception noted above)
59	Repealed
60–65F	Substituted for ss 60–65 by Education (Scotland) Act 1981, s 4(1), Sch 8 (qv)
65G	Inserted by Self-Governing Schools etc (Scotland) Act 1989, s 71(2) (qv)
66	1 Sep 1980 (except so far as relating to junior colleges) (s 137(2), (3))
	Not in force (exception noted above)
67	1 Sep 1980 (s 137(2))
68	1 Sep 1980 (except so far as relating to junior colleges) (s 137(2), (3))
	Not in force (exception noted above)
69–71	1 Sep 1980 (s 137(2))
72(1)	1 Sep 1980 (s 137(2))
(2)	1 Sep 1980 (except so far as relating to junior colleges) (s 137(2), (3))
	Not in force (exception noted above)
73–75	1 Sep 1980 (s 137(2))
75A, 75B	Inserted by Education (Scotland) Act 1981, s 5(1) (qv)
76	1 Sep 1980 (s 137(2))
77	Repealed
78–85	1 Sep 1980 (s 137(2))
86, 87	1 Sep 1980 (except so far as relating to junior colleges) (s 137(2), (3))
	Not in force (exception noted above)
87A, 87B	Inserted by Self-Governing Schools etc (Scotland) Act 1989, s 74 (qv)
88	Repealed
89, 90	1 Sep 1980 (s 137(2))
91–93	Substituted for ss 91–97 together with ss 97A–97D by Education (Scotland) Act 1981, s 14(1), Sch 8 (qv)
94–97	See ss 91–93 above
97A–97D	Substituted for ss 91–97 together with ss 91–93 by Education (Scotland) Act 1981, s 14(1), Sch 8 (qv)
98–107	1 Sep 1980 (s 137(2))
108(1)	1 Sep 1980 (s 137(2))
(2)	1 Sep 1980 (s 137(2)); renumbered s 108A by Education (Scotland) Act 1981, Sch 6, para 7(b) (qv)
108A	See s 108(2) above
109–112	1 Sep 1980 (s 137(2))
113	Repealed
114	1 Sep 1980 (s 137(2))

Education (Scotland) Act 1980 (c 44)—*cont*

s 115, 116	Repealed
117	1 Sep 1980 (s 137(2))
118	Substituted by Education (Scotland) Act 1981, Sch 6, para 16, Sch 8 (qv)
118A	Inserted by Education (Scotland) Act 1981, Sch 6, para 17 (qv)
119–123	1 Sep 1980 (s 137(2))
124	Repealed
125	1 Sep 1980 (s 137(2))
126–128	Repealed
129–137	1 Sep 1980 (s 137(2))
Sch A1	Inserted by Education (Scotland) Act 1981, s 1(2), Sch 1 (qv)
A2	Inserted by Education (Scotland) Act 1981, s 4(3), Schs 3, 8 (qv)
1	1 Sep 1980 (s 137(2))
1A	Inserted by Education (Scotland) Act 1981, s 5(3), Sch 4 (qv)
1B	Inserted by Education (Scotland) Act 1981, s 14(2), Sch 5 (qv)
2–6	1 Sep 1980 (s 137(2))

Employment Act 1980 (c 42)

RA: 1 Aug 1980

Commencement provisions: s 21(2); Employment Act 1980 (Commencement No 1) Order 1980, SI 1980/1170; Employment Act 1980 (Commencement No 2) Order 1980, SI 1980/1926

s 1–5	Repealed
6	1 Oct 1980 (SI 1980/1170)
7	Repealed
8, 9	1 Oct 1980 (SI 1980/1170)
10	Repealed
11	1 Oct 1980 (SI 1980/1170); prospectively repealed by Trade Union Reform and Employment Right Act 1993, s 51, Sch 10 (qv)
12–14	1 Oct 1980 (SI 1980/1170)
15–19	Repealed
20(1)	1 Aug 1980 (RA)
(2)	See Sch 1 below
(3)	See Sch 2 below
21	1 Aug 1980 (RA)
Sch 1, para 1	15 Aug 1980 (SI 1980/1170)
2–7	Repealed
8	1 Oct 1980 (SI 1980/1170)
9, 10	Repealed
11	1 Oct 1980 (SI 1980/1170)
12	Repealed
13	1 Oct 1980 (SI 1980/1170)
14, 15	Repealed
16	8 Sep 1980 (SI 1980/1170)
17	8 Sep 1980 (so far as relates to s 4) (SI 1980/1170) 1 Oct 1980 (otherwise) (SI 1980/1170)

Employment Act 1980 (c 42)—*cont*

Sch 1, para 18	1 Oct 1980 (SI 1980/1170)
19	Repealed
20	15 Aug 1980 (SI 1980/1170)
21	Repealed
22, 23	1 Oct 1980 (SI 1980/1170)
24	Repealed
25	1 Oct 1980 (SI 1980/1170)
26	8 Sep 1980 (SI 1980/1170)
27	1 Oct 1980 (SI 1980/1170)
28, 29	8 Sep 1980 (SI 1980/1170)
30	Repealed
31	1 Oct 1980 (SI 1980/1170)
32	Repealed
33	1 Oct 1980 (SI 1980/1170)
2	15 Aug 1980 (except repeals of or in Trade Union and Labour Relations Act 1974; Employment Protection Act 1975, s 127(1)(g); Trade Union and Labour Relations (Amendment) Act 1976, s 2; Employment Protection (Consolidation) Act 1978, ss 23, 25(1), 33(3), 66(1), 73(1)(c), (8), 135(1), 154(1)) (SI 1980/1170)
	8 Sep 1980 (repeals of Trade Union and Labour Relations Act 1974, s 13(3); Employment Protection (Consolidation) Act 1978, ss 23, 25(1), 135(1)) (SI 1980/1170)
	1 Oct 1980 (otherwise except repeals of or in Trade Union and Labour Relations Act 1974; Trade Union and Labour Relations (Amendment) Act 1976, s 2) (SI 1980/1170)
	22 Dec 1980 (exceptions noted above) (SI 1980/1926)

Note transitional provisions in SI 1980/1170

Films Act 1980 (c 41)

Whole Act repealed

Finance Act 1980 (c 48)

Budget Day: 26 Mar 1980

RA: 1 Aug 1980

See the note concerning Finance Acts at the front of this book

---

Foster Children Act 1980 (c 6)

Whole Act repealed

Gaming (Amendment) Act 1980 (c 8)

RA: 20 Mar 1980

20 Mar 1980 (RA)

Gas Act 1980 (c 37)

Whole Act repealed

Health Services Act 1980 (c 53)

RA: 8 Aug 1980

Commencement provisions: s 26(2), (3); Health Services Act 1980 (Commencement
No 1) Order 1980, SI 1980/1257; Health Services Act 1980 (Commencement No 2)
Order 1981, SI 1981/306; Health Services Act 1980 (Commencement No 3) Order
1981, SI 1981/884; Health Services Act 1980 (Commencement No 4) Order 1983,
SI 1983/303

s 1	8 Aug 1980 (RA)
2	Repealed
3	8 Aug 1980 (RA)
4	Repealed
5–9	8 Aug 1980 (RA)
10–15	Repealed
16	1 Aug 1981 (SI 1981/884)
17–19	Repealed
20	8 Aug 1980 (RA)
21	1 Apr 1983 (SI 1983/303)
22	Repealed
23, 24	8 Aug 1980 (RA)
25(1)	8 Aug 1980 (RA)
(2)	1 Apr 1981 (SI 1981/306)
(3)	8 Aug 1980 (RA)
(4)	See Sch 7 below
26	8 Aug 1980 (RA)
Sch 1, 2	8 Aug 1980 (RA)
3	Repealed
4	1 Aug 1981 (SI 1981/884)
5	1 Apr 1981 (SI 1981/306)
6	8 Aug 1980 (RA)
7	8 Aug 1980 (except repeals in Nursing Homes Registration (Scotland) Act 1938; Nursing Homes Act 1975; Nurses, Midwives and Health Visitors Act 1979) (RA)
	1 Aug 1981 (exception noted above) (SI 1981/884)

Highlands and Islands Air Services (Scotland) Act 1980 (c 19)

RA: 3 Apr 1980

Commencement provisions: s 5(2)

15 Dec 1980 (s 5(2))

Highways Act 1980 (c 66)

RA: 13 Nov 1980

Commencement provisions: s 345(2)

1 Jan 1981 (s 345(2))

Housing Act 1980 (c 51)

RA: 8 Aug 1980

Whole Act repealed (S)

Commencement provisions: s 153; Housing Act 1980 (Commencement No 1) Order
1980, SI 1980/1406; Housing Act 1980 (Commencement No 2) Order 1980,
SI 1980/1466; Housing Act 1980 (Commencement No 3) Order 1980, SI 1980/
1557; Housing Act 1980 (Commencement No 4) Order 1980, SI 1980/1693;
Housing Act 1980 (Commencement No 5) Order 1980, SI 1980/1706; Housing Act
1980 (Commencement No 6) Order 1980, SI 1980/1781; Housing Act 1980
(Commencement No 7) Order 1981, SI 1981/119; Housing Act 1980
(Commencement No 8) Order 1981, SI 1981/296; Rent Rebates and Rent
Allowances (England and Wales) (Appointed Day) Order 1981, SI 1981/297

s 1–24, 24A–24D, 25–50	Repealed
51	28 Nov 1980 (SI 1980/1706)
52	Repealed (subject to saving)
53–55	28 Nov 1980 (SI 1980/1706)
56, 56A–56D, 57, 58	Repealed (subject to saving)
59(1)	Repealed
(2)	28 Nov 1980 (SI 1980/1706)
(3)	See Sch 6 below
60	Repealed
61–77	28 Nov 1980 (SI 1980/1706)
78, 79	20 Oct 1980 (SI 1980/1557)
80	Repealed
81–86	3 Oct 1980 (SI 1980/1406)
87	Repealed
88, 89	3 Oct 1980 (SI 1980/1406)
90–137	Repealed
138	8 Aug 1980 (s 153(3))
139, 140	Repealed
141	3 Oct 1980 (except in relation to Sch 21, para 7) (SI 1980/1406)
	Not in force (exception noted above)
142	31 Mar 1981 (SI 1981/119)
143	3 Oct 1980 (SI 1980/1406)
144–147	Repealed
148	3 Oct 1980 (SI 1980/1406)
149	Repealed
150, 151	8 Aug 1980 (s 153(3))
152(1), (3)	See Sch 25 below
(2)	8 Aug 1980 (s 153(3))
153	8 Aug 1980 (RA)
154, 155	8 Aug 1980 (s 153(3))
Sch 1, 1A–4A	Repealed
5	6 Oct 1980 (SI 1980/1466)
6	*Not in force*—amendments made by this Schedule will not be brought into operation (DoE statement)
7–10	28 Nov 1980 (SI 1980/1706)
11–20	Repealed
21, para 1, 2	3 Oct 1980 (SI 1980/1406)
3	Repealed
4–6	3 Oct 1980 (SI 1980/1706)
7	*Not in force*

Housing Act 1980 (c 51)—*cont*

Sch 21, para 8	3 Oct 1980 (SI 1980/1406)
22	31 Mar 1981 (SI 1981/119)
23, 24	Repealed
25, para 1–3	28 Nov 1980 (SI 1980/1706)
4–6	Spent
7–31	Repealed
32, 33	28 Nov 1980 (SI 1980/1706)
34	Repealed
35	28 Nov 1980 (SI 1980/1706)
36	Repealed
37–45	28 Nov 1980 (SI 1980/1706)
46	Repealed
47–60	28 Nov 1980 (SI 1980/1706)
61	3 Oct 1980 (SI 1980/1406)
62, 63	Repealed
64–68	8 Aug 1980 (s 153(3))
69	Repealed
70	Spent
71	Repealed
72, 73	Spent
74	Repealed
75	8 Aug 1980 (s 153(3))
76	Repealed
77, 78	8 Aug 1980 (s 153(3))
26	3 Oct 1980 (repeals of or in Housing Act 1957, ss 5, 43(4), 113(5), 119(3); Housing (Financial Provisions) Act 1958, s 43(1); Housing Act 1961, s 20; Housing Act 1964, ss 65(1A), 66; Housing Subsidies Act 1967, ss 24(5), 26A; Leasehold Reform Act 1967, Sch 1, para 7(1)(b); Housing Act 1969, s 61(6); Housing Finance Act 1972, ss 90–91A; Local Government Act 1972, Sch 22, para 2; Housing Act 1974, ss 5(3), 13(4), (5)(a), 14, 19(1), 30(5), 31, 32(1), (4), (8), 33(6), 104, 114(1), (6), (7); Criminal Law Act 1977, Schs 6, 12) (SI 1980/1406)
	27 Oct 1980 (repeals of or in Housing Act 1961, s 16; Housing Act 1969, s 60; Housing Act 1974, ss 56(1)(d), 57(6), 62(3), 64(7), 67(2)(b), (4), 84) (SI 1980/1557)
	28 Mar 1980 (repeals of or in Landlord and Tenant Act 1927, s 16; Reserve and Auxiliary Forces (Protection of Civil Interests) Act 1951, ss 16(2)(c), 19(5); Landlord and Tenant Act 1954, s 43(1)(c); Housing Act 1964, Sch 4, para 2; Tribunals and Inquiries Act 1971, ss 7(3), 13(1), Sch 1, para 28(a); Rent (Agriculture) Act 1976, Sch 4, Case X, Sch 6, paras 1, 7; Rent Act 1977 except repeals in Sch 12, paras 4, 9) (SI 1980/1706)
	15 Dec 1980 (repeals of or in Housing Act 1957, s 96(e); Housing (Financial Provisions) Act 1958, ss 14, 15; Housing Act 1969, ss 28A, 29B, 30, 35(1), (3)–(7), 38, 86(5); Chronically Sick and Disabled Persons Act 1970, s 3(1); Local Employment Act 1972, Sch 3; Housing (Amendment) Act 1973, ss 1(1), 2; Housing Act 1974, ss 38(2)(a), 42, 50, 52–55, 56(2)(d), 71(3)(a), Sch 5, Pt I, Pt II, para 4; Housing Rents and Subsidies Act 1975, Sch 1,

Housing Act 1980 (c 51)—*cont*
Sch 26—*cont*   paras 1–11, 12(4)(a), Sch 5, paras 8(3), 18;
                                       Remuneration, Charges and Grants Act 1975, s 9;
                                       Local Land Charges Act 1975, Sch 1) (SI 1980/1781)
                                       31 Mar 1981 (repeal of Leasehold Reform Act 1967,
                                          s 21(5), Sch 2, para 8(2)) (SI 1981/119)
                                       1 Apr 1981 (repeals of Housing Finance Act 1972, ss 8,
                                          20(5), (7), 24(5), 26(1), Sch 3, Pt II, Sch 4,
                                          paras 1(3)(a), 16, 17) (SI 1981/296)
                                       Not in force (repeals of or in Housing Act 1957, ss 91,
                                          105, 106; Housing (Financial Provisions) Act 1958,
                                          s 45; New Towns Act 1959, s 4; Housing Subsidies
                                          Act 1967, ss 24, 24B, 26, 28A; Town and Country
                                          Planning Act 1968, s 39; Housing Act 1974, s 79,
                                          Schs 8, 11; Housing Rents and Subsidies Act 1975,
                                          ss 1(3), 2, 4; New Towns (Amendment) Act 1976,
                                          s 9; Supplementary Benefits Act 1976, Sch 7,
                                          para 28; Development of Rural Wales Act 1976,
                                          ss 18, 22, Sch 5; Rent Act 1977, Sch 12, paras 4, 9)

Import of Live Fish (England and Wales) Act 1980 (c 27)
RA: 15 May 1980

15 May 1980 (RA)

Imprisonment (Temporary Provisions) Act 1980 (c 57)
RA: 29 Oct 1980

29 Oct 1980 (RA)

Industry Act 1980 (c 33)
RA: 30 Jun 1980

30 Jun 1980 (RA)

Insurance Companies Act 1980 (c 25)
RA: 1 May 1980

Commencement provisions: s 5(2); Insurance Companies Act 1980 (Commencement)
   Order 1980, SI 1980/678

Whole Act repealed except ss 4(1), 5, Sch 3, paras 4, 9, 15(b), 16–20 which came into
   force on 1 Jun 1980 (SI 1980/678)

Iran (Temporary Powers) Act 1980 (c 28)
Whole Act repealed

Law Reform (Miscellaneous Provisions) (Scotland) Act 1980 (c 55)

RA: 29 Oct 1980

Commencement provisions: s 29(2); Law Reform (Miscellaneous Provisions)
(Scotland) Act 1980 (Commencement) Order 1980, SI 1980/1726

s 1–11	22 Dec 1980 (SI 1980/1726)
12	Repealed
13, 14	22 Dec 1980 (SI 1980/1726)
15	Repealed
16–25	22 Dec 1980 (SI 1980/1726)
26	Repealed
27, 28	22 Dec 1980 (SI 1980/1726)
29	29 Oct 1980 (RA)
Sch 1, 2	22 Dec 1980 (SI 1980/1726)
3	Repealed

Licensed Premises (Exclusion of Certain Persons) Act 1980 (c 32)

RA: 30 Jun 1980

30 Jun 1980 (RA)

Licensing (Amendment) Act 1980 (c 40)

RA: 17 Jul 1980

Commencement provisions: s 4(2); Licensing (Amendment) Act 1980 (Commencement)
Order 1982, SI 1982/1383

s 1	17 Jul 1980 (RA)
2, 3	1 Oct 1982 (SI 1982/1383)
4	17 Jul 1980 (RA)

Limitation Act 1980 (c 58)

RA: 13 Nov 1980

Commencement provisions: s 41(2), (3); Limitation Act 1980 (Commencement) Order
1981, SI 1981/588

1 May 1981 (s 41(2); note that s 35 also came into force on that date by virtue of
SI 1981/588)

Limitation Amendment Act 1980 (c 24)

RA: 1 May 1980

Whole Act repealed except ss 10, 14(1), (5) which came into force on 1 Aug 1980
(s 14(3) (repealed))

Local Government, Planning and Land Act 1980 (c 65)

RA: 13 Nov 1980

Commencement provisions: ss 23(3), 47, 68(8), 85, 86(8)–(11), 178; Local
Government, Planning and Land Act 1980 (Commencement No 1) Order 1980,
SI 1980/1871; Local Government, Planning and Land Act 1980 (Commencement
No 2) Order 1980, SI 1980/1893; Local Government, Planning and Land Act
1980 (Commencement No 3) Order 1980, SI 1980/2014; Local Government,
Planning and Land Act 1980 (Commencement No 4) Order 1981, SI 1981/194;
Local Government, Planning and Land Act 1980 (Commencement No 5) Order
1981, SI 1981/341; Local Government, Planning and Land Act 1980
(Commencement No 6) Order 1981, SI 1981/1251; Local Government, Planning
and Land Act 1980 (Commencement No 7) Order 1981, SI 1981/1618; Local
Government, Planning and Land Act 1980 (Commencement No 8) (Scotland)
Order 1982, SI 1982/317; Local Government, Planning and Land Act 1980
(Commencement No 8) Order 1983, SI 1983/94; Community Land Act 1975
(Appointed Day for Repeal) Order 1983, SI 1983/673; Local Government,
Planning and Land Act 1980 (Commencement No 9) Order 1984, SI 1984/1493

s 1–4	13 Nov 1980 (RA)
5–14	1 Apr 1981 (EW) (SI 1981/341)
	1 Apr 1982 (S) (SI 1982/317)
15(1)	1 Apr 1981 (EW) (SI 1981/341)
	1 Apr 1982 (S) (SI 1982/317)
(2), (3)	1 Apr 1981 (EW) (SI 1981/341); *not in force* (S)
16(1)	1 Apr 1981 (EW) (but in its application to relevant work, 1 Apr 1982) (SI 1981/341)
(1A)	Prospectively inserted by Local Government Act 1992, s 11, Sch 1, para 4(2) (qv)
(2), (3)	1 Apr 1981 (EW) (SI 1981/341); prospectively repealed by Local Government Act 1992, s 29(2), Sch 4, Pt I (qv)
(4)–(6)	Repealed
	Whole section 1 Apr 1982 (S) (SI 1982/317)
17	Repealed, subject to transitional provisions, by Local Government Act 1988, ss 32, 41, Sch 6, para 7, Sch 7, Pt III (qv)
18, 19	1 Apr 1981 (EW) (SI 1981/341)
	1 Apr 1982 (S) (SI 1982/317)
19A, 19B	Inserted by Local Government Act 1988, s 32, Sch 6, para 9 (qv)
20–22	1 Apr 1981 (EW) (SI 1981/341)
	1 Apr 1982 (S) (SI 1982/317)
23–27	13 Nov 1980 (RA)
28	13 Nov 1980 (S) (s 47(7)); repealed (EW), with savings, by the Local Government Finance (Repeals, Savings and Consequential Amendments) Order 1990, SI 1990/776, art 3, Sch 1
29(1), (2)	Effective for rate periods beginning with date after 13 Nov 1980, on which new valuation lists come into operation (S) (s 47(4)); repealed (EW), with savings, by the Local Government Finance (Repeals, Savings and Consequential Amendments) Order 1990, SI 1990/776, art 3, Sch 1
(3)	Repealed

Local Government, Planning and Land Act 1980 (c 65)—*cont*

s 29(4), (5)	13 Nov 1980 (S) (s 47(7)); repealed (EW), with savings, by the Local Government Finance (Repeals, Savings and Consequential Amendments) Order 1990, SI 1990/776, art 3, Sch 1
30	13 Nov 1980 (S) (s 47(7)); repealed (EW), with savings, by the Local Government Finance (Repeals, Savings and Consequential Amendments) Order 1990, SI 1990/776, art 3, Sch 1
31	Effective for rate periods beginning after 30 Apr 1981 (S) (s 47(2)); repealed (EW), with savings, by the Local Government Finance (Repeals, Savings and Consequential Amendments) Order 1990, SI 1990/776, art 3, Sch 1
32	13 Nov 1980 (s 47(7))
33, 34	Effective for any rate passed beginning after 31 Mar 1981 (S) (s 47(1); SI 1980/2014); repealed (EW), with savings, by the Local Government Finance (Repeals, Savings and Consequential Amendments) Order 1990, SI 1990/776, art 3, Sch 1
35, 36	13 Nov 1980 (S) (s 47(7)); repealed (EW), with savings, by the Local Government Finance (Repeals, Savings and Consequential Amendments) Order 1990, SI 1990/776, art 3, Sch 1
37	Effective for any rate period beginning after 31 Mar 1981 (S) (s 47(1); SI 1980/2014); repealed (EW), with savings, by the Local Government Finance (Repeals, Savings and Consequential Amendments) Order 1990, SI 1990/776, art 3, Sch 1
38–40	13 Dec 1980 (S) (s 47(3)); repealed (EW), with savings, by the Local Government Finance (Repeals, Savings and Consequential Amendments) Order 1990, SI 1990/776, art 3, Sch 1
41–43	13 Nov 1980 (S) (s 47(7)); repealed (EW), with savings, by the Local Government Finance (Repeals, Savings and Consequential Amendments) Order 1990, SI 1990/776, art 3, Sch 1
44	Effective for rate periods beginning after 31 Mar 1981 (S) (s 47(1); SI 1980/2014); repealed (EW), with savings, by the Local Government Finance (Repeals, Savings and Consequential Amendments) Order 1990, SI 1990/776, art 3, Sch 1
45, 46	Repealed
47	13 Nov 1980 (RA)
48–63	13 Nov 1980 (RA) but the commencing year for purposes of Part VI of this Act was that beginning 1 Apr 1981 (SI 1980/1893)
63A	Inserted by the Local Government Act 1985, s 83(2) (qv)
64	Repealed

Local Government, Planning and Land Act 1980 (c 65)—*cont*

s 65	Substituted by Local Government Finance Act 1987, s 11(1), Sch 4, para 4 (with effect as noted in para 12(3) of that Schedule) (qv)
66, 67	13 Nov 1980 (RA) but see the note to ss 48–63 above
68(1)	13 Nov 1980 (RA) but see the note to ss 48–63 above
(2)	11 Dec 1980 (s 68(8); SI 1980/1893)
(3), (4)	Repealed
(5)	11 Dec 1980 (s 68(8); SI 1980/1893)
(6)	Repealed
(7)–(9)	13 Nov 1980 (RA)
69, 70	13 Nov 1980 (RA)
71–79, 79A, 79B, 80, 80A, 80B–85	Repealed
86(1)–(7)	Repealed
(8)–(11)	13 Nov 1980 (RA)
87	13 Nov 1980 (S) (RA); repealed (EW)
88	Repealed
89, 90	Repealed
91, 92	13 Nov 1980 (RA)
93–96	Brought into force area by area on different dates as follows: 31 Dec 1980 (Birmingham, Bradford, Bristol, Coventry, Dudley, Ealing, Gateshead, Leeds, Liverpool, Manchester, Middlesborough, Newcastle-under-Lyme, Newcastle-upon-Tyne, Preston, Salford, Sefton, Stockport, Stoke, Trafford, Wandsworth, Wirral) (SI 1980/1871) 19 Mar 1981 (Derby, Leicester, Newham, North Bedfordshire, Nottingham, Portsmouth, Sandwell, Sheffield, South Staffordshire, Southwark, Tower Hamlets, Walsall) (SI 1981/194) 2 Oct 1981 (Knowsley, St Helens) (SI 1981/1251) 11 Dec 1981 (areas of all other councils of districts in England, all other London boroughs and the City of London) (SI 1981/1618) 3 Mar 1983 (Alyn and Deeside, Cardiff, Newport, Swansea, Vale of Glamorgan, Wrexham, Maelor) (SI 1983/94) 24 Oct 1984 (areas of all other district councils in Wales) (SI 1984/1493)
96A	Inserted by Local Government Act 1988, s 31, Sch 5, para 2(1) (qv)
97	Substituted by Local Government Act 1988, s 31, Sch 5, para 3 (qv)
98, 99	See ss 93–96 above
99A	Inserted by Local Government Act 1988, s 31, Sch 5, para 6 (qv)
100	See ss 93–96 above
101	See Sch 17 below
102–104	13 Nov 1980 (RA)
105	Repealed
106–116	13 Nov 1980 (RA)
117	Repealed
118	13 Nov 1980 (RA)

Local Government, Planning and Land Act 1980 (c 65)—*cont*

s 119	Repealed
120	13 Nov 1980 (RA)
121	13 Nov 1980 (RA) but effective from 12 Dec 1975 (s 121(1))
122	13 Nov 1980 (RA)
123	13 Nov 1980 (RA) but effective from 12 Dec 1975 (s 123(1))
124, 125	13 Nov 1980 (RA)
126–130	Repealed
131–149	13 Nov 1980 (RA)
150	Repealed
151–153	13 Nov 1980 (RA)
154	Substituted by Social Security and Housing Benefits Act 1982, s 48(5), Sch 4, para 36 (qv)
155, 156	13 Nov 1980 (RA)
157, 157A, 157B	Substituted for original s 157 by Leasehold Reform, Housing and Urban Development Act 1993, s 178 (qv)
158	Repealed
159–165	13 Nov 1980 (RA)
165A	Inserted by Leasehold Reform, Housing and Urban Development Act 1993, s 180 (qv)
166–172	13 Nov 1980 (RA)
173(a)	13 Dec 1980 (s 178(3))
(b)	13 Dec 1981 (s 178(2))
174	13 Feb 1981 (s 178(1))
175–178	13 Dec 1980 (s 178(3))
179, 180	13 Nov 1980 (RA)
181, 182	Repealed
183–186	13 Nov 1980 (RA)
187–190	Repealed
191–197	13 Nov 1980 (RA)
Sch 1–10	13 Nov 1980 (RA)
11–15	Repealed
16	13 Nov 1980 (RA)
17, Pt I	13 Nov 1980 (RA)
II	13 Nov 1980 (repeals of Community Land Act 1975, except as noted below) (RA)
	1 Jun 1983 (repeals of Community Land Act 1975, ss 1, 2, 6(1) (part) (6), 7, 26, 40, 43, 44 (except part of sub-s (3)), 51–58 of, and Sch 2 to, 1975 Act) (SI 1983/673)
III, IV	13 Nov 1980 (RA)
18–24	13 Nov 1980 (RA)
25, Pt I	Repealed
II–IV	13 Nov 1980 (RA)
26–32	13 Nov 1980 (RA)
33, para 1–3	13 Nov 1980 (RA)
4	Effective when power to prescribe multipliers exercised (s 47(5))
5	13 Nov 1980 (RA)
6	Repealed
7	13 Nov 1980 (RA)
8	Repealed
9	13 Nov 1980 (S) (RA); repealed (EW), with savings, by the Local Government Finance (Repeals,

Local Government, Planning and Land Act 1980 (c 65)—*cont*

Sch 33, para 9—*cont*	Savings and Consequential Amendments) Order 1990, SI 1990/776, art 3, Sch 1
10	Effective for rate period beginning on 1 Apr 1990 and subsequent rating periods
11	13 Nov 1980 (S) (RA); repealed (EW), with savings, by the Local Government Finance (Repeals, Savings and Consequential Amendments) Order 1990, SI 1990/776, art 3, Sch 1
12	Repealed
13	13 Nov 1980 (RA) but note para 13(2) only effective for applications after 12 Dec 1975
14	Effective when power to prescribe multipliers is exercised (s 47(5)) (It is thought that the coming into force of the Landlord and Tenant Act 1954 (Appropriate Multiplier) Regulations 1981, SI 1981/69, brought this paragraph into effect on 25 Mar 1981)
34, Pt I–VIII	13 Nov 1980 (RA)
IX	Rate periods beginning after 31 Mar 1981 (repeals of General Rate Act 1967, ss 4(2), 5(1)(g), 48(4), 50(2), Sch 10; Decimal Currency Act 1969; GLC (General Powers) Act 1973; Local Government Act 1974) (s 47(1); SI 1980/2014)
	Rate periods beginning after first date after 13 Nov 1980 on which new valuation lists in force (repeals of General Rate Act 1967, ss 19, 30) (s 47(4)(d))
	13 Nov 1980 (repeals of General Rate Act 1967, s 20, Schs 1, 2; General Rate Act 1975; Rating (Caravan Sites) Act 1976) (RA)
X	13 Nov 1980 (RA)
XI	13 Nov 1980 (RA) but note Sch 17 above in relation to repeal of Community Land Act 1975
XII–XVI	13 Nov 1980 (RA)

Magistrates' Courts Act 1980 (c 43)

RA: 1 Aug 1980

Commencement provisions: s 155(7)

6 Jul 1981 (s 155(7))

Married Women's Policies of Assurance (Scotland) (Amendment) Act 1980 (c 56)

RA: 29 Oct 1980

29 Oct 1980 (RA)

National Health Service (Invalid Direction) Act 1980 (c 15)

Whole Act repealed

National Heritage Act 1980 (c 17)

RA: 31 Mar 1980

31 Mar 1980 (RA)

New Hebrides Act 1980 (c 16)

RA: 20 Mar 1980

Commencement provisions: s 4(2); New Hebrides Order 1980, SI 1980/1079

s 1	Repealed
2	30 Jul 1980 (SI 1980/1079)
3	Repealed
4	20 Mar 1980 (RA)
Sch 1, 2	30 Jul 1980 (SI 1980/1079)

New Towns Act 1980 (c 36)

Whole Act repealed

Overseas Development and Co–operation Act 1980 (c 63)

RA: 13 Nov 1980

Commencement provisions: s 19(2)

14 Dec 1980 (s 19(2))

Papua New Guinea, Western Samoa and Nauru (Miscellaneous Provisions) Act 1980 (c 2)

RA: 31 Jan 1980

Commencement provisions: s 3(3)

s 1(1)	Repealed
(2), (3)	31 Jan 1980 (RA)
2	Repealed
3(1)	See Schedule below
(2)	Repealed
(3)	See Schedule below
4	31 Jan 1980 (RA)
Sch, para 1	16 Sep 1975 (retrospective; s 3(3))
2	31 Jan 1980 (RA)
3	16 Sep 1975 (retrospective; s 3(3))
4	31 Jan 1980 (RA)
5	16 Sep 1975 (retrospective; s 3(3))
6–14	31 Jan 1980 (RA)

Petroleum Revenue Tax Act 1980 (c 1)

RA: 31 Jan 1980

Commencement provisions: s 3(3)

s 1, 2(1), (2)	Effective for chargeable periods ending on or after 31 Dec 1979 (s 3(3))
2(3)	Repealed
3	31 Jan 1980 (RA); repealed in relation to chargeable periods beginning on or after 18 Aug 1989
Schedule	Effective for chargeable periods ending on or after 31 Dec 1979 (s 3(3))

Police Negotiating Board Act 1980 (c 10)

RA: 20 Mar 1980

Commencement provisions: s 3(2)

20 May 1980 (s 3(2))

Port of London (Financial Assistance) Act 1980 (c 31)

Whole Act repealed

Protection of Trading Interests Act 1980 (c 11)

RA: 20 Mar 1980

20 Mar 1980 (RA)

Representation of the People Act 1980 (c 3)

Whole Act repealed

Reserve Forces Act 1980 (c 9)

RA: 20 Mar 1980

Commencement provisions: s 158(4)

20 Apr 1980 (s 158(4))

Residential Homes Act 1980 (c 7)

Whole Act repealed

Sea Fish Industry Act 1980 (c 35)

Whole Act repealed

Slaughter of Animals (Scotland) Act 1980 (c 13)

RA: 20 Mar 1980

20 Mar 1980 (RA)

Social Security Act 1980 (c 30)

RA: 23 May 1980

Commencement provisions: s 21(5); Social Security Act 1980 (Commencement No 1)
Order 1980, SI 1980/729; Social Security Act 1980 (Commencement No 2)
Order 1981, SI 1981/1438; Social Security Act 1980 (Commencement No 3)
Order 1983, SI 1983/1002; Social Security Act 1980 (Commencement No 4)
Order 1984, SI 1984/1492

s 1, 2	Repealed
3, 4	23 May 1980 (s 21(5))
5	Repealed or spent
6(1)	24 Nov 1980 (SI 1980/729)
(2)	Repealed
(3)	24 Nov 1980 (SI 1980/729)
(4)	Spent
7	Repealed
8	23 May 1980 (SI 1980/729)
9	24 Nov 1980 (SI 1980/729)
10, 11	Repealed
12	23 May 1980 (s 21(5))
13–15	Repealed
16	23 May 1980 (s 21(5))
17, 18	Repealed
19–21	23 May 1980 (s 21(5))
Sch 1	Repealed
2	24 Nov 1980 (SI 1980/729)
3	Repealed
4, para 1, 2	24 Nov 1980 (SI 1980/729)
3	Spent
4	Repealed
5–7	24 Nov 1980 (SI 1980/729)
8	Spent
9, 10	Repealed
11–13	24 Nov 1980 (SI 1980/729)
14	Repealed
5, Pt I	23 May 1980 (s 21(5))
II	14 Jul 1980 (repeals of or in Social Security Act 1975, ss 44(5)(b), 47(2)(b), Sch 4, Pt IV; Social Security (Miscellaneous Provisions) Act 1977, s 8(3)) (SI 1980/729)
	24 Nov 1980 (repeals of or in Polish Resettlement Act 1947; National Assistance Act 1948; Legal Aid (Scotland) Act 1967; Social Work (Scotland)

Social Security Act 1980 (c 30)—*cont*

Sch 5, Pt II—*cont* Act 1968; Merchant Shipping Act 1970; Family Income Supplements Act 1970, ss 7(2), 10(2)(h); Housing (Financial Provisions) (Scotland) Act 1972; Housing Finance Act 1972; Legal Aid Act 1974; Social Security Act 1975, ss 138, 139, 142(5), 168(4), Sch 15; Social Security (Consequential Provisions) Act 1975; House of Commons Disqualification Act 1975; Northern Ireland Assembly Disqualification Act 1975; Social Security Pensions Act 1975; Child Benefit Act 1975; Supplementary Benefits Act 1976; National Insurance Surcharge Act 1976; Social Security (Miscellaneous Provisions) Act 1977, ss 14(1)–(4), (7)–(10), 15, 24(4); Employment Protection (Consolidation) Act 1978; Social Security Act 1979; Legal Aid Act 1979; Reserve Forces Act 1980) (SI 1980/729)

23 Nov 1981 (repeals of or in Social Security Act 1975, ss 44(3)(b), (6), 47 (so far as not already repealed), 66(1)(c), (8)) (SI1981/1438)

21 Nov 1983 (repeals of Social Security Act 1975, ss 44(5) (so far as not already repealed), 66(1)(b), Sch 20; Family Income Supplements Act 1970, s 17(1)) (SI 1983/1002)

26 Nov 1984 (repeal of Social Security Act 1975, ss 41(1), 65(4), 158, Sch 19) (SI 1984/1492)

Social Security (No 2) Act 1980 (c 39)

Whole Act repealed

Solicitors (Scotland) Act 1980 (c 46)

RA: 1 Aug 1980

Commencement provisions: s 67(3)

1 Sep 1980 (s 67(3))

Statute Law Revision (Northern Ireland) Act 1980 (c 59)

RA: 13 Nov 1980

13 Nov 1980 (RA)

Tenants' Rights, Etc (Scotland) Act 1980 (c 52)

RA: 8 Aug 1980

Commencement provisions: s 86(4); Tenants' Rights, etc (Scotland) Act 1980 (Commencement) Order 1980, SI 1980/1387

s 1–36	Repealed
37	1 Dec 1980 (SI 1980/1387)
38	Repealed

Tenants' Rights, Etc (Scotland) Act 1980 (c 52)—*cont*

s 39	1 Dec 1980 (SI 1980/1387)
40	Repealed
41	1 Dec 1980 (SI 1980/1387)
42–45	Repealed
46	1 Dec 1980 (SI 1980/1387)
47, 48	Repealed
49	1 Dec 1980 (SI 1980/1387)
50–63	Repealed
64, 65	1 Dec 1980 (SI 1980/1387)
66–73	Repealed
74	3 Oct 1980 (SI 1980/1387)
75–85	Repealed
86	3 Oct 1980 (SI 1980/1387)
Sch A1, 1–4	Repealed
5	3 Oct 1980 (except repeals of or in Reserve and Auxiliary Forces (Protection of Civil Interests) Act 1951, ss 16(1), (2)(c), (4)(b), 17(2)(a), (b), 18(2)(a), (b), 19(5); Rent (Scotland) Act 1971, ss 4(1), 5(4), (5), 7(1), (2), 9(1), 24, 25(1), 29, 30, 36, Pt V, ss 70–76, 80(2), 81, 82, 84, 85, 97(2), 100, 106(8), 110(1)(b), (2), 111(1), 113–115, 122(1)(b), 123(2), (3), 125(2), 129(2), 133, 135(1), Sch 2, Sch 3, Case 5, Case 6, Case 9, Schs 8, 10–12, 14, 16, 17, 19, paras 9, 10, 14(1) (c), 19(1); Fire Precautions Act 1971, Sch, Pt III, paras 1(1), (2)(a), (6), (7), 4; Housing (Financial Provisions) (Scotland) Act 1972, ss 61(3), 62(2), (4), 64, 65, Sch 7, paras 1–7; Local Government (Scotland) Act 1973, Sch 13, paras 4, 5, 7; Housing Act 1974, s 18(2), (5); Rent Act 1974, s 1(3); Criminal Procedure (Scotland) Act 1975, Sch 7C; Housing Rents and Subsidies (Scotland) Act 1975, ss 7–11, Schs 2, 3, para 5) (SI 1980/1387) 1 Dec 1980 (exceptions noted above) (SI 1980/1387)

Tenants' Rights, Etc (Scotland) (Amendment) Act 1980 (c 61)

Whole Act repealed

Transport Act 1980 (c 34)

RA: 30 Jun 1980

Commencement provisions: s 70; Transport Act 1980 (Commencement No 1) Order 1980, SI 1980/913; Transport Act 1980 (Commencement No 2) Order 1980, SI 1980/1353; Transport Act 1980 (Commencement No 3) Order 1980, SI 1980/1424; Transport Act 1980 (Commencement No 4) Order 1981, SI 1981/256

s 1–31	Repealed
32(1)–(4)	Repealed
(5)	6 Oct 1980 (SI 1980/1353)
33	Repealed
34	Spent

Transport Act 1980 (c 34)—*cont*

s 35–41	Repealed
42	Repealed except for sub-ss (1), (2)(b)(ii), which came into force on 6 Oct 1980 (SI 1980/1353)
43(1)	See Sch 5, Pt II below
(2)	Repealed
44	Repealed
45–50	30 Jun 1980 (s 70(3), but generally of no effect until 1 Oct 1980, the day appointed under s 45(2) by SI 1980/1380)
51(1)	30 Jun 1980 (s 70(3))
(2)	1 Oct 1980 (appointed day under SI 1980/1380)
52	30 Jun 1980 (s 70(3))
52A	Inserted by Railways Act 1993, s 134(1), Sch 11, para 9(2), (qv)
52B, 52C	Prospectively inserted by Railways Act 1993, s 134(1), Sch 11, para 9(3), (qv)
52D	Inserted (sub-ss (1)–(5), (9) prospectively) by Railways Act 1993, s 134(1), Sch 11, para 9(3) (qv)
	Not in force (exception noted above)
53–60	30 Jun 1980 (s 70(3))
61	Repealed
62	6 Oct 1980 (SI 1980/1353)
63	Repealed
64	31 Jul 1980 (SI 1980/913)
65	6 Oct 1980 (SI 1980/913)
66–68	30 Jun 1980 (s 70(3))
69	See Sch 9 below
70	30 Jun 1980 (s 70(3))
Sch 1–3	Repealed
4	6 Oct 1980 (SI 1980/913)
5, Pt I	Repealed
II	6 Oct 1980 (amendments of Local Government (Miscellaneous Provisions) Act 1953; Transport Act 1962; Road Traffic Act 1972; Road Traffic (Foreign Vehicles) Act 1972 (paras 1(b), 2 only); Local Government (Miscellaneous Provisions) Act 1976 (para 2 only); Energy Act 1976 (sub-paras (a) and (c) only)) (SI 1980/913)
	1 Apr 1981 (amendments of Road Traffic (Foreign Vehicles) Act 1972 (paras 1(a), 3); Road Traffic Act 1974; Local Government (Miscellaneous Provisions) Act 1976 (para 1); Energy Act 1976 (sub-para (b))) (SI 1981/256)
	Remainder repealed
6	30 Jun 1980 (s 70(3); but not generally effective until 1 Oct 1980, the date appointed under s 45(2) by SI 1980/1380)
7	1 Oct 1980 (appointed day under SI 1980/1380)
8	30 Jun 1980 (s 70(3))
9, Pt I	31 Jul 1980 (repeals of Road Traffic Act 1960, ss 144, 145(1), 147(1)(d), 154, 155, 158, 160(1)(f), 163(1); Transport (London) Act 1969, s 24(2), (3); Local Government (Scotland) Act 1973, Sch 18, para 30; Road Traffic Act 1974, Sch 6, para 2; Energy Act 1976, Sch 1, para 2) (SI 1980/913)

Transport Act 1980 (c 34)—*cont*

Sch 9, Pt I—*cont*
6 Oct 1980 (repeals of Education (Miscellaneous
Provisions) Act 1953, s 12; Transport Charges &c
(Miscellaneous Provisions) Act 1954, s 2, Sch 1;
Public Service Vehicles (Travel Concessions) Act
1955, s 1(7); Local Government (Omnibus
Shelters and Queue Barriers) (Scotland) Act 1958,
s 7(1); Road Traffic Act 1960, ss 117, 118,
119(3)(a), 128(2), 134–139, 139A, 140, 143(1)–(3),
(4), (9) (in so far as relate to road service licences),
149, 156(1), 160 (repeals in heads (a) and (c)), 234,
240, 247(2), 257(1), (definition of 'road service
licence'), 258, Schs 12, 17; Transport Act 1962,
Sch 2, Part I; London Government Act 1963,
ss 9(6)(b), 14(6)(d), Sch 5, Part I, para 25; Finance
Act 1965, s 92(8); Road Traffic Regulation Act
1967, s 1(3), Sch 6; Transport Act 1968, ss 21(1),
30, 138(1)(a), (3)(a), 145(1), 159(1); Transport
(London) Act 1969, ss 23(6), (7), 24(4)(b), (d),
Sch 3, paras 8, 11; Tribunals and Inquiries Act
1971, s 13(5), (6)(a), Sch 1, para 30(a) (in so far as
relate to road service licences); European
Communities Act 1972, Sch 4, para 10; Local
Government Act 1972, s 186(3); Local
Government (Scotland) Act 1973, Sch 18, paras
26, 31–35; Road Traffic Act 1974, Sch 5, Part I
(except the entries relating to the Road Traffic
Act 1960, ss 127, 128(3), 132(3), 148(2), 239),
Sch 6, para 1, Sch 7; Transport Act 1978, ss 6,
7(1), (2), 8, Schs 1, 2) (SI 1980/1353)

1 Apr 1981 (repeal of Road Traffic Act 1960, ss 127,
129, 130(2), 132, 133, 133A, 143 (so far as
unrepealed), 153(2), 257(1) (definition of
'owner'); Transport Act 1968, s 35(1), (2), (3)(a);
Tribunals and Inquiries Act 1971, s 13(5),
(6)(a), Sch 1, para 30(a) (so far as unrepealed);
Road Traffic Act 1972, s 44(4); Road Traffic Act
1974, Sch 2, paras 1, 3–5, Sch 5, Pt I (entries
relating to Road Traffic Act 1960, ss 127, 128(3),
132(2)); Transport Act 1978, s 5(10)) (SI 1981/256)

II
30 Jun 1980 (s 70(3))

III
1 Oct 1980 (date appointed by SI 1980/1380)

IV
1 Apr 1981 (SI 1981/256)

Water (Scotland) Act 1980 (c 45)

RA: 1 Aug 1980

1 Aug 1980 (RA)

1981

Acquisition of Land Act 1981 (c 67)

RA: 30 Oct 1981

Commencement provisions: s 35(2)

30 Jan 1982 (s 35(2))

Animal Health Act 1981 (c 22)

RA: 11 Jun 1981

Commencement provisions: s 97(3)

11 Jul 1981 (s 97(3))

Appropriation Act 1981 (c 51)

Whole Act repealed

Armed Forces Act 1981 (c 55)

RA: 28 Jul 1981

Commencement provisions: ss 1(5), 29(1)–(3), (5), Sch 5, Pt II, para 1; Armed Forces Act 1981 (Commencement No 1) Order 1981, SI 1981/1503; Armed Forces Act 1981 (Commencement No 2) Order 1982, SI 1982/497

s 1	Repealed
2–5	1 May 1982 (SI 1982/497)
6	1 Nov 1981 (SI 1981/1503)
7	28 Jul 1981 (s 29(4))
8	1 May 1982 (SI 1982/497)
9	Repealed
10–13	1 May 1982 (SI 1982/497)
14	1 May 1982 (SI 1982/497); prospectively repealed by Armed Forces Act 1991, ss 19(7), 26(2), Sch 3 (qv)
15–17	28 Jul 1981 (s 29(4))
18	1 May 1982 (SI 1982/497)
19–22	28 Jul 1981 (s 29(4))
23, 24	1 May 1982 (SI 1982/497)
25–27	28 Jul 1981 (s 29(4))
28(1)	1 May 1982 (SI 1982/497)
(2)	28 Jul 1981 (s 29(4))
29, 30	28 Jul 1981 (s 29(4))
Sch 1, 2	1 May 1982 (SI 1982/497)
3	28 Jul 1981 (s 29(4))

Armed Forces Act 1981 (c 55)—*cont*
Sch 4   1 May 1982 (SI 1982/497)
    5, Pt I   28 Jul 1982 (s 29(5), Sch 5, para 2)
      II   28 Jul 1982 (repeals of or in Naval Agency and
                      Distribution Act 1864, s 17; Naval and Marine Pay
                      and Pensions Act 1865, s 12; Army Pensions Act
                      1914; Naval Discipline Act 1957, s 93; Armed
                      Forces Act 1976, Sch 9) (s 29(5), Sch 5, para 1)
                  1 Sep 1981 (repeal of Armed Forces Act 1976, s 1)
                      (s 29(5), Sch 5, para 2)
                  1 May 1982 (repeals of or in Greenwich Hospital Act
                      1885, s 4; Colonial Naval Defence Act 1931, s 2(1);
                      Colonial Naval Defence Act 1949, s 1(4); Army Act
                      1955, ss 82(2)(b), 99(2), 131(2), 153(3), 209(3),
                      Sch 7, para 6; Air Force Act 1955, ss 82(2)(b), 99(2),
                      131(2), 153(3), 209(3); Naval Discipline Act 1957,
                      ss 51(1), (2), 101(2); Army and Air Force Act 1961,
                      s 26(3); Criminal Justice (Scotland) Act 1963, s 9(3),
                      (4); Armed Forces Act 1976, Sch 9, para 12) (s 29(1);
                      SI 1982/497)

Atomic Energy (Miscellaneous Provisions) Act 1981 (c 48)

RA: 27 Jul 1981

27 Jul 1981 (RA)

Belize Act 1981 (c 52)

RA: 28 Jul 1981

Commencement provisions: s 6(2); Belize Independence Order 1981, SI 1981/1107

21 Sep 1981 (Independence Day; SI 1981/1107)

Betting and Gaming Duties Act 1981 (c 63)

RA: 30 Oct 1981

30 Oct 1981 (RA)

British Nationality Act 1981 (c 61)

RA: 30 Oct 1981

Commencement provisions: s 53(2), (3); British Nationality Act 1981 (Commencement)
  Order 1982, SI 1982/933

    s 1–48   1 Jan 1983 (SI 1982/933)
      49   Repealed
      50–52   1 Jan 1983 (SI 1982/933)
      53   30 Oct 1981 (s 53(3))

Sch 1–9   1 Jan 1983 (SI 1982/933)

British Telecommunications Act 1981 (c 38)

RA: 27 Jul 1981

27 Jul 1981 (RA; note, however, that many provisions of the Act did not come into force until 1 Oct 1981, the date appointed by British Telecommunications Act 1981 (Appointed Day) Order 1981, SI 1981/1274, made under s 1(2) (repealed))

Broadcasting Act 1981 (c 68)

Whole Act repealed

Companies Act 1981 (c 62)

Whole Act repealed

Consolidated Fund Act 1981 (c 4)

Whole Act repealed

Consolidated Fund (No 2) Act 1981 (c 70)

Whole Act repealed

Compulsory Purchase (Vesting Declarations) Act 1981 (c 66)

RA: 30 Oct 1981

Commencement provisions: s 17(2)

30 Jan 1982 (s 17(2))

Contempt of Court Act 1981 (c 49)

RA: 27 Jul 1981

Commencement provisions: s 21(2), (3)

27 Aug 1981 (s 21(3) with the exception of the provisions relating to legal aid, which are *not in force* and are now, in part, repealed)

Countryside (Scotland) Act 1981 (c 44)

RA: 27 Jul 1981

Commencement provisions: s 18(2); Countryside (Scotland) Act 1981
(Commencement) Order 1981, SI 1981/1614

s 1	1 Apr 1982 (SI 1981/1614)
2–4	5 Nov 1981 (SI 1981/1614)
5	Repealed
6–14	5 Nov 1981 (SI 1981/1614)
15	See Sch 2 below
16–18	5 Nov 1981 (SI 1981/1614)
Sch 1	5 Nov 1981 (SI 1981/1614)
2	5 Nov 1981 (except repeal of Countryside (Scotland) Act 1967, ss 67, 68) (SI 1981/1614) 1 Apr 1982 (exception noted above) (SI 1981/1614)

Criminal Attempts Act 1981 (c 47)

RA: 27 Jul 1981

Commencement provisions: s 11(1)

27 Aug 1981 (s 11(1))

Criminal Justice (Amendment) Act 1981 (c 27)

RA: 2 Jul 1981

Commencement provisions: s 2(2)

2 Oct 1981 (s 2(2))

Deep Sea Mining (Temporary Provisions) Act 1981 (c 53)

RA: 28 Jul 1981

Commencement provisions: s 18(2); Deep Sea Mining (Temporary Provisions) Act 1981
(Appointed Day) Order 1982, SI 1982/52

25 Jan 1982 (SI 1982/52)

Disabled Persons Act 1981 (c 43)

RA: 27 Jul 1981

Commencement provisions: ss 6(6), 9(2)

s 1	27 Oct 1981 (s 9(2))
2, 3	Repealed
4, 5	27 Oct 1981 (s 9(2))
6	*Not in force*
7–9	27 Oct 1981 (s 9(2))

Disused Burial Grounds (Amendment) Act 1981 (c 18)

RA: 21 May 1981

21 May 1981 (RA)

Education Act 1981 (c 60)

RA: 31 Jul 1981

Commencement provisions: s 20(2); Education Act 1981 (Commencement No 1) Order 1981, SI 1981/1711; Education Act 1981 (Commencement No 2) Order 1983, SI 1983/7

Whole Act prospectively repealed except ss 2(1), 11(1), 17, 20(1), (2), (3), 21, Sch 2, para 1, Sch 3 paras 3, 4, 6, 7, 8(1), (2)(b), (d) 11, 12, 14, Sch 4 by Education Act 1993, s 307(1), Sch 21 (qv)

s 1	Repealed
2, 3	1 Apr 1983 (SI 1983/7)
3A	Inserted by Children Act 1989, s 108(4), Sch 12, para 36 (qv)
4–13	1 Apr 1983 (SI 1983/7)
14	5 Jan 1982 (SI 1981/1711)
15–19	1 Apr 1983 (SI 1983/7)
20	5 Jan 1982 (SI 1981/1711)
21(1), (2)	5 Jan 1982 (SI 1981/1711)
(3), (4)	1 Apr 1983 (SI 1983/7)
(5)	5 Jan 1982 (SI 1981/1711)
Sch 1–4	1 Apr 1983 (SI 1983/7)

Education (Scotland) Act 1981 (c 58)

RA: 30 Oct 1981

Commencement provisions: s 22(2), (3); Education (Scotland) Act 1981 (Commencement No 1) Order 1981, SI 1981/1557; Education (Scotland) Act 1981 (Commencement No 2) Order 1982, SI 1982/951; Education (Scotland) Act 1981 (Commencement No 3) Order 1982, SI 1982/1737; Education (Scotland) Act 1981 (Commencement No 4) Order 1983, SI 1983/371

s 1(1)	15 Feb 1982 (so far as inserts Education (Scotland) Act 1980, ss 28A, 28B (except s 28B(1)(d)), and s 28G so far as relates to those sections) (SI 1981/1557)
	15 Mar 1982 (so far as inserts Education (Scotland) Act 1980, ss 28C, 28D, 28E (except s 28E(2)), 28F and s 28G in so far as it relates to those sections) (SI 1981/1557)
	1 Jan 1983 (so far as inserts Education (Scotland) Act 1980, ss 28B(1)(d), 28E(2)) (SI 1982/951)
	9 Mar 1983 (so far as inserts Education (Scotland) Act 1980, s 28G so far as relates to ss 28B(1)(d), 28E(2) and Sch A1) (SI 1983/371)
	5 Apr 1983 (so far as inserts Education (Scotland) Act 1980, s 28H) (SI 1982/1737)

Education (Scotland) Act 1981 (c 58)—*cont*

s 1(2)	15 Mar 1982 (SI 1981/1557)
(3), (4)	15 Feb 1982 (SI 1981/1557)
2	15 Feb 1982 (SI 1981/1557)
3, 4	1 Jan 1983 (SI 1982/951)
5	16 Aug 1982 (SI 1982/951)
6–8	1 Dec 1981 (SI 1981/1557)
9–12	30 Oct 1981 (SI 1981/1557)
13(1)–(7)	1 Jan 1982 (SI 1981/1557)
(8)	16 Aug 1982 (SI 1982/951)
14	1 Jan 1982 (SI 1981/1557)
15	10 Nov 1981 (SI 1981/1557)
16	1 Jan 1983 (SI 1982/1737)
17–20	30 Oct 1981 (SI 1981/1557)
21(1)	See Sch 7 below
(2)	See Sch 8 below
(3)	See Sch 9 below
22	30 Oct 1981 (SI 1981/1557)

Sch 1	15 Mar 1982 (SI 1981/1557)
2, 3	1 Jan 1983 (SI 1982/951)
4	16 Aug 1982 (SI 1982/951)
5	1 Jan 1982 (SI 1981/1557)
6	10 Nov 1981 (SI 1981/1557)
7, para 1–3	30 Oct 1981 (SI 1981/1557)
4	1 Dec 1981 (SI 1981/1557)
5	30 Oct 1981 (SI 1981/1557)
6	15 Feb 1982 (so far as relates to Education (Scotland) Act 1980, ss 50, 51) (SI 1981/1557)
	1 Jan 1983 (so far as relates to Education (Scotland) Act 1980, ss 1(5)(c), (d), 28A(1) (as it has effect under the 1980 Act, Sch A2), 60–65F) (SI 1982/951)
7	15 Feb 1982 (SI 1981/1557)
8, para 1	1 Jan 1983 (SI 1982/951)
2	15 Feb 1982 (SI 1981/1557)
3	15 Mar 1982 (SI 1981/1557)
4	1 Jan 1983 (SI 1982/951)
5	30 Oct 1981 (SI 1981/1557)
6	1 Jan 1982 (SI 1981/1557)
7	30 Oct 1981 (SI 1981/1557)
9	30 Oct 1981 (repeals of or in Education (Scotland) Act 1980, ss 98(1), 132(1), Sch 2, paras 1, 3, 4) (SI 1981/1557)
	10 Nov 1981 (repeals of or in Education (Scotland) Act 1980, ss 104(2), 105(5), 108(2), 110(3), 111(1), (2), (3), (4), (5), 112(6), 113, 114(1), 115, 116, 117 (proviso), 121(b)) (SI 1981/1557)
	1 Dec 1981 (repeals of or in Education (Scotland) Act 1980, ss 7(1)(c), (8), 17(1), 22(1), (4), proviso (ii), 29) (SI 1981/1557)
	1 Jan 1982 (repeals in Education (Scotland) Act 1980, s 129(3), (4)(e), (5)) (SI 1981/1557)
	15 Feb 1982 (repeals of or in Education (Scotland) Act 1980, ss 23(2), proviso, 28(2)) (SI 1981/1557)
	16 Aug 1982 (repeal of Education (Scotland) Act 1980, s 129(6)) (SI 1982/951)

Education (Scotland) Act 1981 (c 58)—*cont*

Sch 9—*cont* 1 Jan 1983 (repeals of or in Education (Scotland) Act 1980, ss 4(b), (c), 5, 59, 135(1)) (SI 1982/951)
1 Jan 1983 (repeal of Education (Scotland) Act 1980, s 66(2)) (SI 1982/1737)

Employment and Training Act 1981 (c 57)

RA: 31 Jul 1981

Commencement provisions: s 11(3); Employment and Training Act 1981 (Commencement) Order 1982, SI 1982/126

s 1–8 Repealed
9–11 31 Jul 1981 (RA)

Sch 1 Repealed
2 31 Jul 1981 (RA)
3 31 Jul 1981 (except entry relating to Industrial Training Act 1964, Schedule) (RA)
1 Apr 1982 (entry relating to Industrial Training Act 1964, Schedule, except for the purposes of specified industrial training boards, but note whole of 1964 Act except s 16 was repealed as from 29 Jun 1982, except as applied to agricultural training boards) (SI 1982/126)

Energy Conservation Act 1981 (c 17)

RA: 21 May 1981

21 May 1981 (RA)

English Industrial Estates Corporation Act 1981 (c 13)

RA: 15 Apr 1981

Commencement provisions: s 10(2)

Whole Act prospectively repealed by Leasehold Reform, Housing and Urban Development Act 1993, s 187(2), Sch 22 (qv)

15 May 1981 (s 10(2))

European Parliamentary Elections Act 1981 (c 8)

RA: 19 Mar 1981

19 Mar 1981 (RA)

Film Levy Finance Act 1981 (c 16)

Whole Act repealed

Finance Act 1981 (c 35)

Budget day: 10 Mar 1981

RA: 27 Jul 1981

See the note about Finance Acts at the front of this book

Fisheries Act 1981 (c 29)

RA: 2 Jul 1981

Commencement provisions: s 46(3), (4); Fisheries Act 1981 (Commencement No 1)
Order 1981, SI 1981/1357; Fisheries Act 1981 (Commencement No 2) Order 1981,
SI 1981/1640

s 1–14	1 Oct 1981 (SI 1981/1357)
15–30	2 Aug 1981 (s 46(3))
31	18 Nov 1981 (SI 1981/1640)
32–45	2 Aug 1981 (s 46(3))
46	2 Aug 1981 (generally) (s 46(3))
	1 Oct 1981 (for the purposes of Sch 5, Pt I) (SI 1981/1357)
Sch 1–3	1 Oct 1981 (SI 1981/1357)
4	2 Aug 1981 (s 46(3))
5, Pt I	1 Oct 1981 (SI 1981/1357)
II	2 Aug 1981 (s 46(3))

Food and Drugs (Amendment) Act 1981 (c 26)

Whole Act repealed

Forestry Act 1981 (c 39)

RA: 27 Jul 1981

27 Jul 1981 (RA)

Forgery and Counterfeiting Act 1981 (c 45)

RA: 27 Jul 1981

Commencement provisions: s 33

28 Oct 1981 (s 33)

Friendly Societies Act 1981 (c 50)

RA: 27 Jul 1981

27 Jul 1981 (RA)

Gas Levy Act 1981 (c 3)

RA: 19 Mar 1981

19 Mar 1981 (RA)

Horserace Betting Levy Act 1981 (c 30)

RA: 2 Jul 1981

2 Jul 1981 (RA)

House of Commons Members' Fund and Parliamentary Pensions Act 1981 (c 7)

RA: 19 Mar 1981

19 Mar 1981 (RA)

Housing (Amendment) (Scotland) Act 1981 (c 72)

Whole Act repealed

Indecent Displays (Control) Act 1981 (c 42)

RA: 27 Jul 1981

Commencement provisions: s 5(5)

27 Oct 1981 (s 5(5))

Industrial Diseases (Notification) Act 1981 (c 25)

RA: 2 Jul 1981

2 Jul 1981 (RA)

Industry Act 1981 (c 6)

RA: 19 Mar 1981

Commencement provisions: s 7(2)

s 1	Repealed
2–4	19 Mar 1981 (RA)
5, 6	Repealed
7	19 Mar 1981 (RA)
Schedule	19 Mar 1981 (RA)

Insurance Companies Act 1981 (c 31)

RA: 2 Jul 1981

Commencement provisions: s 37(1); Insurance Companies Act 1981 (Commencement) Order 1981, SI 1981/1657

Insurance Companies Act 1981 (c 31)—*cont*
1 Jan 1982 (SI 1981/1657)

Whole Act repealed except ss 36(1), 38, Sch 4, Pt II (which make minor and
consequential amendments)

International Organisations Act 1981 (c 9)

RA: 15 Apr 1981

15 Apr 1981 (RA)

Iron and Steel Act 1981 (c 46)

Whole Act repealed

Iron and Steel (Borrowing Powers) Act 1981 (c 2)

Whole Act repealed

Judicial Pensions Act 1981 (c 20)

RA: 21 May 1981

Commencement provisions: s 37(2)

21 Jun 1981 (s 37(2))

Licensing (Alcohol Education and Research) Act 1981 (c 28)

RA: 2 Jul 1981

Commencement provisions: s 13(3); Licensing (Alcohol Education and Research) Act
1981 (Commencement) Order 1981, SI 1981/1324

1 Oct 1981 (SI 1981/1324)

Licensing (Amendment) Act 1981 (c 40)

RA: 27 Jul 1981

Commencement provisions: s 3(2); Licensing (Amendment) Act 1981 (Commencement)
Order 1982, SI 1982/1383

1 Oct 1982 (SI 1982/1383)

Local Government and Planning (Amendment) Act 1981 (c 41)

Whole Act repealed

Local Government (Miscellaneous Provisions) (Scotland) Act 1981 (c 23)

RA: 11 Jun 1981

Commencement provisions: s 43(2)–(4); Local Government (Miscellaneous Provisions) (Scotland) Act 1981 (Commencement No 1) Order 1981, SI 1981/1402

s 1	11 Jun 1981 (RA)
2–4	Repealed
5–8	1 Apr 1982 (s 43(3))
9, 10	Repealed
11	1 Jan 1982 (s 43(2))
12, 13	11 Jun 1981 (RA)
14, 15	Repealed
16, 17	11 Jun 1981 (RA); repealed as from 1 Apr 1994 by the Abolition of Domestic Rates etc (Scotland) Act 1987, Sch 6 (qv)
18, 19	Repealed
20	11 Jun 1981 (RA); repealed as from 1 Apr 1994 by the Abolition of Domestic Rates etc (Scotland) Act 1987, Sch 6 (qv)
21–23	Repealed
24–28	11 Jun 1981 (RA)
29	1 Oct 1981 (SI 1981/1402)
30–33	11 Jun 1981 (RA)
34, 35	Repealed
36	11 Jun 1981 (RA)
37	*Not in force*
38–40	11 Jun 1981 (RA)
41	See Sch 4 below
42, 43	11 Jun 1981 (RA)
Sch 1–3	11 Jun 1981 (RA)
4	11 Jun 1981 (except repeals of Local Government (Financial Provisions etc) (Scotland) Act 1962, s 4(2); Social Work (Scotland) Act 1968, s 7) (RA)
	1 Oct 1981 (repeal of Social Work (Scotland) Act 1968, s 7) (SI 1981/1402)
	1 Apr 1982 (repeal of Local Government (Financial Provisions etc) (Scotland) Act 1962, s 4(2)) (s 43(3))

Matrimonial Homes and Property Act 1981 (c 24)

RA: 2 Jul 1981

Commencement provisions: s 9; Matrimonial Homes and Property Act 1981 (Commencement No 1) Order 1981, SI 1981/1275; Matrimonial Homes and Property Act 1981 (Commencement No 2) Order 1983, SI 1983/50

s 1–3	Repealed
4(1)	14 Feb 1983 (SI 1983/50)
(2)–(4)	Repealed
5, 6	Repealed

Matrimonial Homes and Property Act 1981 (c 24)—*cont*

s 7–9	1 Oct 1981 (SI 1981/1275)
10(1)	1 Oct 1981 (SI 1981/1275)
(2)	14 Feb 1983 (SI 1983/50)
(3)	1 Oct 1981 (SI 1981/1275)
Sch 1, 2	Repealed
3	14 Feb (SI 1983/50)

Matrimonial Homes (Family Protection) (Scotland) Act 1981 (c 59)

RA: 30 Oct 1981

Commencement provisions: s 23(3); Matrimonial Homes (Family Protection) (Scotland) Act 1981 (Commencement) Order 1982, SI 1982/972

s 1–9	1 Sep 1982 (SI 1982/972)
10	Repealed
11–22	1 Sep 1982 (SI 1982/972)
23	30 Oct 1981 (RA)

Merchant Shipping Act 1981 (c 10)

RA: 15 Apr 1981

Commencement provisions: s 5(4); Merchant Shipping Act 1981 (Commencement No 1) Order 1981, SI 1981/1677; Merchant Shipping Act 1981 (Commencement No 2) Order 1983, SI 1983/1906; Merchant Shipping Act 1981 (Commencement No 3) Order 1984, SI 1984/1695

s 1	29 Nov 1984 (SI 1984/1695)
2	4 Feb 1984 (SI 1983/1906)
3	4 Feb 1984 (for purposes of Article IV of Rules set out in Schedule to Carriage of Goods by Sea Act 1971, as amended by s 2) (SI 1983/1906)
	29 Nov 1984 (for purposes of s 1) (SI 1984/1695)
4(1)	4 Feb 1984 (SI 1983/1906)
(2)	23 Dec 1981 (SI 1981/1677)
5(1), (2)	23 Dec 1981 (SI 1981/1677)
(3)	See the Schedule below
(4), (5)	23 Dec 1981 (SI 1981/1677)
(6)	4 Feb 1984 (SI 1983/1906)
Schedule	4 Feb 1984 (repeal of Carriage of Goods by Sea Act 1971, s 1(5)) (SI 1983/1906)
	29 Nov 1984 (repeals of or in Merchant Shipping (Liability of Shipowners and Others) Act 1958, s 1(1)–(4)) (SI 1984/1695)

National Film Finance Corporation Act 1981 (c 15)

Whole Act repealed

New Towns Act 1981 (c 64)

RA: 30 Oct 1981

Commencement provisions: s 82(4)

30 Nov 1981 (s 82(4))

Nuclear Industry (Finance) Act 1981 (c 71)

Whole Act repealed

Parliamentary Commissioner (Consular Complaints) Act 1981 (c 11)

RA: 15 Apr 1981

15 Apr 1981 (RA)

Ports (Financial Assistance) Act 1981 (c 21)

RA: 11 Jun 1981

11 Jun 1981 (RA)

Public Passenger Vehicles Act 1981 (c 14)

RA: 15 Apr 1981

Commencement provisions: s 89(2); Public Passenger Vehicles Act 1981
(Commencement) Order 1981, SI 1981/1387

s 1	30 Oct 1981 (s 89(2); SI 1981/1387)
2	Repealed
3	30 Oct 1981 (s 89(2); SI 1981/1387)
4, 5	Substituted by Transport Act 1985, s 3(2) (qv)
6	30 Oct 1981 (s 89(2); SI 1981/1387)
7	Repealed
8(1), (1A), (2)	Repealed
(3)	30 Oct 1981 (s 89(2); SI 1981/1837)
9	Repealed
9A	Inserted by Transport Act 1985, s 33 (qv)
10–14	30 Oct 1981 (s 89(2); SI 1981/1387)
14A	Inserted by Transport Act 1985, s 25 (qv)
15–17	30 Oct 1981 (s 89(2); SI 1981/1387)
17A	Inserted by Transport Act 1985, s 5 (qv)
18–21	30 Oct 1981 (s 89(2); SI 1981/1387)
22–23A	Repealed
24–27	30 Oct 1981 (s 89(2); SI 1981/1387)
28	Repealed
29	30 Oct 1981 (s 89(2); SI 1981/1387)
30–35	Repealed
35A	Inserted by London Regional Transport Act 1984, s 45(1) (qv)
36–45	Repealed
46	30 Oct 1981 (s 89(2); SI 1981/1387)
47–49	Repealed

Public Passenger Vehicles Act 1981 (c 14)—*cont*

s 50, 51	Substituted by Transport Act 1985, s 31 (qv))
52, 53	30 Oct 1981 (s 89(2); SI 1981/1387)
54	Substituted by Transport Act 1985, s 4 (qv)
55–61	30 Oct 1981 (s 89(2); SI 1981/1387)
62	Repealed
63–66	30 Oct 1981 (s 89(2); SI 1981/1387)
66A	Inserted by Transport Act 1982, s 24(4) (qv)
67–89	30 Oct 1981 (s 89(2), SI 1981/1387)
Sch 1	30 Oct 1981 (s 89(2); SI 1981/1387)
2	Substituted by Transport Act 1985, s 3(3), Sch 2, Pt I (qv)
3	30 Oct 1981 (s 89(2); SI 1981/1387)
4, 5	Repealed
6–8	30 Oct 1981 (s 89(2); SI 1981/1387)

Redundancy Fund Act 1981 (c 5)

Whole Act repealed

Representation of the People Act 1981 (c 34)

RA: 2 Jul 1981

2 Jul 1981 (RA)

Social Security Act 1981 (c 33)

RA: 2 Jul 1981

Commencement provisions: s 8(3); Social Security Act 1981 Commencement Order 1981, SI 1981/953

s 1	Repealed
2, 3	10 Aug 1981 (SI 1981/953)
4–6	Repealed
7	10 Aug 1981 (SI 1981/953)
8(1)	2 Jul 1981 (RA)
(2)	Repealed
(3)	2 Jul 1981 (RA)
(4), (5)	10 Aug 1981 (SI 1981/953)
(6)	2 Jul 1981 (RA)
Sch 1, 2	10 Aug 1981 (SI 1981/953)

Social Security (Contributions) Act 1981 (c 1)

Whole Act repealed

Statute Law (Repeals) Act 1981 (c 19)

RA: 21 May 1981

21 May 1981 (RA)

Supreme Court Act 1981 (c 54)

RA: 28 Jul 1981

Commencement provisions: s 153(2), (3)

s 1–28	1 Jan 1982 (s 153(2))
28A	Inserted by Statute Law (Repeals) Act 1993, s 1(2), Sch 2, para 9 (qv)
29–32	1 Jan 1982 (s 153(2))
32A	Inserted by Administration of Justice Act 1982, s 6(1) (qv)
33–35	1 Jan 1982 (s 153(2)); repealed so far as apply to County Courts
35A	Inserted by Administration of Justice Act 1982, s 15(1), Sch 1, Pt I (qv)
36–40	1 Jan 1982 (s 153(2))
40A	Inserted by Administration of Justice Act 1982, s 55(1), Sch 4, Pt I (qv)
41–43	1 Jan 1982 (s 153(2))
43A	Inserted by Courts and Legal Services Act 1990, s 100 (qv)
44–50	1 Jan 1982 (s 153(2))
51	Substituted by Courts and Legal Services Act 1990, s 4(1) (qv)
52–71	1 Jan 1982 (s 153(2))
72	28 Jul 1981 (s 153(3))
73–82	1 Jan 1982 (s 153(2))
83	Substituted by Courts and Legal Services Act 1990, s 67 (qv)
84–93	1 Jan 1982 (s 153 (2))
94	Repealed
95–102	1 Jan 1982 (s 153(2))
103	1 Jan 1982 (s 153(2)); prospectively repealed by Judicial Pensions and Retirement Act 1993, s 31(4), Sch 9 (qv)
104–125	1 Jan 1982 (s 153(2))
126	1 Jan 1982 (s 153(2)); prospectively repealed by Administration of Justice Act 1982, s 75, Sch 9, Pt I (qv)
127–138	1 Jan 1982 (s 153(2))
138A, 138B	Inserted by Statute Law (Repeals) Act 1989, s 1(2), Sch 2, Pt I, para 4 (qv)
139–142	1 Jan 1982 (s 153(2))
143, 144	Repealed
145–148	1 Jan 1982 (s 153(2))
149	Repealed
150, 151	1 Jan 1982 (s 153(2))
152(1)	1 Jan 1982 (s 153(2))
(2)	Spent
(3)–(5)	1 Jan 1982 (s 153(2))
153	28 Jul 1981 (s 153(3))
Sch 1	1 Jan 1982 (s 153(2))
2	Substituted by Courts and Legal Services Act 1990, s 71(2), Sch 10, para 49 (qv)
3	Repealed
4–7	1 Jan 1982 (s 153(2))

Town and Country Planning (Minerals) Act 1981 (c 36)

Whole Act repealed or spent

Transport Act 1962 (Amendment) Act 1981 (c 32)

RA: 2 Jul 1981

Commencement provisions: s 2(2)

Whole Act prospectively repealed by Railways Act 1993, s 152(3), Sch 14 (qv)

2 Aug 1981 (s 2(2))

Transport Act 1981 (c 56)

RA: 31 Jul 1981

Commencement provisions: ss 5, 15(1), (2), 18(3), 31, 32(2), 35(5), 40(4); Transport Act
   1981 (Commencement No 1) Order 1981, SI 1981/1331; Transport Act 1981
   (Dissolution of National Ports Council) (Appointed Day) Order 1981, SI 1981/
   1364; Transport Act 1981 (Commencement No 2) Order 1981, SI 1981/1617;
   Transport Act 1981 (Dissolution of National Ports Council) (Final) Order 1981,
   SI 1981/1665; Transport Act 1981 (Commencement No 3) Order 1982, SI 1982/
   300; Transport Act 1981 (Commencement No 4) Order 1982, SI 1982/310;
   Transport Act 1981 (Commencement No 5) Order 1982, SI 1982/866; Transport
   Act 1981 (Commencement No 6) Order 1982, SI 1982/1341; Transport Act 1981
   (Commencement No 7) Order 1982, SI 1982/1451; Transport Act 1981
   (Commencement No 8) Order 1982, SI 1982/1803; Transport Act 1981
   (Commencement No 9) Order 1983, SI 1983/576; Transport Act 1981
   (Commencement No 10) Order 1983, SI 1983/930; Transport Act 1981
   (Commencement No 11) Order 1983, SI 1983/1089; Transport Act 1981
   (Commencement No 12) Order 1988, SI 1988/1037; Transport Act 1981
   (Commencement No 13) Order 1988, SI 1988/1170

s 1–4	31 Jul 1981 (RA)
	31 Dec 1982 (appointed day for reconstitution of the British Transport Docks Board) (s 5; SI 1982/1887); prospectively repealed by Railways Act 1993, s 152(3), Sch 14 (qv)
5	31 Jul 1981 (RA)
	31 Dec 1982 (appointed day for reconstitution of the British Transport Docks Board (s 5; SI 1982/1887)
6–15	31 Jul 1981 (RA)
	1 Oct 1981 (date on which the functions of the National Ports Council were determined) (s 15(1); SI 1981/1364)
	1 Dec 1981 (date on which the National Ports Council was dissolved) (s 15(2); SI 1981/1665)
16, 17	31 Jul 1981 (RA)
18	See Sch 6 below
19–31	Repealed
32	25 Aug 1983 (EW) (s 32(2); SI 1983/1089); repealed (S)
33, 34	Repealed
35(1), (2)	1 Apr 1982 (s 35(5); SI 1982/310)
(3)–(5)	12 Oct 1981 (s 35(5); SI 1981/1331)

Transport Act 1981 (c 56)—*cont*
s 36	31 Jul 1981 (RA); prospectively repealed by Railways Act 1993, s 140(8) (qv)
37–43	31 Jul 1981 (RA)
Sch 1	31 Jul 1981 (RA); prospectively repealed by Railways Act 1993, s 152(3), Sch 14 (qv)
2–5	31 Jul 1981 (RA)
6, para 1–9	1 Oct 1981 (s 18(2); SI 1981/1364)
10	2 Aug 1983 (s 18(3); SI 1983/930)
11–15	1 Oct 1986 (s 18(2); SI 1981/1364)
7, 8	Repealed
9, para 1–24	Repealed
25	6 May 1983 (s 31; SI 1983/576)
10	25 Aug 1983 (EW) (s 32(2); SI 1983/1089); repealed (S)
11	Repealed
12, Pt I	31 Dec 1982 (ss 5(4), 40(2))
II	1 Oct 1981 (except repeal of entry for National Ports Council in House of Commons Disqualification Act 1975, Sch 1, Pt II) (ss 5(3), 15(1))
	1 Dec 1981 (exception noted above) (s 15(1))
III	31 Jul 1981 (repeals of or in Railway Fires Act (1905) Amendment Act 1923; Public Passenger Vehicles Act 1981) (s 40(4))
	12 Oct 1981 (repeal of Town Police Clauses Act 1847, s 39) (s 40(4); SI 1981/1331)
	1 Apr 1982 (repeal in Metropolitan Public Carriage Act 1869) (s 40(4); SI 1982/310)
	1 Nov 1982 (repeals of or in Road Traffic Act 1972, ss 93(3), (5), 177(2)) (s 40(4); SI 1982/1451)
	6 May 1983 (repeals of or in Road Traffic Act 1972, ss 89, 90, 189, Sch 4, Pt V, para 1) (s 40(4); SI 1983/576)
	25 Aug 1983 (repeal of entry relating to Road Traffic Act 1974, s 17) (EW) (s 40(4); SI 1983/1089)
	Not in force (repeals of or in Road Traffic Act 1974, Sch 3; British Railways (No 2) Act 1975, s 21; London Transport Act 1977, s 13(1); British Railways Act 1977, s 14(1); Criminal Justice (Scotland) Act 1980, Sch 7, para 22)

Trustee Savings Banks Act 1981 (c 65)

Whole Act repealed

Water Act 1981 (c 12)

RA: 15 Apr 1981

Commencement provisions: ss 2(5), 6(8); Water Act 1981 (Commencement No 1) Order 1981, SI 1981/1755

s 1	15 Apr 1981 (RA)
2–6	Repealed
7	15 Apr 1981 (RA)

Wildlife and Countryside Act 1981 (c 69)

RA: 30 Oct 1981

Commencement provisions: s 74(2), (3); Wildlife and Countryside Act 1981 (Commencement No 1) Order 1982, SI 1982/44; Wildlife and Countryside (Commencement No 2) Order 1982, SI 1982/327; Wildlife and Countryside Act 1981 (Commencement No 3) Order 1982, SI 1982/990; Wildlife and Countryside Act 1981 (Commencement No 4) Order 1982, SI 1982/1136; Wildlife and Countryside Act 1981 (Commencement No 5) Order 1982, SI 1982/1217; Wildlife and Countryside Act 1981 (Commencement No 6) Order 1983, SI 1983/20; Wildlife and Countryside Act 1981 (Commencement No 7) Order 1983, SI 1983/87

s 1–11	28 Sep 1982 (SI 1982/1217)
12	16 Feb 1982 (SI 1982/44)
13–19	28 Sep 1982 (SI 1982/1217)
19A	Inserted (S) by Prisoners and Criminal Proceedings (Scotland) Act 1993, s 36 (qv)
20–27	28 Sep 1982 (SI 1982/1217)
27A	Inserted by Environmental Protection Act 1990, s 132 (qv)
28	30 Nov 1981 (s 74(2))
29–31	6 Sep 1982 (SI 1982/1136)
32	28 Feb 1983 (SI 1983/87)
33–37	30 Nov 1981 (s 74(2))
38	Repealed
39, 40	30 Nov 1981 (s 74(2))
41	28 Feb 1983 (SI 1983/87)
42–45	30 Nov 1981 (s 74(2))
46	19 Aug 1982 (SI 1982/990)
47	1 Apr 1982 (SI 1982/327)
48	Repealed
49–52	30 Nov 1981 (s 74(2))
53–59	28 Feb 1983 (SI 1983/20)
60, 61	Repealed
62–66	28 Feb 1983 (SI 1983/20)
67–70	30 Nov 1981 (s 74(2))
70A	Inserted by Wildlife and Countryside (Service of Notices) Act 1985 s 1(1) (qv)
71	30 Nov 1981 (s 74(2))
72(1)	Repealed
(2), (3)	30 Nov 1981 (s 74(2))
(4)	28 Sep 1982 (SI 1982/1217)
(5)	30 Nov 1981 (s 74(2))
(6)	28 Sep 1982 (SI 1982/1217)
(7)–(13)	30 Nov 1981 (s 74(2))
(14)	28 Sep 1982 (SI 1982/1217)
73(1)	See Sch 17
(2), (3)	30 Nov 1981 (s 74(2))
(4)	Repealed
74	30 Nov 1981 (s 74(2))
Sch 1–6	28 Sep 1982 (SI 1982/1217)
7	16 Feb 1982 (SI 1982/44)
8–10	28 Sep 1982 (SI 1982/1217)
11	30 Nov 1981 (so far as relates to orders under s 34) (s 74(2))
	6 Sep 1982 (so far as relates to orders under s 29) (SI 1982/1136)

Wildlife and Countryside Act 1981 (c 69)—*cont*

Sch 12	30 Nov 1981 (s 74(2))
13	1 Apr 1982 (SI 1982/327)
14–16	28 Feb 1983 (SI 1983/20)
17, Pt I	30 Nov 1981 (s 74(2))
II	16 Feb 1982 (repeals of or in Deer Act 1963, Sch 2; Conservation of Seals Act 1970, s 10(1); Badgers Act 1973, ss 6, 7, 8(2)(c), 11) (SI 1982/44)

1 Apr 1982 (repeals of or in National Parks and Access to the Countryside Act 1949, ss 2, 4, 95; Countryside Act 1968, s 3) (SI 1982/327)

28 Sep 1982 (repeals of or in Protection of Animals (Scotland) Act 1912, s 9; Protection of Birds Act 1954 (Amendment) Act 1964; Protection of Birds Act 1967; Countryside Act 1968, s 1; Local Government Act 1972, Sch 29, para 37; Water Act 1973, Sch 8, para 67; Nature Conservancy Council Act 1973, s 5(3), Sch 1, paras 3, 5, 7, 12; Local Government (Scotland) Act 1973, Sch 27, Pt II, paras 115, 168; Criminal Procedure (Scotland) Act 1975, Sch 7C; Conservation of Wild Creatures and Wild Plants Act 1975; Statute Law (Repeals) Act 1976, Sch 2, Pt II; Endangered Species (Import and Export) Act 1976, s 13(6); Criminal Law Act 1977, Sch 6; Customs and Excise Management Act 1979, Sch 4, para 12; Animal Health Act 1981, Sch 5, para 1; Zoo Licensing Act 1981, s 4(5)) (SI 1982/1217)

28 Feb 1983 (repeals of or in National Parks and Access to the Countryside Act 1949, ss 27–35, 38; London Government Act 1963, s 60(1)–(4); Countryside Act 1968, Sch 3; Courts Act 1971, Sch 8, para 31, Sch 9, Pt II; Town and Country Planning Act 1971, Sch 20; Local Government Act 1972, Sch 17; Highways Act 1980, ss 31(10), 340(2)(d)) (SI 1983/20)

Zoo Licensing Act 1981 (c 37)

RA: 27 Jul 1981

Commencement provisions: s 23(2); Zoo Licensing Act 1981 (Commencement) Order 1984, SI 1984/423

30 Apr 1984 (SI 1984/423)

1982

Administration of Justice Act 1982 (c 53)

RA: 28 Oct 1982

Commencement provisions: s 76; Administration of Justice Act 1982 (Commencement No 1) Order 1983, SI 1983/236; Administration of Justice Act 1982 (Commencement No 2) Order 1984, SI 1984/1142; Administration of Justice Act 1982 (Commencement No 3) Order 1984, SI 1984/1287; Administration of Justice Act 1982 (Commencement No 4) Order 1985, SI 1985/858; Administration of Justice Act 1982 (Commencement No 5) Order 1986, SI 1986/ 2259; Administration of Justice Act 1982 (Commencement No 6) Order 1991, SI 1991/1245; Administration of Justice Act 1982 (Commencement No 7) Order 1991, SI 1991/1786

s 1–5	1 Jan 1983 (s 76(11))
6	1 Jul 1985 (SI 1985/858)
7–11	1 Jan 1983 (s 76(11))
12	1 Sep 1984 (SI 1984/1287)
13	1 Jan 1983 (s 76(11))
14(1)	1 Jan 1983 (s 76(11))
(2)	1 Sep 1984 (SI 1984/1287)
(3), (4)	1 Jan 1983 (s 76(11))
15, 16	1 Apr 1983 (SI 1983/236)
17–22	1 Jan 1983 (s 76(11))
23–25	*Not in force*
26	1 Jan 1983 (s 76(11))
27, 28	*Not in force*
29–33	Repealed
34	1 Sep 1984 (SI 1984/1142)
35	Spent
36	Repealed
37	1 Jan 1983 (s 76(11))
38–47	2 Jan 1987 (SI 1986/2259)
48	*Not in force*
49–51	1 Jan 1983 (s 76(11))
52	28 Oct 1982 (s 76(9), (10))
53	1 Jan 1983 (s 76(11))
54	1 Apr 1983 (SI 1983/236)
55, 56	1 Jan 1983 (s 76(11))
57	1 Apr 1983 (SI 1983/236)
58, 59	1 Jan 1983 (s 76(11))
60	Repealed
61	1 Jan 1983 (s 76(11))
62	Repealed
63	1 Jan 1983 (s 76(11))
64, 65	28 Oct 1982 (s 76(9), (10))
66, 67	1 Jan 1983 (s 76(11))
68	See Sch 6 below

Administration of Justice Act 1982 (c 53)—*cont*

s 69	1 Jun 1983 (SI 1983/236)
70	See Sch 8 below
71	Repealed
72	1 Jan 1983 (s 76(11))
73(1)–(7)	1 Jan 1983 (s 76(11))
(8)	Spent
(9)	1 Jan 1983 (s 76(11))
74	Repealed
75	See Sch 9 below
76–78	28 Oct 1982 (s 76(9), (10))
Sch 1	1 Apr 1983 (SI 1983/236)
2	*Not in force*
3–5	1 Jan 1983 (s 76(11))
6, para 1–9	1 Jan 1983 (s 76(11))
10	1 Sep 1991 (SI 1991/1786)
7	1 Jun 1983 (SI 1983/236)
8, para 1–5	1 Jan 1983 (s 76(11))
6–8	13 Jun 1991 (SI 1991/1245)
9–12	1 Jan 1983 (s 76(11))
9, Pt I	1 Jan 1983 (except repeals noted below) (s 76(11))
	1 Apr 1983 (repeal in Judicial Trustees Act 1896) (SI 1983/236)
	1 Jun 1983 (repeal of Law Reform (Miscellaneous Provisions) Act (Northern Ireland) 1937, s 17) (SI 1983/236)
	1 Sep 1984 (repeal in County Courts Act 1959, s 148) (SI 1984/1142)
	1 Sep 1984 (repeal in Damages (Scotland) Act 1976) (SI 1984/1287)
	2 Jan 1987 (repeal of County Courts Act 1959, ss 99(3), 168–174A, 176) (SI 1986/2259)
	13 Jun 1991 (repeals of Administration of Justice Act 1965, ss 1–16; Judicature (Northern Ireland) Act 1978, s 83) (SI 1991/1245)
	Not in force (repeals of or in Prevention of Fraud (Investments) Act 1958; Administration of Justice Act 1977; Supreme Court Act 1981, s 126)
II	1 Jan 1983 (revocation of or in SI 1967/761; SI 1977/1251) (s 76(11))
	Not in force (revocation in SI 1979/1575)

Agricultural Training Board Act 1982 (c 9)

RA: 29 Mar 1982

Commencement provisions: s 12(3)

29 Jun 1982 (s 12(3))

Appropriation Act 1982 (c 40)

Whole Act repealed

Aviation Security Act 1982 (c 36)

RA: 23 Jul 1982

Commencement provisions: s 41(2)

23 Oct 1982 (s 41(2))

Canada Act 1982 (c 11)

RA: 29 Mar 1982

29 Mar 1982 (RA)

Children's Homes Act 1982 (c 20)

Whole Act repealed

Cinematograph (Amendment) Act 1982 (c 33)

Whole Act repealed

Civic Government (Scotland) Act 1982 (c 45)

RA: 28 Oct 1982

Commencement provisions: s 137(2)–(4); Civic Government (Scotland) Act 1982 (Commencement) Order 1983, SI 1983/201 (as amended by SI 1984/573, SI 1984/774)

s 1–8	1 Apr 1983 (for purpose only of enabling preliminary arrangements to be made for when provisions fully effective in operation) (SI 1983/201)
	1 July 1984 (otherwise) (SI 1983/201)
9–23	1 Apr 1983 (for purpose only of enabling preliminary arrangements to be made for when provisions fully effective in operation) (SI 1983/201)
	1 July 1984 (otherwise, except in relation to areas of local authorities noted below) (SI 1983/201, as amended by SI 1984/744)
	2 Aug 1984 (as respects the area of Lochaber District Council) (SI 1984/744)
	20 Aug 1984 (as respects the area of the City of Glasgow District Council) (SI 1984/744)
	20 Sep 1984 (as respects the area of Wigtown District Council) (SI 1984/744)
	1 Nov 1984 (as respects the area of Cunninghame District Council) (SI 1984/744)
24–27	As noted to ss 9–23 above, and in addition:
	1 Jan 1985 (as respects the area of Monklands District Council) (SI 1984/744)

Civic Government (Scotland) Act 1982 (c 45)—*cont*

s 28–37	1 Apr 1983 (for purpose only of enabling preliminary arrangements to be made for when provisions fully effective in operation) (SI 1983/201)
	1 July 1984 (otherwise) (SI 1983/201)
38–40	As noted to ss 9–23, 24–27 above
41A	Inserted by the Fire Safety and Safety of Places of Sport Act 1987, s 44 (qv)
42–44	As noted to ss 9–23, 24–27 above
45–52	1 Apr 1983 (SI 1983/201)
52A	Inserted by Criminal Justice Act 1988, s 161 (qv)
53–61	1 Apr 1983 (SI 1983/201)
62–66	1 Apr 1983 (for purpose only of enabling preliminary arrangements to be made for when provisions fully effective in operation) (SI 1983/201)
	1 July 1984 (otherwise) (SI 1983/201)
67–109	1 Apr 1983 (SI 1983/201)
110(1)	1 Apr 1983 (so far as relates to s 110(2)) (SI 1983/201)
	1 July 1984 (otherwise) (SI 1983/201)
(2)	1 Apr 1983 (SI 1983/201)
(3)	1 July 1984 (SI 1983/201)
111–118	1 Apr 1983 (SI 1983/201)
119	18 Apr 1984 (for purpose only of enabling preliminary arrangements to be made for when provisions fully effective in operation) (SI 1983/201, as amended by SI 1984/573)
	1 July 1984 (otherwise) (SI 1983/201)
120–123	1 Apr 1983 (SI 1983/201)
124, 125	Prospectively repealed, subject to transitional and saving provisions by the Environmental Protection Act 1990, s 162(1), (2), Sch 16, Pt II (qv)
126(1)	Repealed
(2)	1 Apr 1983 (SI 1983/201)
(3)	Repealed
127	1 Apr (SI 1983/201)
128(1)	Repealed
(2), (3)	1 Apr 1983 (SI 1983/201)
129–133	1 Apr 1983 (SI 1983/201)
134–136	28 Oct 1982 (s 137(2))
137(1)–(6)	28 Oct 1982 (s 137(2))
(7)	See Sch 3 below
(8)	See Sch 4 below
(9)	28 Oct 1982 (s 137(2))
Sch 1	1 Apr 1983 (for purpose only of enabling preliminary arrangements to be made for when provisions fully effective in operation) (SI 1983/201)
	1 July 1984 (otherwise) (SI 1983/201)
2	1 Apr 1983 (SI 1983/201)
3, para 1	Repealed
2, 3	1 Apr 1983 (SI 1983/201)
4	Repealed
5	1 July 1984 (SI 1983/201)
4	1 Apr 1983 (repeals of or in Vagrancy Act 1824, s 4; Prevention of Crime Act 1871, ss 7, 15; Licensing

Civic Government (Scotland) Act 1982 (c 45)—*cont*
Sch 4—*cont*   (Scotland) Act 1903; Dogs Act 1906, s 3(6), (7);
                            Countryside (Scotland) Act 1967, ss 56, 57(1), (2);
                            Theatres Act 1968, s 2(4)(c); Sexual Offences
                            (Scotland) Act 1976, s 13(3)) (SI 1983/201)
                            1 July 1984 (otherwise) (SI 1983/201)

Civil Aviation Act 1982 (c 16)

RA: 27 May 1982

Commencement provisions: s 110(2)

27 Aug 1982 (s 110(2))

Civil Aviation (Amendment) Act 1982 (c 1)

RA: 2 Feb 1982

2 Feb 1982 (RA)

Civil Jurisdiction and Judgments Act 1982 (c 27)

RA: 13 Jul 1982

Commencement provisions: s 53(1), Sch 13, Pt I; Civil Jurisdiction and Judgments Act
    1982 (Commencement No 1) Order 1984, SI 1984/1553; Civil Jurisdiction and
    Judgments Act 1982 (Commencement No 2) Order 1986, SI 1986/1781; Civil
    Jurisdiction and Judgments Act 1982 (Commencement No 3) Order 1986,
    SI 1986/2044

s 1–3	1 Jan 1987 (SI 1986/2044)
3A, 3B	Inserted by Civil Jurisdiction and Judgments Act 1991, s 1(1) (qv)
4–23	1 Jan 1987 (SI 1986/2044)
24(1)(a)	24 Aug 1982 (s 53(1), Sch 13, Pt I)
(b)	1 Jan 1987 (SI 1986/2044)
(2)(a)	24 Aug 1982 (s 53(1), Sch 13, Pt I)
(b)	1 Jan 1987 (SI 1986/2044)
(3)	24 Aug 1982 (s 53(1), Sch 13, Pt I)
25	1 Jan 1987 (SI 1986/2044)
26	1 Nov 1984 (SI 1984/1553)
27, 28	1 Jan 1987 (SI 1986/2044)
29–34	24 Aug 1982 (s 53(1), Sch 13, Pt I)
35(1)	14 Nov 1986 (SI 1986/1781)
(2)	1 Jan 1987 (SI 1986/2044)
(3)	24 Aug 1982 (s 53(1), Sch 13, Pt I)
36, 37	1 Jan 1987 (SI 1986/2044)
38	24 Aug 1982 (s 52(1), Sch 13, Pt I)
39	1 Jan 1987 (SI 1986/2044)
40	24 Aug 1982 (s 53(1), Sch 13, Pt I)
41–48	1 Jan 1987 (SI 1986/2044)
49–52	24 Aug 1982 (s 53(1), Sch 13, Pt I)
53(1)	13 Jul 1982 (s 53(1), Sch 13, Pt I)
(2)	24 Aug 1982 (so far as relates to Sch 13, Pt II, paras 7–10) (s 53(1), Sch 13, Pt I)

Civil Jurisdiction and Judgments Act 1982 (c 27)—*cont*
s 53(2)—*cont*	1 Nov 1984 (so far as relates to Sch 13, Pt II, para 6) (SI 1984/1553)
	1 Jan 1987 (otherwise) (SI 1986/2044)
54	24 Aug 1982 (so far as relates to repeal in Foreign Judgments (Reciprocal Enforcement) Act 1933, s 4) (s 53(1), Sch 13, Pt I)
	1 Jan 1987 (otherwise) (SI 1986/2044)
55	13 Jul 1982 (s 53(1), Sch 13, Pt I).
Sch 1–3	Substituted by Civil Jurisdiction and Judgments Act 1982 (Amendment) Order 1990, SI 1990/2591, art 12(1)–(3), Schs 1–3
3A	Inserted by Civil Jurisdiction and Judgments Act 1982 (Amendment) Order 1989, SI 1989/1346, art 9(3), Sch 3
3B	Inserted by Civil Jurisdiction and Judgments Act 1982 (Amendment) Order 1990, SI 1990/2591, art 12(4), Sch 4
3C	Inserted by Civil Jurisdiction and Judgements Act 1991, s 1(3), Sch 1 (qv)
4–12	1 Jan 1987 (SI 1986/2044)
13, Pt I	13 Jul 1982 (s 53(1), Sch 13, Pt I, para 2)
II para 1–5	1 Jan 1987 (SI 1986/2044)
6	1 Nov 1984 (SI 1984/1553)
7–10	24 Aug 1982 (s 53(1), Sch 13, Pt I, para 2)
14	24 Aug 1982 (repeals in Foreign Judgments (Reciprocal Enforcement) Act 1933, s 4) (s 53(1), Sch 13, Pt I)
	1 Jan 1987 (otherwise) (SI 1986/2044)

Clergy Pensions (Amendment) Measure 1982 (No 2)

RA: 23 Jul 1982

23 Jul 1982 (RA)

Coal Industry Act 1982 (c 15)

RA: 7 Apr 1982

7 Apr 1982 (RA)

Commonwealth Development Corporation Act 1982 (c 54)

RA: 22 Dec 1982

22 Dec 1982 (RA)

Consolidated Fund Act 1982 (c 8)

Whole Act repealed

Copyright Act 1956 (Amendment) Act 1982 (c 35)

Whole Act repealed

Criminal Justice Act 1982 (c 48)

RA: 28 Oct 1982

Commencement provisions: s 80; Criminal Justice Act 1982 (Commencement No 1) Order 1982, SI 1982/1857; Criminal Justice Act 1982 (Scotland) (Commencement No 1) Order 1983, SI 1983/24; Criminal Justice Act 1982 (Commencement No 2) Order 1983, SI 1983/182; Criminal Justice Act 1982 (Scotland) (Commencement No 2) Order 1983, SI 1983/758

s 1	24 May 1983 (SI 1983/182)
1A–1C	Inserted by Criminal Justice Act 1988, s 123(1), (4) (qv)
2	Repealed
3	24 May 1983 (SI 1983/182)
4–7	Repealed
8–13	24 May 1983 (SI 1983/182)
14	Repealed
15	Repealed
16–21	24 May 1983 (SI 1983/182)
22–25	Repealed
26	21 Jan 1983 (SI 1982/1857)
27	Repealed
28	21 Jan 1983 (SI 1982/1857)
29	24 May 1983 (SI 1983/182)
30, 31	31 Jan 1983 (SI 1982/1857)
32	28 Oct 1982 (s 80(1))
33, 34	Repealed
35–40	11 Apr 1983 (SI 1982/1857)
41, 42	11 Apr 1983 (SI 1982/1857; SI 1983/24)
43	Repealed
44, 45	11 Apr 1983 (SI 1982/1857; SI 1983/24)
46	11 Apr 1983 (SI 1982/1857)
47(1)	11 Apr 1983 (SI 1982/1857)
(2)	11 Apr 1983 (SI 1982/1857; SI 1983/24)
48	11 Apr 1983 (SI 1982/1857)
49, 50	11 Apr 1983 (SI 1982/1857; SI 1983/24)
51	24 May 1983 (SI 1983/182)
52	31 Jan 1983 (SI 1982/1857)
53–56	11 Apr 1983 (SI 1983/24)
57	28 Oct 1982 (s 80(1))
58	24 May 1983 (SI 1983/182; SI 1983/758)
59–61	24 May 1983 (SI 1983/182)
62	Repealed
63	31 Jan 1983 (SI 1982/1857)
64	31 Jan 1983 (SI 1982/1857; SI 1983/24)
65	Repealed (with savings)
66, 67	31 Jan 1983 (SI 1982/1857)
68(1)	24 May 1983 (SI 1983/182)
(2)	24 May 1983 (SI 1983/182; SI 1983/758)
69	24 May 1983 (SI 1983/182)
70, 71	31 Jan 1983 (SI 1982/1857)
72	24 May 1983 (SI 1983/182)
73	31 Jan 1983 (SI 1983/24)

Criminal Justice Act 1982 (c 48)—*cont*

s 74, 75	Repealed (except in relation to Channel Islands and Isle of Man)
76	28 Oct 1982 (s 80(1))
77	See Schs 14, 15 below
78	See Sch 16 below
79	See Sch 17 below
80, 81	28 Oct 1982 (s 80(1))
Sch 1	28 Oct 1982 (s 80(1))
2–4	11 Apr 1983 (SI 1982/1857)
5	Repealed
6, 7	11 Apr 1983 (SI 1983/24)
8	24 May 1983 (SI 1983/182; SI 1983/758)
9	24 May 1983 (SI 1983/182)
10	31 Jan 1983 (SI 1982/1857; SI 1983/24))
11	Repealed
12	24 May 1983 (SI 1983/182)
13	24 May 1983 (SI 1983/182; SI 1983/758)
14, para 1	31 Jan 1983 (SI 1982/1857)
2	11 Apr 1983 (SI 1982/1857)
3	31 Jan 1983 (SI 1983/24)
4	24 May 1983 (SI 1983/182)
5	31 Jan 1983 (SI 1982/1857)
6, 7	24 May 1983 (SI 1983/182)
8(a)	24 May 1983 (SI 1983/182; SI 1983/758)
(b), (c)	24 May 1983 (SI 1983/182)
9	24 May 1983 (SI 1983/182)
10(a)	31 Jan 1983 (SI 1982/1857)
(b)	24 May 1983 (SI 1983/182)
11–13	24 May 1983 (SI 1983/182; SI 1983/758)
14	24 May 1983 (SI 1983/182)
15–17	24 May 1983 (SI 1983/182; SI 1983/758)
18(a)	24 May 1983 (SI 1983/182; SI 1983/758); repealed (S)
(b)	31 Jan 1983 (SI 1982/1857; SI 1983/24); repealed (S)
(c)	24 May 1983 (SI 1983/182; SI 1983/758); repealed (S)
19	24 May 1983 (SI 1983/182; SI 1983/758); repealed (S)
20	28 Oct 1982 (s 80(1)); repealed (S)
21	31 Jan 1983 (SI 1982/1857; SI 1983/24); repealed (S)
22	31 Jan 1983 (SI 1982/1857)
23	24 May 1983 (SI 1983/182)
24	24 May 1983 (SI 1983/182; SI 1983/758)
25	Repealed
26–28	24 May 1983 (SI 1983/182)
29	24 May 1983 (SI 1983/182; SI 1983/758)
30	24 May 1983 (SI 1983/182)
31	31 Jan 1983 (SI 1982/1857; SI 1983/24)
32	Repealed
33, 34	24 May 1983 (SI 1983/182)
35	Spent
36, 37	24 May 1983 (SI 1983/182; SI 1983/758)
38	24 May 1983 (SI 1983/182)
39	24 May 1983 (SI 1983/182; SI 1983/758)
40, 41	31 Jan 1983 (SI 1982/1857)
42, 43	31 Jan 1983 (SI 1982/1857; SI 1983/24)
44	Spent
45, 46	Repealed
47–56	24 May 1983 (SI 1983/182)

Criminal Justice Act 1982 (c 48)—*cont*

Sch 14, para 57	Spent
58–60	24 May 1983 (SI 1983/182)
15, para 1	11 Apr 1983 (SI 1983/24)
2	Repealed
3–5	31 Jan 1983 (SI 1983/24)
6–13	11 Apr 1983 (SI 1983/24)
14	Repealed
15	31 Jan 1983 (SI 1983/24)
16	Repealed
17	11 Apr 1983 (SI 1983/24)
18, 19	31 Jan 1983 (SI 1983/24)
20, 21	11 Apr 1983 (SI 1983/24)
22	Repealed
23–29	11 Apr 1983 (SI 1983/24)
30	31 Jan 1983 (SI 1983/24)
16	28 Oct 1982 (repeal of Imprisonment (Temporary Provisions) Act 1980) (s 80(1))
	31 Jan 1983 (repeals of or in Merchant Shipping Act 1894, s 680(1); Prison Act 1952, s 55(3); Criminal Justice Act 1967, s 95(1); Immigration Act 1971, s 6(5); Powers of Criminal Courts Act 1973, ss 2, 4, 23(1), 47(d), 48–51, 57(1), Sch 1, para 7, Sch 3; Criminal Procedure (Scotland) Act 1975, s 421(1); Criminal Law Act 1977, Sch 9, para 10, Sch 12 (repeals in the entry relating to Powers of Criminal Courts Act 1973 only); Customs and Excise Management Act 1979, ss 147(5), 156(3); Criminal Justice (Scotland) Act 1980, s 55; Magistrates' Courts Act 1980, s 108(3)(a); Animal Health Act 1981, s 70) (SI 1982/1857; SI 1983/24)
	11 Apr 1983 (repeals of or in Sea Fisheries (Scotland) Amendment Act 1885, s 4; Electric Lighting (Clauses) Act 1899, Sch; Housing (Scotland) Act 1966, s 185(2); Criminal Procedure (Scotland) Act 1975, ss 8(2), 289D(2), (3A), 291(1); Criminal Law Act 1977, s 31; National Health Service (Scotland) Act 1978, Sch 9, para 1(1), Sch 10, para 7(2)(b); Electricity (Scotland) Act 1979, s 41(1)(b); Merchant Shipping Act 1979, s 43; Water (Scotland) Act 1980, Sch 4, para 10(3); Criminal Justice (Scotland) Act 1980, ss 7(3), 8, 46(1), Sch 7, para 50) (SI 1982/1857; SI 1983/24)
	24 May 1983 (otherwise except as noted below) (SI 1983/182; SI 1983/758)
	Not in force (repeal of Criminal Justice Act 1961, s 38(5)(c), (d))
17, para 1–14	24 May 1983 (SI 1983/182)
15	28 Oct 1982 (s 80(1))
16, 17	Repealed
18	31 Jan 1983 (SI 1983/24)

Currency Act 1982 (c 3)

RA: 2 Feb 1982

2 Feb 1982 (RA)

Deer Amendment (Scotland) Act 1982 (c 19)

RA: 28 Jun 1982

Commencement provisions: s 16(3), (4); commencement order made 27 Jun 1984 (not a statutory instrument)

s 1–10	28 Jul 1982 (s 16(3))
11	1 Jan 1985 (commencement order made 27 Jun 1984)
12–16	28 Jul 1982 (s 16(3))
Sch 1, 2	28 Jul 1982 (s 16(3))
3	28 Jul 1982 (except repeal of Sale of Venison (Scotland) Act 1968) (s 16(3))
	1 Jan 1985 (exception noted above) (commencement order made 27 Jun 1984)

Derelict Land Act 1982 (c 42)

RA: 30 Jul 1982

Commencement provisions: s 5(3)

30 Aug 1982 (s 5(3))

Duchy of Cornwall Management Act 1982 (c 47)

RA: 28 Oct 1982

28 Oct 1982 (RA)

Electricity (Financial Provisions) (Scotland) Act 1982 (c 56)

Whole Act repealed

Employment Act 1982 (c 46)

RA: 28 Oct 1982

Commencement provisions: s 22; Employment Act 1982 (Commencement) Order 1982, SI 1982/1656

s 1–19	Repealed
20	2 Jan 1983 (SI 1982/1656; but note the amendments made by Sch 2 do not apply in the circumstances set out in sub-ss (2)–(4))
21(1)	Substituted by Trade Union and Labour Relations (Consolidation) Act 1992, s 300(2), Sch 2, para 30 (qv)
(2)	See Sch 3 below
(3)	See Sch 4 below
22	1 Dec 1982 (SI 1982/1656)
Sch 1	Repealed
2	2 Jan 1983 (SI 1982/1656; see the note to s 20 above)
3	1 Dec 1982 (subject to transitional and supplementary provisions) (SI 1982/1656)

Employment Act 1982 (c 46)—*cont*
Sch 4   1 Dec 1982 (subject to transitional and
                                       supplementary provisions) (except repeals noted
                                       below) (SI 1982/1656)
                                     2 Jan 1983 (repeals of or in Employment Protection
                                       (Consolidation) Act 1978, ss 3, 4(4)(b), 5, 7,
                                       73(3), 81(4), 143, 147, 149, Sch 4, paras 2, 7,
                                       Sch 13, para 13, Sch 16, para 23(9)) (SI 1982/1656)

Finance Act 1982 (c 39)

Budget day: 9 Mar 1982

RA: 30 Jul 1982

See the note concerning Finance Acts at the front of this book

Fire Service College Board (Abolition) Act 1982 (c 13)

Whole Act repealed

Firearms Act 1982 (c 31)

RA: 13 Jul 1982

Commencement provisions: s 4(3); Firearms Act 1982 (Commencement) Order 1983,
  SI 1983/1440

1 Nov 1983 (SI 1983/1440)

Food and Drugs (Amendment) Act 1982 (c 26)

Whole Act repealed

Forfeiture Act 1982 (c 34)

RA: 13 Jul 1982

Commencement provisions: s 7(2); Forfeiture Act 1982 Commencement Order 1982,
  SI 1982/1731

s 1–3	13 Oct 1982 (s 7(2))
4	31 Dec 1982 (SI 1982/1731)
5	13 Oct 1982 (s 7(2))
6, 7	13 Jul 1982 (RA)

Gaming (Amendment) Act 1982 (c 22)

RA: 28 Jan 1982

Commencement provisions: s 3(2)

28 Aug 1982 (s 3(2))

Harbours (Scotland) Act 1982 (c 17)

RA: 27 May 1982

27 May 1982 (RA)

Hops Marketing Act 1982 (c 5)

RA: 25 Feb 1982

25 Feb 1982 (RA); note that for practical purposes the majority of the Act came into effect on 1 Apr 1982, the day appointed for the revocation of the Hops Marketing Scheme under s 1(2)

Industrial Development Act 1982 (c 52)

RA: 28 Oct 1982

Commencement provisions: s 20(2)

28 Jan 1983 (s 20(2))

Industrial Training Act 1982 (c 10)

RA: 29 Mar 1982

Commencement provisions: s 21(3)

29 Jun 1982 (s 21(3))

Industry Act 1982 (c 18)

Whole Act repealed

Insurance Companies Act 1982 (c 50)

RA: 28 Oct 1982

Commencement provisions: s 100(2)

s 1–21	28 Jan 1983 (s 100(2))
21A	Inserted by Financial Services Act 1986, s 135(1) (qv)
22–31	28 Jan 1983 (s 100(2))
31A	Inserted by Financial Services Act 1986, s 136(1) (qv)
32–35	28 Jan 1983 (s 100(2))
36	*Not in force*
37–44	28 Jan 1983 (s 100(2))
44A	Inserted by Companies Act 1989, s 77(3) (qv)
45–47	28 Jan 1983 (s 100(2))
47A, 47B	Inserted by Companies Consolidation (Consequential Provisions) Act 1985, s 25 (qv)
48, 49	28 Jan 1983 (s 100(2))
49A	Inserted by Friendly Societies Act 1992, s 120(1), Sch 21, Pt I, para 6(2) (qv)

Insurance Companies Act 1982 (c 50)—*cont*

s 49B	Inserted as s 49A by Insurance Companies (Amendment) Regulations 1993/174, reg 3(3); renumbered by Insurance Companies (Cancellation) Regulations 1993, SI 1993/1327, reg 3(1)
50–52	28 Jan 1983 (s 100(2))
52A	Inserted by Insurance Companies (Amendment) Regulations 1990, SI 1990/1333, reg 9(2)
53–63	28 Jan 1983 (s 100(2))
63A	Inserted by Insurance Companies (Amendment) Regulations 1992, SI 1992/2890, reg 5
64–72	28 Jan 1983 (s 100(2))
73	Repealed
74–78	28 Jan 1983 (s 100(2))
79	Repealed
80, 81	28 Jan 1983 (s 100(2))
81A–81C	Inserted by Insurance Companies (Amendment) Regulations 1990, SI 1990/1333, reg 10
81CC	Inserted by Insurance Companies (Amendment) Regulations 1992, SI 1992/2890, reg 7(6)
81D–81J	Inserted by Insurance Companies (Amendment) Regulations 1990, SI 1990/1333, reg 10
82, 83	28 Jan 1983 (s 100(2))
83A	Inserted by Insurance Companies (Amendment) Regulations 1992, SI 1992/2890, reg 8
84–94	28 Jan 1983 (s 100(2))
94A	Inserted by Insurance Fees Act 1985, s 1 (qv)
94B	Inserted as s 94A by Insurance Companies (Amendment) Regulations 1990, SI 1990/1333, reg 6(1); renumbered by Insurance Companies (Amendment) Regulations 1992, SI 1992/2890, reg 9(2).
95, 96	28 Jun 1983 (s 100(2))
96A	Inserted by Insurance Companies (Amendment) Regulations 1990, SI 1990/1333, reg 2(1)
96B	Inserted by Insurance Companies (Amendment) Regulations 1990, SI 1990/1333, reg 4
97–100	28 Jan 1983 (s 100(2))
Sch 1–3	28 Jan 1983 (s 100(2))
3A, Pt I	Inserted as Sch 3A by Insurance Companies (Amendment) Regulations 1990, SI 1990/1333, reg 6(2); renumbered by Insurance Companies (Amendment) Regulations 1993, SI 1993/174, reg 5(4)
Pt II	Inserted by Insurance Companies (Amendment) Regulations 1993, SI 1993/174, reg 5(5)
4–6	28 Jan 1983 (s 100(2)

Iron and Steel Act 1982 (c 25)

RA: 13 Jul 1982

Commencement provisions: s 39(2)

13 Oct 1982 (s 39(2))

Iron and Steel Act 1982 (c 25)—*cont*
Whole Act repealed, partly prospectively (s 1, Sch 1), except ss 33 (part), 34 (part), by British Steel Act 1988, s 16(3), Sch 2 (qv)

Lands Valuation Amendment (Scotland) Act 1982 (c 57)

RA: 22 Dec 1982

22 Dec 1982 (RA)

Legal Aid Act 1982 (c 44)

Whole Act repealed

Local Government and Planning (Scotland) Act 1982 (c 43)

RA: 30 Jul 1982

Commencement provisions: s 69(2); Local Government and Planning (Scotland) Act 1982 (Commencement No 1) Order 1982, SI 1982/1137; Local Government and Planning (Scotland) Act 1982 (Commencement No 2) Order 1982, SI 1982/1397; Local Government and Planning (Scotland) Act 1982 (Commencement No 3) Order 1984, SI 1984/239

s 1–3	Repealed
4, 5	1 Sep 1982 (SI 1982/1137)
6	1 Apr 1983 (SI 1982/1397)
7	1 Nov 1982 (so far as inserts Local Government (Scotland) Act 1973, s 154B) (SI 1982/1397)
	1 Apr 1983 (so far as inserts Local Government (Scotland) Act 1973, s 154A) (SI 1982/1397)
8	1 Sep 1982 (SI 1982/1137)
9–28	1 Apr 1983 (SI 1982/1397)
29	1 Nov 1982 (SI 1982/1397)
30, 31	1 Apr 1983 (SI 1982/1397)
32	1 Nov 1982 (SI 1982/1397)
33–35	1 Sep 1982 (SI 1982/1137)
36–40	1 Nov 1982 (SI 1982/1397)
41	14 May 1984 (SI 1984/239)
42, 43	1 Nov 1982 (SI 1982/1397)
44	14 May 1984 (SI 1984/239)
45, 46	1 Nov 1982 (SI 1982/1397)
47(a)	14 May 1984 (SI 1984/239)
(b), (c)	1 Nov 1982 (SI 1982/1397)
48	See Sch 2 below
49, 50	1 Sep 1982 (SI 1982/1137)
51–55	Repealed
56	1 Sep 1982 (SI 1982/1137)
57	1 Apr 1983 (SI 1982/1397)
58–60	1 Nov 1982 (SI 1982/1397)
61–65	1 Sep 1982 (SI 1982/1137)
66(1)	See Sch 3 below
(2)	See Sch 4 below
67, 68	1 Sep 1982 (SI 1982/1137)
69	30 Jul 1982 (RA)

Local Government and Planning (Scotland) Act 1982 (c 43)—*cont*

Sch 1	1 Apr 1983 (SI 1982/1397)
2, para 1–4	1 Nov 1982 (SI 1982/1397)
5	14 May 1984 (SI 1984/239)
6, 7	1 Nov 1982 (SI 1982/1397)
8–12	14 May 1984 (SI 1984/239)
13–16	1 Nov 1982 (SI 1982/1397)
17–20	14 May 1984 (SI 1984/239)
21, 22	1 Nov 1982 (SI 1982/1397)
23	14 May 1984 (SI 1984/239)
24	1 Nov 1982 (SI 1982/1397)
25–27	14 May 1984 (SI 1984/239)
28–41	1 Nov 1982 (SI 1982/1397)
42	14 May 1984 (SI 1984/239)
43	1 Nov 1982 (SI 1982/1397)
3, para 1, 2	1 Apr 1983 (SI 1982/1397)
3(a)	1 Sep 1982 (SI 1982/1137)
(b)	1 Apr 1983 (SI 1982/1397)
4	1 Nov 1982 (SI 1982/1397)
5–7	Repealed
8–11	1 Nov 1982 (SI 1982/1397)
12	1 Apr 1983 (SI 1982/1397)
13–15	1 Nov 1982 (SI 1982/1397)
16	1 Apr 1983 (SI 1982/1397)
17	1 Sep 1982 (SI 1982/1137)
18–20	Repealed
21	1 Apr 1983 (SI 1982/1397)
22, 23	1 Nov 1982 (SI 1982/1397)
24	14 May 1984 (SI 1984/239)
25–28	1 Nov 1982 (SI 1982/1397)
29–33	Repealed
34	1 Nov 1982 (SI 1982/1397)
35, 36	Repealed
37, 38	1 Apr 1983 (SI 1982/1397)
39, 40	Repealed
41	1 Apr 1983 (SI 1982/1397)
42	1 Sep 1982 (SI 1982/1137)
43	Repealed
4	1 Sep 1982 (repeals of or in Local Government (Scotland) Act 1966, s 5(1), Sch 1, Pt II, paras 2, 3; Local Government (Scotland) Act 1973, ss 216(2)–(5), 218, 221, 224(1)–(4), (6); Local Government (Scotland) Act 1975, Sch 1, paras 2, 2A, 3, 4, 4A; Electricity (Scotland) Act 1979, Sch 4, paras 1, 3, 5, 6; Tenants' Rights, Etc (Scotland) Act 1980, ss 1(1), 4(3)) (SI 1982/1137)
	1 Nov 1982 (repeals of or in Requisitioned Land and War Works Act 1945, s 52; Civic Restaurants Act 1947; Requisitioned Land and War Works Act 1948, Sch, para 10; Highlands and Islands Development (Scotland) Act 1965, s 10(1), (3); Countryside (Scotland) Act 1967, ss 14(5), 34(5), 35A, Sch 3, paras 1(2), 2(1)–(3), 4; Social Work (Scotland) Act 1968, s 6(1)(d); Town and Country Planning (Scotland) Act 1972, ss 12(1), (2), 37(1), 54(2), 61(7), 84(6), 85(8), 92(1), 93(5)(b), 154(2), 164(6), 167C(2)(b), 215(1), 231(1)(b), (3)(f), 262(2), (3), 262A(3), (4), 262(B)(3), Sch 10, para

Local Government and Planning (Scotland) Act 1982 (c 43)—*cont*

Sch 4—*cont*

11(1); Local Government (Scotland) Act 1973, ss 49(2)(a), 164, Sch 22, Pt II, para 5, 8, 9; Safety of Sports Grounds Act 1975, s 11; Scottish Development Agency Act 1975, s 10(1); Refuse Disposal (Amenity) Act 1978, s 8(1); Water (Scotland) Act 1980, Sch 3, para 7(5), Sch 4, para 23; Countryside (Scotland) Act 1981, s 5) (SI 1982/1397)

1 Apr 1983 (repeals of or in Public Parks (Scotland) Act 1878; Burgh Police (Scotland) Act 1892, ss 107, 110, 112, 116, 277, 288, 307, 308; Public Health (Scotland) Act 1897, ss 29, 39; Burgh Police (Scotland) Act 1903, s 44; Physical Training and Recreation Act 1937, ss 4(1)–(4), 5, 7, 10(4)–(7), (11); Food and Drugs (Scotland) Act 1956, s 26(3); Physical Training and Recreation Act 1958; Caravan Sites and Control of Development Act 1960, s 32(1)(h)(iii); Social Work (Scotland) Act 1968, s 85; Agriculture Act 1970, ss 95, 96; Local Government (Scotland) Act 1973, ss 55, 91, 137(2), 139, 158, 162, 178, 219, 220, Sch 23, para 2(a); Control of Pollution Act 1974, ss 22, 23, Sch 4; Education (Scotland) Act 1980, s 1(3)(b), (5)(b)(iii); Local Government, Planning and Land Act 1980, s 70(4)) (SI 1982/1397)

14 May 1984 (otherwise) (SI 1984/239)

Local Government Finance Act 1982 (c 32)

RA: 13 Jul 1982

Commencement provisions: See notes to individual provisions below

s 1

Repealed, with savings, by the Local Government Finance (Repeals, Savings and Consequential Amendments) Order 1990, SI 1990/776, art 3, Sch 1

2–5

13 Jul 1982 (RA; ss 1–3 (and Sch 1) only effective for financial years 1 Apr 1982 onwards)

6

Repealed, with savings, by the Local Government Finance (Repeals, Savings and Consequential Amendments) Order 1990, SI 1990/776, art 3, Sch 1

7

13 Jul 1982 (RA)

8–10

13 Jul 1982 (RA; s 8 only effective in relation to block grant for years 1 Apr 1982 onwards, except s 8(2) so far as relates to consultation; s 8(4A) effective in relation to years 1 Apr 1987 onwards; s 8(8) which only applies to years 1 Apr 1983 onwards; s 10 (and Sch 2) only effective for years 1 Apr 1983 onwards)

11–18

13 Jul 1982 (RA, s 11 (and Sch 3) only effective from 21 Jan 1983 (s 33(2); Accounts and Audit (First Appointed Day) Order 1982, SI 1982/1881); ss 12–18 only effective for periods beginning on or after 1 Apr 1983 (s 33(3); Accounts and Audit (Second Appointed Day) Order 1983, SI 1983/165))

Local Government Finance Act 1982 (c 32)—*cont*

s 18A	Inserted (EW) by Local Government Finance (Publicity for Auditors' Reports) Act 1991, s 1(1), (2) (qv)
19–25	13 Jul 1982 (RA; ss 19–25 only effective for periods beginning on or after 1 Apr 1983 (s 33(3); Accounts and Audit (Second Appointed Day) Order 1983, SI 1983/165))
25A	Inserted by Local Government Act 1988, s 30, Sch 4 (qv)
25AA	Inserted by Local Government Finance Act 1988, s 137, Sch 12, Pt I, para 3(1), (3) (qv)
25B–25D	Inserted by Local Government Act 1988, s 30, Sch 4 (qv)
26–28	13 Jul 1982 (RA; s 11 (and Sch 3) only effective from 21 Jan 1983 (s 33(2); Accounts and Audit (First Appointed Day) Order 1982, SI 1982/1881)
28A	Inserted by Local Government and Housing Act 1989, s 184(1) (qv)
29–31	13 Jul 1982 (RA; s 11 (and Sch 3) only effective from 21 Jan 1983 (s 33(2); Accounts and Audit (First Appointed Day) Order 1982, SI 1982/1881); s 31 (so far as it relates to ss 12–25) only effective for periods beginning on or after 1 Apr 1983 (s 33(3); Accounts and Audit (Second Appointed Day) Order 1983, SI 1983/165)
32	Repealed
33–36	13 Jul 1982 (RA; s 11 (and Sch 3) only effective from 21 Jan 1983 (s 33(2); Accounts and Audit (First Appointed Day) Order 1982, SI 1982/1881))
37–39	13 Jul 1982 (RA)
Sch 1	See ss 1–7 above
2	See ss 8–10 above
3	See ss 11–36 above
4	Repealed
5	13 Jul 1982 (RA; only effective for periods 1 Apr 1983 onwards)
6, Pt I	Effective for financial years 1 Apr 1982 onwards (s 38(2))
II	Effective for financial years 1 Apr 1981 onwards (s 38(3))
III	Effective for financial years 1 Apr 1983 onwards (s 38(4))
IV	Effective for periods 1 Apr 1983 onwards (s 38(5))

Local Government (Miscellaneous Provisions) Act 1982 (c 30)

RA: 13 Jul 1982

Commencement provisions: ss 1(12), 7(3), 25(3), 40(10), 47(3), Sch 3, para 30(1); Local Government (Miscellaneous Provisions) Act 1982 (Commencement No 1) Order 1982, SI 1982/1119; Local Government (Miscellaneous Provisions) Act 1982 (Commencement No 2) Order 1982, SI 1982/1160

Note

Certain provisions of this Act must be adopted by local authority resolution to have effect in particular areas

Local Government (Miscellaneous Provisions) Act 1982 (c 30)—*cont*

s 1	1 Jan 1983 (s 1(12))
2–6	13 Jul 1982 (RA)
7(1), (2)	13 Oct 1982 (s 7(3))
(3), (4)	13 Jul 1982 (RA)
8–17	13 Jul 1982 (RA)
18, 19	Repealed
20–23	13 Jul 1982 (RA)
24–26	Repealed
27	13 Jul 1982 (RA)
28	Repealed
29–34	13 Jul 1982 (RA)
35, 36	Repealed
37–39	13 Jul 1982 (RA)
40	13 Sep 1982 (s 40(10))
41	13 Jul 1982 (RA)
42	Repealed
43–46	13 Jul 1982 (RA)
47(1)	13 Jul 1982 (RA)
(2), (3)	See Sch 7 below
(4)	13 Jul 1982 (RA)
48, 49	13 Jul 1982 (RA)
Sch 1, 2	1 Jan 1983 (s 1(12))
3	13 Jul 1982 (except in relation to sex cinemas) (RA)
	13 Oct 1982 (in relation to sex cinemas) (SI 1982/ 1119)
4–6	13 Jul 1982 (RA)
7, Pt I, II	1 Jan 1983 (s 47(3))
III–XV	13 Jul 1982 (RA)
XVI	13 Jul 1982 (except as noted below) (RA)
	1 Sep 1982 (repeal of Health and Safety at Work etc Act 1974, s 63) (SI 1982/1160)

Mental Health (Amendment) Act 1982 (c 51)

RA: 28 Oct 1982

Commencement provisions: s 69

s 1–33	Repealed
34	30 Sep 1983 (s 69(1))
35–63	Repealed
64	30 Sep 1983 (s 69(1))
65(1)	See Sch 3 below
(2)	See Sch 4 below
66	Repealed
67–69	30 Sep 1983 (s 69(1))
Sch 1, 2	Repealed
3, Pt I	30 Sep 1983 (s 69(1))
II	Repealed
4, Pt I	30 Sep 1983 (s 69(1))
II	28 Oct 1984 (s 69(4))
5, para 1	30 Sep 1983 (s 69(1))
2–15	Repealed

Merchant Shipping (Liner Conferences) Act 1982 (c 37)

RA: 23 Jul 1982

Commencement provisions: s 15(2); Merchant Shipping (Liner Conferences) Act 1982 (Commencement) Order 1985, SI 1985/182

14 Mar 1985 (SI 1985/182)

National Insurance Surcharge Act 1982 (c 55)

Whole Act repealed (with respect to earnings paid on or after 6 April 1985)

New Towns Act 1982 (c 7)

Whole Act repealed

Northern Ireland Act 1982 (c 38)

RA: 23 Jul 1982

23 Jul 1982 (RA)

Oil and Gas (Enterprise) Act 1982 (c 23)

RA: 28 Jun 1982

Commencement provisions: s 38(2); Oil and Gas (Enterprise) Act 1982 (Commencement No 1) Order 1982, SI 1982/895; Oil and Gas (Enterprise) Act 1982 (Commencement No 2) Order 1982, SI 1982/1059; Oil and Gas (Enterprise) Act 1982 (Commencement No 3) Order 1982, SI 1982/1431; Oil and Gas (Enterprise) Act 1982 (Commencement No 4) Order 1987, SI 1987/2272

s 1–7	Repealed
8	1 Apr 1983 (SI 1982/1431)
9–17	Repealed
18	23 Jul 1982 (SI 1982/895)
19, 20	1 Oct 1982 (SI 1982/1059)
21	Repealed
22	1 Feb 1988 (SI 1987/2272)
23(1), (5)	1 Feb 1988 (SI 1987/2272)
(2)–(4), (6)	31 Dec 1982 (amendments to Social Security Act 1975, Patents Act 1977 and Social Security and Housing Benefits Act 1982) (SI 1982/1431)
	1 Feb 1988 (otherwise) (SI 1987/2272)
24	1 Nov 1982 (SI 1982/1431)
25	1 Oct 1982 (SI 1982/1059)
26	1 Nov 1982 (SI 1982/1431)
27(1)(a)	1 Feb 1988 (SI 1987/2272)
(b)	1 Oct 1982 (SI 1982/1059)
(c)	1 Oct 1982 (SI 1982/1059)
(d)	Repealed
(2)	1 Oct 1982 (SI 1982/1059)
(3)	1 Oct 1982 (SI 1982/1059); repealed, so far as relates to prosecutions for offences under Mineral Workings (Offshore Installations) Act 1971 or Petroleum Act 1987, s 23, by Offshore Safety Act 1992, s 3(1)(d) (qv)

Oil and Gas (Enterprise) Act 1982 (c 23)—*cont*

s 27(4)	1 Oct 1982 (SI 1982/1059); repealed so far as relates to prosecutions for offences under Mineral Workings (Offshore Installations) Act 1971 or Petroleum Act 1987, s 23, by Offshore, and Pipelines, Safety (Northern Ireland) Order 1992, SI 1992/1728, art 8, Sch 2
(5)–(7)	1 Oct 1982 (SI 1982/1059)
28	1 Oct 1982 (SI 1982/1059)
29	23 Jul 1982 (SI 1982/895)
30, 31	1 Oct 1982 (SI 1982/1059)
32	2 Jul 1982 (SI 1982/895)
33, 34	Repealed
35, 36	2 Jul 1982 (SI 1982/895)
37	See Schs 3, 4 below
38	2 Jul 1982 (SI 1982/895)
Sch 1	Repealed
2	1 Oct 1982 (SI 1982/1059)
3, para 1	1 Oct 1982 (SI 1982/1059)
2, 3	1 Feb 1988 (SI 1987/2272)
4	1 Oct 1982 (SI 1982/1059)
5, 6	Repealed
7–11	1 Nov 1982 (SI 1982/1431)
12–21	Repealed
22	18 Aug 1982 (SI 1982/1059)
23	Repealed
24	*Not in force*
25–29	Repealed
30, 31	1 Nov 1982 (SI 1982/1431)
32, 33	Repealed
34	1 Feb 1988 (SI 1987/2272)
35, 36	*Not in force*
37	18 Aug 1982 (SI 1982/1059)
38	*Not in force*
39	31 Dec 1982 (SI 1982/1431)
40	*Not in force*; substituted by Trade Union and Labour Relations (Consolidation) Act 1992, s 300(2), Sch 2, para 29(1), (2) (qv)
40	*Not in force*
41	Repealed
42, 43	1 Feb 1988 (SI 1987/2272)
44	Repealed
45	*Not in force;* added by Trade Union and Labour Relations (Consolidation) Act 1992, s 300(2), Sch 2, para 29(1), (3), (4) (qv)
4	18 Aug 1982 (repeals in Petroleum (Production) Act 1934; Gas Act 1972 (except repeal in s 7(2)); Oil Taxation Act 1975; Energy Act 1976; Gas Act 1980) (SI 1982/1059)
	1 Oct 1982 (repeals in Continental Shelf Act 1964, s 2; Mineral Workings (Offshore Installations) Act 1971, s 10 (except in relation to offences within sub-s (1)(a)); Petroleum and Submarine Pipe-lines Act 1975, ss 22, 26, 41; Customs and Excise Management Act 1979) (SI 1982/1059)
	1 Nov 1982 (repeals of or in Mineral Workings

Oil and Gas (Enterprise) Act 1982 (c 23)—*cont*
Sch 4—*cont*   (Offshore Installations) Act 1971, ss 6(2), 12(1);
                                                Petroleum and Submarine Pipe-lines Act 1975,
                                                ss 1(3)(c), 3(3), 44(1)–(4), 45(3)) (SI1982/1431)
                                                31 Dec 1982 (repeals of or in Petroleum and
                                                Submarine Pipe-lines Act 1975, ss 2(4)(d), 7(2),
                                                14(4)(b), 40(2)(a), (c), (3)(a), (c)) (SI 1982/1431)
                                                1 Apr 1983 (repeals of Petroleum and Submarine
                                                Pipe-lines Act 1975, s 40(1), (4), 40(3) (so far as not
                                                brought into force on 31 Dec 1982)) (SI 1982/1431)
                                                1 Feb 1988 (repeals of Continental Shelf Act 1964, ss 3,
                                                11(3); Mineral Workings (Offshore Installations)
                                                Act 1971, ss 8, 9(5), 10 (so far as not already
                                                repealed)) (SI 1987/2272)
                                                Not in force (otherwise)

Pastoral (Amendment) Measure 1982 (No 1)

Whole Measure repealed

Planning Inquiries (Attendance of Public) Act 1982 (c 21)

Whole Act repealed

Reserve Forces Act 1982 (c 14)

RA: 7 Apr 1982

7 Apr 1982 (RA)

Shipbuilding Act 1982 (c 4)

Whole Act repealed

Social Security and Housing Benefits Act 1982 (c 24)

RA: 28 Jun 1982

Commencement provisions: s 48(3); Social Security and Housing Benefits Act 1982
    (Commencement No 1) Order 1982, SI 1982/893; Social Security and Housing
    Benefits Act 1982 (Commencement No 2) Order 1982, SI 1982/906

s 1–9	Repealed
10	6 Apr 1983 (SI 1982/893)
11–23, 23A, 24–38	Repealed
39	6 Apr 1983 (SI 1982/893)
40	28 Jun 1982 (s 48(3)); prospectively repealed by Pension Schemes Act 1993, s 188(1), Sch 5 (qv)
41	Repealed
42	28 Jun 1982 (s 48(3))
43	30 Aug 1982 (SI 1982/893)
44	Repealed
45–47	28 Jun 1982 (s 48(3))
48(1)	28 Jun 1982 (s 48(3))

Social Security and Housing Benefits Act 1982 (c 24)—*cont*

s 48(2)	Repealed
(3), (4)	28 Jun 1982 (s 48(3))
(5), (6)	See Schs 4, 5 below
(7)	28 Jun 1982 (s 48(3))
Sch 1	Repealed
2	6 Apr 1983 (SI 1982/893)
3	Repealed
4, para 1–19	Repealed or spent
20	30 Jun 1982 (SI 1982/893); prospectively repealed by Pension Schemes Act 1993, s 188(1), Sch 5 (qv)
21	28 Jun 1982 (s 48(3)); prospectively repealed by Pension Schemes Act 1993, s 188(1), Sch 5 (qv)
22	Repealed
23–28	Repealed
29	Spent
30–34	Repealed
35(1), (2)	Repealed
(3)	4 Apr 1983 (SI 1982/906)
36	4 Apr 1983 (SI 1982/906)
37	28 Jun 1982 (RA)
38, 39	Repealed
5	30 Jun 1982 (repeals of or in Social Security Act 1975, s 4(2), Sch 11, para 2) (SI 1982/893)
	6 Apr 1983 (remaining repeals in Social Security Act 1975, except words in s 65(4); repeals of or in Child Benefit Act 1975, Sch 4, para 39; Social Security Act 1980, Sch 1; Social Security (No 2) Act 1980, s 3(2)) (SI 1982/893)
	4 Apr 1983 (otherwise except repeals in Social Security Act 1975, s 65(4); Social Security Pensions Act 1975, Sch 4, para 22) (SI 1982/906)

Note: It is unclear why the outstanding repeals were not brought into force

---

Social Security (Contributions) Act 1982 (c 2)

Whole Act repealed

Stock Transfer Act 1982 (c 41)

RA: 30 Jul 1982

Commencement provisions: s 6(2); Stock Transfer Act 1982 (Commencement) Order 1985, SI 1985/1137

s 1–3	23 Jul 1985 (SI 1985/1137)
4–6	30 Oct 1982 (s 6(2))
Sch 1, 2	23 Jul 1985 (SI 1985/1137)

Supply of Goods and Services Act 1982 (c 29)

RA: 13 Jul 1982

Commencement provisions: s 20(3); Supply of Goods and Services Act 1982 (Commencement) Order 1982, SI 1982/1770

Supply of Goods and Services Act 1982 (c 29)—*cont*

s 1–11	4 Jan 1983 (s 20(3))
12–16	4 Jul 1983 (SI 1982/1770)
17	4 Jan 1983 (s 20(3))
18, 19	4 Jan 1983 (so far as relate to ss 1–11) (s 20(3))
	4 Jul 1983 (so far as relate to ss 12–16) (SI 1982/1770)
20	13 Jul 1982 (RA)
Schedule	Spent

Taking of Hostages Act 1982 (c 28)

RA: 13 Jul 1982

Commencement provisions: s 6; Taking of Hostages Act 1982 (Commencement) Order 1982, SI 1982/1532

26 Nov 1982 (SI 1982/1532)

Transport Act 1982 (c 49)

RA: 28 Oct 1982

Commencement provisions: s 76; Transport Act 1982 (Commencement No 1) Order 1982, SI 1982/1561; Transport Act 1982 (Commencement No 2) Order 1982, SI 1982/1804; Transport Act 1982 (Commencement No 3) Order 1983, SI 1983/ 276; Transport Act 1982 (Commencement No 4) Order 1983, SI 1983/577; Transport Act 1982 (Scotland) (Commencement No 1) Order 1983, SI 1983/650; Transport Act 1982 (Commencement No 5) Order 1984, SI 1984/175; Transport Act 1982 (Commencement No 6) Order 1986, SI 1986/1326; Transport Act 1982 (Scotland) (Commencement No 2) Order 1986, SI 1986/1874

s 1–7	Repealed
8–15	*Not in force*
16	Repealed
17, 18	*Not in force*
19	Repealed
20	*Not in force*: substituted by Road Traffic Act 1991, s 48, Sch 4, para 20 (qv)
21–26	*Not in force*
27–51	Repealed
52	1 Jun 1984 (SI 1984/175)
53–64	Repealed
65	11 Apr 1983 (SI 1983/276)
66	*Not in force*
67	20 Dec 1982 (SI 1982/1804)
68	1 Nov 1982 (SI 1982/1561)
69	Repealed
70	1 Nov 1982 (SI 1982/1561)
71	20 Dec 1982 (SI 1982/1804)
72(a)	*Not in force*
(b)	Repealed
73	30 Jun 1983 (S) (SI 1983/650)
	1 Oct 1986 (EW) (SI 1986/1326)
74	See Schs 5, 6 below
75, 76	30 Jun 1983 (S) (SI 1983/650)
	1 Oct 1986 (EW) (SI 1986/1326)

Transport Act 1982 (c 49)—*cont*

Sch 1–3	Repealed
4	1 Jun 1984 (SI 1984/175)
5, para 1–4	Repealed
5	*Not in force*
6	1 Jun 1984 (SI 1984/175)
7–16	Repealed
17	*Not in force*
18, 19	Repealed
20	*Not in force*
21	Repealed
22–24	*Not in force*
25, 26	Repealed
6	1 Nov 1982 (repeal of Road Traffic Regulation Act 1967, s 72(2), (4)) (SI 1982/1561)
	1 Jun 1984 (repeals in Transport Act 1968) (SI 1984/175)

Transport (Finance) Act 1982 (c 6)

RA: 25 Feb 1982

25 Feb 1982 (RA)

Whole Act prospectively repealed by Railways Act 1993, s 152, Sch 14 (qv)

Travel Concessions (London) Act 1982 (c 12)

Whole Act repealed

1983

Agricultural Holdings (Amendment) (Scotland) Act 1983 (c 46)
Whole Act repealed

Agricultural Marketing Act 1983 (c 3)
RA: 1 Mar 1983

Commencement provisions: s 9(3); Agricultural Marketing Act 1983 (Commencement) Order 1983, SI 1983/366

23 Mar 1983 (SI 1983/366)

Appropriation Act 1983 (c 27)
Whole Act repealed

Appropriation (No 2) Act 1983 (c 48)
Whole Act repealed

British Fishing Boats Act 1983 (c 8)
RA: 28 Mar 1983

28 Mar 1983 (RA)

British Nationality (Falkland Islands) Act 1983 (c 6)
RA: 28 March 1983

Commencement provisions: s 5(2)

1 Jan 1983 (retrospective: s 5(2))

British Shipbuilders Act 1983 (c 15)
RA: 9 May 1983

Commencement provisions: s 3(4)

9 Jul 1983 (s 3(4))

British Shipbuilders (Borrowing Powers) Act 1983 (c 58)

RA: 21 Dec 1983

21 Dec 1983 (RA)

Car Tax Act 1983 (c 53)

RA: 26 Jul 1983

Commencement provisions: s 11(2)

26 Oct 1983 (s 11(2))

Church of England (Miscellaneous Provisions) Measure 1983 (No 2)

RA: 9 May 1983

Commencement provisions: s 13(3)

9 Jun 1983 (s 13(3))

Civil Aviation (Eurocontrol) Act 1983 (c 11)

RA: 11 Apr 1983

Commencement provisions: s 4(2); Civil Aviation (Eurocontrol) Act 1983
(Commencement No 1) Order 1983, SI 1983/1886; Civil Aviation (Eurocontrol)
Act 1983 (Commencement No 2) Order 1985, SI 1985/1915

s 1, 2	1 Jan 1986 (SI 1985/1915)
3(1)	1 Jan 1986 (SI 1985/1915)
(2)	1 Jan 1984 (s 4(2); SI 1983/1886)
4	1 Jan 1984 (s 4(2); SI 1983/1886)

Coal Industry Act 1983 (c 60)

RA: 21 Dec 1983

21 Dec 1983 (RA)

Companies (Beneficial Interests) Act 1983 (c 50)

Whole Act repealed

Consolidated Fund Act 1983 (c 1)

Whole Act repealed

Consolidated Fund (No 2) Act 1983 (c 5)

Whole Act repealed

Consolidated Fund (No 3) Act 1983 (c 57)

Whole Act repealed

Conwy Tunnel (Supplementary Powers) Act 1983 (c 7)

Local application only

Copyright (Amendment) Act 1983 (c 42)

Whole Act repealed

Coroners' Juries Act 1983 (c 31)

Whole Act repealed

County Courts (Penalties for Contempt) Act 1983 (c 45)

RA: 13 May 1983

13 May 1983 (RA)

Currency Act 1983 (c 9)

RA: 28 Mar 1983

28 Mar 1983 (RA)

Dentists Act 1983 (c 38)

Whole Act repealed

Diseases of Fish Act 1983 (c 30)

RA: 13 May 1983

Commencement provisions: s 11(2); Diseases of Fish Act 1983 (Commencement) Order 1984, SI 1984/302

s 1–10	1 Apr 1984 (SI 1984/302)
11	13 May 1983 (RA)
Schedule	1 Apr 1984 (SI 1984/302)

Divorce Jurisdiction, Court Fees and Legal Aid (Scotland) Act 1983 (c 12)

RA: 11 Apr 1983

Commencement provisions: s 7(2), (3); Divorce Jurisdiction, Court Fees and Legal Aid (Scotland) Act 1983 (Commencement) Order 1984, SI 1984/253

Divorce Jurisdiction, Court Fees and Legal Aid (Scotland) Act 1983 (c 12)—*cont*

s 1	1 May 1984 (SI 1984/253)
2, 3	Repealed
4, 5	1 Apr 1984 (SI 1984/253)
6(1)	See Sch 1 below
(2)	See Sch 2 below
7	11 Jun 1983 (s 7(2))

Sch 1, para 1	1 May 1984 (SI 1984/253)
2–5	Repealed
6	1 Apr 1984 (certain purposes) (SI 1984/253)
	1 May 1984 (otherwise) (SI 1984/253)
7, 8	Repealed
9, 10	1 Apr 1984 (SI 1984/253)
11	Repealed
12	1 May 1984 (SI 1984/253)
13–17	Repealed
18–20	1 May 1984 (SI 1984/253)
21	Repealed
22	1 May 1984 (SI 1984/253)
23	Repealed
24	1 May 1984 (SI 1984/253)
2	1 Apr 1984 (repeals of or in the Court of Session Act 1821, s 31; Sheriff Courts (Scotland) Act 1907, s 40; Church of Scotland (Property and Endowments) Act 1925, s 1(3); Juries Act 1949, s 26(1); Legal Aid (Scotland) Act 1967, s 16(1)(b)(i), (2), (4); Legal Advice and Assistance Act 1972, ss 3(3), 5(6)) (SI 1984/253)
	1 May 1984 (otherwise) (SI 1984/253)

Education (Fees and Awards) Act 1983 (c 40)

RA: 13 May 1983

13 May 1983 (RA)

Energy Act 1983 (c 25)

RA: 9 May 1983

Commencement provisions: s 37(1); Energy Act 1983 (Commencement No 1) Order 1983, SI 1983/790; Energy Act 1983 (Commencement No 2) Order 1988, SI 1988/1587

s 1–26	Repealed
27–34	1 Sep 1983 (SI 1983/790)
35(a)	1 Jun 1983 (SI 1983/790)
(b)	1 Sep 1983 (SI 1983/790)
36	See Sch 4 below
37(1), (2)	1 Jun 1983 (SI 1983/790)
(3)	1 Sep 1983 (SI 1983/790)

Energy Act 1983 (c 25)—*cont*
s 38   1 Jun 1983 (SI 1983/790)

Sch 1–3   Repealed
4, Pt I   1 Jun 1983 (repeals of or in Electric Lighting
                          (Clauses) Act 1899, Schedule, ss 2, 52, 54(2);
                          Electric Lighting Act 1909, s 23; Electricity
                          (Supply) Act 1919, ss 11, 36; Electricity (Supply)
                          Act 1922, s 23; Electricity Supply (Meters) Act
                          1936, s 1(1), (3); Acquisition of Land
                          (Authorisation Procedure) Act 1946, Sch 4;
                          Electricity Act 1947 (except for s 60, in Sch 4, Pt I,
                          the entry relating to the Electricity (Supply) Act
                          1946, s 24, and in Sch 4, Pt III, the entry relating
                          to the Electric Lighting (Clauses) Act 1899,
                          Schedule, s 60); South of Scotland Electricity
                          Order Confirmation Act 1956, s 40; Electricity
                          Act 1957 (except in Sch 4, Pt I, the entry relating
                          to the Electricity Act 1947, s 60); North of
                          Scotland Electricity Order Confirmation Act
                          1958, s 27; Post Office Act 1969, Sch 4, para 11;
                          Energy Act 1976, s 14(6)(b); Electricity (Scotland)
                          Act 1979 (except reference to Electricity Act
                          1947, s 60 in Sch 10, para 13); Acquisition of Land
                          Act 1981, Sch 4, para 1) (SI 1983/790)
                          1 Oct 1988 (repeals of or in Electric Lighting
                          (Clauses) Act 1899, Schedule, ss 10, 38, 60, 69(1),
                          (2); Electricity Act 1947, s 60, in Sch 4, Pt III, the
                          entry relating to the Electric Lighting (Clauses)
                          Act 1899, Schedule, s 60; Electricity Act 1957, in
                          Sch 4, Pt I, the entry relating to Electricity Act
                          1947, s 60; Post Office Act 1969, Sch 4, para 8 (c),
                          (g); Electricity (Scotland) Act 1979, in Sch 10,
                          para 13, the reference to the Electricity Act 1947,
                          s 60) (SI 1988/1587)
                          Not in force (repeals of or in Electric Lighting
                          Act 1888; Electricity (Supply) Act 1926, s 24;
                          Electricity Act 1947, in Sch 4, Pt I, the entry
                          relating to Electricity (Supply) Act 1926, s 24;
                          Electricity Reorganisation (Scotland) Act 1954,
                          s 1(3), Sch 1, Pt III; Post Office Act 1969, Sch 4,
                          para 8(b))
                          (*Note*: Certain of the above repeals will become
                          spent on coming into force of Electricity Act
                          1989, s 112(4), Sch 18 (qv))
II   1 Sep 1983 (SI 1983/790)

Finance Act 1983 (c 28)

Budget day: 15 Mar 1983

RA: 13 May 1983

See the note about Finance Acts at the front of this book

Finance (No 2) Act 1983 (c 49)

RA: 26 Jul 1983

See the note about Finance Acts at the front of this book

Health and Social Services and Social Security Adjudications Act 1983 (c 41)

RA: 13 May 1983

Commencement provisions: s 32(1), (2); Health and Social Services and Social Security Adjudications Act 1983 (Commencement No 1) Order 1983, SI 1983/974; Health and Social Services and Social Security Adjudications Act 1983 (Commencement No 2) Order 1983, SI 1983/1862; Health and Social Services and Social Security Adjudications Act 1983 (Commencement No 3) Order 1984, SI 1984/216; Health and Social Services and Social Security Adjudications Act 1983 (Commencement No 4) Order 1984, SI 1984/957; Health and Social Services and Social Security Adjudications Act 1984 (Commencement No 5) Order 1984, SI 1984/1347; Health and Social Services and Social Security Adjudications Act 1983 (Scotland) (Commencement No 1) Order 1985, SI 1985/704; Health and Social Services and Social Security Adjudications Act 1983 (Commencement No 6) Order 1992, SI 1992/2974

s 1	15 Aug 1983 (so far as relates to (i) National Health Service Act 1977, s 28A(2)(a)–(d), but only for the purpose of giving effect to s 28B(1)(a) of that Act, and (ii) s 28B of the 1977 Act) (SI 1983/974)
	1 Apr 1984 (so far as relates to new s 28A of the 1977 Act) (SI 1984/216)
2	1 May 1985 (SI 1985/704)
3	15 Aug 1983 (SI 1983/974)
4	1 Jan 1984 (SI 1983/974)
5, 6	Repealed
7(1)	15 Aug 1983 (SI 1983/974)
(2), (3)	30 Jan 1984 (SI 1983/1862)
8	30 Jan 1984 (SI 1983/1862)
9	See Sch 2 below
10	1 Apr 1984 (SI 1983/974)
11	1 Oct 1984 (so far as relates to Sch 4, para 24 (repealed)) (SI 1984/957)
	1 Jan 1985 (otherwise) (SI 1984/1347))
12	See Sch 5 below
13, 14	15 Aug 1983 (SI 1983/974)
15, 16	1 Oct 1984 (SI 1983/974)
17–19	1 Jan 1984 (SI 1983/974)
20	15 Aug 1983 (SI 1983/974)
21–24	12 Apr 1993 (SI 1992/2974)
25	See Sch 8 below
26–28	15 Aug 1983 (SI 1983/974)
29(1)	See Sch 9, Pt I below
(2)	See Sch 9, Pt II below
30(1)	See Sch 10, Pt I below
(2)	See Sch 10, Pt II below
(3)	Repealed
31	15 Aug 1983 (SI 1983/974)
32–34	13 May 1983 (s 32(1))

**Health and Social Services and Social Security Adjudications Act 1983
(c 41)**—*cont*

Sch 1		Repealed
	2, para 1–3	Repealed
	4–8	15 Aug 1983 (SI 1983/974)
	9–14	Repealed
	15, 16	15 Aug 1983 (SI 1983/974)
	17, 18	1 Jan 1984 (SI 1983/974)
	19	15 Aug 1983 (SI 1983/974)
	20–24	Repealed
	25, 26	Spent
	27, 28	Repealed
	29–33	15 Aug 1983 (SI 1983/974)
	34	Repealed
	35	15 Aug 1983 (SI 1983/974) (only in force as from 27 May 1984; SI 1983/1946)
	36	15 Aug 1983 (SI 1983/974)
	37	Repealed
	38–45	15 Aug 1983 (SI 1983/974)
	46–62	Repealed
3		1 Apr 1984 (SI 1983/974)
4		Repealed
5, para 1		15 Aug 1983 (SI 1983/974)
	2	1 Apr 1984 (SI 1984/216)
	3	15 Aug 1983 (SI 1983/974)
6, 7		15 Aug 1983 (SI 1983/974)
8		Repealed (except paras 1(3)(a), 29, which came into force on 23 Apr 1984 (SI 1984/216))
9, Pt I, para 1		Repealed
	2	15 Aug 1983 (SI 1983/974)
	3	1 Apr 1984 (SI 1983/974)
	4–6	Repealed
	7, 8	15 Aug 1983 (SI 1983/974)
	9–17	Repealed
	18	23 Apr 1984 (SI 1984/216)
	19	1 Jan 1985 (SI 1984/1347)
	20	Repealed
	21	15 Aug 1983 (SI 1983/974)
	22	1 Jan 1984 (SI 1983/974)
	23	1 Apr 1984 (SI 1983/974)
	24, 25	15 Aug 1983 (SI 1983/974)
	26	Repealed
	27	1 Jan 1985 (SI 1984/1347)
	28	15 Aug 1983 (SI 1983/974)
	II	1 Jan 1984 (SI 1983/974)
10, Pt I		15 Aug 1983 (repeals of or in Public Health Act 1936; Food and Drugs Act 1955; Health Services and Public Health Act 1968, ss 48(2), 64 (so far as relates to Scotland); Social Work (Scotland) Act 1968, s 31(2); Radiological Protection Act 1970; Powers of Criminal Courts Act 1973; Children Act 1975, s 109(3); Adoption Act 1976; Criminal Law Act 1977; National Health Service Act 1977, ss 8(1A), 9, 100(2), 128(1), Sch 5; Adoption (Scotland) Act 1978; Employment Protection (Consolidation) Act 1978; Child Care Act 1980, ss 71, 79(5)(h); Health Services Act 1980, ss 1, 4(1) (but only for the purpose of giving effect to new

Health and Social Services and Social Security Adjudications Act 1983 (c 41)—*cont*

Sch 10, Pt I—*cont*

s 28B(1)(a) of National Health Service Act 1977), Sch 1; Overseas Development and Co-operation Act 1980) (SI 1983/974, as partly revoked by SI 1983/1862)

1 Jan 1984 (repeals of or in National Assistance Act 1948; Local Government Act 1966; Health Services and Public Health Act 1968, s 45(2); Social Work (Scotland) Act 1968, ss 14(2), 78(1)(b); Children and Young Persons Act 1969; Local Government Act 1972; National Health Service Act 1977, Sch 8; Domestic Proceedings and Magistrates' Courts Act 1978; Child Care Act 1980, ss 10(2), 36(1), 39(2), 43(3), 44(5), 45(1)(ii), 87(1), Schs 1, 5; Residential Homes Act 1980 (but only for the purposes of the repeal of s 8 of that Act); Criminal Justice Act 1982) (SI 1983/974, as partly revoked by SI 1983/1862)

30 Jan 1984 (repeals of or in Social Work (Scotland) Act 1968, s 59A(1), (3); Children Act 1975, s 72) (SI 1983/1862)

1 Apr 1984 (repeals of or in Health Visiting and Social Work (Training) Act 1962; Local Authority Social Services Act 1970; National Health Service Act 1977, Sch 15; Nurses, Midwives and Health Visitors Act 1979) (SI 1983/974, as partly revoked by SI 1983/1862)

1 Apr 1984 (repeal of Health Services Act 1980, s 4(1) for remaining purposes) (SI 1984/216)

23 Apr 1984 (repeals of or in Family Income Supplements Act 1970; Tribunals and Inquiries Act 1971; Social Security Act 1975; House of Commons Disqualification Act 1975; Child Benefit Act 1975; Supplementary Benefits Act 1976; Social Security (Miscellaneous Provisions) Act 1977; Social Security and Housing Benefits Act 1982) (SI 1984/216)

1 Jan 1985 (repeals of or in Nursing Homes Act 1975; Child Care Act 1980, s 58, Sch 3; Residential Homes Act 1980 (except s 8, repealed on 1 Jan 1984); Children's Homes Act 1982) (SI 1984/1347, as amended by SI 1984/1767)

1 May 1985 (repeal of Health Services Act 1980, s 4(2)) (SI 1985/704)

II   15 Aug 1983 (SI 1983/974)

Importation of Milk Act 1983 (c 37)

Whole Act repealed

International Monetary Arrangements Act 1983 (c 51)

RA: 26 Jul 1983

Commencement provisions: s 3(2); International Monetary Arrangements Act 1983 (Commencement) Order 1983, SI 1983/1643

International Monetary Arrangements Act 1983 (c 51)—*cont*
s 1   14 Nov 1983 (SI 1983/1643)
  2, 3   26 Jul 1983 (RA)

International Transport Conventions Act 1983 (c 14)

RA: 11 Apr 1983

Commencement provisions: s 11(3); International Transport Convention Act 1983
  (Certification of Commencement of Convention) Order 1985, SI 1985/612

s 1   1 May 1985 (SI 1985/612)
  2–10   11 Apr 1983 (RA)
  11   11 Apr 1983 (RA; sub-s (2) effective from 1 May 1985,
                         the day on which the Convention comes into force
                         as regards the United Kingdom) (s 11(3); SI 1985/
                         612)

Sch 1, 2   11 Apr 1983 (RA)
  3   1 May 1985 (SI 1985/612)

Level Crossings Act 1983 (c 16)

RA: 9 May 1983

Commencement provisions: s 2(2)

9 Aug 1983 (s 2(2))

Licensing (Occasional Permissions) Act 1983 (c 24)

RA: 9 May 1983

Commencement provisions: s 5(2)

9 Aug 1983 (s 5(2))

Litter Act 1983 (c 35)

RA: 13 May 1983

Commencement provisions: s 13(2), (3)

s 1, 2   Repealed
  3   13 Aug 1983 (s 13(3))
  4   *Not in force*
  5–11   13 Aug 1983 (s 13(3))
  12(1)   Repealed
    (2)   13 Aug 1983 (s 13(3))
    (3)   See Sch 2 below
  13   13 Aug 1983 (s 13(3))

Sch 1   13 Aug 1983 (s 13(3))
  2   13 Aug 1983 (except repeal of Control of Pollution
                         Act 1974, s 24(1)–(3)) (s 13(2))
                       Not in force (exception noted above)

Local Authorities (Expenditure Powers) Act 1983 (c 52)

Whole Act repealed

Marriage Act 1983 (c 32)

RA: 13 May 1983

Commencement provisions: s 12(5); Marriage Act 1983 (Commencement) Order 1984, SI 1984/413

1 May 1984 (SI 1984/413)

Matrimonial Homes Act 1983 (c 19)

RA: 9 May 1983

Commencement provisions: s 13(2)

9 Aug 1983 (s 13(2))

Medical Act 1983 (c 54)

RA: 26 Jul 1983

Commencement provisions: s 57(2)

26 Oct 1983 (s 57(2))

Mental Health Act 1983 (c 20)

RA: 9 May 1983

Commencement provisions: s 149(2), (3); Mental Health Act 1983 Commencement Order 1984, SI 1984/1357

s 1–26	30 Sep 1983 (s 149(2))
27	Substituted by Children Act 1989, s 108(5), Sch 13, para 48 (qv)
28–34	30 Sep 1983 (s 149(2))
35, 36	1 Oct 1984 (SI 1984/1357)
37	30 Sep 1983 (s 149(2))
38	1 Oct 1984 (SI 1984/1357)
39	30 Sep 1983 (s 149(2))
39A	Inserted by Criminal Justice Act 1991, s 27(1) (qv)
40(1), (2)	30 Sep 1983 (s 149(2))
(3)	1 Oct 1984 (SI 1984/1357)
(4), (5)	30 Sep 1983 (s 149(2))
41–54	30 Sep 1983 (s 149(2))
54A	Inserted by Criminal Justice Act 1991, s 27(2) (qv)
55–123	30 Sep 1983 (s 149(2)
124	Repealed
125–149	30 Sep 1983 (s 149(2))
Sch 1–6	30 Sep 1983 (s 149(2))

Mental Health (Amendment) (Scotland) Act 1983 (c 39)

RA: 13 May 1983

Commencement provisions: s 41(2) (repealed); Mental Health (Amendment) (Scotland) Act 1983 (Commencement No 1) Order 1983, SI 1983/1199; Mental Health (Amendment) (Scotland) Act 1983 (Commencement No 2) Order 1983, SI 1983/1920

Whole Act repealed, subject to savings for the provisions mentioned below

s 7(2)	16 Aug 1983 (SI 1983/1199)
22(2)	30 Sep 1984 (SI 1983/1920)
34–36	30 Sep 1984 (SI 1983/1920)
Sch 2, para 1	30 Sep 1984 (SI 1983/1920)
38	31 Mar 1984 (SI 1983/1920)

Merchant Shipping Act 1983 (c 13)

Whole Act repealed

Miscellaneous Financial Provisions Act 1983 (c 29)

RA: 13 May 1983

Commencement provisions: s 9(^{1}), (2); Miscellaneous Financial Provisions Act 1983 (Commencement of Provisions) Order 1983, SI 1983/1338

s 1	1 Apr 1984 (SI 1983/1338)
2	13 Jul 1983 (s 9(2))
3	Repealed
4–7	13 Jul 1983 (s 9(2))
8	1 Apr 1984 (SI 1983/1338)
9–11	13 Jul 1983 (s 9(2))
Sch 1	1 Apr 1984 (SI 1983/1338)
2	13 Jul 1983 (s 9(2))
3	1 Apr 1984 (SI 1983/1338)

Mobile Homes Act 1983 (c 34)

RA: 13 May 1983

Commencement provisions: s 6(3)

20 May 1983 (s 6(3))

National Audit Act 1983 (c 44)

RA: 13 May 1983

Commencement provisions: s 15(2), (3)

s 1–15	1 Jan 1984 (s 15(2))
Sch 1–4	1 Jan 1984 (s 15(2))

National Audit Act 1983 (c 44)—*cont*

Sch 5   1 Jan 1984 (repeal of Exchequer and Audit
                                                        Departments Act 1866, s 24; Exchequer and Audit
                                                        Departments Act 1921, in s 1(2), the proviso,
                                                        ss 3(3), (4), 8(1)) (s 15(2))
                                                      1 Oct 1984 (repeal of Exchequer and Audit
                                                        Departments Act 1921, s 8(2)) (s 15(3))

National Heritage Act 1983 (c 47)

RA: 13 May 1983

Commencement provisions: s 41(1)–(3); National Heritage Act 1983 (Commencement
No 1) Order 1983, SI 1983/1062; National Heritage Act 1983 (Commencement No
2) Order 1983, SI 1983/1183; National Heritage Act 1983 (Commencement No 3)
Order 1983, SI 1983/1437; National Heritage Act 1983 (Commencement No 4)
Order 1984, SI 1984/208, National Heritage Act 1983 (Commencement No 5)
Order 1984, SI 1984/217; National Heritage Act 1983 (Commencement No 6)
Order 1984, SI 1984/225

s 1(1)	30 Sep 1983 (SI 1983/1062)
(2)	See Sch 1, Pt I below
2, 3	1 Apr 1984 (SI 1984/225)
4(1)–(4)	1 Apr 1984 (SI 1984/225)
(5)	13 Jul 1983 (s 41(3))
(6)	1 Apr 1984 (SI 1984/225)
(7)	13 Jul 1983 (s 41(3))
(8)	1 Apr 1984 (SI 1984/225)
5–7	1 Apr 1984 (SI 1984/225)
8	Repealed
9(1)	30 Sep 1983 (SI 1983/1062)
(2)	See Sch 1, Pt II below
10, 11	1 Apr 1984 (SI 1984/225)
12(1)–(4)	1 Apr 1984 (SI 1984/225)
(5), (6)	13 Jul 1983 (s 41(3))
(7)	1 Apr 1984 (SI 1984/225)
13–15	1 Apr 1984 (SI 1984/225)
16	Repealed
17	1 Oct 1983 (SI 1983/1437)
18	1 Apr 1984 (SI 1984/208)
18A	Inserted by Museums and Galleries Act 1992, s 11(2), Sch 8, Pt II, para 13(4) (qv)
19(1)–(3)	1 Apr 1984 (SI 1984/208)
(4), (5)	13 Jul 1983 (s 41(3))
(6)	1 Apr 1984 (SI 1984/208)
20, 21	1 Apr 1984 (SI 1984/208)
22	1 Oct 1983 (SI 1983/1437)
23	8 Aug 1983 (SI 1983/1183)
24–28	1 Apr 1984 (SI 1984/217)
29	8 Aug 1983 (SI 1983/1183)
30, 31	13 Jul 1983 (s 41(3))
32	1 Oct 1983 (SI 1983/1437)
33(1), (2)	1 Apr 1984 (SI 1984/208)
(2A)	Inserted by Planning and Compensation Act 1991, s 29(1) (qv)

National Heritage Act 1983 (c 47)—*cont*

s 33(2B)	Inserted by Leasehold Reform, Housing and Urban Development Act 1993, s 187(1), Sch 21, para 9 (qv)
(3), (4)	1 Apr 1984 (SI 1984/208)
(5)	1 Oct 1983 (SI 1983/1437)
(6)–(8)	1 Apr 1984 (SI 1984/208)
34	1 Apr 1984 (SI 1984/208)
35	1 Oct 1983 (SI 1983/1437)
36, 37	1 Apr 1984 (SI 1984/208)
38	1 Oct 1983 (SI 1983/1437)
39	1 Apr 1984 (SI 1984/208)
40(1)	See Sch 5 below
(2)	See Sch 6 below
41–43	13 Jul 1983 (s 41(3))
Sch 1, Pt I, para 1–8	30 Sep 1983 (SI 1983/1062)
9	Repealed
10	30 Sep 1983 (SI 1983/1062)
II 11–18	30 Sep 1983 (SI 1983/1062)
19	Repealed
20	30 Sep 1983 (SI 1983/1062)
III 21–30	1 Oct 1983 (SI 1983/1437)
IV 31–40	8 Aug 1983 (SI 1983/1183)
2	13 Jul 1983 (s 41(3))
3	1 Oct 1983 (SI 1983/1437)
4, para 1–11	1 Apr 1984 (SI 1984/208)
12	Spent
13–21	Repealed
22	1 Apr 1984 (SI 1984/208)
23, 24	Repealed
25–71	1 Apr 1984 (SI 1984/208)
5, para 1, 2	Repealed
3	8 Aug 1983 (so far as relates to Royal Botanic Gardens, Kew) (SI 1983/1183)
	30 Sep 1983 (so far as relates to the Science Museum and the Victoria and Albert Museum) (SI 1983/1062)
	1 Oct 1983 (so far as relates to Armouries, the Historic Buildings and Monuments Commission for England and the Board of Trustees of the Armouries) (SI 1983/1437)
4–7	Repealed
6	3 Aug 1983 (repeal in National Gallery and Tate Gallery Act 1954, s 4(2)) (SI 1983/1062)
	1 Apr 1984 (repeals in Historic Buildings and Ancient Monuments Act 1953; Town and Country Planning (Amendment) Act 1972; Ancient Monuments and Archaeological Areas Act 1979) (SI 1984/208)
	1 Apr 1984 (repeals in Patents and Designs Act 1907, s 47(1); Public Records Act 1958, Sch 1, para 3 (entries in Pt I of the Table relating to the Victoria and Albert Museum and the Science Museum) (SI 1984/225)

Nuclear Material (Offences) Act 1983 (c 18)

RA: 9 May 1983

Commencement provisions: s 8(2); Nuclear Material (Offences) Act 1983
(Commencement) Order 1991, SI 1991/1716

s 1–4	2 Oct 1991 (SI 1991/1716)
5	Repealed
6	2 Oct 1991 (SI 1991/1716)
7(1)	Repealed
(2)	24 Jul 1991 (in relation to any Order in Council) (SI 1991/1716)
	2 Oct 1991 (otherwise) (SI 1991/1716)
8	2 Oct 1991 (SI 1991/1716)

Oil Taxation Act 1983 (c 56)

RA: 1 Dec 1983

1 Dec 1983 (RA) (though largely effective from 1 Jul 1982)

Pastoral Measure 1983 (No 1)

RA: 9 May 1983

Commencement provisions: s 94(4)

1 Nov 1983 (s 94(4))

Pet Animals Act 1951 (Amendment) Act 1983 (c 26)

RA: 9 May 1983

Commencement provisions: s 2(2)

9 Nov 1983 (s 2(2))

Petroleum Royalties (Relief) Act 1983 (c 59)

RA: 21 Dec 1983

Commencement provisions: s 2(2)

21 Feb 1984 (s 2(2))

Pig Industry Levy Act 1983 (c 4)

RA: 1 Mar 1983

1 Mar 1983 (RA)

Pilotage Act 1983 (c 21)

Whole Act repealed

Plant Varieties Act 1983 (c 17)

RA: 9 May 1983

Commencement provisions: s 6(3)

9 Jul 1983 (s 6(3))

Ports (Reduction of Debt) Act 1983 (c 22)

RA: 9 May 1983

9 May 1983 (RA)

Representation of the People Act 1983 (c 2)

RA: 8 Feb 1983

Commencement provisions: s 207(2); Representation of the People Act 1983 (Commencement) Order 1983, SI 1983/153

15 Mar 1983 (SI 1983/153)

Road Traffic (Driving Licences) Act 1983 (c 43)

Whole Act repealed

Social Security and Housing Benefits Act 1983 (c 36)

Whole Act repealed

Solvent Abuse (Scotland) Act 1983 (c 33)

RA: 13 May 1983

Commencement provisions: s 3(2)

13 July 1983 (s 3(2))

Transport Act 1983 (c 10)

RA: 28 Mar 1983

Commencement provisions: s 10(1)(a)–(c)

This Act came into force on Royal Assent, subject to certain provisions of Pt I taking effect; see the relevant provisions as noted below:

s 1	28 Mar 1983 (s 10(1))
2	Effective in relation to any accounting period of an Executive ending after 31 Mar 1983 (s 10(1)(a))
3, 4	1 Apr 1983 (s 10(1)(b))
5	Effective in relation to any year beginning on or after 1 Apr 1984 (s 10(1)(c))
6(1), (2)	1 Apr 1983 (s 10(1)(b))

Transport Act 1983 (c 10)—*cont*

s 6(3), (4)	Repealed
(5), (6)	1 Apr 1983 (s 10(1)(b))
(7)	Effective in relation to any accounting period of an Executive ending after 31 Mar 1983 (s 10(1)(a))
7, 8	28 Mar 1983 (s 10(1))
9(1)	See Schedule below
(2)	Repealed
(3)	Effective in relation to any accounting period of an Executive ending after 31 Mar 1983 (s 10(1)(a))
(4), (5)	Repealed
10	28 Mar 1983 (s 10(1))
11, 12	28 Mar 1983 (RA)
Schedule	31 Mar 1983 (repeals in Transport (London) Act 1969, ss 5, 7) (s 10(1)(a))
	1 Apr 1983 (repeals in Transport (London) Act 1969, s 11) (s 10(1)(b))

Value Added Tax Act 1983 (c 55)

RA: 26 Jul 1983

Commencement provisions: s 51(2)

26 Oct 1983 (s 51(2))

Water Act 1983 (c 23)

RA: 9 May 1983

Commencement provisions: ss 3(1), 9(2), 11(4), (5); Water Act 1983 (Commencement No 1) Order 1983, SI 1983/1173; Water Act 1983 (Water Space Amenity Commission Appointed Day) Order 1983, SI 1983/1174; Water Act 1983 (Commencement No 2) Order 1983, SI 1983/1234; Water Act 1983 (National Water Council Appointed Day) Order 1983, SI 1983/1235; Water Act 1983 (Dissolution of the National Water Council) Order 1983, SI 1983/1927; Water Act 1983 (Representation of Consumers' Interests) (Appointed Date) Order 1984, SI 1984/71

s 1(1)	Repealed
(2)	1 Oct 1983 (SI 1983/1234; prospectively repealed by Water Act 1989, s 190(3), Sch 27, Pt II (qv))
(3)	Repealed
2	Repealed
3, 4	9 May 1983 (s 11(4))
5–7	Repealed
8	10 Aug 1983 (SI 1983/1173)
9, 10	9 May 1983 (s 11(4))
11(1)	9 May 1983 (s 11(4))
(2), (3)	See Schs 4, 5 below
(4)–(7)	9 May 1983 (s 11(4))
Sch 1	Repealed
2	9 May 1983 (s 11(4))
3	Repealed

Water Act 1983 (c 23)—*cont*

Sch 4, para 1–6	Repealed
7	1 Oct 1983 (SI 1983/1234)
8, 9	9 May 1983 (s 11(4))
5, Pt I	10 Aug 1983 (repeals of or in Development of Rural Wales Act 1976, Sch 7, para 11; Water Charges Equalisation Act 1977; Local Government Planning and Land Act 1980, s 158(1), (2); New Towns Act 1981, Sch 12, para 12) (SI 1983/1173)
	1 Oct 1983 (repeals of or in Water Act 1973, ss 23, 24(12)(a), 25(5)(a), Sch 3, para 40, sub-para (1)(b) and word 'and' immediately preceding it, and sub-para (5)) (SI 1983/1174)
	1 Oct 1983 (repeals of or in Public Bodies (Admission to Meetings) Act 1960; Local Government Act 1972; Water Act 1973, ss 6, 17(5); House of Commons Disqualification Act 1975, Sch 1, Pt III; Local Government, Planning and Land Act 1980, s 25(4)) (SI 1983/1234)
	1 Oct 1983 (repeals of or in Public Health Act 1961, s 9(3); Water Act 1973, ss 4, 5(3), 26(2)–(4), 29(2), 30(6), 38(1), Sch 3, Sch 8, para 90; House of Commons Disqualification Act 1975, Sch 1, Pt III; Land Drainage Act 1976, Sch 5, para 8(1); Water (Scotland) Act 1980, Sch 10) (SI 1983/1235)
	Not in force (Local Government (Scotland) Act 1973, Sch 17, para 64)
II	9 May 1983 (revocation of SI 1982/944) (s 11(4))
	1 Oct 1983 (otherwise) (SI 1983/1234)

1984

Agricultural Holdings Act 1984 (c 41)

Whole Act repealed

Agriculture (Amendment) Act 1984 (c 20)

RA: 24 May 1984

Commencement provisions: s 3(2)

24 Jul 1984 (s 3(2))

Anatomy Act 1984 (c 14)

RA: 24 May 1984

Commencement provisions: s 13(3); Anatomy Act 1984 (Commencement) Order 1988, SI 1988/81

14 Feb 1988 (SI 1988/81)

Animal Health and Welfare Act 1984 (c 40)

RA: 12 Jul 1984

Commencement provisions: s 17(2)–(4); Animal Health and Welfare Act 1984 (Commencement No 1) Order 1985, SI 1985/1267

s 1–4	12 Sep 1984 (s 17(2))
5(1)	12 Sep 1984 (except in relation to slaughter of poultry chicks within meaning of Slaughter of Poultry Act 1967, s 1(2B)) (s 17(2))
	Not in force (exception noted above) (s 17(4))
(2)–(7)	12 Sep 1984 (s 17(2))
6–12	12 Sep 1984 (s 17(2))
13	16 Aug 1985 (SI 1985/1267)
14–17	12 Sep 1984 (s 17(2))
Sch 1, para 1, 2	12 Sep 1984 (s 17(2))
3	16 Aug 1985 (SI 1985/1267)
4	12 Sep 1984 (s 17(2))
2	12 Sep 1984 (except repeals in Medicines Act 1968) (s 17(2))
	16 Aug 1985 (exception noted above) (SI 1985/1267)

Appropriation Act 1984 (c 44)

Whole Act repealed

Betting, Gaming and Lotteries (Amendment) Act 1984 (c 25)

RA: 26 Jun 1984

Commencement provisions: s 4(2); Betting, Gaming and Lotteries (Amendment) Act 1984 (Commencement) Order 1986, SI 1986/102

s 1	26 Aug 1984 (s 4(2))
2	10 Mar 1986 (SI 1986/102)
3	26 Aug 1984 (s 4(2))
4	26 Jun 1984 (RA)

Building Act 1984 (c 55)

RA: 31 Oct 1984

Commencement provisions: s 134; Building Act 1984 (Commencement No 1) Order 1985, SI 1985/1602; Building Act 1984 (Appointed Day and Repeal) Order 1985, SI 1985/1603

s 1–11	1 Dec 1984 (s 134(2))
12, 13	1 Dec 1984 (so far as enable regulations to be made) (s 134(1)(a))
	Not in force (otherwise)
14, 15	1 Dec 1984 (s 134(2))
16	1 Dec 1984 (11 Nov 1985 being the appointed day under sub-s (13)) (SI 1985/1603)
17–19	1 Dec 1984 (s 134(2))
20	*Not in force*
21–25	1 Dec 1984 (s 134(2))
26–30	Repealed
31	1 Dec 1984 (far as enables regulations to be made) (s 134(1)(a))
	Not in force (otherwise)
32	1 Dec 1984 (s 134(2))
33	*Not in force*
34–37	1 Dec 1984 (s 134(2))
38	1 Dec 1984 (so far as enables regulations to be made) (s 134(1)(a))
	Not in force (otherwise)
39–41	1 Dec 1984 (s 134(2))
42(1)–(3)	*Not in force*
(4)–(6)	1 Dec 1984 (so far as enable regulations to be made) (s 134(1)(a))
	Not in force (otherwise)
(7)	1 Dec 1984 (but no day appointed)
43(1), (2)	*Not in force*
(3)	*Not in force* (except so far as enables regulations to be made) (s 134(1)(a))
44, 45	*Not in force*
46–49	1 Dec 1984 (s 134(2))
50(1)	1 Dec 1984 (s 134(2))
(2), (3)	11 Nov 1985 (SI 1985/1602)
(4)–(8)	1 Dec 1984 (s 134(2))
51–68	1 Dec 1984 (s 134(2))

Building Act 1984 (c 55)—*cont*

s 69	Repealed (for savings see Water Act 1989, s 190(2), Sch 26, Pt II, para 20(2))
70–108	1 Dec 1984 (s 134(2))
109	Repealed
110–132	1 Dec 1984 (s 134(2))
133(1)	1 Dec 1984 (s 134(2))
133(2)	1 Dec 1984 (except so far as relates to Town and Country Planning Act 1947 and Atomic Energy Authority Act 1954) (s 134(2))
	Not in force (otherwise)(s 134(1)(c))
134	1 Dec 1984 (s 134(2))
135	1 Dec 1984 (s 134(2))
Sch 1, para 1–8	1 Dec 1984 (s 134(2))
9	*Not in force*
10, 11	1 Dec 1984 (s 134(2))
2–6	1 Dec 1984 (s 134(2))
7	*Not in force* (repeals of or in Town and Country Planning Act 1947; Atomic Energy Authority Act 1954) (s 134(1)(c))
	1 Dec 1984 (otherwise) (s 134(2))

Cable and Broadcasting Act 1984 (c 46)

Whole Act repealed

Capital Transfer Tax Act 1984 (c 51)

RA: 31 Jul 1984

Commencement provisions: s 274(1)

1 Jan 1985 (s 274(1))

Notes

This Act does not apply to transfers of value made before 1985 or to other events before then on which tax is or would be chargeable. Note also s 275 of, and Sch 7 to, the Act in relation to continuity and construction of references to old and new law

On and after 25 Jul 1986 the tax charged under this Act is known as inheritance tax and this Act may be cited as the Inheritance Tax Act 1984 (Finance Act 1986, s 100)

Child Abduction Act 1984 (c 37)

RA: 12 Jul 1984

Commencement provisions: s 13(2)

12 Oct 1984 (s 13(2))

Consolidated Fund Act 1984 (c 1)

Whole Act repealed

Consolidated Fund (No 2) Act 1984 (c 61)

Whole Act repealed

Co-operative Development Agency and Industrial Development Act 1984 (c 57)

RA: 31 Oct 1984

Commencement provisions: s 7(1); Co-operative Development Agency and Industrial Development Act 1984 (Commencement) Order 1984, SI 1984/1845

s 1, 2	Repealed
3	31 Oct 1984 (s 7(1))
4, 5	29 Nov 1984 (SI 1984/1845)
6	See Sch 2 below
7, 8	31 Oct 1984 (s 7(1))
Sch 1	29 Nov 1984 (SI 1984/1845)
2, Pt I	31 Oct 1984 (s 7(1))
II	31 Dec 1990 (see note below)
III	29 Nov 1984 (SI 1984/1845)

Note

The day appointed for the winding up of the Co-operative Development Agency by the Co-operative Development Agency (Winding up and Dissolution) Order 1990 (SI 1990/279)

County Courts Act 1984 (c 28)

RA: 26 Jun 1984

Commencement provisions: s 150

1 Aug 1984 (s 150)

Cycle Tracks Act 1984 (c 38)

RA: 12 Jul 1984

Commencement provisions: s 9(2)

12 Sep 1984 (s 9(2))

Data Protection Act 1984 (c 35)

RA: 12 Jul 1984

Commencement provisions: s 42; Data Protection Act 1984 (Appointed Day) Order 1985, SI 1985/1055

12 Jul 1984 (RA)

Note

Although this Act in general came into force on the date of Royal Assent, no application for registration under Pt II of the Act is to be made until a day to be appointed by order and certain provisions of the Act are not to apply, or fully apply, until six months, or two years, after the day so appointed (s 42). The appointed day for the purposes of s 42(1) is 11 Nov 1985 (SI 1985/1055)

Dentists Act 1984 (c 24)

RA: 26 Jun 1984

Commencement provisions: s 55(1)–(3); Dentists Act 1984 (Commencement) Order
  1984, SI 1984/1815

s 1	1 Oct 1984 (s 55(1))
2(1)–(3)	1 Oct 1984 (s 55(1))
(4), (5)	1 Jan 1985 (SI 1984/1815)
3–27	1 Oct 1984 (s 55(1))
28	1 Jan 1985 (SI 1984/1815)
29, 30	1 Jan 1985 (so far as relate to proceedings before Health Committee or any direction or order given or made by that Committee) (SI 1984/1815)
	1 Oct 1984 (otherwise) (s 55(1))
31	1 Jan 1985 (SI 1984/1815)
32	1 Oct 1984 (s 55(1))
33	As noted to ss 29, 30 above
34–48	1 Oct 1984 (s 55(1))
49	26 Jul 1984 (s 55(2))
50–53	1 Oct 1984 (s 55(1))
54(1)	See Sch 5 below
(2)	See Sch 6, Pt I below
(3)	See Sch 6, Pt II below
55, 56	1 Oct 1984 (s 55(1))
Sch 1, para 1–7	1 Oct 1984 (s 55(1))
8(1)	1 Oct 1984 (s 55(1))
(2)	1 Jan 1985 (SI 1984/1815)
(3)–(12)	1 Oct 1984 (s 55(1))
2	1 Oct 1984 (s 55(1))
3, para 1, 2	As noted to ss 29, 30 above
3	1 Jan 1985 (SI 1984/1815)
4, 5	As noted to ss 29, 30 above
6	1 Jan 1985 (SI 1984/1815)
7, 8	As noted to ss 29, 30 above
9	Repealed
4, 5	1 Oct 1984 (s 55(1))
6, Pt I	26 Jul 1984 (repeal of Dentists Act 1983, s 29) (s 55(2))
	1 Oct 1984 (otherwise) (s 55(1))
II	1 Oct 1984 (s 55(1))
7	1 Oct 1984 (s 55(1))

Education (Amendment) (Scotland) Act 1984 (c 6)

RA: 13 Mar 1984

Commencement provisions: s 2

13 May 1984 (s 2)

Education (Grants and Awards) Act 1984 (c 11)

RA: 12 Apr 1984

Commencement provisions: s 6(2)

12 Jun 1984 (s 6(2))

Finance Act 1984 (c 43)

Budget Day: 13 Mar 1984

RA: 26 Jul 1984

See the note concerning Finance Acts at the front of this book

---

Food Act 1984 (c 30)

RA: 26 Jun 1984

Commencement provisions: s 136(4)

26 Sep 1984 (s 136(4))

Foreign Limitation Periods Act 1984 (c 16)

RA: 24 May 1984

Commencement provisions: s 7(2); Foreign Limitation Periods Act 1984
    (Commencement) Order 1985, SI 1985/1276

1 Oct 1985 (SI 1985/1276)

Fosdyke Bridge Act 1984 (c 17)

Local application only

Foster Children (Scotland) Act 1984 (c 56)

RA: 31 Oct 1984

Commencement provisions: s 23(2)

31 Jan 1985 (s 23(2))

Friendly Societies Act 1984 (c 62)

RA: 20 Dec 1984

20 Dec 1984 (RA)

Health and Social Security Act 1984 (c 48)

RA: 26 Jul 1984

Commencement provisions: s 27; Health and Social Security Act 1984 (Commencement No 1) Order 1984, SI 1984/1302; Health and Social Security Act 1984 (Commencement No 1) Amendment Order 1984, SI 1984/1467; Health and Social Security Act 1984 (Commencement No 2) Order 1986, SI 1986/974

s 1(1), (2)	Repealed
(3)	1 Jul 1986 (SI 1986/974)
(4)	1 Apr 1985 (SI 1984/1302)
(5)(a)	1 Jul 1986 (SI 1986/974)
(b)	1 Apr 1985 (SI 1984/1302)
(6), (7)	1 Jul 1986 (SI 1986/974)
2–4	Repealed
5(1)	26 Sep 1984 (SI 1984/1302)
(2), (3)	1 Apr 1985 (SI 1984/1302)
(4)	See Sch 3 below
(5)–(8)	26 Sep 1984 (SI 1984/1302)
6(1)	26 Sep 1984 (SI 1984/1302)
(2)	1 Apr 1985 (SI 1984/1302)
(3)	26 Sep 1984 (SI 1984/1302)
(4)	26 Jul 1984 (s 27(2))
7(1)–(3)	*Not in force*
(4)	26 Jul 1984 (s 27(2))
8	Repealed
9, 10	26 Jul 1984 (s 27(2))
11–14	Repealed
15	26 Jul 1984 (s 27(2))
16–18	Repealed
19	26 Sep 1984 (s 27(3)); prospectively repealed by Pension Schemes Act 1993, s 188, Sch 5, Pt I (qv)
20	1 Jan 1985 (SI 1984/1302); prospectively repealed by Pension Schemes Act 1993, s 188, Sch 5, Pt I (qv)
21	See Sch 7 below
22	Repealed
23	26 Jul 1984 (s 27(2))
24	See Sch 8 below
25–29	26 Jul 1984 (s 27(2))
Sch 1	1 Jul 1986 (SI 1986/974)
2	Repealed
3, para 1	26 Sep 1984 (SI 1984/1302)
2–6	1 Apr 1985 (SI 1984/1302)
7(a)	1 Apr 1985 (SI 1984/1302)
(b)(i)	1 Apr 1985 (SI 1984/1302)
(ii)	26 Sep 1984 (SI 1984/1302)
(c)	26 Sep 1984 (SI 1984/1302)
8–11	1 Apr 1985 (SI 1984/1302)
12	26 Sep 1984 (SI 1984/1302); prospectively repealed by National Health Service and Community Care Act 1990, s 66(2), Sch 10 (qv)
13–17	1 Apr 1985 (SI 1984/1302)
4, 5	Repealed
6	1 Jan 1985 (SI 1984/1302); prospectively repealed by Pension Schemes Act 1993, s 188, Sch 5, Pt I (qv)
7, para 1–3	Repealed

Health and Social Security Act 1984 (c 48)—*cont*

Sch 7, para 4, 5   26 Sep 1984 (s 27(3)); prospectively repealed by
                         Pension Schemes Act 1993, s 188, Sch 5, Pt I (qv)

         6–8   Repealed

         9   Spent

8   26 Sep 1984 (repeal in Social Security Pensions Act
                         1975, s 38(3)) (s 27(3))

                         26 Sep 1984 (repeals of or in National Health
                         Service Act 1977, ss 45(2), (3), 97(1)(a), (c), (2);
                         National Health Service (Scotland) Act 1978,
                         s 85(1); Health Services Act 1980, s 18, Sch 1,
                         paras 30, 79, 88, 99; Social Security Act 1980,
                         s 3(5)) (SI 1984/1302)

                         1 Nov 1984 (repeal in Opticians Act 1958, s 13(3))
                         (spent) (SI 1984/1302)

                         26 Nov 1984 (repeals of or in Social Security Act
                         1975, ss 12(1)(d), 41(2)(d), (3), Sch 4, Pt IV, para
                         3) (SI 1984/1302)

                         28 Nov 1984 (repeal of Child Benefit Act 1975,
                         Sch 4, para 25) (SI 1984/1302)

                         29 Nov 1984 (repeals of or in Social Security Act
                         1975, s 57(2), Sch 4, Pt IV, para 1(a), (c); Social
                         Security (Miscellaneous Provisions) Act 1977,
                         s 22(2); Social Security and Housing Benefits Act
                         1982, Sch 4, para 18(4)) (SI 1984/1302)

                         1 Apr 1985 (repeals of or in Tribunals and Inquiries
                         Act 1971, Sch 1 (repealed); National Health
                         Service Act 1977, ss 12(b), 15(1), (2), 39(c), 98(2),
                         Sch 5, paras 9(1)–(3), 10; National Health Service
                         (Scotland) Act 1978, s 26(2)(c); Health Services
                         Act 1980, ss 1(6), 2, Sch 1, paras 35, 37, 56, 57,
                         69, 77(b), 82(2), (3), 87, 89–98) (SI 1984/1302)

                         6 Apr 1985 (repeal in Social Security Pensions Act
                         1975, s 4(1)) (SI 1984/1302)

                         1 Jul 1986 (repeals of or in National Health Service Act
                         1977, ss 44, 46, 72, 81–83, Sch 5, paras 1, 2, 6(3)(e),
                         (5)(iv), Sch 12; National Health Service (Scotland)
                         Act 1978, ss 26 (except sub-s (2)(c)), 29, 64, 73–75,
                         Schs 8, 11; Health Services Act 1980, Sch 5)
                         (SI 1986/974)

                         Not in force (otherwise)

Housing and Building Control Act 1984 (c 29)

RA: 26 Jun 1984

Commencement provisions: s 66(3)

26 Aug 1984 (s 66(3))

Housing Defects Act 1984 (c 50)

Whole Act repealed

Inheritance Tax Act 1984 (c 51)

See entry for Capital Transfer Tax Act 1984 ante

Inshore Fishing (Scotland) Act 1984 (c 26)

RA: 26 Jun 1984

Commencement provisions: s 11(2); Inshore Fishing (Scotland) Act 1984 (Commencement) Order 1985, SI 1985/961

26 Jul 1985 (SI 1985/961)

Juries (Disqualification) Act 1984 (c 34)

RA: 12 Jul 1984

Commencement provisions: s 2(3); Juries (Disqualification) Act 1984 (Commencement) Order 1984, SI 1984/1599

1 Dec 1984 (SI 1984/1599)

Law Reform (Husband and Wife) (Scotland) Act 1984 (c 15)

RA: 24 May 1984

Commencement provisions: s 10(2)

24 Jul 1984 (s 10(2))

Local Government (Interim Provisions) Act 1984 (c 53)

RA: 31 Jul 1984

Commencement provisions: s 1(1); Local Government (Interim Provisions) Act 1984 (Appointed Day) Order 1985, SI 1985/2

Whole Act repealed, except ss 4, 6(3), 10, 11 and 13, which came into force on 31 Jul 1984 (RA)

London Regional Transport Act 1984 (c 32)

RA: 26 Jun 1984

Commencement provisions: s 72(2)–(6); London Regional Transport (Appointed Day) Order 1984, SI 1984/877

s 1–12	29 Jun 1984 (SI 1984/877)
13, 14	Repealed by Local Government Finance Act 1988, s 149, Sch 13, Pt III, in accordance with s 127 of that Act (qv) and subject to any regulations made under that section
15–31	29 Jun 1984 (SI 1984/877)

London Regional Transport Act 1984 (c 32)—*cont*

s 31A	Prospectively inserted by Railways Act 1993, s 152(1), Sch 12, para 17 (qv)
32–35	29 Jun 1984 (SI 1984/877)
36	29 Jun 1984 (SI 1984/877); prospectively repealed by Railways Act 1993, s 152(1), Sch 14 (qv)
37, 38	29 Jun 1984 (SI 1984/877; note that these sections apply only if brought into effect by order under s 36(1)); prospectively repealed by Railways Act 1993, s 152(1), Sch 14 (qv)
39	29 Jun 1984 (SI 1984/877); prospectively repealed by Railways Act 1993, s 152(1), Sch 14 (qv)
40(1)	26 Jun 1984 (s 72(4))
(2)	26 Jun 1984 (s 72(4)); prospectively substituted by Railways Act 1993, s 152(1), Sch 12, para 18(2) (qv)
(3)	26 Jun 1984 (s 72(4))
(4), (5)	29 Jun 1984 (SI 1984/877)
(6)	29 Jun 1984 (SI 1984/877); prospectively repealed by Railways Act 1993, s 152(1), (3), Sch 12, para 18(5), Sch 14 (qv)
(7)–(11)	29 Jun 1984 (SI 1984/877)
(12)	See Sch 3 below
41	29 Jun 1984 (SI 1984/877); prospectively repealed by Railways Act 1993, s 152(1), (3), Sch 12, para 19, Sch 14 (qv)
42	29 Jun 1984 (SI 1984/877)
43–45	Repealed
46–59	29 Jun 1984 (SI 1984/877)
60	26 Jun 1984 (s 72(3))
61–67	29 Jun 1984 (SI 1984/877)
68, 69	26 Jun 1984 (s 72(3))
70	29 Jun 1984 (SI 1984/877)
71(1)	29 Jun 1984 (SI 1984/877)
(2)	See Sch 5 below
(3)	See Schs 6, 7 below
(4)–(7)	29 Jun 1984 (SI 1984/877)
72	26 Jun 1984 (s 72(3))
Sch 1, 2	29 Jun 1984 (SI 1984/877)
3	26 Jun 1984 (s 72(4))
4	29 Jun 1984 (SI 1984/877)
5, para 1–6	29 Jun 1984 (SI 1984/877)
7	26 Jun 1984 (s 72(3))
8(1)–(5)	26 Jun 1984 (s 72(3))
(6)–(8)	29 Jun 1984 (SI 1984/877)
(9)	26 Jun 1984 (s 72(3))
(10)(a)	26 Jun 1984 (s 72(3))
(b)	29 Jun 1984 (SI 1984/877)
9–19	29 Jun 1984 (SI 1984/877)
6	29 Jun 1984 (SI 1984/877)
7	1 Apr 1985 (repeals of or in London Government Act 1963, Sch 2; Local Government, Planning and Land Act 1980, Sch 13, para 9) (s 72(6))
	29 Jun 1984 (otherwise) (SI 1984/877)

Lotteries (Amendment) Act 1984 (c 9)

RA: 12 Apr 1984

Commencement provisions: s 2(2)

12 Jun 1984 (s 2(2))

Matrimonial and Family Proceedings Act 1984 (c 42)

RA: 12 Jul 1984

Commencement provisions: s 47; Matrimonial and Family Proceedings Act 1984 (Commencement No 1) Order 1984, SI 1984/1589; Matrimonial and Family Proceedings Act 1984 (Commencement No 2) Order 1985, SI 1985/1316; Matrimonial and Family Proceedings Act 1984 (Commencement No 3) Order 1986, SI 1986/635; Matrimonial and Family Proceedings Act 1984 (Commencement No 4) Order 1986, SI 1986/1049; Matrimonial and Family Proceedings Act 1984 (Commencement No 3) (Scotland) Order 1986, SI 1986/1226; Matrimonial and Family Proceedings Act 1984 (Commencement No 5) Order 1991, SI 1991/1211

s 1–9	12 Oct 1984 (s 47(1))
10	1 Oct 1986 (SI 1986/1049)
11	12 Oct 1984 (s 47(1))
12–25	16 Sep 1985 (SI 1985/1316)
26	Repealed
27	16 Sep 1985 (SI 1985/1316)
28, 29	1 Sep 1986 (SI 1986/1226)
29A	Inserted (S) by the Family Law (Scotland) Act 1985, Sch 1, para 12 (qv)
30, 31	1 Sep 1986 (SI 1986/1226)
32–39	28 Apr 1986 (SI 1986/635)
40, 41	14 Oct 1991 (SI 1991/1211)
42, 43	28 Apr 1986 (SI 1986/635)
44	12 Oct 1984 (SI 1984/1589)
45	*Not in force*
46	See Schs 1–3 below
47, 48	12 Jul 1984 (s 47(1))
Sch 1, para 1(a)	16 Sep 1985 (SI 1985/1316)
(b)	1 Sep 1986 (SI 1986/1226)
2	12 Oct 1984 (SI 1984/1589)
3	28 Apr 1986 (SI 1986/635)
4	12 Oct 1984 (SI 1984/1589)
5	16 Sep 1985 (SI 1985/1316)
6, 7	1 Sep 1986 (SI 1986/1226)
8	16 Sep 1985 (SI 1985/1316)
9	Repealed
10–13	12 Oct 1984 (SI 1984/1589)
14	Repealed
15	16 Sep 1985 (SI 1985/1316)
16, 17	28 Apr 1986 (SI 1986/635)
18, 19	Repealed
20(a)	*Not in force*
(b)	28 Apr 1986 (SI 1986/635)

Matrimonial and Family Proceedings Act 1984 (c 42)—*cont*

Sch 1, para 21	1 Oct 1986 (SI 1986/1049)
22	12 Oct 1984 (SI 1984/1589)
23	Repealed
24–26	1 Oct 1986 (SI 1986/1049)
27	12 Oct 1984 (SI 1984/1589)
28	1 Sep 1986 (SI 1986/1226)
29	Repealed
30	28 Apr 1986 (SI 1986/635)
31	Repealed
2, para 1, 2	12 Oct 1984 (s 47(1))
3	*Not in force*
3	12 Oct 1984 (repeal of Matrimonial Causes Act 1973, ss 43(9), 44(6)) (SI 1984/1589)
	28 Apr 1986 (repeals of or in Matrimonial Causes Act 1967; Guardianship of Minors Act 1971; Courts Act 1971; Matrimonial Causes Act 1973, s 45, Sch 2; Domicile and Matrimonial Proceedings Act 1973; Children Act 1975; Adoption Act 1976; Domestic Proceedings and Magistrates' Courts Act 1978; Matrimonial Homes and Property Act 1981; Matrimonial Homes Act 1983; County Courts Act 1984) (SI 1986/635)
	14 Oct 1991 (otherwise) (SI 1991/1211)

Mental Health (Scotland) Act 1984 (c 36)

RA: 12 Jul 1984

Commencement provisions: s 130

30 Sep 1984 (s 130)

Merchant Shipping Act 1984 (c 5)

RA: 13 Mar 1984

Commencement provisions: s 14(5)

13 May 1984 (s 14(5))

Occupiers' Liability Act 1984 (c 3)

RA: 13 Mar 1984

Commencement provisions: s 4(2)

13 May 1984 (s 4(2))

Ordnance Factories and Military Services Act 1984 (c 59)

RA: 31 Oct 1984

31 Oct 1984 (RA)

Parliamentary Pensions etc Act 1984 (c 52)

RA: 31 Jul 1984

Commencement provisions: ss 1(5), 2(8), 4(5), 5(6)

s 1–11	Repealed*
12	31 Jul 1984 (RA)
13	Repealed
14, 15	31 Jul 1984 (RA)
16	Repealed*
17	31 Jul 1984 (RA)
Schedule	Repealed*

* Ss 1–11, 16 and the Schedule repealed, with savings, by Parliamentary and other Pensions Act 1987, ss 2(9), 6(2), Schs 2, 4 (qv)

Pensions Commutation Act 1984 (c 7)

RA: 13 Mar 1984

Commencement provisions: s 3(2); Pensions Commutation Act 1984 (Commencement) Order 1984, SI 1984/1140

20 Aug 1984 (SI 1984/1140)

Police and Criminal Evidence Act 1984 (c 60)

RA: 31 Oct 1984

Commencement provisions: s 121; Police and Criminal Evidence Act 1984 (Commencement No 1) Order 1984, SI 1984/2002; Police and Criminal Evidence Act 1984 (Commencement No 2) Order 1984, SI 1985/623; Police and Criminal Evidence Act 1984 (Commencement No 3) Order 1985/1934; Police and Criminal Evidence Act 1984 (Commencement No 4) Order 1991, SI 1991/2686; Police and Criminal Evidence Act 1984 (Commencement No 5) Order 1992, SI 1992/2802

s 1	1 Jan 1985 (so far as relates to search for stolen articles in localities in which, on 31 Dec 1984, an enactment (other than one contained in a public general Act or one relating to statutory undertakers) applies conferring power on a constable to search for stolen or unlawfully obtained goods) (SI 1984/2002)
	1 Jan 1986 (otherwise) (SI 1985/1934)
2–6	1 Jan 1986 (SI 1985/1934)
7(1)	1 Jan 1986 (SI 1985/1934)
(2)(a)	1 Jan 1986 (SI 1985/1934)
(b)	1 Jan 1985 (SI 1984/2002)
(3)	1 Jan 1985 (SI 1984/2002)
8–22	1 Jan 1986 (SI 1985/1934)
23	1 Jan 1985 (SI 1984/2002)
24–36	1 Jan 1986 (SI 1985/1934)
37(1)–(10)	1 Jan 1986 (SI 1985/1934)
(11)–(14)	Repealed
(15)	1 Jan 1986 (SI 1985/1934)
38–51	1 Jan 1986 (SI 1985/1934)

Police and Criminal Evidence Act 1984 (c 60)—*cont*

s 52	Repealed
53–58	1 Jan 1986 (SI 1985/1934)
59	Repealed
60(1)(a)	1 Jan 1986 (SI 1985/1934)
(b)	29 Nov 1991 (in the following police areas: Avon and Somerset, Bedfordshire, Cambridgeshire, Cheshire, City of London, Cleveland, Cumbria, Derbyshire, Devon and Cornwall, Dorset, Durham, Dyfed-Powys, Essex, Gloucestershire, Greater Manchester, Gwent, Hampshire, Hertfordshire, Humberside, Kent, Lancashire, Leicestershire, Lincolnshire, Merseyside, Metropolitan Police District, Norfolk, Northamptonshire, Northumbria, North Wales, North Yorkshire, Nottinghamshire, South Wales, South Yorkshire, Staffordshire, Suffolk, Surrey, Sussex, Warwickshire, West Mercia, West Midlands, West Yorkshire, Wiltshire) (SI 1991/2686)
	9 Nov 1992 (in the Thames Valley police area) (SI 1992/2802)
(2)	29 Nov 1991 (SI 1991/2686)
61–65	1 Jan 1986 (SI 1985/1934)
66, 67	1 Jan 1985 (SI 1984/2002)
68	Repealed
69–82	1 Jan 1986 (SI 1985/1934)
83–105	29 Apr 1985 (SI 1985/623)
106	1 Jan 1985 (SI 1984/2002)
107	1 Jan 1986 (SI 1985/1934)
108	1 Mar 1985 (SI 1984/2002)
109(a), (b)	29 Apr 1985 (SI 1985/623)
(c)	1 Jan 1985 (SI 1984/2002)
110, 111	1 Mar 1985 (SI 1984/2002)
112	1 Jan 1985 (SI 1984/2002)
113(1), (2)	1 Jan 1986 (SI 1985/1934)
(3)–(13)	1 Jan 1985 (SI 1984/2002)
114	1 Jan 1986 (SI 1985/1934)
115	1 Jan 1985 (SI 1984/2002)
116	29 Apr 1985 (SI 1985/623)
117	1 Jan 1986 (SI 1985/1934)
118	1 Jan 1985 (SI 1984/2002)
119	See Schs 6, 7 below
120–122	31 Oct 1984 (RA)
Sch 1–3	1 Jan 1986 (SI 1985/1934)
4, 5	29 Apr 1985 (SI 1985/623)
6, para 1–12	1 Jan 1986 (SI 1985/1934)
13	Repealed
14, 15	1 Mar 1985 (SI 1984/2002)
16	Repealed
17–21	1 Jan 1986 (SI 1985/1934)
22, 23	Repealed
24–26	1 Jan 1986 (SI 1985/1934)
27	Repealed
28, 29	1 Jan 1986 (SI 1985/1934)
30–33	1 Mar 1985 (SI 1984/2002)
34	1 Jan 1986 (SI 1985/1934)

Police and Criminal Evidence Act 1984 (c 60)—*cont*

Sch 6, para 35	29 Apr 1985 (SI 1985/623)
36–41	1 Jan 1986 (SI 1985/1934)
7	1 Mar 1985 (repeals in Police (Scotland) Act 1967) (SI 1984/2002, as amended by SI 1985/623)
	29 Apr 1985 (repeals of or in Police Act 1964; Superannuation Act 1972; House of Commons Disqualification Act 1975; Northern Ireland Assembly Disqualification Act 1975; Police Act 1976) (SI 1985/623)
	1 Jan 1986 (otherwise) (SI 1985/1934)

Prescription and Limitation (Scotland) Act 1984 (c 45)

RA: 26 Jul 1984

Commencement provisions: s 7(2)

26 Sep 1984 (s 7(2))

Prevention of Terrorism (Temporary Provisions) Act 1984 (c 8)

Whole Act repealed

Public Health (Control of Disease) Act 1984 (c 22)

RA: 26 Jun 1984

Commencement provisions: s 79(2)

26 Sep 1984 (s 79(2))

Rates Act 1984 (c 33)

RA: 26 Jun 1984

Commencement provisions: s 18

s 1–8	26 Jun 1984 (RA) (but maximum rate or precept may only be prescribed from financial year 1 Apr 1985 onwards (s 18(1)))
9	26 Jun 1984 (RA)
10, 11	*Not in force*
12	26 Jun 1984 (RA)
13	Repealed
14	26 Jun 1984 (RA)
15	Repealed, with savings, by the Local Government Finance (Repeals, Savings and Consequential Amendments) Order 1990, SI 1990/776, art 3, Sch 1
16(1)	See Sch 1 below
(2)	See Sch 2 below
(3)	26 Jun 1984 (RA)
17–19	26 Jun 1984 (RA)
Sch 1, para 1	26 Jun 1984 (RA)

Rates Act 1984 (c 33)—*cont*

Sch 1, para 2–22	Repealed, with savings, by Local Government Finance (Repeals, Savings and Consequential Amendments) Order 1990, SI 1990/776, art 3, Sch 1
23	Effective for any financial year from 1 Apr 1983 (para 23(2))
24	Effective for any financial year from 1 Apr 1984 (para 24(2))
2	Repealed, with savings, by Local Government Finance (Repeals, Savings and Consequential Amendments) Order 1990, SI 1990/776, art 3, Sch 1

Rating and Valuation (Amendment) (Scotland) Act 1984 (c 31)

RA: 26 Jun 1984

Commencement provisions: s 23(1)

s 1(1)	26 Jun 1984 (s 23(1)(a)); repealed as from 1 Apr 1994 by the Abolition of Domestic Rates Etc (Scotland) Act 1987, Sch 6 (qv)
(2)	Repealed
2–4	Repealed
5, 6	26 Aug 1984 (s 23(1)(c))
7	1 Apr 1985 (s 23(1)(b))
8	Repealed
9–13	1 Apr 1985 (s 23(1)(b))
14	26 Aug 1984 (s 23(1)(c))
15	Repealed
16	26 Aug 1984 (s 23(1)(c))
17–19	1 Apr 1985 (s 23(1)(b))
20	26 Aug 1984 (s 23(1)(c))
21(1)	See Sch 2 below
(2)	Repealed
22	26 Aug 1984 (s 23(1)(c))
23	26 Jun 1984 (s 23(1)(a))
Sch 1	Repealed
2, para 1–8	26 Aug 1984 (s 23(1)(c))
9	1 Apr 1985 (s 23(1)(b))
10, 11	26 Aug 1984 (s 23(1)(c))
12	Repealed
13–15	1 Apr 1985 (s 23(1)(b))
16	26 Aug 1984 (s 23(1)(c))
17	1 Apr 1985 (s 23(1)(b))
18	Repealed
3	Repealed

Registered Homes Act 1984 (c 23)

RA: 26 Jun 1984

Commencement provisions: s 59(2); Registered Homes Act 1984 (Commencement) Order 1984, SI 1984/1348

1 Jan 1985 (except s 1 so far as relates to an establishment which is a school referred to in s 1(5)(f), for which the date is 1 Jan 1986) (SI 1984/1348)

Rent (Scotland) Act 1984 (c 58)

RA: 31 Oct 1984

Commencement provisions: s 118(2)

31 Jan 1985 (s 118(2))

Repatriation of Prisoners Act 1984 (c 47)

RA: 26 Jul 1984

Commencement provisions: s 9(2); Repatriation of Prisoners (Commencement) Order
  1985, SI 1985/550

15 Apr 1985 (SI 1985/550)

Restrictive Trade Practices (Stock Exchange) Act 1984 (c 2)

Whole Act repealed

Road Traffic (Driving Instruction) Act 1984 (c 13)

Whole Act repealed

Road Traffic Regulation Act 1984 (c 27)

RA: 26 Jun 1984

Commencement provisions: s 145(1), (2); Road Traffic Regulation Act 1984
  (Commencement No 1) Order 1986, SI 1986/1147

s 1–13	26 Sep 1984 (s 145(1))
13A	Inserted by Road Traffic Act 1991, s 81, Sch 7, para 4 (qv)
14, 15	Substituted by Road Traffic (Temporary Restrictions) Act 1991, s 1(1), Sch 1 (qv)
16, 17	26 Sep 1984 (s 145(1))
17A	Inserted by New Roads and Street Works Act 1991, s 168(1), Sch 8, Pt II, para 29 (qv)
18–28	26 Sep 1984 (s 145(1))
29	Substituted for original ss 29, 30 by New Roads and Street Works Act 1991, s 168(1), Sch 8, Pt II, para 37 (qv)
30	See note to s 29 above
31–35	26 Sep 1984 (s 145(1))
35A, 35B	Inserted by Parking Act 1989, ss 2, 3 (qv)
35C	Prospectively inserted by Road Traffic Act 1991, s 41 (qv)
36–46	26 Sep 1984 (s 145(1))
46A	Prospectively inserted by Road Traffic Act 1991, s 42 (qv)
47–50	26 Sep 1984 (s 145(1))
51	Substituted by Road Traffice Regulation (Parking) Act 1986, s 2(1) (qv)
52–63	26 Sep 1984 (s 145(1))

Road Traffic Regulation Act 1984 (c 27)—*cont*

s 63A	Inserted by Road Traffic Act 1991, s 44(1) (qv)
64–77	26 Sep 1984 (s 145(1))
78	Repealed
79–89	26 Sep 1984 (s 145(1))
90, 91	Repealed
92, 93	26 Sep 1984 (s 145(1))
94	Substituted by Local Government Act 1985, s 8, Sch 5, para 4 (qv)
95–97	26 Sep 1984 (s 145(1))
98	Repealed
99–106	26 Sep 1984 (s 145(1))
106A	Inserted by Road Traffic Act 1991, s 75 (qv)
107–112	26 Sep 1984 (s 145(1))
113, 114	Repealed
115–117	26 Sep 1984 (s 145(1))
118	Repealed
119	26 Sept 1984 (s 145(1))
120, 121	Repealed
121A	Inserted by New Roads and Street Works Act 1991, s 168(1), Sch 8, Pt II, para 70 (qv)
122	26 Sep 1984 (s 145(1))
122A	Inserted by New Roads and Street Works Act 1991, ss 24 (EW), 44 (S) (qv)
123	Repealed
124–132	26 Sep 1984 (s 145(1))
132A	Repealed
133–140	26 Sep 1984 (s 145(1))
141	Repealed
141A	Inserted by Road Traffic Act 1991, s 46(1) (qv)
142–147	26 Sep 1984 (s 145(1))
Sch 1, 2	26 Sep 1984 (s 145(1))
3	Repealed
4–6	26 Sep 1984 (s 145(1))
7	Repealed
8, para 1, 2	26 Sep 1984 (s 145(1))
3	*Not in force*
4–6	26 Sep 1984 (s 145(1))
9–14	26 Sep 1984 (s 145(1))

Roads (Scotland) Act 1984 (c 54)

RA: 31 Oct 1984

Commencement provisions: s 157(2), (3); Roads (Scotland) Act 1984 (Commencement No 1) Order 1985, SI 1985/1953; Roads (Scotland) Act 1984 (Commencement No 2) Order 1989, SI 1989/1094; Roads (Scotland) Act 1984 (Commencement No 3) Order 1990, SI 1990/2622

s 1–35	1 Jan 1985 (s 157(2))
36–39	1 Aug 1989 (so far as relates to areas of Tayside and Lothian Regional Councils) (SI 1989/1084)
	8 Jan 1991 (otherwise) (SI 1990/2622)
39A–39C	Inserted by Traffic Calming Act 1992, s 2(1), Sch 2 (qv)

Roads (Scotland) Act 1984 (c 54)—*cont*

s 40	1 Aug 1989 (so far as relates to areas of Tayside and Lothian Regional Councils) (SI 1989/1084)
	8 Jan 1991 (otherwise) (SI 1990/2622)
41–61	1 Jan 1985 (s 157(2))
61A	Inserted by New Roads and Street Works Act 1991, s 168(1), Sch 8, Pt III, para 88 (qv)
62–125	1 Jan 1985 (s 157(2))
126	1 Jan 1986 (SI 1985/1953)
127	Repealed
128–132	1 Jan 1985 (s 157(2))
133	Repealed
134–155	1 Jan 1985 (s 157(2))
156(1), (2)	1 Jan 1985 (s 157(2))
(3)	See Sch 11 below
157	31 Oct 1984 (RA)
Sch 1–6	1 Jan 1985 (s 157(2))
7	1 Jan 1986 (SI 1985/1953)
8–10	1 Jan 1985 (s 157(2))
11	1 Jan 1985 (except repeal of Road Traffic Regulation Act 1984, Sch 10, paras 14–16) (s 157(2))
	1 Jan 1986 (exception noted above) (SI 1985/1953)

Somerset House Act 1984 (c 21)

RA: 26 Jun 1984

26 Jun 1984 (RA)

Telecommunications Act 1984 (c 12)

RA: 12 Apr 1984

Commencement provisions: s 110(2)–(5); Telecommunications Act 1984 (Appointed Day) (No 1) Order 1984, SI 1984/749; Telecommunications Act 1984 (Appointed Day) (No 2) Order 1984, SI 1984/876

s 1	18 Jun 1984 (SI 1984/749)
2–12	5 Aug 1984 (SI 1984/876)
13	Repealed, with savings, by Local Government Finance (Repeals, Savings and Consequential Amendments) Order 1990, SI 1990/776, art 3, Sch 1
14–21	5 Aug 1984 (SI 1984/876)
22	5 Aug 1984 (SI 1984/876); repealed in relation to applicable terminal equipment by Telecommunications Terminal Equipment Regulations 1992, SI 1992/2423, reg 2(1), as from 6 Nov 1992
23–27	5 Aug 1984 (SI 1984/876)
27A, 27B	Inserted by Competition and Service (Utilities) Act 1992, s 1 (qv)
27C	Inserted by Competition and Service (Utilities) Act 1992, s 2 (qv)
27D	Inserted by Competition and Service (Utilities) Act 1992, s 3 (qv)

Telecommunications Act 1984 (c 12)—*cont*

s 27E	Inserted by Competition and Service (Utilities) Act 1992, s 4 (qv)
27F	Inserted by Competition and Service (Utilities) Act 1992, s 5(1) (qv)
27G	Inserted, partly prospectively, by Competition and Service (Utilities) Act 1992, s 6(1) (qv)
27H	Inserted, partly prospectively, by Competition and Service (Utilities) Act 1992, s 7 (qv)
27I	Inserted by Competition and Service (Utilities) Act 1992, s 7 (qv)
27J	Inserted by Competition and Service (Utilities) Act 1992, s 8 (qv)
27K	Inserted by Competition and Service (Utilities) Act 1992, s 9 (qv)
27L	Inserted by Competition and Service (Utilities) Act 1992, s 10 (qv)
28–44	5 Aug 1984 (SI 1984/876)
45	Substituted by Interception of Communications Act 1985, s 11(1), Sch 2 (qv)
46	5 Aug 1984 (SI 1984/876)
46A	Inserted by Competition and Service (Utilities) Act 1992, s 49 (qv)
47–55	5 Aug 1984 (SI 1984/876)
56–59	Repealed
60–73	6 Aug 1984 (SI 1984/876)
74, 75	16 Jul 1984 (SI 1984/876)
76	Repealed
77	16 Jul 1984 (SI 1984/876)
78	Repealed
79–93	16 Jul 1984 (SI 1984/876)
84	16 Jul 1984 (SI 1984/876); repealed in relation to applicable terminal equipment by Telecommunications Terminal Equipment Regulations 1992, SI 1992/2423, reg 2(1), as from 6 Nov 1992
85–92	16 Jul 1984 (SI 1984/876)
93–95	5 Aug 1984 (SI 1984/876)
96	*Not in force*
97–107	5 Aug 1984 (SI 1984/876)
108	18 Jun 1984 (SI 1984/749)
109(1)	5 Aug 1984 (SI 1984/876)
(2), (3)	5 Aug 1984 (SI 1984/876)
(4)	See Sch 5 below
(5)	5 Aug 1984 (SI 1984/876)
(6)	See Sch 7 below
(7)	5 Aug 1984 (SI 1984/876)
110	18 Jun 1984 (SI 1984/749)
Sch 1	18 Jun 1984 (SI 1984/749)
2	5 Aug 1984 (SI 1984/876)
3	16 Jul 1984 (SI 1984/876)
4	5 Aug 1984 (SI 1984/876)
5, Pt I	5 Aug 1984 (SI 1984/876)
II	6 Aug 1984 (SI 1984/876)
6	6 Aug 1984 (SI 1984/876)
7, Pt I	5 Aug 1984 (SI 1984/876)
II	6 Aug 1984 (SI 1984/876)

Telecommunications Act 1984 (c 12)—*cont*
Sch 7, Pt III   *Not in force*
     IV   16 Jul 1984 (SI 1984/876)

Tenant's Rights, Etc (Scotland) Amendment Act 1984 (c 18)

Whole Act repealed

Tourism (Overseas Promotion) (Scotland) Act 1984 (c 4)

RA: 13 Mar 1984

Commencement provisions: s 3

13 May 1984 (s 3)

Town and Country Planning Act 1984 (c 10)

RA: 12 Apr 1984

Commencement provisions: s 7(2)

12 Aug 1984 (s 7(2)); *whole Act repealed (EW)*

Trade Marks (Amendment) Act 1984 (c 19)

RA: 24 May 1984

Commencement provisions: s 2(2); Trade Marks (Amendment) Act 1984
   (Commencement) Order 1986, SI 1986/1273

1 Oct 1986 (SI 1986/1273)

Trade Union Act 1984 (c 49)

Whole Act repealed

Video Recordings Act 1984 (c 39)

RA: 12 Jul 1984

Commencement provisions: s 23(2); Video Recordings Act 1984 (Commencement No 1)
   Order 1985, SI 1985/883; Video Recordings Act 1984 (Scotland) (Commencement
   No 1) Order 1985, SI 1985/904; Video Recordings Act 1984 (Commencement
   No 2) Order 1985, SI 1985/1264; Video Recordings Act 1984 (Scotland)
   (Commencement No 2) Order 1985, SI 1985/1265; Video Recordings Act 1984
   (Commencement No 3) Order 1986, SI 1986/1125; Video Recordings Act 1984
   (Scotland) (Commencement No 3) Order 1986, SI 1986/1182; Video Recordings
   Act 1984 (Commencement No 4) Order 1987, SI 1987/123; Video Recordings Act
   1984 (Scotland) (Commencement No 4) Order 1987, SI 1987/160; Video
   Recordings Act 1984 (Commencement No 5) Order 1987, SI 1987/1142; Video
   Recordings Act 1984 (Scotland) (Commencement No 5) Order 1987, SI 1987/1249;
   Video Recordings Act 1984 (Commencement No 6) Order 1987, SI 1987/2155;
   Video Recordings Act 1984 (Scotland) (Commencement No 6) Order 1987,
   SI 1987/2273; Video Recordings Act 1984 (Commencement No 7) Order 1988,

Video Recordings Act 1984 (c 39)—*cont*
SI 1988/1018; Video Recordings Act 1984 (Scotland) (Commencement No 7)
Order 1988, SI 1988/1079

s 1	10 Jun 1985 (SI 1985/883; SI 1985/904)
2, 3	1 Sep 1985 (SI 1985/1264; SI 1985/1265)
4, 5	10 Jun 1985 (SI 1985/883; SI 1985/904)
6	1 Sep 1985 (SI 1985/1264; SI 1985/1265)
7, 8	10 Jun 1985 (SI 1985/883; SI 1985/904)
9, 10	1 Sep 1985 (for the purpose of prohibiting the supply, the offer to supply or the possession for the purpose of supply of a video recording containing a video work where—

(a) a video recording containing such video work has not been sold, let on hire or offered for sale or hire in the United Kingdom to the public before 1 Sep 1985; and

(b) no classification certificate in respect of such video work has been issued) (SI 1985/1264; SI 1985/1265)

1 Sep 1986 (for the purpose of prohibiting the supply, the offer to supply or the possession for the purpose of supply of a video recording which has been sold, let on hire or offered for sale in the UK to the public in video form before 1 September 1985 where—

(a) its visual images, when shown as a moving picture, are not substantially the same as the moving picture produced on showing a film registered, or deemed to have been registered, under the Films Act 1960, Pt II, on or after 1 Jan 1940;

(b) its visual images are accompanied by sound which comprises or includes words predominantly in the English language; and

(c) no classification certificate has been issued in respect of it.

Where such a video recording also contains another video work which does not satisfy the above requirements these sections are only brought into force for the above purpose in respect of the video work which does satisfy the requirements) (SI 1986/1125; SI 1986/1182)

1 Mar 1987 (for the purpose of prohibiting the supply, the offer to supply, or the possession for the purpose of supply of a video recording which has been sold, let on hire or offered for sale in the UK to the public in video form before 1 September 1985 where—

(a) its visual images, when shown as a moving picture, are substantially the same as the moving picture produced on showing a film registered, or deemed to have been registered, under Part II of the Films Act 1960 on or after 1 January 1980;

(b) its visual images are accompanied by sound which comprises or includes words predominantly in the English language; and

Video Recordings Act 1984 (c 39)—*cont*

s 9, 10—*cont*
    (c) no classification certificate has been issued in respect of it

Where such a video recording also contains another video work which does not satisfy the above requirements these sections are only brought into force for the above purpose in respect of the video work which does satisfy the requirements) (SI 1987/123; SI 1987/160)

1 Sep 1987 (for the purpose of prohibiting the supply, the offer to supply or the possession for the purpose of supply of a video recording which has been sold, let on hire or offered for sale in the UK to the public in video form before 1 September 1985 where—

    (a) its visual images, when shown as a moving picture, are substantially the same as the moving picture produced on showing a film registered, or deemed to have been registered, under Part II of the Films Act 1960 on or after 1 January 1975;

    (b) its visual images are accompanied by sound which comprises or includes words predominantly in the English language; and

    (c) no classification certificate has been issued in respect of it.

Where such a video recording also contains another video work which does not satisfy the above requirements these sections are only brought into force for the above purposes in respect of the video work which does satisfy the requirements) (SI 1987/1142; SI 1987/1249)

1 Mar 1988 (for the purpose of prohibiting the supply, the offer to supply or the possession for the purpose of supply of a video recording which has been sold, let on hire or offered for sale in the UK to the public in video form before 1 September 1985 where—

    (a) its visual images, when shown as a moving picture, are substantially the same as the moving picture produced on showing a film registered under Part II of the Films Act 1960 on or after 1 January 1970;

    (b) its visual images are accompanied by sound which comprises or includes words predominantly in the English language; and

    (c) no classification certificate has been issued in respect of it.

Where such a video recording also contains another video work which does not satisfy the above requirements these sections are only brought into force for the above purposes in respect of the video work which does satisfy the requirements) (SI 1987/2155; SI 1987/2273)

1 Sep 1988 (otherwise) (SI 1988/1018; SI 1988/1079)

11–14   1 Sep 1985 (SI 1985/1264; SI 1985/1265)
14A   Inserted by Video Recordings Act 1993, s 2 (qv)
15, 16   1 Sep 1985 (SI 1985/1264; SI 1985/1265)

Video Recordings Act 1984 (c 39)—*cont*

s 16A	Inserted by Criminal Justice Act 1988, s 162 (qv)
17	1 Sep 1985 (SI 1985/1264; SI 1985/1265)
18	Repealed
19	1 Sep 1985 (SI 1985/1264)
20	1 Sep 1985 (SI 1985/1265)
21	1 Sep 1985 (SI 1985/1264; SI 1985/1265)
22, 23	10 Jun 1985 (SI 1985/883; SI 1985/904)

1985

Administration of Justice Act 1985 (c 61)

RA: 30 Oct 1985

Commencement provisions: s 69(2)–(4); Administration of Justice Act 1985 (Commencement No 1) Order 1986, SI 1986/364; Administration of Justices Act 1985 (Commencement No 2) Order 1986, SI 1986/1503; Administration of Justice Act 1985 (Commencement No 3) Order 1986, SI 1986/2260; Administration of Justice Act 1985 (Commencement No 4) Order 1987, SI 1987/787; Administration of Justice Act 1985 (Commencement No 5) Order 1988, SI 1988/1341; Administration of Justice Act 1985 (Commencement No 6) Order 1989, SI 1989/287; Administration of Justice Act 1985 (Commencement No 7) Order 1991, SI 1991/2683

s 1	Repealed
2	12 Mar 1986 (except so far as relates to the investigation of any complaint made to the Law Society relating to the quality of any professional services provided by a solicitor) (SI 1986/364)
	1 Jan 1987 (exception noted above) (SI 1986/2260)
3	Repealed
4, 5	12 Mar 1986 (SI 1986/364)
6(1)–(3)	11 May 1987 (SI 1987/787)
(4)	1 Dec 1987 (SI 1987/787)
(5)	11 May 1987 (SI 1987/787)
7, 8	12 Mar 1986 (SI 1986/364)
9, 10	1 Jan 1992 (SI 1991/2683)
11	11 May 1987 (SI 1987/787)
12	12 Mar 1986 (SI 1986/364)
13	1 Oct 1986 (SI 1986/1503)
14–21	11 May 1987 (SI 1987/787)
22, 23	1 Oct 1986 (SI 1986/1503)
24–33	11 May 1987 (SI 1987/787)
34(1), (2)	11 May 1987 (SI 1987/787)
(3)	*Not in force*
35–37	11 May 1987 (SI 1987/787)
38	1 Oct 1986 (SI 1986/1503)
39	11 May 1987 (SI 1987/787)
40	1 Apr 1989 (SI 1989/287)
41, 42	Substituted by Legal Aid Act 1988, s 33 (qv)
43, 44	1 Apr 1989 (SI 1989/287)
45, 46	Repealed
47	1 Oct 1986 (SI 1986/1503)
48	1 Jan 1987 (SI 1986/2260)
49	30 Dec 1985 (s 69(4))
50	28 Apr 1986 (SI 1986/364)
51	1 Oct 1986 (SI 1986/1503)
52	30 Dec 1985 (s 69(4))

Administration of Justice Act 1985 (c 61)—*cont*
s 53	1 Oct 1988 (SI 1988/1341)
54	30 Dec 1985 (s 69(4))
55	1 Oct 1986 (SI 1986/1503)
56–59	30 Dec 1985 (s 69(4))
60	Repealed
61, 62	30 Dec 1985 (s 69(4))
63	Repealed
64, 65	30 Dec 1985 (s 69(4))
66	Repealed
67(1)	See Sch 7 below
(2)	See Sch 8 below
68, 69	30 Oct 1985 (s 69(3))
Sch 1	12 Mar 1986 (SI 1986/364)
2	1 Jan 1992 (SI 1991/2683)
3	12 Mar 1986 (SI 1986/364)
4–6	11 May 1987 (SI 1987/787)
7, para 1–3	Repealed
4	*Not in force*
5	Repealed
6	*Not in force*
7	1 Oct 1986 (SI 1986/1503)
8	30 Dec 1985 (s 69(4))
8, Pt I	30 Oct 1985 (s 69(3))
II	30 Dec 1985 (s 69(4))
III	12 Mar 1986 (repeals in Solicitors Act 1974) (SI 1986/364)
	1 Oct 1986 (repeals in Supreme Court Act 1981; County Courts Act 1984) (SI 1986/1503)
	Not in force (otherwise)
9	30 Oct 1985 (s 69(3))

Agricultural Training Board Act 1985 (c 36)

RA: 16 Jul 1985

Commencement provisions: s 4(2)

16 Sep 1985 (s 4(2))

Appropriation Act 1985 (c 55)

Whole Act repealed

Bankruptcy (Scotland) Act 1985 (c 66)

RA: 30 Oct 1985

Commencement provisions: s 78(2); Bankruptcy (Scotland) Act 1985 (Commencement) Order 1985, SI 1985/1924; Bankruptcy (Scotland) Act 1985 (Commencement No 2) Order 1986, SI 1986/1913

s 1–1C	Substituted for original s 1 by Bankruptcy (Scotland) Act 1993, s 1 (qv)
2	Substituted by Bankruptcy (Scotland) Act 1993, s 2 (qv)

Bankruptcy (Scotland) Act 1985 (c 66)—*cont*

s 3–12	1 Apr 1986 (SI 1985/1924)
13	Substituted by Bankruptcy (Scotland) Act 1993, s 11, Sch 1, para 2 (qv)
14–18	1 Apr 1986 (SI 1985/1924)
19	Substituted by Bankruptcy (Scotland) Act 1993, s 11, Sch 1, para 7 (qv)
20	1 Apr 1986 (SI 1985/1924)
20A	Inserted by Bankruptcy (Scotland) Act 1993, s 11, Sch 1, para 9 (qv)
21	1 Apr 1986 (SI 1985/1924)
21A	Inserted by Bankruptcy (Scotland) Act 1993, s 5 (qv)
22, 23	1 Apr 1986 (SI 1985/1924)
23A	Inserted by Bankruptcy (Scotland) Act 1993, s 6(1) (qv)
24, 25	1 Apr 1986 (SI 1985/1924)
25A	Inserted by Bankruptcy (Scotland) Act 1993, s 7 (qv)
26	1 Apr 1986 (SI 1985/1924)
26A	Inserted by Bankruptcy (Scotland) Act 1993, s 11, Sch 1, para 15 (qv)
27–50	1 Apr 1986 (SI 1985/1924)
51(1)	1 Apr 1986 (SI 1985/1924)
(2)	29 Dec 1986 (SI 1986/1913)
(3)–(7)	1 Apr 1986 (SI 1985/1924)
52–58	1 Apr 1986 (SI 1985/1924)
58A	Inserted by Bankruptcy (Scotland) Act 1993, s 11, Sch 1, para 26 (qv)
59–69	1 Apr 1986 (SI 1985/1924)
69A	Inserted by Bankruptcy (Scotland) Act 1993, s 8 (qv)
70, 71	1 Apr 1986 (SI 1985/1924)
72	1 Feb 1986 (SI 1985/1924)
72A	Inserted by Bankruptcy (Scotland) Act 1993, s 11, Sch 1, para 28 (qv)
73(1)	1 Feb 1986 (except definition of 'preferred debt') (SI 1985/1924)
	29 Dec 1986 (definition of 'preferred debt') (SI 1986/1913)
(2)–(5)	1 Feb 1986 (SI 1985/1924)
(6)	Added by Bankruptcy (Scotland) Act 1993, s 11, Sch 1, para 29 (qv)
74, 75	1 Apr 1986 (SI 1985/1924)
76	1 Feb 1986 (SI 1985/1924)
77	1 Apr 1986 (SI 1985/1924)
78	30 Oct 1985 (RA)
Sch 1, 2	1 Apr 1986 (SI 1985/1924)
2A	Inserted by Bankruptcy (Scotland) Act 1993, s 6(2) (qv)
3	29 Dec 1986 (SI 1986/1913)
4–6	1 Apr 1986 (SI 1985/1924)
7, para 1	1 Apr 1986 (SI 1985/1924)
2	Repealed
3–6	1 Apr 1986 (SI 1985/1924)
7	Repealed
8, 9	1 Apr 1986 (SI 1985/1924)
10	Repealed
11, 12	1 Apr 1986 (SI 1985/1924)

Bankruptcy (Scotland) Act 1985 (c 66)—*cont*

Sch 7, para 13	29 Dec 1986 (SI 1986/1913); prospectively repealed by Pension Schemes Act 1993, s 188(1), Sch 5 (qv)
14(1), (2)	1 Apr 1986 (SI 1985/1924)
(3)	Repealed
(4)	1 Apr 1986 (SI 1985/1924)
15–18	1 Apr 1986 (SI 1985/1924)
19–22	Repealed
23–25	1 Apr 1986 (SI 1985/1924)
8	1 Apr 1986 (repeals of or in Bankruptcy Act 1621; Bankruptcy Act 1696; Titles to Land Consolidation (Scotland) Act 1868; Married Women's Property (Scotland) Act 1881; Judicial Factors (Scotland) Act 1889; Merchant Shipping Act 1894; Bankruptcy (Scotland) Act 1913 (except repeal of s 118); Married Women's Property (Scotland) Act 1920; Conveyancing (Scotland) Act 1924; Third Parties (Rights Against Insurers) Act 1930; Industrial Assurance and Friendly Societies Act 1948; Post Office Act 1969; Road Traffic Act 1972; Insolvency Act 1976; Banking Act 1979; Sale of Goods Act 1979; Law Reform (Miscellaneous Provisions) (Scotland) Act 1980; Matrimonial Homes (Family Protection) (Scotland) Act 1981; Companies Act 1985) (SI 1985/1924)
	29 Dec 1986 (otherwise) (SI 1986/1913)

Betting, Gaming and Lotteries (Amendment) Act 1985 (c 18)

RA: 9 May 1985

Commencement provisions: s 3(2), (3); Betting, Gaming and Lotteries (Amendment) Act 1985 (Commencement) Order 1985, SI 1985/1475

s 1	9 Jul 1985 (s 3(2))
2(1), (2)	9 Jul 1985 (s 3(2))
(3), (4)	28 Oct 1985 (SI 1985/1475)
(5)	9 Jul 1985 (s 3(2))
(6)	28 Oct 1985 (SI 1985/1475)
3	9 Jul 1985 (s 3(2))
Schedule	9 Jul 1985 (s 3(2))

Brunei and Maldives Act 1985 (c 3)

RA: 11 Mar 1985

11 Mar 1985 (RA)

Business Names Act 1985 (c 7)

RA: 11 Mar 1985

Commencement provisions: s 10

1 Jul 1985 (s 10)

Charities Act 1985 (c 20)

Whole Act repealed (with savings)

Charter Trustees Act 1985 (c 45)

RA: 16 Jul 1985

16 Jul 1985 (RA)

Child Abduction and Custody Act 1985 (c 60)

RA: 25 Jul 1985

Commencement provisions: s 29(2); Child Abduction and Custody Act 1985
   (Commencement) Order 1986, SI 1986/1048

1 Aug 1986 (SI 1986/1048)

Cinemas Act 1985 (c 13)

RA: 27 Mar 1985

Commencement provisions: s 25(2)

27 Jun 1985 (s 25(2))

Coal Industry Act 1985 (c 27)

RA: 13 Jun 1985

13 Jun 1985 (RA)

Companies Act 1985 (c 6)

RA: 11 Mar 1985

Commencement provisions: ss 243(6), 746

1 Jul 1985 (s 746), except s 243(3), (4) (which provision has now been replaced)

Companies Consolidation (Consequential Provisions) Act 1985 (c 9)

RA: 11 Mar 1985

Commencement provisions: s 34

1 Jul 1985 (s 34)

Company Securities (Insider Dealing) Act 1985 (c 8)

RA: 11 Mar 1985

Commencement provisions: s 18

1 Jul 1985 (s 18)

Whole Act prospectively repealed by Criminal Justice Act 1993, s 79(4), Sch 6, Pt I
   (qv)

Consolidated Fund Act 1985 (c 1)

Whole Act repealed

Consolidated Fund (No 2) Act 1985 (c 11)

Whole Act repealed

Consolidated Fund (No 3) Act 1985 (c 74)

Whole Act repealed

Controlled Drugs (Penalties) Act 1985 (c 39)

RA: 16 Jul 1985

Commencement provisions: s 2(1)

16 Sep 1985 (s 2(1))

Copyright (Computer Software) (Amendment) Act 1985 (c 41)

Whole Act repealed

Dangerous Vessels Act 1985 (c 22)

RA: 23 May 1985

Commencement provisions: s 8(2)

23 Jul 1985 (s 8(2))

Elections (Northern Ireland) Act 1985 (c 2)

RA: 24 Jan 1985

Commencement provisions; s 7(2), (3); Elections (Northern Ireland) Act 1985
    (Commencement) Order 1985, SI 1985/1221

s 1–3	24 Jan 1985 (so far as gives effect to s 5(1)) (s 7(3))
	6 Aug 1985 (otherwise) (SI 1985/1221)
4	6 Aug 1985 (SI 1985/1221)
5(1)	24 Jan 1985 (s 7(3))
(2), (3)	6 Aug 1985 (SI 1985/1221)
6, 7	24 Jan 1985 (s 7(3))

Enduring Powers of Attorney Act 1985 (c 29)

RA: 26 Jun 1985

Commencement provisions: s 14(2); Enduring Powers of Attorney Act 1985
    (Commencement) Order 1986, SI 1986/125

10 Mar 1986 (SI 1986/125)

European Communities (Finance) Act 1985 (c 64)

Whole Act repealed

European Communities (Spanish and Portuguese Accession) Act 1985 (c 75)

RA: 19 Dec 1985

19 Dec 1985 (RA)

Family Law (Scotland) Act 1985 (c 37)

RA: 16 Jul 1985

Commencement provisions: s 29(2), (3); Family Law (Scotland) Act 1985
(Commencement No 1) Order 1986, SI 1986/1237; Family Law (Scotland) Act
1985 (Commencement No 2) Order 1988, SI 1988/1887

s 1–24	1 Sep 1986 (SI 1986/1237)
25	30 Nov 1988 (SI 1988/1887)
26–29	1 Sep 1986 (SI 1986/1237)
Sch 1, 2	1 Sep 1986 (SI 1986/1237)

Films Act 1985 (c 21)

RA: 23 May 1985

Commencement provisions: s 8(2)

s 1	23 May 1985 (RA)
2	Repealed
3	23 May 1985 (RA)
4	Repealed
5	23 May 1985 (RA)
6	23 Jul 1985 (s 8(2))
7(1)	See Sch 2 below
(2)	Repealed
(3), (4)	23 May 1985 (RA)
(5), (6)	Repealed
(7)	23 May 1985 (RA)
8	23 May 1985 (RA)
Sch 1	23 Jul 1985 (s 8(2))
2	23 May 1985 (except repeals noted below) (RA)
	23 Jul 1985 (repeals in Finance Act 1982; Finance Act 1984) (s 8(2))

Finance Act 1985 (c 54)

Budget Day: 19 Mar 1985

RA: 25 Jul 1985

See the note concerning Finance Acts at the front of this book

Food and Environment Protection Act 1985 (c 48)

RA: 16 Jul 1985

Commencement provisions: s 27; Food and Environment Protection Act 1985
  (Commencement No 1) Order 1985, SI 1985/1390; Food and Environment
  Protection Act 1985 (Commencement No 2) Order 1985, SI 1985/1698

s 1–4	16 Jul 1985 (s 27(2))
5–13	1 Jan 1986 (SI 1985/1698)
14	Substituted by Environmental Protection Act 1990, s 147 (qv)
15	1 Jan 1986 (SI 1985/1698)
16, 17	5 Sep 1985 (SI 1985/1390)
18	Substituted by Pesticides (Fees and Enforcement) Act 1989, s 1(2) (qv)
19	5 Sep 1985 (SI 1985/1390)
20–26	16 Jul 1985 (so far as relate to Pt I (ss 1–4)) (s 27(2))
	1 Jan 1986 (otherwise) (SI 1985/1698)
27, 28	16 Jul 1985 (s 27(2))
Sch 1	16 Jul 1985 (s 27(2))
2	16 Jul 1985 (so far as relates to Pt I (ss 1–4)) (s 27(2))
	5 Sep 1985 (so far as relates to Pt III (ss 16–19)) (SI 1985/1390)
	1 Jan 1986 (otherwise) (SI 1985/1698)
3	1 Jan 1986 (SI 1985/1698)
4	1 Jan 1986 (SI 1985/1698; prospectively repealed by Environmental Protection Act 1990, s 162(2), Sch 16, Pt VIII (qv))
5	5 Sep 1985 (SI 1985/1390)

Further Education Act 1985 (c 47)

RA: 16 Jul 1985

Commencement provisions: s 7; Further Education Act 1985 (Commencement) (No 1)
  Order 1985, SI 1985/1429; Further Education Act 1985 (Commencement No 2)
  (Scotland) Order 1987, SI 1987/1335

s 1–3	16 Sep 1985 (s 7(3))
4	16 Sep 1985 (EW) (SI 1985/1429)
	17 Aug 1987 (S) (SI 1987/1335)
5–8	16 Jul 1985 (s 7(2))

Gaming (Bingo) Act 1985 (c 35)

RA: 16 Jul 1985

Commencement provisions: s 5(2); Gaming (Bingo) Act 1985 (Commencement) Order
  1986, SI 1986/832

9 Jun 1986 (SI 1986/832)

Hill Farming Act 1985 (c 32)

RA: 26 Jun 1985

Commencement provisions: s 2(3)

26 Aug 1985 (s 2(3))

Hong Kong Act 1985 (c 15)

RA: 11 Mar 1985

11 Mar 1985 (RA)

Hospital Complaints Procedure Act 1985 (c 42)

RA: 16 Jul 1985

Commencement provisions: s 2(2); Hospital Complaints Procedure Act 1985
    (Commencement) Order 1989, SI 1989/1191

11 Jul 1989 (SI 1989/1191)

Housing Act 1985 (c 68)

RA: 30 Oct 1985

Commencement provisions: s 625(2)

1 Apr 1986 (s 625(2))

Housing Associations Act 1985 (c 69)

RA: 30 Oct 1985

Commencement provisions: s 107(2)

1 Apr 1986 (s 107(2))

Housing (Consequential Provisions) Act 1985 (c 71)

RA: 30 Oct 1985

Commencement provisions: s 6(2)

1 Apr 1986 (s 6(2))

Industrial Development Act 1985 (c 25)

RA: 13 Jun 1985

Commencement provisions: s 6(4)

s 1, 2   13 Aug 1985 (s 6(4)); prospectively repealed by
                                Leasehold Reform, Housing and Urban
                                Development Act 1993, s 187(2), Sch 22 (qv)

Industrial Development Act 1985 (c 25)—*cont*

s 3	1 Apr 1986 (s 6(4)); prospectively repealed by Leasehold Reform, Housing and Urban Development Act 1993, s 187(2), Sch 22 (qv)
4	13 Aug 1985 (s 6(4)); prospectively repealed by Leasehold Reform, Housing and Urban Development Act 1993, s 187(2), Sch 22 (qv)
5, 6	13 Aug 1985 (s 6(4))
Schedule	13 Aug 1985 (s 6(4))

Insolvency Act 1985 (c 65)

RA: 30 Oct 1985

Commencement provisions: s 236(2); Insolvency Act 1985 (Commencement No 1) Order 1986, SI 1986/6; Insolvency Act 1985 (Commencement No 2) Order 1986, SI 1986/185; Insolvency Act 1985 (Commencement No 3) Order 1986, SI 1986/463; Insolvency Act 1985 (Commencement No 4) Order 1986, SI 1986/840; Insolvency Act 1985 (Commencement No 5) Order 1986, SI 1986/1924

s 1–216	Repealed
217(1)–(3)	Repealed
(4)	29 Dec 1986 (SI 1986/1924)
218–220	29 Dec 1986 (SI 1986/1924)
221–234	Repealed
235(1)	1 Mar 1986 (SI 1986/185)
(2)–(5)	Repealed
236(1), (2)	1 Feb 1986 (SI 1986/6)
(3)–(5)	Repealed
Sch 1, para 1–5	Repealed
6	1 Jul 1986 (SI 1986/840)
2–5	Repealed
6, para 1, 2	Repealed
3, 4	28 Apr 1986 (SI 1986/463)
5–7	Repealed
8	29 Dec 1986 (SI 1986/1924)
9	Repealed
10–13	29 Dec 1986 (SI 1986/1924)
14–17	Repealed
18, 19	29 Dec 1986 (SI 1986/1924)
20–23	Repealed
24	1 Mar 1986 (so far as relates to the making of rules under s 106 in relation to England and Wales) (SI 1986/185) 29 Dec 1986 (otherwise) (SI 1986/1924)
25–45	Repealed
46, 47	29 Dec 1986 (SI 1986/1924)
48–52	Repealed
7	Repealed
8, para 1–7	29 Dec 1986 (SI 1986/1924)
8, 9	Repealed
10–16	29 Dec 1986 (SI 1986/1924)
17	Spent
18–23	29 Dec 1986 (SI 1986/1924)
24	Repealed
25	29 Dec 1986 (SI 1986/1924)

Insolvency Act 1985 (c 65)—*cont*

Sch 8, para 26	29 Dec 1986 (SI 1986/1924); prospectively repealed by Pension Schemes Act 1993, s 188(1), Sch 5 (qv)
27	1 Apr 1986 (so far as relates to the awarding by a court in Scotland of the sequestration of an individual's estate) (SI 1986/463)
	29 Dec 1986 (otherwise) (SI 1986/1924)
28	Repealed
29, 30	Repealed
31	29 Dec 1986 (SI 1986/1924)
32	Spent
33–35	29 Dec 1986 (SI 1986/1924)
36	1 Apr 1986 (SI 1986/185)
37(1)–(3)	29 Dec 1986 (SI 1986/1924)
(4)	1 Mar 1986 (so far as relates to the making of rules under s 106 in relation to England and Wales) (SI 1986/185)
	29 Dec 1986 (otherwise) (SI 1986/1924)
38–40	29 Dec 1986 (SI 1986/1924)
9, 10	Repealed

Insurance (Fees) Act 1985 (c 46)

RA: 16 Jul 1985

16 Jul 1985 (RA)

Interception of Communications Act 1985 (c 56)

RA: 25 Jul 1985

Commencement provisions: s 12(2); Interception of Communications Act 1985 (Commencement) Order 1986, SI 1986/384

10 Apr 1986 (SI 1986/384)

Intoxicating Substances (Supply) Act 1985 (c 26)

RA: 13 Jun 1985

Commencement provisions: s 2(2)

13 Aug 1985 (s 2(2))

Landlord and Tenant Act 1985 (c 70)

RA: 30 Oct 1985

Commencement provisions: s 40(2)

1 Apr 1986 (s 40(2))

Law Reform (Miscellaneous Provisions) (Scotland) Act 1985 (c 73)

RA: 30 Oct 1985

Commencement provisions: s 60(3), (4); Law Reform (Miscellaneous Provisions) (Scotland) Act 1985 (Commencement No 1) Order 1985, SI 1985/1908; Law Reform (Miscellaneous Provisions) (Scotland) Act 1985 (Commencement No 2) Order 1985, SI 1985/2055; Law Reform (Miscellaneous Provisions) (Scotland) Act 1985 (Commencement No 3) Order 1986, SI 1986/1945; Law Reform (Miscellaneous Provisions) (Scotland) Act 1985 (Commencement No 4) Order 1988, SI 1988/1819

s 1–13	30 Dec 1985 (s 60(3))
14, 15	8 Dec 1986 (SI 1986/1945)
16	Repealed
17	30 Dec 1985 (s 60(3))
18	30 Nov 1988 (SI 1988/1819)
19	8 Dec 1986 (SI 1986/1945)
20–25	30 Dec 1985 (s 60(3))
26–29	30 Oct 1985 (s 60(3))
30–32	Repealed
33, 34	30 Dec 1985 (s 60(3))
35	1 Jan 1986 (SI 1985/1908)
36	1 Jan 1986 (SI 1985/2055)
37	30 Dec 1985 (s 60(3))
38, 39	Repealed
40, 41	30 Dec 1985 (s 60(3))
42	Repealed
43	30 Dec 1985 (s 60(3))
44, 45	Repealed
46–49	30 Dec 1985 (s 60(3))
50	1 Feb 1986 (SI 1985/1908)
51–53	30 Dec 1985 (s 60(3))
54	30 Oct 1985 (s 60(3))
55–58	30 Dec 1985 (s 60(3))
59(1)	See Sch 2 below
(2)	30 Dec 1985 (s 60(3))
60	30 Oct 1985 (s 60(3))
Sch 1	30 Dec 1985 (s 60(3))
2, para 1–7	30 Dec 1985 (s 60(3))
8	Repealed
9–11	30 Dec 1985 (s 60(3))
12, 13	8 Dec 1986 (SI 1986/1945)
14–23	30 Dec 1985 (s 60(3))
24	8 Dec 1986 (SI 1986/1945)
25	30 Dec 1985 (s 60(3))
26, 27	Repealed
28–30	30 Oct 1985 (s 60(3))
31	30 Dec 1985 (s 60(3))
32	30 Oct 1985 (s 60(3))
3	30 Oct 1985 (s 60(3))
4	30 Dec 1985 (s 60(3))

Licensing (Amendment) Act 1985 (c 40)

RA: 16 Jul 1985

16 Jul 1985 (RA)

Local Government Act 1985 (c 51)

RA: 16 Jul 1985

This Act largely came into force on the date of Royal Assent, but the effective date of operation for many of its provisions (except as otherwise provided) is 1 Apr 1986 (the date of abolition of the Greater London Council and the metropolitan county councils). In addition certain provisions come into force in different areas on dates appointed by order before and after 1 Apr 1986

Local Government (Access to Information) Act 1985 (c 43)

RA: 16 Jul 1985

Commencement provisions: s 5

1 Apr 1986 (s 5)

London Regional Transport (Amendment) Act 1985 (c 10)

RA: 11 Mar 1985

11 Mar 1985 (RA)

Milk (Cessation of Production) Act 1985 (c 4)

RA: 11 Mar 1985

Commencement provisions: s 7(2)

s 1–5	11 May 1985 (s 7(2))
6	11 Mar 1985 (RA)
7	11 May 1985 (s 7(2))

Mineral Workings Act 1985 (c 12)

RA: 27 Mar 1985

Commencement provisions: s 11(2)–(4)

s 1	1 Apr 1985 (s 11(2))
2	Repealed
3–6	1 Apr 1985 (s 11(2))
7, 8	27 May 1985 (s 11(3))
9, 10	1 Apr 1985 (s 11(2))
11	27 Mar 1985 (s 11(4))
Sch 1, 2	1 Apr 1985 (s 11(2))

Motor-Cycle Crash-Helmets (Restriction of Liability) Act 1985 (c 28)

Whole Act repealed

National Heritage (Scotland) Act 1985 (c 16)

RA: 4 Apr 1985

Commencement provisions: s 25(1); National Heritage (Scotland) Act 1985
Commencement Order 1985, SI 1985/851

s 1	4 Jun 1985 (SI 1985/851)
2–5	1 Oct 1985 (SI 1985/851)
6(1)–(4)	1 Oct 1985 (SI 1985/851)
(5)–(7)	4 Jun 1985 (SI 1985/851)
7–9	1 Oct 1985 (SI 1985/851)
10	4 Jun 1985 (SI 1985/851)
11–15	1 Apr 1986 (SI 1985/851)
16	4 Jun 1985 (SI 1985/851)
17	4 Jun 1985 (so far as adds paras 1–7, 9 of Schedule to the National Galleries of Scotland Act 1906) (SI 1985/851)
	1 Apr 1986 (so far as adds para 8 of that Schedule) (SI 1985/851)
18(1)–(5)	4 Jun 1985 (SI 1985/851)
(6)	1 Apr 1986 (SI 1985/851)
19(1)	1 Oct 1985 (SI 1985/851)
(2), (3)	4 Jun 1985 (SI 1985/851)
20–23	4 Jun 1985 (SI 1985/851)
24	See Sch 2 below
25	4 Apr 1985 (RA)
Sch 1, Pt I, para 1–3	4 Jun 1985 (SI 1985/851)
4(1)–(5)	4 Jun 1985 (SI 1985/851)
(6)	1 Oct 1985 (SI 1985/851)
5–10	4 Jun 1985 (SI 1985/851)
Pt II	4 Jun 1985 (SI 1985/851)
2, Pt I, para 1	1 Apr 1986 (SI 1985/851)
2	Repealed
3, 4	1 Oct 1985 (SI 1985/851)
Pt II	4 Jun 1985 (repeal of words in the National Library of Scotland Act 1925, s 2(f)) (SI 1985/851)
	1 Oct 1985 (repeal of or in National Museum of Antiquities of Scotland Act 1954; National Gallery and Tate Gallery Act 1954, Sch 1) (SI 1985/851)
	1 Apr 1986 (repeal of National Library of Scotland Act 1925, s 10) (SI 1985/851)

New Towns and Urban Development Corporations Act 1985 (c 5)

RA: 11 Mar 1985

Commencement provisions: s 15(2)

s 1, 2	11 May 1985 (s 15(2))
3, 4	11 May 1985 (s 15(2)); prospectively repealed by Local Government and Housing Act 1989, s 194(4), Sch 12, Pt II (qv)
5	11 Mar 1985 (RA)
6–11	11 May 1985 (s 15(2))
12	Repealed

New Towns and Urban Development Corporations Act 1985 (c 5)—*cont*

s 13–15	11 May 1985 (s 15(2))
Sch 1, 2	11 May 1985 (s 15(2))
3, para 1–6	11 May 1985 (s 15(2))
7	11 Mar 1985 (RA); prospectively repealed by Local Government and Housing Act 1989, s 194(4), Sch 12, Pt II (qv)
8–16	11 May 1985 (s 15(2))

Northern Ireland (Loans) Act 1985 (c 76)

RA: 19 Dec 1985

19 Dec 1985 (RA)

Oil and Pipelines Act 1985 (c 62)

RA: 30 Oct 1985

Commencement provisions: s 8(2), (3); Oil and Pipelines Act 1985 (Commencement) Order 1985, SI 1985/1748; Oil and Pipelines Act 1985 (Appointed Day) Order 1985, SI 1985/1749; British National Oil Corporation (Dissolution) Order 1986, SI 1986/585

s 1, 2	1 Dec 1985 (SI 1985/1748)
3	1 Dec 1985 (SI 1985/1749)
4–8	1 Dec 1985 (SI 1985/1748)
Sch 1	1 Dec 1985 (SI 1985/1748)
2	1 Dec 1985 (SI 1985/1749)
3	1 Dec 1985 (SI 1985/1748)
4, Pt I	1 Dec 1985 (SI 1985/1749)
II	27 Mar 1986 (SI 1986/585)

Ports (Finance) Act 1985 (c 30)

RA: 26 Jun 1985

Commencement provisions: s 7(2); Ports (Finance) Act 1985 (Commencement) Order 1985, SI 1985/1153

s 1	Repealed
2	5 Aug 1985 (SI 1985/1153)
3–5	1 Jan 1986 (SI 1985/1153)
6, 7	5 Aug 1985 (SI 1985/1153)
Schedule	5 Aug 1985 (SI 1985/1153)

Prohibition of Female Circumcision Act 1985 (c 38)

RA: 16 Jul 1985

Commencement provisions: s 4(2)

16 Sep 1985 (s 4(2))

Prosecution of Offences Act 1985 (c 23)

RA: 23 May 1985

Commencement provisions: s 31(2); Prosecution of Offences Act 1985 (Commencement
No 1) Order 1985, SI 1985/1849; Prosecution of Offences Act 1985
(Commencement No 2) Order 1986, SI 1986/1029; Prosecution of Offences Act
1985 (Commencement No 3) Order 1986, SI 1986/1334

s 1, 2	1 Apr 1986 (in the counties of Durham, Greater Manchester, Merseyside, Northumberland, South Yorkshire, Tyne and Wear, West Midlands and West Yorkshire only) (SI 1985/1849)
	1 Oct 1986 (otherwise) (SI 1986/1029)
3	1 Apr 1986 (in the counties noted to ss 1, 2 above only; but s 3(2) (a), (c), (d) shall not apply in relation to proceedings transferred (whether on appeal or otherwise) to an area where those provisions are in force from an area where they are not) (SI 1985/1849)
	1 Oct 1986 (otherwise) (SI 1986/1029)
4–7	1 Apr 1986 (in the counties noted to ss 1, 2 above only) (SI 1985/1849)
	1 Oct 1986 (otherwise) (SI 1986/1029)
7A	Inserted by Courts and Legal Services Act 1990, s 114 (qv)
8	1 Apr 1986 (in the counties noted to ss 1, 2 above only) (SI 1985/1849)
	1 Oct 1986 (otherwise) (SI 1986/1029)
9	5 Apr 1987 (SI 1986/1029)
10	1 Apr 1986 (in the counties noted to ss 1, 2 above only) (SI 1985/1849)
	1 Oct 1986 (otherwise) (SI 1986/1029)
11–13	23 May 1985 (s 31(2))
14	1 Apr 1986 (in the counties noted to ss 1, 2 above only) (SI 1985/1849)
	1 Oct 1986 (otherwise) (SI 1986/1029)
15	23 May 1985 (so far as applies in relation to ss 11–13) (s 31(2))
	1 Oct 1986 (otherwise) (SI 1986/1029)
16–19	1 Oct 1986 (SI 1986/1334)
19A	Inserted by Courts and Legal Services Act 1990, s 111 (qv)
20, 21	1 Oct 1986 (SI 1986/1334)
22	1 Oct 1986 (SI 1986/1029)
23	1 Apr 1986 (in the counties noted to ss 1, 2 above only) (SI 1985/1849)
	1 Oct 1986 (otherwise) (SI 1986/1029)
24	1 Apr 1986 (SI 1985/1849)
25, 26	1 Apr 1986 (in the counties noted to ss 1, 2 above only) (SI 1985/1849)
	1 Oct 1986 (otherwise) (SI 1986/1029)
27	Repealed
28	1 Apr 1986 (SI 1985/1849)
29, 30	23 May 1985 (s 31(2))
31(1)–(4)	23 May 1985 (s 31(2))
(5), (6)	1 Apr 1986 (SI 1985/1849)
(7)	23 May 1985 (s 31(2))

Prosecution of Offences Act 1985 (c 23)—*cont*

Sch 1, para 1–3	1 Apr 1986 (in the counties noted to ss 1, 2 above only) (SI 1985/1849)
	1 Oct 1986 (otherwise) (SI 1986/1029)
4, 5	1 Apr 1986 (SI 1985/1849)
6–10	1 Oct 1986 (otherwise) (SI 1986/1334)
11	*Not in force*
2	1 Apr 1986 (repeals of or in Perjury Act 1911; Administration of Justice (Miscellaneous Provisions) Act 1933; Industrial Development Act 1966; Transport Act 1968; European Communities Act 1972; Bail Act 1976; Representation of the People Act 1983) (SI 1985/1849)
	1 Apr 1986 (in the counties noted to ss 1, 2 above only) (repeals of or in Prosecution of Offences Act 1979; Magistrates' Courts Act 1980, s 25) (SI 1985/1849)
	1 Oct 1986 (in counties other than those noted above) (repeals of or in Prosecution of Offences Act 1979; Magistrates' Courts Act 1980, s 25) (SI 1986/1029)
	1 Oct 1986 (repeals of or in Indictments Act 1915; Criminal Justice Act 1967; Criminal Appeal Act 1968; Administrtaion of Justice Act 1970; Costs in Criminal Cases Act 1973; Administration of Justice Act 1973; Magistrates' Courts Act 1980, s 30(3); Legal Aid Act 1982) (SI 1986/1334)
	Not in force (repeal in Supreme Court Act 1981, s 77)

Rating (Revaluation Rebates) (Scotland) Act 1985 (c 33)

RA: 26 Jun 1985

Commencement provisions: s 3(1)

26 Aug 1985 (s 3(1))

Rent (Amendment) Act 1985 (c 24)

RA: 23 May 1985

23 May 1985 (RA)

Representation of the People Act 1985 (c 50)

RA: 16 Jul 1985

Commencement provisions: s 29(2), (3); Representation of the People Act 1985 (Commencement No 1) Order 1985, SI 1985/1185; Representation of the People Act 1985 (Commencement No 2) Order 1986, SI 1986/639; Representation of the People Act 1985 (Commencement No 3) Order 1986, SI 1986/1080; Representation of the People Act 1985 (Commencement No 4) Order 1987, SI 1987/207

s 1–4	11 Jul 1986 (SI 1986/1080)
5–11	16 Feb 1987 (SI 1986/1080)
12(1), (2)	11 Jul 1986 (SI 1986/1080)
(3)	16 Feb 1987 (SI 1986/1080)

Representation of the People Act 1985 (c 50)—*cont*

s 12(4)	11 Jul 1986 (SI 1986/1080)
13, 14	1 Oct 1985 (SI 1985/1185)
15, 16	16 Feb 1987 (SI 1986/1080)
17	1 Sep 1985 (SI 1985/1185)
18	1 Oct 1985 (SI 1985/1185)
19(1)–(5)	16 Feb 1987 (SI 1986/1080)
(6)(a)	1 Oct 1985 (SI 1985/1185)
(b), (c)	16 Feb 1987 (SI 1986/1080)
20	1 Oct 1985 (SI 1985/1185)
21	16 Feb 1987 (SI 1986/1080)
22	Substituted by Welsh Language Act 1993, s 34(5) (qv)
23, 24	1 Oct 1985 (SI 1985/1185)
25(1)	16 Jul 1985 (s 29(3))
(2)	1 Oct 1985 (SI 1985/1185)
26	1 Oct 1985 (SI 1985/1185)
27(1)	16 Jul 1985 (s 29(3))
(2), (3)	1 Oct 1985 (SI 1985/1185)
28	1 Oct 1985 (SI 1985/1185)
29	16 Jul 1985 (s 29(3))
Sch 1	*Not in force*
2	16 Feb 1987 (SI 1986/1080)
3	1 Oct 1985 (SI 1985/1185)
4, para 1–6	1 Oct 1985 (SI 1985/1185)
7	16 Feb 1987 (SI 1986/1080)
8	1 Oct 1985 (SI 1985/1185)
9	16 Feb 1987 (SI 1986/1080)
10–17	1 Oct 1985 (SI 1985/1185)
18	16 Jul 1985 (s 29(3))
19–33	1 Oct 1985 (SI 1985/1185)
34	30 Mar 1987 (except for the purposes of an election, notice of which is published before that date) (SI 1987/207)
35–68	1 Oct 1985 (SI 1985/1185)
69	21 Apr 1986 (SI 1986/639)
70–72	1 Oct 1985 (SI 1985/1185)
73	16 Feb 1987 (SI 1986/1080)
74–78	1 Oct 1985 (SI 1985/1185)
79, 80	16 Feb 1987 (SI 1986/1080)
81–83	1 Oct 1985 (SI 1985/1185)
84–86	16 Feb 1987 (SI 1986/1080)
87–89	1 Oct 1985 (SI 1985/1185)
90	Repealed
5	16 Jul 1985 (repeals in Police and Criminal Evidence Act 1984) (s 29(3))
	1 Oct 1985 (repeals of or in Meeting of Parliament Act 1797, ss 3–5; Representation of the People Act 1918; Local Government Act 1972, s 243(3); Representation of the People Act 1983, ss 18(2)(b), (6)(b), 39(8), 49(1)(d), (2)(c), 51, 52(2), 53(2), 55, 56(1)(c), (6), 76(3), 103(2), 104(b), 106(4), 108(3), (4), 124(a), (b), 125(a), 126(3), 136(4), (5), (7), 140(5), (7), 141(3), (4), 142, 148(4)(a), 156(2)–(4), 161, 162, 163(1)(b), 168(5), (6), 169, 171, 172, 173(a), 176(1), (3), 181(3), (6), 187(1), 190, 191(1)(a), 192, 196, 199, 202(1), 203(4)(a), Sch 1,

Representation of the People Act 1985 (c 50)—*cont*

Sch 5—*cont*   rule 5, para (1), rule 23, para (2)(c), (3), Appendix of
                               Forms, Sch 2, para 9, Sch 7, paras 8, 9) (SI 1985/
                               1185)
                               16 Feb 1987 (repeals of or in City of London (Various
                               Powers) Act 1957; Representation of the People Act
                               1983, ss 19–22, 32–34, 38, 40(1), 43(2)(b), 44, 49(3),
                               61, Sch 1, rr 2(3), 27, 40(1)(b), Sch 2, para 5(4),
                               Sch 8) (SI 1986/1080)
                               Not in force (otherwise)

Reserve Forces (Safeguard of Employment) Act 1985 (c 17)

RA: 9 May 1985

Commencement provisions: s 23(3)

9 Aug 1985 (s 23(3))

Road Traffic (Production of Documents) Act 1985 (c 34)

Whole Act repealed

Sexual Offences Act 1985 (c 44)

RA: 16 Jul 1985

Commencement provisions: s 5(4)

16 Sep 1985 (s 5(4))

Shipbuilding Act 1985 (c 14)

RA: 27 Mar 1985

27 Mar 1985 (RA)

Whole Act repealed by Statute Law (Repeals) Act 1993, s 1, Sch 1, Pt IX (qv) partly
    (s 1) prospectively

Social Security Act 1985 (c 53)

RA: 22 Jul 1985

Commencement provisions: s 32; Social Security Act 1985 (Commencement No 1)
    Order 1985, SI 1985/1125; Social Security Act 1985 (Commencement No 2) Order
    1985, SI 1985/1364

s 1, 2   1 Jan 1986 (SI 1985/1364); prospectively repealed by
                               Pension Schemes Act 1993, s 188(1), Sch 5 (qv)
3   See Sch 2 below; prospectively repealed by Pension
                               Schemes Act 1993, s 188(1), Sch 5 (qv)
4   See Sch 3 below; prospectively repealed by Pension
                               Schemes Act 1993, s 188(1), Sch 5 (qv)

Social Security Act 1985 (c 53)—*cont*

s 5	1 Jan 1986 (SI 1985/1364); prospectively repealed by Pension Schemes Act 1993, s 188(1), Sch 5 (qv)
6(1)–(4)	1 Jan 1986 (SI 1985/1364); prospectively repealed by Pension Schemes Act 1993, s 188(1), Sch 5 (qv)
(5), (6)	22 Jul 1985 (s 32(2)); prospectively repealed by Pension Schemes Act 1993, s 188(1), Sch 5 (qv)
7	Repealed
8	22 Jul 1985 (s 32(2))
9–20	Repealed
21	See Sch 4 below
22	Repealed
23–25	22 Jul 1985 (s 32(2))
26	22 Jul 1985 (s 32(2)); prospectively repealed by Pension Schemes Act 1993, s 188(1), Sch 5 (qv)
27	Repealed
28	22 Jul 1985 (s 32(2))
29(1)	See Sch 5 below
(2)	See Sch 6 below
30	Repealed
31–33	22 Jul 1985 (s 32(2))
Sch 1	1 Jan 1986 (SI 1985/1364); prospectively repealed by Pension Schemes Act 1993, s 188(1), Sch 5 (qv)
2	1 Jan 1986 (insertion in Social Security Pensions Act 1985 of s 56A, 56E(1) (except para (c)), (2)–(8), 56L(1) (except words "or (c)" in para (a), and para (b)), (2)–(4), (5)(a), (c) (except so far as applies to the registrar), (d), (6)–(8)) (SI 1985/1364); prospectively repealed by Pension Schemes Act 1993, s 188(1), Sch 5 (qv)
	Repealed (otherwise)
3, Pt I	22 Jul 1985 (s 32(2)); prospectively repealed by Pension Schemes Act 1993, s 188(1), Sch 5 (qv)
II	1 Jan 1986 (SI 1985/1364); prospectively repealed by Pension Schemes Act 1993, s 188(1), Sch 5 (qv)
4, para 1	16 Sep 1985 (SI 1985/1125)
2–7	Repealed
5, para 1–4	1 Jan 1986 (SI 1985/1364)
5	Repealed
6	6 Oct 1985 (SI 1985/1125); repealed, in part prospectively, by Social Security Act 1986, s 86(2), Sch 11 (qv)
7–15	Repealed
16	6 Oct 1985 (SI 1985/1125); prospectively repealed by Social Security Act 1986, s 86(2), Sch 11 (qv)
17	6 Oct 1985 (SI 1985/1125); prospectively repealed by Pension Schemes Act 1993, s 188(1), Sch 5 (qv)
18	1 Jan 1986 (SI 1985/1364); prospectively repealed by Pension Schemes Act 1993, s 188(1), Sch 5 (qv)
19	Repealed
20, 21	1 Jan 1986 (SI 1985/1364); prospectively repealed by Pension Schemes Act 1993, s 188(1), Sch 5 (qv)
22	Repealed
23, 24	1 Jan 1986 (SI 1985/1364); prospectively repealed by Pension Schemes Act 1993, s 188(1), Sch 5 (qv)
25	6 Apr 1986 (SI 1985/1364); prospectively repealed by Pension Schemes Act 1993, s 188(1), Sch 5 (qv)

Social Security Act 1985 (c 53)—*cont*

Sch 5, para 26	6 Oct 1985 (SI 1985/1364); prospectively repealed by Pension Schemes Act 1993, s 188(1), Sch 5 (qv)
27	1 Jan 1986 (SI 1985/1364); prospectively repealed by Pension Schemes Act 1993, s 188(1), Sch 5 (qv)
28	Repealed
29	6 Oct 1985 (SI 1985/1364); prospectively repealed by Pension Schemes Act 1993, s 188(1), Sch 5 (qv)
30, 31	1 Jan 1986 (SI 1985/1364)
32	1 Jan 1986 (SI 1985/1364); prospectively repealed by Social Security Act 1989, s 31(2), Sch 9 (qv) and Pension Schemes Act 1993, s 188(1), Sch 5 (qv)
33	6 Oct 1985 (SI 1985/1364)
34	22 Jul 1985 (s 32(2)); prospectively repealed by Pension Schemes Act 1993, s 188(1), Sch 5 (qv)
35	Repealed
36	22 Jul 1985 (s 32(2)); prospectively repealed by Pension Schemes Act 1993, s 188(1), Sch 5 (qv)
37, 38	Repealed
39	6 Oct 1985 (SI 1985/1125)
40	6 Oct 1985 (SI 1985/1364)
6	22 Jul 1985 (repeals of or in Social Security Pensions Act 1975, s 41D; Social Security (Miscellaneous Provisions) Act 1977, s 22(7); Social Security Act 1981; Health and Social Security Act 1984) (s 32(2))
	23 Jul 1985 (repeals of or in Social Security Act 1975, s 28(2); Social Security Act 1979, Sch 1, para 11) (SI 1985/1125)
	5 Aug 1985 (repeals of or in Social Security Act 1975, ss 79, 82, 90) (s 32(3))
	16 Sep 1985 (repeals of or in Social Security Act 1975, ss 45(3), (4), 125(1), 126A(1); Social Security (Miscellaneous Provisions) Act 1977, s 5(1); Social Security and Housing Benefits Act 1982, s 24, Sch 2, paras 7–11) (SI 1985/1125; SI 1985/1364)
	6 Oct 1985 (repeals of or in Social Security Pensions Act 1975, ss 41B(4), 59(5)(b), Sch 4, para 36(b); Social Security (Contributions) Act 1982, s 1(5), Sch 1, para 1(3)) (SI 1985/1125; SI 1985/1364)
	25 Nov 1985 (repeals of or in Social Security Act 1975, s 39(2), Sch 4, Pt III, para 5) (SI 1985/1125)
	1 Jan 1986 (repeals of or in Social Security Act 1973, Sch 16, para 6(1)(a); Social Security Pensions Act 1975, ss 26(2), 34(4), 41A(4)(i), 66; Social Security (Miscellaneous Provisions) Act 1977, s 22(9)–(11); Social Security Act 1980, s 3(6), (7)) (SI 1985/1364)
	6 Apr 1986 (remaining repeals in Social Security and Housing Benefits Act 1982) (SI 1985/1125)

Sporting Events (Control of Alcohol etc) Act 1985 (c 57)

RA: 25 Jul 1985

25 Jul 1985 (RA)

Surrogacy Arrangements Act 1985 (c 49)

RA: 16 Jul 1985

16 Jul 1985 (RA)

Town and Country Planning (Amendment) Act 1985 (c 52)

RA: 22 Jul 1985

Commencement provisions: s 3(3)

22 Sep 1985 (s 3(3))

Town and Country Planning (Compensation) Act 1985 (c 19)

RA: 9 May 1985

9 May 1985 (RA)

Transport Act 1985 (c 67)

RA: 30 Oct 1985

Commencement provisions: s 140(2); Transport Act 1985 (Commencement No 1) Order
1985, SI 1985/1887; Transport Act 1985 (Commencement No 2) Order 1986,
SI 1986/80; Transport Act 1985 (Commencement No 3) Order 1986, SI 1986/414;
Transport Act 1985 (Commencement No 4) Order 1986, SI 1986/1088; Transport
Act 1985 (Commencement No 5) Order 1986, SI 1986/1450; Transport Act 1985
(Commencement No 6) Order 1986, SI 1986/1794 (as amended by SI 1988/2294);
Transport Act 1985 (Commencement No 7) Order 1987, SI 1987/1228

s 1(1), (2)	26 Oct 1986 (SI 1986/1794)
(3)	See Sch 1 below
2, 3	6 Jan 1986 (SI 1985/1887)
4	6 Jan 1986 (to extent necessary to replace Public Passenger Vehicles Act 1981, s 54 with sub-ss (1), (2) only of the new s 54) (SI 1985/1887)
	26 Oct 1986 (otherwise) (SI 1986/1794)
5	6 Jan 1986 (SI 1985/1887)
6	26 Oct 1986 (SI 1986/1794)
7–9	14 Jul 1986 (SI 1986/1088)
10, 11	1 Aug 1986 (SI 1986/1088)
12	6 Jan 1986 (SI 1985/1887)
13	6 Jan 1986 (to the extent that supplements s 12 of this Act) (SI 1985/1887)
	1 Aug 1986 (otherwise) (SI 1986/1088)
14, 15	1 Jan 1987 (SI 1986/1794)
16	6 Jan 1986 (SI 1985/1887)
17	1 Aug 1986 (SI 1986/1088)
18	1 Aug 1986 (so far as relates to the use of any vehicle under a permit granted under s 22 or the driving of any vehicle so used) (SI 1986/1088)
	13 Aug 1987 (otherwise) (SI 1987/1228)
19, 21	13 Aug 1987 (SI 1987/1228)
22, 23	1 Aug 1986 (SI 1986/1088)

Transport Act 1985 (c 67)—*cont*

s 24–28	26 Oct 1986 (SI 1986/1794)
29, 30	6 Jan 1986 (SI 1985/1887)
31	15 Sep 1986 (SI 1986/1450)
32	6 Jan 1986 (to the extent that applies to Public Passenger Vehicles Act 1981, s 28) (SI 1985/1887)
	26 Oct 1986 (otherwise) (SI 1986/1794)
33	1 Aug 1986 (SI 1986/1088)
34	6 Jan 1986 (SI 1985/1887)
35–46	26 Oct 1986 (SI 1986/1794)
47–53	Repealed
54–56	6 Jan 1986 (SI 1985/1887)
57(1)–(5)	6 Jan 1986 (SI 1985/1887)
(6)	See Sch 3 below
58	30 Oct 1985 (s 140(2))
59–84	6 Jan 1986 (SI 1985/1887)
85, 86	13 Aug 1987 (SI 1987/1228)
87–92	6 Jan 1986 (SI 1985/1887)
93(1)–(7), (8)(a)	14 Feb 1986 (SI 1986/80)
(8)(b)	1 Apr 1986 (SI 1986/414)
(9), (10)	14 Feb 1986 (SI 1986/80)
94–101	14 Feb 1986 (SI 1986/80))
102	1 Apr 1986 (SI 1986/414)
103	14 Feb 1986 (SI 1986/80)
104	15 Sep 1986 (SI 1986/1450)
105	14 Feb 1986 (SI 1986/80)
106	6 Jan 1986 (SI 1985/1887)
107	1 Apr 1986 (SI 1985/1887)
108, 109	1 Apr 1986 (SI 1986/414)
110	6 Jan 1986 (SI 1985/1887)
111	26 Oct 1986 (SI 1986/1794)
112, 113	6 Jan 1986 (SI 1985/1887)
114, 115	26 Jul 1986 (SI 1986/1088)
116(1)	1 Apr 1986 (SI 1986/414)
(2), (3)	26 Jul 1986 (SI 1986/1088)
117	15 Sep 1986 (SI 1986/1450)
118–125	6 Jan 1986 (SI 1985/1887)
126(1), (2)	1 Aug 1986 (so far as relate to fees chargeable in respect of applications for, and the grant of, permits under s 22) (SI 1986/1088)
	26 Oct 1986 (otherwise, except so far as sub-s (1) relates to applications for and the grant of permits under s 19) (SI 1986/1794)
	13 Aug 1987 (otherwise) (SI 1987/1228)
(3)(a)	26 Oct 1986 (SI 1986/1794)
(b)	14 Jul 1986 (SI 1986/1088)
(c)	26 Oct 1986 (SI 1986/1794)
127(1), (2)	1 Aug 1986 (SI 1986/1088)
(3)	6 Jan 1986 (SI 1985/1887)
(4)	6 Jan 1986 (so far as relates to s 30(2)) (SI 1985/1887)
	1 Aug 1986 (so far as relates to s 23(5)) (SI 1986/1088)
	26 Oct 1986 (otherwise) (SI 1986/1794)
(5)–(7)	6 Jan 1986 (SI 1985/1887)
128–138	6 Jan 1986 (SI 1985/1887)
139(1)–(3)	See Schs 6–8 below
(4), (5)	6 Jan 1986 (SI 1985/1887)
140	30 Oct 1985 (s 140(2))

Transport Act 1985 (c 67)—*cont*

Sch 1, para 1, 2	6 Jan 1986 (SI 1985/1887)
3(1), (2)	6 Jan 1986 (SI 1985/1887)
(3)	26 Oct 1986 (SI 1986/1794)
(4)	6 Jan 1986 (except omission of words 'or Part III') (SI 1985/1887)
	26 Oct 1986 (exception noted above) (SI 1986/1794)
(5)	6 Jan 1986 (SI 1985/1887)
4	6 Jan 1986 (SI 1985/1887)
5	Repealed
6	6 Jan 1986 (SI 1985/1887)
7–11	26 Oct 1986 (SI 1986/1794)
12	6 Jan 1986 (SI 1985/1887)
13	6 Jan 1986 (except omission of definitions of 'excursion or tour', 'road service licence', 'trial area') (SI 1985/1887)
	26 Oct 1986 (exceptions noted above) (SI 1986/1794)
14	6 Jan 1986 (SI 1985/1887)
15(1)	6 Jan 1986 (SI 1985/1887)
(2), (3)	26 Oct 1986 (SI 1986/1794)
(4), (5)	6 Jan 1986 (SI 1985/1887)
16	6 Jan 1986 (SI 1985/1887)
2	6 Jan 1986 (SI 1985/1887)
3, para 1–7	6 Jan 1986 (SI 1985/1887)
8	1 Apr 1986 (SI 1986/414)
9–23	6 Jan 1986 (SI 1985/1887)
24	6 Jan 1986 (to the extent that relates to Local Government Act 1972, s 202(1), (4)–(7) only) (SI 1985/1887)
	1 Apr 1986 (otherwise) (SI 1986/414)
25	6 Jan 1986 (SI 1985/1887)
26	1 Apr 1986 (SI 1986/414)
27, 28	6 Jan 1986 (SI 1985/1887)
29	Repealed
30–33	6 Jan 1986 (SI 1985/1887)
4	15 Sep 1986 (SI 1986/1450)
5	6 Jan 1986 (SI 1985/1887)
6, para 1–5	Spent
6–11	6 Jan 1986 (SI 1985/1887)
12	30 Oct 1985 (s 140(2))
13	6 Jan 1986 (SI 1985/1887)
14	26 Oct 1986 (SI 1986/1794)
15	6 Jan 1986 (SI 1985/1887)
16–18	26 Oct 1986 (SI 1986/1794)
19	6 Jan 1986 (SI 1985/1887)
20	Spent
21	6 Jan 1986 (SI 1985/1887)
22, 23	14 Feb 1986 (SI 1986/80) (also purportedly brought into force, to the extent that not already in force, by SI 1986/414)
24, 25	15 Sep 1986 (SI 1986/1450)
26	6 Jan 1986 (SI 1985/1887)
7, para 1	6 Jan 1986 (SI 1985/1887)
2	1 Aug 1986 (SI 1986/1088)
3	1 Apr 1986 (SI 1986/414)
4	6 Jan 1986 (SI 1985/1887)
5	26 Oct 1986 (SI 1986/1794)
6	6 Jan 1986 (SI 1985/1887)

Transport Act 1985 (c 67)—*cont*

Sch 7, para 7, 8	15 Sep 1986 (SI 1986/1450)
9	1 Apr 1986 (SI 1986/414)
10–14	6 Jan 1986 (SI 1985/1887)
15	Repealed
16	26 Oct 1986 (SI 1986/1794)
17	1 Apr 1986 (SI 1986/414)
18	6 Jan 1986 (SI 1985/1887)
19	1 Apr 1986 (SI 1986/414)
20	6 Jan 1986 (SI 1985/1887)
21(1)	6 Jan 1986 (SI 1985/1887)
(2), (3)	Repealed
(4)	6 Jan 1986 (except words 'sub-section (1A) below and') (SI 1985/1887)
	26 Oct 1986 (exception noted above) (SI 1986/1794)
(5)	26 Oct 1986 (SI 1986/1794)
(6)	6 Jan 1986 (SI 1985/1887)
(7)	Repealed
(8)	6 Jan 1986 (SI 1985/1887)
(9), (10)	26 Oct 1986 (SI 1986/1794)
(11)	15 Sep 1986 (SI 1986/1450)
(12)	6 Jan 1986 (SI 1985/1887)
22	1 Apr 1986 (SI 1986/414)
23	6 Jan 1986 (SI 1985/1887)
24	1 Apr 1986 (SI 1986/414)
25, 26	26 Oct 1986 (SI 1986/1794)
8	6 Jan 1986 (repeals of or in Road Traffic Act 1930; Transport Act 1962, ss 4, 92; Finance Act 1965; Transport Act 1968, ss 9, 10(2), 11(1), 12(3)(d), 14(3), 15, 15(A)(1), 16(2), 17–19, 20, 21, 22, 24(3), 29(4), 34, 36, 54, 59(3), 90, 103(1), 159(1), Sch 5; Post Office Act 1969; Local Government Act 1972, ss 80(4), 202, Sch 24, Pt II; Local Government Act 1974; Energy Act 1976, Sch 1, para 1(2); Transport Act 1978; Transport Act 1980; Public Passenger Vehicles Act 1981, ss 1, 2, 28, 46, 53(1) (word 'the' before words 'traffic commissioners'), 56, 60, 61(2), 62, 81(2), 82(1) (definitions of 'contract carriage', 'express carriage', 'express carriage service', 'stage carriage' and 'stage carriage service'), 83, Sch 1, paras 3, 4; Transport Act 1982, s 73(4); Transport Act 1983, s 9(2); Road Traffic Regulation Act 1984, Sch 13, para 49; London Regional Transport Act 1984, s 28, Sch 6, paras 3, 6) (SI 1985/1887)
	1 Apr 1986 (repeals of or in Finance Act 1970; Local Government Act 1972, s 202(2), (3); Local Government (Scotland) Act 1973, s 150; Transport Act 1983, s 3; Local Government Act 1985) (SI 1986/414)
	26 Jul 1986 (repeal of London Regional Transport Act 1984, Sch 6, para 15(1)(a)) (SI 1986/1088)
	15 Sep 1986 (repeals of or in Transport Act 1962, s 57, Sch 10; Transport Act 1968, s 88, Sch 10) (SI 1986/1450)
	26 Oct 1986 (otherwise except those of or in Town Police Clauses Act 1847; Public Passenger Vehicles Act 1981, ss 42–44, 52, 67, 76 (words 'except

Transport Act 1985 (c 67)—*cont*

Sch 8—*cont*   sections 42 to 44' and word 'thereof')) (SI 1986/
                                          1794)
                                          13 Aug 1987 (otherwise except repeal of words 'such
                                          number of' and 'as they think fit' in Town Police
                                          Clauses Act 1847, s 37 (which repeal entry is now
                                          itself repealed)) (SI 1987/1228)

Trustee Savings Banks Act 1985 (c 58)

RA: 25 Jul 1985

Commencement provisions: ss 4(3)–(5), 7(2); Trustee Savings Banks Act 1985
(Appointed Day) (No 2) Order 1986, SI 1986/1220; Trustee Savings Banks Act
1985 (Appointed Day) (No 4) Order 1986, SI 1986/1223; Trustee Savings Banks
Act 1985 (Appointed Day) (No 6) Order 1988, SI 1988/1168

s 1–5	25 Sep 1985 (s 7(2))
6	Repealed
7	25 Sep 1985 (s 7(2))
Sch 1, 2	25 Sep 1985 (s 7(2))
3	Repealed
4	20 Jul 1986 (repeals of or in Finance Act 1921; Finance Act 1946; Finance Act 1969; National Savings Bank Act 1971; Trustee Savings Banks Act 1981, Sch 7, para 10, para 12(a) (words '4 to 7')) (SI 1986/1220)
	21 Jul 1986 (repeals of or in Bankers' Books Evidence Act 1879; Consolidated Fund (Permanent Charges Redemption) Act 1883; Savings Banks Act 1887; Bankruptcy Act 1914; Agricultural Credits Act 1928; Agricultural Credits (Scotland) Act 1929; Government Annuities Act 1929; Payment of Wages Act 1960; Companies Act (Northern Ireland) 1960; Trustee Investments Act 1961; Clergy Pensions Measure 1961; Building Societies Act 1962; Administration of Estates (Small Payments) Act 1965; Building Societies Act (Northern Ireland) 1967; Payment of Wages Act (Northern Ireland) 1970; Friendly Societies Act (Northern Ireland) 1970; Northern Ireland Constitution Act 1973; Pensions (Increase) Act 1974; Friendly Societies Act 1974; Solicitors Act 1974; Financial Provisions (Northern Ireland) Order 1976; Home Purchase Assistance and Housing Corporation Guarantee Act 1978; Credit Unions Act 1979, s 31(1)(b) in definition of 'authorised bank'; Banking Act 1979; Solicitors (Scotland) Act 1980; British Telecommunications Act 1981; Trustee Savings Banks Act 1981, ss 1, 2, 3(1), (2), 4, 5, 6(1), 7(3), (5), (6), 8–11, 13 (words 'to the Central Board and' and ', and shall furnish such particulars of that person as the Central Board may direct'), 14, 15(1)–(8), (11), 16(1), (3), (4), 17, 18, 19(1)–(4), 20–22, 25(1) (the words 'to the Central Board and'), (2), 26–50, 52, 55(1), (3), Schs 1, 2, paras 1(a), (c), (3), (4), 4, 11, 13–16, Schs 4, 6, Sch 7,

Trustee Savings Banks Act 1985 (c 58)—*cont*

Sch 4—*cont*	para 5–8, 9(1), 11, 12, (so far as unrepealed), 13–15, Sch 8; Housing (Northern Ireland) Order 1981; Companies (Northern Ireland) Order 1982; Companies Act 1985) (SI 1986/1223)
	5 Jul 1988 (repeal of Trustee Savings Banks Act 1981, ss 12, 13 (so far as unrepealed), 23, 24, 25 (so far as unrepealed), 51, 53, Schs 3, 5, Sch 7, para 9(2)) (SI 1988/1168)

Water (Fluoridation) Act 1985 (c 63)

RA: 30 Oct 1985

30 Oct 1985 (RA); *Whole Act repealed (S)*

Weights and Measures Act 1985 (c 72)

RA: 30 Oct 1985; Weights and Measures Act 1985 (Commencement) Order 1992, SI 1992/770 (revoked); Weights and Measures Act 1985 (Revocation) Order 1993, SI 1993/2698 (revoking)

Commencement provisions: ss 43(2), 99(2)

s 1–42	30 Jan 1986 (s 99(2))
43	*Not in force*★
44–59	30 Jan 1986 (s 99(2))
60, 61	Repealed
62–99	30 Jan 1986 (s 99(2))
Sch 1–8	30 Jan 1986 (s 99(2))
9	Repealed
10–13	30 Jan 1986 (s 99(2))

★ The Weights and Measure Act 1985 (Commencement) Order 1992 (SI 1992/770) appointed 1 Apr 1994 as the date on which s 43 was to come into force; the Weights and Measures Act 1985 (Revocation) Order 1993 (SI 1993/2698) revoked that Commencement Order but did not appoint a new date for s 43

Wildlife and Countryside (Amendment) Act 1985 (c 31)

RA: 26 Jun 1985

Commencement provisions: s 5(3)

26 Aug 1985 (s 5(3))

Wildlife and Countryside (Service of Notices) Act 1985 (c 59)

RA: 25 Jul 1985

25 Jul 1985 (RA)

1986

Advance Petroleum Revenue Tax Act 1986 (c 68)

RA: 18 Dec 1986

18 Dec 1986 (RA)

Agricultural Holdings Act 1986 (c 5)

RA: 18 Mar 1986

Commencement provision: s 102(2)

18 Jun 1986 (s 102(2))

Agriculture Act 1986 (c 49)

RA: 25 Jul 1986

Commencement provisions: s 24(2), (3); Agriculture Act 1986 (Commencement) (No 1) Order 1986, SI 1986/1484; Agriculture Act 1986 (Commencement) (No 2) (Scotland) Order 1986, SI 1986/1485; Agriculture Act 1986 (Commencement No 3) Order 1986, SI 1986/1596; Agriculture Act 1986 (Commencement No 4) Order 1986, SI 1986/2301; Agriculture Act 1986 (Commencement No 5) Order 1991, SI 1991/2635

s 1–7	25 Sep 1986 (s 24(2))
8(1)	*Not in force*
(2)	8 Sep 1986 (SI 1986/1596)
(3)–(6)	*Not in force*
9	25 Sep 1986 (s 24(2))
10	31 Dec 1986 (SI 1986/2301)
11	25 Sep 1986 (s 24(2))
12	25 Jul 1986 (RA)
13	25 Sep 1986 (SI 1986/1484)
14	25 Sep 1986 (SI 1986/1485)
15	25 Sep 1986 (SI 1986/1484)
16	25 Sep 1986 (SI 1986/1485)
17	25 Sep 1986 (s 24(2))
18(1)–(12)	25 Sep 1986 (s 24(2))
(13)	25 Jul 1986 (RA)
19, 20	25 Sep 1986 (s 24(2))
21	Repealed
22, 23	25 Sep 1986 (s 24(2))
23A	Inserted (S) by Agricultural Holdings (Scotland) Act 1991, s 88(1), Sch 11, para 45 (qv)
24	25 Sep 1986 (s 24(2))

Agriculture Act 1986 (c 49)—*cont*

Sch 1	25 Sep 1986 (SI 1986/1484)
2	25 Sep 1986 (SI 1986/1485)
3	25 Sep 1986 (s 24(2))
4	25 Sep 1986 (except repeals consequential on ss 8–10) (s 24(2))
	31 Dec 1986 (repeals consequential on ss 9, 10) (SI 1986/2301)
	21 Nov 1991 (repeals in House of Commons Disqualification Act 1975; Northern Ireland Assembly Disqualification Act 1975) (SI 1991/2635)
	Not in force (repeals consequential on s 8)

Airports Act 1986 (c 31)

RA: 8 Jul 1986

Commencement provisions: s 85(2)–(6); Airports Act 1986 (Commencement No 1 and Appointed Day) Order 1986, SI 1986/1228; Airports Act 1986 (Commencement No 2) Order 1986, SI 1986/1487

s 1	8 Jul 1986 (s 85(2))
2	1 Aug 1986 (SI 1986/1228)
3	8 Jul 1986 (s 85(2))
4–9	1 Aug 1986 (SI 1986/1228)
10	Repealed
11	1 Aug 1986 (SI 1986/1228)
12–35	8 Sep 1986 (s 85(4))
36–56	1 Oct 1986 (SI 1986/1487)
57–62	31 Jul 1986 (SI 1986/1228)
63–66	1 Apr 1986 (SI 1986/1228)
67	1 Oct 1986 (SI 1986/1487)
68	8 Sep 1986 (SI 1986/1228)
69	1 Oct 1986 (SI 1986/1487)
70	8 Sep 1986 (s 85(4))
71	Repealed
72	8 Sep 1986 (s 85(4))
73, 74	1 Oct 1986 (SI 1986/1487)
75	8 Jul 1986 (s 85(2))
76(1), (2)	Repealed
(3), (4)	8 Jul 1986 (s 85(2))
(5)	Repealed
77(1)–(4)	1 Aug 1986 (SI 1986/1228)
(5), (6)	8 Jul 1986 (s 85(2))
78	8 Sep 1986 (s 85(4))
79–82	8 Jul 1986 (s 85(2))
83(1)	See Sch 4 below
(2)	1 Aug 1986 (SI 1986/1228)
(3)	1 Oct 1986 (SI 1986/1487)
(4)	1 Aug 1986 (SI 1986/1228)
(5)	See Sch 6 below
84	8 Sep 1986 (s 85(4))
85	8 Jul 1986 (s 85(2))
Sch 1	1 Oct 1986 (SI 1986/1487)
2	31 Jul 1986 (SI 1986/1228)

Airports Act 1986 (c 31)—*cont*

Sch 3	1 Aug 1986 (SI 1986/1228)
4, para 1	Repealed
2	31 Jul 1986 (SI 1986/1228)
3–8	1 Oct 1986 (SI 1986/1487)
9	1 Aug 1986 (SI 1986/1228)
10	1 Aug 1986 (except the expression '60(3)(o)') (SI 1986/1228)
	1 Apr 1987 (exception noted above) (SI 1986/1487)
5	1 Aug 1986 (SI 1986/1228)
6, Pt I	1 Aug 1986 (SI 1986/1228)
II	1 Aug 1986 (repeals of or in Civil Aviation Act 1982, ss 27, 29, 32, 33, 37, 40, 58, 99, Sch 5, Sch 13, Pt II (entries relating to ss 32(5), 33(1), 37, 40(2)), Sch 14; Criminal Justice Act 1982) (SI 1986/1228)
	1 Oct 1986 (repeal in Fair Trading Act 1973) (SI 1986/1487)
	1 Apr 1987 (repeals of or in Local Government, Planning and Land Act 1980; Civil Aviation Act 1982, s 38, Sch 13, Pt II, entry relating to s 61(6)) (SI 1986/1487)

Animals (Scientific Procedures) Act 1986 (c 14)

RA: 20 May 1986

Commencement provisions: s 30(3); Animals (Scientific Procedures) Act (Commencement) Order 1986, SI 1986/2088; Animals (Scientific Procedures) Act 1986 (Commencement No 1) Order 1986, SR 1986/364 (NI); Animals (Scientific Procedures) Act (Commencement No 2) Order 1989, SI 1989/2306; Animals (Scientific Procedures) (1986 Act) (Commencement No 2) Order (Northern Ireland) 1989, SR 1989/496

s 1–6	1 Jan 1987 (SI 1986/2088)
7	1 Jan 1990 (SI 1989/2306; SR 1989/496)
8, 9	1 Jan 1987 (SI 1986/2088)
10(1), (2)	1 Jan 1987 (SI 1986/2088)
(3)	1 Jan 1990 (SI 1989/2306; SR 1989/496)
(3A)	Inserted by Animals (Scientific Procedures) Act 1986 (Amendment) Regulations 1993, SI 1992/2102, reg 2(2)
(4)–(7)	1 Jan 1987 (SI 1986/2088)
11–28	1 Jan 1987 (SI 1986/2088)
29	1 Jan 1987 (SR 1986/364) (NI)
30	1 Jan 1987 (SI 1986/2088)
Sch 1	1 Jan 1987 (SI 1986/2088)
2	1 Jan 1990 (SI 1989/2306; SR 1989/496)
3, 4	1 Jan 1987 (SI 1986/2088)

Appropriation Act 1986 (c 42)

Whole Act repealed

Armed Forces Act 1986 (c 21)

RA: 26 Jun 1986

Commencement provisions: s 17(2), (3); Armed Forces Act 1986 (Commencement No 1) Order 1986, SI 1986/2071; Armed Forces Act 1986 (Commencement No 2) Order 1986, SI 1986/2124; Armed Forces Act 1986 (Commencement No 3) Order 1987, SI 1987/1998

s 1	Repealed
2–8	1 Jan 1987 (SI 1986/2124)
9	31 Dec 1987 (SI 1987/1998)
10–12	1 Jan 1987 (SI 1986/2124)
13	1 Jan 1987 (SI 1986/2124); prospectively repealed by Armed Forces Act 1991, s 26, Sch 3 (qv)
14	30 Dec 1986 (SI 1986/2071)
15	26 Jun 1986 (RA)
16(1)	1 Jan 1987 (SI 1986/2124)
(2)	See Sch 2 below
(3)	1 Jan 1987 (SI 1986/2124)
17	26 Jun 1986 (RA)
Sch 1	1 Jan 1987 (SI 1986/2124)
2	1 Sep 1986 (repeal of Armed Forces Act 1981, s 1) (s 17(3))
	30 Dec 1986 (repeal of Army Act 1955, s 213(a)) (SI 1986/2071)
	1 Jan 1987 (otherwise) (SI 1986/2124)

Atomic Energy Authority Act 1986 (c 3)

RA: 19 Feb 1986

Commencement provisions: s 10(2)

1 Apr 1986 (s 10(2))

Australia Act 1986 (c 2)

RA: 17 Feb 1986

Commencement provisions: s 17(2); Australia Act 1986 (Commencement) Order 1986, SI 1986/319

3 Mar 1986 (at 5 am GMT) (SI 1986/319)

Bishops (Retirement) Measure 1986 (No 1)

RA: 18 Mar 1986

Commencement provisions: s 13(3)

1 Jun 1986 (the day appointed by the Archbishops of Canterbury and York under s 13(3))

British Council and Commonwealth Institute Superannuation Act 1986 (c 51)

RA: 25 Jul 1986

Commencement provisions: s 3(2); British Council and Commonwealth Institute Superannuation Act 1986 (Commencement No 1) Order 1986, SI 1986/1860; British Council and Commonwealth Institute Superannuation Act 1986 (Commencement No 2) Order 1987, SI 1987/588

10 Nov 1986 (in relation to British Council) (SI 1986/1860)

1 Apr 1987 (in relation to Commonwealth Institute) (SI 1987/588)

British Shipbuilders (Borrowing Powers) Act 1986 (c 19)

Whole Act repealed

Building Societies Act 1986 (c 53)

RA: 25 Jul 1986

Commencement provisions: s 126(2)–(4); Building Societies Act 1986 (Commencement No 1) Order 1986, SI 1986/1560; Building Societies Act 1986 (Commencement No 2) Order 1989, SI 1989/1083

s 1–4	25 Sep 1986 (s 126(2))
5, 6	1 Jan 1987 (SI 1986/1560)
7	25 Sep 1986 (so far as relates to orders under s 7(9)) (SI 1986/1560)
	1 Jan 1987 (otherwise) (SI 1986/1560)
8, 9	1 Jan 1987 (SI 1986/1560)
10–17	1 Jan 1987 (SI 1986/1560)
18	25 Sep 1986 (so far as relates to designation orders under s 18(2)(c)) (SI 1986/1560)
	1 Jan 1987 (otherwise, except so far as empowers building societies to invest in, or support, corresponding European bodies) (SI 1986/1560)
	1 Jan 1988 (exception noted above) (SI 1986/1560)
19–23	1 Jan 1987 (SI 1986/1560)
24–34	1 Jan 1987 (SI 1986/1560)
35	*Not in force*; prospectively repealed by Courts and Legal Services Act 1990, s 125(7), Sch 20 (qv)
36(1)–(4)	1 Jan 1987 (SI 1986/1560)
(5), (6)	1 Jan 1988 (SI 1986/1560)
(7)	1 Jan 1987 (SI 1986/1560)
(8), (9)	1 Jan 1988 (SI 1986/1560)
(10)	1 Jan 1987 (SI 1986/1560)
(11)(a)	1 Jan 1987 (SI 1986/1560)
(b), (c)	1 Jan 1988 (SI 1986/1560)
(d)	1 Jan 1987 (SI 1986/1560)
(e), (f)	1 Jan 1988 (SI 1986/1560)
(12)	1 Jan 1988 (SI 1986/1560)
37	1 Jan 1987 (SI 1986/1560)
38–40	25 Sep 1986 (so far as relate to procedure following directions under Sch 20, para 11(5)(c)) (SI 1986/1560)
	1 Jan 1987 (otherwise) (SI 1986/1560)

Building Societies Act 1986 (c 53)—*cont*

s 41–45	1 Jan 1987 (SI 1986/1560)
45A	Inserted by Banking Coordination (Second Council Directive) Regulations 1992, SI 1992/3218, reg 74
46–82	1 Jan 1987 (SI 1986/1560)
83(1)–(5)	1 Jul 1987 (SI 1986/1560)
(6)–(15)	1 Jan 1987 (SI 1986/1560)
84(1)–(7)	1 Jan 1987 (SI 1986/1560)
(8)–(10)	1 Jul 1987 (SI 1986/1560)
(11)	1 Jan 1987 (SI 1986/1560)
85	1 Jan 1987 (SI 1986/1560)
86–89	1 Jan 1988 (SI 1986/1560)
90	1 Jan 1987 (so far as relates to Sch 15, paras 58, 59) (SI 1986/1560)
	1 Jan 1988 (otherwise) (SI 1986/1560)
91, 92	1 Jan 1988 (SI 1986/1560)
93–96	1 Jan 1987 (SI 1986/1560)
97–102	1 Jan 1988 (SI 1986/1560)
103(1)	1 Jan 1987 (so far as relates to societies dissolved by ss 93(5) or 94(10)) (SI 1986/1560)
	1 Jan 1988 (otherwise) (SI 1986/1560)
(2)–(9)	1 Jan 1987 (SI 1986/1560)
104–108	1 Jan 1987 (SI 1986/1560)
109(1)	25 Sep 1986 (so far as it relates to the exemption from stamp duties of any instrument referred to in s 109(1)(e) and required or authorised to be given, issued, signed, made or produced in pursuance of this Act) (SI 1986/1560)
	1 Jan 1987 (otherwise) (SI 1986/1560)
	(Formerly s 109, renumbered as s 109(1) by Finance Act 1988, s 145, Sch 12, para 8 (qv))
(2)	Added by Finance Act 1988, s 145, Sch 12, para 8 (qv)
110, 111	1 Jan 1987 (SI 1986/1560)
112(1)	25 Sep 1986 (SI 1986/1560)
(2)	1 Jan 1987 (SI 1986/1560)
(3), (4)	25 Sep 1986 (SI 1986/1560)
113	25 Sep 1986 (so far as relates to a memorandum or rules agreed upon under Sch 20, para 2) (SI 1986/1560)
	1 Jan 1987 (otherwise) (SI 1986/1560)
114	1 Jan 1987 (SI 1986/1560)
115, 116	25 Sep 1986 (SI 1986/1560)
117	1 Jan 1987 (SI 1986/1560)
118	25 Sep 1986 (SI 1986/1560)
118A	Inserted by Banking Coordination (Second Council Directive) Regulations 1992, SI 1992/3218, reg 80
119	25 Sep 1986 (SI 1986/1560)
120(1)	1 Jan 1987 (SI 1986/1560)
(2)	See Sch 19 below
(3)	1 Jan 1987 (SI 1986/1560)
(4)	See Sch 20 below
121	25 Jul 1986 (s 126(3))
122, 123	25 Sep 1986 (SI 1986/1560)
124	*Not in force*; prospectively repealed by Courts and Legal Services Act 1990, s 125(7), Sch 20 (qv)
125, 126	25 Jul 1986 (s 126(3))

Building Societies Act 1986 (c 53)—*cont*

Sch 1	25 Sep 1986 (s 126(2))
2, para 1–29	1 Jan 1987 (SI 1986/1560)
30	1 Jan 1988 (SI 1986/1560)
31–36	1 Jan 1987 (SI 1986/1560)
3–7	1 Jan 1987 (SI 1986/1560)
8	Substituted by Building Societies (Commercial Assets and Services) Order 1988, SI 1988/1141
9–14	1 Jan 1987 (SI 1986/1560)
15, para 1–33	1 Jan 1988 (SI 1986/1560)
34–55E	Substituted for original paras 34–55 by Insolvency (Northern Ireland) Order 1989, SI 1989/2405, art 381, Sch 9, Pt II
56, 57	1 Jan 1988 (SI 1986/1560)
58, 59	1 Jan 1987 (SI 1986/1560)
16	1 Jan 1987 (SI 1986/1560)
17	1 Jan 1988 (SI 1986/1560)
18	1 Jan 1987 (SI 1986/1560)
19, Pt I	1 Jan 1987 (except repeals of or in Building Societies Act 1874; Building Societies Act 1894; Building Societies Act 1960, Sch 5; Building Societies Act 1962, ss 28–31, Pt VII) (SI 1986/1560)
	1 Jan 1988 (otherwise, except repeal of 1962 Act, ss 28–31) (SI 1986/1560)
	17 Jul 1989 (repeal of 1962 Act, ss 28–31) (SI 1989/1083)
II	1 Jan 1987 (SI 1986/1560)
III	1 Jan 1987 (except repeal of Building Societies Act (Northern Ireland) 1967, ss 28–31, Pt VII) (SI 1986/1560)
	1 Jan 1988 (repeal of 1967 Act, Pt VII) (SI 1986/1560)
	17 Jul 1989 (repeal of 1967 Act, ss 28–31) (SI 1989/1083)
20, para 1, 2	25 Sep 1986 (SI 1986/1560)
3–6	1 Jan 1987 (SI 1986/1560)
7	25 Jul 1986 (s 126(3))
8–11	25 Sep 1986 (SI 1986/1560)
12	Ceased to have effect
13–16	1 Jan 1987 (SI 1986/1560)
17	25 Sep 1986 (SI 1986/1560)
18	1 Jan 1987 (SI 1986/1560)
21	*Not in force*; prospectively repealed by virtue of Courts and Legal Services Act 1990, s 125(7), Sch 20 (qv)

Children and Young Persons (Amendment) Act 1986 (c 28)

Whole Act repealed

Civil Protection in Peacetime Act 1986 (c 22)

RA: 26 Jun 1986

Commencement provisions: s 3(2)

26 Aug 1986 (s 3(2))

Commonwealth Development Corporation Act 1986 (c 25)

RA: 26 Jun 1986

26 Jun 1986 (RA)

Company Directors Disqualification Act 1986 (c 46)

RA: 25 Jul 1986

Commencement provisions: s 25

29 Dec 1986 (s 25)

Consolidated Fund Act 1986 (c 4)

Whole Act repealed

Consolidated Fund (No 2) Act 1986 (c 67)

Whole Act repealed

Consumer Safety (Amendment) Act 1986 (c 29)

Whole Act repealed

Corneal Tissue Act 1986 (c 18)

RA: 26 Jun 1986

Commencement provisions: s 2(2)

26 Aug 1986 (s 2(2))

Crown Agents (Amendment) Act 1986 (c 43)

RA: 25 Jul 1986

25 Jul 1986 (RA)

Deacons (Ordination of Women) Measure 1986 (No 4)

RA: 7 Nov 1986

Commencement provisions: s 5(2)

16 Feb 1987 (the day appointed by the Archbishops of Canterbury and York under
s 5(2))

Disabled Persons (Services, Consultation and Representation Act 1986 (c 33)

RA: 8 Jul 1986

Commencement provisions: s 18(2); Disabled Persons (Services, Consultation and Representation) Act 1986 (Commencement No 1) Order 1987, SI 1987/564; Disabled Persons (Services, Consultation and Representation) Act 1986 (Commencement No 2) Order 1987, SI 1987/729; Disabled Persons (Services, Consultation and Representation) Act 1986 (Commencement No 3) (Scotland) Order 1987, SI 1987/911; Disabled Persons (Services, Consultation and Representation) Act 1986 (Commencement No 4) Order 1988, SI 1988/51; Disabled Persons (Services, Consultation and Representation) Act 1986 (Commencement No 5) (Scotland) Order 1988, SI 1988/94; Disabled Persons (Services, Consultation and Representation) Act 1986 (Commencement No 5) Order 1989, SI 1989/2425

s 1–3	*Not in force*
4(a)	1 Apr 1987 (EW) (SI 1987/564)
	1 Oct 1987 (S) (SI 1987/911)
(b)	*Not in force*
(c)	1 Apr 1987 (EW) (SI 1987/564)
	1 Oct 1987 (S) (SI 1987/911)
5, 6	1 Feb 1988 (SI 1988/51)
7	*Not in force*
8(1)	1 Apr 1987 (EW) (SI 1987/564)
	1 Oct 1987 (S) (SI 1987/911)
(2), (3)	*Not in force*
9, 10	1 Apr 1987 (EW) (SI 1987/564)
	1 Jun 1987 (S) (SI 1987/911)
11	1 Jun 1987 (S) (SI 1987/911)
	18 Dec 1989 (EW) (SI 1989/2425)
12	1 Jun 1987 (SI 1987/911)
13	1 Feb 1988 (SI 1988/94)
14	1 Jun 1987 (SI 1987/911)
15	*Not in force*
16–18	17 Apr 1987 (EW) (SI 1987/729)
	1 Jun 1987 (S) (SI 1987/911)

Dockyard Services Act 1986 (c 52)

RA: 25 Jul 1986

Commencement provisions: s 5(2)

25 Sep 1986 (s 5(2))

Drainage Rates (Disabled Persons) Act 1986 (c 17)

Whole Act repealed

Drug Trafficking Offences Act 1986 (c 32)

RA: 8 Jul 1986

Commencement provisions: s 40(2); Drug Trafficking Offences Act 1986 (Commencement No 1) Order 1986, SI 1986/1488; Drug Trafficking Offences

Drug Trafficking Offences Act 1986 (c 32)—*cont*
Act 1986 (Commencement No 2) (Scotland) Order 1986, SI 1986/1546; Drug
Trafficking Offences Act 1986 (Commencement No 3) Order 1986, SI 1986/
2145, Drug Trafficking Offences Act 1986 (Commencement No 4) (Scotland)
Order 1986, SI 1986/2266

s 1(1), (2)	12 Jan 1987 (SI 1986/2145)
(3)	30 Sep 1986 (SI 1986/1488)
(4)–(6)	12 Jan 1987 (SI 1986/2145)
(7A)	Prospectively inserted by Criminal Justice Act 1993, s 7(2) (qv)
(8)	12 Jan 1987 (SI 1986/2145); prospectively repealed by Criminal Justice Act 1993, s 79(14), Sch 6, Pt I (qv)
1A	Prospectively inserted by Criminal Justice Act 1993, s 8 (qv)
2(1)	30 Sep 1986 (SI 1986/1488)
(2)	12 Jan 1987 (SI 1986/2145)
(2A), (2B)	Prospectively inserted by Criminal Justice Act 1993, s 9(3) (qv)
(3)–(5)	12 Jan 1987 (SI 1986/2145)
3	12 Jan 1987 (SI 1986/2145)
3A	Prospectively inserted by Criminal Justice Act 1993, s 10(5) (qv)
4	12 Jan 1987 (SI 1986/2145)
4A, 4B	Prospectively inserted by Criminal Justice Act 1993, s 14(1) (qv)
5	12 Jan 1987 (SI 1986/2145)
5A–5C	Prospectively inserted by Criminal Justice Act 1993, s 12 (qv)
6	12 Jan 1987 (SI 1986/2145)
7(1), (2)	12 Jan 1987 (SI 1986/2145); prospectively substituted by Criminal Justice Act 1993, s 13(3), (4) (qv)
(3), (4)	12 Jan 1987 (SI 1986/2145); repealed (S)
(5), (6)	Prospectively inserted by Criminal Justice Act 1993, s 13(5) (qv)
8	12 Jan 1987 (SI 1986/2145); repealed (S)
9, 10	12 Jan 1987 (SI 1986/2145)
11–13	12 Jan 1987 (SI 1986/2145); repealed (S)
14	12 Jan 1987 (SI 1986/2145)
15–17	12 Jan 1987 (SI 1986/2145; SI 1986/2266)
17A	Inserted by Criminal Justice Act 1988, s 103(1), Sch 5, Pt I, paras 1, 10 (qv)
18(1)	12 Jan 1987 (SI 1986/2145; SI 1986/2266)
(2)	12 Jan 1987 (SI 1986/2145)
19	12 Jan 1987 (SI 1986/2145)
19A–19C	Prospectively inserted by Criminal Justice Act 1993, s 15 (qv)
20–23	Repealed
23A	Inserted by Criminal Justice Act 1993, s 16 (qv)
24(1), (2)	30 Sep 1986 (SI 1986/1488)
(3)(a)	30 Sep 1986 (SI 1986/1488); repealed (S)
(b)	30 Sep 1986 (SI 1986/1488)
(4)	30 Sep 1986 (SI 1986/1488)
(4A)	Prospectively inserted by Criminal Justice Act 1993, s 18(3) (qv)

Drug Trafficking Offences Act 1986 (c 32)—*cont*

s 24(5)	30 Sep 1986 (SI 1986/1488)
(5A)	Repealed
(6)	30 Sep 1986 (SI 1986/1488)
24A	Inserted by Criminal Justice (Scotland) Act 1987, s 31 (qv)
25	12 Jan 1987 (SI 1986/2145)
26, 26A	Substituted for original s 26 by Criminal Justice Act 1988, s 103(1), Sch 5, Pt I, paras 1, 15 (qv)
26B, 26C	Prospectively inserted by Criminal Justice Act 1993, s 18(1) (qv)
27–29	30 Dec 1986 (EW) (SI 1986/2145); repealed (S)
30	12 Jan 1987 (SI 1986/2145; SI 1986/2266)
31	30 Dec 1986 (SI 1986/2145)
32	12 Jan 1987 (SI 1986/2145)
33	Repealed
34	30 Sep 1986 (SI 1986/1488; SI 1986/1546)
35	8 Jul 1986 (s 40(2))
36	12 Jan 1987 (SI 1986/2145)
36A	Prospectively inserted by Criminal Justice Act 1993, s 20(1) (qv)
36B	Prospectively inserted by Criminal Justice Act 1993, s 77, Sch 4, para 1 (qv)
37	12 Jan 1987 (SI 1986/2145)
38	30 Sep 1986 (SI 1986/1488; SI 1986/1546)
39(1), (2)	12 Jan 1987 (SI 1986/2145)
(3), (4)	12 Jan 1987 (SI 1986/2145; SI 1986/2266)
(5)	12 Jan 1987 (SI 1986/2145)
(6)	12 Jan 1987 (SI 1986/2145; SI 1986/2266)
40	30 Sep 1986 (SI 1986/1488; SI 1986/1546)

Ecclesiastical Fees Measure 1986 (No 2)

RA: 18 Mar 1986

Commencement provisions: s 12(3)

1 Sep 1986 (the day appointed by the Archbishops of Canterbury and York under s 12(3))

Education Act 1986 (c 40)

RA: 18 Jul 1986

Commencement provisions: s 6(2)

s 1	18 Sep 1986 (s 6(2))
2–6	18 Jul 1986 (RA)

Education (No 2) Act 1986 (c 61)

RA: 7 Nov 1986

Commencement provisions: s 66(1)–(4); Education (No 2) Act 1986 (Commencement No 1) Order 1986, SI 1986/2203; Education (No 2) Act 1986 (Commencement

Education (No 2) Act 1986 (c 61)—*cont*
No 2) Order 1987, SI 1987/344; Education (No 2) Act 1986 (Commencement
No 3) Order 1987, SI 1987/1159

s 1–4	1 Sep 1987 (SI 1987/344)
4A	Inserted by Education Act 1993, s 271(1) (qv)
5–16	1 Sep 1987 (SI 1987/344)
16A	Inserted by Further and Higher Education Act 1992, s 12(3) (qv)
17	7 Jan 1987 (SI 1986/2203)
18, 19	1 Sep 1987 (SI 1987/344)
20	Repealed
21	Substituted by Education Reform Act 1988, s 115 (qv)
22–28	1 Sep 1987 (SI 1987/344)
29	Repealed
30, 31	7 Jan 1987 (SI 1986/2203)
32	1 Sep 1987 (SI 1987/344)
33	7 Jan 1987 (SI 1986/2203)
34–41	1 Sep 1987 (SI 1987/344)
42	Substituted by Education Act 1993, s 238(9), Sch 13, para 5 (qv)
43	1 Sep 1987 (SI 1987/344)
44–46	7 Jan 1987 (SI 1986/2203)
46A	Inserted by Education Reform Act 1988, s 237(1), Sch 12, Pt I, para 34 (qv)
47(1)	15 Aug 1987 (SI 1987/344)
(1A), (1B)	Inserted by Education Act 1993, s 293(2) (qv)
(2)–(10)	15 Aug 1987 (SI 1987/344)
(11)	7 Jan 1987 (SI 1986/2203)
48	15 Aug 1987 (SI 1987/344)
49	7 Jan 1987 (s 66(2))
50–53	7 Jan 1987 (SI 1986/2203)
54, 55	1 Apr 1987 (SI 1986/2203)
56	7 Jan 1987 (SI 1986/2203)
57, 58	1 Sep 1987 (SI 1987/344)
59	7 Jan 1987 (s 66(2))
60	7 Nov 1986 (s 66(1))
61, 62	1 Sep 1987 (SI 1987/344)
63–66	7 Nov 1986 (s 66(1))
67(1)–(3)	7 Nov 1986 (s 66(1)
(4)	See Sch 4 below
(5)	See Sch 5 below
(6)	See Sch 6 below
(7)	7 Nov 1986 (s 66(1))
Sch 1–3	1 Sep 1987 (SI 1987/344)
4, para 1	1 Apr 1987 (SI 1986/2203)
2, 3	1 Sep 1987 (SI 1987/344)
4	Repealed
5	7 Jan 1987 (SI 1986/2203)
6, 7	Repealed
5	1 Sep 1987 (SI 1987/344)
6, Pt I	7 Jan 1987 (repeals of or in Education Act 1944, ss 4, 5, 67; London Government Act 1963, s 31(7)(a); Education Act 1980, ss 31, 32, Sch 6; Education (Scotland) Act 1980; Local Government, Planning and Land Act 1980) (SI 1986/2203)

Education (No 2) Act 1986 (c 61)—*cont*

Sch 6, Pt I—*cont*
1 Sep 1987 (repeals of or in Education Act 1944, ss 17–21, 23, 24(1), 27(3); Education Act 1962; Education (No 2) Act 1968; Education Act 1980, ss 2–4, 35(1)) (SI 1987/344)

1 Sep 1987 (repeals of or in London Government Act 1963, s 31(8); Local Government Act 1966, Sch 5, para (6)) (SI 1987/1159)

II
7 Jan 1987 (SI 1986/2203)

Education (Amendment) Act 1986 (c 1)

Whole Act repealed

European Communities (Amendment) Act 1986 (c 58)

RA: 7 Nov 1986

7 Nov 1986 (RA; but note that the repeals and revocations in the Schedule took effect on 1 July 1987, the day on which the Single European Act came into force, see Art 33(2) thereof, Cmnd 9758)

Family Law Act 1986 (c 55)

RA: 7 Nov 1986

Commencement provisions: s 69(2), (3); Family Law Act 1986 (Commencement No 1) Order 1988, SI 1988/375

s 1	4 Apr 1988 (SI 1988/375)
2, 2A	Substituted for original s 2 by Children Act 1989, s 108(5), Sch 13, para 64 (qv)
3	4 Apr 1988 (SI 1988/375)
4	Repealed
5, 6	4 Apr 1988 (SI 1988/375)
7	Substituted by Children Act 1989, s 108(5), Sch 13, para 67 (qv)
8–55	4 Apr 1988 (SI 1988/375)
56	Substituted by Family Law Reform Act 1987, s 22 (qv)
57–63	4 Apr 1988 (SI 1988/375)
64	Repealed
65–67	7 Jan 1987 (s 69(2))
68, 69	4 Apr 1988 (SI 1988/375)
Sch 1, para 1	Repealed
2–9	4 Apr 1988 (SI 1988/375)
10, 11	Repealed
12	4 Apr 1988 (SI 1988/375)
13	Repealed
14, 15	4 Apr 1988 (SI 1988/375)
16, 17	Repealed
18, 19	Spent
20	Repealed

Family Law Act 1986 (c 55)—*cont*

Sch 1, para 21, 22	4 Apr 1988 (SI 1988/375)
23	Repealed
24–34	4 Apr 1988 (SI 1988/375)
2	4 Apr 1988 (SI 1988/375)

Finance Act 1986 (c 41)

Budget Day: 18 Mar 1986

RA: 25 Jul 1986

See the note concerning Finance Acts at the front of this book

Financial Services Act 1986 (c 60)

RA: 7 Nov 1986

Commencement provisions: s 211(1), (2); Financial Services Act 1986
(Commencement No 1) Order 1986, SI 1986/1940; Financial Services Act 1986
(Commencement No 2) Order 1986, SI 1986/2031; Financial Services Act 1986
(Commencement No 3) Order 1986, SI 1986/2246; Financial Services Act 1986
(Commencement) (No 4) Order 1987, SI 1987/623; Financial Services Act 1986
(Commencement) (No 5) Order 1987, SI 1987/907; Financial Services Act 1986
(Commencement) (No 6) Order 1987, SI 1987/1997; Financial Services Act 1986
(Commencement) (No 7) Order 1987, SI 1987/2158; Financial Services Act 1986
(Commencement) (No 8) Order 1988, SI 1988/740; Financial Services Act 1986
(Commencement) (No 9) Order 1988, SI 1988/995; Financial Services Act 1986
(Commencement) (No 10) Order 1988, SI 1988/1960; Financial Services Act
1986 (Commencement) (No 11) Order 1988, SI 1988/2285; Financial Services
Act 1986 (Commencement) (No 12) Order 1989, SI 1989/1583

s 1	See Sch 1 below
2	18 Dec 1986 (SI 1986/2246)
3, 4	29 Apr 1988 (SI 1988/740)
5	12 Jan 1987 (so far as necessary to identify agreements to which s 5(1) applies for the purposes of s 132, so far as that section is in force by virtue of this Order) (SI 1986/2246)
	29 Apr 1988 (otherwise) (SI 1988/740)
6, 7	29 Apr 1988 (SI 1988/740)
8–11	4 Jun 1987 (SI 1987/907)
12	1 Dec 1987 (SI 1987.1997)
13, 14	4 Jun 1987 (SI 1987/907)
15	4 Jun 1987 (except so far as has effect of conferring authorisation) (SI 1987/907)
	29 Apr 1988 (otherwise) (SI 1988/740)
16–19	4 Jun 1987 (SI 1987/907)
20	1 Dec 1987 (SI 1987/1997)
21	4 Jun 1987 (SI 1987/907)
22	29 Apr 1988 (SI 1988/740)
23	Substituted by Friendly Societies Act 1992, s 98(a), Sch 18, Pt I, para 1 (qv)
24	29 Apr 1988 (for purposes of Sch 15, para 10) (SI 1988/740)
	1 Oct 1989 (otherwise) (SI 1989/1583)

Financial Services Act 1986 (c 60)—*cont*

s 25	29 Apr 1988 (SI 1988/740)
26–30	1 Jan 1988 (SI 1987/2158)
31(1)–(3)	29 Apr 1988 (SI 1988/740)
(4)	1 Jan 1988 (so far as necessary to enable the Secretary of State to issue and revoke certificates) (SI 1987/2158)
	29 Apr 1988 (otherwise) (SI 1988/740)
(5)	29 Apr 1988 (SI 1988/740)
32–34	29 Apr 1988 (SI 1988/740)
35	18 Dec 1986 (so far as relevant for the purposes of s 105) (SI 1986/2246)
	29 Apr 1988 (otherwise) (SI 1988/740)
36(1)	29 Apr 1988 (SI 1988/740)
(2), (3)	4 Jun 1987 (SI 1987/907)
37	4 Jun 1987 (except so far as has effect in relation to a body or association of the kind described in s 40(1)) (SI 1987/907)
	23 Nov 1987 (exception noted above) (SI 1987/1997)
38(1)	29 Apr 1988 (SI 1988/740)
(2), (3)	4 Jun 1987 (SI 1987/907)
39	4 Jun 1987 (except so far as has effect in relation to a body or association of the kind described in s 40(1)) (SI 1987/907)
	23 Nov 1987 (exception noted above) (SI 1987/1997)
40	23 Nov 1987 (SI 1987/1997)
41	4 Jun 1987 (SI 1987/907)
42	18 Dec 1986 (for purposes of s 105) (SI 1986/2246)
	29 Apr 1988 (otherwise) (SI 1988/740)
43	1 Jan 1988 (SI 1987/2158)
44	29 Apr 1988 (SI 1988/740)
45	18 Dec 1986 (for purposes of s 105) (SI 1986/2246)
	29 Apr 1988 (otherwise) (SI 1988/740)
46	4 Jun 1987 (SI 1987/907)
47	29 Apr 1988 (SI 1988/740)
47A	Inserted by Companies Act 1989, s 192 (qv)
47B	Prospectively inserted by Companies Act 1989, s 192 (qv)
48–52	4 Jun 1987 (SI 1987/907)
53	*Not in force*
54, 55	4 Jun 1987 (SI 1987/907)
56	4 Jun 1987 (so far as necessary in order to enable regulations to be made under s 56(1)) (SI 1987/907)
	29 Apr 1988 (otherwise) (SI 1988/740)
57	29 May 1988 (so far as it relates to an advertisement issued for valuable consideration in a newspaper, journal, magazine or other periodical publication which is published at intervals of less than seven days *except* in relation to an advertisement issued on or after 29 May 1988 in an edition of a newspaper, magazine, journal or other publication first issued before that date) (SI 1988/740)
	29 Jul 1988 (so far as relates to an advertisement issued for valuable consideration either (i) in any

Financial Services Act 1986 (c 60)—*cont*

s 57—*cont*
newspaper, journal, magazine or other publication which is published at intervals of seven or more days; or (ii) by way of sound broadcasting or television, by the exhibition of cinematographic films or by the distribution of recordings *except* in relation to an advertisement issued on or after 29 July 1988 in an edition of a newspaper, magazine, journal or other publication first issued before that date) (SI 1988/740)

6 May 1988 (so far as relates to an advertisement which is *neither* (a) issued for valuable consideration in a newspaper, journal, magazine or other periodical published at intervals of less than seven days, *nor* (b) issued for valuable consideration either (i) in any newspaper, journal, magazine or other publication published at intervals of seven or more days, or (ii) by way of sound broadcasting or television by the exhibition of cinematographic films or by the distribution of recordings, and which is issued or caused to be issued by a person who is not an authorised person *except* in relation to an advertisement issued on or after 6 May 1988 in an edition of a newspaper, magazine, journal or other publication first issued before 6 May 1988) (SI 1988/740)

29 Apr 1988 (exception noted above) (SI 1988/740)

58(1)(a)–(c)
29 Apr 1988 (SI 1988/740)

(d)(i)
29 Apr 1988 (SI 1988/740)

(ii)
29 Apr 1988 (except so far as relates to an advertisement required or permitted to be published by an approved exchange under Pt V of the Act) (SI 1988/740)

Not in force (exception noted above)

(2)
Not in force

(3)–(6)
29 Apr 1988 (SI 1988/740)

59–61
29 Apr 1988 (SI 1988/740)

62(1)
1 Dec 1987 (except so far as s 62(1) applies to a contravention such as is mentioned in s 62(2)) (SI 1987/1997)

3 Oct 1988 (exception noted above) (SI 1987/1997)

(2)–(4)
1 Dec 1987 (SI 1987/1997)

62A
Inserted by Companies Act 1989, s 193(1) (qv)

63
23 Apr 1987 (SI 1987/623)

63A, 63B
Inserted by Companies Act 1989, s 194 (qv)

63C
Inserted by Companies Act 1989, s 195 (qv)

64–75
29 Apr 1988 (SI 1988/740)

76
29 Apr 1988 (except so far as has effect in relation to (a) a collective investment scheme which takes the form of an open-ended investment company units in which are either included in the Official List of The International Stock Exchange of the United Kingdom and the Republic of Ireland Limited or are offered on terms such that any agreement for their acquisition is conditional upon their admission to that List; or (b) any prospectus

Financial Services Act 1986 (c 60)—*cont*

s 76—*cont*   issued by or on behalf of an open-ended
investment company which complies with
Chapter II of Part III of the Companies Act 1985
or the corresponding provisions of the
Companies (Northern Ireland) Order 1986 and
the issue of which in the United Kingdom does
not contravene s 74 or 75 of the Companies Act
1985 or the corresponding provisions of the
Companies (Northern Ireland) Order 1986 as the
case may be) (SI 1988/740)

31 Dec 1988 (otherwise, except so far as has effect in
relation to (a) an open-ended investment
company units in which are either included in the
Official List of The International Stock Exchange
of the United Kingdom and the Republic of
Ireland Limited or are offered on terms such that
any agreement for their acquisition is conditional
upon such listing being an open-ended
investment company which either (i) is managed
in and authorised under the law of a country or
territory in respect of which an order under s 87
of the Financial Services Act 1986 is in force on 31
Dec 1988 and which is of a class specified in that
order; or (ii) is constituted in a member State in
respect of which an order under para 10 of Sch 15
to the Financial Services Act 1986 is in force on 31
Dec 1988 and which meets the requirements
specified in that order; or (b) any prospectus
issued by or on behalf of an open-ended
investment company which fulfils the conditions
described in head (a)(i) or (a)(ii) immediately
above being a prospectus which complies with
Chapter II of Part III of the Companies Act 1985
or the corresponding provisions of the
Companies (Northern Ireland) Order 1986 and
the issue of which in the United Kingdom does
not contravene s 74 or 75 of the Companies Act
1985 or the corresponding provisions of the
Companies (Northern Ireland) Order 1986 as the
case may be) (SI 1988/1960, as amended by SI
1988/2285)

(and also except so far as has effect in relation to (a)
an open-ended investment company managed in
and authorised under the law of Bermuda units in
which are, on 31 Dec 1988, included in the
Official List of The International Stock Exchange
of the United Kingdom and the Republic of
Ireland Limited; or (b) any prospectus issued by
or on behalf of an open-ended investment
company which fulfils the conditions described in
head (a) immediately above, being a prospectus
which complies with Chapter II of Part III of the
Companies Act 1985 or the corresponding
provisions of the Companies (Northern Ireland)
Order 1986 and the issue of which in the United
Kingdom does not contravene s 74 or 75 of the
Companies Act 1985 or the corresponding

Financial Services Act 1986 (c 60)—*cont*

s 76—*cont*

provisions of the Companies (Northern Ireland) Order 1986 (as the case may be) (SI 1988/2285)

28 Feb 1989 (so far as has effect in relation to an open-ended investment company falling within head (a) immediately above but which is not a scheme of a class specified in the Schedule to the Financial Services (Designated Countries and Territories) (Overseas Collective Investment Schemes) (Bermuda) Order 1988, SI 1988/2284, or to any prospectus which falls within head (b) immediately above issued by or on behalf of any such company) (SI 1988/2285)

1 Mar 1989 (otherwise, except so far as has effect in relation to (a) an open-ended investment company which fulfils the conditions described in head (a) immediately above and which is a scheme of a class specified in the Schedule to the Financial Services (Designated Countries and Territories) (Overseas Collective Investment Schemes) (Bermuda) Order 1988, SI 1988/2284, or (b) any prospectus issued by or on behalf of such an open-ended investment company, being a prospectus which fulfils the conditions described in head (b) immediately above) (SI 1988/1960)

1 May 1989 (exception noted above) (SI 1988/2285)

77–85	29 Apr 1988 (SI 1988/740)
86	29 Apr 1988 (for purposes of Sch 15, para 10) (SI 1988/740)
	1 Oct 1989 (otherwise) (SI 1989/1583)
87–95	29 Apr 1988 (SI 1988/740)
96	1 Dec 1987 (SI 1987/1997)
97–101	29 Apr 1988 (SI 1988/740)
102, 103	4 Jun 1987 (SI 1987/9907)
104(1)	29 Apr 1988 (SI 1988/740)
(2), (3)	4 Jun 1987 (SI 1987/907)
(4)	29 Apr 1988 (SI 1988/740)
105, 106	18 Dec 1986 (SI 1986/2246)
107	4 Jun 1987 (SI 1987/907)
107A	Inserted by Companies Act 1989, s 206(1), Sch 23, para 11 (qv)
108, 109	29 Apr 1988 (SI 1988/740)
110	4 Jun 1987 (SI 1987/907)
111	29 Apr 1988 (SI 1988/740)
112(1)–(4)	4 Jun 1987 (SI 1987/907)
(5)	1 Jan 1988 (so far as has effect in relation to applications under s 26) (SI 1987/2158)
	29 Apr 1988 (otherwise) (SI 1988/740)
113(1)	4 Jun 1987 (SI 1987/907)
(2)	29 Apr 1988 (SI 1988/740)
(3)	Substituted by Friendly Societies Act 1992, s 98(a), Sch 18, Pt I, para 2 (qv)
(4)–(8)	29 Apr 1988 (SI 1988/740)
114–118	12 Jan 1987 (SI 1986/2246)
119, 120	4 Jun 1987 (SI 1987/907)
121	12 Jan 1987 (SI 1986/2246)
122	12 Jan 1987 (for purposes of s 121) (SI 1986/2246)
	4 Jun 1987 (otherwise) (SI 1987/907)

Financial Services Act 1986 (c 60)—*cont*

s 123	12 Jan 1987 (for purposes of any provision brought into force by SI 1986/2246) (SI 1986/2246)
	4 Jun 1987 (otherwise) (SI 1987/907)
124	12 Jan 1987 (SI 1986/2246)
125(1)–(7)	4 Jun 1987 (SI 1987/907)
(8)	1 Jul 1988 (SI 1988/995)
126	12 Jan 1987 (SI 1986/2246)
127	4 Jun 1987 (SI 1987/907)
128	12 Jan 1987 (SI 1986/2246)
128A–128C	Inserted by Companies Act 1989, s 196 (qv)
129	See Sch 10 below
130, 131	29 Apr 1988 (SI 1988/740)
132(1)–(5)	12 Jan 1987 (SI 1986/2246)
(6)(first part)	12 Jan 1987 (for purposes of any contract of insurance which is not an agreement to which s 5(1) applies) (SI 1986/2246)
	29 Apr 1988 (otherwise) (SI 1988/740)
(second part)	12 Jan 1987 (for purposes of any re–insurance contract entered into in respect of a contract of insurance which is not an agreement to which s 5(1) applies) (SI 1986/2246)
	29 Apr 1988 (otherwise) (SI 1988/740)
133	29 Apr 1988 (SI 1988/740)
134	12 Jan 1987 (for the purpose of a person who, on 12 Jan 1987, is not entitled (either alone or with any associate or associates) to exercise, or control the exercise of, 15% or more of the voting power at any general meeting of an applicant under Insurance Companies Act 1982, s 3, or of an insurance company in relation to which applicant or insurance company the question of who is its controller under that Act arises, or of a body corporate of which such an applicant or such an insurance company is a subsidiary. 'Associate' has the meaning given in Insurance Companies Act 1982, s 7(8), and 'body corporate' and 'subsidiary' have the meanings which they have for the purposes of s 7(4)(c)(ii) of that Act as set out in s 96(1) of that Act) (SI 1986/2246)
	Not in force (otherwise)
135, 136	29 Apr 1988 (SI 1988/740)
137	12 Jan 1987 (SI 1986/2246)
138(1), (2)	4 Jun 1987 (SI 1987/907)
(3)	12 Jan 1987 (SI 1986/2246)
(4)	29 Apr 1988 (SI 1988/740)
(5)	12 Jan 1987 (SI 1986/2246)
(6)	4 Jun 1987 (SI 1987/907)
139(1)(a)	29 Apr 1988 (SI 1988/740)
(b)	12 Jan 1987 (SI 1986/2246)
(2)	29 Apr 1988 (SI 1988/740)
(3), (4)	Repealed
(5)	29 Apr 1988 (SI 1988/740)
140	See Sch 11 below
141	12 Jan 1987 (SI 1986/2246)
142–153	12 Jan 1987 (for all purposes relating to the admission of securities offered by or on behalf of a Minister of the Crown or a body corporate

Financial Services Act 1986 (c 60)—*cont*

s 142–153—*cont*	controlled by a Minister of the Crown or a subsidiary of such a body corporate to the Official List in respect of which an application is made after that date) (SI 1986/2246)
	16 Feb 1987 (for purposes relating to the admission of securities in respect of which an application is made after that date, other than those referred to in the preceding paragraph, and otherwise for all purposes) (SI 1986/2246)
154(1)	12 Jan 1987 (for all purposes relating to the admission of securities offered by or on behalf of a Minister of the Crown or a body corporate controlled by a Minister of the Crown or a subsidiary of such a body corporate to the Official List in respect of which an application is made after that date) (SI 1986/2246)
	16 Feb 1987 (for purposes relating to the admission of securities in respect of which an application is made after that date, other than those referred to in the preceding paragraph, and otherwise for all purposes) (SI 1986/2246)
(2)–(4)	29 Apr 1988 (SI 1988/740)
(5)	12 Jan 1987 (for all purposes relating to the admission of securities offered by or on behalf of a Minister of the Crown or a body corporate controlled by a Minister of the Crown or a subsidiary of such a body corporate to the Official List in respect of which an application is made after that date) (SI 1986/2246)
	16 Feb 1987 (for purposes relating to the admission of securities in respect of which an application is made after that date, other than those referred to in the preceding paragraph, and otherwise for all purposes) (SI 1986/2246)
155, 156	12 Jan 1987 (for all purposes relating to the admission of securities offered by or on behalf of a Minister of the Crown or a body corporate controlled by a Minister of the Crown or a subsidiary of such a body corporate to the Official List in respect of which an application is made after that date) (SI 1986/2246)
	16 Feb 1987 (for purposes relating to the admission of securities in respect of which an application is made after that date, other than those referred to in the preceding paragraph, and otherwise for all purposes) (SI 1986/2246)
157	Repealed
158, 159	*Not in force*
160	29 Apr 1988 (so far as necessary to enable the Secretary of State to make an order under this section) (SI 1988/740)
	Not in force (otherwise)
160A	Inserted by Companies Act 1989, s 198 (qv)
161	*Not in force*
162	29 Apr 1988 (so far as necessary to enable the Secretary of State to make rules under this section

Financial Services Act 1986 (c 60)—*cont*

s 162—*cont*	and so far as necessary for the purposes of s 169) (SI 1988/740)
	Not in force (otherwise)
163–168	*Not in force*
169	29 Apr 1988 (SI 1988/740)
170	29 Apr 1988 (so far as necessary to enable the Secretary of State to make an order under this section) (SI 1988/740)
	Not in force (otherwise)
171	*Not in force*
172	30 Apr 1987 (SI 1986/2246)
(ss 173–176	Prospectively repealed by Criminal Justice Act 1993, s 79(14), Sch 6, Pt I (qv))
173	12 Jan 1987 (SI 1986/2246)
174(1), (2)	18 Dec 1986 (SI 1986/2246)
(3)	29 Apr 1988 (SI 1988/740)
(4)(a)	*Not in force*
(b)	29 Apr 1988 (SI 1988/740)
175	29 Apr 1988 (SI 1988/740)
176	12 Jan 1987 (SI 1986/2246)
177	15 Nov 1986 (SI 1986/1940)
178(1)	15 Nov 1986 (SI 1986/1940)
(2)(a)	15 Nov 1986 (SI 1986/1940)
(b)	29 Apr 1988 (SI 1988/740)
(3)–(9)	29 Apr 1988 (SI 1988/740)
(10)	12 Jan 1987 (SI 1986/2246)
179	15 Nov 1986 (for purposes of information obtained by a person mentioned in s 179(3)(h) so far as that provision applies to a person appointed or authorised to exercise any powers under s 177, or by a person mentioned in s 179(3)(i) who is an officer or servant of any such person) (SI 1986/1940)
	18 Dec 1986 (otherwise) (SI 1986/2246)
180	15 Nov 1986 (SI 1986/2246)
181	12 Jan 1987 (SI 1986/2246)
182	See Sch 13 below
183	23 Apr 1987 (so far as relates to notices relating to the carrying on of insurance business or of a deposit–taking business as a recognised bank or licensed institution within the meaning of the Banking Act 1979) (SI 1987/623)
	29 Apr 1988 (otherwise) (SI 1988/740)
184(1)–(3)	23 Apr 1987 (so far as relate to notices relating to the carrying on of insurance business) (SI 1987/623)
	29 Apr 1988 (otherwise) (SI 1988/740)
(4)	29 Apr 1988 (SI 1988/740)
(5)	23 Apr 1987 (SI 1987/623)
(6)	29 Apr 1988 (SI 1988/740)
(7)	23 Apr 1987 (SI 1987/623)
(8)	29 Apr 1988 (SI 1988/740)
185	23 Apr 1987 (SI 1987/623)
186(1)–(5)	23 Apr 1987 (so far as relate to provisions brought into force by SI 1987/623) (SI 1987/623)
	29 Apr 1988 (otherwise) (SI 1988/740)
(6)	29 Apr 1988 (SI 1988/740)

Financial Services Act 1986 (c 60)—*cont*

s 186(7)	23 Apr 1987 (so far as relates to provisions brought into force by SI 1987/623) (SI 1987/623)
	29 Apr 1988 (otherwise) (SI 1988/740)
187(1), (2)	4 Jun 1987 (SI 1987/907)
(3), (4)	12 Jan 1987 (SI 1986/2246)
(5), (7)	4 Jun 1987 (SI 1987/907)
188	Substituted by Companies Act 1989, s 200(1) (qv)
189	See Sch 14 below
190, 191	4 Jun 1987 (SI 1987/907)
192	Substituted by Companies Act 1989, s 201 (qv)
193	Repealed
194	29 Apr 1988 (SI 1988/740)
195	7 Nov 1986 (s 211(2)); prospectively repealed by s 212(3) of, and Sch 17 to, this Act (qv)
196	1 Dec 1987 (SI 1987/1997)
197	29 Apr 1988 (SI 1988/740)
198(1)	Repealed
(2)(a)	15 Nov 1986 (SI 1986/1940)
(b)	18 Dec 1986 (SI 1986/2246)
(3)(a)	29 Apr 1988 (SI 1988/740)
(b)	4 Jun 1987 (SI 1987/907)
199(1)	Substituted by Companies Act 1989, s 76(2) (qv); prospectively substituted by Criminal Justice Act 1993, s 79(13), Sch 5, para 12(1) (qv)
(2)	Substituted by Companies Act 1989, s 76(2) (qv);
(3)–(6)	15 Nov 1986 (for purposes relating to offences under Company Securities (Insider Dealing) Act 1985, ss 1, 2, 4, 5) (SI 1986/1940)
	29 Apr 1988 (otherwise) (SI 1988/740)
(7)	12 Jan 1987 (SI 1986/2246)
(8)	Substituted by Companies Act 1989, s 76(7) (qv)
(8A)	Prospectively inserted by Criminal Justice Act 1993, s 79(13), Sch 5, para 12(2) (qv)
(9)	15 Nov 1986 (for purposes relating to offences under Company Securities (Insider Dealing) Act 1985, ss 1, 2, 4, 5) (SI 1986/1940)
	29 Apr 1988 (otherwise) (SI 1988/740)
200(1)(a)	4 Jun 1987 (so far as has effect in relation to an application for a recognition order under Ch III or IV of Pt 1) (SI 1987/907)
	1 Jan 1988 (so far as has effect in relation to an application for authorisation under s 26) (SI 1987/2158)
	29 Apr 1988 (otherwise) (SI 1988/740)
(b)	15 Nov 1986 (so far as relates to a requirement imposed by or under s 177) (SI 1986/2246)
	12 Jan 1987 (so far as relates to a requirement imposed by or under any provision brought into force on 12 Jan 1987 by SI 1986/2246) (SI 1986/2246)
	4 Jun 1987 (so far as relates to a requirement imposed by or under any provision brought into force by SI 1987/907) (SI 1987/907)
	1 Jan 1988 (so far as relates to a requirement imposed by or under any provision brought into force by SI 1987/2158) (SI 1987/2158)
	29 Apr 1988 (otherwise) (SI 1988/740)

Financial Services Act 1986 (c 60)—*cont*

s 200(2)	29 Apr 1988 (SI 1988/740)
(3), (4)	4 Jun 1987 (SI 1987/907)
(5)	15 Nov 1986 (so far as relates to a requirement imposed by or under s 177) (SI 1986/1940)
	18 Dec 1986 (so far as relates to a requirement imposed by or under s 105) (SI 1986/2246)
	12 Jan 1987 (so far as relates to a requirement imposed by or under any provision brought into force on 12 Jan 1987 by SI 1986/2246) (SI 1986/2246)
	4 Jun 1987 (so far as relates to a provision brought into force by SI 1987/907) (SI 1987/907)
	1 Jan 1988 (so far as has relates to any provision brought into force by SI 1987/2158 (SI 1987/2158)
	29 Apr 1988 (otherwise) (SI 1988/740)
(6)–(8)	4 Jun 1987 (so far as relates to a provision brought into force by SI 1987/907) (SI 1987/907)
	29 Apr 1988 (otherwise) (SI 1988/740)
201(1)	15 Nov 1986 (so far as relates to a provision brought into force by SI 1986/1940) (SI 1986/1940)
	18 Dec 1986 (otherwise) (SI 1986/2246)
(2)	29 Apr 1988 (SI 1988/740)
(3)	23 Apr 1987 (SI 1987/623)
(4)	12 Jan 1987 (SI 1986/2246)
202, 203	15 Nov 1986 (for purposes of any provision brought into force by SI 1986/1940) (SI 1986/1940)
	18 Dec 1986 (otherwise) (SI 1986/2246)
204	12 Jan 1987 (SI 1986/2246)
205, 205A	Substituted for original s 205 by Companies Act 1989, s 206(1), Sch 23, para 18 (qv)
206(1)–(3)	4 Jun 1987 (SI 1987/907)
(4)	15 May 1987 (SI 1987/907)
207	15 Nov 1986 (for purposes of any provision brought into force by SI 1986/1940) (SI 1986/1940)
	18 Dec 1986 (otherwise) (SI 1986/2246)
208	29 Apr 1988 (so far as has effect in relation to the application of s 130) (SI 1988/740)
	Not in force (otherwise)
209, 210	15 Nov 1986 (for purposes of any provision brought into force by SI 1986/1940) (SI 1986/1940)
	18 Dec 1986 (otherwise) (SI 1986/2246)
211(1), (2)	7 Nov 1986 (RA)
(3)	See Sch 15 below
212(1)	27 Nov 1986 (SI 1986/2031)
(2)	See Sch 16 below
(3)	See Sch 17 below
Sch 1, para 1–22	18 Dec 1986 (SI 1986/2246)
23	1 Dec 1987 (SI 1987/1997)
24	18 Dec 1986 (SI 1986/2246)
25(1)	18 Dec 1986 (SI 1986/2246)
(2), (3)	18 Jan 1988 (SI 1987/2158)

Financial Services Act 1986 (c 60)—*cont*

Sch 1, para 25A	Inserted by Financial Services Act 1986 (Restriction of Scope of Act) Order 1988, SI 1988/318; substituted by Financial Services Act 1986 (Extension of Scope of Act) Order 1992, SI 1992/273
25B	Inserted by Financial Services Act 1986 (Restriction of Scope of Act) Order 1988, SI 1988/318
26–29	18 Dec 1986 (SI 1986/2246)
30	Substituted by Companies Act 1989, s 23, Sch 10, Pt II, para 36 (qv)
31–33	18 Dec 1986 (SI 1986/2246)
34, 35	Inserted by Financial Services Act 1986 (Restriction of Scope of Act and Meaning of Collective Investment Scheme) Order 1990, SI 1990/349
2–4	4 Jun 1987 (SI 1987/907)
5	1 Jan 1988 (SI 1987/2158)
6	1 Dec 1987 (SI 1987/1997)
7–9	12 Jan 1987 (SI 1986/2246)
10, para 1	12 Jan 1987 (SI 1986/2246)
2	29 Apr 1988 (SI 1988/740)
3(1), (2)	4 Jun 1987 (SI 1987/907)
(3)	12 Jan 1987 (SI 1986/2246)
(4)	4 Jun 1987 (SI 1987/907)
4(1), (2)	4 Jun 1987 (SI 1987/907)
(2A)	Inserted by Companies Act 1989, s 206(1), Sch 23, para 25 (qv)
(3), (4)	4 June 1987 (SI 1987/907)
(5)	29 Apr 1988 (SI 1988/740)
(6)	12 Jan 1987 (SI 1986/2246)
5(1), (2)	29 Apr 1988 (SI 1988/740)
(3), (4)	1 Jul 1988 (SI 1988/995)
6, 7	29 Apr 1988 (SI 1988/740)
8(1)–(5)	29 Apr 1988 (SI 1988/740)
(6)	12 Jan 1987 (SI 1986/2246)
9	29 Apr 1988 (SI 1988/740)
10	12 Jan 1987 (SI 1986/2246)
11, para 1	12 Jan 1987 (SI 1986/2246)
2–5	4 Jun 1987 (SI 1987/907)
6	1 Dec 1987 (SI 1987/1997)
7	Repealed
8–13	4 Jun 1987 (SI 1987/907)
13A	Inserted by Companies Act 1989, s 206(1), Sch 23, para 32 (qv)
13B	Prospectively inserted by Companies Act 1989, s 206(1), Sch 23, para 32 (qv)
14–16	4 Jun 1987 (SI 1987/907)
17	*Not in force*
18, 19	4 Jun 1987 (SI 1987/907)
20	Substituted by Companies Act 1989, s 206(1), Sch 23, para 35 (qv)
21	29 Apr 1988 (SI 1988/740)
22(1)–(3)	29 Apr 1988 (SI 1988/740)
(4)	1 Dec 1987 (except for purposes of making a contravention of the kind described in para 22(4)(d) actionable at the suit of a person of the kind described in that paragraph) (SI 1987/1997)
	3 Oct 1988 (exception noted above) (SI 1987/1997)

Financial Services Act 1986 (c 60)—*cont*

Sch 11, para 22(5)	1 Dec 1987 (SI 1987/1997)
22A	Inserted by Companies Act 1989, s 193(3) (qv)
22B–22D	Inserted by Companies Act 1989, s 206(1), Sch 23, para 36 (qv)
23	29 Apr 1988 (SI 1988/740)
24	4 Jun 1987 (SI 1987/907)
25, 26	29 Apr 1988 (SI 1988/740)
27	Repealed
28	12 Jan 1987 (SI 1986/2246)
29	Substituted by Companies Act 1989, s 206(1), Sch 23, para 37 (qv)
30, 31	12 Jan 1987 (SI 1986/2246)
31A	Prospectively inserted by Friendly Societies Act 1992, s 98(a), Sch 18, Pt II, para 19 (qv)
32, 33	12 Jan 1987 (SI 1986/2246)
34	Substituted by Companies Act 1989, s 206(1), Sch 23, para 40 (qv)
35–37	12 Jan 1987 (SI 1986/2246)
38	4 Jun 1987 (SI 1987/907)
39	1 Jan 1988 (SI 1987/2158)
40	12 Jan 1987 (SI 1986/2246)
40A	Inserted by Friendly Societies Act 1992, s 98(a), Sch 18, Pt II, para 21 (qv)
41	12 Jan 1987 (SI 1986/2246)
42	4 Jun 1987 (SI 1987/907)
43	Repealed
44	12 Jan 1987 (SI 1986/2246)
45	Substituted by Friendly Societies Act 1992, s 98(a), Sch 18, Pt II, para 22 (qv)
12	30 Apr 1987 (SI 1986/2246)
13, para 1, 2	18 Dec 1986 (SI 1986/2246)
3, 4	Repealed
5	18 Dec 1986 (SI 1986/2246)
6	15 Nov 1986 (for purposes of anything done or which may be done under or by virtue of any provision brought into force by SI 1986/1940) (SI 1986/1940)
	18 Dec 1986 (otherwise) (SI 1986/2246)
7	15 Nov 1986 (for purposes of anything done or which may be done under or by virtue of any provision brought into force by SI 1986/1940) (SI 1986/1940)
	27 Nov 1986 (otherwise) (SI 1986/2031)
8	27 Nov 1986 (SI 1986/2031)
9	15 Nov 1986 (for purposes of anything done or which may be done under or by virtue of any provision brought into force by SI 1986/1940) (SI 1986/1940)
	27 Nov 1986 (otherwise) (SI 1986/2031)
10	Spent
11	15 Nov 1986 (for purposes of anything done or which may be done under or by virtue of any provision brought into force by SI 1986/1940) (SI 1986/1940)
	27 Nov 1986 (otherwise) (SI 1986/2031)
12	27 Nov 1986 (SI 1986/2031)

Financial Services Act 1986 (c 60)—*cont*

Sch 13, para 13, 14   15 Nov 1986 (for purposes of anything done or
which may be done under or by virtue of any
provision brought into force by SI 1986/1940) (SI
1986/1940)
27 Nov 1986 (otherwise) (SI 1986/2031)

14   12 Jan 1987 (so far as makes provision as to the
application of:
    (i)   Rehabilitation of Offenders Act 1974,
s 4(1), in relation to the determination of
proceedings of the kind specified in Sch 14,
Pt I, para 4;
    (ii) s 4(2) of the 1974 Act in relation to a
question put by or on behalf of a person
specified in Sch 14, Pt II, para 5, first
column;
    (iii) s 4(3)(b) of the 1974 Act in relation to
action taken by the competent authority or
by a person specified in Sch 14, Pt III, para 3,
first column) (SI 1986/2246)
1 Dec 1987 (so far as makes provision as to the
application of:
    (i)   Rehabilitation of Offenders Act 1974,
s 4(1), in relation to the determination of
proceedings of the kind described in Sch 14,
Pt 1, paras 2, 3 and 6; Rehabilitation of
Offenders (Northern Ireland) Order 1978, art
5(1), in relation to the determination of
proceedings of the kind described in those
paras and in Sch 14, Pt I, para 4;
    (ii) s 4(2) of the 1974 Act, in relation to a
question put by or on behalf of a person
specified in Sch 14, Pt II, para 6, first
column; Rehabilitation of Offenders
(Northern Ireland) Order 1978, art 5(2) in
relation to a question put by or on behalf of a
person specified in Sch 14, Pt II, para 5 or 6,
first column;
    (iii) s 4(2) of the 1974 Act and art 5(2) of the
1978 Order, in relation to a question put by
or on behalf of a person specified in Sch 14,
Pt II, para 2 or 3, first column; or to a
question put by or on behalf of a person
specified in Sch 14, Pt II, para 4, first column
insofar as it relates to persons described in
paras 2(a), (b) or (c) or 3(a), (b) or (c) or to a
question put by or on behalf of a person
specified in para 8 of that column;
    (iv) s 4(3)(b) of the 1974 Act in relation to
action taken by a person of a kind described
in sub-para (c) above and art 5(3)(b) of the
1978 Order in relation to action taken by a
person described in sub-para (c) above or
specified in Sch 14, Pt III, para 3, first
column (SI 1987/1977)
1 Jan 1988 (otherwise, except for the purposes of
Rehabilitation of Offenders Act 1974 (Exceptions)
(Amendment No 2) Order 1986, art 1(2)(b), and

Financial Services Act 1986 (c 60)—*cont*

Sch 14—*cont*	Rehabilitation of Offenders (Exceptions) (Amendment) Order (Northern Ireland) 1987, art 1(2)(b)) (SI 1987/2158)
	Not in force (exception noted above)
15, para 1(1)–(3)	27 Feb 1988 (SI 1987/2158)
(4)	29 Apr 1988 (SI 1988/740)
(5)	27 Feb 1988 (SI 1987/2158)
2, 3	29 Apr 1988 (SI 1988/740)
4–6	4 Jun 1987 (SI 1987/907)
7–11	29 Apr 1988 (SI 1988/740)
12	12 Jan 1987 (SI 1986/2246)
13	27 Nov 1986 (SI 1986/2031)
14, 15	29 Apr 1988 (SI 1988/740)
16	27 Feb 1988 (in relation to Sch 15, para 1(1)–(3), (5)) (SI 1987/2158)
	29 Apr 1988 (otherwise) (SI 1988/740)
16, para 1	Repealed
2	29 Apr 1988 (SI 1988/740)
3	Spent
4–9	29 Apr 1988 (SI 1988/740)
10	Repealed
11, 12	29 Apr 1988 (SI 1988/740)
13	30 Apr 1987 (SI 1986/2246)
14	Spent
15	29 Apr 1988 (SI 1988/740)
16	*Not in force*
17(a), (b)	29 Apr 1988 (SI 1988/740)
(c)	12 Jan 1987 (so far as relates to Companies Act 1985, s 173(2)(a)) (SI 1986/2246)
	29 Apr 1988 (otherwise) (SI 1988/740)
(d)	29 Apr 1988 (SI 1988/740)
18–21	29 Apr 1988 (SI 1988/740)
22	Repealed
23–26	29 Apr 1988 (SI 1988/740)
27(a)	29 Apr 1988 (SI 1988/740)
(b)	4 Jun 1987 (SI 1987/907)
28(a), (b)	12 Jan 1987 (SI 1986/2246); prospectively repealed by Criminal Justice Act 1993, s 79(14), Sch 6, Pt I (qv)
(c)	29 Apr 1988 (SI 1988/740); prospectively repealed by Criminal Justice Act 1993, s 79(14), Sch 6, Pt I (qv)
29, 30	29 Apr 1988 (SI 1988/740)
31	*Not in force*
32(a), (b)	29 Apr 1988 (SI 1988/740)
(c)	12 Jan 1987 (so far as it relates to the Companies (Northern Ireland) Order 1986, art 173(2)(a)) (SI 1986/2246)
	29 Apr 1988 (otherwise) (SI 1988/740)
(d)	29 Apr 1988 (SI 1988/740)
33–42	29 Apr 1988 (SI 1988/740)
43	29 Apr 1988 (SI 1988/740); prospectively repealed by Criminal Justice Act 1993, s 79(14), Sch 6, Pt I (qv)
17	27 Nov 1986 (repeals of or in Banking Act 1979, s 20; Companies Act 1985, ss 433, 446(5); Companies Consolidation (Consequential Provisions) Act 1985, Sch 2 (entry relating to

Financial Services Act 1986 (c 60)—*cont*

Sch 17—*cont*   Banking Act 1979, s 20); Companies
                               (Consequential Provisions) (Northern Ireland)
                               Order 1986, Sch 2 (entry relating to Banking Act
                               1979, s 20)) (SI 1986/2031)
                               12 Jan 1987 (repeals of or in Banking Act 1979,
                               Sch 1; Company Securities (Insider Dealing) Act
                               1985, s 3) (SI 1986/2246)
                               12 Jan 1987 (for all purposes relating to the
                               admission of securities offered by or on behalf of
                               a Minister of the Crown or a body corporate
                               controlled by a Minister of the Crown or a
                               subsidiary of such a body corporate, to the
                               Official List in respect of which an application is
                               made after that date) (repeals of or in Companies
                               Act 1985, Pt III, ss 81–87, 97, 693, 709, Schs 3,
                               22, 24 and corresponding provisions of
                               Companies (Northern Ireland) Order 1986, to the
                               extent which they would apply in relation to any
                               investment which is listed or the subject of an
                               application for listing in accordance with Pt IV of
                               the Act) (SI 1986/2246)
                               16 Feb 1987 (repeals noted above for all other
                               purposes) (SI 1986/2246)
                               30 Apr 1987 (repeals of or in Industry Act 1975;
                               Scottish Development Agency Act 1975; Welsh
                               Development Agency Act 1975; Aircraft and
                               Shipbuilding Industries Act 1977) (SI 1986/2246)
                               29 Apr 1988 (otherwise, except repeals of or in such
                               provisions of Prevention of Fraud (Investments)
                               Act (Northern Ireland) 1940 as are necessary for
                               the purposes of Sch 15, para 1(3) to this Act as it
                               applies by virtue of para 16 of that Schedule; such
                               provisions of Prevention of Fraud (Investments)
                               Act 1958 as are necessary for the purposes of
                               Sch 15, para 1(3) to this Act; Tribunals and
                               Inquiries Act 1971; House of Commons
                               Disqualification Act 1975; Restrictive Trade
                               Practices (Stock Exchange) Act 1984; Company
                               Securities (Insider Dealing) Act 1985, s 13; to the
                               extent not yet repealed, and except insofar as is
                               necessary to have the effect that those provisions
                               cease to apply to a prospectus offering for
                               subscription, or to any form of application for,
                               units in a body corporate which is a recognised
                               scheme, Companies Act 1985, Pt III, ss 81 to 87,
                               97, 449(1)(d), 693, 709, 744, so far as relates to
                               the definition 'prospectus issued generally',
                               Schs 3, 22, 24, and corresponding provisions of
                               Companies (Northern Ireland) Order 1986; s 195
                               of this Act) (SI 1988/740)
                               1 Jul 1988 (repeal of Restrictive Trade Practices
                               (Stock Exchange) Act 1984) (SI 1988/995)
                               31 Dec 1988 (so far as necessary to have the effect
                               that, to the extent that they do apply, Companies
                               Act 1985, Pt III, s 693, Sch 3, and corresponding
                               provisions of Companies (Northern Ireland)
                               Order 1986 cease to apply to a prospectus

Financial Services Act 1986 (c 60)—*cont*

Sch 17—*cont*

offering for subscription, or to any application form for, units in an open-ended investment company which does not fulfil the conditions described in head (a)(i) or (a)(ii) mentioned against s 76 above, except in relation to a prospectus offering for subscription, or to any application form for, units in an open-ended investment company which is managed in and authorised under the law of Bermuda units in which are, on 31 Dec 1988, included in the Official List of The International Stock Exchange of the United Kingdom and the Republic of Ireland Limited) (SI 1988/1960 (amending SI 1988/740); SI 1988/2285)

28 Feb 1989 (so far as necessary to have the effect that, to the extent that they do apply, Companies Act 1985, Pt III, s 693, Sch 3, and corresponding provisions of Companies (Northern Ireland) Order 1986 cease to apply to a prospectus offering for subscription, or to any application form for, units in an open-ended investment company managed in and authorised under the law of Bermuda units in which are, on 31 Dec 1988, included in the Official List of The International Stock Exchange of the United Kingdom and the Republic of Ireland Limited but which is not a scheme of a class specified in the Schedule to the Financial Services (Designated Countries and Territories) (Overseas Collective Investment Schemes) (Bermuda) Order 1988, SI 1988/2284) (SI 1988/2285)

1 Mar 1989 (so far as necessary to have the effect that to the extent that they do apply, Companies Act 1985, Pt III, s 693, Sch 3, and corresponding provisions of Companies (Northern Ireland) Order 1986 cease to apply to a prospectus offering for subscription, or to any application form for, units in an open-ended investment company which does fulfil the conditions described in head (a)(i) or (a)(ii) mentioned against s 76 above) (SI 1988/1960 (amending SI 1988/740), as amended by SI 1988/2285)

1 May 1989 (so far as necessary to have the effect that, to the extent that they do apply, Companies Act 1985, Pt III, s 693, Sch 3, and corresponding provisions of Companies (Northern Ireland) Order 1986 cease to apply to a prospectus offering for subscription, or to any application form for, units in an open-ended investment company managed in and authorised under the law of Bermuda units in which are, on 31 Dec 1988, included in the Official List of The International Stock Exchange of the United Kingdom and the Republic of Ireland Limited and which is a scheme of a class specified in Financial Services (Designated Countries and Territories) (Overseas Collective Investment Schemes)

Financial Services Act 1986 (c 60)—*cont*
Sch 17—*cont*   (Bermuda) Order 1988, SI 1988/2284, Schedule)
                                       (SI 1988/2285)
                                       1 Oct 1989 (repeals of or in Prevention of Fraud
                                       (Investments) Act (Northern Ireland) 1940 (for all
                                       remaining purposes); Prevention of Fraud
                                       (Investments) Act 1958 (for all remaining
                                       purposes); Tribunals and Inquiries Act 1971;
                                       House of Commons Disqualification Act 1975)
                                       (SI 1989/1583)
                                       Not in force (otherwise)

Forestry Act 1986 (c 30)

RA: 8 Jul 1986

Commencement provisions: s 2(1)

8 Sep 1986 (s 2(1))

Gaming (Amendment) Act 1986 (c 11)

RA: 2 May 1986

Commencement provisions: s 3(3); Gaming (Amendment) Act 1986 (Commencement)
    Order 1988, SI 1988/1250

19 Sep 1988 (SI 1988/1250)

Gas Act 1986 (c 44)

RA: 25 Jul 1986

Commencement provisions: s 68(2)–(5); Gas Act 1986 (Commencement No 1) Order
    1986, SI 1986/1315; Gas Act 1986 (Appointed Day) Order 1986, SI 1986/1316;
    Gas Act 1986 (Transfer Date) Order 1986, SI 1986/1318; Gas Act 1986
    (Commencement No 2) Order 1986, SI 1986/1809

s 1	18 Aug 1986 (SI 1986/1315)
2	23 Aug 1986 (SI 1986/1315)
3, 4	23 Aug 1986 (s 68(2); SI 1986/1316)
5	23 Aug 1986 (s 68(2); SI 1986/1316); prospectively substituted by Gas (Exempt Supplies) Act 1993, s 1 (qv)
6	23 Aug 1986 (s 68(2); SI 1986/1316)
6A	Prospectively inserted by Gas (Exempt Supplies) Act 1993, s 2 (qv)
7, 8	23 Aug 1986 (s 68(2); SI 1986/1316)
8A	Inserted by Competition and Service (Utilities) Act 1992, s 37 (qv)
9–14	23 Aug 1986 (s 68(2); SI 1986/1316)
14A	Inserted by Competition and Service (Utilities) Act 1992, s 16 (qv)
15	23 Aug 1986 (s 68(2); SI 1986/1316)

Gas Act 1986 (c 44)—*cont*

s 15A	Prospectively inserted by Competition and Service (Utilities) Act 1992, s 17 (qv)
15B	Inserted by Competition and Service (Utilities) Act 1992, s 15 (qv)
16–32	23 Aug 1986 (s 68(2); SI 1986/1316)
32A	Inserted by Competition and Service (Utilities) Act 1992, s 18 (qv)
33	23 Aug 1986 (s 68(2); SI 1986/1316)
33A, 33B	Inserted by Competition and Service (Utilities) Act 1992, s 11 (qv)
33C	Inserted by Competition and Service (Utilities) Act 1992, s 12 (qv)
33D	Inserted by Competition and Service (Utilities) Act 1992, s 13 (qv)
33E	Inserted by Competition and Service (Utilities) Act 1992, s 14 (qv)
34–48	23 Aug 1986 (s 68(2); SI 1986/1316)
49–57	24 Aug 1986 (s 68(3); SI 1986/1318)
58	Repealed
59–61	24 Aug 1986 (s 68(3); SI 1986/1318)
62	14 Nov 1986 (SI 1986/1809)
63, 64	23 Aug 1986 (SI 1986/1315)
65	18 Aug 1986 (SI 1986/1315)
66	23 Aug 1986 (s 68(2); SI 1986/1316)
67(1), (2)	23 Aug 1986 (s 68(2); SI 1986/1316)
(3)	See Sch 8 below
(4)	See Sch 9 below
68	18 Aug 1986 (SI 1986/1315)
Sch 1	18 Aug 1986 (SI 1986/1315)
2	23 Aug 1986 (SI 1986/1315)
3–5	23 Aug 1986 (s 68(2); SI 1986/1316)
6	24 Aug 1986 (s 68(3); SI 1986/1318)
7	23 Aug 1986 (s 68(2); SI 1986/1316)
8, Pt I	23 Aug 1986 (s 68(3); SI 1986/1316)
II	24 Aug 1986 (s 68(3); SI 1986/1318)
9, Pt I	23 Aug 1986 (s 68(2); SI 1986/1316)
II	24 Aug 1986 (s 68(3); SI 1986/1318)
III	*Not in force*

Health Service Joint Consultative Committee (Access to Information) Act 1986 (c 24)

RA: 26 Jun 1986

Commencement provisions: s 4(2)

26 Aug 1986 (s 4(2))

Highways (Amendment) Act 1986 (c 13)

RA: 2 May 1986

Commencement provisions: s 2(2)

2 Jul 1986 (s 2(2))

Horticultural Produce Act 1986 (c 20)

RA: 26 Jun 1986

Commencement provisions: s 7(3)

26 Aug 1986 (s 7(3))

Housing and Planning Act 1986 (c 63)

RA: 7 Nov 1986

Commencement provisions: s 57(1), (2); Housing and Planning Act 1986
(Commencement No 1) Order 1986, SI 1986/2262; Housing and Planning Act
1986 (Commencement No 2) Order 1987, SI 1987/178 (revoked); Housing and
Planning Act 1986 (Commencement No 3) Order 1987, SI 1987/304; Housing
and Planning Act 1986 (Commencement No 4) Order 1987, SI 1987/348;
Housing and Planning Act 1986 (Commencement No 5) Order 1987, SI 1987/
754; Housing and Planning Act 1986 (Commencement No 6) Order 1987, SI
1987/1554 (revoking); Housing and Planning Act 1986 (Commencement No 7)
(Scotland) Order 1987, SI 1987/1607; Housing and Planning Act 1986
(Commencement No 8) Order 1987, SI 1987/1759; Housing and Planning Act
1986 (Commencement No 9) Order 1987, SI 1987/1939; Housing and Planning
Act 1986 (Commencement No 10) Order 1987, SI 1987/2277; Housing and
Planning Act 1986 (Commencement No 11) Order 1988, SI 1988/283; Housing
and Planning Act 1986 (Commencement No 12) Order 1988, SI 1988/1787;
Housing and Planning Act 1986 (Commencement No 13) Order 1989, SI 1989/
430; Housing and Planning Act 1986 (Commencement No 14) Order 1990, SI
1990/511; Housing and Planning Act 1986 (Commencement No 15) Order 1990,
SI 1990/614; Housing and Planning Act 1986 (Commencement No 16) Order
1990, SI 1990/797 (bringing into force enabling provision in relation to Sch 11,
paras 39, 40 only); Housing and Planning Act 1986 (Commencement No 17 and
Transitional Provisions) Order 1992, SI 1992/1753; Housing and Planning Act
1986 (Commencement No 18 and Transitional Provisions) (Scotland) Order
1993, SI 1993/273

s 1	Repealed
2	7 Jan 1987 (SI 1986/2262)
3	Repealed
4	7 Jan 1987 (SI 1986/2262)
5	13 Jul 1992 (SI 1992/1753)
6	11 Mar 1988 (SI 1988/283)
7	Repealed
8	5 Apr 1989 (SI 1989/430)
9	13 May 1987 (SI 1987/754)
10, 11	7 Jan 1987 (SI 1986/2262)
12	Repealed
13, 14	7 Jan 1987 (SI 1986/2262)
15	17 Feb 1988 (SI 1987/2277); prospectively repealed by Local Government and Housing Act 1989, s 194, Sch 12, Pt II (qv)
16, 17	7 Jan 1987 (SI 1986/2262)
18	See Sch 4 below
19	Repealed
20	7 Jan 1987 (SI 1986/2262); prospectively repealed by Local Government and Housing Act 1989, s 194, Sch 12, Pt II (qv)

Housing and Planning Act 1986 (c 63)—*cont*

s 21	7 Nov 1986 (s 57(1))
22, 23	7 Jan 1987 (SI 1986/2262)
24(1), (2)	See Sch 5 below (note sub-s (1)(j) came into force on 7 Nov 1986 (s 57(1))
(3)	See Sch 12, Pt I below
25	Repealed
26	1 Oct 1987 (SI 1987/1607)
27	Substituted by Leasehold Reform, Housing and Urban Development Act 1993, s 174 (qv)
28, 29	7 Jan 1987 (SI 1986/2262)
30–34	Repealed
35, 36	18 Feb 1993 (so far as confers power or imposes duty on Secretary of State to make regulations, or makes provision with respect to exercise of any such power or duty) (SI 1993/273)
	1 May 1993 (otherwise) (subject to transitional provisions) (SI 1993/273)
37	See Sch 7, Pt II below
38	18 Feb 1993 (so far as confers power or imposes duty on Secretary of State to make regulations, or makes provision with respect to exercise of any such power or duty) (SI 1993/273)
	1 May 1993 (otherwise) (SI 1993/273)
39	11 Dec 1987 (SI 1987/1939)
40	1 Apr 1987 (SI 1987/348)
41	Repealed
42	17 Nov 1988 (SI 1988/1787)
43	31 Mar 1990 (SI 1990/614)
44–46	Repealed
47, 48	7 Jan 1987 (SI 1986/2262)
49(1)	See Sch 11, Pt I below
(2)	See Sch 12, Pt III below
50, 51	1 Oct 1987 (SI 1987/1607)
52	7 Nov 1986 (s 57(1))
53(1)	See Sch 11, Pt II below
(2)	See Sch 12, Pt IV below
54, 55	7 Jan 1987 (SI 1986/2262)
56–59	7 Nov 1986 (s 57(1))
Sch 1	11 Mar 1988 (SI 1988/283)
2	5 Apr 1989 (SI 1989/430)
3	17 Feb 1988 (SI 1988/2277); prospectively repealed by Local Government and Housing Act 1989, s 194, Sch 12, Pt II (qv)
4, para 1–9	11 Dec 1987 (SI 1987/1939)
10	Repealed
11	11 Dec 1987 (SI 1987/1939)
5, para 1–4	7 Jan 1987 (SI 1986/2262)
5	Repealed
6, 7	7 Jan 1987 (SI 1986/2262)
8	Repealed
9	17 Feb 1988 (SI 1987/2277)
10–13	7 Nov 1986 (s 57(1))
14	Repealed
15	7 Jan 1987 (SI 1986/2262)
16	*Not in force*

Housing and Planning Act 1986 (c 63)—*cont*

Sch 5, para 17		Repealed
	18–20	17 Aug 1992 (SI 1992/1753)
	21–26	7 Jan 1987 (SI 1986/2262)
	27	17 Aug 1992 (so far as relates to definitions 'consent' and 'management agreement and manager') (SI 1992/1753)
		Not in force (otherwise)
	28	7 Jan 1987 (SI 1986/2262)
	29	17 Aug 1992 (subject to transitional provisions) (SI 1992/1753)
	30	7 Jan 1987 (SI 1986/2262)
	31	17 Aug 1992 (SI 1992/1753)
	32, 33	7 Jan 1987 (SI 1986/2262)
	34–38	17 Aug 1992 (subject to transitional provisions) (SI 1992/1753)
	39	7 Jan 1987 (SI 1986/2262)
	40	17 Aug 1992 (subject to transitional provisions) (SI 1992/1753)
	41, 42	7 Jan 1987 (SI 1986/2262)
6, Pt I, II		Repealed
III, IV		1 Oct 1987 (SI 1987/1607)
7, Pt I		Repealed
II, para 1–3		1 May 1993 (SI 1993/273)
4		18 Feb 1993 (SI 1993/273)
5–8		1 May 1993 (SI 1993/273)
8		11 Dec 1987 (SI 1987/1939)
9, Pt I, para 1–5		Repealed
6		1 Apr 1987 (SI 1987/348)
7–12		Repealed
II		1 Oct 1987 (SI 1987/1607)
10		Repealed
11, Pt I, para 1–24		Repealed
25		7 Jan 1987 (SI 1986/2262)
26, 27		Repealed
II 28–38		7 Jan 1987 (SI 1986/2262)
39, 40		31 Mar 1990 (SI 1990/511)
41–56		7 Jan 1987 (SI 1986/2262)
57, 58		*Not in force*
59–62		7 Jan 1987 (SI 1986/2262)
12, Pt I		7 Nov 1986 (repeals in Housing (Consequential Provisions) Act 1985 specified in first part of Sch 12, Pt I) (s 57(1))
		7 Jan 1987 (repeals of or in Housing Rents and Subsidies (Scotland) Act 1975; Rent Act 1977, s 70; Housing Act 1980, s 56; New Towns Act 1981; Housing Act 1985, ss 30, 46, 127, Schs 4, 6; Housing (Consequential Provisions) Act 1985, Sch 2, paras 27, 35(3), 45(2)) (SI 1986/2262)
		11 Dec 1987 (repeals of or in Housing Act 1980, s 140; Local Government Planning and Land Act 1980, s 156(3); Local Government Act 1985, Sch 13, para 14(d), Sch 14, para 58(e)) (SI 1987/1939)
		Not in force (otherwise)
II		11 Dec 1987 (SI 1987/1939)
III		7 Jan 1987 (repeals of or in Electric Lighting (Clauses) Act 1899; Electricity (Supply) Act 1926;

Housing and Planning Act 1986 (c 63)—*cont*

Sch 12, Pt III—*cont*	Requisitioned Land and War Works Act 1945; Town and Country Planning Act 1947; Electricity Act 1947; Requisitioned Land and War Works Act 1948; Electricity Act 1957; Town and Country Planning Act 1971, ss 29A, B, 66–86, 88B, 105, 147, 151, 165, 169, 180, 185, 191, 237, 250–252, 260, 287(4), (5), (7), 290, Schs 12, 13, 21, 24; Town and Country Planning (Amendment) Act 1972; Local Government Act 1972, s 182; Local Government Act 1974; Town and Country Amenities Act 1974, s 3; Control of Office Development Act 1977; Local Government, Planning and Land Act 1980 (except s 88); Industrial Development Act 1982; Local Government Act 1985, s 3) (SI 1986/2262)
	1 Apr 1987 (repeals of or in Town and Country Planning Act 1971, s 55(4); Town and Country Amenities Act 1974, s 5; National Heritage Act 1983; Local Government Act 1985, Sch 2, para 1(8)) (SI 1987/348)
	2 Nov 1987 (repeals of or in Local Government Act 1972, s 183(2), Sch 16, paras 1–3; Local Government, Planning and Land Act 1980, s 88; Local Government (Miscellaneous Provisions) Act 1982, Sch 6, para 7(b)) (SI 1987/1759)
	17 Nov 1988 (repeals of or in Public Expenditure and Receipts Act 1968; Local Government Act 1972, s 250(4); Land Drainage Act 1976; Road Traffic Regulation Act 1984) (SI 1988/1787)
	31 Mar 1990 (repeal in Acquisition of Land Act 1981, Sch 4, para 1) (SI 1990/614)
	Not in force (otherwise)
IV	7 Jan 1987 (repeals of or in Town and Country Planning (Scotland) Act 1972, ss 29, 63, 64–83, 85, 136, 140, 154, 164, 174, 180, 226, 231, 233, 237–239, 247, 273 (4), (5), (7), (8), 275, Schs 19, 22; Local Government Planning and Land Act 1980; Industrial Development Act 1982) (SI 1986/2262)
	Not in force (otherwise)

Housing (Scotland) Act 1986 (c 65)

RA: 7 Nov 1986

Commencement provisions: s 26(2); Housing (Scotland) Act 1986 (Commencement) Order 1986, SI 1986/2137

s 1–12	Repealed
13	7 Jan 1987 (SI 1986/2137)
14–16	Repealed
17	7 Jan 1987 (SI 1986/2137)
18	Repealed
19, 20	7 Jan 1987 (SI 1986/2137)
21	Repealed

Housing (Scotland) Act 1986 (c 65)—*cont*

s 22–25	7 Jan 1987 (SI 1986/2137)
26	7 Nov 1986 (RA)
Sch 1	Repealed
2, para 1	7 Jan 1987 (SI 1986/2137)
2	Repealed
3, 4	7 Jan 1987 (SI 1986/2137)
3	7 Jan 1987 (SI 1986/2137)

Incest and Related Offences (Scotland) Act 1986 (c 36)

RA: 18 Jul 1986

Commencement provisions: s 3(2); Incest and Related Offences (Scotland) Act 1986 (Commencement) Order 1986, SI 1986/1803

1 Nov 1986 (SI 1986/1803)

Industrial Training Act 1986 (c 15)

RA: 20 May 1986

Commencement provisions: s 2(2)

20 Jul 1986 (s 2(2))

Insolvency Act 1986 (c 45)

RA: 25 Jul 1986

Commencement provisions: s 443; Insolvency Act 1985 (Commencement No 5) Order 1986, SI 1986/1924

29 Dec 1986 (s 443; SI 1986/1924)

Land Registration Act 1986 (c 26)

RA: 26 Jun 1986

Commencement provisions: s 6(4); Land Registration Act 1986 (Commencement) Order 1986, SI 1986/2117

1 Jan 1987 (SI 1986/2117)

Latent Damage Act 1986 (c 37)

RA: 18 Jul 1986

Commencement provisions: s 5(3)

18 Sep 1986 (s 5(3))

Law Reform (Parent and Child) (Scotland) Act 1986 (c 9)

RA: 26 Mar 1986

Commencement provisions: s 11(2); Law Reform (Parent and Child) (Scotland) Act 1986 (Commencement) Order 1986, SI 1986/1983

8 Dec 1986 (SI 1986/1983)

Legal Aid (Scotland) Act 1986 (c 47)

RA: 25 Jul 1986

Commencement provisions: s 46(2); Legal Aid (Scotland) Act 1986 (Commencement No 1) Order 1986, SI 1986/1617; Legal Aid (Scotland) Act 1986 (Commencement No 2) Order 1987, SI 1987/289; Legal Aid (Scotland) Act 1986 (Commencement No 3) Order 1992, SI 1992/1226

s 1(1)	1 Oct 1986 (SI 1986/1617)
(2)	1 Apr 1987 (SI 1987/289)
(3)–(6)	1 Oct 1986 (SI 1986/1617)
2(1)	1 Apr 1987 (SI 1987/289)
(2), (3)	1 Oct 1986 (SI 1986/1617)
3(1), (2)	1 Oct 1986 (SI 1986/1617)
(3)	1 Apr 1987 (SI 1987/289)
(4)–(6)	1 Oct 1986 (SI 1986/1617)
4–25	1 Apr 1987 (SI 1987/289)
26–28	*Not in force*
29	1 Apr 1987 (SI 1987/289)
30	1 Jul 1992 (SI 1992/1226)
31–39	1 Apr 1987 (SI 1987/289)
40(1)(a)	1 Apr 1987 (SI 1987/289)
(b)	1 Oct 1986 (SI 1986/1617)
(2)(a)	1 Apr 1987 (SI 1987/289)
(b)	1 Oct 1986 (SI 1986/1617)
(3), (4)	1 Apr 1987 (SI 1987/289)
41	1 Oct 1986 (SI 1986/1617)
42, 43	1 Apr 1987 (SI 1987/289)
43A	Inserted by Law Reform (Miscellaneous Provisions) (Scotland) Act 1990, s 38 (qv)
44	1 Apr 1987 (SI 1987/289)
45(1)	See Sch 3 below
(2), (3)	1 Apr 1987 (SI 1987/289)
46	25 Jul 1986 (RA)
Sch 1	1 Oct 1986 (SI 1986/1617)
2	1 Apr 1987 (SI 1987/289)
3, para 1, 2	1 Apr 1987 (SI 1987/289)
3, 4	1 Oct 1986 (SI 1986/1617)
5–9	1 Apr 1987 (SI 1987/289)
4, 5	1 Apr 1987 (SI 1987/289)

Local Government Act 1986 (c 10)

RA: 26 Mar 1986

Commencement provisions: s 12(2); Local Government Act 1986 (Commencement) Order 1987, SI 1987/2003

Local Government Act 1986 (c 10)—*cont*

s 1	26 Mar 1986 (s 12(2)); repealed by Local Government Finance Act 1988, s 149, Sch 13, Pt I (qv), with effect for financial years beginning in or after 1990
2	1 Apr 1986 (s 12(2))
2A	Inserted by Local Government Act 1988, s 28 (qv)
3, 4	1 Apr 1986 (s 12(2))
5	1 Apr 1988 (SI 1987/2003)
6	1 Apr 1986 (s 12(2))
7	26 Mar 1986 (s 12(2))
8	Repealed
9, 10	26 Mar 1986 (s 12(2))
11	Repealed
12	26 Mar 1986 (s 12(2))

Marriage (Prohibited Degrees of Relationship) Act 1986 (c 16)

RA: 20 May 1986

Commencement provisions: s 6(5); Marriage (Prohibited Degrees of Relationship) Act 1986 (Commencement) Order 1986, SI 1986/1343

1 Nov 1986 (SI 1986/1343)

Marriage (Wales) Act 1986 (c 7)

RA: 18 Mar 1986

18 Mar 1986 (RA)

Museum of London Act 1986 (c 8)

RA: 26 Mar 1986

Commencement provisions: s 7(2)

1 Apr 1986 (RA)

National Health Service (Amendment) Act 1986 (c 66)

RA: 7 Nov 1986

Commencement provisions: s 8(4), (5); National Health Service (Amendment) Act 1986 (Commencement No 1) Order 1987, SI 1987/399

s 1, 2	Repealed
3	1 Apr 1987 (SI 1987/399)
4	7 Nov 1986 (RA)
5	7 Nov 1986 (except so far as inserts National Health Service (Scotland) Act 1978, s 13B) (RA)
	Not in force (exception noted above)
6–8	7 Nov 1986 (RA)

Outer Space Act 1986 (c 38)

RA: 18 Jul 1986

Commencement provisions: s 15(2); Outer Space Act 1986 (Commencement) Order 1989, SI 1989/1097

31 Jul 1989 (SI 1989/1097)

Parliamentary Constituencies Act 1986 (c 56)

RA: 7 Nov 1986

Commencement provisions: s 9(2)

7 Feb 1986 (s 9(2))

Patents, Designs and Marks Act 1986 (c 39)

RA: 18 Jul 1986

Commencement provisions: s 4(6), (7); Patents, Designs and Marks Act 1986 (Commencement No 1) Order 1986, SI 1986/1274; Patents, Designs and Marks Act 1986 (Commencement No 2) Order 1988, SI 1988/1824

s 1	See Sch 1 below
2	1 Oct 1986 (s 4(7))
3	See Sch 3 below
4	18 Jul 1986 (RA)
Sch 1, para 1, 2	1 Oct 1986 (SI 1986/1274)
3, 4	1 Jan 1989 (SI 1988/1824)
2	1 Oct 1986 (s 4(7))
3, Pt I	1 Oct 1986 (repeals in Trade Marks Act 1938) (SI 1986/1274)
	1 Jan 1989 (repeals of Registered Designs Act 1949, s 24; Patents Act 1977, s 35) (SI 1988/1824)
II	1 Oct 1986 (s 4(7))

Patronage (Benefices) Measure 1986 (No 3)

RA: 18 Jul 1986

Commencement provisions: s 42(3)

The provisions of this Measure are brought into force on the following dates by an appointed day notice signed by the Archbishops of Canterbury and York and dated 31 December 1986 (made under s 42(3))

s 1, 2	1 Oct 1987
3–5	1 Jan 1989
6	1 Oct 1987
7–25	1 Jan 1989
26, 27	1 Jan 1987
28–34	1 Jan 1989

Patronage (Benefices) Measure 1986 (No 3)—*cont*

s 35(1)–(3)	1 Oct 1987
(4)–(9)	1 Jan 1989
36, 37	1 Oct 1987
38, 39	1 Jan 1987
40	1 Oct 1987
41	1 Jan 1989
42	1 Jan 1987
Sch 1	1 Oct 1987
2	1 Jan 1989
3	1 Jan 1987
4	1 Jan 1989
5	1 Jan 1987 (repeal of Benefices (Diocesan Boards of Patronage) Measure 1932)
	1 Jan 1989 (otherwise)

Prevention of Oil Pollution Act 1986 (c 6)

RA: 18 Mar 1986

Commencement provisions: s 2(2)

18 May 1986 (s 2(2))

Protection of Children (Tobacco) Act 1986 (c 34)

RA: 8 Jul 1986

Commencement provisions: s 3(3)

8 Oct 1986 (s 3(3))

Protection of Military Remains Act 1986 (c 35)

RA: 8 Jul 1986

Commencement provisions: s 10(2)

8 Sep 1986 (s 10(2))

Public Order Act 1986 (c 64)

RA: 7 Nov 1986

Commencement provisions: s 41(1); Public Order Act 1986 (Commencement No 1) Order 1986, SI 1986/2041; Public Order Act 1986 (Commencement No 2) Order 1987, SI 1987/198; Public Order Act 1986 (Commencement No 3) Order 1987, SI 1987/852

s 1–10	1 Apr 1987 (SI 1987/198)
11	1 Jan 1987 (SI 1986/2041)
12–15	1 Apr 1987 (SI 1987/198)
16	1 Jan 1987 (SI 1986/2041)

Public Order Act 1986 (c 64)—*cont*

s 17–29	1 Apr 1987 (SI 1987/198)
30–37	Repealed (with savings)
38	1 Jan 1987 (SI 1986/2041)
39	1 Apr 1987 (SI 1987/198)
40(1)	See Sch 1 below
(2)	See Sch 2 below
(3)	See Sch 3 below
(4), (5)	1 Apr 1987 (SI 1987/198)
41–43	1 Jan 1987 (SI 1986/2041)
Sch 1	1 Jan 1987 (SI 1986/2041)
2, para 1	Repealed
2	1 Apr 1987 (SI 1987/198)
3(1), (2)	1 Jan 1987 (SI 1986/2041)
(3)–(6)	1 Apr 1987 (SI 1987/198)
4	1 Apr 1987 (SI 1987/198)
5, 6	Repealed
7	1 Apr 1987 (SI 1987/198)
3	1 Jan 1987 (repeals in Erith Tramways and Improvement Act 1903; Middlesex County Council Act 1944; County of South Glamorgan Act 1976; County of Merseyside Act 1980; West Midlands County Council Act 1980; Cheshire County Council Act 1980; Isle of Wight Act 1980; Greater Manchester Act 1981; East Sussex Act 1981; Civic Government (Scotland) Act 1982, s 62; Sporting Events (Control of Alcohol etc) Act 1985) (SI 1986/2041) 1 Apr 1987 (otherwise) (SI 1987/198)

Public Trustee and Administration of Funds Act 1986 (c 57)

RA: 7 Nov 1986

Commencement provisions: s 6(2); Public Trustee and Administration of Funds Act 1986 Commencement Order 1986, SI 1986/2261

2 Jan 1987 (SI 1986/2261)

Rate Support Grants Act 1986 (c 54)

RA: 21 Oct 1986

21 Oct 1986 (RA)

Road Traffic Regulation (Parking) Act 1986 (c 27)

RA: 8 Jul 1986

Commencement provisions: s 3(3)

8 Sep 1986 (s 3(3))

Safety at Sea Act 1986 (c 23)

RA: 26 Jun 1986

Commencement provisions: s 15(3), (4); Safety at Sea Act 1986 (Commencement No
1) Order 1986, SI 1986/1759

s (ss 1–6	Repealed by Merchant Shipping (Registration, etc) Act 1993, s 8(4), Sch 5, Pt II, as from 1 May 1994(qv))
1–9	*Not in force*
10, 11	30 Oct 1986 (SI 1986/1759)
12, 13	*Not in force*
(s 14	Repealed by Merchant Shipping (Registration, etc) Act 1993, s 8(4), Sch 5, Pt II, as from 1 May 1994(qv))
14(1)	*Not in force*
(2), (3)	30 Oct 1986 (SI 1986/1759)
(4)	30 Oct 1986 (so far as relates to s 14(2), (3)) (SI 1986/1759)
	Not in force (otherwise)
15	30 Oct 1986 (SI 1986/1759)

Salmon Act 1986 (c 62)

RA: 7 Nov 1986

Commencement provisions: s 43(1), (2); Salmon Act 1986 (Commencement and
Transitional Provisions) Order 1992, SI 1992/1973

s 1–3	7 Jan 1987 (s 43(1))
4	Repealed
5–20	7 Jan 1987 (s 43(1))
21	1 Jan 1993 (subject to transitional provisions) (SI 1992/1973)
22–43	7 Jan 1987 (s 43(1))
Sch 1–5	7 Jan 1987 (s 43(1))

Sex Discrimination Act 1986 (c 59)

RA: 7 Nov 1986

Commencement provisions: s 10(2)–(4); Sex Discrimination Act (Commencement)
Order 1986, SI 1986/2313; Sex Discrimination Act 1986 (Commencement No 2)
Order 1988, SI 1988/99

s 1	7 Feb 1987 (s 10(2))
2, 3	7 Nov 1987 (s 10(4))
4, 5	7 Nov 1986 (RA)
6	7 Feb 1987 (s 10(2))
7	Repealed
8	27 Feb 1987 (SI 1986/2313)
9(1)	7 Feb 1987 (s 10(2))
(2)	7 Nov 1986 (RA)
(3)	7 Feb 1987 (s 10(2))
10	7 Nov 1986 (RA)

Sex Discrimination Act 1986 (c 59)—*cont*

Sch Pt I	7 Nov 1986 (RA)
II	7 Feb 1987 (s 10(2))
III	27 Feb 1987 (repeals of or in Baking Industry (Hours of Work) Act 1954; Mines and Quarries Act 1954, ss 125, 126, 128, 131; Factories Act 1961; Civil Evidence Act 1968; Health and Safety at Work etc Act 1974; Sex Discrimination Act 1975; Companies Consolidation (Consequential Provisions) Act 1985) (SI 1986/2313)
	26 Feb 1988 (repeals in Hours of Employment (Conventions) Act 1936; Mines and Quarries Act 1954, Sch 4) (SI 1988/99)

Social Security Act 1986 (c 50)

RA: 25 Jul 1986

Commencement provisions: s 88; Social Security Act 1986 (Commencement No 1) Order 1986, SI 1986/1609; Social Security Act 1986 (Commencement No 2) Order 1986, SI 1986/1719; Social Security Act (Commencement No 3) Order 1986, SI 1986/1958; Social Security Act 1986 (Commencement No 4) Order 1986, SI 1986/1959 (as amended SI 1986/1959); Social Security Act 1986 (Commencement No 5) Order 1987, SI 1987/354 (also amending SI 1986/1959); Social Security Act 1986 (Commencement No 6) Order 1987, SI 1987/543; Social Security Act 1986 (Commencement No 7) Order 1987, SI 1987/1096 (as amended by SI 1987/1853); Social Security Act 1986 (Commencement No 8) Order 1987, SI 1987/1853 (also amending SI 1987/1096); Social Security Act 1986 (Commencement No 9) Order 1988, SI 1988/567 (also amending SI 1987/1096)

s (ss 1–8, 10–17A	Prospectively repealed by Pension Schemes Act 1993, s 188(1), Sch 5, Pt I (qv))
1	4 Jan 1988 (SI 1987/543)
2	11 May 1987 (SI 1987/543)
3–5	4 Jan 1988 (SI 1987/543)
6, 7	6 Apr 1988 (SI 1987/543)
8	1 Nov 1986 (SI 1986/1719)
9, 10	6 Apr 1988 (SI 1987/543)
11	6 Apr 1987 (SI 1986/1719)
12	4 Jan 1988 (so far as relates to personal pension schemes) (SI 1987/543)
	6 Apr 1988 (so far as relates to occupational pension schemes) (SI 1987/543)
13, 14	1 May 1987 (SI 1987/543)
15	4 Jan 1988 (so far as relates to personal pension schemes) (SI 1987/543)
	6 Apr 1988 (so far as relates to occupational pension schemes) (SI 1987/543)
16	1 Nov 1986 (SI 1986/1719)
17	1 May 1987 (SI 1987/543)
17A	Inserted by Social Security Act 1989, s 24, Sch 6, para 17 (qv)
18–22, 22A, 22B, 23, 23A, 24, 24A, 24B, 25–29	Repealed
30(1)–(9)	Repealed

Social Security Act 1986 (c 50)—*cont*

s 30(10)	25 Jul 1986 (s 88(5))
31, 31A–31G, 32–36	Repealed
37	25 Jul 1986 (s 88(5))
38	Repealed
39	See Sch 3 below
40–51	Repealed
51A, 51B	Inserted by Local Government Finance Act 1988, s 135, Sch 10, paras 1, 8 (qv)
51C	Repealed
52	6 Apr 1987 (SI 1986/1958)
53	Repealed
54(1)	6 Apr 1987 (SI 1986/1958)
(2)	Repealed
55	Repealed
56, 57	6 Apr 1987 (SI 1986/1959)
58	Repealed
59, 60	6 Apr 1987 (SI 1986/1959); prospectively repealed by Pension Schemes Act 1993, s 188(1), Sch 5, Pt I (qv)
61	25 Jul 1986 (s 88(5)); prospectively repealed by Pension Schemes Act 1993, s 188(1), Sch 5, Pt I (qv)
62, 63, 63A, 64, 64A, 64B, 65–69	Repealed
70	25 Jul 1986 (s 88(5))
71–74	Repealed
75	See Sch 8 below; prospectively repealed by Pension Schemes Act 1993, s 188(1), Sch 5, Pt I (qv)
76	25 Jul 1986 (s 88(5))
77	11 Apr 1988 (SI 1987/1853)
(ss 78–80	Prospectively repealed by Pension Schemes Act 1993, s 188(1), Sch 5, Pt I (qv))
78	11 Apr 1988 (SI 1987/1096)
79(1), (2)	1 May 1987 (SI 1987/543)
(3)–(5)	Repealed
(6)	6 Apr 1987 (SI 1986/1959)
80	6 Apr 1987 (except in its application to Pt I (ss 1–19) of this Act) (SI 1986/1959)
	1 May 1987 (exception noted above) (SI 1987/543)
81	Repealed
82	6 Apr 1987 (SI 1986/1958)
83–85	25 Jul 1986 (s 88(5))
86(1)	See Sch 10 below
(2)	See Sch 11 below
87–90	25 Jul 1986 (s 88(5))
Sch 1	1 May 1987 (SI 1987/543); prospectively repealed by Pension Schemes Act 1993, s 188(1), Sch 5, Pt I (qv)
2	6 Apr 1988 (SI 1987/543); prospectively repealed by Pension Schemes Act 1993, s 188(1), Sch 5, Pt I (qv)
3, para 1–16	Repealed
17	1 Oct 1986 (SI 1986/1609)
4	Repealed
5, Pt I, para 1	6 Apr 1987 (SI 1986/1958); prospectively repealed by Pension Schemes Act 1993, s 188(1), Sch 5, Pt I (qv)

Social Security Act 1986 (c 50)—*cont*

Sch 5, Pt I, para 2–20	Repealed
II	6 Apr 1987 (SI 1986/1958)
6, 7	Repealed
8, para 1–3	Repealed
4	6 Apr 1987 (SI 1986/1959, as amended by SI 1987/354); prospectively repealed by Pension Schemes Act 1993, s 188(1), Sch 5, Pt I (qv)
5–7	Repealed
8–11	6 Apr 1987 (SI 1986/1959, as amended by SI 1987/354); prospectively repealed by Pension Schemes Act 1993, s 188(1), Sch 5, Pt I (qv)
9	6 Apr 1987 (SI 1986/1958)
10, para 1	6 Apr 1987 (SI 1987/354)
(paras 2–9	Prospectively repealed by Pension Schemes Act 1993, s 188(1), Sch 5, Pt I (qv))
2	25 Jul 1986 (s 88(5))
3	1 Nov 1986 (SI 1986/1719)
4–8	1 May 1987 (SI 1987/543)
9	1 Nov 1986 (SI 1986/1719)
10	Repealed
11	6 Apr 1987 (SI 1987/354)
(paras 12–31	Prospectively repealed by Pension Schemes Act 1993, s 188(1), Sch 5, Pt I (qv))
12	1 Nov 1986 (SI 1986/1719)
13	6 Apr 1987 (SI 1986/1719)
14(a)	6 Apr 1988 (SI 1987/543)
(b)(i)	1 May 1987 (SI 1987/543)
(ii)	6 Apr 1988 (SI 1987/543)
15–19	1 Nov 1986 (SI 1986/1719)
20, 21	6 Apr 1988 (1987/543)
22	25 Jul 1986 (s 88(5))
23(1), (2)	1 Nov 1986 (SI 1986/1719)
(3)	25 Jul 1986 (s 88(5))
(4), (5)	1 Nov 1986 (SI 1986/1719)
24, 25	1 Nov 1986 (SI 1986/1719)
26(1), (2)	25 Jul 1986 (s 88(5))
(3)	1 Nov 1986 (SI 1986/1719)
27	25 Jul 1986 (s 88(5))
28, 29	1 May 1987 (SI 1987/543)
30(a)	6 Apr 1988 (SI 1987/543)
(b), (c)	25 Jul 1986 (s 88(5))
(d)(i)	6 Apr 1988 (SI 1987/543)
(ii)	25 Jul 1986 (s 88(5))
(iii)	6 Apr 1988 (SI 1987/543)
31	4 Jan 1988 (SI 1987/543)
32, 33	11 Apr 1988 (SI 1987/1853)
34	Repealed
35–39	11 Apr 1988 (SI 1987/1853)
40	Repealed
41–43	11 Apr 1988 (SI 1987/1853)
44	1 Apr 1988 (so far as relates to housing benefit in a case where rent is payable at intervals of one month or any other interval which is not a week or a multiple thereof or in a case where payments by way of rates are not made together with payments of rent at weekly intervals or multiples thereof) (SI 1987/1853)

Social Security Act 1986 (c 50)—*cont*

Sch 10, para 44—*cont*	4 Apr 1988 (otherwise) (SI 1987/1853)
45–48	Repealed
49	1 Apr 1988 (so far as relates to housing benefit in a case where rent is payable at intervals of one month or any other interval which is not a week or a multiple thereof or in a case where payments by way of rates are not made together with payments of rent at weekly intervals or multiples thereof) (SI 1987/1853)
	4 Apr 1988 (otherwise) (SI 1987/1853)
50	11 Apr 1988 (SI 1987/1853)
51	Repealed
52, 53	1 Apr 1988 (so far as relates to housing benefit in a case where rent is payable at intervals of one month or any other interval which is not a week or a multiple thereof or in a case where payments by way of rates are not made together with payments of rent at weekly intervals or multiples thereof) (SI 1987/1853)
	4 Apr 1988 (otherwise) (SI 1987/1853)
54	Repealed
55	11 Apr 1988 (SI 1987/1853)
56	Repealed
57	11 Apr 1988 (SI 1987/1853)
58–60	1 Apr 1988 (so far as relates to housing benefit in a case where rent is payable at intervals of one month or any other interval which is not a week or a multiple thereof or in a case where payments by way of rates are not made together with payments of rent at weekly intervals or multiples thereof) (SI 1987/1853)
	4 Apr 1988 (otherwise) (SI 1987/1853)
61	11 Apr 1988 (SI 1987/1853)
62–68	Repealed
69–74	Repealed
75	6 Apr 1987 (SI 1986/1959); prospectively repealed by Trade Union Reform and Employment Rights Act 1993, s 51, Sch 10 (qv)
76	6 Apr 1987 (SI 1986/1959)
77, 78	Repealed
79–81	6 Apr 1987 (SI 1986/1959)
82	25 Jul 1986 (s 88(5)); prospectively repealed by Pension Schemes Act 1993, s 188(1), Sch 5, Pt I (qv)
83–92	Repealed
93	1 Oct 1986 (SI 1986/1609)
94(a)	25 Jul 1986 (s 88(5))
(b)	26 Jun 1987 (SI 1987/1096)
95–101	Repealed
102	26 Jun 1987 (SI 1987/1096)
103	6 Apr 1987 (SI 1986/1959)
104–107	Repealed
108(a)	Repealed
(b)	11 Apr 1988 (except so far as substitutes words for reference in Forfeiture Act 1982, s 4(5), to Family Income Supplements Act 1970 and Supplementary Benefits Act 1976) (SI 1987/1096)

Social Security Act 1986 (c 50)—*cont*

Sch 10, para 108(b)—*cont*
    11

11 Apr 1988 (exception noted above) (SI 1987/1853)

25 Jul 1986 (repeals of or in Social Security Act 1975, ss 37, 141; Social Security Pensions Act 1975, s 52D, Sch 1A; Social Security (Miscellaneous Provisions) Act 1977, s 22(2) (reference to Social Security Act 1975, s 37(3)(b)); Social Security Act 1980, s 10; Social Security and Housing Benefits Act 1982, s 29) (s 88(5))

1 Oct 1986 (repeals of or in Statute Law Revision (Consequential Repeals) Act 1965; Social Security Act 1975, ss 12(3), 28, 34, 37A, 57, 60, 124–126A, Schs 14, 20 (definition of 'Up–rating Order'); Social Security Pensions Act 1975, ss 22, 23; Child Benefit Act 1975, ss 5, 17(3), (4); Social Security Act 1979, s 13, Social Security Act 1980, s 1; Social Security (No 2) Act 1980, ss 1, 2; Social Security Act 1981, s 1; Social Security and Housing Benefits Act 1982, ss 7, 42; Social Security and Housing Benefits Act 1983; Social Security Act 1985, ss 15, 16, Sch 5, para 10) (SI 1986/1609)

1 Nov 1986 (repeals of or in Social Security Act 1973, s 99; Social Security Pensions Act 1975, ss 30, 32–34, 36, 37, 39, 41, 44A, 46, 49, 66, Schs 2, 4, paras 31, 32(a); Social Security Act 1985, Sch 5, paras 19, 28) (SI 1986/1719)

6 Apr 1987 (repeals of or in Supplementary Benefit Act 1966; Social Work (Scotland) Act 1968; Income and Corporation Taxes Act 1970; Family Income Supplements Act 1970, ss 8(5), (6), 12; Local Government Act 1972; Social Security Act 1973, s 92, Sch 23; National Insurance Act 1974, s 6(1) (the words 'or the Social Security and Housing Benefits Act 1982'); Social Security Act 1975, ss 13(1), 21, 32, 92, 95, 100, 104, 106, 107. 110, 114, 119(1)–(2A), (5), (6), 135(2)(g), 136, 144, 145, 146(3)(c), (5), 147, 164, Sch 3, Pt I, para 7, Pt II, paras 8(3), 12, Sch 4, Pt II, Sch 8, Sch 16, para 4; Industrial Injuries and Diseases (Old Cases) Act 1975, ss 9, 10; Social Security (Consequential Provisions) Act 1975, Sch 2, paras 5, 35; Social Security Pensions Act 1975, s 19, Sch 4, para 17; Child Benefit Act 1975, ss 9–11, 24, Sch 4, paras 11, 31; Adoption Act 1976; Supplementary Benefits Act 1976, s 20 (1), (2), (5)–(7); Social Security (Miscellaneous Provisions) Act 1977, s 19; Social Security Act 1979, ss 6, 8; Child Care Act 1980; Social Security Act 1980, ss 5, 14, 15, 17, 20, Sch 1, paras 9, 10, Sch 2, paras 19(a), (b), (d), 21, Sch 3, Pt II, paras 16–18; Social Security Act 1981, Sch 1, paras 1–5; Social Security and Housing Benefits Act 1982, ss 8, 9, 11–16, 19–21, 25, 41, Schs 2, 3, Sch 4, paras 26, 38; Health and Social Services and Social Security Adjudications Act 1983, Sch 8, paras 18, 31, Sch 9; Public Health (Control of Disease) Act 1984; Health and Social Security Act

Social Security Act 1986 (c 50)—*cont*

Sch 11—*cont*

1984, Sch 4, para 12; Social Security Act 1985, s 17, Sch 4, Sch 5, paras 37, 38; Insolvency Act 1985; Bankruptcy (Scotland) Act 1985) (SI 1986/1959, as amended by SI 1987/354)

6 Apr 1987 (repeals of or in Social Security Act 1975, ss 1(1)(b), 122(4), 134(5)(b); Employment Protection Act 1975, s 40(2), (4); Supplementary Benefits Act 1976, s 26; Social Security (Miscellaneous Provisions) Act 1977, s 18(1)(c), (2)(a), (b); Employment Protection (Consolidation) Act 1978 (except ss 123(5), 127(3), 132(6)); Social Security Act 1979, ss 3(2), 12, Sch 3, para 16; Social Security Act 1985, Sch 5, para 7) (SI 1987/354)

7 Apr 1987 (repeals of or in Family Income Supplement Act 1970, s 8(3), (4); Social Security Act 1975, ss 86, 119(3), (4)(b)–(d); Social Security (Consequential Provisions) Act 1975, Sch 2, para 41; Social Security Pensions Act 1975, Sch 4, para 13; Child Benefit Act 1975, ss 7, 8 (except in relation to Social Security Act 1975, ss 82(3)), 17(5), (6), Sch 4, paras 5, 29, 33; Supplementary Benefits Act 1979, s 7, Sch 3, para 9; Social Security Act 1980, s 4, Sch 1, para 12, Sch 2, paras 11, 19(c); Social Security and Housing Benefits Act 1982; Sch 4, para 22; Health and Social Services and Social Security Adjudications Act 1983, Sch 8, para 17) (SI 1986/1959)

26 Jun 1987 (repeals of or in Attachment of Earnings Act 1971; Social Security (Consequential Provisions) Act 1975, Sch 2, para 44; Social Security and Housing Benefits Act 1982, s 45(2)(a)) (SI 1987/1096)

4 Jan 1988 (repeals of or in Social Security Act 1975, ss 146(1), 151(1), 152(8); Employment Protection (Consolidation) Act 1978, ss 123(5), 127(3)) (SI 1987/543)

1 Apr 1988 or 4 Apr 1988 (see s 20(1)) (repeals of or in Social Security Act 1980, Sch 3, Pt II, para 15B; Social Security and Housing Benefits Act 1982, Pt II, ss 45(1), (2)(b), (c), (3), 47, Sch 4, paras 5, 19, 27, 28, 35(1), (2); Social Security Act 1985, ss 22, 32(2)) (SI 1987/1853)

6 Apr 1988 (repeal of or in Social Security Pensions Act 1975, s 6(2)) (SI 1987/543)

11 Apr 1988 (repeals of or in Pensioners and Family Income Supplement Payments Act 1972 (except s 3 and s 4 so far as it refers to expenses attributable to s 3); Pensioners' Payments and National Insurance Contributions Act 1972; Pensioners' Payments and National Insurance Act 1973 (except s 7 and the Schedule); Pensioners' Payments Act 1974; Social Security Act 1975, ss 12(1)(h), (2), 13(1) (entry relating to widow's allowance), (5)(a), 25(3), 26(3), 41(2)(e), (2C), 50(2), 79–81, 82, 84(3), 88(a), 90, 101(3), Sch 3, Pt II, paras 8(2), 9, 10, Sch 4, Pt I, para 5, Pt IV, para

Social Security Act 1986 (c 50)—*cont*

Sch 11—*cont*   4, Pt V, paras 6, 11, Sch 20 (definitions of
                             'Relative'. 'Short–term benefit'); Industrial
                             Injuries and Diseases (Old Cases) Act 1975, s 4(4);
                             Social Security Pensions Act 1975, s 56K(4),
                             Sch 4, para 51; Child Benefit Act 1975, ss 6, 8 (so
                             far as not already in force), 15(1), Sch 4, paras 3,
                             4, 6, 27; Social Security (Miscellaneous
                             Provisions) Act 1977, ss 9, 17(2), 22(2), (reference
                             to Social Security Act 1975, s 24(2)); Pensioners'
                             Payments Act 1977; Pensioners' Payments Act
                             1978; Pensioners' Payments and Social Security
                             Act 1979; Social Security (No 2) Act 1980, s 4(2);
                             Social Security and Housing Benefits Act 1982,
                             s 44(1)(f), Sch 4, para 14; Health and Social
                             Security Act 1984, ss 22, 27(2), Sch 4, paras 3, 14,
                             Sch 5, paras 5, 6; Social Security Act 1985, ss 27,
                             32(2) ('section 15'), Sch 5, para 6(a)) (SI 1987/
                             1096)

                             11 Apr 1988 (repeals of or in National Assistance
                             Act 1948; Family Income Supplements Act 1970
                             (so far as it is not already repealed); Pensioners
                             and Family Income Supplement Payments Act
                             1972 (so far as it is not already repealed); National
                             Insurance Act 1974, s 6(1); Social Security Act
                             1975, ss 67(2)(b), 143(1); Supplementary Benefits
                             Act 1976, ss 1–11, 13–19, 21, 24, 25, 27, 31–34,
                             Sch 1, Sch 5, para 1(2), Sch 7, paras 1(b), (d), 3(a),
                             5, 19, 21, 23, 24, 31, 33, 37; Social Security
                             (Miscellaneous Provisions) Act 1977, s 18(1);
                             Employment Protection (Consolidation) Act
                             1978, s 132(6); Social Security Act 1979, Sch 3,
                             paras 1, 2, 24–27; Social Security Act 1980, ss 7,
                             8(1), 9(7), 18(1), Sch 2, paras 1–10, 12–18, 22–30,
                             Sch 3, Pt II, paras 11, 15; Social Security (No 2)
                             Act 1980, s 6; Social Security Act 1981, s 4, Sch 1,
                             paras 8, 9; Social Security and Housing Benefits
                             Act 1982, ss 38, 44(1)(a), Sch 4, paras 2, 4, 23–25;
                             Health and Social Services and Social Security
                             Adjudications Act 1983, s 19(2), Sch 8, Pt III, Pt
                             IV (so far as that Pt is not already repealed); Law
                             Reform (Parent and Child) (Scotland) Act 1986)
                             (SI 1987/1853)

                             11 Apr 1988 (repeals of or in Social Security Act
                             1975, ss 67, 68, 70–75, 117(4), (5)) (SI 1988/567)

                             Not in force (otherwise)

Statute Law (Repeals) Act 1986 (c 12)

RA: 2 May 1986

2 May 1986 (RA)

Wages Act 1986 (c 48)

RA: 25 Jul 1986

Wages Act 1986 (c 48)—*cont*

Commencement provisions: s 33(2)–(5); Wages Act 1986 (Commencement) Order
1986, SI 1986/1998

s 1–11	1 Jan 1987 (SI 1986/1998)
12–27	Repealed (with savings in relation to ss 16, 19, 20)
28	1 Aug 1986 (s 33(5))
29	25 Jul 1986 (s 33(2))
30	1 Jan 1987 (so far as relates to Pt 1 (ss 1–11)) (SI 1986/1998)
	25 Sep 1986 (so far as relates to Pt II (ss 12–26)) (s 33(4))
31	25 Jul 1986 (s 33(2))
32(1)	See Sch 4 below
(2)	See Sch 5 below
(3)	25 Jul 1986 (s 33(2))
33	25 Jul 1986 (s 33(2))
Sch 1	1 Jan 1987 (SI 1986/1998)
2, 3	Repealed
4, para 1–3	1 Jan 1987 (SI 1986/1998); prospectively repealed by Coal Industry Act 1992, s 3(3), Schedule, Pt II (qv)
4	25 Sep 1986 (s 33(4))
5–8	Repealed
9, 10	1 Jan 1987 (SI 1986/1998)
11	Repealed
5, Pt I	1 Aug 1986 (s 33(3))
II	25 Sep 1986 (s 33(4))
III	1 Jan 1987 (SI 1986/1998)
6	25 Jul 1986 (s 33(2))

1987

Abolition of Domestic Rates etc (Scotland) Act 1987 (c 47)

RA: 15 May 1987

Commencement provisions: s 35(2); Abolition of Domestic Rates etc (Scotland) Act 1987 Commencement Order 1987, SI 1987/1489

Whole Act prospectively repealed by Local Government Finance Act 1992, s 117(2), Sch 14 (qv)

s 1, 2	14 Sep 1987 (SI 1987/1489)
3A	Repealed
3B	Substituted for s 3A by Local Government and Housing Act 1989, s 141(1) (qv)
4, 5	14 Sept 1987 (SI 1987/1489)
6–8	14 Sept 1987 (certain purposes) (SI 1987/1489)
	1 Apr 1989 (remaining purposes) (SI 1987/1489)
	Prospectively repealed by Local Government Finance Act 1992, s 117(2), Sch 14 (qv)
9	Repealed
9A	Inserted by Local Government and Housing Act, s 143(1) (qv)
10, 11	14 Sept 1987 (certain purposes) (SI 1987/1489)
	1 Apr 1989 (remaining purposes) (SI 1987/1489)
	Prospectively repealed by Local Government Finance Act 1992, s 117(2), Sch 14 (qv)
11A	Inserted by Local Government Finance Act 1988, s 137, Sch 12, Pt II, para 21 (qv)
11B	Repealed
12–17	14 Sept 1987 (SI 1987/1489)
18	1 Oct 1988 (SI 1987/1489)
18A	Inserted by Local Government Finance Act 1988, s 137, Sch 12, Pt II, para 28 (qv)
19, 20	1 Oct 1988 (SI 1987/1489)
20A	Inserted by Local Government Finance Act 1988, s 137, Sch 12, Pt II, para 30 (qv)
20B	Inserted by Local Government Finance Act 1988, s 137, Sch 12, Pt II, para 31 (qv)
20C	Inserted by Local Government and Housing Act 1989, s 145, Sch 6, para 27 (qv)
21–23	14 Sep 1987 (SI 1987/1489)
23A	Inserted by Local Government and Housing Act 1989, s 144 (qv)
24	Repealed
25(1)	14 Sep 1987 (SI 1987/1489)
(2), (3)	14 Sep 1987 (certain purposes) (SI 1987/1489)
	1 Apr 1989 (remaining purposes) (SI 1987/1489)
	Prospectively repealed by Local Government Finance Act 1992, s 117(2), Sch 14 (qv)

Abolition of Domestic Rates etc (Scotland) Act 1987 (c 47)—*cont*

s 26(1)	14 Sep 1987 (SI 1987/1489)
(2)	14 Sep 1987 (certain purposes) (SI 1987/1489)
	1 Apr 1989 (remaining purposes) (SI 1987/1489)
	Prospectively repealed by Local Government
	Finance Act 1992, s 117(2), Sch 14 (qv)
27	14 Sep 1987 (SI 1987/1489)
28	Repealed
29–33	14 Sep 1987 (SI 1987/1489)
34	14 Sep 1987 (certain purposes) (SI 1987/1489)
	1 Apr 1989 (certain purposes) (SI 1987/1489)
	1 Apr 1994 (remaining purposes) (SI 1987/1489)
	Prospectively repealed by Local Government
	Finance Act 1992, s 117(2), Sch 14 (qv)
35	14 Sep 1987 (SI 1987/1489)
Sch 1, para 1–14	14 Sep 1987 (SI 1987/1489)
15	14 Sep 1987 (certain purposes) (SI 1987/1489)
	1 Apr 1989 (remaining purposes) (SI 1987/1489)
16	1 Apr 1989 (SI 1987/1489)
17	14 Sep 1987 (certain purposes) (SI 1987/1489)
	1 Apr 1989 (remaining purposes) (SI 1987/1489)
18	1 Apr 1989 (SI 1989/1489)
19	Repealed
20	14 Sep 1987 (SI 1987/1489)
21	14 Sep 1987 (certain purposes) (SI 1987/1489)
	1 Apr 1989 (remaining purposes) (SI 1987/1489)
22	14 Sep 1987 (SI 1987/1489)
23(a)	14 Sep 1987 (certain purposes) (SI 1987/1489)
	1 Apr 1989 (remaining purposes) (SI 1987/1489)
(b)	14 Sep 1987 (SI 1987/1489)
24	1 Apr 1989 (SI 1987/1489)
25, 26	14 Sep 1987 (SI 1987/1489)
27	1 Apr 1989 (SI 1987/1489)
28	14 Sep 1987 (certain purposes) (SI 1987/1489)
	1 Apr 1989 (remaining purposes) (SI 1987/1489)
29–31	1 Apr 1989 (SI 1987/1489)
32	14 Sep 1987 (certain purposes) (SI 1987/1489)
	1 Apr 1989 (remaining purposes) (SI 1987/1489)
33	14 Sep 1987 (SI 1987/1489)
34–36	1 Apr 1989 (SI 1987/1489)
37, 38	14 Sep 1987 (certain purposes) (SI 1987/1489)
	1 Apr 1989 (remaining purposes) (SI 1987/1489)
39	1 Apr 1989 (SI 1987/1489)
1A	Inserted by Local Government Finance Act 1988,
	s 137, Sch 12, Pt II, para 35 (qv)
2–4	14 Sep 1987 (SI 1987/1489)
5, para 1	14 Sep 1987 (certain purposes) (SI 1987/1489)
	1 Apr 1989 (remaining purposes) (SI 1987/1489)
2–5	Repealed
6–8	14 Sep 1987 (certain purposes) (SI 1987/1489)
	1 Apr 1989 (remaining purposes) (SI 1987/1489)
9, 10	Repealed
11–13	14 Sep 1987 (certain purposes) (SI 1987/1489)
	1 Apr 1989 (remaining purposes) (SI 1987/1489)
14, 15	Repealed
16	14 Sep 1987 (certain purposes) (SI 1987/1489)
	1 Apr 1989 (remaining purposes) (SI 1987/1489)

Abolition of Domestic Rates etc (Scotland) Act 1987 (c 47)—*cont*

Sch 5, para 17–19	Repealed
19A	Inserted by Local Government and Housing Act 1989, s 145, Sch 6, para 21 (qv)
20	14 Sep 1987 (certain purposes) (SI 1987/1489)
	1 Apr 1989 (remaining purposes) (SI 1987/1489)
21	Repealed
22	14 Sep 1987 (certain purposes) (SI 1987/1489)
	1 Apr 1989 (remaining purposes) (SI 1987/1489)
23, 24	1 Apr 1989 (SI 1987/1489)
25	Repealed
26	14 Sep 1987 (certain purposes) (SI 1987/1489)
	1 Apr 1989 (remaining purposes) (SI 1987/1489)
27	1 Apr 1989 (SI 1987/1489)
28, 29	14 Sep 1987 (certain purposes) (SI 1987/1489)
	1 Apr 1989 (remaining purposes) (SI 1987/1489)
30(a)	14 Sep 1987 (certain purposes) (SI 1987/1489)
	1 Apr 1989 (remaining purposes) (SI 1987/1489)
(b), (c)	1 Apr 1989 (SI 1987/1489)
31–37	14 Sep 1987 (certain purposes) (SI 1987/1489)
	1 Apr 1989 (remaining purposes) (SI 1987/1489)
	1 Apr 1989 (SI 1987/1489)
39–41	14 Sep 1987 (certain purposes) (SI 1987/1489)
	1 Apr 1989 (remaining purposes) (SI 1987/1489)
42–46	1 Apr 1989 (SI 1987/1489)
47–49	14 Sep 1987 (certain purposes) (SI 1987/1489)
	1 Apr 1989 (remaining purposes) (SI 1987/1489)
6	14 Sep 1987 (certain purposes) (SI 1987/1489)
	1 Apr 1989 (certain purposes) (SI 1987/1489)
	1 Apr 1994 (remaining purposes) (SI 1987/1489)

Access to Personal Files Act 1987 (c 37)

RA: 15 May 1987

15 May 1987 (RA)

Agricultural Training Board Act 1987 (c 29)

RA: 15 May 1987

Commencement provisions: s 2(2)

15 Jul 1987 (s 2(2))

AIDS (Control) Act 1987 (c 33)

RA: 15 May 1987

15 May 1987 (RA)

Animals (Scotland) Act 1987 (c 9)

RA: 9 Apr 1987

Commencement provisions: s 9(2)

9 June 1987 (s 9(2))

Appropriation Act 1987 (c 17)

Whole Act repealed

Appropriation (No 2) Act 1987 (c 50)

Whole Act repealed

Banking Act 1987 (c 22)

RA: 15 May 1987

Commencement provisions: s 110(2); Banking Act 1987 (Commencement No 1) Order 1987, SI 1987/1189; Banking Act 1987 (Commencement No 2) Order 1987, SI 1987/1664; Banking Act 1987 (Commencement No 3) Order 1988, SI 1988/502; Banking Act 1987 (Commencement No 4) Order 1988, SI 1988/644

s 1–12	1 Oct 1987 (SI 1987/1664)
12A	Inserted by Banking (Second Council Directive) Regulations 1992, SI 1992/3218, reg 29
13–26	1 Oct 1987 (SI 1987/1664)
26A	Inserted by Banking (Second Council Directive) Regulations 1992, SI 1992/3218, reg 32(1)
27–36	1 Oct 1987 (SI 1987/1664)
36A	Inserted by Banking (Second Council Directive) Regulations 1992, SI 1992/3218, reg 33
37	1 Oct 1987 (SI 1987/1664)
37A	Inserted by Banking (Second Council Directive) Regulations 1992, SI 1992/3218, reg 35
38	1 Apr 1988 (SI 1988/502)
39–81	1 Oct 1987 (SI 1987/1664)
82–85	15 Jul 1987 (SI 1987/1189)
86	Substituted by Banking (Second Council Directive) Regulations 1992, SI 1992/3218, reg 41
87	15 Jul 1987 (SI 1987/1189)
88–90	1 Oct 1987 (SI 1987/1664)
91	15 May 1987 (s 110(2))
92–101	1 Oct 1987 (SI 1987/1664)
102	15 Jul 1987 (SI 1987/1189)
103–105	1 Oct 1987 (SI 1987/1664)
105A	Inserted by Companies Act 1989, s 23, Sch 10, Pt II, para 37(3) (qv)
106	15 Jul 1987 (SI 1987/1189)
107	See Sch 5 below
108(1)	See Sch 6 below
(2)	See Sch 7 below
109, 110	15 Jul 1987 (SI 1987/1189)

Banking Act 1987 (c 22)—*cont*

Sch 1–4	1 Oct 1987 (SI 1987/1664)
5, para 1–13	1 Oct 1987 (SI 1987/1664)
14	15 Jul 1987 (SI 1987/1189)
6, para 1–3	1 Oct 1987 (SI 1987/1664)
4	Repealed
5	1 Oct 1987 (SI 1987/1664)
6	Substituted by Banking (Second Council Directive) Regulations 1992, SI 1992/3218, reg 27(4)
7–12	1 Oct 1987 (SI 1987/1664)
13	Repealed
14, 15	1 Oct 1987 (SI 1987/1664)
16	Repealed
17–23	1 Oct 1987 (SI 1987/1664)
24	Repealed
25	1 Oct 1987 (SI 1987/1664)
26(1)–(4)	1 Oct 1987 (SI 1987/1189)
(5)	15 Jul 1987 (SI 1987/1189)
(6)–(8)	1 Oct 1987 (SI 1987/1664)
27–28	1 Oct 1987 (SI 1987/1664)
7	15 Jul 1987 (repeals of or in Banking Act 1979, s 20; Building Societies Act 1986, s 54(4), (5); Financial Services Act 1986, Sch 13, para 4) (SI 1987/1189)
	1 Oct 1987 (otherwise, except repeal of Financial Services Act 1986, s 193) (SI 1987/1664)
	29 Apr 1988 (exception noted above) (SI 1988/644)

Billiards (Abolition of Restrictions) Act 1987 (c 19)

Whole Act repealed

British Shipbuilders (Borrowing Powers) Act 1987 (c 52)

RA: 23 Jul 1987

23 Jul 1987 (RA)

Broadcasting Act 1987 (c 10)

Whole Act repealed

Channel Tunnel Act 1987 (c 53)

RA: 23 Jul 1987

23 Jul 1987 (RA)

Chevening Estate Act 1987 (c 20)

RA: 15 May 1987

Commencement provisions: s 5(2); Chevening Estate Act 1987 (Commencement) Order 1987, SI 1987/1254

1 Sep 1987 (SI 1987/1254)

Coal Industry Act 1987 (c 3)

RA: 5 Mar 1987

Commencement provisions: s 10(2)

s 1–5	5 Mar 1987 (RA)
6–8	5 May 1987 (s 10(2))
9, 10	5 Mar 1987 (RA)
Sch 1	5 Mar 1987 (RA)
2, 3	5 Mar 1987 (RA)

Consolidated Fund Act 1987 (c 8)

Whole Act repealed

Consolidated Fund (No 2) Act 1987 (c 54)

Whole Act repealed

Consolidated Fund (No 3) Act 1987 (c 55)

Whole Act repealed

Consumer Protection Act 1987 (c 43)

RA: 15 May 1987

Commencement provisions: s 50(2), (4), (5); Consumer Protection Act 1987 (Commencement No 1) Order 1987, SI 1987/1680; Consumer Protection Act 1987 (Commencement No 2) Order 1988, SI 1988/2041; Consumer Protection Act 1987 (Commencement No 3) Order 1988, SI 1988/2076

s 1–9	1 Mar 1988 (SI 1987/1680)
10–19	1 Oct 1987 (SI 1987/1680)
20–26	1 Mar 1989 (subject to transitional provisions in relation to s 20(1), (2)) (SI 1988/2076)
27–35	1 Oct 1987 (for purposes of or in relation to Pt II) (SI 1987/1680)
	1 Mar 1989 (otherwise) (SI 1988/2076)
36	1 Mar 1988 (SI 1987/1680)
37–40	1 Oct 1987 (for purposes of or in relation to Pt II) (SI 1987/1680)
	1 Mar 1989 (otherwise) (SI 1988/2076)
41(1)	1 Oct 1987 (for purposes of or in relation to Pt II) (SI 1987/1680)
	1 Mar 1989 (otherwise) (SI 1988/2076)
(2)	1 Oct 1987 (for purposes of or in relation to Pt II) (SI 1987/1680)
	1 Mar 1988 (for purposes of or in relation to Pt I) (SI 1987/1680)
	1 Mar 1989 (otherwise) (SI 1988/2076)

Consumer Protection Act 1987 (c 43)—*cont*

s 41(3)–(5)	1 Oct 1987 (for purposes of or in relation to Pt II) (SI 1987/1680)
	1 Mar 1989 (otherwise) (SI 1988/2076)
(6)	1 Oct 1987 (for purposes of or in relation to Pt II) (SI 1987/1680)
	1 Mar 1988 (for purposes of or in relation to Pt I) (SI 1987/1680)
	1 Mar 1989 (otherwise) (SI 1988/2076)
42–44	1 Oct 1987 (so far as have effect for purposes of or in relation to Pt II) (SI 1987/1680)
	1 Mar 1989 (otherwise) (SI 1988/2076)
45, 46	1 Oct 1987 (so far as have effect for purposes of or in relation to Pt II) (SI 1987/1680)
	1 Mar 1988 (so far as have effect for purposes of or in relation to Pt I) (SI 1987/1680)
	1 Mar 1989 (otherwise) (SI 1988/2076)
47	1 Oct 1987 (for purposes of or in relation to Pt II) (SI 1987/1680)
	1 Mar 1989 (otherwise) (SI 1988/2076)
48(1)	See Sch 4 below
(2)(a)	31 Dec 1988 (SI 1988/2041)
(b)	1 Oct 1987 (SI 1987/1680)
(3)	See Sch 5 below
49, 50	1 Oct 1987 (SI 1987/1680)
Sch 1	1 Mar 1988 (SI 1987/1680)
2	1 Oct 1987 (SI 1987/1680)
3	1 Mar 1988 (SI 1987/1680)
4, para 1, 2	1 Oct 1987 (SI 1987/1680)
3	1 Mar 1989 (SI 1988/2076)
4	1 Oct 1987 (SI 1987/1680)
5	1 Mar 1988 (SI 1987/1680)
6, 7	1 Oct 1987 (SI 1987/1680)
8	Repealed
9–11	1 Oct 1987 (SI 1987/1680)
12	1 Mar 1988 (SI 1987/1680)
13	1 Oct 1987 (SI 1987/1680)
5	1 Oct 1987 (repeals of or in Fabrics (Misdescription) Act 1913; Criminal Justice Act 1967; Fines Act (Northern Ireland) 1967; Local Government Act 1972; Local Government (Scotland) Act 1973; Explosives (Age of Purchase etc) Act 1976; Consumer Safety Act 1978; Magistrates' Courts Act 1980; Telecommunications Act 1984; Food Act 1984; Consumer Safety (Amendment) Act 1986; Airports Act 1986; Gas Act 1986) (SI 1987/1680)
	1 Mar 1988 (repeals of or in Prescription and Limitation (Scotland) Act 1973; Health and Safety at Work etc Act 1974) (SI 1987/1680)
	31 Dec 1988 (repeal of Trade Descriptions Act 1972) (SI 1988/2041)
	1 Mar 1989 (repeal of Trade Descriptions Act 1968, s 11) (SI 1988/2076)

Criminal Justice Act 1987 (c 38)

RA: 15 May 1987

Commencement provisions: s 16; Criminal Justice Act 1987 (Commencement No 1)
Order 1987, SI 1987/1061; Criminal Justice Act 1987 (Commencement No 2)
Order 1988, SI 1988/397; Criminal Justice Act 1987 (Commencement No 3)
Order 1988, SI 1988/1564

s 1	20 Jul 1987 (for purposes of appointment of person to be Director of the Serious Fraud Office, staff for Office and doing of such other things necessary or expedient for establishment of Office) (SI 1987/1061)
	6 Apr 1988 (otherwise) (SI 1988/397)
2, 3	6 Apr 1988 (SI 1988/397)
4, 5	31 Oct 1988 (SI 1988/1564)
6	Substituted by Criminal Justice Act 1988, s 144(1), (5) (qv)
7–11	31 Oct 1988 (SI 1988/1564)
12	20 Jul 1987 (except in relation to things done before that date) (SI 1987/1061)
13	15 May 1987 (s 16(3))
14	20 Jul 1987 (SI 1987/1061)
15	See Sch 2 below
16–18	15 May 1987 (s 16(3))
Sch 1	See s 1 above
2, para 1–5	31 Oct 1988 (SI 1988/1564)
6	6 Apr 1988 (SI 1988/397)
7, 8	Repealed
9–12	31 Oct 1988 (SI 1988/1564)
13	6 Apr 1988 (SI 1988/397)
14–16	31 Oct 1988 (SI 1988/1564)

Criminal Justice (Scotland) Act 1987 (c 41)

RA: 15 May 1987

Commencement provisions: s 72(2); Criminal Justice (Scotland) Act 1987
(Commencement No 1) Order 1987, SI 1987/1468; Criminal Justice (Scotland)
Act 1987 (Commencement No 2) Order 1987, SI 1987/1594; Criminal Justice
(Scotland) Act 1987 (Commencement No 3) Order 1987, SI 1987/2119; Criminal
Justice (Scotland) Act 1987 (Commencement No 4) Order 1988, SI 1988/483;
Criminal Justice (Scotland) Act 1987 (Commencement No 5) Order 1988, SI
1988/482; Criminal Justice (Scotland) Act 1987 (Commencement No 6) Order
1988, SI 1988/1710

s 1–29	1 Apr 1988 (SI 1988/482)
30, 30A	Substituted for original s 30 by Law Reform (Miscellaneous Provisions) (Scotland) Act 1990, s 63 (qv)
31	1 Apr 1988 (SI 1988/483)
32–40	1 Apr 1988 (SI 1988/482)
40A	Prospectively inserted by Criminal Justice Act 1993, s 20(2) (qv)
41, 42	1 Apr 1988 (SI 1988/482)
42A	Inserted by Criminal Justice Act 1993, s 17 (qv)

Criminal Justice (Scotland) Act 1987 (c 41)—*cont*

s 43	1 Apr 1988 (SI 1988/482)
43A, 43B	Prospectively inserted by Criminal Justice Act 1993, s 19 (qv)
44	1 Apr 1988 (SI 1988/482)
45(1)	1 Apr 1988 (SI 1988/483)
(2), (3)	1 Apr 1988 (SI 1988/482)
(4)	1 Apr 1988 (SI 1988/483)
(5), (6)	1 Apr 1988 (SI 1988/482)
(7)(a), (b)	1 Apr 1988 (SI 1988/483)
(c)	1 Apr 1988 (SI 1988/482)
(d), (e)	1 Apr 1988 (SI 1988/483)
(f)	1 Apr 1988 (SI 1988/482)
46	1 Apr 1988 (SI 1988/482)
46A	Prospectively inserted by Criminal Justice Act 1993, s 77, Sch 4, paras 1, 2 (qv)
47	1 Apr 1988 (SI 1988/482)
48, 49	1 Oct 1987 (SI 1987/1594)
50	1 Apr 1988 (SI 1988/482)
51–56	1 Jan 1988 (SI 1987/2119)
57	1 Sep 1987 (SI 1987/1468)
58	1 Jan 1988 (SI 1987/2119)
59	1 Apr 1988 (SI 1988/482)
60	1 Oct 1987 (SI 1987/1594)
61–63	1 Jan 1988 (SI 1987/2119)
64	1 Oct 1987 (SI 1987/1594)
65	1 Jan 1988 (SI 1987/2119)
66	12 Oct 1988 (SI 1988/1710)
67	1 Apr 1988 (SI 1988/482)
68	1 Jan 1988 (SI 1987/2119)
69	1 Oct 1987 (SI 1987/1594)
70	See Schs 1, 2 below
71	1 Apr 1988 (SI 1988/482)
72	15 May 1987 (s 72(2))
Sch 1, para 1, 2	1 Sep 1987 (SI 1987/1468)
3	Repealed
4–6	1 Sep 1987 (SI 1987/1468)
7–9	1 Jan 1988 (SI 1987/2119)
10(a)	1 Jan 1988 (SI 1987/2119)
(b)	1 Oct 1987 (SI 1987/1594)
11–14	1 Oct 1987 (SI 1987/1594)
15	12 Oct 1988 (SI 1988/1710)
16–18	1 Oct 1987 (SI 1987/1594)
19	Repealed
2	1 Sep 1987 (repeals of or in Circuit Courts (Scotland) Act 1709; Heritable Jurisdiction (Scotland) Act 1746; Circuit Courts (Scotland) Act 1828; Justiciary (Scotland) Act 1848; Circuit Clerks (Scotland) Act 1898; Criminal Procedure (Scotland) Act 1975, ss 5(1), 87, 88, 113, 115–119) (SI 1987/1468)
	1 Oct 1987 (repeals of or in Road Traffic Act 1974, Sch 3, para 10(4); Criminal Procedure (Scotland) Act 1975, s 263(2)) (SI 1987/1594)
	1 Jan 1988 (repeals of or in Road Traffic Act 1972; Criminal Procedure (Scotland) Act 1976, s 300(5); Sexual Offences (Scotland) Act 1976; Community

Criminal Justice (Scotland) Act 1987 (c 41)—*cont*

Sch 2—*cont*	Service by Offenders (Scotland) Act 1978) (SI 1987/2119)
	1 Apr 1988 (repeals of or in Children and Young Persons (Scotland) Act 1937; Social Work (Scotland) Act 1968; Criminal Procedure (Scotland) Act 1975, s 193B; Law Reform (Miscellaneous Provisions) (Scotland) Act 1985; Drug Trafficking Offences Act 1986) (SI 1988/482)
	12 Oct 1988 (repeals of or in Criminal Procedure (Scotland) Act 1975, ss 289B(3), (4), 289D(1A), (2)–(4)) (SI 1988/1710)

Crossbows Act 1987 (c 32)

RA: 15 May 1987

Commencement provisions: s 8(2)

| s 1–6 | 15 Jul 1987 (s 8(2)) |
| 7, 8 | 15 May 1987 (RA) |

Crown Proceedings (Armed Forces) Act 1987 (c 25)

RA: 15 May 1987

15 May 1987 (RA)

Debtors (Scotland) Act 1987 (c 18)

RA: 15 May 1987

Commencement provisions: s 109(2); Debtors (Scotland) Act 1987 (Commencement No 1) Order 1987, SI 1987/1838; Debtors (Scotland) Act 1987 (Commencement No 2) Order 1988, SI 1988/1818

s 1–67	30 Nov 1988 (SI 1988/1818)
68	Repealed
69–74	30 Nov 1988 (SI 1988/1818)
75, 76	2 Nov 1987 (SI 1987/1838)
77–96	30 Nov 1988 (SI 1988/1818)
97	2 Nov 1987 (SI 1987/1838)
98–108	30 Nov 1988 (SI 1988/1818)
109	15 May 1987 (RA)
Sch 1–8	30 Nov 1988 (SI 1988/1818)

Deer Act 1987 (c 28)

Whole Act repealed

Diplomatic and Consular Premises Act 1987 (c 46)

RA: 15 May 1987

Commencement provisions: s 9(2); Diplomatic and Consular Premises Act 1987 (Commencement No 1) Order 1987, SI 1987/1022; Diplomatic and Consular Premises Act 1987 (Commencement No 2) Order 1987, SI 1987/2248; Diplomatic and Consular Premises Act 1987 (Commencement No 3) Order 1987, SI 1988/106

s 1–5	1 Jan 1988 (SI 1987/2248)
6, 7	11 Jun 1987 (SI 1987/1022)
8	1 Jan 1988 (SI 1987/2248)
9	3 Feb 1988 (SI 1988/106)
Sch 1	1 Jan 1988 (SI 1987/2248)
2	11 Jun 1987 (SI 1987/1022)

Family Law Reform Act 1987 (c 42)

RA: 15 May 1987

Commencement provisions: s 34(2); Family Law Reform Act 1987 (Commencement No 1) Order 1988, SI 1988/425; Family Law Reform Act 1987 (Commencement No 2) Order 1989, SI 1989/382

s 1	4 Apr 1988 (SI 1988/425)
2	1 Apr 1989 (SI 1989/382)
3–7	Repealed
8	1 Apr 1989 (SI 1989/382)
9–16	Repealed
17	1 Apr 1989 (SI 1989/382)
18–22	4 Apr 1988 (SI 1988/425)
23	*Not in force*
24, 25	1 Apr 1989 (SI 1989/382)
26–29	4 Apr 1988 (SI 1988/425)
30	1 Apr 1989 (SI 1989/382)
31	4 Apr 1988 (SI 1988/425)
32	*Not in force*★
33	See Schs 2–4 below
34	4 Apr 1988 (SI 1988/425)
Sch 1	Spent
2, para 1	1 Apr 1989 (SI 1989/382)
2–4	4 Apr 1988 (SI 1988/425)
5–8	1 Apr 1989 (SI 1989/382)
9, 10	4 Apr 1988 (SI 1988/425)
11	Repealed
12, 13	1 Apr 1989 (SI 1989/382)
	Repealed
	1 Apr 1989 (SI 1989/382)
16(a), (b)	1 Apr 1989 (SI 1989/382)
(c)	4 Apr 1988 (SI 1988/425)
17, 18	1 Apr 1989 (SI 1989/382)
19	4 Apr 1988 (SI 1988/425)
20	Repealed
21–25	*Not in force*

Family Law Reform Act 1987 (c 42)—*cont*

Sch 2, para 26, 27		1 Apr 1989 (SI 1989/382)
	28–43	Spent
	44, 45	1 Apr 1989 (SI 1989/382)
	46	Repealed
	47–50	1 Apr 1989 (SI 1989/382)
	51	Repealed
	52	1 Apr 1989 (SI 1989/382)
	53–58	Spent
	59	Repealed
	60–66	Spent
	67, 68	Repealed
	69–72	1 Apr 1989 (SI 1989/382)
	73, 74	4 Apr 1988 (SI 1988/425)
	75–79	Spent
	80–90	1 Apr 1989 (SI 1989/382)
	91–95	Repealed
	96	4 Apr 1988 (SI 1988/425)
3, para 1		4 Apr 1988 (SI 1988/425)
	2–7	1 Apr 1988 (SI 1989/382)
	8–10	4 Apr 1988 (SI 1988/425)
	11, 12	Repealed
4		4 Apr 1988 (repeals of or in Domestic and Appellate Proceedings (Restrictions of Publicity) Act 1968, s 2(1); Family Law Reform Act 1969, ss 14, 15, 17; Interpretation Act 1978, Sch 2, para 4) (SI 1988/425)
		1 Apr 1989 (otherwise) (SI 1989/382)

* Provisions not brought into force consequent on errors in Sch 1

Finance Act 1987 (c 16)

RA: 15 May 1987

See the note concerning Finance Acts at the front of this book

---

Finance (No 2) Act 1987 (c 51)

RA: 23 Jul 1987

See the note concerning Finance Acts at the front of this book

---

Fire Safety and Safety of Places of Sport Act 1987 (c 27)

RA: 15 May 1987

Commencement provisions: s 50(2); Fire Safety and Safety of Places of Sport Act 1987 (Commencement No 1) Order 1987, SI 1987/1762; Fire Safety and Safety of Places of Sport Act 1987 (Commencement No 2) Order 1988, SI 1988/485; Fire Safety and Safety of Places of Sport Act 1987 (Commencement No 3) (Scotland) Order 1988, SI 1988/626; Fire Safety and Safety of Places of Sport Act 1987 (Commencement No 4) Order 1988, SI 1988/1806; Fire Safety and Safety of Places of Sport Act 1987 (Commencement No 5) Order 1989, SI 1989/75; Fire

Fire Safety and Safety of Places of Sport Act 1987 (c 27)—*cont*
Safety and Safety of Places of Sport Act 1987 (Commencement No 6) Order
1990, SI 1990/1984; Fire Safety and Safety of Places of Sport Act 1987
(Commencement No 7) Order 1993, SI 1993/1411

s 1, 2	1 Apr 1989 (SI 1989/75)
3, 4	1 Jan 1988 (SI 1987/1762)
5–7	1 Apr 1989 (SI 1989/75)
8, 9	1 Jan 1988 (SI 1987/1762)
10	*Not in force*
11–14	1 Jan 1988 (SI 1987/1762)
15	1 Aug 1993 (SI 1993/1411)
16(1)	1 Jan 1988 (SI 1987/1762)
(2)	See Sch 1 below
(3)	1 Jan 1988 (SI 1987/1762)
17	1 Jan 1988 (SI 1987/1762)
18(1)	See s 18(2)–(4) below
(2)	1 Jan 1988 (so far as it amends Fire Precautions Act 1971, s 40(1)(a), by the insertion of a reference to '5(2A)') (SI 1987/1762)
	1 Apr 1989 (otherwise) (SI 1989/75)
(3)	1 Jan 1988 (so far as amends Fire Precautions Act 1971, s 40(1)(b), by the insertion of references to '8B' and '10B') (SI 1987/1762)
	1 Apr 1989 (otherwise) (SI 1989/75)
(4)	1 Apr 1989 (SI 1989/75)
19–25	1 Jan 1988 (SI 1987/1762)
26–41	1 Jan 1989 (SI 1988/1806)
42, 43	1 Jun 1988 (SI 1988/485)
44	1 Jun 1988 (SI 1988/626)
45	1 Jun 1988 (SI 1988/485)
46	1 Jan 1988 (SI 1987/1762)
47	31 Dec 1990 (SI 1990/1984)
48	1 Jun 1988 (SI 1988/626)
49	See Schs 4, 5 below
50(1)–(3)	1 Jan 1988 (SI 1987/1762)
(4)–(7)	1 Jan 1988 (so far as have effect in relation to Pt II of this Act) (SI 1987/1762)
	1 Jan 1989 (otherwise) (SI 1988/1806)
Sch 1	1 Jan 1988 (so far as gives effect to Fire Precautions Act 1971, Sch 2, Pt I, Pt II, para 3(1), (2), (3) (so far as para 3(3) has effect in relation to the references to the occupier in ss 5(2A), 7(3A), 7(4), 8B(1) of the 1971 Act)) (SI 1987/1762)
	1 Apr 1989 (otherwise) (SI 1989/75)
2	1 Jan 1988 (SI 1987/1762)
3	1 Jun 1988 (SI 1988/485)
4	1 Jan 1988 (repeals of or in Fire Precautions Act 1971, ss 2, 12(1), 43(1), (2); Safety of Sports Grounds Act 1975) (SI 1987/1762)
	1 Jun 1988 (repeals in London Government Act 1963, Sch 12) (SI 1988/485)
	1 Apr 1989 (repeal of Health and Safety at Work etc Act 1974, s 78(4)) (SI 1989/75)
	1 Aug 1993 (repeals in Fire Precautions Act 1971, ss 5(3)(c), 6(1)(d)) (SI 1993/1411)

Fire Safety and Safety of Places of Sport Act 1987 (c 27)—*cont*

Sch 5, para 1	1 Jan 1988 (SI 1987/1762)
2	1 Apr 1989 (SI 1989/75)
3–7	1 Jan 1988 (SI 1987/1762)
8	1 Jun 1988 (SI 1988/485)
9	1 Jan 1988 (SI 1987/1762)
10	1 Jun 1988 (SI 1988/485)

Gaming (Amendment) Act 1987 (c 11)

RA: 9 Apr 1987

Commencement provisions: s 2(2); Gaming (Amendment) Act 1987 (Commencement) Order 1987, SI 1987/1200

1 Aug 1987 (SI 1987/1200)

Housing (Scotland) Act 1987 (c 26)

RA: 15 May 1987

Commencement provisions: s 340(2)

15 Aug 1987 (s 340(2))

Immigration (Carriers' Liability) Act 1987 (c 24)

RA: 15 May 1987

Commencement provisions: s 2(3)

Act has effect in relation to persons arriving in UK after 4 Mar 1987 except persons arriving by voyage or flight for which they embarked before that date (s 2(3))

Irish Sailors and Soldiers Land Trust Act 1987 (c 48)

Local application only

Landlord and Tenant Act 1987 (c 31)

RA: 15 May 1987

Commencement provisions: s 62(2); Landlord and Tenant Act 1987 (Commencement No 1) Order 1987, SI 1987/2177; Landlord and Tenant Act 1987 (Commencement No 2) Order 1988, SI 1988/480; Landlord and Tenant Act 1987 (Commencement No 3) Order 1988, SI 1988/1283)

s 1–20	1 Feb 1988 (SI 1987/2177)
21–40	18 Apr 1988 (SI 1988/480)
41	1 Sep 1988 (SI 1988/1283)
42	1 Apr 1989 (SI 1988/1283)
43, 44	1 Sep 1988 (SI 1988/1283)
45	Repealed
46–50	1 Feb 1988 (SI 1987/2177)

Landlord and Tenant Act 1987 (c 31)—*cont*

s 51	Repealed
52–60	1 Feb 1988 (so far as relate to ss 1–20, 45–51) (SI 1987/2177)
	18 Apr 1988 (so far as relate to ss 21–40) (SI 1988/480)
	1 Sep 1988 (otherwise) (SI 1988/1283)
61(1)	See Sch 4 below
(2)	See Sch 5 below
62	1 Feb 1988 (SI 1987/2177)
Sch 1, Pt I	1 Feb 1988 (SI 1987/2177)
II	18 Apr 1988 (SI 1988/480)
2, 3	1 Sep 1988 (SI 1988/1283)
4, para 1, 2	18 Apr 1988 (SI 1988/480)
3(a)	1 Sep 1988 (SI 1988/1283)
(b)	1 Feb 1988 (SI 1987/2177)
4–6	1 Sep 1988 (SI 1988/1283)
7	Repealed
5	1 Sep 1988 (SI 1988/1283)

Licensing (Restaurant Meals) Act 1987 (c 2)

Whole Act repealed

Local Government Act 1987 (c 44)

RA: 15 May 1987

Commencement provisions: ss 1, 2(3), (4), 3(7)

s 1, 2	Repealed
3	15 Jul 1987 (s 3(7))
4	15 May 1987 (RA)
Schedule	Repealed

Local Government Finance Act 1987 (c 6)

RA: 12 Mar 1987

12 Mar 1987 (RA)

Ministry of Defence Police Act 1987 (c 4)

RA: 5 Mar 1987

Commencement provisions: s 8(2)

5 May 1987 (s 8(2))

Minors' Contracts Act 1987 (c 13)

RA: 9 Apr 1987

Commencement provisions: s 5(2)

9 June 1987 (s 5(2))

Motor Cycle Noise Act 1987 (c 34)

RA: 15 May 1987

Commencement provisions: s 2(3)

Not in force

Northern Ireland (Emergency Provisions) Act 1987 (c 30)

Whole Act repealed

Parliamentary and Health Service Commissioners Act 1987 (c 39)

RA: 15 May 1987

Commencement provisions: s 10(3)

15 Jul 1987 (s 10(3))

Parliamentary and other Pensions Act 1987 (c 45)

RA: 15 May 1987

Commencement provisions: s 7(2); Parliamentary and other Pensions Act 1987
(Commencement No 1) Order 1987, SI 1987/1311; Parliamentary and other
Pensions Act 1987 (Commencement No 2) Order 1989, SI 1989/892

s 1–3	24 May 1989 (SI 1989/892)
4(1)	23 Jul 1987 (SI 1987/1311)
(2)	24 May 1989 (SI 1989/892)
(3)	23 Jul 1987 (SI 1987/1311)
5–7	24 May 1989 (SI 1989/892)
Sch1–4	24 May 1989 (SI 1989/892)

Petroleum Act 1987 (c 12)

RA: 9 Apr 1987

Commencement provisions: s 31(1), (2); Petroleum Act 1987 (Commencement No 1)
Order 1987, SI 1987/820; Petroleum Act 1987 (Commencement No 2) Order
1987, SI 1987/1330

s 1–16	9 Apr 1987 (s 31(1))
17, 18	30 Jun 1987 (SI 1987/820)

Petroleum Act 1987 (c 12)—*cont*

s 19, 20	9 Apr 1987 (s 31(1))
21–24	1 Sep 1987 (SI 1987/1330)
25–32	9 Apr 1987 (s 31(1))
Sch 1, 2	30 Jun 1987 (SI 1987/820)
3	9 Apr 1987 (except repeals of or in Oil and Gas (Enterprise) Act 1982, ss 21, 27) (s 31(1))
	1 Sep 1987 (exception noted above) (SI 1987/1330)

Pilotage Act 1987 (c 21)

RA: 15 May 1987

Commencement provisions: s 33(2), (3); Pilotage Act 1987 (Commencement No 1) Order 1987, SI 1987/1306; Pilotage Act 1987 (Commencement No 2) Order 1987, SI 1987/2138; Pilotage Act 1987 (Commencement No 3) Order 1988, SI 1988/1137; Pilotage Act 1987 (Commencement No 4) Order 1991, SI 1991/1029

s 1–23	1 Oct 1988 (SI 1988/1137)
24, 25	1 Sep 1987 (SI 1987/1306)
26	1 Oct 1988 (SI 1988/1137)
27	Repealed
28	1 Sep 1987 (SI 1987/1306)
29	1 Aug 1988 (SI 1988/1137)
30, 31	1 Sep 1987 (SI 1987/1306)
32(1)–(3)	1 Sep 1987 (SI 1987/1306)
(4)	1 Oct 1988 (SI 1988/1137)
(5)	See Sch 3 below
33	1 Sep 1987 (SI 1987/1306)
Sch 1, para 1–4	1 Sep 1987 (SI 1987/1306)
5, 6	1 Oct 1988 (SI 1988/1137)
2	1 Oct 1988 (SI 1988/1137)
3	1 Feb 1988 (repeal of Pilotage Act 1983, s 15(1)(i)) (SI 1987/2138)
	1 Oct 1988 (otherwise, except repeal of Pilotage Act 1983, ss 1(1), 2, 4, 5(4), 8, Sch 1) (SI 1988/1137)
	30 Apr 1991 (exception noted above) (SI 1991/1029)

Prescriptions (Scotland) Act 1987 (c 36)

RA: 15 May 1987

15 May 1987 (RA)

Protection of Animals (Penalties) Act 1987 (c 35)

RA: 15 May 1987

Commencement provisions: s 2(3)

15 Jul 1987 (s 2(3))

Rate Support Grants Act 1987 (c 5)

RA: 12 Mar 1987

12 Mar 1987 (RA)

Recognition of Trusts Act 1987 (c 14)

RA: 9 Apr 1987

Commencement provisions: s 3(2); Recognition of Trusts Act 1987 (Commencement) Order 1987, SI 1987/1177

1 Aug 1987 (SI 1987/1177)

Register of Sasines (Scotland) Act 1987 (c 23)

RA: 15 May 1987

Commencement provisions: s 3(1)

15 Jul 1987 (s 3(1))

Registered Establishments (Scotland) Act 1987 (c 40)

RA: 15 May 1987

Commencement provisions: s 8(2); commencement order dated 26 Sep 1988 (not a statutory instrument)

17 Oct 1988 (commencement order dated 26 September 1988)

Reverter of Sites Act 1987 (c 15)

RA: 9 Apr 1987

Commencement provisions: s 9(2); Reverter of Sites (Commencement) Order 1987, SI 1987/1260

17 Aug 1987 (SI 1987/1260)

Scottish Development Agency Act 1987 (c 56)

Whole Act repealed

Social Fund (Maternity and Funeral Expenses) Act 1987 (c 7)

Whole Act repealed

Teachers' Pay and Conditions Act 1987 (c 1)

Whole Act repealed

Territorial Sea Act 1987 (c 49)

RA: 15 May 1987

Commencement provisions: s 4(2); Territorial Sea Act 1987 (Commencement) Order 1987, SI 1987/1270

1 Oct 1987 (SI 1987/1270)

Urban Development Corporation (Financial Limits) Act 1987 (c 57)

RA: 17 Dec 1987

Commencement provisions: s 2(2)

17 Feb 1988 (s 2(2))

1988

Access to Medical Reports Act 1988 (c 28)

RA: 29 Jul 1988

Commencement provisions: s 10(2)

1 Jan 1989 (s 10(2))

Appropriation Act 1988 (c 38)

RA: 29 Jul 1988

29 Jul 1988 (RA)

Arms Control and Disarmament (Privileges and Immunities) Act 1988 (c 2)

RA: 9 Feb 1988

9 Feb 1988 (RA)

British Steel Act 1988 (c 35)

RA: 29 Jul 1988

Commencement provisions: s 17(2)–(4); British Steel Act 1988 (Appointed Day) Order 1988, SI 1988/1375

s 1	5 Sep 1988 (SI 1988/1375)
2	29 Jul 1988 (s 17(2))
3–14	5 Sep 1988 (SI 1988/1375)
15(1)	29 Jul 1988 (s 17(2))
(2)	5 Sep 1988 (SI 1988/1375)
16(1), (2)	5 Sep 1988 (SI 1988/1375)
(3)	See Sch 2 below
(4)	5 Sep 1988 (SI 1988/1375)
17	29 Jul 1988 (RA)
Sch 1	5 Sep 1988 (SI 1988/1375)
2, Pt I	5 Sep 1988 (SI 1988/1375)
II	*Not in force*
3	5 Sep 1988 (SI 1988/1375)

Church Commissioners (Assistance for Priority Areas) Measure 1988 (No 2)

RA: 3 May 1988

Commencement provisions: s 4(3)

4 May 1988 (the day appointed by the Archbishops of Canterbury and York under s 4(3))

Church of England (Ecumenical Relations) Measure 1988 (No 3)

PA: 29 Jul 1988

Commencement provisions: s 9(3)

1 Nov 1988 (the day appointed by the Archbishops of Canterbury and York under s 9(3))

Church of England (Legal Aid and Miscellaneous Provisions) Measure 1988 (No 1)

RA: 9 Feb 1988

Commencement provisions: s 15(2)

The provisions of this measure are brought into force on the following dates by an appointed day notice signed by the Archbishops of Canterbury and York and dated 19 Apr 1988 (made under s 15(2))

Pt I (ss 1–4)	1 Aug 1988
Pt II (ss 5–13)	1 May 1988
Pt III (ss 14, 15)	1 May 1988
Sch 1	1 Aug 1988
2, para 1, 2	1 Aug 1988
3	1 May 1988
4	1 Aug 1988
3	1 May 1988 (repeals of or in Pluralities Act 1838, ss 97, 98; Parochial Church Councils (Powers) Measure 1956, s 7; Clergy (Ordination and Miscellaneous Provisions) Measure 1964, ss 10, 12)
	1 Aug 1988 (otherwise)

Church of England (Pensions) Measure 1988 (No 4)

RA: 27 Oct 1988

Commencement provisions: s 19(2)

The provisions of this measure are brought into force on the following dates by an appointed day notice signed by the Archbishops of Canterbury and York and dated 31 Oct 1988 (made under s 19(2))

s 1–4	Repealed
5	1 Dec 1988

Church of England (Pensions) Measure 1988 (No 4)—*cont*

s 6	Repealed
7–14	1 Dec 1988
15	Repealed
16	1 Nov 1988
17–19	1 Dec 1988
Sch 1	Repealed
2, 3	1 Dec 1988

Civil Evidence (Scotland) Act 1988 (c 32)

RA: 29 Jul 1988

Commencement provisions: s 11(2); Civil Evidence (Scotland) Act 1988 (Commencement) Order 1989, SI 1989/556

3 Apr 1989 (SI 1989/556)

Community Health Councils (Access to Information) Act 1988 (c 24)

RA: 29 Jul 1988

Commencement provisions: s 3(2)

1 Apr 1989 (s 3(2))

Consolidated Fund Act 1988 (c 6)

Whole Act repealed

Consolidated Fund (No 2) Act 1988 (c 55)

Whole Act repealed

Consumer Arbitration Agreements Act 1988 (c 21)

RA: 28 Jun 1988

Commencement provisions: s 9(2); Consumer Arbitration Agreements Act 1988 (Appointed Day No 1) Order 1988, SI 1988/1598; Consumer Arbitration Agreements Act 1988 (Appointed Day No 2) Order 1988, SI 1988/2291

s 1–5	Have effect in relation to contracts made on or after 1 Oct 1988 (SI 1988/1598)
6–8	Have effect in relation to contracts made on or after 1 Feb 1989 (SI 1988/2291)
9	28 Jun 1988 (RA)

Copyright, Designs and Patents Act 1988 (c 48)

RA: 15 Nov 1988

Commencement provisions: s 305; Copyright, Designs and Patents Act 1988
(Commencement No 1) Order 1989, SI 1989/816 (as amended by SI 1989/1303);
Copyright, Designs and Patents Act 1988 (Commencement No 2) Order 1989,
SI 1989/955 (as amended by SI 1989/1032); Copyright, Designs and Patents Act
1988 (Commencement No 3) Order 1989, SI 1989/1032 (amends SI 1989/955);
Copyright, Designs and Patents Act 1988 (Commencement No 4) Order 1989,
SI 1989/1303 (amends SI 1989/816); Copyright, Designs and Patents Act 1988
(Commencement No 5) Order 1990, SI 1990/1400; Copyright, Designs and
Patents Act 1988 (Commencement No 6) Order 1990, SI 1990/2168

s 1–36	1 Aug 1989 (SI 1989/816)
37–43	9 Jun 1989 (for purposes of making regulations) (SI 1989/955; SI 1989/1032)
	1 Aug 1989 (otherwise) (SI 1989/816)
44–46	1 Aug 1989 (SI 1989/816)
47	9 Jun 1989 (for purposes of making orders) (SI 1989/955; SI 1989/1032)
	1 Aug 1989 (otherwise) (SI 1989/816)
48–50	1 Aug 1990 (SI 1989/816)
50A–50C	Inserted in relation to agreements entered into on or after 1 Jan 1993 by Copyright (Computer Programs) Regulations 1992, SI 1992/3233, regs 2, 8, 12(2)
51	1 Aug 1990 (SI 1989/816)
52	9 Jun 1989 (for purposes of making orders) (SI 1989/955; SI 1989/1032)
	1 Aug 1989 (otherwise) (SI 1989/816)
53–60	1 Aug 1989 (SI 1989/816)
61	9 Jun 1989 (for purposes of making orders) (SI 1989/955; SI 1989/1032)
	1 Aug 1989 (otherwise) (SI 1989/816)
62–73	1 Aug 1989 (SI 1989/816)
74, 75	9 Jun 1989 (for purposes of making orders) (SI 1989/955; SI 1989/1032)
	1 Aug 1989 (otherwise) (SI 1989/816)
76–99	1 Aug 1989 (SI 1989/816)
100	9 Jun 1989 (for purposes of making orders) (SI 1989/955; SI 1989/1032)
	1 Aug 1989 (otherwise) (SI 1989/816)
101–111	1 Aug 1989 (SI 1989/816)
112	9 Jun 1989 (for purposes of making regulations) (SI 1989/955; SI 1989/1032)
	1 Aug 1989 (otherwise) (SI 1989/816)
113–135	1 Aug 1989 (SI 1989/816)
135A–135G	Inserted by Broadcasting Act 1990, s 175 (qv)
136–149	1 Apr 1989 (SI 1989/816)
150	9 Jun 1989 (for purposes of making rules) (SI 1989/955; SI 1989/1032)
	1 Aug 1989 (otherwise) (SI 1989/816)
151	1 Aug 1989 (SI 1989/816)
152	9 Jun 1989 (for purposes of making rules) (SI 1989/955; SI 1989/1032)
	1 Aug 1989 (otherwise) (SI 1989/816)

Copyright, Designs and Patents Act 1988 (c 48)—*cont*

s 153–158	1 Aug 1989 (SI 1989/816)
159	9 Jun 1989 (for purposes of making orders) (SI 1989/955; SI 1989/1032)
	1 Aug 1989 (otherwise) (SI 1989/816)
160–167	1 Aug 1989 (SI 1989/816)
168	9 Jun 1989 (for purposes of making orders) (SI 1989/955; SI 1989/1032)
	1 Aug 1989 (otherwise) (SI 1989/816)
169	1 Aug 1989 (SI 1989/816)
170	See Sch 1 below
171–173	1 Aug 1989 (SI 1989/816)
174	9 Jun 1989 (for purposes of making orders) (SI 1989/955; SI 1989/1032)
	1 Aug 1989 (otherwise) (SI 1989/816)
175–188	1 Aug 1989 (SI 1989/816)
189	See Sch 2 below
190–195	1 Aug 1989 (SI 1989/816)
196	9 Jun 1989 (for purposes of making orders) (SI 1989/955; SI 1989/1032)
	1 Aug 1989 (otherwise) (SI 1989/816)
197–207	1 Aug 1989 (SI 1989/816)
208	9 Jun 1989 (for purposes of making orders) (SI 1989/955; SI 1989/1032)
	1 Aug 1989 (otherwise) (SI 1989/816)
209–249	1 Aug 1989 (SI 1989/816)
250	9 Jun 1989 (for purposes of making rules) (SI 1989/955; SI 1989/1032)
	1 Aug 1989 (otherwise) (SI 1989/816)
251–255	1 Aug 1989 (SI 1989/816)
256	9 Jun 1989 (for purposes of making orders) (SI 1989/955; SI 1989/1032)
	1 Aug 1989 (otherwise) (SI 1989/816)
257–271	1 Aug 1989 (SI 1989/816)
272	See Sch 3 below
273	See Sch 4 below
274–286	10 Jul 1990 (for the purpose of making rules expressed to come into force on or after 13 Aug 1990) (SI 1990/1400)
	13 Aug 1990 (otherwise) (SI 1990/1400)
287–289	1 Aug 1989 (SI 1989/816)
290	1 Aug 1989 (SI 1989/816); prospectively repealed by Courts and Legal Services Act 1990, s 125(7), Sch 20 (qv)
291, 292	1 Aug 1989 (SI 1989/816)
293, 294	15 Jan 1989 (s 305(2))
295	See Sch 5 below
296	1 Aug 1989 (SI 1989/816)
296A	Inserted in relation to agreements entered into on or after 1 Jan 1993 by Copyright (Computer Programs) Regulations 1992, SI 1992/3233, regs 2, 11, 12(2)
297	1 Aug 1989 (SI 1989/816)
297A	Inserted by Broadcasting Act 1990, s 179 (qv)
298–300	1 Aug 1989 (SI 1989/816)
301	See Sch 6 below
302	1 Aug 1989 (SI 1989/816)
303(1)	See Sch 7 below

Copyright, Designs and Patents Act 1988 (c 48)—*cont*

s 303(2)	See Sch 8 below
304(1)–(3)	1 Aug 1989 (SI 1989/816)
(4)	28 Jul 1989 (SI 1989/816; SI 1989/1303)
(5)	1 Aug 1989 (SI 1989/816)
(6)	28 Jul 1989 (SI 1989/816; SI 1989/1303)
305	15 Nov 1988 (RA)
306	1 Aug 1989 (SI 1989/816)
Sch 1, para 1–33	1 Aug 1989 (SI 1989/816)
34	9 Jun 1989 (for purposes of making rules) (SI 1989/955; SI 1989/1032)
	1 Aug 1989 (otherwise) (SI 1989/816)
35–46	1 Aug 1989 (SI 1989/816)
2	1 Aug 1989 (SI 1989/816)
3, para 1–20	1 Aug 1989 (SI 1989/816)
21	13 Aug 1990 (SI 1990/1400)
22–38	1 Aug 1989 (SI 1989/816)
4	13 Aug 1990 (SI 1990/1400)
5, para 1–11	1 Nov 1990 (for purposes of making rules) (SI 1990/2168)
	7 Jan 1991 (otherwise) (SI 1990/2168)
12–16	1 Aug 1989 (SI 1989/816)
17–23	1 Nov 1990 (for purposes of making rules) (SI 1990/2168)
	7 Jan 1991 (otherwise) (SI 1990/2168)
24	Repealed
25, 26	1 Nov 1990 (for purposes of making rules) (SI 1990/2168)
	7 Jan 1991 (otherwise) (SI 1990/2168)
27	13 Aug 1990 (SI 1990/1400)
28	1 Nov 1990 (for purposes of making rules) (SI 1990/2168)
	7 Jan 1991 (otherwise) (SI 1990/2168)
29	15 Nov 1988 (s 305(1))
30	1 Nov 1990 (for purposes of making rules) (SI 1990/2168)
	7 Jan 1991 (otherwise) (SI 1990/2168)
6	15 Nov 1988 (s 305(1))
7, para 1–13	1 Aug 1989 (SI 1989/816)
14	Repealed
15	13 Aug 1990 (SI 1990/1400)
16, 17	1 Aug 1989 (SI 1989/816)
18(1)	1 Aug 1989 (SI 1989/1400)
(2)	13 Aug 1990 (SI 1990/1400)
(3)	1 Aug 1989 (SI 1989/816)
19, 20	1 Aug 1989 (SI 1989/816)
21	13 Aug 1990 (SI 1990/1400)
22–25	1 Aug 1989 (SI 1989/816)
26	Repealed
27, 28	1 Aug 1989 (SI 1989/816)
29, 30	Repealed
31	1 Aug 1989 (SI 1989/816); prospectively repealed by Companies Act 1989, s 212, Sch 24 (qv)
32–36	1 Aug 1989 (SI 1989/816)
8	1 Aug 1989 (except repeals of or in of Registered Designs Act 1949, s 32; Patents Act 1977 (other than s 49(3), Sch 5, para 1, 3)) (SI 1989/816)

Copyright, Designs and Patents Act 1988 (c 48)—*cont*

Sch 8—*cont*   13 Aug 1990 (repeals of or in Registered Design Act
                               1949, s 32; Patents Act 1977, ss 84, 85, 104, 105,
                               114, 115, 123(2)(k), 130(1)) (SI 1990/1400)
                               7 Jan 1991 (repeals of or in Patents Act 1977 (so far
                               as not already in force)) (SI 1990/2168)

Coroners Act 1988 (c 13)

RA: 10 May 1988

Commencement provisions: s 37(2)

10 Jul 1988 (s 37(2))

Court of Session Act 1988 (c 36)

RA: 29 Jul 1988

Commencement provisions: s 53(2)

29 Sep 1988 (s 53(2))

Criminal Justice Act 1988 (c 33)

RA: 29 Jul 1988

Commencement provisions: ss 166(4), 171; Criminal Justice Act 1988
(Commencement No 1) Order 1988, SI 1988/1408; Criminal Justice Act 1988
(Commencement No 2) Order 1988, SI 1988/1676; Criminal Justice Act 1988
(Commencement No 3) Order 1988, SI 1988/1817; Criminal Justice Act 1988
(Commencement No 4) Order 1988, SI 1988/2073; Criminal Justice Act 1988
(Commencement No 5) Order 1989, SI 1989/1; Criminal Justice Act 1988
(Commencement No 6) Order 1989, SI 1989/50; Criminal Justice Act 1988
(Commencement No 7) Order 1989, SI 1989/264; Criminal Justice Act 1988
(Commencement No 8) Order 1989, SI 1989/1085; Extradition Act 1989, s 38(4);
Criminal Justice Act 1988 (Commencement No 9) Order 1989, SI 1989/1595;
Criminal Justice Act 1988 (Commencement No 10) Order 1990, SI 1990/220;
Criminal Justice Act 1988 (Commencement No 11) Order 1990, SI 1990/1145;
Criminal Justice Act 1988 (Commencement No 12) Order 1990, SI 1990/2084

s 1–21	Repealed
22	5 Jun 1990 (SI 1990/1145)
23–28	3 Apr 1989 (except in relation to a trial, or proceedings before a magistrates' court acting as examining justices, which began before that date) (SI 1989/264)
29	Repealed
30, 31	3 Apr 1989 (except in relation to a trial, or proceedings before a magistrates' court acting as examining justices, which began before that date) (SI 1989/264)
32(1)(a)	26 Nov 1990 (in relation only to proceedings for murder, manslaughter or any other offence of killing any person; proceedings being conducted

Criminal Justice Act 1988 (c 33)—*cont*

s 32(1)(a)—*cont*	by the Director of the Serious Fraud Office under Criminal Justice Act 1987, s 1(5); and proceedings for serious and complex fraud where there has been given a notice of transfer under s 4 of that Act) (subject to transitional provisions set out in SI 1990/2084, art 3) (SI 1990/2084)
	Not in force (otherwise)
(b)	Substituted by Criminal Justice Act 1991, s 55(2) (qv)
(1A)	Inserted by Criminal Justice Act 1991, s 55(3) (qv)
(2)	5 Jan 1989 (SI 1988/2073)
(3)	26 Nov 1990 (in relation only to proceedings for murder, manslaughter or any other offence of killing any person; proceedings being conducted by the Director of the Serious Fraud Office under Criminal Justice Act 1987, s 1(5); and proceedings for serious and complex fraud where there has been given a notice of transfer under s 4 of that Act) (subject to transitional provisions set out in SI 1990/2084, art 3) (SI 1990/2084)
	Not in force (otherwise)
(3A), (3B)	Inserted by Criminal Justice Act 1991, s 55(4) (qv)
(4), (5)	5 Jan 1989 (SI 1988/2073)
(6)	Added by Criminal Justice Act 1991, s 55(6) (qv)
32A	Inserted by Criminal Justice Act 1991, s 54 (qv)
33	12 Oct 1988 (SI 1988/1676)
33A	Inserted by Criminal Justice Act 1991, s 52(1) (qv)
34	12 Oct 1988 (SI 1988/1676)
34A	Inserted by Criminal Justice Act 1991, s 55(7) (qv)
35, 36	1 Feb 1989 (SI 1989/1)
37–42	12 Oct 1988 (SI 1988/1676)
43	31 Jul 1989 (SI 1989/1085)
44–47	29 Sep 1988 (s 171(6))
48	Repealed
49	12 Oct 1988 (SI 1988/1676)
50	5 Jan 1989 (SI 1988/2073)
51–57	12 Oct 1988 (SI 1988/1676)
58	29 Sep 1988 (s 171(6)); prospectively repealed by Environmental Protection Act 1990, s 162, Sch 16, Pt IX (qv)
59	12 Oct 1988 (SI 1988/1676)
60–62	5 Jan 1989 (SI 1988/2073)
63	Repealed
64	29 Sep 1988 (s 171(6))
65	5 Jun 1990 (SI 1990/1145)
66, 67	29 Jul 1988 (s 171(5))
68	Repealed
69	29 Sep 1988 (s 171(6))
70	12 Oct 1988 (SI 1988/1676)
71, 72	3 Apr 1989 (SI 1989/264)
72A	Prospectively inserted (EW) by Criminal Justice Act 1993, s 28 (qv)
73–93	3 Apr 1989 (SI 1989/264)
93A	Inserted (EWS) by Criminal Justice Act 1993, s 29 (qv)
93B	Inserted (EWS) by Criminal Justice Act 1993, s 30 (qv)

Criminal Justice Act 1988 (c 33)—*cont*

s 93C	Inserted (EWS) by Criminal Justice Act 1993, s 31 (qv)
93D	Prospectively inserted (EWS) by Criminal Justice Act 1993, s 32 (qv)
93E	Inserted (S) by Criminal Justice Act 1993, s 33 (qv)
93F	Prospectively inserted (EWS) by Criminal Justice Act 1993, s 35 (qv)
93G	Prospectively inserted (EWS) by Criminal Justice Act 1993, s 77, Sch 4, paras 1, 3 (qv)
94, 95	3 Apr 1989 (SI 1989/264)
96, 97	12 Oct 1988 (SI 1988/1676)
98	Repealed
99–102	3 Apr 1989 (SI 1989/264)
103	See Sch 5 below
104–107	12 Oct 1988 (SI 1988/1676)
108–117	*Not in force*
118	5 Jan 1989 (SI 1988/2073)
119	15 Feb 1990 (SI 1989/1085)
120	5 Jan 1989 (SI 1988/2073)
121, 122	12 Oct 1988 (SI 1988/1676)
123	1 Oct 1988 (SI 1988/1408)
124	1 Nov 1988 (SI 1988/1817)
125–128	1 Oct 1988 (SI 1988/1408)
129	29 Jul 1988 (s 171(5))
130	5 Jan 1989 (SI 1988/2073)
131	12 Oct 1988 (SI 1988/1676)
132	Repealed
133	12 Oct 1988 (SI 1988/1676)
134, 135	29 Sep 1988 (s 171(6))
136, 137	Repealed
138(1)	29 Sep 1988 (s 171(6))
(2), (3)	Repealed
139, 140	29 Sep 1988 (s 171(6))
141–144	29 Jul 1988 (s 171(5))
145	12 Oct 1988 (SI 1988/1676)
146	See Sch 13 below
147, 148	12 Oct 1988 (SI 1988/1676)
149	Repealed
150	*Not in force*
151(1)–(4)	*Not in force*
(5)	3 Apr 1989 (SI 1989/264)
152–154	5 Jan 1989 (SI 1988/2073)
155–157	12 Oct 1988 (SI 1988/1676)
158	29 Sep 1988 (s 171(6))
159	31 Jul 1989 (SI 1989/1085)
160, 161	29 Sep 1988 (s 171(6))
162	1 Sep 1988 (s 171(7))
163–165	12 Oct 1988 (SI 1988/1676)
166(1)	29 Jul 1988 (s 171(5))
(2), (3)	1 Oct 1986 (retrospective; s 166(4))
(4), (5)	29 Jul 1988 (s 171(5))
167–169	29 Jul 1988 (s 171(5))
170(1)	See Sch 15 below
(2)	See Sch 16 below
171–173	29 Jul 1988 (s 171(5))
Sch 1	Repealed

Criminal Justice Act 1988 (c 33)—*cont*

Sch 2		3 Apr 1989 (except in relation to a trial, or proceedings before a magistrates' court acting as examining justices, which began before that date) (SI 1989/264)
3		1 Feb 1989 (SI 1989/1)
4		3 Apr 1989 (SI 1989/264)
5, Pt I, para 1		29 Jul 1988 (so far as relating to paras 3(2), 13, 15) (s 171(5))
		23 Jan 1989 (so far as relating to paras 2, 3(1), 4–11, 16, 17) (SI 1989/50)
		3 Apr 1989 (otherwise) (SI 1989/264)
	2	23 Jan 1989 (SI 1989/50)
	3(1)	23 Jan 1989 (SI 1989/50)
	(2)	29 Jul 1988 (s 171(5))
	4–11	23 Jan 1989 (SI 1989/50)
	12	3 Apr 1989 (SI 1989/264)
	13	Repealed
	14	3 Apr 1989 (SI 1989/264)
	15	29 Jul 1988 (s 171(5))
	16, 17	23 Jan 1989 (SI 1989/50)
II, para 18–23		23 Jan 1989 (SI 1989/50)
6, 7		*Not in force*
8		1 Oct 1988 (SI 1988/1408)
9		1 Nov 1988 (SI 1988/1817)
10		1 Oct 1988 (SI 1988/1408)
11		Repealed
12		12 Oct 1988 (SI 1988/1676)
13		31 Jul 1989 (SI 1989/1085)
14		Repealed
15, para 1–4		12 Oct 1988 (SI 1988/1676)
	5, 6	3 Apr 1989 (SI 1989/264)
	7	29 Jul 1988 (s 171(5))
	8	12 Oct 1988 (SI 1988/1676)
	9	29 Jul 1988 (s 171(5))
	10	12 Oct 1988 (SI 1988/1676)
	11, 12	1 Oct 1988 (SI 1988/1408)
	13–15	29 Jul 1988 (s 171(5))
	16	*Not in force*
	17	29 Jul 1988 (so far as relating to para 19) (s 171(5))
		12 Oct 1988 (so far as relating to para 18) (SI 1988/1676)
	18	12 Oct 1988 (SI 1988/1676); repealed (S)
	19	29 Jul 1988 (s 171(5))
	20	12 Oct 1988 (so far as relating to paras 21–24, 26–29, 31) (SI 1988/1676)
		31 Jul 1989 (so far as relating to paras 25, 30, 32) (SI 1989/1085)
	21–24	12 Oct 1988 (SI 1988/1676)
	25	31 Jul 1989 (SI 1989/1085)
	26–29	12 Oct 1988 (SI 1988/1676)
	30	31 Jul 1989 (SI 1989/1085)
	31	12 Oct 1988 (SI 1988/1676)
	32	31 Jul 1989 (SI 1989/1085)
	33	12 Oct 1988 (SI 1988/1676)
	34	Repealed
	35	1 Oct 1988 (SI 1988/1408)
	36	29 Jul 1988 (s 171(5))

Criminal Justice Act 1988 (c 33)—*cont*

Sch15, para 37	Repealed
38	1 Oct 1988 (so far as relating to para 38) (SI 1988/1408)
	12 Oct 1988 (so far as relating to paras 39, 41) (SI 1988/1676)
	Not in force (so far as relating to para 40)
39	12 Oct 1988 (SI 1988/1676)
40	*Not in force*
41	12 Oct 1988 (SI 1988/1676)
42	Repealed
43	12 Oct 1988 (SI 1988/1676)
44	31 Jul 1989 (except in relation to any register of electors or any part of any such register required to be used for elections in the twelve months ending on 15 Feb 1990) (SI 1990/1085)
45	29 Jul 1988 (s 171(5))
46	5 Jan 1989 (SI 1988/2073)
47	3 Apr 1989 (SI 1989/264)
48	29 Jul 1988 (s 171(5))
49	12 Oct 1988 (SI 1988/1676)
50, 51	29 Jul 1988 (s 171(5))
52	12 Oct 1988 (SI 1988/1676)
53	29 Sep 1988 (s 171(6))
54, 55	Repealed
56	1 Feb 1989 (SI 1989/1)
57	Repealed
58, 59	12 Oct 1988 (SI 1988/1676)
60–62	29 Sep 1988 (s 171(6))
63	12 Oct 1988 (SI 1988/1676)
64	29 Jul 1988 (s 171(5))
65	29 Jul 1988 (so far as relating to paras 67, 70) (s 171(5))
	29 Sep 1988 (so far as relating to para 66) (s 171(6))
	12 Oct 1988 (otherwise) (SI 1988/1676)
66	29 Sep 1988 (s 171(6))
67	29 Jul 1988 (s 171(5))
68, 69	12 Oct 1988 (SI 1988/1676)
70	29 Jul 1988 (s 171(5))
71	1 Feb 1989 (so far as relating to para 76) (SI 1989/1)
	3 Apr 1989 (so far as relating to paras 72, 74, 75, 77) (SI 1989/264)
	31 Jul 1989 (so far as relating to para 73) (SI 1989/1085)
72	3 Apr 1989 (SI 1989/264)
73	31 Jul 1989 (SI 1989/1085)
74, 75	3 Apr 1989 (SI 1989/264)
76	1 Feb 1989 (SI 1989/1)
77	3 Apr 1989 (SI 1989/264)
78	31 Jul 1989 (SI 1989/1085)
79	31 Jul 1989 (SI 1989/1085); but note already in force 1 Feb 1989 (SI 1989/1)
80	1 Feb 1989 (SI 1989/1)
81	Repealed
82	12 Oct 1988 (SI 1988/1676)
83–88	Repealed
89–91	29 Jul 1988 (s 171(5))
92–96	Repealed

Criminal Justice Act 1988 (c 33)—*cont*

Sch 15, para 97–104   29 Jul 1988 (s 171(5))
             105   Repealed
             106–110   3 Apr 1989 (SI 1989/264)
             111–117   29 Jul 1988 (s 171(5))
             118   12 Oct 1988 (SI 1988/1676)

       16   29 Jul 1988 (repeals of or in Criminal Justice Act 1967, s 49; Children and Young Persons Act 1969, s 29; Criminal Justice Act 1987) (s 171(5))

29 Sep 1988 (repeals of or in Prevention of Corruption Act 1916; Criminal Justice Act 1967, Sch 3; Criminal Justice Act 1972, s 28(3); Sexual Offences (Amendment) Act 1976; Protection of Children Act 1978; Cable and Broadcasting Act 1984; Police and Criminal Evidence Act 1984, s 24(2)(e)) (s 171(6))

1 Oct 1988 (repeals of or in Prison Act 1952; Criminal Justice Act 1961; Firearms Act 1968 (EW only); Children and Young Persons Act 1969, ss 16(10), 22(5), 34(1)(f); Powers of Criminal Courts Act 1973, s 57(3); Criminal Law Act 1977, Sch 12; Reserve Forces Act 1980; Criminal Justice Act 1982, ss 4–7, 12(1)–(5), (8), (9), 14, 20(1), Sch 8, paras 3(c), 7(d); Repatriation of Prisoners Act 1984 (EW only)) (SI 1988/1408)

12 Oct 1988 (repeals of or in Criminal Law Act 1826, s 30; Offences Against the Person Act 1861, ss 42–44; Criminal Justice Act 1925, s 39; Children and Young Persons Act 1933, ss 1(5), (6), 38(1), Sch 1; Children and Young Persons (Scotland) Act 1937, s 12(5), (6); Criminal Appeal Act 1968, ss 10(3)(d), 42; Road Traffic Act 1972, s 100; Criminal Justice Act 1972, Sch 5; Powers of Criminal Courts Act 1973, ss 22(5), 34A(1)(c), Sch 3, paras 2(4)(b), 7, Sch 5, para 29; Juries Act 1974, s 16(2); Criminal Law Act 1977, Sch 5, para 2, Sch 6; Magistrates' Courts Act 1980; Criminal Justice Act 1982, ss 43, 74, 75, 80(1); Video Recordings Act 1984, s 15(2), (4), (5); Police and Criminal Evidence Act 1984, s 65; Cinemas Act 1985, Sch 2, para 11; Local Government Act 1985, s 15(5); Coroners Act 1988, Sch 3, para 14) (SI 1988/1676)

1 Nov 1988 (repeals of or in the Prisons (Scotland) Act 1952; Firearms Act 1968 (S only); Fire Precautions Act 1971, s 40(2)(b); Repatriation of Prisoners Act 1984 (S only)) (SI 1988/1817)

5 Jan 1989 (repeals of or in Offences Against the Person Act 1861, ss 46, 47; Juries Act 1974, s 12(1)(a); Criminal Law Act 1977, s 43; Drug Trafficking Offences Act 1986, s 6(1)(b), (3), (5)) (SI 1988/2073)

23 Jan 1989 (repeals of or in Drug Trafficking Offences Act 1986, ss 10(1), 15(5)(b), (c), 17(1), 38(11)) (SI 1989/50)

3 Apr 1989 (repeals of or in Police and Criminal Evidence Act 1984, s 68, Sch 3, paras 1–7, 13) (except in relation to a trial, or proceedings before

Criminal Justice Act 1988 (c 33)—*cont*

Sch 16—*cont*   a magistrates' court acting as examining justices,
                                  which began before that date) (SI 1989/264)
                                  3 Apr 1989 (repeals of or in Administration of
                                  Justice Act 1970, s 41(8); Insolvency Act 1985,
                                  Sch 8, para 24; Drug Trafficking Offences Act
                                  1986, ss 19, 25) (SI 1989/264)
                                  31 Jul 1989 (repeal in Criminal Appeal Act 1968,
                                  s 7(1)) (SI 1989/1085)
                                  Not in force (otherwise)

Dartford–Thurrock Crossing Act 1988 (c 20)

Local application only

Duchy of Lancaster Act 1988 (c 10)

RA: 3 May 1988

3 May 1988 (RA)

Education Reform Act 1988 (c 40)

RA: 29 Jul 1988

Commencement provisions: s 236; Education Reform Act 1988 (Commencement No
  1) Order 1988, SI 1988/1459; Education Reform Act 1988 (Commencement No
  2) Order 1988, SI 1988/1794; Education Reform Act 1988 (Commencement No
  3) Order 1988, SI 1988/2002; Education Reform Act 1988 (Commencement No
  4) Order 1988, SI 1988/2271 (as amended by SI 1989/501, SI 1990/391);
  Education Reform Act 1988 (Commencement No 5) Order 1989, SI 1989/164;
  Education Reform Act 1988 (Commencement No 6) Order 1989, SI 1989/501
  (also amends SI 1988/2271); Education Reform Act 1988 (Commencement No
  7) Order 1989, SI 1989/719; Education Reform Act 1988 (Commencement No 8
  and Amendment) Order 1990, SI 1990/391 (also amends SI 1988/2271);
  Education Reform Act 1988 (Commencement No 8) Order 1991, SI 1991/409

s 1	29 Jul 1988 (s 236(1))
2(1)(a)	29 Sep 1988 (s 236(3))
(aa), (ab)	Prospectively inserted by Education Act 1993, s 241(1) (qv)
(b)	29 Jul 1988 (s 236(1))
(2)	29 Jul 1988 (s 236(1))
(3)	29 Sep 1988 (s 236(3))
3, 4	29 Jul 1988 (s 236(1))
5	1 Aug 1989 (SI 1989/164)
6	29 Sep 1988 (s 236(3))
7	1 Aug 1989 (except in relation to ILEA schools) (SI 1988/2271)
	1 Aug 1990 (exception noted above) (SI 1988/2271)
8, 9	29 Sep 1988 (s 236(3))
10(1)	29 Sep 1988 (s 236(3))
(2)	1 Aug 1989 (SI 1989/164)

Education Reform Act 1988 (c 40)—*cont*

s 10(3)	1 Aug 1989 (in relation to pupils at schools in England in the first, second and third key stage who do not have a statement of special education needs) (SI 1989/164)
	1 Aug 1989 (so far as regards the core subjects, in relation to pupils at schools in Wales in the first, second and third key stage who do not have a statement of special educational needs) (SI 1989/501)
	1 Aug 1990 (in relation to pupils at schools in England in the first, second and third key stage who have a statement of special educational needs and, so far as regards the core subjects, in relation to pupils at such schools in the first year of the fourth key stage) (SI 1989/164)
	1 Aug 1990 (so far as regards the core subjects and other foundation subjects, in relation to pupils at schools in Wales in the first, second and third key stage (and who, in the former case, have a statement of special educational needs); and, so far as regards the core subjects in relation to pupils at schools in Wales in the first year of the fourth key stage) (SI 1989/501)
	1 Aug 1991 (so far as regards the core subjects, in relation to pupils at schools in England in the second year of the fourth key stage) (SI 1989/164)
	1 Aug 1991 (so far as regards the core subjects, in relation to pupils at schools in Wales in the second year of the fourth key stage) (SI 1989/501)
11	29 Sep 1988 (s 236(3))
12	1 Mar 1989 (except in relation to ILEA county schools) (SI 1989/164)
	1 Apr 1990 (exception noted above) (SI 1989/164)
12A	Prospectively inserted by Education Act 1993, s 257 (qv)
13	29 Sep 1988 (s 236(3))
14, 15	29 Jul 1988 (s 236(1))
16	1 Aug 1989 (SI 1989/164)
17	1 Nov 1988 (SI 1988/1794)
17A	Prospectively inserted by Education Act 1993, s 241(3) (qv)
18, 19	1 Nov 1988 (SI 1988/1794)
20–22	29 Jul 1988 (s 236(1))
23(1)	29 Jul 1988 (s 236(1))
(2)	1 Sep 1989 (except in relation to ILEA schools) (SI 1989/164)
	1 Apr 1990 (exception noted above) (SI 1989/164)
24	31 Mar 1990 (SI 1990/391)
25	29 Jul 1988 (s 236(1))
26	1 Sep 1989 (for the purpose of enabling proposals to be made under s 26(4)–(6) for fixing the number of pupils in any age group which it is intended to admit to a secondary school in school year beginning next after 4 Aug 1990, and for purposes of s 26(7), (8), (10)) (SI 1988/1459)
	4 Aug 1990 (remaining purposes so far as relate to secondary schools) (SI 1988/1459)

Education Reform Act 1988 (c 40)—*cont*

s 26	1 Sep 1991 (for the purpose of enabling proposals to be made under s 26(4)–(6) for fixing the number of pupils in any age group which it is intended to admit to a primary school in the school year beginning next after 1 Aug 1992, and for the purposes of s 26(7), (8), (10)) (SI 1991/409)
	1 Aug 1992 (for remaining purposes so far as relate to primary schools) (SI 1991/409)
27(1)–(3)	1 Sep 1988 (so far as relate to secondary schools) (SI 1988/1459)
	12 Mar 1991 (so far as relate to primary schools and subject, in the case of s 27(2), to transitional provisions) (SI 1991/409)
(4)–(8)	1 Sep 1988 (for purpose of enabling orders reducing any standard number applying to a secondary school to be made under s 27(5) and applications for such orders to be made as mentioned in s 27(6)) (SI 1988/1459)
	1 Sep 1989 (for purpose of enabling orders increasing any standard number applying to a secondary school to be made under s 27(5) and applications for such orders to be made as mentioned in s 27(7)) (SI 1988/1459)
	4 Aug 1990 (remaining purposes, so far as relate to secondary schools) (SI 1988/1459)
	1 May 1991 (for purpose of enabling orders reducing any standard number applying to a primary school to be made under s 27(5) and applications for such orders to be made as mentioned under s 27(6)) (SI 1991/409)
	1 Sep 1991 (for purpose of enabling orders increasing any standard numbers applying to a primary school to be made under s 27(5) and applications for such orders to be made as mentioned in s 27(7)) (SI 1991/409)
	12 Mar 1991 (for remaining purposes, so far as relate to primary schools) (SI 1991/409)
(9)	1 Sep 1988 (so far as relates to secondary schools) (SI 1988/1459)
	12 Mar 1991 (so far as relates to primary schools) (SI 1991/409)
28	1 Sep 1988 (so far as relates to secondary schools) (SI 1988/1459)
	12 Mar 1991 (so far as relates to primary schools) (SI 1991/409)
29	1 May 1991 (SI 1991/409)
30	1 Sep 1988 (SI 1988/1459)
31(1)	4 Aug 1990 (so far as relates to secondary schools) (SI 1988/1459)
	1 Aug 1992 (so far as relates to primary schools) (SI 1991/409)
(2)	1 Sep 1989 (so far as relates to the publication of admission arrangements for secondary schools for the school year beginning next after 4 Aug 1990 and subsequent school years) (SI 1988/1459)
	1 Sep 1991 (so far as relates to publication of admission arrangements for primary schools for

Education Reform Act 1988 (c 40)—*cont*

s 31(2)—*cont*	the school year beginning next after 1 Aug 1992 and subsequent school years) (SI 1991/409)
(3)	1 Aug 1991 (SI 1991/409)
(4)–(6)	1 May 1991 (SI 1991/409)
32	1 Sep 1988 (so far as relates to secondary schools) (SI 1988/1459)
	12 Mar 1991 (so far as relates to primary schools) (SI 1991/409)
33, 34	29 Jul 1988 (s 236(1))
35	Substituted by Education Act 1993, s 274(1) (qv)
36–42	29 Jul 1988 (s 236(1))
42A	Inserted by Education Act 1993, s 275(2) (qv)
43	Substituted by Education Act 1993, s 276 (qv)
44–51	29 Jul 1988 (s 236(1))
52	29 Jul 1988 (s 236(1)); repealed, in part (sub-ss (1), (2)) prospectively by Education Act 1993, s 307(3), Sch 21, Pt I (qv)
53–56	Repealed
57	29 Jul 1988 (s 236(1)); prospectively repealed by Education Act 1993, s 307(3), Sch 21, Pt I (qv)
58–72	Repealed
73	29 Jul 1988 (s 236(1)); prospectively repealed by Education Act 1993, s 307(3), Sch 21, Pt I (qv)
74–78	Repealed
79–99	29 Jul 1988 (s 236(1)); prospectively repealed by Education Act 1993, s 307(3), Sch 21, Pt I (qv)
100	29 Jul 1988 (s 236(1))
101	29 Jul 1988 (s 236(1)); prospectively repealed by Education Act 1993, s 307(3), Sch 21, Pt I (qv)
102, 103	Repealed
104	29 Jul 1988 (s 236(1)); repealed, in part (sub-ss (1)(c)–(e), (i), (j), (3) in part, (4)–(6)) prospectively by Education Act 1993, s 307(3), Sch 21, Pt I (qv)
105	29 Jul 1988 (s 236(1))
106–111	1 Apr 1989 (SI 1988/1794)
112, 113	29 Jul 1988 (s 236(1))
114	30 Nov 1988 (SI 1988/2002)
115	1 May 1989 (SI 1989/164)
116	29 Jul 1988 (s 236(1))
117, 118	1 Apr 1989 (SI 1988/1794)
119	29 Jul 1988 (s 236(1))
120	1 Apr 1989 (SI 1988/2271)
121	21 Nov 1988 (except Southampton Institute of Higher Education) (SI 1988/1794)
	1 Feb 1989 (exception noted above) (SI 1988/2271)
122	21 Nov 1988 (SI 1988/1794)
122A	Inserted by Further and Higher Education Act 1992, s 74(1) (qv)
123, 124	21 Nov 1988 (SI 1988/1794)
124A–124D	Inserted by Further and Higher Education Act 1992, s 71(1) (qv)
125–129	21 Nov 1988 (SI 1988/1794)
129A, 129B	Inserted by Further and Higher Education Act 1992, s 73(1) (qv)
130	21 Nov 1988 (SI 1988/1794)
131, 132	Repealed

Education Reform Act 1988 (c 40)—*cont*

s 133	1 Nov 1988 (SI 1988/1794)
134	Repealed
135	21 Nov 1988 (SI 1988/1794)
136	1 Nov 1988 (SI 1988/1794)
137, 138	29 Jul 1988 (s 236(1))
139–155	Repealed
156	29 Jul 1988 (s 236(1)); repealed in relation to designated institutions by Further and Higher Education Act 1992, ss 73(2), 85(1), 93(2), Sch 9 (qv)
157–199	29 Jul 1988 (s 236(1))
200	Repealed
201–208	29 Jul 1988 (s 236(1))
209	31 Mar 1990 (SI 1990/391)
210, 211	1 May 1989 (SI 1989/719)
212, 213	29 Jul 1988 (s 236(1))
214–216	30 Nov 1988 (SI 1988/2002)
217	29 Jul 1988 (s 236(1))
218	1 Apr 1989 (SI 1988/2002)
219(1)	1 Jan 1989 (SI 1988/2271)
(2)(a)	1 Jan 1989 (SI 1988/2271)
(b)	29 Jul 1988 (s 236(1))
(c), (d)	1 Jan 1989 (SI 1988/2271)
(e)	21 Nov 1988 (SI 1988/1794)
(3)(a)	1 Jan 1989 (SI 1988/2271)
(b)	29 Jul 1988 (s 236(1))
(c)	1 Jan 1989 (SI 1989/2271)
220	1 Nov 1988 (SI 1988/1794)
221–225	29 Jul 1988 (s 236(1))
226	21 Nov 1988 (SI 1988/1794)
227(1)	29 Jul 1988 (s 236(1))
(2)–(4)	Repealed
228, 229	21 Nov 1988 (SI 1988/1794)
230–236	29 Jul 1988 (s 236(1))
237(1)	See Sch 12 below
(2)	See Sch 13 below
238	29 Jul 1988 (s 236(1))
Sch 1	29 Sep 1988 (s 236(3))
2–4	29 Jul 1988 (s 236(1))
5	Repealed
6	29 Jul 1988 (s 236(1))
7	21 Nov 1988 (SI 1988/1794)
7A	Inserted by Further and Higher Education Act 1992, s 71(4), Sch 6 (qv)
8	29 Jul 1988 (so far as relating to the Education Assets Board) (s 236(1))
	1 Nov 1988 (otherwise) (SI 1988/1794)
(8	Repealed, in relation to Universities Funding Council and Polytechnics and Colleges Funding Council, by Further and Higher Education Act 1992, s 93(1), Sch 8, Pt I, paras 27, 60 (qv))
9–11	29 Jul 1988 (s 236(1))
12, para 1–8	29 Jul 1988 (s 236(1))
9, 10	Repealed
11	29 Jul 1988 (s 236(1))
12	Repealed

Education Reform Act 1988 (c 40)—*cont*

Sch 12, para 13–25	29 Jul 1988 (s 236(1))
26–28	29 Jul 1988 (s 236(1)); prospectively repealed by Education Act 1993, s 307(1), (3), Sch 19, para 145, Sch 21, Pt I (qv)
29–32	29 Jul 1988 (s 236(1))
33	29 Jul 1988 (s 236(1)); prospectively repealed by Education Act 1993, s 307(1), (3), Sch 19, para 145, Pt I (qv)
34–37	9 Jul 1988 (s 236(1))
38–40	Repealed
41–46	1 Apr 1990 (s 236(4))
47–49	Repealed
50–53	1 Apr 1990 (s 236(4))
54–57	1 Apr 1989 (SI 1988/2271)
58	1 Mar 1989 (SI 1989/164)
59	1 Apr 1989 (SI 1988/2271)
60	29 Jul 1988 (s 236(1))
61, 62	1 Apr 1989 (SI 1988/2271)
63, 64	Repealed
65, 66	1 Apr 1989 (SI 1988/2271)
67	29 Jul 1988 (s 236(1)) (NB also brought into force on 1 Jan 1989 by SI 1988/2271)
68	Repealed
69	1 Apr 1989 (SI 1988/2271)
70	Repealed
71–76	1 Apr 1989 (SI 1988/2271)
77	*Not in force* (by virtue of amendment made to SI 1988/2271) (SI 1989/501)
78, 79	1 Apr 1989 (SI 1988/2271)
80	21 Nov 1988 (SI 1988/1794)
81, 82	29 Jul 1988 (s 236(1))
83–85	1 Nov 1988 (SI 1988/1794); prospectively repealed by Education Act 1993, s 307(1), (3), Sch 19, para 145, Sch 21, Pt I (qv)
86–98	1 Apr 1989 (SI 1988/2271)
99	1 Aug 1989 (SI 1988/2271)
100, 101	1 Apr 1989 (SI 1988/2271)
102	29 Jul 1988 (s 236(1))
103–105	1 Apr 1989 (SI 1988/2271)
106	31 Mar 1990 (SI 1990/391)
107	1 Apr 1989 (SI 1988/2271)
13, Pt I	1 Apr 1990 (s 236(5))
II	30 Nov 1988 (repeals of Education Act 1967, s 3; Education Act 1980, Sch 3, para 14) (SI 1988/2002)
	1 Jan 1989 (repeals of Education Act 1944, ss 25, 29(2)–(4); Education Act 1946, s 7; Education (No 2) Act 1968 (subject to transitional provisions)) (SI 1988/2271)
	1 Apr 1989 (repeal of Education Act 1944, s 61) (SI 1988/1794)
	1 Apr 1989 (repeals of Education Act 1980, s 27; Education Act 1981, Sch 3, para 5) (SI 1988/2002)
	1 Apr 1989 (repeals of or in Education Act 1944, ss 8(1)(b), 42–46, 50, 52(1), 54, 60, 62(2), 69, 84, 114; Education Act 1946, s 8(3); London Government Act 1963, s 31(1), (4); Industrial

Education Reform Act 1988 (c 40)—*cont*

Sch 13, Pt II—*cont*	Training Act 1964, s 16; Local Government Act 1972, ss 81(4)(a), 104(2); Sex Discrimination Act 1975, ss 24(2)(a), 25(6)(c)(ii); Race Relations Act 1976, ss 19(6)(c)(ii), 78(1); Education (No 2) Act 1986, s 56) (SI 1988/2271)
	1 Aug 1989 (repeals of or in Education (No 2) Act 1986, ss 17(1), (4), 18(3), (4), (6), (8), 19(3), 20) (SI 1988/2271)
	1 May 1989 (repeals of or in Education Act 1946, s 1(1); Employment Protection (Consolidation) Act 1978, s 29(1)(e); Education Act 1980, s 35(5), Sch 1, para 25; Local Government, Planning and Land Act 1980, Sch 10, Pt I; Local Government Act 1985, s 22; Education (No 2) Act 1986, ss 29, 47(5)(a)(ii), Sch 4, para 4; Local Government Act 1987, s 2) (SI 1989/719)
	31 Mar 1990 (repeals in Local Government Act 1974) (SI 1990/391)
	Not in force (otherwise)

Electricity (Financial Provisions) (Scotland) Act 1988 (c 37)

Whole Act repealed

Employment Act 1988 (c 19)

RA: 26 May 1988

Commencement provisions: s 34(2); Employment Act 1988 (Commencement No 1) Order 1988, SI 1988/1118; Employment Act 1988 (Commencement No 2) Order 1988, SI 1988/2042

s 1–24	Repealed
25, 26	26 May 1988 (RA)
27	Repealed
28, 29	26 May 1988 (RA)
30	Repealed
31, 32	26 May 1988 (RA)
33(1)	See Sch 3 below
(2)	See Sch 4 below
34	26 May 1988 (RA)
Sch 1	Repealed
2	26 May 1988 (RA)
3, Pt I	Repealed
II	26 May 1988 (RA) (mostly repealed)
4	26 May 1988 (repeals of or in Parliamentary Commissioner Act 1967, Sch 2; Employment and Training Act 1973, ss 4(2), 5(1), (4), 11(3), 12(4); Social Security Act 1975, s 20(1); House of Commons Disqualification Act 1975, Sch 1, Pt III; Northern Ireland Assembly Disqualification Act 1975, Sch 1, Pt III; Employment Protection Act 1975, Sch 14, para 2(1); Social Security (Miscellaneous Provisions) Act 1977, s 22(6); Social Security (No 2) Act 1980, s 7(7)) (RA)

Employment Act 1988 (c 19)—*cont*

Sch 4—*cont*	26 Jul 1988 (repeals of or in Trade Union Act 1913, s 4(1F); Trade Union (Amalgamations, etc) Act 1964, s 4(6), Sch 1; Employment Protection (Consolidation) Act 1978, ss 23(1), 58(1), 58A, 153(1); Employment Act 1980, s 15(2); Employment Act 1982, s 10(1), (2), Sch 3, para 16; Trade Union Act 1984, ss 3, 6(6), 9(1)) (SI 1988/1118) 26 Jul 1989 (repeals of or in Trade Union Act 1984, ss 1(1)–(3), 8(1)) (SI 1988/1118) *Not in force* (repeal of Employment Protection (Consolidation) Act 1978, s 58(3)–(12))

Environment and Safety Information Act 1988 (c 30)

RA: 29 Jul 1988

Commencement provisions: s 5(2)

1 Apr 1989 (s 5(2))

European Communities (Finance) Act 1988 (c 46)

RA: 15 Nov 1988

15 Nov 1988 (RA)

Farm Land and Rural Development Act 1988 (c 16)

RA: 10 May 1988

10 May 1988 (RA)

Finance Act 1988 (c 39)

RA: 29 Jul 1988

See the note concerning Finance Acts at the front of this book

Firearms (Amendment) Act 1988 (c 45)

RA: 15 Nov 1988

Commencement provisions: s 27(3); Firearms (Amendment) Act 1988 (Commencement No 1) Order 1988, SI 1988/2209; Firearms (Amendment) Act 1988 (Commencement No 2) Order 1989, SI 1989/853 (amended by SI 1989/1673); Firearms (Amendment) Act 1988 (Commencement No 3) Order 1990, SI 1990/2620

s 1	1 Feb 1989 (subject to transitional provisions) (SI 1988/2209)

Firearms (Amendment) Act 1988 (c 45)—*cont*

s 2(1), (2)	1 Jul 1989 (subject to transitional provisions) (SI 1989/853)
(3)	1 Jul 1989 (SI 1989/853)
3(1)	1 Jul 1989 (SI 1989/853)
(2)	1 Jul 1989 (subject to transitional provisions) (SI 1989/853)
4(1)	1 Jul 1989 (SI 1989/853)
(2)(a)	1 Jul 1989 (SI 1989/853)
(b)	1 Jul 1989 (subject to transitional provisions) (SI 1989/853)
(3)	1 Jul 1989 (subject to transitional provisions) (SI 1989/853)
(4), (5)	1 Jul 1989 (SI 1989/853)
5, 6	1 Jul 1990 (SI 1989/853)
7(1)	1 Feb 1989 (subject to transitional provisions) (SI 1988/2209)
(2)	1 Jul 1989 (subject to transitional provisions) (SI 1989/853)
(3)	1 Jul 1989 (SI 1989/853)
8–10	1 Feb 1988 (SI 1988/2209)
11	1 Jul 1989 (SI 1989/853)
12	1 Feb 1989 (SI 1989/2209)
13(1)	1 Jul 1989 (SI 1989/853)
(2)–(5)	1 Feb 1989 (SI 1988/2209)
14	1 Feb 1989 (SI 1988/2209)
15	1 Jul 1989 (SI 1989/853)
16	1 Feb 1989 (SI 1988/2209)
17, 18	1 Oct 1989 (SI 1989/853)
18A	Inserted by Firearms Acts (Amendment) Regulations 1992, SI 1992/2823, reg 9
19	See Schedule below
20(1), (2)	1 Jul 1989 (for purpose of enabling the Secretary of State to make an order under the Firearms Act 1968, s 6(1A), which is to come into force on the date on which this section comes into force for all other purposes) (SI 1989/853 as amended by Firearms (Amendment) Act 1988 (Commencement No 2) Order (Amendment) Order 1989, SI 1989/1673, art 3)
	2 Apr 1991 (otherwise) (SI 1990/2620)
(3)	2 Apr 1991 (SI 1990/2620)
21, 22	1 Feb 1989 (SI 1988/2209)
23(1)–(3)	1 Feb 1989 (SI 1988/2209)
(4)–(6)	1 Jul 1989 (SI 1989/853)
(7)	1 Feb 1989 (SI 1988/2209)
(8)	1 Oct 1989 (except in relation to a person who is in Great Britain on 1 Oct 1989) (SI 1989/853)
	31 Oct 1989 (exception noted above) (SI 1989/853)
24(1)	1 Feb 1989 (SI 1988/2209)
(2)	1 Jul 1989 (SI 1989/853)
25	1 Feb 1989 (SI 1988/2209)
26, 27	15 Nov 1988 (s 27(3))
Schedule	1 Jul 1989 (SI 1989/853)

Foreign Marriage (Amendment) Act 1988 (c 44)

RA: 2 Nov 1988

Commencement provisions: s 7(3); Foreign Marriage (Amendment) Act 1988 (Commencement) Order 1990, SI 1990/522

12 Apr 1990 (SI 1990/522)

Health and Medicines Act 1988 (c 49)

RA: 15 Nov 1988

Commencement provisions: ss 19(2), 26(1)–(5); Health and Medicines Act 1988 (Commencement No 1) Order 1988, SI 1988/2107; Health and Medicines Act 1988 (Commencement No 2) Order 1989, SI 1989/111; Health and Medicines Act 1988 (Commencement No 3) Order 1989, SI 1989/337; Health and Medicines Act 1988 (Commencement No 4) Order 1989, SI 1989/826 ; Health and Medicines Act 1988 (Commencement No 5) Order 1989, SI 1989/1174 (revoked); Health and Medicines Act 1988 (Commencement No 6) Order 1989, SI 1989/1229 (revoking SI 1989/1174); Health and Medicine Act 1988 (Commencement No 7) Order 1989, SI 1989/1896; Health and Medicines Act 1988 (Commencement No 8) Order 1989, SI 1989/1984

s 1–6	15 Nov 1988 (s 26(3), (4))
7	15 Jan 1989 (s 26(1)–(5))
8(1)(a)	15 Oct 1989 (except words 'or section 19 of the National Health Service (Scotland) Act 1978') (SI 1989/1896)
	31 Oct 1989 (exception noted above) (SI 1989/1984)
(b)	9 Jun 1989 (SI 1989/826)
(2)	9 Jun 1989 (except words '(a) or') (SI 1989/826)
	15 Oct 1989 (words '(a) or' except so far as they have effect for the purposes of any list maintained under National Health Service (Scotland) Act 1978, s 19) (SI 1989/1896)
	31 Oct 1989 (exception noted above) (SI 1989/1984)
(3)–(7)	9 Jun 1989 (SI 1989/826)
9	1 Apr 1990 (SI 1989/826)
10	15 Jan 1989 (s 26(1)–(5))
11(1)	7 Mar 1989 (SI 1989/337)
(2)	1 Apr 1989 (SI 1989/337)
(3)	7 Mar 1989 (for purposes of regulations as to charges authorised by National Health Service Act 1977, s 78(1A)) (SI 1989/337)
	1 Apr 1989 (otherwise) (SI 1989/337)
(4)	7 Mar 1989 (SI 1989/337)
(5)	1 Apr 1989 (SI 1989/337)
(6)	7 Mar 1989 (for purposes of regulations as to charges authorised by National Health Service (Scotland) Act 1978, s 70(1A)) (SI 1989/337)
	1 Apr 1989 (otherwise) (SI 1989/337)
(7)	1 Jan 1989 (SI 1989/2107)
(8)	1 Apr 1989 (SI 1989/337)
12	1 Apr 1989 (SI 1989/337)

Health and Medicines Act 1988 (c 49)—*cont*

s 13(1)	7 Mar 1989 (for purposes of adding National Health Service Act 1977, s 38(2)–(6) and of adding s 38(7) thereof up to the words 'are to be made' thereto) (SI 1989/337)
	1 Apr 1989 (otherwise) (SI 1989/337)
(2)	7 Mar 1989 (for purposes of any regulations made to come into force on or after 1 Apr 1989) (SI 1989/337)
	1 Apr 1989 (otherwise) (SI 1989/337)
(3)	7 Mar 1989 (SI 1989/337)
(4)	7 Mar 1989 (for purposes of adding National Health Service (Scotland) Act 1978, s 26(1A)–(1E) and of adding s 26(1F) thereof up to the words 'are to be made' thereto) (SI 1989/337)
	1 Apr 1989 (otherwise) (SI 1989/337)
(5)	7 Mar 1989 (SI 1989/337)
(6), (7)	Repealed
14	Repealed
15, 16	15 Jan 1989 (s 26(1)–(5))
17(1), (2)	15 Jan 1989 (s 26(1)–(5))
(3)	15 Nov 1988 (s 26(3), (4))
18	15 Jan 1989 (s 26(1)–(5))
19	26 Nov 1987 (retrospective; s 192))
20	15 Jan 1989 (s 26(1)–(5))
21, 22	15 Nov 1988 (s 26(3), (4))
23, 24	15 Jan 1989 (s 26(1)–(5))
25(1)	See Sch 2 below
(2)	See Sch 3 below
26–28	15 Nov 1988 (s 26(3), (4))
Sch 1	15 Nov 1988 (s 26(3), (4))
2, para 1	15 Jan 1989 (so far as relates to paras 2, 6, 7) (s 26(1)–(5))
	7 Mar 1989 (so far as relates to para 8(1), (2)) (SI 1989/337)
	1 Apr 1989 (so far as relates to paras 5, 8(3)) (SI 1989/337)
	9 Jun 1989 (so far as relates to para 4) (SI 1989/826)
	15 Oct 1989 (so far as relates to para 3) (SI 1989/1896)
2	15 Jan 1989 (s 26(1)–(5))
3	15 Oct 1989 (SI 1989/1896)
4	9 Jun 1989 (SI 1989/826)
5	1 Apr 1989 (SI 1989/337)
6, 7	15 Jan 1989 (s 26(1)–(5))
8(1)	7 Mar 1989 (for purposes of any regulations made to come into force on or after 1 Apr 1989) (SI 1989/337)
	1 Apr 1989 (otherwise) (SI 1989/337)
(2)	7 Mar 1989 (SI 1989/337)
(3)	1 Apr 1989 (SI 1989/337)
9	15 Jan 1989 (so far as relates to paras 13, 14) (s 26(1)–(5)
	7 Mar 1989 (so far as relates to para 15(1), (2)) (SI 1989/337)
	1 Apr 1989 (so far as it relates to paras 12, 15(3)) (SI 1989/337)

Health and Medicines Act 1988 (c 49)—*cont*

Sch 2, para 9—*cont*		9 Jun 1989 (so far as relates to para 11) (SI 1989/826)
		31 Oct 1989 (so far as relates to para 10) (SI 1989/1984)
	10	31 Oct 1989 (SI 1989/1984)
	11	Repealed
	12	1 Apr 1989 (SI 1989/337)
	13, 14	15 Jan 1989 (s 26(1)–(5))
	15(1)	7 Mar 1989 (for purposes of any regulations made to come into force on or after 1 Apr 1989) (SI 1989/337)
		1 Apr 1989 (otherwise) (SI 1989/337)
	(2)	7 Mar 1989 (SI 1989/337)
	(3)	1 Apr 1989 (SI 1989/337)
3		15 Nov 1988 (repeal of National Health Service Act 1977, s 28(4)) (s 26(3), (4))
		1 Jan 1989 (repeals of or in National Health Service Act 1977, s 79(1)(d) and word 'or' preceding it; National Health Service (Scotland) Act 1978, s 71(1)(d) and word 'or' preceding it) (SI 1989/2107)
		15 Jan 1989 (repeals of or in Health Services and Public Health Act 1968, s 63(3); National Health Service Act 1977, ss 5(1)(a), 58, 61, 62, 63(2), 66A; National Health Service (Scotland) Act 1978, ss 39, 50, 53, 54, 55(2), 58A; Health Services Act 1980, ss 10, 11) (s 26(1)–(5))
		27 Feb 1989 (repeals of or in National Health Service Act 1966; Superannuation Act 1972; Health Services Act 1980, ss 17, 19; Health and Social Security Act 1984, s 8; Companies Consolidation (Consequential Provisions) Act 1985) (SI 1989/111)
		1 Apr 1989 (otherwise) (SI 1989/337)

Housing Act 1988 (c 50)

RA: 15 Nov 1988

Commencement provisions: ss 132(8), 141(2), (3); Housing Act 1988 (Commencement No 1) Order 1988, SI 1988/2056; Housing Act 1988 (Commencement No 2) Order 1988, SI 1988/2152; Housing Act 1988 (Commencement No 3) Order 1989, SI 1989/203; Housing Act 1988 (Commencement No 4) Order 1989, SI 1989/404; Housing Act 1988 (Commencement No 5 and Transitional Provisions) Order 1991, SI 1991/954; Housing Act 1988 (Commencement No 6) Order 1992, SI 1992/324

s 1–14	15 Jan 1989 (s 141(3))
14A, 14B	Inserted by Local Government Finance (Housing) (Consequential Amendments) Order 1993, SI 1993/651, art 2(2), Sch 2, para 8
15–41	15 Jan 1989 (s 141(3))
41A	Inserted by Social Security (Consequential Provisions) Act 1992, s 4, Sch 2, para 103 (qv)
41B	Inserted by Local Government Finance (Housing) (Consequential Amendments) Order 1993, SI 1993/651, art 2(1), Sch 1, para 18 (as substituted

Housing Act 1988 (c 50)—*cont*

s 41B—*cont*	by Local Government Finance (Housing) (Consequential Amendments) (Amendment) Order 1993, SI 1993/1120, art 2)
42–45	15 Jan 1989 (s 141(3))
46(1)	1 Dec 1988 (SI 1988/2056)
(2)	See Sch 5 below
(3)–(5)	1 Apr 1989 (SI 1989/404)
47(1)	1 Apr 1989 (SI 1989/404)
(2)	1 Dec 1988 (SI 1988/2056)
(3)–(5)	1 Apr 1989 (SI 1989/404)
(6)	1 Dec 1988 (so far as relates to s 47(2)) (SI 1988/ 2056)
	1 Apr 1989 (otherwise) (SI 1989/404)
48	1 Apr 1989 (SI 1989/404)
49	15 Jan 1989 (SI 1988/2152)
50–56	1 Apr 1989 (SI 1989/404)
57	15 Jan 1989 (SI 1988/2152)
58	1 Apr 1989 (SI 1989/404)
59(1)	15 Jan 1989 (SI 1988/2152)
(2), (3)	See Sch 6 below
(4)	1 Apr 1989 (SI 1989/404)
60–84	15 Nov 1988 (RA)
84A	Inserted by Leasehold Reform, Housing and Urban Development Act 1993, s 125(5) (qv)
93	5 Apr 1989 (SI 1989/404)
94	15 Jan 1989 (SI 1988/2152)
95–105	5 Apr 1989 (SI 1989/404)
106	15 Jan 1989 (SI 1988/2152)
107	5 Apr 1989 (SI 1989/404)
108	See Sch 12 below
109–110	5 Apr 1989 (SI 1989/404)
111–114	15 Jan 1989 (SI 1988/2152)
115–118	15 Jan 1989 (s 141(3))
119	See Sch 13 below
120, 121	15 Jan 1989 (s 141(3))
122	10 Mar 1989 (SI 1989/203)
123	15 Jan 1989 (s 141(3))
124	10 Mar 1989 (SI 1989/203)
125, 126	15 Jan 1989 (s 141(3))
127	5 Apr 1989 (SI 1989/404)
128	21 Feb 1992 (SI 1992/324)
129	1 Apr 1989 (SI 1989/404)
130	15 Jan 1989 (s 141(3))
131	15 Jan 1989 (s 141(3)); prospectively repealed by Local Government and Housing Act 1989, s 194, Sch 12, Pt II (qv)
132	9 Jun 1988 (retrospective; s 132(8))
133, 134	15 Nov 1988 (RA; s 141(2), (3))
135(1)	21 Feb 1992 (SI 1992/324)
(2)	See Sch 16 below
(3)	21 Feb 1992 (SI 1992/324)
136	Repealed
137	15 Jan 1989 (s 141(3))
138, 139	15 Nov 1988 (RA; s 141(2), (3))
140(1)	See Sch 17 below
(2)	See Sch 18 below
141	15 Nov 1988 (RA; s 141(2), (3))

Housing Act 1988 (c 50)—*cont*

Sch 1–4		15 Jan 1989 (s 141(3))
5		1 Dec 1988 (SI 1988/2056)
6, para 1		15 Jan 1989 (for the purposes only of s 59(1) of the Act and Housing Associations Act 1985, s 36A) (SI 1988/2152)
		1 Apr 1989 (otherwise) (SI 1989/404)
	2–7	1 Apr 1989 (SI 1989/404)
	8(1)	1 Apr 1989 (SI 1989/404)
	(2)	15 Jan 1989 (SI 1988/2152)
	9–24	1 Apr 1989 (SI 1989/404)
	25	15 Jan 1989 (SI 1988/2152)
	26(a)	15 Jan 1989 (SI 1988/2152)
	(b), (c)	1 Apr 1989 (SI 1989/404)
	27	*Not in force*
	28	1 Apr 1989 (SI 1989/404)
	29	1 Apr 1989 (except for purposes of hostel deficit grant payable under Housing Associations Act 1985, s 55) (SI 1989/404)
	30–37	1 Apr 1989 (SI 1989/404)
7–11		15 Nov 1988 (RA)
12		5 Apr 1989 (SI 1989/404)
13		15 Jan 1989 (subject to transitional provisions) (SI 1988/2152)
14, 15		15 Jan 1989 (s 141(3))
16		21 Feb 1992 (SI 1992/324)
17, para 1–16		15 Jan 1989 (SI 1988/2152)
	17(1)	5 Apr 1989 (SI 1989/404)
	(2)	15 Jan 1989 (SI 1988/2152)
	18	Repealed
	19–37	15 Jan 1989 (subject to transitional provision for para 21) (SI 1988/2152)
	38, 39	5 Apr 1989 (SI 1989/404)
	40	15 Jan 1989 (SI 1988/2152)
	41	10 Mar 1989 (SI 1989/203)
	42–65	15 Jan 1989 (SI 1988/2152)
	66	1 Apr 1989 (SI 1989/404)
	67–76	15 Jan 1989 (SI 1988/2152)
	77, 78	2 Jan 1989 (SI 1988/2152)
	79	*Not in force*
	80–84	15 Jan 1989 (SI 1988/2152)
	85–88	2 Jan 1989 (SI 1988/2152)
	89	1 Apr 1989 (SI 1989/404)
	90	2 Jan 1989 (SI 1988/2152)
	91, 92	1 Dec 1988 (SI 1988/2056)
	93	Repealed (retrospectively to 1 Dec 1988)
	94–96	1 Dec 1988 (SI 1988/2056)
	97	1 Apr 1989 (SI 1989/404)
	98–102	1 Dec 1988 (SI 1988/2056)
	103	1 Apr 1989 (SI 1989/404)
	104, 105	1 Dec 1988 (SI 1988/2056)
	106–113	1 Apr 1989 (SI 1989/404)
	114–116	1 Dec 1988 (SI 1988/2056)
18		2 Jan 1989 (repeal in Housing (Scotland) Act 1988, s 38) (SI 1988/2152)
		15 Jan 1989 (repeals of or in Reserve and Auxiliary Forces (Protection of Civil Interests) Act 1951; Rent (Agriculture) Act 1976; Rent Act 1977;

Housing Act 1988 (c 50)—*cont*

Sch 18—*cont*	Protection from Eviction Act 1977; Housing Act 1980; Local Government Act 1985; Housing Act 1985; Housing and Planning Act 1986, ss 7, 12, 13, Sch 4; Landlord and Tenant Act 1987, ss 3, 4, 60; Housing (Scotland) Act 1988, Sch 9, para 6) (subject to transitional provisions) (SI 1988/2152)
	1 Apr 1989 (repeals of or in Housing Associations Act 1985, except s 55 and ss 56, 57 in relation to hostel deficit grants; Housing and Planning Act 1986 (so far as not yet in force); Housing (Scotland) Act 1986; Landlord and Tenant Act 1987 (so far as not yet in force); Local Government Act 1988; Housing (Scotland) Act 1988 (so far as not yet in force)) (SI 1989/404)
	1 Apr 1991 (repeals of or in Housing Associations Act 1985, ss 55–57, except in relation to hostel deficit grant payable to an association for a period which expires before 1 Apr 1991) (SI 1991/954)
	Not in force (otherwise)

Housing (Scotland) Act 1988 (c 43)

RA: 2 Nov 1988

Commencement provisions: s 74(2); Housing (Scotland) Act 1988 Commencement Order 1988, SI 1988/2038

s 1(1)	1 Dec 1988 (SI 1988/2038)
(2)	See Sch 1 below
(3)	1 Dec 1988 (SI 1988/2038)
2	1 Dec 1988 (SI 1988/2038)
3(1)	1 Dec 1988 (SI 1988/2038)
(2)	1 Apr 1989 (SI 1988/2038)
(3)	See Sch 2 below
(4)	1 Dec 1988 (SI 1988/2038)
4(1)–(3)	1 Dec 1988 (SI 1988/2038)
(4)	Repealed
(5)–(7)	1 Dec 1988 (SI 1988/2038)
5–11	1 Dec 1988 (SI 1988/2038)
12(1)	2 Jan 1989 (SI 1988/2038)
(2)	See Sch 4 below
13–24	2 Jan 1989 (SI 1988/2038)
25A, 25B	Inserted by Local Government Finance (Housing) (Consequential Amendments) (Scotland) Order 1993, SI 1993/658, art 2, Sch 2, para 5
36–40	2 Jan 1989 (s 74(2)(b))
41–45	2 Jan 1989 (SI 1988/2038)
46(1), (2)	2 Jan 1989 (SI 1988/2038)
(3), (4)	See Sch 6 below
47, 48	2 Jan 1989 (SI 1988/2038)
48A	Inserted by Social Security (Consequential Provisions) Act 1992, s 4, Sch 2, para 102 (qv)
49–55	2 Jan 1989 (SI 1988/2038)
56–64	1 Apr 1989 (SI 1988/2038)
65	2 Jan 1989 (s 74(2)(b))
66	2 Jan 1989 (SI 1988/2038)

Housing (Scotland) Act 1988 (c 43)—*cont*

s 67	2 Jan 1989 (s 74(2)(b))
68	2 Jan 1989 (SI 1988/2038)
69	2 Nov 1988 (s 74(2)(a))
70	2 Jan 1989 (SI 1988/2038)
71	2 Jan 1989 (s 74(2)(b))
72(1)	See Schs 7, 8 below
(2)	See Sch 9 below
(3)	See Sch 10 below
73	1 Dec 1988 (SI 1988/2038)
74	2 Nov 1988 (s 74(2)(a))
Sch 1	1 Dec 1988 (SI 1988/2038)
2, para 1, 2	1 Apr 1989 (SI 1988/2038)
3(a)	1 Dec 1988 (SI 1988/2038)
(b)	1 Apr 1989 (SI 1988/2038)
4–17	1 Apr 1989 (SI 1988/2038)
3	Repealed
4–6	2 Jan 1989 (SI 1988/2038)
7	2 Nov 1988 (s 74(2)(a))
8	2 Jan 1989 (s 74(2)(b))
9, para 1–6	2 Jan 1989 (SI 1988/2038)
7	Repealed
8–16	2 Jan 1989 (SI 1988/2038)
17	1 Apr 1989 (SI 1988/2038)
18–21	2 Apr 1989 (SI 1988/2038)
10	2 Jan 1989 (repeals of or in Housing (Scotland) Act 1987, ss 62(11)–(13), 151) (s 74(2)(b))
	1 Apr 1989 (repeal of Housing (Scotland) Act 1987, Sch 16, para 1(b)) (s 74(2)(c))
	2 Jan 1989 (repeals of or in Rent (Scotland) Act 1984, ss 66(1), 68, 70(2), 71(1)) (SI 1988/2038)
	1 Apr 1989 (otherwise) (SI 1988/2038)

Immigration Act 1988 (c 14)

RA: 10 May 1988

Commencement provisions: s 12(3), (4); Immigration Act 1988 (Commencement No 1) Order 1988, SI 1988/1133; Immigration Act 1988 (Commencement No 2) Order 1991, SI 1991/1001

s 1–5	1 Aug 1988 (subject to exceptions in relation to ss 1, 2, 4) (SI 1988/1133)
6	10 Jul 1988 (s 12(3))
7(1)	*Not in force*
(2), (3)	10 Jul 1988 (s 12(3))
8–12	10 Jul 1988 (s 12(3))
Schedule, para 1	1 May 1991 (SI 1991/1001)
2–10	10 Jul 1988 (s 12(3))

Income and Corporation Taxes Act 1988 (c 1)

RA: 9 Feb 1988

Commencement provisions: as provided for by s 843. Note also ss 96, 380–384, 393, 394, 400; s 470(3) (spent); Income and Corporation Taxes Act 1988 (Appointed Day) Order 1988, SI 1988/745; s 703; s 729(12); Income and Corporation Taxes Act 1988 (Appointed Day No 2) Order 1988, SI 1988/1002; s 812

Appointed day for the purposes of s 470(3) 29 Apr 1988 (SI 1988/745)
Appointed day for the purposes of s 729(12) 9 Jun 1988 (SI 1988/1002)

Landlord and Tenant Act 1988 (c 26)

RA: 29 Jul 1988

Commencement provisions: s 7(2)

29 Sep 1988 (s 7(2))

Land Registration Act 1988 (c 3)

RA: 15 Mar 1988

Commencement provisions: s 3(2); Land Registration Act 1988 (Commencement) Order 1990, SI 1990/1359

3 Dec 1990 (SI 1990/1359)

Legal Aid Act 1988 (c 34)

RA: 29 Jul 1988

Commencement provisions: s 47; Legal Aid Act 1988 (Commencement No 1) Order 1988, SI 1988/1361; Legal Aid Act 1988 (Commencement No 2) (Scotland) Order 1988, SI 1988/1388; Legal Aid Act 1988 (Commencement No 3) Order 1989, SI 1989/288; Legal Aid Act 1988 (Commencement No 4) Order 1991, SI 1991/790

s 1, 2	1 Apr 1989 (SI 1989/288)
3(1)	20 Aug 1988 (SI 1988/1361)
(2)–(4)	1 Apr 1989 (SI 1989/288)
(5)–(10)	20 Aug 1988 (SI 1988/1361)
4–26	1 Apr 1989 (SI 1989/288)
27, 28	Repealed
29	1 May 1991 (SI 1991/790)
30(1), (2)	Repealed
(3)	1 May 1991 (SI 1991/790)
31–34	1 Apr 1989 (SI 1989/288)
35	29 Jul 1988 (s 47(4))
36–43	1 Apr 1989 (SI 1989/288)
44	See Sch 4 below
45(1)	See Sch 5 below
(2)	See Sch 6 below
(3)	See Schs 5, 6 below
(4)	See Sch 7 below

Legal Aid Act 1988 (c 34)—*cont*
s 46	29 Jul 1988 (s 47(4))
47	29 Jul 1988 (RA)
Sch 1	20 Aug 1988 (SI 1988/1361)
2, 3	1 Apr 1989 (SI 1989/288)
4, para 1, 2	29 Jul 1988 (SI 1988/1388)
3	*Not in force*
4	29 Jul 1988 (SI 1988/1388)
5	*Not in force*
6–9	29 Jul 1988 (SI 1988/1388)
5	1 Apr 1989 (SI 1989/288)
6	29 Jul 1988 (repeal of Legal Aid Act 1974, s 21) (s 47(4))
	1 Apr 1989 (otherwise) (SI 1989/288)
7, para 1–5	1 Apr 1989 (SI 1989/288)
6–8	20 Aug 1988 (SI 1988/1361)
9–11	1 Apr 1989 (SI 1989/288)
8	29 Jul 1988 (s 47(4))

Licensing Act 1988 (c 17)

RA: 19 May 1988

Commencement provisions: s 20(3); Licensing Act 1988 (Commencement No 1) Order 1988, SI 1988/1187; Licensing Act 1988 (Commencement No 2) Order 1988, SI 1988/1333

s 1	22 Aug 1988 (SI 1988/1333)
2	1 Aug 1988 (SI 1988/1187)
3	22 Aug 1988 (SI 1988/1333)
4	1 Aug 1988 (SI 1988/1187)
5	22 Aug 1988 (SI 1988/1333)
6–8	1 Aug 1988 (SI 1988/1187)
9	22 Aug 1988 (SI 1988/1333)
10	1 Aug 1988 (SI 1988/1187)
11	22 Aug 1988 (SI 1988/1333)
12	1 Mar 1989 (SI 1988/1333)
13, 14	22 Aug 1988 (SI 1988/1333)
15	1 Mar 1989 (SI 1988/1333)
16–18	1 Aug 1988 (SI 1988/1187)
19(1)	See Sch 3 below
(2)	See Sch 4 below
20	1 Aug 1988 (SI 1988/1187)
Sch 1, 2	22 Aug 1988 (SI 1988/1333)
3, para 1	22 Aug 1988 (SI 1988/1333)
2	1 Aug 1988 (SI 1988/1187)
3–6	1 Mar 1989 (SI 1988/1333)
7	22 Aug 1988 (SI 1988/1333)
8(a)	22 Aug 1988 (SI 1988/1333)
(b)	1 Aug 1988 (SI 1988/1187)
9	22 Aug 1988 (SI 1988/1333)
10	1 Aug 1988 (SI 1988/1187)
11–14	22 Aug 1988 (SI 1988/1333)
15(a)	22 Aug 1988 (SI 1988/1333)
(b)	1 Mar 1989 (SI 1988/1333)

Licensing Act 1988 (c 17)—*cont*

Sch 3, para 16–18	1 Aug 1988 (SI 1988/1187)
19	22 Aug 1988 (SI 1988/1333)
4	1 Aug 1988 (repeals of or in Licensing Act 1964, ss 9(5), 71(3), 72(2), 73(1), 92(4), 169) (SI 1988/1187)
	22 Aug 1988 (repeals of or in Licensing Act 1964, ss 2(3)(b), 6(4), 7, 60, 62(2), 80(2), 95, 151(5), Sch 2, para 9; Finance Act 1967; Criminal Law Act 1977; Magistrates' Courts Act 1980; Licensing (Restaurant Meals) Act 1987) (SI 1988/1333)

Licensing (Retail Sales) Act 1988 (c 25)

RA: 29 Jul 1988

Commencement provisions: s 4(2); Licensing (Retail Sales) Act 1988 (Commencement) Order 1988, SI 1988/1670

1 Nov 1988 (SI 1988/1670)

Local Government Act 1988 (c 9)

RA: 24 Mar 1988

Commencement provisions: passim; Local Government Act 1988 (Commencement No 1) Order 1988, SI 1988/979; Local Government Act 1988 (Commencement No 2) (Scotland) Order 1988, SI 1988/1043

s 1–3	24 Mar 1988 (RA)
4	24 Mar 1988 (RA; but applies only where it is proposed to enter into the works contract on or after 1 Apr 1989: s 4(7))
5–8	24 Mar 1988 (RA) (in relation to s 6, see s 6(3))
9–11	24 Mar 1988 (RA; apply in relation to work carried out in or after financial year beginning in 1989: ss 9(1), 10(1), 11(1))
12–16	24 Mar 1988 (RA)
17–22	7 Apr 1988 (s 23)
23–26	24 Mar 1988 (RA)
27–30	24 May 1988 (ss 27(3), 28(2), 29(2), 30(3))
31	See Sch 5 below
32	24 May 1988 (RA); but see Sch 6 below
33	11 Feb 1988 (s 33(4))
34	The day any authority or body concerned was established (s 34(2))
35	24 May 1988 (s 35(5))
36	Repealed
37	24 Mar 1988 (RA))
38	24 May 1988 (s 38(4))
39	24 May 1988 (s 39(6))
40	24 Mar 1988 (RA)
41	24 Mar 1988 (RA); but see Sch 7 below
42	24 Mar 1988 (RA)
Sch 1	24 Mar 1988 (RA)

Local Government Act 1988 (c 9)—*cont*

Sch 2	7 Apr 1988 (s 23)
3	24 May 1988 (s 29(2))
4	24 May 1988 (s 30(3))
5, para 1	24 May 1988 (s 31(2))
2	*Not in force*
3–6	24 May 1988 (s 31(2))
6, para 1–3	24 Jun 1988 (SI 1988/979; SI 1988/1043)
4	1 Oct 1988 (SI 1988/979; SI 1988/1043)
5–7	24 Jun 1988 (SI 1988/979; SI 1988/1043)
8(1)	24 Mar 1988 (s 32(3))
(2)	24 Jun 1988 (SI 1988/979; SI 1988/1043)
(3)	24 Mar 1988 (s 32(3))
(4)	24 Jun 1988 (SI 1988/979; SI 1988/1043)
9	24 Jun 1988 (SI 1988/979; SI 1988/1043)
10(1)	24 Jun 1988 (SI 1988/979; SI 1988/1043)
(2)	1 Oct 1988 (SI 1988/979; SI 1988/1043)
(3), (4)	24 Jun 1988 (SI 1988/979; SI 1988/1043)
(5)	Repealed
(6)	24 Jun 1988 (so far as inserts Local Government, Planning and Land Act 1980, s 20(5)) (SI 1988/ 979; SI 1988/1043)
	1 Oct 1988 (so far as inserts Local Government, Planning and Land Act 1980, s 20(6)) (SI 1988/ 979; SI 1988/1043)
(7)	24 Jun 1988 (SI 1988/979; SI 1988/1043)
11	24 Mar 1988 (s 32(3))
7, Pt I	7 Apr 1988 (s 23)
II	24 May 1988 (s 29(2))
III	24 Jun 1988 or 1 Oct 1988 (dependent on relationship to s 32 and Sch 6 noted above) (SI 1988/979; SI 1988/1043)
IV	29 May 1988 (Sch 7, Pt IV)

Local Government Finance Act 1988 (c 41)

RA: 29 Jul 1988

Commencement provisions: ss 111(5), 131(8), 132(6), 143(1), (2), 150, Schs 12, 13; Local Government Finance Act 1988 (Commencement) (Scotland) Order 1988, SI 1988/1456 (partially revoked by SI 1990/573); Local Government Finance Act 1988 Commencement (Scotland) Amendment Order 1990, SI 1990/573 (partially revokes SI 1988/1456)

s 1–35, 35A–35C, 36–40	Repealed
41–44	29 Jul 1988 (RA)
44A	Inserted by Local Government and Housing Act 1989, s 139, Sch 5, para 22 (qv)
45, 46	29 Jul 1988 (RA)
46A	Inserted by Local Government and Housing Act 1989, s 139, Sch 5, para 25 (qv)
47–56	29 Jul 1988 (RA)
57	Substituted by Local Government and Housing Act 1989, s 139, Sch 5, para 31 (qv)
58	29 Jul 1988 (RA)
59	Substituted by Local Government and Housing Act 1989, s 139, Sch 5, para 32 (qv)

Local Government Finance Act 1988 (c 41)—*cont*

s 60–67	29 Jul 1988 (RA)
68–73	Repealed
74	29 Jul 1988 (RA)
74A	Repealed
75	29 Jul 1988 (RA)
75A	Repealed
76	29 Jul 1988 (RA)
77	Repealed (see Local Government and Housing Act 1989, Sch 5, paras 57(1), 79(3))
78	29 Jul 1988 (RA)
78A	Inserted by Local Government Finance Act 1992, s 104, Sch 10, Pt II, para 10 (qv)
79	29 Jul 1988 (RA)
80, 81	Repealed
82	29 Jul 1988 (RA)
82A	Inserted by Local Government Finance Act 1992, s 104, Sch 10, Pt II, para 13 (qv)
83	29 Jul 1988 (RA)
84	Repealed
84A–84C	Inserted by Local Government Finance Act 1992, s 104, Sch 10, Pt II, para 15 (qv)
85–88	29 Jul 1988 (RA)
88A, 88B	Substituted for s 88A (as inserted by Local Government and Housing Act 1989, s 139, Sch 5, para 61), by Local Government Finance Act 1992, s 104, Sch 10, Pt II, para 18 (qv)
89	29 Jul 1988 (RA)
90	Substituted by Local Government Finance Act 1992, s 104, Sch 10, Pt III, para 20 (qv)
91–94	29 Jul 1988 (RA)
95, 96	Repealed
97	Substituted by Local Government Finance Act 1992, s 104, Sch 10, Pt III, para 22 (qv)
98	29 Jul 1988 (RA)
99	Substituted by Local Government Finance Act 1992, s 104, Sch 10, Pt III, para 24 (qv)
100–110	Repealed
111–116	29 Sep 1988 (s 111(5))
117, 118	29 Jul 1988 (RA)
119	29 Jul 1988 (RA); prospectively repealed by Local Government and Housing Act 1989, s 194, Sch 12, Pt II (qv)
120–126	29 Jul 1988 (RA)
127	29 Jul 1988 (RA) (subject to prescribed savings made under s 127(2); section forbids levies under London Regional Transport Act 1984, s 13, after 31 Mar 1990)
128	22 Aug 1988 (SI 1988/1456)
129–134	Repealed
135–139	29 Jul 1988 (RA)
139A	Inserted by Local Government and Housing Act 1989, s 139, Sch 5, para 68 (qv)
140, 141	29 Jul 1988 (RA)
141A, 141B	Repealed
142–145	29 Jul 1988 (RA)
145A	Repealed
146–149	29 Jul 1988 (RA)

Local Government Finance Act 1988 (c 41)—*cont*

s 150	22 Aug 1988 (SI 1988/1456)
151, 152	29 Jul 1988 (RA)
Sch 1–4	Repealed
4A	Inserted by Local Government and Housing Act 1989, s 139, Sch 5, para 36 (qv)
5–7	29 Jul 1988 (RA)
7A	Inserted by Local Government and Housing Act 1989, s 139, Sch 5, para 40 (qv)
8–11	29 Jul 1988 (RA)
12, Pt I, para 1	31 Mar 1990 (as regards qualifying dates after that date) (Sch 12, Pt I, para 1(2))
2	31 Mar 1990 (as regards any time after that date) (Sch 12, Pt I, para 2(2))
3(1)	29 Jul 1988 (RA)
(2)	1 Apr 1990 (Sch 12, Pt I, para 3(5))
(3)	29 Jul 1988 (RA)
(4)	1 Apr 1990 (Sch 12, Pt I, para 3(5))
(5)	29 Jul 1988 (RA)
II, para 4	22 Aug 1988 (SI 1988/1456)
5	Repealed
6	22 Aug 1988 (SI 1988/1456)
7	1 Apr 1990 (SI 1988/1456)
8	22 Aug 1988 (SI 1988/1456); prospectively repealed by Local Government Finance Act 1992, s 117(2), Sch 14 (qv)
9	22 Aug 1988 (SI 1988/1456)
10	Repealed
11, 12	1 Apr 1990 (SI 1988/1456)
13	Repealed
14	22 Aug 1988 (SI 1988/1456)
15	15 Sep 1988 (SI 1988/1456); prospectively repealed by Local Government Finance Act 1992, s 117(2), Sch 14 (qv)
16	Repealed
17	22 Aug 1988 (SI 1988/1456); prospectively repealed by Local Government Finance Act 1992, s 117(2), Sch 14 (qv)
18–21	22 Aug 1988 (only for the purposes of and in relation to the community charge and the community water charge in respect of the financial year 1989–90 and each subsequent financial year) (SI 1988/1456) 1 Apr 1989 (otherwise) (SI 1988/1456)
(18–21	Prospectively repealed by Local Government Finance Act 1992, s 117(2), Sch 14 (qv))
22–26	22 Aug 1988 (SI 1988/1456); prospectively repealed by Local Government Finance Act 1992, s 117(2), Sch 14 (qv)
27	1 Oct 1988 (SI 1988/1456); prospectively repealed by Local Government Finance Act 1992, s 117(2), Sch 14 (qv)
28	22 Aug 1988 (SI 1988/1456); prospectively repealed by Local Government Finance Act 1992, s 117(2), Sch 14 (qv)

Local Government Finance Act 1988 (c 41)—*cont*

Sch 12, Pt II, para 29, 30		1 Oct 1988 (SI 1988/1456); prospectively repealed by Local Government Finance Act 1992, s 117(2), Sch 14 (qv)
	31–34	22 Aug 1988 (SI 1988/1456); prospectively repealed by Local Government Finance Act 1992, s 117(2), Sch 14 (qv)
	35	22 Aug 1988 (only for the purposes of and in relation to the personal community charge and the personal community water charge in respect of the financial year 1989–90 and each subsequent financial year) (SI 1988/1456)
		1 Apr 1989 (otherwise) (SI 1988/1456)
	(35	Prospectively repealed by Local Government Finance Act 1992, s 117(2), Sch 14 (qv))
	36	22 Aug 1988 (SI 1988/1456); prospectively repealed by Local Government Finance Act 1992, s 117(2), Sch 14 (qv)
	37	Repealed
	38	22 Aug 1988 (SI 1988/1456); prospectively repealed by Local Government Finance Act 1992, s 117(2), Sch 14 (qv)
III, para 39		1 Apr 1989 (S); 1 Apr 1990 (EW) (Sch 12, Pt III, para 39(2), (3))
	40	29 Jul 1988 (RA)
	41	Repealed
	42	1 Apr 1989 (S); 1 Apr 1990 (EW) (Sch 12, Pt III, para 42(2), (3))
12A		Repealed
13, Pt I		1 Apr 1990 (subject to any saving under s 117(8)) (Sch 13, Pt I)
II		1 Apr 1990 (Sch 13, Pt II)
III		(See s 127 above)
IV		22 Aug 1988 (repeals of or in Abolition of Domestic Rates Etc (Scotland) Act 1987, ss 4(1), 11(11), 17(5), 30(2), Sch 2) (SI 1988/1456)
		15 Sep 1988 (repeals in s 2 of 1987 Act) (SI 1988/1456)
		1 Oct 1988 (repeals in s 20 of 1987 Act) (SI 1988/1456)
		1 Apr 1989 (repeal in Acquisition of Land (Authorisation Procedure) (Scotland) Act 1947, s 5) (SI 1988/1456)
		1 Apr 1990 (otherwise, except repeal in Abolition of Domestic Rates Act (Scotland) Act 1987, s 24) (SI 1988/1456, as amended by SI 1990/573)
		Not in force (exception noted above)

Malicious Communications Act 1988 (c 27)

RA: 29 Jul 1988

Commencement provisions: s 3(2)

s 1	29 Sep 1988 (s 3(2))
2, 3	29 Jul 1988 (RA)

Matrimonial Proceedings (Transfers) Act 1988 (c 18)

RA: 19 May 1988

19 May 1988 (RA)

Merchant Shipping Act 1988 (c 12)

RA: 3 May 1988

Commencement provisions: s 58(2), (3); Merchant Shipping Act 1988
(Commencement No 1) Order 1988, SI 1988/1010; Merchant Shipping Act 1988
(Commencement No 2) Order 1988, SI 1988/1907; Merchant Shipping
(Registration of Fishing Vessels) Regulations 1988, SI 1988/1926; Merchant
Shipping Act 1988 (Commencement No 3) Order 1989, SI 1989/353

s 1–10	Repealed
11	4 Jul 1988 (SI 1988/1010)
12–25	Repealed
26–30	4 Jul 1988 (SI 1988/1010)
30A	Inserted by Merchant Shipping (Registration, etc) Act 1993, s 8(3), Sch 4, para 12(2) as from 1 May 1994 (qv)
31–33	4 Jul 1988 (SI 1988/1010)
34	*Not in force*; repealed by Merchant Shipping (Registration, etc) Act 1993, s 8(4), Sch 5, Pt II as from 1 May 1994 (qv)
35–47	4 Jul 1988 (SI 1988/1010)
48	See Sch 5 below
49	4 Jul 1988 (SI 1988/1010)
50, 51	4 Jul 1988 (SI 1988/1010); repealed by Merchant Shipping (Registration, etc) Act 1993, s 8(4), Sch 5, Pt II as from 1 May 1994 (qv)
52	1 Apr 1989 (SI 1989/353)
53	4 Jul 1988 (SI 1988/1010)
54	1 Dec 1988 (so far as relates to notices under Pt II) (SI 1988/1907)
	1 Apr 1989 (otherwise) (SI 1989/353); repealed by Merchant Shipping (Registration, etc) Act 1993, s 8(4), Sch 5, Pt II as from 1 May 1994 (qv)
55	4 Jul 1988 (SI 1988/1010)
56	4 Jul 1988 (SI 1988/1010)); repealed by Merchant Shipping (Registration, etc) Act 1993, s 8(4), Sch 5, Pt II as from 1 May 1994 (qv)
57(1)–(3)	4 Jul 1988 (SI 1988/1010)
(4)	See Sch 6 below
(5)	See Sch 7 below
58(1)–(3)	4 Jul 1988 (SI 1988/1010)
(4)	See Sch 8 below
(5)	4 Jul 1988 (SI 1988/1010)
Sch 1	Repealed (except para 48)
	1 Apr 1989 (SI 1989/353) (exception noted above)
2, 3	Repealed
4	*Not in force*; repealed by Merchant Shipping (Registration, etc) Act 1993, s 8(4), Sch 5, Pt II as from 1 May 1994 (qv)

Merchant Shipping Act 1988 (c 12)—*cont*

Sch 5   4 Jul 1988 (except entry for Merchant Shipping 1906; para 7 of entry for Merchant Shipping Act 1970) (SI 1988/1010)

1 Apr 1989 (entry for Merchant Shipping Act 1906) (SI 1989/353)

Not in force (otherwise)

6   4 Jul 1988 (entries relating to Merchant Shipping Act 1894; Merchant Shipping (Amendment) Act 1920; Merchant Shipping Act 1965; paras 1–4, 5(a) of entry for Merchant Shipping Act 1970; Merchant Shipping Act 1979; Supreme Court Act 1981; para 2 of entry for Merchant Shipping Act 1983; Merchant Shipping Act 1984) (SI 1988/1010)

1 Dec 1988 (entries relating to Sea Fisheries Act 1868; Contracts of Employment and Redundancy Payments Act (Northern Ireland) 1965; Sea Fish (Conservation) Act 1967; Sea Fisheries Act 1968; Fishing Vessels (Safety Provisions) Act 1970; para 5(b) of entry for Merchant Shipping Act 1970; Fishery Limits Act 1976; Employment Protection (Consolidation) Act 1978; Customs and Excise Management Act 1979; British Fishing Boats Act 1983; para 1(b) of entry for Merchant Shipping Act 1983; Inshore Fishing (Scotland) Act 1984; Safety at Sea Act 1986) (SI 1988/1907)

1 Apr 1989 (entries relating to Merchant Shipping Act 1906; Merchant Shipping Act 1965 (already in force as from 4 Jul 1988 (SI 1988/1010); Merchant Shipping Act 1983 (already mostly in force under previous orders)) (SI 1989/353)

7   4 Jul 1988 (repeals of or in Merchant Shipping Act 1894, ss 463, 648(1), 652(4), 663, 676(1), para (i), 677, para (i), 731, 744; Merchant Shipping Act 1897; Merchant Shipping (Mercantile Marine Fund) Act 1898; Merchant Shipping Act 1906, ss 2(1), 83; Merchant Shipping Act 1950; National Loans Act 1968; Merchant Shipping Act 1970 (except entries for ss 73, 75(1)(c), 89, 95(1)); Trade Union and Labour Relations Act 1974; Merchant Shipping Act 1979 (except entries for ss 31, 38, Sch 6, Pt I, Sch 6, Pt II (entry relating to s 44(11) of 1894 Act), Sch 6, Pt VI); Merchant Shipping Act 1983 (except entries relating to ss 5, 6)) (SI 1988/1010)

1 Dec 1988 (repeals of or in Sea Fishing Boats (Scotland) Act 1886; Merchant Shipping Act 1894, ss 370, 372–374; Sea Fisheries Act 1968, Sch 1, paras 23, 32, 33; Fishery Limits Act 1976, s 2(8)(b), Sch 2, para 3; British Fishing Boats Act 1983, s 11(2); Inshore Fishing (Scotland) Act 1984, Sch 1 (entry relating to 1894 Act)) (SI 1988/1907)

1 Apr 1989 (repeals of or in Merchant Shipping Act 1894, ss 1–3, 4(2), 6, 7(1), (2), 9(iii), 11, 13, 19, 23, 26, 27(1)(b), (2), 32, 33, 38(1), (2), 39–46, 47(4), (5), 48(1), 54, 55, 56, 57, 61(1), 62, 63(1), (2), 64(2)(a), (d), 65(1)–(4), 71, 73(1)–(3), 76(1),

Merchant Shipping Act 1988 (c 12)—*cont*

Sch 7—*cont*	85, 88–91, 695(2)(a), Sch 1, Pts I, II; Merchant Shipping Act 1906, ss 51, 52; Fees (Increase) Act 1923, s 2(1); Merchant Shipping Act 1965, s 19(2)(c), Sch 1; Merchant Shipping Act 1979, s 31, Sch 6, Pt I (entry relating to s 374(4) of 1894 Act), Pt II (entry relating to s 44(11) of 1894 Act), Pt VI; Merchant Shipping Act 1983, ss 5(5), 6) (SI 1989/353)
	Not in force (otherwise)
8, para 1	4 Jul 1988 (SI 1988/1010)
2	1 Apr 1989 (SI 1989/353)
3	4 Jul 1988 (SI 1988/1010)
4	1 Dec 1988 (SI 1988/1807)
5	1 Apr 1989 (SI 1989/353)

Motor Vehicles (Wearing of Rear Seat Belts by Children) Act 1988 (c 23)

RA: 28 Jun 1988

Commencement provisions: s 3(2)

s 1	Repealed
2, 3	28 Jun 1988 (RA)

Multilateral Investment Guarantee Agency Act 1988 (c 8)

RA: 24 Mar 1988

Commencement provisions: s 9(2); Multilateral Investment Guarantee Agency Act 1988 (Commencement) Order 1988, SI 1988/715

12 Apr 1988 (SI 1988/715)

Norfolk and Suffolk Broads Act 1988 (c 4)

Local application only

Protection Against Cruel Tethering Act 1988 (c 31)

RA: 29 Jul 1988

Commencement provisions: s 2(2)

29 Sep 1988 (s 2(2))

Protection of Animals (Amendment) Act 1988 (c 29)

RA: 29 Jul 1988

Commencement provisions: s 3(4)

29 Sep 1988 (s 3(4))

Public Utility Transfers and Water Charges Act 1988 (c 15)

RA: 10 May 1988

Commencement provisions: s 8(2); Public Utility Transfers and Water Charges Act 1988 (Commencement No 1) Order 1988, SI 1988/879; Public Utility Transfers and Water Charges Act 1988 (Commencement No 2) Order 1988, SI 1988/1165

s 1	10 May 1988 (RA); prospectively repealed by Water Act 1989, s 190(3), Sch 27, Pt II (qv)
2–7	Repealed (for savings see Water Act 1989, s 190(2), Sch 26, Pt I, para 16(5)–(7), Pt VIII, para 54(3))
8(1)	10 May 1988 (RA); prospectively repealed by Water Act 1989, s 190(3), Sch 27, Pt II (qv)
(2)	Repealed (for savings see Water Act 1989, s 190(2), Sch 26, Pt I, para 16(5)–(7), Pt VIII, para 54(3))
(3)	10 May 1988 (RA); prospectively repealed by Water Act 1989, s 190(3), Sch 27, Pt II (qv)
Sch 1–3	Repealed (for savings see Water Act 1989, s 190(2), Sch 26, Pt I, para 16(5)–(7), Pt VIII, para 54(3))

Rate Support Grants Act 1988 (c 51)

RA: 15 Nov 1988

15 Nov 1988 (RA)

Regional Development Grants (Termination) Act 1988 (c 11)

RA: 3 May 1988

3 May 1988 (RA)

Road Traffic Act 1988 (c 52)

RA: 15 Nov 1988

Commencement provisions: s 197(2)

15 May 1989 (subject to transitory provisions in Road Traffic (Consequential Provisions) Act 1988, Sch 5 (qv) (s 197(2))

Road Traffic (Consequential Provisions) Act 1988 (c 54)

RA: 15 Nov 1988

Commencement provisions: s 8(2), (3)

Appointed day orders: Road Traffic Act 1988 (Appointed Day for Section 15) Order 1989, SI 1989/1086; Road Traffic Act 1988 (Appointed Day for Section 15) (No 2) Order 1989, SI 1989/1260

s 1–3	15 May 1989 (s 8(2), (3))
4	See Schs 2, 3 below

Road Traffic (Consequential Provisions) Act 1988 (c 54)—*cont*

s 5	15 May 1989 (s 8(2), (3))
6	Repealed
7, 8	15 May 1989 (s 8(2), (3))
Sch 1	15 May 1989 (s 8(2), (3))
2, para 1	Repealed
2–7	15 May 1989 (s 8(2), (3))
8, 9	Repealed
10–14	15 May 1989 (s 8(2), (3))
15–20	*Not in force*
21–23	Repealed
24–39	*Not in force*
3, 4	15 May 1989 (s 8(2), (3))
5	Repealed

Road Traffic Offenders Act 1988 (c 53)

RA: 15 Nov 1988

Commencement provisions: s 99(2)–(5)

s 1–19	15 May 1989 (s 99(2)–(5))
20	Substituted by Road Traffic Act 1991, s 23 (qv)
21–23	15 May 1989 (s 99(2)–(5))
24	Substituted by Road Traffic Act 1991, s 24 (qv)
25	15 May 1989 (s 99(2)–(5))
26	Substituted by Road Traffic Act 1991, s 25 (qv)
27(1)	15 May 1989 (s 99(2)–(5))
(2)	Repealed
(3)	15 May 1989 (s 99(2)–(5))
(4)	15 May 1989 (EW) (s 99(2)–(5))
	Not in force (S)
28	Substituted by Road Traffic Act 1991, s 27 (qv)
29	Substituted by Road Traffic Act 1991, s 28 (qv)
30	15 May 1989 (EW) (s 99(2)–(5))
	15 May 1989 (so far as relates to ss 75–77) (S) (s 99(2)–(5))
	Not in force (otherwise) (S)
31–34	15 May 1989 (s 99(2)–(5))
34A–34C	Inserted by Road Traffic Act 1991, s 30 (qv)
35	15 May 1989 (s 99(2)–(5))
36	Substituted by Road Traffic Act 1991, s 32 (qv)
37–41	15 May 1989 (s 99(2)–(5))
41A	Inserted by Road Traffic Act 1991, s 48, Sch 4, para 97 (qv)
42–47	15 May 1989 (s 99(2)–(5))
48	Substituted by Road Traffic Act 1991, s 48, Sch 4, para 101 (qv)
49–51	15 May 1989 (s 99(2)–(5))
52(1)–(3)	15 May 1989 (s 99(2)–(5))
(4)	15 May 1989 (EW) (s 99(2)–(5))
	Not in force (S)
53	Substituted by Road Traffic Act 1991, s 48, Sch 4, para 102 (qv)
54–58	15 May 1989 (EW) (s 99(2)–(5))
	Not in force (S)

Road Traffic Offenders Act 1988 (c 53)—*cont*

s 59	*Not in force*
60	Repealed
61	15 May 1989 (s 99(2)–(5)); *not in force* (S)
62–74	15 May 1989 (s 99(2)–(5))
75–77	Substituted by Road Traffic Act 1991, s 34 (qv)
78	15 May 1989 (s 99(2)–(5))
79	15 May 1989 (EW) (s 99(2)–(5))
	Not in force (S)
80, 81	15 May 1989 (s 99(2)–(5))
82	15 May 1989 (EW) (s 99(2)–(5))
	Not in force (S)
83–99	15 May 1989 (s 99(2)–(5))
Sch 1–5	15 May 1989 (s 99(2)–(5))

School Boards (Scotland) Act 1988 (c 47)

RA: 15 Nov 1988

Commencement provisions: s 24(2); School Boards (Scotland) Act 1988
(Commencement) Order 1989, SI 1989/272

s 1–23	1 Apr 1989 (SI 1989/272)
24	15 Nov 1988 (RA)
Sch 1–3	1 Apr 1989 (SI 1989/272)
4, para 1–5	1 Nov 1989 (SI 1989/272)
6	1 Apr 1989 (SI 1989/272)
7	1 Nov 1989 (SI 1989/272)

Scotch Whisky Act 1988 (c 22)

RA: 28 Jun 1988

Commencement provisions: s 5(2); Scotch Whisky Act 1988 (Commencement and
Transitional Provisions) Order 1990, SI 1990/997

s 1–3	30 Apr 1990 (SI 1990/997)
4, 5	28 Jun 1988 (RA; note that SI 1990/997 also purports to bring s 5 into force on 30 Apr 1990)

Social Security Act 1988 (c 7)

RA: 15 Mar 1988

Commencement provisions: s 18(1)–(4); Social Security Act 1988 (Commencement No
1) Order 1988, SI 1988/520; Social Security Act 1988 (Commencement No 2)
Order 1988, SI 1988/1226; Social Security Act 1988 (Commencement No 3)
Order 1988, SI 1988/1857

s 1–8	Repealed
9	6 Apr 1988 (SI 1988/520); prospectively repealed by Pension Schemes Act 1993, s 188, Sch 5, Pt I (qv)
10, 11	Repealed
12	15 Mar 1988 (s 18(1), (2))

Social Security Act 1988 (c 7)—*cont*

s 13, 14	17 Mar 1988 (SI 1988/520)
15	15 Mar 1988 (s 18(1), (2))
15A	Inserted by Social Security Act 1990, s 21(1), Sch 6, para 8(10) (qv)
16(1)	See Sch 4 below
(2)	See Sch 5 below
17	Repealed
18–20	15 Mar 1988 (s 18(1), (2))
Sch 1	Repealed
2	6 Apr 1988 (SI 1988/520); repealed in part by Social Security (Consequential Provisions) Act 1992, s 3, Sch 1 (qv), remainder prospectively repealed by Pension Schemes Act 1993, s 188, Sch 5, Pt I (qv)
3	Repealed
4, para 1	6 Apr 1988 (SI 1988/520)
2	12 Sep 1988 (SI 1988/1226)
3–20	Repealed
21	6 Apr 1988 (SI 1988/520)
22	6 Apr 1988 (SI 1988/520); prospectively repealed by Pension Schemes Act 1993, s 188(1), Sch 5, Pt I (qv)
23–30	Repealed
5	15 Mar 1988 (repeals of or in Social Security Act 1975, ss 45, 45A, 46, 47B, 66; Social Security Act 1980, Sch 1; Social Security Act 1985, s 13(4)(a)) (s 18(1), (2))
	6 Apr 1988 (repeals in Social Security Act 1986, s 50(1)) (SI 1988/520)
	11 Apr 1988 (repeals of or in Emergency Laws (Re–enactments and Repeals) Act 1964; Health Services and Public Health Act 1968; Social Security Act 1975, ss 59A, 69; Adoption Act 1976; National Health Service Act 1977; Adoption (Scotland) Act 1978; National Health Service (Scotland) Act 1978; Social Security Act 1985, s 14; Social Security Act 1986, ss 20(6), 23(8), 32, 33(1), 34(1)(a), 51(2), 52(6), 53(10), 63(7), 84(1), Sch 3) (SI 1988/520)
	2 Oct 1988 (repeals in Social Security Act 1975, Sch 3) (SI 1988/520)
	12 Sep 1988 (repeal of Social Security Act 1986, Sch 10, para 45) (SI 1988/1226)

Solicitors (Scotland) Act 1988 (c 42)

RA: 29 Jul 1988

Commencement provisions: s 7(2)

29 Jan 1989 (s 7(2))

Welsh Development Agency Act 1988 (c 5)

Whole Act repealed

1989

Antarctic Minerals Act 1989 (c 21)

RA: 21 Jul 1989

Commencement provisions: s 20(2)

Not in force

Appropriation Act 1989 (c 25)

Whole Act repealed

Atomic Energy Act 1989 (c 7)

RA: 25 May 1989

Commencement provisions: s 7(2); Atomic Energy Act 1989 (Commencement) Order 1989, SI 1989/1317

1 Sept 1989 (SI 1989/1317)

Brunei Appeals Act 1989 (c 36)

RA: 16 Nov 1989

Commencement provisions: s 2(2); Brunei Appeals Act 1989 (Commencement) Order 1989, SI 1989/2445

1 Feb 1990 (SI 1989/2445)

Children Act 1989 (c 41)

RA: 16 Nov 1989

Commencement provisions: s 108(2), (3); Children Act 1989 (Commencement and Transitional Provisions) Order 1991, SI 1991/828; Children Act 1989 (Commencement No 2—Amendment and Transitional Provisions) Order 1991, SI 1991/1990

s 1–4	14 Oct 1991 (SI 1991/828)
5(1)–(10)	14 Oct 1991 (SI 1991/828)
(11), (12)	1 Feb 1992 (SI 1991/828, SI 1991/1990)
(13)	14 Oct 1991 (SI 1991/828)
6–87	14 Oct 1991 (SI 1991/828)
88(1)	See Sch 10 below

Children Act 1989 (c 41)—*cont*

s 88(2)	14 Oct 1991 (SI 1991/828)
89	16 Nov 1989 (s 108(2))
90–95	14 Oct 1991 (SI 1991/828)
96(1), (2)	14 Oct 1991 (SI 1991/828)
(3)–(7)	16 Nov 1989 (s 108(2))
97–107	14 Oct 1991 (SI 1991/828)
108	16 Nov 1989 (RA)
Sch 1–9	14 Oct 1991 (SI 1991/828)
10, para 1–20	14 Oct 1991 (SI 1991/828)
21	1 May 1991 (SI 1991/828)
22–46	14 Oct 1991 (SI 1991/828)
11	14 Oct 1991 (SI 1991/828)
12, para 1–3	14 Oct 1991 (SI 1991/828)
4	Repealed
5–7	14 Oct 1991 (SI 1991/828)
8	Repealed
9	14 Oct 1991 (SI 1991/828)
10	Repealed
11–17	14 Oct 1991 (SI 1991/828)
18	Repealed
19, 20	14 Oct 1991 (SI 1991/828)
21	Repealed
22, 23	14 Oct 1991 (SI 1991/828)
24, 25	Repealed
26–34	14 Oct 1991 (SI 1991/828)
35	16 Nov 1989 (s 108(2))
36	16 Jan 1990 (s 108(2)); prospectively repealed by Education Act 1993, s 307(1), (3), Sch 19, para 154, Sch 21, Pt I (qv)
37–45	14 Oct 1991 (SI 1991/828)
13–15	14 Oct 1991 (SI 1991/828)

Civil Aviation (Air Navigation Charges) Act 1989 (c 9)

RA: 25 May 1989

25 May 1989 (RA)

Common Land (Rectification of Registers) Act 1989 (c 18)

RA: 21 Jul 1989

21 Jul 1989 (RA)

Companies Act 1989 (c 40)

RA: 16 Nov 1989

Commencement provisions: s 215(1)–(3); Companies Act 1989 (Commencement No 1) Order 1990, SI 1990/98; Companies Act 1989 (Commencement No 2) Order 1990, SI 1990/142; Companies Act 1989 (Commencement No 3, Transitional Provisions and Transfer of Functions under the Financial Services Act 1986) Order 1990, SI 1990/354 (which contains transitional provisions in relation to

Companies Act 1989 (c 40)—*cont*
self-regulating organisations and professional bodies); Companies Act 1989
(Commencement No 4, Transitional and Saving Provisions) Order 1990, SI
1990/355, as amended by SI 1990/1707, SI 1990/2569, SI 1993/3246; Companies
Act 1989 (Commencement No 5 and Transitional and Saving Provisions) Order
1990, SI 1990/713; Companies Act 1989 (Commencement No 6 and Transitional
and Savings Provisions) Order 1990, SI 1990/1392, as amended by SI 1990/1707;
Companies Act 1989 (Commencement No 7, Transitional and Saving
Provisions) Order 1990, SI 1990/1707; Companies Act 1989 (Commencement
No 8 and Transitional and Saving Provisions) Order 1990, SI 1990/2569;
Companies Act 1989 (Commencement No 9 and Saving and Transitional
Provisions) Order 1991, SI 1991/488; Companies Act 1989 (Commencement No
10 and Saving Provisions) Order 1991, SI 1991/878; Companies Act 1989
(Commencement No 11) Order 1991, SI 1991/1452; Companies Act 1989
(Commencement No 12 and Transitional Provision) Order 1991, SI 1991/1996;
Companies Act 1989 (Commencement No 13) Order 1991, SI 1991/2173;
Companies Act 1989 (Commencement No 14 and Transitional Provision) Order
1991, SI 1991/2945

s 1	1 Mar 1990 (so far as relates to s 15 below) (SI 1990/ 142)
	1 Apr 1990 (so far as relates to any section or part thereof brought into force by SI 1990/355) (SI 1990/355)[1]
	7 Jan 1991 (so far as relates to any section or part thereof brought into force by SI 1990/2569)
	1 Jul 1992 (so far as relates to s 11) (subject to transitional provisions) (SI 1991/2945)
2–6	1 Apr 1990 (SI 1990/355)[1]
7	1 Apr 1990 (except so far as relates to Companies Act 1985, s 233(5)) (SI 1990/355)[1]
	7 Jan 1991 (exception noted above) (SI 1990/2569)[8]
8–10	1 Apr 1990 (SI 1990/355)[1]
11	1 Apr 1990 (except so far as relates to Companies Act 1985, s 242A) (SI 1990/355)[1]
	1 Jul 1992 (exception noted above) (subject to transitional provisions) (SI 1991/2945)
12	7 Jan 1991 (SI 1990/2569)[8]
13, 14	1 Apr 1990 (SI 1990/355)[1]
15	1 Mar 1990 (SI 1990/142)
16–22	1 Apr 1990 (SI 1990/355)[1]
23	See Sch 10 below
24	1 Mar 1990 (for purposes of ss 30–33, 37–40, 41(1), (3)–(6), 42–45, 47(1), 48(1), (2), 49–54, Schs 11, 12, 14) (SI 1990/142)
	1 Oct 1991 (otherwise) (SI 1991/1996)
25–27	1 Oct 1991 (SI 1991/1996)
28	1 Oct 1991 (subject to transitional provisions in SI 1991/1996, art 4) (SI 1991/1996)
29	1 Oct 1991 (SI 1991/1996)
30	1 Mar 1990 (SI 1990/142)
31	1 Mar 1990 (so far as relates to recognition of supervisory bodies under Sch 11 and for the purpose of enabling the Secretary of State to approve a qualification under s 31(4), (5)) (SI 1990/142)
	1 Oct 1991 (otherwise) (SI 1991/1996)
32, 33	1 Mar 1990 (SI 1990/142)

Companies Act 1989 (c 40)—*cont*

s 34	1 Oct 1991 (SI 1991/1996)
35, 36	26 Jun 1991 (SI 1991/1452)
37–40	1 Mar 1990 (SI 1990/142)
41(1)	1 Mar 1990 (for purposes of an application under this section or under provisions specified under s 24 above or of any requirement imposed under such provisions) (SI 1990/142)
	1 Oct 1991 (otherwise) (SI 1991/1996)
(2)	1 Oct 1991 (SI 1991/1996)
(3)	1 Mar 1990 (SI 1990/142)
(4)	1 Mar 1990 (for purposes of an application under this section or under provisions specified under s 24 above or of any requirement imposed under such provisions) (SI 1990/142)
	1 Oct 1991 (otherwise) (SI 1991/1996)
(5), (6)	1 Mar 1990 (for purposes of s 41(3)) (SI 1990/142)
	1 Oct 1991 (otherwise) (SI 1991/1996)
42–44	1 Mar 1990 (for purposes of ss 30–33, 37–40, 41(1), (3)–(6), 42–45, 47(1), 48(1), (2), 49–54, Schs 11, 12, 14) (SI 1990/142)
	1 Oct 1991 (otherwise) (SI 1991/1996)
45	1 Mar 1990 (SI 1990/142)
46	*Not in force*
47(1)	1 Mar 1990 (SI 1990/142)
(2)–(6)	*Not in force*
48(1), (2)	1 Mar 1990 (SI 1990/142)
(3)	*Not in force*
49	1 Mar 1990 (for purposes of ss 30–33, 37–40, 41(1), (3)–(6), 42–45, 47(1), 48(1), (2), 49–54, Schs 11, 12, 14) (SI 1990/142)
	1 Oct 1991 (otherwise) (SI 1991/1996)
50, 51	1 Mar 1990 (SI 1990/142)
52–54	1 Mar 1990 (for purposes of ss 30–33, 37–40, 41(1), (3)–(6), 42–45, 47(1), 48(1), (2), 49–54, Schs 11, 12, 14) (SI 1990/142)
	1 Oct 1991 (otherwise) (SI 1991/1996)
55–64	21 Feb 1990 (SI 1990/142)
65(1)	21 Feb 1990 (SI 1990/142)
(2)	21 Feb 1990 (except so far as refers to Part VII (ss 154–191) and so far as s 65(2)(g) refers to a body established under s 46) (SI 1990/142)
	25 Apr 1991 (so far as not already in force, except so far as s 65(2)(g) refers to a body established under s 46) (SI 1991/878)
	Not in force (exception noted above)
(3)–(7)	21 Feb 1990 (SI 1990/142)
66–74	21 Feb 1990 (SI 1990/142)
75(1)	21 Feb 1990 (SI 1990/142)
(2)	25 Jan 1990 (SI 1990/98)
(3)(a)–(c)	21 Feb 1990 (except so far as refers to Part VII (ss 154–191) and so far as s 75(3)(c) refers to a body established under s 46) (SI 1990/142)
	25 Apr 1991 (so far as not already in force, except so far as s 75(3)(c) refers to a body established under s 46) (SI 1991/878)
	Not in force (exception noted above)
(d)	25 Jan 1990 (SI 1990/98)

Companies Act 1989 (c 40)—*cont*

s 75(3)(e), (f)	21 Feb 1990 (except so far as refers to Part VII (ss 154–191)) (SI 1990/142)
	25 Apr 1991 (exception noted above) (SI 1991/878)
(4)	25 Jan 1990 (so far as relates to s 75(3)(d) above) (SI 1990/98)
	21 Feb 1990 (otherwise) (SI 1990/142)
(5), (6)	21 Feb 1990 (SI 1990/142)
(7)	25 Jan 1990 (SI 1990/98)
76–79	21 Feb 1990 (SI 1990/142)
80	21 Feb 1990 (except so far as refers to Pt VII (ss 154–191)) (SI 1990/142)
	25 Apr 1991 (exception noted above) (SI 1991/878)
81(1)	21 Feb 1990 (SI 1990/142)
(2)	21 Feb 1990 (except so far as refers to Part VII (ss 154–191)) (SI 1990/142)
	25 Apr 1991 (exception noted above) (SI 1991/878)
(3), (4)	21 Feb 1990 (SI 1990/142)
(5)	21 Feb 1990 (except so far as refers to Pt VII (ss 154–191)) (SI 1990/142)
	25 Apr 1991 (exception noted above) (SI 1991/878)
82–86	21 Feb 1990 (SI 1990/142)
87(1)–(3)	21 Feb 1990 (SI 1990/142)
(4)	21 Feb 1990 (except so far as refers to Pt VII (ss 154–191)) (SI 1990/142)
	25 Apr 1991 (exception noted above) (SI 1991/878)
(5), (6)	21 Feb 1990 (SI 1990/142)
88–91	21 Feb 1990 (SI 1990/142)
92–107	*Not in force*
108–110	4 Feb 1991 (SI 1990/2569)[8]
111	Repealed
112	4 Feb 1991 (SI 1990/2569)[8]
113, 114	1 Apr 1990 (SI 1990/355)
115	1 Apr 1990 (SI 1990/355)[2]
116, 117	1 Apr 1990 (SI 1990/355)
118–123	1 Apr 1990 (SI 1990/355)[2]
124	Repealed
125	7 Jan 1991 (SI 1990/2569)
126	1 Jul 1991 (SI 1991/488)[9]
127(1), (2)	7 Jan 1991 (SI 1990/2569)
(3)	1 Jul 1991 (SI 1991/488)
(4)	7 Jan 1991 (SI 1990/2569)
(5), (6)	1 Jul 1991 (SI 1991/488)
(7)	7 Jan 1991 (so far as inserts in Companies Act 1985, Sch 22, a reference to ss 706, 707, 715A of the 1985 Act, as inserted by ss 125, 127(1) of this Act) (SI 1990/2569)
	1 Jul 1991 (otherwise) (SI 1991/488)
128	*Not in force*
129	1 Nov 1990 (SI 1990/1392)
130	31 Jul 1990 (SI 1990/1392)
131	1 Apr 1990 (not to be construed as affecting any right, privilege, obligation or liability acquired, accrued or incurred before 1 Apr 1990; see SI 1990/355, art 11) (SI 1990/355)
132	1 Apr 1990 (SI 1990/355)
133	*Not in force*
134(1)–(3)	31 May 1990 (SI 1990/713)

Companies Act 1989 (c 40)—*cont*

s 134(4)	1 Nov 1991 (SI 1991/1996)
(5), (6)	31 May 1990 (SI 1990/713)
135	7 Jan 1991 (SI 1990/2569)
136	1 Apr 1990 (SI 1990/355; see, however, saving in art 12 thereof)
137(1)	1 Apr 1990 (SI 1990/355)
(2)	1 Apr 1990 (for the purposes of a director's report of a company within the meaning of the Companies Act 1985, s 735 (except in relation to a financial year commencing before 23 Dec 1989; see SI 1990/355, art 13) (SI 1990/355)
	Not in force (otherwise)
138	31 Jul 1990 (SI 1990/1392)[4]
139	1 Oct 1990 (SI 1990/1707)[7]
140	*Not in force*
141	16 Nov 1989 (s 215(1))
142	*Not in force*
143	1 Nov 1991 (SI 1991/1996)
144	1 Nov 1990 (SI 1990/1392)[5]
145	See Sch 19 below
146	1 Apr 1990 (SI 1990/142)
147–150	16 Nov 1989 (s 215(1))
151	1 Apr 1990 (SI 1990/142)
152	1 Mar 1990 (SI 1990/142)
153	See Sch 20 below
154–156	25 Mar 1991 (Pt VII (ss 154–191, Schs 21, 22) brought into force only insofar as is necessary to enable regulations to be made under ss 155(4), (5), 156(1) (so far as it relates to Sch 21), 158(4), (5), 160(5), 173(4), (5), 174(2)–(4), 185, 186, 187(3), Sch 21, para 2(3)) (SI 1991/488)
	25 Apr 1991 (otherwise) (SI 1991/878)
157	25 Mar 1991 (see note to ss 154–156) (SI 1991/488)
	25 Apr 1991 (otherwise) (SI 1991/878)[10]
158, 159	25 Mar 1991 (see note to ss 154–156) (SI 1991/488)
	25 Apr 1991 (otherwise) (SI 1991/878)
160	25 Mar 1991 (see note to ss 154–156) (SI 1991/488)
	25 Apr 1991 (so far as not already in force, except insofar as imposing a duty (i) on any person where conflict with enactments in force in Northern Ireland relating to insolvency would arise, and (ii) on a relevant office-holder appointed under the general law of insolvency for the time being in force in Northern Ireland) (SI 1991/878)[10]
	1 Oct 1991 (exception noted above) (SI 1991/2173)
161	25 Mar 1991 (see note to ss 154–156) (SI 1991/488)
	25 Apr 1991 (otherwise) (SI 1991/878)
162	25 Mar 1991 (see note to ss 154–156) (SI 1991/488)
	25 Apr 1991 (otherwise, except so far as would require an exchange or clearing house to supply a copy of a report to any relevant office-holder appointed under the general law of insolvency for the time being in force in Northern Ireland) (SI 1991/878)
	1 Oct 1991 (exception noted above) (SI 1991/2173)

Companies Act 1989 (c 40)—*cont*

s 185, 186	25 Mar 1991 (see note to ss 154–156) (SI 1991/488)
	Not in force (otherwise)
187–191	25 Mar 1991 (see note to ss 154–156) (SI 1991/488)
	25 Apr 1991 (otherwise) (SI 1991/878)
192	15 Mar 1990 (so far as relates to Financial Services Act 1986, s 47A) (SI 1990/354)
	Not in force (otherwise)
193(1)	15 Mar 1990 (so far as relates to regulations under Financial Services Act 1986, s 62A) (SI 1990/354)
	1 Apr 1991 (otherwise) (SI 1991/488)[9]
(2)	1 Apr 1991 (SI 1991/488)[9]
(3)	15 Mar 1990 (so far as relates to regulations under Financial Services Act 1986, Sch 11, para 22A) (SI 1990/354)
	1 Apr 1991 (otherwise) (SI 1991/488)[9]
(4)	1 Apr 1991 (SI 1991/488)[9]
194–200	15 Mar 1990 (SI 1990/354)
201	25 Apr 1991 (SI 1991/878)[10]
202	16 Nov 1989 (s 215(1))
203–205	15 Mar 1990 (SI 1990/354)
206(1)	See Sch 23 below
(2)–(4)	15 Mar 1990 (SI 1990/354)
207	1 Nov 1990 (SI 1990/1392 as amended by SI 1990/1707)
208	1 Mar 1990 (SI 1990/142)
209	21 Feb 1990 (SI 1990/142); prospectively repealed by Criminal Justice Act 1993, s 79(14), Sch 6, Pt I (qv)
210	1 Apr 1990 (SI 1990/142)
211(1)	1 Oct 1991 (SI 1991/1996)
(2)	31 Jul 1990 (SI 1990/1392)[6]
(3)	31 Jul 1990 (SI 1990/1392)
212	See Sch 24 below
213, 214	2 Feb 1990 (SI 1990/142)
215, 216	16 Nov 1989 (RA; see however SI 1990/98 which purports to bring s 216 into force on 25 Jan 1990)
Sch 1–9	1 Apr 1990 (SI 1990/355)[1]
10[3], para 1–18	1 Apr 1990 (SI 1990/355)[1]
19	1 Aug 1990 (SI 1990/355)[1]
20–23	1 Apr 1990 (SI 1990/355)[1]
24(1)	1 Apr 1990 (SI 1990/355)[1]
(2)	1 Apr 1990 (except so far as relates to Companies Act 1985, s 245(1), (2)) (SI 1990/355)[1]
	7 Jan 1991 (exception noted above)[1] (SI 1990/2569)[8]
(3)	1 Apr 1990 (except so far as relates to Companies Act 1985, s 233(5)) (SI 1990/355)[1]
	7 Jan 1991 (exception noted above)[1] (SI 1990/2569)
(4)	1 Apr 1990 (SI 1990/355)[1]
25–34	1 Apr 1990 (SI 1990/355)[1]
35(1)	1 Apr 1990 (SI 1990/355)[1]
(2)(a)	1 Apr 1990 (SI 1990/355)[1]
(b)	7 Jan 1991 (SI 1990/2569)
(3)	1 Apr 1990 (SI 1990/355)[1]
36–39	1 Apr 1990 (SI 1990/355)[1]
11, 12	1 Mar 1990 (SI 1990/142)

Companies Act 1989 (c 40)—*cont*

Sch 13		*Not in force*
14		1 Mar 1990 (SI 1990/142)
15–16		*Not in force*
17		31 Jul 1990 (SI 1990/1392)
18		1 Nov 1990 (SI 1990/1392)[5]
19, para 1		1 Mar 1990 (SI 1990/142)
	2–6	1 Oct 1990 (SI 1990/1707)[7]
	7	1 Oct 1990 (SI 1990/1707)
	8, 9	1 Mar 1990 (SI 1990/142)
	10	7 Jan 1991 (SI 1990/2569)
	11	4 Feb 1991 (SI 1990/2569)
	12	1 Mar 1990 (SI 1990/142)
	13	*Not in force*
	14	1 Oct 1990 (SI 1990/1707)
	15–18	1 Apr 1990 (SI 1990/355)
	19	1 Mar 1990 (SI 1990/142)
	20	*Not in force*
	21	1 Mar 1990 (SI 1990/142)
20, para 1		1 Apr 1990 (SI 1990/142)
	2–12	16 Nov 1989 (s 215(1))
	13	1 Apr 1990 (SI 1990/142)
	14–16	16 Nov 1989 (s 215(1))
	17	1 Apr 1990 (SI 1990/142)
	18–20	16 Nov 1989 (s 215(1))
	21	1 Apr 1990 (SI 1990/142)
	22–25	16 Nov 1989 (s 215(1))
	26	1 Apr 1990 (SI 1990/142)
21, 22		25 Mar 1991 (see note to ss 154–156) (SI 1991/488)
		25 Apr 1991 (otherwise) (SI 1991/878)
23, para 1–31		15 Mar 1990 (SI 1990/354)
	32	15 Mar 1990 (so far as relates to Financial Services Act 1986, Sch 11, para 13A) (SI 1990/354)
		Not in force (otherwise)
	33–43	15 Mar 1990 (SI 1990/354)
24		16 Nov 1989 (repeals of or in Fair Trading Act 1973, ss 71, 74, 88, 89, Sch 9) (s 215(1))
		21 Feb 1990 (repeals of or in Companies Act 1985, ss 435, 440, 443, 446, 447, 449, 452, 735A; Financial Services Act 1986, ss 94, 105, 179, 180, 198(1); Banking Act 1987, s 84(1)) (SI 1990/142)
		1 Mar 1990 (repeals of or in Company Directors Disqualification Act 1986, s 21(2)) (SI 1990/142)
		1 Mar 1990 (repeal in Financial Services Act 1986, s 199(9)) (SI 1990/355)
		15 Mar 1990 (repeals of or in Financial Services Act 1986, ss 48, 55, 119, 159, 160, Sch 11, paras 4, 10, 14) (SI 1990/354)
		1 Apr 1990 (repeals of or in Fair Trading Act 1973, ss 46(3), 85) (SI 1990/142)
		1 Apr 1990 (repeals of or in Harbours Act 1964, s 42(6) (subject to transitional or saving provisions); Companies Act 1985, ss 716, 717, 744 (definition of 'authorised institution'), 746, Schs 2, 4, 9, 11, 22 (entry relating to ss 384–393), 24 (except entries relating to ss 245(1), (2), 365(3), 389(10))) (subject to transitional or saving provisions); Insolvency Act 1985, Sch 6, paras 23,

Companies Act 1989 (c 40)—*cont*

Sch 24—*cont*   45; Insolvency Act 1986, Sch 13, Pt 1 (entries relating to ss 222(4), 225); Financial Services Act 1986, Sch 16, para 22) (SI 1990/355)

31 May 1990 (repeals of or in Companies Act 1985, ss 201, 202(1), 209(1)(j)) (SI 1990/713)

31 Jul 1990 (repeals of or in Companies Act 1985, s 651(1), Sch 22 (entry relating to s 36(4)); Building Societies Act 1986, Schs 15, 18) (SI 1990/1392)

1 Oct 1990 (repeals of or in Companies Act 1985, ss 466(2), 733(3), Sch 22 (entries relating to ss 363–365), Sch 24 (entries relating to s 365(3)); Insolvency Act 1986, Sch 13, Pt I (entry relating to s 733(3)) (SI 1990/1707)[7]

7 Jan 1991 (repeals of or in Companies Act 1985, s 708(1)(b), Sch 15, 24 (entries relating to s 245(1), (2))) (SI 1990/2569)[7, 8]

1 Jul 1991 (repeal of Companies Act 1985, ss 712, 715) (SI 1991/488)

1 Oct 1991 (repeals of or in Companies Act 1985, ss 389, 460(1); Financial Services Act 1986, s 196(3); Income and Corporation Taxes Act 1988, s 565(6)(b)) (SI 1991/1996)

1 Nov 1991 (repeals of or in Companies Act 1985, ss 169(5), 175(6)(b), 191(1), (3)(a), (b), 219(1), 288(3), 318(7), 356(1), (2), (4), 383(1)–(3), Sch 13, para 25) (SI 1991/1996)

Not in force (otherwise)

Note: Erroneous repeal of Financial Services Act 1986, s 199(1), by s 212, Sch 24, brought into force on 21 Feb 1990 by SI 1990/142, art 7(d), is revoked by SI 1990/355, art 16, as from 1 March 1990

[1] subject to transitional and saving provisions set out in SI 1990/355, arts 6–9, Sch 2, as amended by SI 1990/2569, art 8, SI 1993/3246, reg 5(2), the principal effect being (with certain exceptions) that the existing rules relating to accounts and reports of companies continue to apply for financial years of a company commencing before 23 December 1989

[2] subject to transitional and saving provisions set out in SI 1990/355, art 10, Sch 4, as amended by SI 1990/1707, art 8, with regard to annual returns and auditors

[3] see, as to transitional and savings provisions, SI 1990/355, art 8, Sch 3

[4] subject to the saving provision set out in SI 1990/1392, art 5

[5] subject to the transitional provisions set out in SI 1990/1392, art 6

[6] subject to the saving provision set out in SI 1990/1392, art 7

[7] subject to transitional and saving provisions set out in SI 1990/1707, arts 4–6

[8] subject to transitional and saving provisions set out in SI 1990/2569, arts 6, 7

[9] subject to the transitional and saving provisions set out in SI 1991/488, arts 3 and 4

[10] subject to saving provisions set out in SI 1991/878, art 3

Consolidated Fund Act 1989 (c 2)

Whole Act repealed

Consolidated Fund (No 2) Act 1989 (c 46)

Whole Act repealed

Continental Shelf Act 1989 (c 35)

RA: 27 Jul 1989

27 Jul 1989 (RA)

Control of Pollution (Amendment) Act 1989 (c 14)

RA: 6 Jul 1989

Commencement provisions: s 11(2); Control of Pollution (Amendment) Act 1989 (Commencement) Order 1991, SI 1991/1618

s 1(1), (2)	1 Apr 1992 (SI 1991/1618)
(3)	16 Jul 1991 (SI 1991/1618)
(4)–(6)	1 Apr 1992 (SI 1991/1618)
2	16 Jul 1991 (SI 1991/1618)
3	16 Jul 1991 (so far as relates to making of regulations) (SI 1991/1618)
	14 Oct 1991 (otherwise) (SI 1991/1618)
4(1)–(5)	14 Oct 1991 (SI 1991/1618)
(6)	16 Jul 1991 (SI 1991/1618)
(7), (8)	14 Oct 1991 (SI 1991/1618)
5(1), (2)	1 Apr 1992 (SI 1991/1618)
(3)	16 Jul 1991 (so far as relates to making of regulations) (SI 1991/1618)
	1 Apr 1992 (otherwise) (SI 1991/1618)
(4), (5)	1 Apr 1992 (SI 1991/1618)
(6)	16 Jul 1991 (so far as relates to making of regulations) (SI 1991/1618)
	1 Apr 1992 (otherwise) (SI 1991/1618)
(7)	1 Apr 1992 (SI 1991/1618)
6	16 Jul 1991 (so far as relates to making of regulations) (SI 1991/1618)
	14 Oct 1991 (otherwise) (SI 1991/1618)
7	14 Oct 1991 (SI 1991/1618)
8–11	16 Jul 1991 (SI 1991/1618)

Control of Smoke Pollution Act 1989 (c 17)

Whole Act repealed

Dangerous Dogs Act 1989 (c 30)

RA: 27 Jul 1989

Commencement provisions: s 2(4)

27 Aug 1989 (s 2(4))

Disabled Persons (Northern Ireland) Act 1989 (c 10)

Local application only

Dock Work Act 1989 (c 13)

RA: 3 Jul 1989

Commencement provisions: s 8(3), (4); National Dock Labour Board (Date of
  Dissolution) Order 1990, SI 1990/1158

s 1–6	3 Jul 1989 (s 8(3))
7(1)	See Sch 1 below
(2)–(5)	3 Jul 1989 (s 8(3))
8	3 Jul 1989 (s 8(3))
Sch 1, Pt I	3 Jul 1989 (s 8(3))
II	30 Jun 1990 (SI 1990/1158)
2	3 Jul 1989 (s 8(3))

Elected Authorities (Northern Ireland) Act 1989 (c 3)

RA: 15 Mar 1989

Commencement provisions: s 13(2); Elected Authorities (Northern Ireland) Act 1989
  (Commencement No 1) Order 1989, SI 1989/1093

s 1(1)	15 Mar 1989 (RA)
(2)	16 Feb 1990 (SI 1989/1093)
(3), (4)	15 Mar 1989 (RA)
2–4	15 Mar 1989 (RA)
5	*Not in force*
6, 7	15 Mar 1989 (RA)
8(1)	15 Mar 1989 (RA)
(2)	*Not in force*
9–13	15 Mar 1989 (RA)
Sch 1	15 Mar 1989 (so far as relates to Representation of the People Act 1983, ss 3, 4) (RA)
	27 Jun 1989 (so far as relates to Representation of the People Act 1983, ss 53, 201, 202(1), Sch 2) (SI 1989/1093)
	16 Feb 1990 (so far as relates to Representation of the People Act 1983, ss 49, 50) (SI 1989/1093)
	1 Aug 1989 (otherwise) (SI 1989/1093)
2, 3	15 Mar 1989 (RA)

Electricity Act 1989 (c 29)

RA: 27 Jul 1989

Commencement provisions: s 113(2); Electricity Act 1989 (Commencement No 1)
  Order 1989, SI 1989/1369; Electricity Act 1989 (Commencement No 2) Order
  1990, SI 1990/117

s 1, 2	1 Sep 1989 (SI 1989/1369)

Electricity Act 1989 (c 29)—*cont*

s 3–5	31 Mar 1990 (SI 1990/117)
6(1)–(8)	31 Mar 1990 (SI 1990/117)
(9)	1 Sep 1989 (for the purpose of the interpretation of s 2(7)) (SI 1989/1369)
	31 Mar 1990 (otherwise) (SI 1990/117)
(10), (11)	31 Mar 1990 (SI 1990/117)
7–42	31 Mar 1990 (SI 1990/117)
42A	Inserted by Competition and Service (Utilities) Act 1992, s 21 (qv)
42B	Inserted by Competition and Service (Utilities) Act 1992, s 22 (qv)
43, 44	31 Mar 1990 (SI 1990/117)
44A	Prospectively inserted by Competition and Service (Utilities) Act 1992, s 23 (qv)
45–63	31 Mar 1990 (SI 1990/117)
64	1 Oct 1989 (definition of 'prescribed' for purposes of Schs 14, 15) (SI 1989/1369)
	31 Mar 1990 (otherwise) (SI 1990/117)
65–69	1 Oct 1989 (SI 1989/1369)
70	See Sch 10 below
71–84	31 Mar 1990 (SI 1990/117)
85	1 Mar 1990 (SI 1990/117)
86	1 Sep 1989 (SI 1989/1369)
87, 88	31 Mar 1990 (SI 1990/117)
89	1 Oct 1989 (SI 1989/1369)
90	31 Mar 1990 (SI 1990/117)
91, 92	1 Oct 1989 (SI 1989/1369)
93	31 Mar 1990 (SI 1990/117)
94, 95	1 Oct 1989 (SI 1989/1369)
96	31 Mar 1990 (SI 1990/117)
97	See Sch 12 below
98–103	31 Mar 1990 (SI 1990/117)
104	See Sch 14 below
105	See Sch 15 below
106, 107	1 Sep 1989 (SI 1989/1369)
108, 109	31 Mar 1990 (SI 1990/117)
110, 111	1 Sep 1989 (SI 1989/1369)
112(1)–(3)	31 Mar 1990 (SI 1990/117)
(4)	See Sch 18 below
113	1 Sep 1989 (SI 1989/1369)
Sch 1, 2	1 Sep 1989 (SI 1989/1369)
3–9	31 Mar 1990 (SI 1990/117)
10	1 Oct 1989 (SI 1989/1369)
11	31 Mar 1990 (SI 1990/117)
12	1 Oct 1989 (SI 1989/1369)
13	31 Mar 1990 (SI 1990/117)
14	1 Oct 1989 (SI 1989/1369)
15	1 Oct 1989 (SI 1989/1369)
16	31 Mar 1990 (SI 1990/117)
17, para 1, 2	31 Mar 1990 (SI 1990/117)
3(a)	31 Mar 1990 (SI 1990/117)
(b)	*Not in force*
4–40	31 Mar 1990 (SI 1990/117)
18	31 Mar 1990 (except repeals of or in Electricity Act 1947, ss 1(2), (3), 3(1), (7), (8), 64(3), (4), 67(1),

Electricity Act 1989 (c 29)—*cont*

Sch 18—*cont*	69, Sch 1, column 1; Electricity Act 1957, ss 2(1), 3(1), (6), (7), 40(1), 42, Sch 4, Pt I; House of Commons Disqualification Act 1975, Sch 1, Pt II; Electricity (Scotland) Act 1979, s 1, Sch 1, paras 2–6; National Audit Act 1983, Sch 4; Income and Corporation Taxes Act 1988, s 511(1)–(3), (6)) (SI 1990/117)
	Not in force (exception noted above)

Employment Act 1989 (c 38)

RA: 16 Nov 1989

Commencement provisions: s 30(2)–(4); Employment Act 1989 (Commencement and Transitional Provisions) Order 1990, SI 1990/189

s 1–7	16 Jan 1990 (s 30(3))
8	16 Nov 1989 (s 30(2))
9(1), (2)	16 Jan 1990 (s 30(3))
(3)	26 Feb 1990 (SI 1990/189)
(4)–(6)	16 Jan 1990 (s 30(3))
10(1), (2)	16 Jan 1990 (s 30(3))
(3)–(6)	16 Nov 1989 (s 30(2))
11, 12	16 Nov 1989 (s 30(2))
13, 14	Repealed
15	26 Feb 1990 (subject to transitional provisions) (SI 1990/189)
16–19	16 Jan 1990 (s 30(3))
20	26 Feb 1990 (SI 1990/189)
21	16 Jan 1990 (s 30(3))
22–28	16 Nov 1989 (s 30(2))
29(1), (2)	16 Nov 1989 (s 30(2))
(3)	See Sch 6 below
(4)	See Sch 7 below
(5)	See Sch 8 below
(6)	See Sch 9 below
30	16 Nov 1989 (s 30(2))
Sch 1, 2	16 Jan 1990 (s 30(3))
3, Pt I, II	16 Jan 1990 (except repeals of or in Employment of Women, Young Persons and Children Act 1920, s 1(3), Sch, Pt II; Factories Act 1961, s 119A) (s 30(3))
	26 Feb 1990 (repeals of or in Employment of Women, Young Persons and Children Act 1920, s 1(3), Sch, Pt II) (SI 1990/189)
	Not in force (otherwise)
III	16 Jan 1990 (s 30(3))
4, 5	16 Nov 1989 (s 30(2))
6, para 1, 2	26 Feb 1990 (SI 1990/189)
3–5	16 Jan 1990 (s 30(3))
6	*Not in force*
7, 8	16 Jan 1990 (s 30(3))
9–15	16 Nov 1989 (s 30(2))
16	16 Jan 1990 (s 30(3))
17	16 Nov 1989 (s 30(2))

Employment Act 1989 (c 38)—*cont*

Sch 6, para 18–20		Repealed
	21–25	16 Jan 1990 (s 30(3))
	26	26 Feb 1990 (SI 1990/189)
	27–29	16 Nov 1989 (s 30(2))
	30	16 Jan 1990 (s 30(3))
7, Pt I		16 Nov 1989 (s 30(2))
	II	16 Jan 1990 (s 30(3))
	III	26 Feb 1990 (except repeals of or in Factories Act 1961, s 119A; Employment Medical Advisory Service Act 1972, s 8(1) (so far as relates to Factories Act 1961, s 119A); Employment and Training Act 1973, Sch 3, para 6) (SI 1990/189)
8		16 Jan 1990 (s 30(3))
9		16 Nov 1989 (s 30(2))

Extradition Act 1989 (c 33)

RA: 27 Jul 1989

Commencement provisions: s 38(2), (3)

s 1–6		27 Sep 1989 (s 38(2))
	7(1), (2)	27 Sep 1989 (s 38(2))
	(3)	27 Jul 1989 (s 38(3))
	(4)–(6)	27 Sep 1989 (s 38(2))
8, 9		27 Sep 1989 (s 38(2))
	10(1), (2)	27 Sep 1989 (s 38(2))
	(3)	27 Jul 1989 (s 38(3))
	(4)–(13)	27 Sep 1989 (s 38(2))
11–13		27 Sep 1989 (s 38(2))
	14(1)	27 Sep 1989 (s 38(2))
	(2), (3)	27 Jul 1989 (s 38(3))
	(4)	27 Sep 1989 (s 38(2))
15–37		27 Sep 1989 (s 38(2))
38		27 Jul 1989 (s 38(3))
Sch 1, para 1–8		27 Sep 1989 (s 38(3))
	9(1)	27 Sep 1989 (s 38(2))
	(2)	27 Jul 1989 (s 38(3))
	(3), (4)	27 Sep 1989 (s 38(2))
	10–20	27 Sep 1989 (s 38(2))
	2	27 Sep 1989 (s 38(2))

Fair Employment (Northern Ireland) Act 1989 (c 32)

RA: 27 Jul 1989

Commencement provisions: Fair Employment (Northern Ireland) Act 1989 (Commencement) Order 1989, SI 1989/1928

s 1(1), (2)	1 Jan 1990 (SI 1989/1928)
(3)	1 Nov 1989 (SI 1989/1928)
2–28	1 Jan 1990 (SI 1989/1928)
29	1 Nov 1989 (SI 1989/1928)
30	Repealed

Fair Employment (Northern Ireland) Act 1989 (c 32)—*cont*

s 31–46	1 Jan 1990 (SI 1989/1928)
47	1 Nov 1989 (SI 1989/1928)
48	1 Jan 1990 (SI 1989/1928)
49	1 Jan 1990 (except for p. rposes of acts done before 1 Jan 1990) (SI 1990/1928)
50–56	1 Jan 1990 (SI 1989/1928)
57	1 Nov 1989 (SI 1989/1928)
58–60	1 Jan 1990 (SI 1989/1928)
Sch 1	1 Jan 1990 (SI 1989/1928)
2, para 1–14	1 Jan 1990 (SI 1989/1928)
15	1 Jan 1990 (except for purposes of any complaint or act to which s 50(2) applies) (SI 1989/1928)
16(1), (2)	1 Jan 1990 (SI 1989/1928)
(3)(a)	1 Jan 1990 (SI 1989/1928)
(b)	1 Jan 1990 (except for purposes of any complaint or act to which s 50(2) applies) (SI 1989/1928)
17	1 Jan 1990 (except for purposes of any complaint or act to which s 50(2) applies) (SI 1989/1928)
18–20	1 Jan 1990 (SI 1989/1928)
21(a), (b)	1 Jan 1990 (SI 1989/1928)
(c)	1 Jan 1990 (except for purposes of any complaint or act to which s 50(2) applies) (SI 1989/1928)
(d)–(f)	1 Jan 1990 (SI 1989/1928)
22, 23	1 Jan 1990 (SI 1989/1928)
24–26	1 Jan 1990 (except for purposes of any complaint or act to which s 50(2) applies) (SI 1989/1928)
27–31	1 Jan 1990 (SI 1989/1928)
32, 33	1 Jan 1990 (except for purposes of any complaint or act to which s 50(2) applies) (SI 1989/1928)
3	1 Jan 1990 (except repeals of or in Fair Employment (Northern Ireland) Act 1976, ss 44–48, 51, 53(4), 57(1) (definitions of 'complainant', 'the county court', 'finding' and 'the injured person'), 59(2), Sch 1, para 11, for the purposes of any complaint or act to which s 50(2) of this Act applies) (SI 1989/1928)

Finance Act 1989 (c 26)

RA: 27 Jul 1989

See the note concerning Finance Acts at the front of this book

---

Football Spectators Act 1989 (c 37)

RA: 16 Nov 1989

Commencement provisions: s 27(2), (3); Football Spectators Act 1989 (Commencement No 1) Order 1990, SI 1990/690; Football Spectators Act 1989 (Commencement No 2) Order 1990, SI 1990/926; Football Spectators Act 1989 (Commencement No 3) Order 1991, SI 1991/1071; Football Spectators Act 1989 (Commencement No 4) Order 1993, SI 1993/1690

s 1(1), (2)	22 Mar 1990 (SI 1990/690)

Football Spectators Act 1989 (c 37)—*cont*

s 1(3)	*Not in force*
(4)(a)	22 Mar 1990 (SI 1990/690)
(b)	*Not in force*
(5), (6)	*Not in force*
(7)–(11)	22 Mar 1990 (SI 1990/690)
2–7	*Not in force*
8	1 Jun 1990 (SI 1990/690)
9	1 Aug 1993 (SI 1993/1690)
10(1)–(5)	1 Jun 1990 (SI 1990/690)
(6), (7)	*Not in force*
(8)(a), (b)	1 Jun 1990 (SI 1990/690)
(c)	*Not in force*
(9)–(11)	1 Jun 1990 (SI 1990/690)
(12)(a), (b)	*Not in force*
(c), (d)	1 Jun 1990 (SI 1990/690)
(13)–(17)	1 Jun 1990 (SI 1990/690)
11, 12	1 Jun 1990 (SI 1990/690)
13	3 Jun 1991 (SI 1991/1071)
14	22 Mar 1990 (SI 1990/690)
15–21	24 Apr 1990 (SI 1990/690)
22(1)	22 Mar 1990 (SI 1990/690)
(2)–(8)	24 Apr 1990 (SI 1990/690)
(9)	22 Mar 1990 (SI 1990/690)
(10), (11))	24 Apr 1990 (SI 1990/690)
(12)	22 Mar 1990 (SI 1990/690)
23–26	24 Apr 1990 (SI 1990/690)
Sch 1	24 Apr 1990 (SI 1990/926)
2	1 Jun 1990 (SI 1990/690)

Hearing Aid Council (Amendment) Act 1989 (c 12)

RA: 3 Jul 1989

Commencement provisions: s 6(2)

s 1–4	3 Sep 1989 (s 6(2))
5	1 Jan 1990 (s 6(2))
6	3 Sep 1989 (s 6(2))

Human Organ Transplants Act 1989 (c 31)

RA: 27 Jul 1989

Commencement provisions: s 7(3); Human Organ Transplants Act 1989 (Commencement) Order 1989, SI 1989/2106

s 1	28 Jul 1989 (s 7(3))
2(1)	1 Apr 1990 (SI 1989/2106)
(2)–(7)	27 Jul 1989 (RA)
3–7	27 Jul 1989 (RA)

International Parliamentary Organisations (Registration) Act 1989 (c 19)

RA: 21 Jul 1989

21 Jul 1989 (RA)

Law of Property (Miscellaneous Provisions) Act 1989 (c 34)

RA: 27 Jul 1989

Commencement provisions: s 5; Law of Property (Miscellaneous Provisions) Act 1989
(Commencement) Order 1990, SI 1990/1175

s 1(1)–(7)	31 Jul 1990 (SI 1990/1175)
(8)	See Sch 1 below
(9)–(11)	31 Jul 1990 (SI 1990/1175)
2, 3	27 Sep 1989 (s 5)
4	See Sch 2 below
5, 6	27 Jul 1989 (RA)
Sch 1	31 Jul 1990 (SI 1990/1175)
2	27 Sep 1989 (repeal of Law of Property Act 1925, s 40) (s 5)
	31 Jul 1990 (otherwise) (SI 1990/1175)

Licensing (Amendment) Act 1989 (c 20)

RA: 21 Jul 1989

Commencement provisions: s 2(2)

21 Sep 1989 (s 2(2))

Local Government and Housing Act 1989 (c 42)

RA: 16 Nov 1989

Commencement provisions: ss 154(3), 195(2), (3) (and individually as noted below:
passim); Local Government and Housing Act 1989 (Commencement No 1)
Order 1989, SI 1989/2180; Local Government and Housing Act 1989
(Commencement No 2) Order 1989, SI 1989/2186; Local Government and
Housing Act 1989 (Commencement No 3) Order 1989, SI 1989/2445; Local
Government and Housing Act 1989 (Commencement No 4) Order 1990, SI
1990/191; Local Government and Housing Act 1989 (Commencement No 5 and
Transitional Provisions) Order 1990, SI 1990/431; Local Government and
Housing Act 1989 (Commencement No 6 and Miscellaneous Provisions) Order
1990, SI 1990/762; Local Government and Housing Act 1989 (Commencement
No 7) Order 1990, SI 1990/961; Local Government and Housing Act 1989
(Commencement No 8 and Transitional Provisions) Order 1990, SI 1990/1274,
as amended by SI 1990/1335; Local Government and Housing Act 1989
(Commencement No 9 and Saving) Order 1990, SI 1990/1552; Local
Government and Housing Act 1989 (Commencement No 10) Order 1990, SI
1990/2581; Local Government and Housing Act 1989 (Commencement No 11
and Savings) Order 1991, SI 1991/344; Local Government and Housing Act 1989
(Commencement No 12) Order 1991, SI 1991/953; Local Government and

Local Government and Housing Act 1989 (c 42)—*cont*
Housing Act 1989 (Commencement No 13) Order 1991, SI 1991/2940; Local
Government and Housing Act 1989 (Commencement No 14) Order 1992, SI
1992/760; Local Government and Housing Act 1989 (Commencement No 15)
Order 1993, SI 1993/105; Local Government and Housing Act 1989
(Commencement No 16) Order 1993, SI 1993/2410

Abbreviation: "orders etc" means "so far as confers on Secretary of State powers to
make orders, regulations or determinations, to give or make directions, to specify
matters, to require information, to impose conditions or to give guidance or
approvals, or make provision with respect to the exercise of any such power"

s 1(1)–(4)	1 Mar 1990 (SI 1989/2445)
(5), (6)	29 Nov 1989 (SI 1989/2186)
(7), (8)	1 Mar 1990 (SI 1989/2445)
2	29 Nov 1989 (SI 1989/2186)
3	16 Nov 1989 (RA)
4–7	16 Jan 1990 (ss 4(7), 5(9), 6(8), 7(3))
8	16 Nov 1989 (RA)
9	16 Jan 1990 (orders etc) (SI 1989/2445)
	1 Aug 1990 (EW) (otherwise) (SI 1990/1552)
	Not in force (S) (otherwise)
10	1 Apr 1990 (SI 1990/431)
11	16 Nov 1989 (RA; note s 11(4))
12	16 Jan 1990 (s 12(3))
13	16 Jan 1990 (orders etc) (SI 1989/2445)
	1 Aug 1990 (so far as not already in force, except in relation to a parish or community council until 1 Jan 1991) (SI 1990/1552)
14	*Not in force*
15	16 Jan 1990 (orders etc) (SI 1989/2445)
	1 Aug 1990 (EW) (otherwise) (SI 1990/1552)
	Not in force (S) (otherwise)
16	1 Aug 1990 (EW) (SI 1990/1552)
	Not in force (S)
17	16 Jan 1990 (orders etc) (SI 1989/2445)
	1 Aug 1990 (EW) (otherwise) (SI 1990/1552)
	Not in force (S) (otherwise)
18	16 Jan 1990 (SI 1989/2445)
19	16 Jan 1990 (orders etc) (SI 1989/2445)
	8 May 1992 (otherwise) (SI 1992/760)
20	16 Jan 1990 (SI 1989/2445)
21	16 Nov 1989 (RA)
22	16 Jan 1990 (SI 1989/2445)
23	1 Apr 1990 (SI 1990/431)
24	16 Nov 1989 (RA) (note s 24(3))
25–29	1 Apr 1990 (SI 1990/431)
30(1)	3 May 1990 (SI 1990/961)
(2)	3 May 1990 (so far as amends the Local Government Act 1972, s 83(1)) (SI 1990/961)
	1 Jan 1991 (otherwise) (SI 1990/2581)
31	16 Jan 1990 (SI 1989/2445)
32	3 May 1990 (SI 1990/961)
33–35	16 Jan 1990 (orders etc) (SI 1989/2445)
	1 Apr 1990 (otherwise) (SI 1990/762)
36	16 Jan 1990 (orders etc) (SI 1989/2445)
	1 Apr 1990 (otherwise) (SI 1990/431)
37, 38	1 Apr 1990 (SI 1990/431)

Local Government and Housing Act 1989 (c 42)—*cont*

s 39–66	16 Jan 1990 (SI 1989/2445)
67–70	16 Jan 1990 (orders etc) (SI 1989/2445)
	7 Oct 1993 (otherwise) (SI 1993/2410)
71	16 Jan 1990 (orders etc) (SI 1989/2445)
	Not in force (otherwise)
72	16 Jan 1990 (orders etc) (SI 1989/2445)
	7 Oct 1993 (otherwise) (SI 1993/2410)
73	7 Oct 1993 (SI 1993/2410)
74	16 Nov 1989 (RA)
75	See Sch 4 below
76–80	16 Nov 1989 (RA)
81	Repealed
82–88	16 Nov 1989 (RA)
89–92	16 Jan 1990 (orders etc) (SI 1989/2445)
	1 Apr 1990 (otherwise) (SI 1990/431)
93, 94	1 Apr 1990 (SI 1990/431)
95, 96	16 Jan 1990 (orders etc) (SI 1989/2445)
	1 Apr 1990 (otherwise) (SI 1990/431)
97	1 Apr 1990 (SI 1990/431)
98	16 Jan 1990 (orders etc) (SI 1989/2445)
	1 Apr 1990 (otherwise) (SI 1990/431)
99	16 Jan 1990 (SI 1989/2445)
100	1 Apr 1990 (SI 1990/431)
101(1)–(4)	1 Jul 1990 (SI 1990/1274)
(5)(a)	1 Jul 1990 (SI 1990/1274)
(b)	*Not in force*
102	16 Jan 1990 (orders etc) (SI 1989/2445)
	1 Jul 1990 (otherwise) (SI 1990/1274)
103	1 Jul 1990 (SI 1990/1274)
104	16 Jan 1990 (orders etc) (SI 1989/2445)
	1 Jul 1990 (otherwise) (SI 1990/1274)
105–108	1 Jul 1990 (SI 1990/1274)
109, 110	16 Jan 1990 (orders etc) (SI 1989/2445)
	1 Jul 1990 (otherwise) (SI 1990/1274)
111, 112	1 Jul 1990 (SI 1990/1274)
113	1 Jul 1990 (subject to transitional provisions) (SI 1990/1274)
114	1 Jul 1990 (SI 1990/1274)
115	16 Jan 1990 (orders etc) (SI 1989/2445)
	1 Jul 1990 (otherwise) (SI 1990/1274)
116–120	1 Jul 1990 (SI 1990/1274)
121	16 Jan 1990 (orders etc) (SI 1989/2445)
	1 Jul 1990 (otherwise) (SI 1990/1274)
122–126	1 Jul 1990 (SI 1990/1274)
127	16 Jan 1990 (orders etc) (SI 1989/2445)
	1 Jul 1990 (otherwise) (SI 1990/1274)
128, 129	1 Jul 1990 (SI 1990/1274)
130	16 Jan 1990 (orders etc) (SI 1989/2445)
	1 Jul 1990 (otherwise) (SI 1990/1274)
131	16 Jan 1990 (orders etc) (SI 1989/2445)
	1 Apr 1990 (otherwise) (SI 1990/431)
132(1)–(4)	16 Jan 1990 (orders etc) (SI 1989/2445)
	1 Apr 1990 (so far as relate to s 131 and not already in force) (SI 1990/431)
(5)	16 Jan 1990 (orders etc) (SI 1989/2445)
	1 Jul 1990 (otherwise, subject to transitional provisions) (SI 1990/1274)

Local Government and Housing Act 1989 (c 42)—*cont*

s 133–136	1 Jul 1990 (SI 1990/1274)
137, 138	16 Jan 1990 (SI 1989/2445)
139	See Sch 5 below
140, 141	Repealed (with savings)
142	1 Dec 1989 (for purposes of, and in relation to, the financial year 1990–91 and each subsequent financial year) (SI 1989/2180)
	Prospectively repealed by Local Government Finance Act 1992, s 117(2), Sch 14 (qv)
143, 144	1 Dec 1989 (SI 1989/2180); prospectively repealed by Local Government Finance Act 1992, s 117(2), Sch 14 (qv)
145	See Sch 6 below
146	Repealed
147–149	16 Nov 1989 (RA)
150–152	16 Jan 1990 (s 152(7))
153	16 Nov 1989 (RA)
154	1 Jan 1992 (SI 1991/2940)
155	1 Apr 1990 (s 155(7))
156	1 Apr 1990 (SI 1990/431)
157, 158	16 Nov 1989 (RA)
159	1 Dec 1989 (SI 1989/2180)
160	See Sch 8 below
161	16 Nov 1989 (RA)
162	16 Jan 1990 (SI 1989/2445)
163	16 Nov 1989 (RA)
164	Repealed
165(1)	See Sch 9 below
(2)	1 Apr 1990 (SI 1990/431)
(3)–(9)	1 Mar 1990 (SI 1990/191)
166	16 Nov 1989 (RA)
167, 168	16 Jan 1990 (SI 1989/2445)
169(1)	1 Apr 1990 (SI 1990/431)
(2)(a)	1 Apr 1990 (SI 1990/431)
(b), (c)	1 Jul 1990 (SI 1990/1274)
(d)	1 Apr 1990 (SI 1990/431)
(3)–(9)	1 Apr 1990 (SI 1990/431)
170	1 Apr 1990 (SI 1989/2180)
171	16 Jan 1990 (SI 1989/2445)
172(1)–(5)	1 Mar 1990 (SI 1989/2445)
(6)–(8)	16 Jan 1990 (SI 1989/2445)
(9)	1 Mar 1990 (SI 1989/2445)
173	1 Mar 1990 (SI 1989/2445)
174	16 Nov 1989 (RA)
175	16 Jan 1990 (SI 1989/2445)
176–178	16 Jan 1990 (SI 1989/2180)
179	1 Dec 1989 (SI 1989/2180)
180	16 Jan 1990 (SI 1989/2445)
181	16 Nov 1989 (RA)
182	16 Jan 1990 (SI 1989/2445)
183	1 Apr 1990 (SI 1990/431)
184	16 Nov 1989 (RA)
185	16 Jan (SI 1989/2180)
186	1 Apr 1990 (SI 1990/431)
187, 188	16 Nov 1989 (RA)
189	16 Nov 1989 (RA); prospectively repealed by Criminal Justice Act 1991, s 101(2), Sch 13 (qv)

Local Government and Housing Act 1989 (c 42)—*cont*

s 190–193	16 Nov 1989 (RA)
194(1)	See Sch 11 below
(2)–(4)	See Sch 12 below
195	16 Nov 1989 (RA)
Sch 1–3	*Not in force*
4	16 Nov 1989 (RA)
5, para 1★	16 Nov 1989 (RA)
2–18	Repealed
19–42★	16 Nov 1989 (RA)
43	Repealed
44–48★	16 Nov 1989 (RA)
49–54	Repealed
55★	16 Nov 1989 (RA)
56	Repealed
57★	16 Nov 1989 (RA)
58, 59	Repealed
60	16 Jan 1990 (SI 1989/2445)
61	Repealed
62★	16 Nov 1989 (RA)
63–65	Repealed
66	16 Jan 1989 (para 79(1))
67–69★	16 Nov 1989 (RA)
70, 71	Repealed
72★	16 Nov 1989 (RA)
73, 74	Repealed
75, 76★	16 Nov 1989 (RA)
77, 78	Repealed
79, 80★	16 Nov 1989 (RA)
6, para 1, 2	1 Apr 1990 (SI 1989/2180)
3, 4	1 Dec 1989 (for purposes of, and in relation to, the financial year 1990–91 and each subsequent financial year) (SI 1989/2180)
5–7	1 Dec 1989 (SI 1989/2180)
8	Repealed
9, 10	1 Apr 1990 (SI 1989/2180)
11, 12	1 Dec 1989 (SI 1989/2180); prospectively repealed by Local Government Finance Act 1992, s 117(2), Sch 14 (qv)
13–15	1 Apr 1990 (SI 1989/2180); prospectively repealed by Local Government Finance Act 1992, s 117(2), Sch 14 (qv)
16, 17	1 Dec 1989 (SI 1989/2180)
18, 19	1 Apr 1990 (SI 1989/2180)
20, 21	Repealed
22	1 Apr 1990 (SI 1989/2180); prospectively repealed by Local Government Finance Act 1992, s 117(2), Sch 14 (qv)
23	1 Dec 1989 (SI 1989/2180)
24–27	1 Dec 1989 (SI 1989/2180); prospectively repealed by Local Government Finance Act 1992, s 117(2), Sch 14 (qv)
28, 29	1 Dec 1989 (for purposes of, and in relation to, the financial year 1990–91 and each subsequent financial year) (SI 1989/2180)
	Prospectively repealed by Local Government Finance Act 1992, s 117(2), Sch 14 (qv)

Local Government and Housing Act 1989 (c 42)—*cont*

Sch 7	16 Nov 1989 (RA)
8	*Not in force*
9, para 1(1)–(5)	1 Apr 1990 (SI 1990/431)
(6)	1 Jul 1990 (SI 1990/1274)
2	1 Apr 1990 (SI 1990/431)
3	1 Jul 1990 (SI 1990/1274)
4–43	1 Apr 1990 (SI 1990/431)
44	16 Jan 1990 (for purposes of Housing Act 1985, s 369) (SI 1989/2445)
	1 Apr 1990 (otherwise) (SI 1990/431)
45–55	1 Apr 1990 (SI 1990/431)
56(1), (2)	16 Jan 1990 (SI 1989/2445)
(3), (4)	1 Apr 1990 (SI 1990/431)
57, 58	1 Jul 1990 (SI 1990/1274)
59	1 Apr 1990 (SI 1990/431)
60	1 Jul 1990 (SI 1990/1274)
61–63	1 Apr 1990 (SI 1990/431)
64, 65	1 Jul 1990 (SI 1990/1274)
66–70	1 Apr 1990 (SI 1990/431)
71(a), (b)	1 Apr 1990 (SI 1990/431)
(c), (d)	1 Jul 1990 (SI 1990/1274)
72–83	1 Apr 1990 (SI 1990/431)
84	16 Jan 1990 (orders etc) (SI 1989/2445)
	1 Apr 1990 (otherwise) (SI 1990/431)
85	1 Apr 1990 (except so far as relating to Housing Act 1985, s 605(1)(e)) (SI 1990/431)
	1 Jul 1990 (exception noted above) (SI 1990/1274)
86–91	1 Apr 1990 (SI 1990/431)
10	1 Apr 1990 (SI 1990/431)
11, para 1, 2	1 Apr 1990 (SI 1990/431)
3	*Not in force*
4	26 Feb 1990 (SI 1990/191); prospectively repealed by Education Act 1993, s 307(3), Sch 21, Pt II (qv)
5–13	1 Apr 1990 (SI 1990/431)
14	25 Jan 1993 (SI 1993/105)
15	*Not in force*
16	1 Apr 1990 (SI 1990/431)
17, 18	*Not in force*
19, 20	Repealed
21	*Not in force*
22, 23	1 Apr 1990 (SI 1990/431)
24, 25	*Not in force*
26	27 Feb 1991 (in relation only to the power to make regulations relating to prescribed amount in Local Government Act 1972, s 173(1)) (SI 1991/344)
	1 Apr 1991 (otherwise) (SI 1991/344)
27	1 Apr 1990 (orders etc) (SI 1990/431)
	1 Apr 1991 (otherwise) (SI 1991/344)
28(1), (2)	1 Jul 1990 (orders etc) (SI 1990/1274)
	1 Apr 1991 (otherwise) (SI 1991/344)
(3)	16 Jan 1990 (orders etc) (SI 1989/2445)
	1 Apr 1991 (otherwise) (SI 1991/344)
(4)	16 Jan 1990 (SI 1989/2445)
29	1 Apr 1991 (SI 1991/344)
30	8 May 1992 (SI 1992/760)
31–33	1 Apr 1990 (SI 1990/431)
34	1 Apr 1991 (SI 1991/344)

Local Government and Housing Act 1989 (c 42)—*cont*

Sch 11, para 35(1), (2)	*Not in force*
(3)	16 Jan 1990 (orders etc) (SI 1989/2445)
	Not in force (otherwise)
(4)	16 Jan 1990 (SI 1989/2445)
36	*Not in force*
37	16 Jan 1990 (SI 1989/2445)
38–41	1 Apr 1990 (SI 1990/431)
42	16 Jan 1990 (SI 1989/2445)
43	*Not in force*
44–48	1 Apr 1990 (SI 1990/431)
49	16 Jan 1990 (SI 1989/2445)
50	1 Apr 1990 (SI 1990/431)
51	Repealed
52	1 Jul 1990 (SI 1990/1274)
53(1)	16 Jan 1990 (SI 1989/2445)
(2)	1 Apr 1990 (SI 1990/431)
54	1 Apr 1990 (SI 1990/431)
55–57	*Not in force*
58	16 Jan 1990 (SI 1989/2445)
59	1 Apr 1990 (SI 1990/431)
60	*Not in force*
61	1 Dec 1989 (SI 1989/2180)
62	1 Apr 1990 (SI 1990/431)
63	1 Jul 1990 (SI 1990/1274)
64, 65	1 Apr 1990 (SI 1990/431)
66–69	1 Jul 1990 (SI 1990/1274)
70–76	1 Apr 1990 (SI 1990/431)
77–84	16 Jan 1990 (SI 1989/2445)
85–87	1 Apr 1990 (SI 1990/431)
88	16 Jan 1990 (orders etc) (SI 1989/2445)
	1 Apr 1990 (otherwise) (SI 1990/431)
89	16 Jan 1990 (SI 1989/2445)
90, 91	1 Jul 1990 (SI 1990/1274)
92	*Not in force*
93, 94	16 Jan 1990 (SI 1989/2180)
95	1 Dec 1989 (SI 1989/2180)
96	1 Apr 1990 (SI 1990/431)
97	*Not in force*
98	Repealed
99, 100	16 Jan 1990 (SI 1989/2180)
101, 102	1 Apr 1990 (SI 1990/431)
103	16 Jan 1990 (SI 1989/2445)
104–106	16 Nov 1989 (RA)
107	16 Jan 1990 (SI 1989/2445)
108	1 Apr 1990 (SI 1990/431)
109–112	16 Jan 1990 (SI 1989/2445)
113	Repealed
12, Pt I	1 Apr 1990 (SI 1990/431)
II	1 Dec 1989 (repeals of or in Valuation and Rating (Scotland) Act 1956, s 22(4); Local Government (Scotland) Act 1973, s 110A(2); Local Government Finance Act 1988, s 128(2), Sch 12, para 16; Housing (Scotland) Act 1988, s 2(6)) (SI 1988/2180)
	16 Jan 1990 (repeals of or in Housing (Scotland) Act 1987, s 61(10)(a)(v)) (SI 1989/2180)
	16 Jan 1990 (repeals of or in Race Relations Act

Local Government and Housing Act 1989 (c 42)—*cont*

Sch 12, Pt II—*cont*

1976, s 47; Housing Act 1985, ss 107, 417–420, 423(2), 434, 459, Sch 14; Social Security Act 1986, s 30(10); Housing and Planning Act 1986, s 1; Housing (Scotland) Act 1987, s 80; Housing Act 1988, s 129(5)(b)) (SI 1989/2445)

1 Mar 1990 (repeals of or in Housing Act 1985, ss 312–314, Sch 12 (in relation to any financial year beginning on or after 1 Apr 1990)) (SI 1990/191)

1 Apr 1990 (repeals of or in Local Government (Financial Provisions etc) (Scotland) Act 1962, s 4(3), (4), Sch 1; Water (Scotland) Act 1980, s 40(7); Local Government Finance Act 1988, Sch 12, para 37) (SI 1989/2180)

1 Apr 1990 (repeals of or in Land Compensation Act 1961, s 10, Sch 2; Local Government Act 1972, ss 101, 110; Land Compensation Act 1973, ss 29, 37, 39, 73; Local Government Act 1974, ss 23, 24, 25, 34; Housing Act 1974, Sch 13; Housing Act 1985, so far as not already in force except those of or in ss 370, 371, 372, 374, 379(1), 381(4) (figure '370'), 460–520, 524–526, 567, 569); Housing (Consequential Provisions) Act 1985, Sch 2; Housing and Planning Act 1986, s 42(1)(d), Sch 5; Local Government Act 1988, s 25, Sch 3; Housing Act 1988, s 130(2)) (SI 1990/431)

1 Jul 1990 (repeals of or in Local Authorities (Expenditure Powers) Act 1983; Housing Act 1985, ss 370–372, 374, 379(1), 381(4) (figure '370'), 460–520, 567, 569) (subject to transitional provisions) (SI 1990/1274)

1 Aug 1990 (repeals of or in Local Government Act 1972, s 102(3) (except in relation to a parish or community council until 1 Jan 1991); Local Government Act 1985, s 33) (SI 1990/1552)

1 Apr 1991 (repeals of or in Local Government Act 1972, ss 177, 177A, 178; Local Government (Scotland) Act 1973, ss 45, 45A, 49A; Education Act 1980; Local Government Planning and Land Act 1980; Local Government Act 1985, Sch 14; Local Government Act 1986; Norfolk and Suffolk Broads Act 1988) (SI 1991/344)

Not in force (otherwise)

★ **Note** Certain amendments made by Sch 5 above (except those made by paras 7, 8, 12, 49(3), 52, 54, 57, 60, 63, 66 or 68) to Local Government Finance Act 1988 are, by virtue of para 79(3) thereof, retrospective in effect

---

National Maritime Museum Act 1989 (c 8)

RA: 5 May 1989

Commencement provisions: s 3(3); National Maritime Museum Act 1989 (Commencement) Order 1989, SI 1989/1028

7 Jul 1989 (SI 1989/1028)

Official Secrets Act 1989 (c 6)

RA: 11 May 1989

Commencement provisions: s 16(6); Official Secrets Act 1989 (Commencement) Order 1990, SI 1990/199

1 Mar 1990 (SI 1990/199)

Opticians Act 1989 (c 44)

RA: 16 Nov 1989

Commencement provisions: s 38

16 Feb 1990 (s 38)

Parking Act 1989 (c 16)

RA: 21 Jul 1989

Commencement provisions: s 5(2); Parking Act 1989 (Commencement) Order 1990, SI 1990/933)

16 May 1990 (SI 1990/933)

Pesticides (Fees and Enforcement) Act 1989 (c 27)

RA: 27 Jul 1989

Commencement provisions: s 39(2)

s 1	27 Jul 1989 (RA)
2	27 Sep 1989 (s 3(2))
3	27 Jul 1989 (RA)

Petroleum Royalties (Relief) and Continental Shelf Act 1989 (c 1)

RA: 7 Feb 1989

7 Feb 1989 (RA)

Police Officers (Central Services) Act 1989 (c 11)

RA: 3 Jul 1989

3 Jul 1989 (RA)

Prevention of Terrorism (Temporary Provisions) Act 1989 (c 4)

RA: 15 Mar 1989

Commencement provisions: s 27(1), (2), (3), (4) (see as to expiry of certain provisions on 22 Mar 1990, s 27(5), (10)–(12)); Prevention of Terrorism (Temporary

Prevention of Terrorism (Temporary Provisions) Act 1989 (c 4)—*cont*
Provisions) Act 1989 (Commencement No 1) Order 1989, SI 1989/1361;
Prevention of Terrorism (Temporary Provisions) Act 1989 (Commencement No
2) Order 1990, SI 1990/215

Continuance orders: Prevention of Terrorism (Temporary Provisions) Act 1989
(Continuance) Order 1991, SI 1991/549; Northern Ireland (Emergency and
Prevention of Terrorism Provisions) (Continuance) Order 1991, SI 1991/779;
Prevention of Terrorism (Temporary Provisions) Act 1989 (Continuance) Order
1992, SI 1992/495; Northern Ireland (Emergency and Prevention of Terrorism
Provisions) (Continuance) Order 1992, SI 1992/1413; Prevention of Terrorism
(Temporary Provisions) Act 1989 (Continuance) Order 1993, SI 1993/747;
Northern Ireland (Emergency and Prevention of Terrorism Provisions)
(Continuance) Order 1993, SI 1993/1522

The provisions of Pts I to V (ss 1–20, Schs 1–7) and s 27(6)(c) (except so far as Pt III
(ss 9–13, Sch 4) and Pt V (ss 17–20, Sch 7) have effect in Northern Ireland and
relate to proscribed organisations for the purposes of, or offences or orders
under, the Northern Ireland (Emergency Provisions) Act 1978, s 21 (repealed))
were continued in force for twelve months from 22 Mar 1991 (SI 1991/549); the
latest relevant Order is SI 1993/747, by which those provisions (except so far as
Pts III, V have effect in Northern Ireland and relate to proscribed organisations
for the purposes of, or offences or orders under, the Northern Ireland
(Emergency Provisions) Act 1991, s 28), are continued in force for twelve
months from 22 Mar 1993

The provisions of Pts III (ss 9–13, Sch 4), V (ss 17–20, Sch 7), so far as they have
effect in Northern Ireland and relate to proscribed organisations for the purposes
of, or offences or orders under, the Northern Ireland (Emergency Provisions)
Act 1978, s 21 (repealed), were continued in force for twelve months from 22
Mar 1991 (SI 1991/779); the latest relevant Order is SI 1993/1522 by which those
provisions, so far as they have effect in Northern Ireland and relate to proscribed
organisations for the purposes of, or offences or orders under, the Northern
Ireland (Emergency Provisions) Act 1991, s 28, are continued in force for twelve
months from 16 Jun 1993

s 1–18	22 Mar 1989 (s 27(1))
18A	Prospectively inserted by Criminal Justice Act 1993, s 51 (qv)
19	22 Mar 1989 (s 27(1))
19A	Prospectively inserted by Criminal Justice Act 1993, s 77, Sch 4, para 4 (qv)
21–24	Repealed
25–28	22 Mar 1989 (s 27(1)) (ss 27(2), 28 in effect in force on 16 Mar 1989 for purposes of ss 22–24)
Sch 1, 2	22 Mar 1989 (s 27(1))
3	1 Sep 1989 (in relation to a person detained under s 14, Sch 2, para 7 or Sch 5, para 6, after 31 Aug 1989, or a person given notice under Sch 5, para 2(4), after 31 Aug 1989 but not detained under Sch 5, para 6) (SI 1989/1361)
	5 Mar 1990 (otherwise) (SI 1990/215)
4, para 1–7	22 Mar 1989 (s 27(1))
8, 9	1 Sep 1989 (SI 1989/1361)
10	5 Mar 1990 (SI 1990/1361)
11–17	22 Mar 1989 (s 27(1))
18–19	1 Sep 1989 (SI 1989/1361)

Prevention of Terrorism (Temporary Provisions) Act 1989 (c 4)—*cont*

Sch 4, para 20		5 Mar 1990 (SI 1990/215)
	21–25	22 Mar 1989 (s 27(1))
	25A, 25B	Inserted by Northern Ireland (Emergency Provisions) Act 1991, s 70(3), Sch 7, para 5(9) (qv)
	26, 27	22 Mar 1989 (s 27(1))
	28, 29	1 Sep 1989 (SI 1989/1361)
	30	5 Mar 1990 (SI 1990/215)
	31–33	22 Mar 1989 (s 27(1))
	34	5 Mar 1990 (SI 1990/215)
	35	22 Mar 1989 (s 27(1))
5–8		22 Mar 1989 (s 27(1))
9		22 Mar 1989 (except repeal of Sch 7, para 9 of this Act) (s 27(1))
		3 Dec 1990 (repeal of Sch 7, para 9 of this Act, which came into force on the coming into force of the Land Registration Act 1988 (qv) (s 27(4)))

Prisons (Scotland) Act 1989 (c 45)

RA: 16 Nov 1989

Commencement provisions: s 46(2)

16 Feb 1990 (s 46(2))

Representation of the People Act 1989 (c 28)

RA: 27 Jul 1989

Commencement provisions: s 8(2); Representation of the People Act 1989 (Commencement No 1) Order 1989, SI 1989/1318; Representation of the People Act 1989 (Commencement No 2) Order 1990, SI 1990/519

s 1–4	1 Apr 1990 (SI 1990/519)
5–8	1 Sep 1989 (SI 1989/1318)

Road Traffic (Driving Licensing and Information Systems) Act 1989 (c 22)

RA: 21 Jul 1989

Commencement provisions: s 17(2); Road Traffic (Driver Licensing and Information Systems) Act 1989 (Commencement No 1) Order 1989, SI 1989/1843; Road Traffic (Driver Licensing and Information Systems) Act 1989 (Commencement No 2) Order 1990, SI 1990/802; Road Traffic (Driver Licensing and Information Systems) Act 1989 (Commencement No 3) Order 1990, SI 1990/2228; Road Traffic (Driver Licensing and Information Systems) Act 1989 (Commencement No 4) Order 1990, SI 1990/2610

s 1(1)–(5)	1 Apr 1991 (SI 1990/2610)
(6)	See Sch 1 below
(7)	1 Jun 1990 (so far as relates to definitions 'the 1981 Act', 'the 1988 Act') (SI 1990/802)
2	1 Apr 1991 (SI 1990/2610)

Road Traffic (Driving Licensing and Information Systems) Act 1989 (c 22)—*cont*

s 3	1 Jun 1990 (SI 1990/802)
4	1 Apr 1991 (SI 1990/2610)
5(1)	1 Jun 1990 (except so far as relates to s 5(5)) (SI 1990/802)
	1 Apr 1991 (exception noted above) (SI 1990/2610)
(2)–(4)	1 Jun 1990 (SI 1990/802)
(5)	1 Apr 1991 (SI 1990/2610)
(6)–(10)	1 Jun 1990 (SI 1990/802)
6	1 Dec 1990 (SI 1990/2228)
7	See Sch 3 below
8–15	1 Jun 1990 (SI 1990/802)
16	See Sch 6 below
17	8 Nov 1989 (SI 1989/1843)
Sch 1, para 1–9	1 Apr 1991 (SI 1990/2610)
10	Repealed
11	1 Jun 1990 (SI 1990/802); prospectively repealed by s 16 of, and Sch 6 to, this Act (qv)
12	1 Apr 1991 (SI 1990/2610)
2	1 Apr 1991 (SI 1990/2610)
3, para 1–5	1 Apr 1991 (SI 1990/2610)
6	1 Dec 1990 (SI 1990/2228)
7	1 Jun 1990 (SI 1990/802)
8(a)	1 Apr 1991 (SI 1991/2610)
(b)(i)	1 Apr 1991 (SI 1990/2610)
(ii), (iii)	1 Jun 1990 (SI 1990/802)
(c)–(e)	1 Apr 1991 (SI 1990/2610)
9(a), (c)	1 Apr 1991 (SI 1990/2610)
(b), (d)	1 Jun 1990 (SI 1990/802)
10	1 Dec 1990 (SI 1990/2228)
11(a)	1 Apr 1991 (SI 1990/2610)
(b)	1 Jun 1990 (SI 1990/2802)
(c)	1 Dec 1990 (SI 1990/2228)
(d)	1 Jun 1990 (SI 1990/802)
12(a)	1 Apr 1991 (SI 1990/2610)
(b), (c)	1 Jun 1990 (SI 1990/802)
13	1 Apr 1991 (SI 1990/2610)
14	1 Jun 1990 (SI 1990/802)
15(a)	1 Jun 1990 (SI 1990/802)
(b)–(d)	1 Apr 1991 (SI 1990/2610)
(e)	1 Jun 1990 (so far as relates to definitions 'NI driving licence', 'NI licence') (SI 1990/802)
	1 Apr 1991 (so far as relates to definition 'passenger carrying vehicle') (SI 1990/2610)
(f)	1 Jun 1990 (SI 1990/802)
(g)	1 Dec 1990 (SI 1990/2228)
16, 17	1 Jun 1990 (SI 1990/802)
18(a)	1 Apr 1991 (SI 1990/2610)
(b)–(d)	1 Dec 1990 (SI 1990/2228)
19	1 Jun 1990 (SI 1990/802)
20	1 Apr 1991 (SI 1990/2610)
21	Repealed
22, 23	1 Apr 1991 (SI 1990/2610)
24, 25	1 Jun 1990 (SI 1990/802)
26	8 Nov 1989 (SI 1989/1843)
27(a)–(c)	1 Apr 1991 (SI 1990/2610)

Road Traffic (Driving Licensing and Information Systems) Act 1989
(c 22)—*cont*

Sch 3, para 27(d)	1 Jun 1990 (SI 1990/802)
(e)	1 Apr 1991 (SI 1990/2610)
28(a), (b)	1 Jun 1990 (SI 1990/802)
(c), (d)	1 Apr 1991 (SI 1990/2610)
29	8 Nov 1989 (so far as relates to offences under Sch 1, para 10(4), (5)) (SI 1989/1843)
	1 Apr 1991 (otherwise) (SI 1990/2610)
30(a)	1 Jun 1990 (SI 1990/802)
(b)–(c)	1 Apr 1991 (SI 1990/2610)
(d)	8 Nov 1989 (so far as relates to offences under Sch 1, para 10(4), (5)) (SI 1989/1843)
	1 Apr 1991 (otherwise) (SI 1990/2610)
4, 5	1 Jun 1990 (SI 1990/802)
6	1 Jun 1990 (repeals of or in Road Traffic Act 1988, s 97(1); Road Traffic Offenders Act 1988, s 45(3), Sch 2, Pt I (entry relating to s 45 of that Act)) (SI 1990/802)
	1 Dec 1990 (repeals in Road Traffic Act 1988, s 97(3)) (SI 1990/2228)
	1 Apr 1991 (otherwise, except repeal of Road Traffic (Driver Licensing and Information Systems) Act 1989, Sch 1, para 11) (SI 1990/2610)
	Not in force (exception noted above)

Security Service Act 1989 (c 5)

RA: 27 Apr 1989

Commencement provisions: s 7(2); Security Service Act 1989 (Commencement) Order 1989, SI 1989/2093

18 Dec 1989 (SI 1989/2093)

Self–Governing Schools etc (Scotland) Act 1989 (c 39)

RA: 16 Nov 1989

Commencement provisions: s 81; Self–Governing Schools etc (Scotland) Act 1989 (Commencement) Order 1990, SI 1990/86; Self–Governing Schools etc (Scotland) Act 1989 (Commencement No 2) Order 1990, SI 1990/1108

s 1–53	16 Nov 1989 (s 81(1))
54–66	Repealed
67	1 Feb 1990 (SI 1990/86)
68	16 Nov 1989 (s 81(1))
69(1), (2)	1 Feb 1990 (SI 1990/86)
(3)	16 Nov 1989 (s 81(1))
70	*Not in force*
71	16 Nov 1989 (s 81(1))
72	1 Jun 1990 (SI 1990/1108)
73–76	1 Feb 1990 (SI 1990/86)
77–81	16 Nov 1989 (s 81(1))
82(1)	16 Nov 1989 (s 81(1))
(2)	1 Feb 1990 (SI 1990/86)
83	16 Nov 1989 (s 81(1))

Self–Governing Schools etc (Scotland) Act 1989 (c 39)—*cont*

Sch 1–9	16 Nov 1989 (s 81(1))
10, para 1, 2	1 Feb 1990 (SI 1990/86)
3	16 Nov 1989 (s 81(1))
4	Repealed
5–7	16 Nov 1989 (s 81(1))
8(1)–(6)	16 Nov 1989 (s 81(1))
(7)	1 Feb 1990 (SI 1990/86)
(8)	16 Nov 1989 (s 81(1))
(9)–(11)	1 Feb 1990 (SI 1990/86)
(12)	16 Nov 1989 (s 81(1))
(13)–(21)	1 Feb 1990 (SI 1990/86)
(22)	16 Nov 1989 (s 81(1))
9, 10	16 Nov 1989 (s 81(1))
11	1 Feb 1990 (SI 1990/86)

Social Security Act 1989 (c 24)

RA: 21 Jul 1989

Commencement provisions: s 33(2), (3); Social Security Act 1989 (Commencement No 1) Order 1989, SI 1989/1238; Social Security Act 1989 (Commencement No 2) Order 1989, SI 1989/1262; Social Security Act 1989 (Commencement No 3) Order 1990, SI 1990/102; Social Security Act 1989 (Commencement No 4) Order 1990, SI 1990/312 (correcting defect in SI 1990/102)

s 1–3	Repealed
4	21 Jul 1989 (RA)
5	9 Oct 1989 (SI 1989/1238)
6	21 Jul 1989 (RA)
7(1)–(5)	Repealed
(6)	See Sch 1 below; prospectively repealed by Pension Schemes Act 1993, s 188(1), Sch 5 (qv)
8–19	Repealed
20	21 Jul 1989 (RA)
21	Repealed
22(1)–(6)	Repealed
(7)	See Sch 4 below
(8)	Repealed
23	See Sch 5 below
24	See Sch 6 below
25(1)–(3)	1 Mar 1990 (for purposes of regulations expressed to come into force on 1 Jan 1991) (SI 1990/102)
	1 Jan 1991 (otherwise) (SI 1990/102)
(4)–(6)	1 Jan 1991 (SI 1990/102)
26	See Sch 7 below
27	Repealed
28–30	21 Jul 1989 (RA)
31(1)	See Sch 8 below
(2)	See Sch 9 below
(3)	21 Jul 1989 (RA)
32	Repealed
33	21 Jul 1989 (RA)
Sch 1, para 1–10	Repealed
11	1 Oct 1989 (SI 1989/1238); prospectively repealed by Pension Schemes Act 1993, s 188(1), Sch 5 (qv)

Social Security Act 1989 (c 24)—*cont*

Sch 2, 3	Repealed
4, para 1–21	Repealed
22, 23	3 Sep 1990 (SI 1990/102)
24	Repealed
5	*Not in force*
6, para 1–5	1 Oct 1989 (SI 1989/1238); prospectively repealed by Pension Schemes Act 1993, s 188(1), Sch 5 (qv)
6, 7	21 Jul 1989 (RA); prospectively repealed by Social Security Act 1990, ss 21(2), 23, Sch 7 (qv)
(8–20	Prospectively repealed by Pension Schemes Act 1993, s 188(1), Sch 5 (qv))
8	21 Jul 1989 (RA)
9–13	1 Oct 1989 (SI 1989/1238)
14	21 Jul 1989 (RA)
15	1 Oct 1989 (SI 1989/1238)
16–21	21 Jul 1989 (RA)
7, para 1	1 Oct 1989 (SI 1989/1238); prospectively repealed by Pension Schemes Act 1993, s 188(1), Sch 5 (qv)
2–20	Repealed
21	1 Oct 1989 (SI 1989/1238); prospectively repealed by Pension Schemes Act 1993, s 188(1), Sch 5 (qv)
22–26	Repealed
27	1 Oct 1989 (SI 1989/1238)
8, para 1–7	Repealed
8(1)	Repealed
(2)	21 Jul 1989 (RA); prospectively repealed by Social Security Act 1990, ss 21(2), 23, Sch 7 (qv)
9	Repealed
10	21 Jul 1989 (RA)
11	Repealed
12, 13	21 Jul 1989 (RA)
14–18	Repealed
19	25 Jul 1989 (SI 1989/1262 superseding SI 1989/1238))
9	21 Jul 1989 (repeals consequential on the bringing into force of provisions listed in s 33(3)(a)–(f) on 21 Jul 1989) (RA)
	1 Oct 1989 (repeals of or in Social Security Act 1973, s 51(7); Social Security Act 1975, ss 14(6), 15(6)(a), 27(3)–(5), 28(1)(a), 29(5)(a), 30(1), (3), (6)(a), 39(1)(b), 41(1), 48(2), (3), Sch 20 (in definition 'week'); Social Security Pensions Act 1975, ss 8(1), 11, 45(3), Sch 4, para 39; Social Security (Miscellaneous Provisions) Act 1977, s 21(1); Social Security Act 1979, Sch 1, para 17; Social Security and Housing Benefits Act 1982; Social Security Act 1986, ss 50(1), 63(1)(a)(ii), Sch 6, para 3, Sch 10, para 96) (SI 1989/1238)
	5 Oct 1989 (repeals of or in Social Security Act 1975, s 4(6F); Social Security Contributions Act 1982, s 4(4), Sch 1, para 1(4)) (SI 1989/1238)
	9 Oct 1989 (repeals of or in Merchant Shipping Act 1970, s 17(10); Social Security Act 1975, ss 20(1A), 26(7); Social Security Act 1986, s 26(3) and second paragraph of rubric at end of Sch 9) (SI 1989/1238)

Social Security Act 1989 (c 24)—*cont*

Sch 9—*cont*   1 Feb 1990 (repeal of Social Security (Contributions)
                                    Act 1982, s 4(4)) (SI 1990/312)
                                 6 Apr 1990 (repeals of or in Social Security Act
                                    1975, ss 100(3), 101(6), (7), 112(4), (5), Sch 10,
                                    para 1(7), 2(2), Sch 11, para 4, Sch 13, para 8, 9,
                                    Sch 20, definition of 'local office') (SI 1990/102)
                                 Not in force (otherwise)

Statute Law (Repeals) Act 1989 (c 43)

RA: 16 Nov 1989

Commencement provisions: s 3(2); Statute law (Repeals) Act 1989 (Commencement)
    Order 1992, SI 1992/1275

  s 1–3   16 Nov 1989 (RA)

Sch 1   16 Nov 1989 (except repeal of Federation of Malaya
                                    Independence Act 1957, s 3; Malaysia Act 1963, s 5)
                                    (RA)
                                 1 Jun 1992 (exceptions noted above) (SI 1992/1275)
  2   16 Nov 1989 (RA)

Transport (Scotland) Act 1989 (c 23)

RA: 21 Jul 1989

Commencement provisions: s 12(2)

  s 1–17   21 Sep 1989 (s 12(2))
  18   21 Jul 1989 (s 12(2))

Water Act 1989 (c 15)

RA: 6 Jul 1989

Commencement provisions: s 194(2)–(5); Water Act 1989 (Commencement No 1)
    Order 1989, SI 1989/1146; Water Authorities (Transfer of Functions) (Appointed
    Day) Order 1989, SI 1989/1530; Water Act 1989 (Commencement No 2 and
    Transitional Provisions) Order 1989, SI 1989/1557; Water Act 1989
    (Commencement No 3) (Scotland) Order 1989, SI 1989/1561; Water Act 1989
    (Commencement No 4) Order 1989, SI 1989/2278

Abbreviation: "rel sub leg" means "so far as relating to the making of subordinate
legislation"

  s 1(1)–(5)   Repealed
    (6)   See Sch 1 below
  2, 3   Repealed
  4   6 Jul 1989 (rel sub leg) (s 194(2))
                                 7 Jul 1989 (otherwise) (EW) (SI 1989/1146)
                                 1 Sep 1989 (otherwise) (NI) (SI 1989/1557)
                                 1 Sep 1989 (otherwise) (S) (SI 1989/1561)
  5(1)–(4)   Repealed
    (5)   See Sch 3 below

Water Act 1989 (c 15)—*cont*

s 6(1)–(7)	Repealed
(8)	1 Sep 1989 (SI 1989/1146; SI 1989/1530; SI 1989/1561)
7–10	Repealed
11(1)–(8)	Repealed
(9)	7 Jul 1989 (EW) (SI 1989/1146)
	1 Sep 1989 (NI) (SI 1989/1557)
12	Repealed
13	6 Jul 1989 (rel sub leg) (S) (s 194(2))
	1 Sep 1989 (so far as relates to schemes under Sch 5) (S) (SI 1989/1561)
	Not in force (otherwise) (S)
	Repealed (EW)
14–22	Repealed
23	1 Sep 1989 (S) (s 194(3))
	Repealed (EW)
24–68	Repealed
69	1 Sep 1989 (s 194(3))
70(1), (2)	1 Sep 1989 (s 194(3))
(3)–(5)	Repealed
71–82	Repealed
83	6 Jul 1989 (rel sub leg) (s 194(2))
	1 Sep 1989 (otherwise) (s 194(3))
84	1 Sep 1989 (s 194(3))
85, 86	6 Jul 1989 (rel sub leg) (s 194(2))
	1 Sep 1989 (otherwise) (s 194(3))
87, 88	1 Sep 1989 (s 194(3))
89	6 Jul 1989 (rel sub leg) (s 194(2))
	1 Sep 1989 (otherwise) (s 194(3))
90, 91	1 Sep 1989 (s 194(3))
92	6 Jul 1989 (rel sub leg) (s 194(2))
	1 Sep 1989 (otherwise) (s 194(3))
93, 94	1 Sep 1989 (s 194(3))
95	6 Jul 1989 (rel sub leg) (s 194(2))
	1 Sep 1989 (otherwise) (s 194(3))
96	1 Sep 1989 (s 194(3))
97–135	Repealed
136	1 Sep 1989 (S) (s 194(3))
	Repealed (EW)
137(1)–(8)	Repealed
(9)	6 Jul 1989 (rel sub leg) (s 194(2))
	1 Sep 1989 (otherwise) (s 194(3))
(10), (11)	Repealed
138	Repealed
139(1)–(5)	Repealed
(6)	1 Sep 1989 (s 194(3))
140	Repealed
141(1)–(4)	1 Sep 1989 (S) (s 194(3))
	Repealed (EW)
(5), (6)	1 Sep 1989 (s 194(3))
(7)	1 Sep 1989 (S) (s 194(3))
	Repealed (EW)
142(1)	Repealed
(2)	1 Sep 1989 (s 194(3))
143–167	Repealed
168	See Sch 22 below
169	See Sch 23 below

Water Act 1989 (c 15)—*cont*

s 170, 171	Repealed
172	1 Sep 1989 (S) (SI 1989/1561)
	Repealed (EW)
173	6 Jul 1989 (rel sub leg) (s 194(2))
	1 Sep 1989 (otherwise) (SI 1989/1146; SI 1989/1530)
174(1)–(7)	6 Jul (rel sub leg) (s 194(2))
	7 Jul 1989 (otherwise) (SI 1989/1146)
(8)	Added by Water Consolidation (Consequential Provisions) Act 1991, s 2(1), Sch 1, para 50(1), (2)(e) (qv)
175	1 Sep 1989 (SI 1989/1146; SI 1989/1530)
176	Repealed
177	7 Jul 1989 (SI 1989/1146)
178–182	Repealed
183, 184	1 Sep 1989 (SI 1989/1146; SI 1989/1530)
185	6 Jul 1989 (s 194(2))
186	Repealed
187	7 Jul 1989 (SI 1989/1146)
188	Repealed
189(1)	6 Jul 1989 (definitions of 'the 1945 Act', 'the 1973 Act', 'the Authority', 'contravention', 'the Director', 'disposal' (and cognate expressions), 'enactment', 'holding company', 'information', 'local statutory provision', 'the Minister', 'modifications' (and cognate expressions), 'sewer', 'statutory water company', 'subordinate legislation', 'successor company', 'transfer date', 'water authority') (rel sub leg) (s 194(2))
	Repealed (otherwise)
	7 Jul 1989 (definitions listed above) (otherwise) (SI 1989/1146)
(2)–(5)	Repealed
(6), (7)	6 Jul 1989 (rel sub leg) (s 194(2))
	7 Jul 1989 (otherwise) (SI 1989/1146)
(8)	Repealed
(9), (10)	6 Jul 1989 (rel sub leg) (s 194(2))
	7 Jul 1989 (otherwise) (SI 1989/1146)
190	See Schs 25–27 below (6 Jul 1989 (rel sub leg) (s 194(2))
191(1)–(5)	6 Jul 1989 (s 194(2))
(6)	7 Jul 1989 (SI 1989/1146)
192	7 Jul 1989 (SI 1989/1146)
193	6 Jul 1989 (rel sub leg) (s 194(2))
	7 Jul 1989 (otherwise) (SI 1989/1146)
194	6 Jul 1989 (s 194(2))
Sch 1, para 1–10	Repealed
11	7 Jul 1989 (EW) (SI 1989/1146)
	1 Sep 1989 (NI) (SI 1989/1557)
	1 Sep 1989 (S) (SI 1989/1561)
12	7 Jul 1989 (SI 1989/1146)
13	7 Jul 1989 (EW) (SI 1989/1146)
	1 Sep 1989 (NI) (SI 1989/1557)
	1 Sep 1989 (S) (SI 1989/1561)
14–23	Repealed
2	6 Jul 1989 (rel sub leg) (s 194(2))
	7 Jul 1989 (otherwise) (EW) (SI 1989/1146)

Water Act 1989 (c 15)—*cont*

2—*cont*	1 Sep 1989 (otherwise) (NI) (SI 1989/1557)
	1 Sep 1989 (otherwise) (S) (SI 1989/1561)
3, para 1–5	Repealed
6, 7	7 Jul 1989 (EW) (SI 1989/1146)
	1 Sep 1989 (NI) (SI 1989/1557)
	1 Sep 1989 (S) (SI 1989/1561)
4, para 1–5	Repealed
6	1 Sep 1989 (SI 1989/1146; SI 1989/1530; SI 1989/ 1557; SI 1989/1561)
5	6 Jul 1989 (rel sub leg) (S) (s 194(2))
	1 Sep 1989 (otherwise) (S) (s 194(3))
	Repealed (EW)
6, 7	Repealed
8, para 1	Repealed
2(1)–(10)	Repealed
(11)	1 Sep 1989 (s 194(3))
(12)	Repealed
3–5	Repealed
6, 7	1 Sep 1989 (s 194(3))
9–14	Repealed
15, para 1	1 Sep 1989 (S) (s 194(3))
	Repealed (EW)
2–13	Repealed
14	1 Sep 1989 (S) (s 194(3))
	Repealed (EW)
15–41	Repealed
16	Repealed
17, para 1	1 Sep 1989 (s 194(3))
2	6 Jul 1989 (s 194(2))
3	1 Sep 1989 (s 194(3))
4	*Not in force*
5–9	1 Sep 1989 (s 194(3))
18–21	Repealed
22	1 Sep 1989 (s 194(3))
23	1 Sep 1989 (except so far as relates to Control of Pollution Act 1974, s 33) (S) (s 194(3))
	31 May 1991 (exception noted above) (S) (SI 1991/ 1172)
	Not in force (so far as relates to Control of Pollution Act 1984, ss 33 (EW), 47, 48)
24	Repealed
25	1 Sep 1989 (for transitional provisions, see SI 1989/ 1557, art 6) (SI 1989/1146; SI 1989/1530; SI 1989/ 1557; SI 1989/1561)
26	6 Jul 1989 (rel sub leg) (s 194(2))
	1 Sep 1989 (otherwise) (s 194(3))
27, Pt I	1 Sep 1989 (s 194(3))
II	1 Sep 1989 (repeals of or in Water Act 1945, s 41(7), Sch 3, ss 75–77; Rating and Valuation (Miscellaneous Provisions) Act 1955, s 11; Trustee Investments Act 1961, Sch 4, para 3; Water Act 1973, ss 34(1), (3), 35(1), (2), Sch 6, Pt I, Sch 8, para 50) (SI 1989/1557; note savings therein)
	1 Apr 1990 (repeals of or in Water Act 1945, s 59(3), Sch 3, ss 74, 81) (SI 1989/1557)
	Not in force (otherwise)

1990

Access to Health Records Act 1990 (c 23)

RA: 13 Jul 1990

Commencement provisions: s 12(2)

1 Nov 1991 (s 12(2))

Agricultural Holdings (Amendment) Act 1990 (c 15)

RA: 29 Jun 1990

Commencement provisions: s 3(2)

29 Jul 1990 (s 3(2))

Appropriation Act 1990 (c 28)

Whole Act repealed

Australian Constitution (Public Record Copy) Act 1990 (c 17)

RA: 29 Jul 1990

29 Jul 1990 (RA)

Aviation and Maritime Security Act 1990 (c 31)

RA: 26 Jul 1990

Commencement provisions: s 54(2)

s 1	26 Sep 1990 (s 54(2))
2–4	26 Jul 1990 (RA)
5	26 Sep 1990 (s 54(2))
6, 7	26 Jul 1990 (RA)
8	See Sch 1 below
9–17	26 Sep 1990 (s 54(2))
18–36	26 Jul 1990 (RA)
37–40	26 Sep 1990 (s 54(2))
41–44	26 Jul 1990 (RA)
45	See Sch 2 below
46–52	26 Jul 1990 (RA)
53(1)	See Sch 3 below
(2)	See Sch 4 below
54	26 Jul 1990 (RA)

Aviation and Maritime Security Act 1990 (c 31)—*cont*

Sch 1, para 1	26 Sep 1990 (s 54(2))
2(1)–(5)	26 Jul 1990 (RA)
(6)	26 Sep 1990 (s 54(2))
(7)	26 Jul 1990 (RA)
3	26 Jul 1990 (RA)
4–6	26 Sep 1990 (s 54(2))
7–10	26 Jul 1990 (RA)
11(1)–(4)	26 Jul 1990 (RA)
(5)	26 Sep 1990 (s 54(2))
2	26 Jul 1990 (RA)
3	26 Sep 1990 (s 54(2))
4	26 Jul 1990 (except repeals of or in Aviation Security Act 1982, ss 11(5)(a), 14(7)(a), 20(5); Extradition Act 1989) (RA)
	26 Sep 1990 (exception noted above) (s 54(2))

British Nationality (Hong Kong) Act 1990 (c 34)

RA: 26 Jul 1990

Commencement provisions: s 6(4); British Nationality (Hong Kong) Act 1990 (Commencement) Order 1990, SI 1990/2210

s 1(1)	See Sch 1 below
(2), (3)	7 Nov 1990 (SI 1990/2210)
(4)	See Sch 2 below
(5)	7 Nov 1990 (SI 1990/2210)
2(1)	7 Nov 1990 (SI 1990/2210)
(2)	*Not in force*
(3)	7 Nov 1990 (SI 1990/2210)
3–6	7 Nov 1990 (SI 1990/2210)
Sch 1, 2	7 Nov 1990 (SI 1990/2210)

Broadcasting Act 1990 (c 42)

RA: 1 Nov 1990

Commencement provisions: s 204(2); Broadcasting Act 1990 (Commencement No 1 and Transitional Provisions) Order 1990, SI 1990/2347

s 1(1), (2)	1 Dec 1990 (SI 1990/2347)
(3)	See Sch 1 below
2(1)	1 Jan 1991 (SI 1990/2347)
(2)–(6)	1 Dec 1990 (SI 1990/2347)
3–9	1 Dec 1990 (SI 1990/2347)
10	1 Jan 1991 (SI 1990/2347)
11	1 Dec 1990 (SI 1990/2347)
12–22	1 Jan 1991 (SI 1990/2347)
23(1)–(5)	1 Jan 1993 (SI 1990/2347)
(6)	See Sch 3 below
24, 25	1 Jan 1993 (SI 1990/2347)
26	1 Jan 1991 (SI 1990/2347)
27	1 Jan 1993 (SI 1990/2347)
28–33	1 Jan 1991 (SI 1990/2347)

Broadcasting Act 1990 (c 42)—*cont*

s 34, 35	1 Jan 1991 (for purposes of enabling conditions of type specified in ss 34(2), 35(1) to be included in a Channel 3 or Channel 5 licence or a licence to provide Channel 4) (SI 1990/2347)
	1 Jan 1993 (otherwise) (SI 1990/2347)
36–42	1 Jan 1991 (SI 1990/2347)
43	1 Dec 1990 (SI 1990/2347)
44	1 Jan 1991 (SI 1990/2347)
45–47	1 Dec 1990 (SI 1990/2347)
48–55	1 Jan 1991 (SI 1990/2347)
56(1), (2)	1 Jan 1991 (SI 1990/2347)
(3)	See Sch 6 below
57–70	1 Jan 1991 (SI 1990/2347)
71	1 Dec 1990 (SI 1990/2347)
72–82	1 Jan 1991 (SI 1990/2347)
83(1), (2)	1 Dec 1990 (SI 1990/2347)
(3)	See Sch 8 below
84–125	1 Jan 1991 (SI 1990/2347)
126, 127	1 Dec 1990 (SI 1990/2347)
128, 129	1 Jan 1991 (SI 1990/2347)
130–133	1 Dec 1990 (SI 1990/2347)
134–140	1 Jan 1991 (SI 1990/2347)
141	1 Dec 1990 (SI 1990/2347)
142(1)–(3)	1 Jan 1991 (SI 1990/2347)
(4)	See Sch 13 below
143–150	1 Jan 1991 (SI 1990/2347)
151(1), (2)	1 Jan 1991 (SI 1990/2347)
(3)	See Sch 14 below
152–161	1 Jan 1991 (SI 1990/2347)
162(1)	1 Jan 1991 (SI 1990/2347)
(2)	See Sch 15 below
163–170	1 Jan 1991 (SI 1990/2347)
171	See Sch 16 below
172–174	1 Jan 1991 (SI 1990/2347)
175	1 Feb 1991 (SI 1990/2347)
176	See Sch 17 below
177–179	1 Jan 1991 (SI 1990/2347)
180	See Sch 18 below
181, 182	1 Jan 1991 (SI 1990/2347)
183	See Sch 19 below
184	1 Jan 1991 (SI 1990/2347)
185	1 Jan 1991 (for purposes of enabling conditions of type specified in s 185(3) to be included in a Channel 3 or Channel 5 licence or a licence to provide Channel 4) (SI 1990/2347)
	1 Jan 1993 (otherwise) (SI 1990/2347)
186	1 Jan 1991 (SI 1990/2347)
187	1 Jan 1993 (SI 1990/2347)
188–197	1 Jan 1991 (SI 1990/2347)
198–202	1 Dec 1990 (SI 1990/2347)
203(1)	See Sch 20 below
(2)	1 Jan 1991 (SI 1990/2347)
(3)	See Sch 21 below
(4)	See Sch 22 below
204	1 Dec 1990 (SI 1990/2347)
Sch 1, 2	1 Dec 1990 (SI 1990/2347)

Broadcasting Act 1990 (c 42)—*cont*

Sch 3	1 Jan 1993 (SI 1990/2347)
4–7	1 Jan 1991 (SI 1990/2347)
8, 9	1 Dec 1990 (SI 1990/2347)
10–16	1 Jan 1991 (SI 1990/2347)
17	1 Jan 1991 (for purposes of enabling publication of information about programmes to be included in a programme service on or after that date) (SI 1990/2347)
	1 Mar 1991 (otherwise) (SI 1990/2347)
18	1 Apr 1991 (SI 1990/2347)
19	1 Jan 1991 (SI 1990/2347)
20, para 1–13	1 Jan 1991 (SI 1990/2347)
14	Repealed
15–21	1 Jan 1991 (SI 1990/2347)
22	Repealed
23–35	1 Jan 1991 (SI 1990/2347)
36	1 Jan 1991 (except so far as replaces the reference to the Independent Broadcasting Authority until that Authority is dissolved by order under s 127(3)) (SI 1990/2347)
	Not in force (exception noted above)
37	1 Jan 1993 (SI 1990/2347)
38–54	1 Jan 1991 (SI 1990/2347)
21	1 Dec 1990 (repeal of or in Cable and Broadcasting Act 1984, s 8(1)(a), (b)) (SI 1990/2347)
	1 Jan 1991 (all remaining repeals except repeals of or in Wireless Telegraphy (Blind Persons) Act 1955; Wireless Telegraphy Act 1967; House of Commons Disqualification Act 1975, Sch 1, Pt II; Northern Ireland Assembly Disqualification Act 1975) (subject to transitional provisions; see SI 1990/2347, art 3(3)) (SI 1990/2347)
	1 Apr 1991 (repeals of or in Wireless Telegraphy (Blind Persons) Act 1955; Wireless Telegraphy Act 1967) (SI 1990/2347)
22, para 1–3	1 Dec 1990 (SI 1990/2347)
4–7	1 Jan 1991 (SI 1990/2347)

Caldey Island Act 1990 (c 44)

RA: 1 Nov 1990

1 Nov 1990 (RA)

Capital Allowances Act 1990 (c 1)

RA: 19 Mar 1990

Commencement provisions: s 164

Act (which is a consolidation) has effect, generally, as respects allowances and charges falling to be made for chargeable periods ending after 5 April 1990 and applies in relation to expenditure incurred in chargeable periods ending before 6 April 1990

Care of Cathedrals Measure 1990 (No 2)

RA: 26 Jul 1990

Commencement provisions: s 21(2)

The provisions of this measure are brought into force on the following dates by an appointed day notice signed by the Archbishops of Canterbury and York and dated 28 Sep 1990 (made under s 21(2))

s 1, 2	1 Mar 1991
3(1), (2)	1 Mar 1991
(3)	See Sch 1 below
4(1), (2)	1 Mar 1991
(3)	See Sch 2 below
5–12	1 Mar 1991
13	1 Oct 1990
14, 15	1 Mar 1991
16	Repealed
17–21	1 Oct 1990
Sch 1, 2	1 Mar 1991

Civil Aviation Authority (Borrowing Powers) Act 1990 (c 2)

RA: 19 Mar 1990

19 Mar 1990 (RA)

Clergy (Ordination) Measure 1990 (No 1)

RA: 22 Feb 1990

22 Feb 1990 (RA)

Coal Industry Act 1990 (c 3)

RA: 19 Mar 1990

Commencement provisions: s 6(2)

s 1	19 Mar 1990 (RA)
2	Repealed
3	19 Mar 1990 (RA)
4	19 May 1990 (s 6(2))
5, 6	19 Mar 1990 (RA)

Computer Misuse Act 1990 (c 18)

RA: 26 Jun 1990

Commencement provisions: s 18(2)

29 Aug 1990 (s 18(2))

Consolidated Fund Act 1990 (c 4)

Whole Act repealed

Consolidated Fund (No 2) Act 1990 (c 46)

Whole Act repealed

Contracts (Applicable Law) Act 1990 (c 36)

RA: 26 Jul 1990

Commencement provisions: s 7; Contracts (Applicable Law) Act 1990
(Commencement No 1) Order 1991, SI 1991/707

s 1	1 Apr 1991 (SI 1991/707)
2(1)	1 Apr 1991 (so far as relates to the Rome Convention and the Luxembourg Convention as defined in s 1) (SI 1991/707)
	Not in force (otherwise)
(1A)	Inserted by Insurance Companies (Amendment) Regulations 1993, SI 1993/174, reg 9; substituted by Friendly Societies (Amendment) Regulations 1993, SI 1993/2519, reg 6(5)
(2), (3)	1 Apr 1991 (SI 1991/707)
(4)	See Schs 1–3 below
3(1), (2)	*Not in force*
(3)(a)	1 Apr 1991 (SI 1991/707)
(b)	*Not in force*
4	1 Apr 1991 (SI 1991/707)
5	See Sch 4 below
6–9	1 Apr 1991 (SI 1991/707)
Sch 1–4	1 Apr 1991 (SI 1991/707)

Courts and Legal Services Act 1990 (c 41)

RA: 1 Nov 1990

Commencement provisions: s 124; Courts and Legal Services Act 1990
(Commencement No 1) Order 1990, SI 1990/2170; Courts and Legal Services
Act 1990 (Commencement No 2) Order 1990, SI 1990/2484; Courts and Legal
Services Act 1990 (Commencement No 3) Order 1991, SI 1991/608; Courts and
Legal Services Act 1990 (Commencement No 4) Order 1991, SI 1991/985;
Courts and Legal Services Act 1990 (Commencement No 5) Order 1991, SI
1991/1364; Courts and Legal Services Act 1990 (Commencement No 6) Order
1991, SI 1991/1883; Courts and Legal Services Act 1990 (Commencement No 7)
Order 1991, SI 1991/2730; Courts and Legal Services Act 1990 (Commencement
No 8) Order 1992, SI 1992/1221; Courts and Legal Services Act 1990
(Commencement No 9) Order 1993, SI 1993/2132

s 1	1 Nov 1990 (RA)
2, 3	1 Jul 1991 (SI 1991/1364)
4	1 Oct 1991 (SI 1991/1883)
5	1 Nov 1990 (RA)

Courts and Legal Services Act 1990 (c 41)—*cont*

s 6	1 Jan 1991 (s 124(2)(a))
7(1)	23 Jul 1993 (except so far as relates to s 7(2)) (SI 1993/2132)
	1 Oct 1993 (exception noted above) (SI 1993/2132)
(2)	1 Oct 1993 (SI 1993/2132)
(3), (4)	23 Jul 1993 (SI 1993/2132)
8	1 Jan 1991 (s 124(2)(a))
9	1 Jan 1991 (SI 1990/2484)
10	1 Jul 1991 (SI 1991/1364)
11	1 Jan 1991 (s 124(2)(a))
12–14	*Not in force*
15	1 Jul 1991 (SI 1991/1364)
16	1 Jan 1991 (s 124(2)(a)
17, 18	1 Apr 1991 (SI 1991/608)
19(1)–(8)	1 Apr 1991 (SI 1991/608)
(9)	See Sch 1 below
20(1)	1 Apr 1991 (SI 1991/608)
(2)	See Sch 2 below
(3)	1 Apr 1991 (SI 1991/608)
21(1)–(5)	1 Jan 1991 (SI 1990/2484)
(6)	See Sch 3 below
22, 23	1 Jan 991 (SI 1990/2484)
24(1), (2)	1 Jan 1991 (SI 1990/2484)
(3)	1 Apr 1991 (SI 1991/608)
25–28	1 Jan 1991 (SI 1990/2484)
29	1 Apr 1991 (SI 1991/608)
30(1), (2)	1 Apr 1991 (SI 1991/608)
(3)	See Sch 4, Pt III below
(4)–(6)	1 Apr 1991 (SI 1991/608)
31(1), (2)	1 Jan 1991 (SI 1990/2484)
(3)–(9)	1 Apr 1991 (SI 1991/608)
32(1), (2)	1 Jan 1991 (SI 1990/2484)
(3)–(9)	1 Apr 1991 (SI 1991/608)
33(1), (2)	1 Jan 1991 (SI 1990/2484)
(3)–(9)	1 Apr 1991 (SI 1991/608)
34(1)–(7)	1 Apr 1991 (SI 1991/608)
(8)	See Sch 5 below
35	1 Apr 1991 (SI 1991/608)
36–39	*Not in force*
40	1 Apr 1991 (SI 1991/608)
41(1)–(10)	*Not in force*
(11)	See Sch 6 below
42	*Not in force*
43(1)–(3)	*Not in force*
(4)	See Sch 7 below
(5)–(12)	*Not in force*
44–52	*Not in force*
53(1)–(6)	1 Apr 1991 (except in relation to exemptions under s 55) (SI 1991/608)
	Not in force (exception noted above)
(7)	See Sch 8 below
(8), (9)	1 Apr 1991 (except in relation to exemptions under s 55) (SI 1991/608)
	Not in force (exception noted above)
54	*Not in force*
55(1)–(3)	*Not in force*
(4)	See Sch 9 below

Courts and Legal Services Act 1990 (c 41)—*cont*

s 56, 57	1 Jul 1991 (SI 1991/1364)
58	23 Jul 1993 (SI 1993/2132)
59	1 Apr 1991 (SI 1991/608)
60–62	1 Jan 1991 (SI 1990/2484)
63(1)(a)	1 Apr 1991 (SI 1991/608)
(b), (c)	*Not in force*
(2)	1 Apr 1991 (SI 1991/608)
(3)	*Not in force*
64, 65	1 Jan 1991 (s 124(2)(a))
66–68	1 Jan 1991 (SI 1990/2484)
69	1 Apr 1991 (SI 1991/608)
70	1 Jan 1991 (except so far as relates to authorised practitioners) (SI 1990/2484)
	Not in force (exception noted above)
71(1)	1 Jan 1991 (SI 1990/2484)
(2)	See Sch 10 below
(3)–(8)	1 Jan 1991 (SI 1990/2484)
72, 73	1 Jan 1991 (s 124(2)(a))
74(1)–(3)	1 Jan 1991 (SI 1990/2484)
(4)–(7)	1 Jul 1991 (SI 1991/1364)
75	See Sch 11 below
76–78	1 Jan 1991 (SI 1990/2484)
79(1)	1 Jan 1992 (SI 1991/2730)
(2)	See Sch 12 below
80	1 Jan 1992 (SI 1991/2730)
81	See Sch 13 below
82	*Not in force*
83, 84	1 Jan 1991 (SI 1990/2484)
85	1 Jan 1991 (s 124(2)(a))
86	1 Jul 1991 (SI 1991/1364)
87, 88	1 Jan 1991 (s 124(2)(a))
89(1)–(7)	14 Oct 1991 (SI 1991/1883)
(8)	See Sch 14 below
(9)	14 Oct 1991 (SI 1991/1883)
90–92	1 Jan 1991 (s 124(2)(a))
93(1), (2)	1 Apr 1991 (SI 1991/608)
(3)	See Sch 15 below
(4)	1 Apr 1991 (SI 1991/608)
94–98	1 Jan 1991 (s 124(2)(a))
99–101	1 Apr 1991 (SI 1991/608)
102	1 Jan 1992 (SI 1991/2730)
103	1 Apr 1991 (SI 1991/608)
104–107	*Not in force*
108–110	1 Jan 1991 (s 124(2)(a))
111	1 May 1991 (SI 1991/985)
112	1 Oct 1991 (SI 1991/1883)
113–115	1 Apr 1991 (SI 1991/608)
116(1)	See Sch 16, Pt I below
(2)	See Sch 16, Pt II below
(3)	1 Jan 1992 (SI 1991/2730)
117	1 Jul 1991 (SI 1991/1364)
118	1 Jan 1991 (SI 1990/2484)
119–124	1 Nov 1990 (RA)
125(1)	1 Nov 1990 (RA)
(2)	See Sch 17 below
(3)	See Sch 18 below
(4), (5)	1 Oct 1991 (SI 1991/1883)

Courts and Legal Services Act 1990 (c 41)—*cont*

s 125(6)	See Sch 19 below
(7)	See Sch 20 below
Sch 1, 2	1 Apr 1991 (SI 1991/608)
3	1 Jan 1991 (SI 1990/2484)
4, 5	1 Apr 1991 (SI 1991/608)
6, 7	*Not in force*
8	1 Apr 1991 (except in relation to exemptions under s 55) (SI 1991/608)
	Not in force (exception noted above)
9	*Not in force*
10, 11	1 Jan 1991 (SI 1990/2484)
12	1 Jan 1992 (SI 1991/2730)
	Not in force
14	14 Oct 1991 (SI 1991/1883)
15	1 Apr 1991 (SI 1991/608)
16, Pt I, para 1–7	14 Oct 1991 (SI 1991/1883)
8	1 Jan 1991 (SI 1990/2484)
9–33	14 Oct 1991 (SI 1991/1883)
II, para 34–42	14 Oct 1991 (SI 1991/1883)
17, para 1	1 Jan 1991 (s 124(2)(b)
2, 3	1 Nov 1990 (RA)
4	1 Apr 1991 (SI 1991/608)
5	*Not in force*
6	1 Jul 1991 (SI 1991/1364)
7, 8	1 Apr 1991 (SI 1991/608)
9	1 Jan 1991 (SI 1990/2484)
10	1 Apr 1991 (SI 1991/608)
11, 12	1 Jan 1991 (s 124(2)(b))
13	1 Apr 1991 (SI 1991/608)
14	14 Oct 1991 (SI 1991/1883)
15	1 Jan 1991 (SI 1990/2484)
16	1 Jan 1991 (s 124(2)(b))
17, 18	1 Jul 1991 (SI 1991/1364)
19	*Not in force*
20	1 Jan 1991 (s 124(2)(b))
18, para 1	1 Jan 1991 (so far as relates to the Legal Services Ombudsman) (SI 1990/2484)
	1 Apr 1991 (so far as relates to Lord Chancellor's Advisory Committee on Legal Education and Conduct) (SI 1991/608)
	Not in force (otherwise)
2	Repealed
3	1 Jan 1991 (SI 1990/2484)
4	*Not in force*
5	1 Apr 1991 (SI 1991/608)
6	*Not in force*
7, 8	1 Jan 1991 (s 124(2)(c))
9, 10	1 Jul 1991 (SI 1991/1364)
11, 12	*Not in force*
13	1 Jun 1992 (SI 1992/1221)
14–16	1 Jan 1991 (s 124(2)(c))
17, 18	1 Jul 1991 (SI 1991/1364)
19	*Not in force*
20	1 Jan 1991 (SI 1990/2484)
21	14 Oct 1991 (SI 1991/1883)
22, 23	*Not in force*

Courts and Legal Services Act 1990 (c 41)—*cont*

Sch 18, para 24	Repealed
25	1 Jan 1991 (SI 1990/2484)
26–30	1 Jan 1992 (SI 1991/2730)
31	*Not in force*
32	1 Jan 1991 (SI 1990/2484)
33–35	1 Jan 1992 (SI 1991/2730)
36–40	1 Jan 1991 (SI 1990/2484)
41	1 Apr 1991 (SI 1991/608)
42	1 Jan 1991 (SI 1990/2484)
43–46	1 Jul 1991 (SI 1991/1364)
47	1 Jan 1991 (SI 1990/2484)
48, 49	1 Apr 1991 (SI 1991/608)
50, 51	1 Jan 1991 (SI 1990/2484)
52	1 Apr 1991 (SI 1991/608)
53	1 May 1991 (SI 1991/985)
54	14 Oct 1991 (SI 1991/1883)
55	1 Jan 1991 (s 124(2)(c))
56	1 Apr 1991 (SI 1991/608)
57	1 Jan 1991 (s 124(2)(c))
58–63	1 Apr 1991 (SI 1991/608)
19, para 1	1 Jan 1991 (s 124(2)(d))
2–8	1 Jan 1991 (SI 1990/2484)
9	1 Jan 1992 (SI 1991/2730)
10, 11	1 Jan 1991 (SI 1990/2484)
12, 13	1 Jul 1991 (SI 1991/1364)
14, 15	1 Apr 1991 (SI 1991/608)
16	1 Jan 1991 (SI 1990/2484)
17	1 Apr 1991 (SI 1991/608)
20	1 Nov 1990 (repeal of Administration of Justice Act 1956, s 53) (SI 1990/2170)
	1 Jan 1991 (repeals of or in Public Notaries Act 1801, ss 10, 14; Summary Jurisdiction Act 1857; Naval Agency and Distribution Act 1864; War Pensions (Administrative Provisions) Act 1919; Pensions Appeal Tribunals Act 1943; Lands Tribunal Act 1949; Courts–Martial (Appeals) Act 1951; Barristers (Qualification for Office) Act 1961; Superannuation (Miscellaneous Provisions) Act 1967; Superannuation (Miscellaneous Provisions) Act (Northern Ireland) 1969; Courts Act 1971; Administration of Justice Act 1973; Solicitors Act 1974, ss 3–5, 7, 20(2)(c), 39, 45, 82, Sch 3, para 7; Social Security Act 1975; House of Commons Disqualification Act 1975; Ministerial and other Salaries Act 1975; Justices of the Peace Act 1979; Social Security Act 1980; Judicial Pensions Act 1981, s 33, Sch 1, Pt I; Supreme Court Act 1981, ss 12(4), 94, 100(5), 101(2), 102(6), 103(6); County Courts Act 1984, ss 10, 60(1), (2); Prosecution of Offences Act 1985, s 4(5); Administration of Justice Act 1985, ss 3(1), 63, Sch 1, paras 4, 11, Sch 2, paras 8, 15, Sch 7, para 4; Coroners Act 1988) (SI 1990/2484)
	1 Apr 1991 (repeals of or in Commissioners for Oaths Act 1889, s 1; Arbitration Act 1950, s 12(6)(b); Solicitors Act 1974, ss 2(2), 44A, 47A, 81(5); County Courts Act 1984, s 143(2);

Courts and Legal Services Act 1990 (c 41)—*cont*

Sch 20—*cont*	Prosecution of Offences Act 1985, s 15(1); Administration of Justice Act 1985, ss 1, 3(2), 26(3), 65(5), Sch 2, para 19, Sch 3, para 8, Sch 7, para 5) (SI 1991/608)
	1 Jul 1991 (repeals of or in Public Notaries Act 1801, ss 1–5, 7–9; Public Notaries Act 1833; Public Notaries Act 1843; Small Debts Act 1845; Welsh Church Act 1914; Administration of Justice Act 1956, s 37; Administration of Justice Act 1969, s 29; County Courts Act 1984, ss 19, 20, 22, 29, 34, 43, 44, 89(3), 105, 106, Sch 1) (SI 1991/1364)
	14 Oct 1991 (repeals of or in Maintenance Orders Act 1950; Family Law Reform Act 1969; Children and Young Persons Act 1969; Administration of Justice Act 1970; Maintenance Orders (Reciprocal Enforcement of Orders) Act 1972; Domestic Proceedings and Magistrates' Courts Act 1978; Magistrates' Courts Act 1980; Matrimonial and Family Proceedings Act 1984; Family Law Reform Act 1987; Children Act 1989) (SI 1991/1883)
	1 Jan 1992 (repeals of or in Judicial Pensions Act 1981, ss 18(3), 20(6), 22(5), 24, 25, Sch 1, para 15(3)) (SI 1991/2730)
	1 Jun 1992 (repeals of or in Solicitors Act 1974, ss 7, 33(4); County Courts Act 1984, s 45; Administration of Justice Act 1985, s 9(8), Sch 2, para 4(2)) (SI 1992/1221)
	1 Oct 1993 (repeal of words in Supreme Court Act 1981, s 18) (SI 1993/2132)
	Not in force (otherwise)

Criminal Justice (International Co-operation) Act 1990 (c 5)

RA: 5 Apr 1990

Commencement provisions: s 32(2); Criminal Justice (International Co-operation) Act 1990 (Commencement No 1) Order 1991, SI 1991/1072; Criminal Justice (International Co-operation) Act 1990 (Commencement No 2) Order 1991, SI 1991/2108

s 1, 2	10 Jun 1991 (SI 1991/1072)
3(1), (2)	10 Jun 1991 (SI 1991/1072)
(3)	23 Apr 1991 (for purpose of making any Order in Council, order, rules, or regulations) (SI 1991/1072)
	10 Jun 1991 (otherwise) (SI 1991/1072)
(4)–(10)	10 Jun 1991 (SI 1991/1072)
4(1)–(5)	10 Jun 1991 (SI 1991/1072)
(6)	See Sch 1 below
5, 6	10 Jun 1991 (SI 1991/1072)
7(1)–(6)	10 Jun 1991 (SI 1991/1072)
(7)	23 Apr 1991 (for purpose of making any Order in Council, order, rules, or regulations) (SI 1991/1072)

Criminal Justice (International Co-operation) Act 1990 (c 5)—*cont*

s 7(7)—*cont*	10 Jun 1991 (otherwise) (SI 1991/1072)
(8), (9)	10 Jun 1991 (SI 1991/1072)
8(1)–(4)	10 Jun 1991 (SI 1991/1072)
(5)	23 Apr 1991 (for purpose of making any Order in Council, order, rules, or regulations) (SI 1991/1072)
	10 Jun 1991 (otherwise) (SI 1991/1072)
(6)	10 Jun 1991 (SI 1991/1072)
9, 10	23 Apr 1991 (for purpose of making any Order in Council, order, rules, or regulations) (SI 1991/1072)
	10 Jun 1991 (otherwise) (SI 1991/1072)
11	10 Jun 1991 (SI 1991/1072)
12(1)–(4)	1 Jul 1991 (SI 1991/1072)
(5)	23 Apr 1991 (for purpose of making any Order in Council, order, rules, or regulations) (SI 1991/1072)
	1 Jul 1991 (otherwise) (SI 1991/1072)
13	23 Apr 1991 (for purpose of making any Order in Council, order, rules, or regulations) (SI 1991/1072)
	1 Jul 1991 (otherwise) (SI 1991/1072)
14–23	1 Jul 1991 (SI 1991/1072)
23A	Prospectively inserted by Criminal Justice Act 1993, s 77, Sch 4, para 5 (qv)
24	1 Jul 1991 (SI 1991/1072)
25, 26	23 Sep 1991 (SI 1991/2108)
26A	Prospectively inserted (EW) by Criminal Justice Act 1993, s 25(1) (qv)
26B	Prospectively inserted (S) by Criminal Justice Act 1993, s 25(1) (qv)
27	23 Sep 1991 (SI 1991/2108)
28(1)	23 Sep 1991 (SI 1991/2108)
(2)	23 Apr 1991 (for purpose of making any Order in Council, order, rules, or regulations) (SI 1991/1072)
	23 Sep 1991 (otherwise) (SI 1991/2108)
(3)	23 Sep 1991 (SI 1991/2108)
29(1)	23 Sep 1991 (SI 1991/2108)
(2)	23 Apr 1991 (for purpose of making any Order in Council, order, rules, or regulations) (SI 1991/1072)
	23 Sep 1991 (otherwise) (SI 1991/2108)
(3)	23 Sep 1991 (SI 1991/2108)
30(1)	10 Jun 1991 (SI 1991/1072)
(2)	23 Sep 1991 (SI 1991/2108)
(3)	Prospectively added (EW) by Criminal Justice Act 1993, s 25(5) (qv)
31(1)	See Sch 4 below
(2)	1 Jul 1991 (SI 1991/1072)
(3)	See Sch 5 below
(4)	1 Jul 1991 (SI 1991/1072)
32(1)–(3)	10 Jun 1991 (SI 1991/1072)
(4)	23 Apr 1991 (for purpose of making any Order in Council, order, rules, or regulations) (SI 1991/1072)
	10 Jun 1991 (otherwise) (SI 1991/1072)

Criminal Justice (International Co-operation) Act 1990 (c 5)—*cont*

Sch 1	10 Jun 1991 (SI 1991/1072)
2	23 Apr 1991 (for purpose of making any Order in Council, order, rules, or regulations) (SI 1991/1072)
	1 Jul 1991 (otherwise) (SI 1991/1072)
3, para 1(1)(a), (b)	1 Jul 1991 (SI 1991/1072)
(c)	23 Apr 1991 (for purpose of making any Order in Council, order, rules, or regulations) (SI 1991/1072)
	1 Jul 1991 (otherwise) (SI 1991/1072)
(2), (3)	1 Jul 1991 (SI 1991/1072)
2–9	1 Jul 1991 (SI 1991/1072)
4, para 1	1 Jul 1991 (SI 1991/1072)
2	10 Jun 1991 (SI 1991/1072)
3–5	1 Jul 1991 (SI 1991/1072)
6–8	10 Jun 1991 (SI 1991/1072)
5	10 Jun 1991 (repeals of or in Extradition Act 1873, s 5; Evidence (Proceedings in Other Jurisdictions) Act 1975, s 5; Suppression of Terrorism Act 1978, s 1(3)(d) (and the word 'and' immediately preceding it), (4), (5)(b) (and the word 'and' immediately preceding it); Criminal Justice Act 1988, s 29) (SI 1991/1072)
	1 Jul 1991 (otherwise) (SI 1991/1072)

Education (Student Loans) Act 1990 (c 6)

RA: 26 Apr 1990

26 Apr 1990 (RA)

Employment Act 1990 (c 38)

RA: 1 Nov 1990

Commencement provisions: s 18(2)–(4); Employment Act 1990 (Commencement and Transitional Provisions) Order 1990, SI 1990/2378; Employment Act 1990 (Commencement and Transitional Provisions) Amendment Order 1991, SI 1991/89 (corrects defect in SI 1990/2378)

s 1–12	Repealed
13	1 Feb 1991 (SI 1990/2378)
14, 15	1 Nov 1990 (s 18(2))
16(1)	See Sch 2 below
(2)	See Sch 3 below
17	1 Nov 1990 (s 18(2))
18	1 Nov 1990 (RA)
Sch 1	Repealed
2, para 1(1)	1 Feb 1991 (SI 1990/2378)
(2)	Repealed
(3)–(6)	1 Jan 1991 (SI 1990/2378)
2, 3	Repealed

Employment Act 1990 (c 38)—*cont*

Sch 3	1 Jan 1991 (repeals of or in Employment Act 1980; Employment Act 1982; Trade Union Act 1984; Employment Act 1988) (subject to transitional provisions) (SI 1990/2378)
	1 Feb 1991 (otherwise) (SI 1990/2378)

Enterprise and New Towns (Scotland) Act 1990 (c 35)

RA: 26 Jul 1990

Commencement provisions: s 39(1), (3); Enterprise and New Towns (Scotland) Act 1990 Commencement Order 1990, SI 1990/1840

s 1	1 Oct 1990 (for purpose of establishing Scottish Enterprise and Highlands and Islands Enterprise, and bringing into force Sch 1) (SI 1990/1840)
	1 Apr 1990 (otherwise) (SI 1990/1840)
2–14	1 Apr 1991 (SI 1990/1840)
14A	Inserted by Trade Union Reform and Employment Rights Act 1993, s 47(5) (qv)
15–18	1 Apr 1991 (SI 1990/1840)
19, 20	26 Jul 1990 (for purposes of Sch 3, paras 4, 5) (s 39(1), (3))
	1 Apr 1991 (otherwise) (SI 1990/1840)
21(1)–(3)	1 Apr 1991 (SI 1990/1840)
(4)	1 Oct 1990 (SI 1990/1840)
22	1 Oct 1990 (SI 1990/1840)
23(1)–(3)	1 Apr 1991 (SI 1990/1840)
(4)	See Sch 3 below
24	1 Apr 1991 (SI 1990/1840)
25(1)	See Sch 2 below
(2)–(4)	1 Apr 1991 (SI 1990/1840)
26(1), (2)	1 Oct 1990 (SI 1990/1840)
(3), (4)	1 Apr 1991 (SI 1990/1840)
27	1 Oct 1990 (SI 1990/1840)
28	1 Apr 1991 (SI 1990/1840)
29, 30	1 Oct 1990 (SI 1990/1840)
31, 32	1 Apr 1991 (SI 1990/1840)
33–35	1 Oct 1990 (SI 1990/1840)
36, 37	26 Jul 1990 (s 39(1), (3))
38(1)	See Sch 4 below
(2)	See Sch 5 below
(3), (4)	1 Apr 1991 (SI 1990/1840)
39	26 Jul 1990 (RA)
40	1 Apr 1991 (SI 1990/1840)
Sch 1	1 Oct 1990 (SI 1990/1840)
2, para 1	1 Oct 1990 (SI 1990/1840)
2–6	1 Apr 1991 (SI 1990/1840)
3, para 1–3	1 Apr 1991 (SI 1990/1840)
4, 5	26 Jul 1990 (s 39(1), (3))
6–9	1 Apr 1991 (SI 1990/1840)
4, para 1	1 Oct 1990 (SI 1990/1840)
2–5	1 Apr 1991 (SI 1990/1840)
6	1 Oct 1990 (SI 1990/1840)
7–18	1 Apr 1991 (SI 1990/1840)
5	26 Jul 1990 (s 39(1), (3))

Entertainments (Increased Penalties) Act 1990 (c 20)

RA: 13 Jul 1990

13 Jul 1990 (RA)

Environmental Protection Act 1990 (c 43)

RA: 1 Nov 1990

Commencement provisions: s 164(2), (3); Environmental Protection Act 1990
(Commencement No 1) Order 1990, SI 1990/2226; Environmental Protection
Act 1990 (Commencement No 2) Order 1990, SI 1990/2243; Environmental
Protection Act 1990 (Commencement No 3) Order 1990, SI 1990/2565;
Environmental Protection Act 1990 (Commencement No 4) Order 1990, SI
1990/2635 (also amends SI 1990/2565); Environmental Protection Act 1990
(Commencement No 5) Order 1991, SI 1991/96; Environmental Protection Act
1990 (Commencement No 6 and Appointed Day) Order 1991, SI 1991/685;
Environmental Protection Act 1990 (Commencement No 7) Order 1991, SI
1991/1042; Environmental Protection Act 1990 (Commencement No 8) Order
1991, SI 1991/1319; Environmental Protection Act 1990 (Commencement No 9)
Order 1991, SI 1991/1577; Environmental Protection Act 1990 (Commencement
No 10) Order 1991, SI 1991/2829; Environmental Protection Act 1990
(Commencement No 11) Order 1992, SI 1992/266; Environmental Protection
Act 1990 (Commencement No 12) Order 1992, SI 1992/3253; Environmental
Protection Act 1990 (Commencement No 13) Order 1993, SI 1993/274

s 1, 2	1 Jan 1991 (SI 1990/2635)
3	19 Dec 1991 (SI 1990/2635)
4, 5	1 Jan 1991 (SI 1990/2635)
6	See Sch 1 below
7–28	1 Jan 1991 (SI 1990/2635)
29–31	31 May 1991 (SI 1991/1319)
32	See Sch 2 below
33(1)(a), (b)	*Not in force*
(c)	1 Apr 1992 (SI 1991/2829)
(2)	1 Apr 1992 (so far as relates to s 33(1)(c)) (SI 1991/ 2829)
	Not in force (otherwise)
(3), (4)	13 Dec 1991 (SI 1991/2829)
(5)	*Not in force*
(6)–(9)	1 Apr 1992 (so far as relates to s 33(1)(c)) (SI 1991/ 2829)
	Not in force (otherwise)
34(1)–(4)	1 Apr 1992 (SI 1991/2829)
(5)	13 Dec 1991 (SI 1991/2829)
(6)	1 Apr 1992 (SI 1991/2829)
(7)–(9)	13 Dec 1991 (SI 1991/2829)
(10)	1 Apr 1992 (SI 1991/2829)
(11)	13 Dec 1991 (SI 1991/2829)
35(1)–(5)	*Not in force*
(6)	18 Feb 1993 (SI 1993/274)
(7)–(12)	*Not in force*
36(1)	18 Feb 1993 (SI 1993/274)
(2)–(10)	*Not in force*
37(1), (2)	*Not in force*
(3)	18 Feb 1993 (so far as enables Secretary of State to give directions) (SI 1993/274)
	Not in force (otherwise)

[handwritten annotation: 1/5/94 SI 1994/1096]

Environmental Protection Act 1990 (c 43)—*cont*

s 37(4)–(6)	*Not in force*
38(1)–(6)	*Not in force*
(7)	18 Feb 1993 (so far as enables Secretary of State to give directions) (SI 1993/274)
	Not in force (otherwise)
(8)–(12)	*Not in force*
39(1), (2)	*Not in force*
(3)	18 Feb 1993 (SI 1993/274)
(4)–(11)	*Not in force*
40(1), (2)	*Not in force*
(3)	18 Feb 1993 (SI 1993/274)
(4)–(6)	*Not in force*
41(1)	*Not in force*
(2)	18 Feb 1993 (SI 1993/274)
(3)	*Not in force*
(4), (5)	18 Feb 1993 (SI 1993/274)
(6)–(8)	*Not in force*
42(1)–(7)	*Not in force*
(8)	18 Feb 1993 (so far as enables Secretary of State to give directions) (SI 1993/274)
	Not in force (otherwise)
43(1)–(7)	*Not in force*
(8)	18 Feb 1993 (SI 1993/274)
44	*Not in force*
45(1)	14 Feb 1992 (so far as enables orders or regulations to be made) (SI 1992/266)
	1 Apr 1992 (otherwise) (SI 1992/266)
(2)	14 Feb 1992 (so far as enables orders or regulations to be made) (SI 1992/266)
	1 Apr 1992 (otherwise) (S) (SI 1992/266)
	Not in force (otherwise) (EW)
(3)–(12)	14 Feb 1992 (so far as enable orders or regulations to be made) (SI 1992/266)
	1 Apr 1992 (otherwise) (SI 1992/266)
46, 47	1 Apr 1992 (SI 1992/266)
48(1)–(6)	1 Apr 1992 (SI 1992/266)
(7)	*Not in force*
(8), (9)	1 Apr 1992 (SI 1992/266)
49	1 Aug 1991 (SI 1991/1577)
50, 51	31 May 1991 (SI 1991/1319)
52(1)	1 Apr 1992 (SI 1992/266)
(2)	*Not in force*
(3)–(7)	1 Apr 1992 (SI 1992/266)
(8)	13 Dec 1991 (so far as relates to s 52(1), (3)) (SI 1991/2829)
	Not in force (otherwise)
(9)–(11)	1 Apr 1992 (SI 1992/266)
53	1 Apr 1992 (SI 1992/266)
54(1)–(13)	*Not in force*
(14)	18 Feb 1993 (SI 1993/274)
(15)–(17)	*Not in force*
55, 56	1 Apr 1992 (SI 1992/266)
57–59	*Not in force*
60	31 May 1991 (so far as relates to anything deposited at a place for the deposit of waste, or in a receptacle for waste, provided by a waste disposal

Environmental Protection Act 1990 (c 43)—*cont*

s 60—*cont*	contractor under arrangements made with a waste disposal authority) (SI 1991/1319)
	Not in force (otherwise)
61, 62	*Not in force*
63(1)	18 Feb 1993 (SI 1993/274)
(2)–(4)	*Not in force*
64(1)	18 Feb 1993 (SI 1993/274)
(2), (3)	*Not in force*
(4)	18 Feb 1993 (SI 1993/274)
(5)–(7)	*Not in force*
(8)	18 Feb 1993 (SI 1993/274)
65(1)	*Not in force*
(2)	18 Feb 1993 (so far as enables Secretary of State to give directions) (SI 1993/274)
	Not in force (otherwise)
(3), (4)	*Not in force*
66(1)–(6)	*Not in force*
(7)	18 Feb 1993 (so far as enables Secretary of State to give directions) (SI 1993/274)
	Not in force (otherwise)
(8)–(11)	*Not in force*
67	*Not in force*
68	31 May 1991 (SI 1991/1319)
69, 70	1 Apr 1992 (SI 1991/2829)
71, 72	31 May 1991 (SI 1991/1319)
73(1)–(5)	1 Apr 1992 (SI 1992/266)
(6)–(9)	*Not in force*
74(1)–(5)	*Not in force*
(6)	18 Feb 1993 (SI 1993/274)
(7)	*Not in force*
75	31 May 1991 (SI 1991/1319)
76	*Not in force*
77	31 May 1991 (SI 1991/1319)
78	13 Dec 1991 (SI 1991/2829)
79, 80	1 Jan 1991 (s 164(2))
80A	Inserted (EW) by Noise and Statutory Nuisance Act 1993, s 3(6) (qv)
81	See Sch 3 below
81A, 81B	Inserted (EW) by Noise and Statutory Nuisance Act 1993, s 10(2) (qv)
82–84	1 Jan 1991 (s 164(2))
85	Repealed
86(1)	13 Feb 1991 (EW) (SI 1991/96)
	1 Apr 1991 (S) (SI 1991/1042)
(2)	14 Jan 1991 (SI 1991/96)
(3)	1 Apr 1991 (SI 1991/1042)
(4), (5)	13 Feb 1991 (EW) (SI 1991/96)
	1 Apr 1991 (S) (SI 1991/1042)
(6)–(8)	14 Jan 1991 (SI 1991/96)
(9)	13 Feb 1991 (EW) (SI 1991/96)
(10)	1 Apr 1991 (SI 1991/1042)
(11)	14 Jan 1991 (SI 1991/96)
(12)	1 Jun 1991 (SI 1991/1042)
(13)	13 Feb 1991 (EW) (SI 1991/96)
	1 Apr 1991 (S) (SI 1991/1042)
(14), (15)	14 Jan 1991 (SI 1991/96)

Environmental Protection Act 1990 (c 43)—*cont*

s 87(1), (2)	13 Feb 1991 (EW) (SI 1991/96)
	1 Apr 1991 (S) (SI 1991/1042)
(3)(a)–(e)	13 Feb 1991 (EW) (SI 1991/96)
	1 Apr 1991 (S) (SI 1991/1042)
(f)	1 Jun 1991 (SI 1991/1042)
(4)–(6)	13 Feb 1991 (EW) (SI 1991/96)
	1 Apr 1991 (S) (SI 1991/1042)
(7)	1 Apr 1991 (SI 1991/1042)
88(1)–(4)	13 Feb 1991 (EW) (SI 1991/96)
	1 Apr 1991 (S) (SI 1991/1042)
(5)	14 Jan 1991 (SI 1991/96)
(6)	13 Feb 1991 (EW) (SI 1991/96)
	1 Apr 1991 (S) (SI 1991/1042)
(7)	14 Jan 1991 (SI 1991/96)
(8)	13 Feb 1991 (EW) (SI 1991/96)
	1 Apr 1991 (S) (SI 1991/1042)
(9)(a)	13 Feb 1991 (EW) (SI 1991/96)
	1 Apr 1991 (S) (SI 1991/1042)
(b)	14 Jan 1991 (SI 1991/96)
(c), (d)	13 Feb 1991 (EW) (SI 1991/96)
	1 Apr 1991 (S) (SI 1991/1042)
(e)	13 Feb 1991 (EW) (SI 1991/96)
(10)	13 Feb 1991 (EW) (SI 1991/96)
	1 Apr 1991 (S) (SI 1991/1042)
89(1)(a)–(f)	1 Apr 1991 (SI 1991/1042)
(g)	1 Jun 1991 (SI 1991/1042)
(2), (3)	1 Apr 1991 (SI 1991/1042)
(4)	14 Jan 1991 (SI 1991/96)
(5), (6)	1 Apr 1991 (SI 1991/1042)
(7)–(9)	13 Nov 1990 (SI 1990/2243)
(10)	1 Apr 1991 (SI 1991/1042)
(11)–(13)	13 Nov 1990 (SI 1990/2243)
(14)	1 Apr 1991 (SI 1991/1042)
90(1), (2)	14 Jan 1991 (SI 1991/96)
(3)–(6)	1 Jun 1991 (SI 1991/1042)
(7)	14 Jan 1991 (SI 1991/96)
91(1)(a)–(f)	1 Apr 1991 (SI 1991/1042)
(g)	1 Jun 1991 (SI 1991/1042)
(2)–(13)	1 Apr 1991 (SI 1991/1042)
92(1)(a)–(c)	1 Apr 1991 (SI 1991/1042)
(d)	1 Jun 1991 (SI 1991/1042)
(2)–(10)	1 Apr 1991 (SI 1991/1042)
93	1 Apr 1991 (SI 1991/1042)
94(1), (2)	14 Jan 1991 (SI 1991/96)
(3)–(9)	1 Apr 1991 (SI 1991/1042)
95	1 Apr 1991 (SI 1991/1042)
96(1)	1 Apr 1991 (SI 1991/1042)
(2), (3)	14 Jan 1991 (SI 1991/96)
97	1 Jan 1991 (s 164(2))
98(1)	13 Feb 1991 (EW) (SI 1991/96)
	1 Apr 1991 (S) (SI 1991/1042)
(2)	13 Feb 1991 (SI 1991/96)
(3), (4)	1 Apr 1991 (SI 1991/1042)
(5), (6)	13 Feb 1991 (EW) (SI 1991/96)
	1 Apr 1991 (S) (SI 1991/1042)
99	See Sch 4 below
100–105	Repealed

Environmental Protection Act 1990 (c 43)—*cont*

s 106(1)–(3)	1 Feb 1993 (SI 1992/3253)
(4), (5)	1 Apr 1991 (SI 1991/1042)
(6), (7)	1 Feb 1993 (SI 1992/3253)
107(1)–(7)	1 Feb 1993 (SI 1992/3253)
(8)	1 Apr 1991 (SI 1991/1042)
(9)–(11)	1 Feb 1993 (SI 1992/3253)
108(1)(a)	1 Feb 1993 (so far as relates to import or acquisition of genetically modified organisms) (SI 1992/3253)
	Not in force (otherwise)
(b)	1 Apr 1991 (SI 1991/1042)
(2)	*Not in force*
(3)(a)	*Not in force*
(b)	1 Apr 1991 (SI 1991/1042)
(4)	*Not in force*
(5)	1 Apr 1991 (SI 1991/1042)
(6)	*Not in force*
(7)	1 Apr 1991 (SI 1991/1042)
(8)	*Not in force*
(9)	1 Apr 1991 (SI 1991/1042)
(10)	1 Jan 1993 (SI 1992/3253)
109	*Not in force*
110	1 Feb 1993 (so far as relates to import, acquisition, release or marketing of genetically modified organisms) (SI 1992/3253)
	Not in force (otherwise)
111(1), (2)	1 Apr 1991 (SI 1991/1042)
(3)	*Not in force*
(4), (5)	1 Apr 1991 (SI 1991/1042)
(6)	1 Feb 1993 (SI 1992/3253)
(6A)	Inserted by Genetically Modified Organisms (Deliberate Release) Regulations 1992, SI 1992/3280, reg 13
(7)	1 Apr 1991 (SI 1991/1042)
(8)–(10)	1 Feb 1993 (SI 1992/3253)
(11)	1 Apr 1991 (SI 1991/1042)
112(1), (2)	1 Feb 1993 (SI 1992/3253)
(3), (4)	*Not in force*
(5)–(7)	1 Feb 1993 (SI 1992/3253)
113	1 Apr 1991 (SI 1991/1042)
114(1)–(3)	1 Apr 1991 (SI 1991/1042)
(4), (5)	1 Feb 1993 (SI 1992/3253)
115(1)–(3)	1 Feb 1993 (SI 1992/3253)
(4)	1 Apr 1991 (SI 1991/1042)
(5)–(10)	1 Feb 1993 (SI 1992/3253)
116	1 Feb 1993 (so far as relates to import, acquisition, release or marketing of genetically modified organisms) (SI 1992/3253)
	Not in force (otherwise)
117	1 Feb 1993 (SI 1992/3253)
118(1)(a)	1 Feb 1993 (SI 1992/3253)
(b)	*Not in force*
(c)	1 Feb 1993 (SI 1992/3253)
(d)	*Not in force*
(e)–(l)	1 Feb 1993 (SI 1992/3253)
(m)	1 Feb 1993 (so far as relates to s 111) (SI 1992/3253)
	Not in force (otherwise)
(n), (o)	1 Feb 1993 (SI 1992/3253)

Environmental Protection Act 1990 (c 43)—*cont*

s 118(2)–(10)	1 Feb 1993 (SI 1992/3253)
119–121	1 Feb 1993 (SI 1992/3253)
122(1)(a), (b)	1 Apr 1991 (so far as empower Secretary of State to make regulations) (SI 1991/1042)
	Not in force (otherwise)
(c)–(h)	1 Apr 1991 (so far as empower Secretary of State to make regulations) (SI 1991/1042)
	1 Feb 1993 (otherwise) (SI 1992/3253)
(2), (3)	1 Feb 1993 (SI 1992/3253)
(4)	1 Apr 1991 (SI 1991/1042)
123(1)–(6)	1 Feb 1993 (SI 1992/3253)
(7)	1 Apr 1991 (SI 1991/1042)
(8)	1 Feb 1993 (SI 1992/3253)
(9)	1 Apr 1991 (SI 1991/1042)
124–126	1 Apr 1991 (SI 1991/1042)
127	1 Feb 1993 (SI 1992/3253)
128(1)–(4)	5 Nov 1990 (save for amendments) (SI 1990/2226)
	1 Apr 1991 (otherwise) (SI 1991/685)
(5)	See Schs 6, 7 below
129	5 Nov 1990 (SI 1990/2226)
130	1 Apr 1991 (SI 1991/685)
131	5 Nov 1990 (SI 1990/2226)
132(1)(a)	1 Apr 1991 (SI 1991/685)
(b)–(e)	5 Nov 1990 (save for amendments) (SI 1990/2226)
	1 Apr 1991 (otherwise) (SI 1991/685)
(2), (3)	5 Nov 1990 (SI 1990/2226)
133, 134	5 Nov 1990 (SI 1990/2226)
135(1), (2)	5 Nov 1990 (SI 1990/2226)
(3)	See Sch 10, Pt I below
136(1), (2)	5 Nov 1990 (SI 1990/2226)
(3)	See Sch 10, Pt II below
137(1)–(3)	5 Nov 1990 (SI 1990/2226)
(4)	See Sch 10, Pt III below
138	5 Nov 1990 (SI 1990/2226)
139	See Sch 11 below
140(1)–(4)	1 Jan 1991 (s 164(2))
(5)	See Sch 12 below
(6)–(11)	1 Jan 1991 (s 164(2))
141	1 Jan 1991 (s 164(2))
142(1), (2)	1 Jan 1991 (s 164(2))
(3)	See Sch 12 below
(4)–(7)	1 Jan 1991 (s 164(2))
143(1)	14 Feb 1992 (EW) (SI 1992/266)
	Not in force (S)
(2)–(4)	*Not in force*
(5), (6)	14 Feb 1992 (EW) (SI 1992/266)
	Not in force (S)
144	See Sch 13 below
145, 146	1 Jan 1991 (s 164(2))
147	31 May 1991 (SI 1991/1319)
148	See Sch 14 below
149–151	14 Feb 1992 (so far as enable orders or regulations to be made) (SI 1992/266)
	1 Apr 1992 (otherwise) (SI 1992/266)
152	10 Jul 1991 (SI 1991/1577)
153–155	1 Jan 1991 (s 164(2))
156	1 Apr 1991 (SI 1991/1042)

Environmental Protection Act 1990 (c 43)—*cont*

s 157	1 Jan 1991 (s 164(2))
158	1 Apr 1991 (SI 1991/1042)
159	*Not in force*
160, 161	1 Jan 1991 (s 164(2))
162(1)	See Sch 15 below
(2)	See Sch 16 below
(3)	1 Apr 1992 (SI 1992/266)
(4)	*Not in force*
(5)	1 Jan 1991 (s 164(2))
163	1 Jan 1991 (s 164(2))
164	1 Nov 1990 (RA)

Sch 1	1 Jan 1991 (SI 1990/2635)
2	31 May 1991 (SI 1991/1319)
3, 4	1 Jan 1991 (s 164(2))
5	Repealed
6–9	5 Nov 1990 (save for amendments) (SI 1990/2226)
	1 Apr 1991 (otherwise) (SI 1991/685)
10, 11	5 Nov 1990 (SI 1990/2226)
12	1 Jan 1991 (s 164(2))
13, Pt I	1 Jan 1992 (SI 1991/2829)
II, para 11, 12	18 Feb 1993 (SI 1993/274)
13	1 May 1993 (SI 1993/274)
14	1 Jan 1991 (s 164(2))
15, para 1	Repealed
2	1 Apr 1991 (SI 1991/1042)
3	1 Apr 1992 (SI 1992/266)
4, 5	1 Jan 1991 (s 164(2))
6–8	Repealed
9	1 Jan 1991 (s 164(2))
10(1), (2)	1 Apr 1992 (SI 1991/2829)
(3)	14 Jan 1991 (SI 1991/96)
11	1 Apr 1991 (SI 1991/1042)
12	Repealed
13, 14	1 Apr 1991 (SI 1991/1042)
15(1), (2)	*Not in force*
(3)–(5)	14 Jan 1991 (SI 1991/96)
(6)–(9)	Repealed
16(1)	1 Apr 1991 (SI 1991/1042)
(2)	1 Apr 1991 (so far as inserts Control of Pollution Act 1974, s 31(2)(b)(v)) (SI 1991/1042)
	Not in force (otherwise)
(3)	1 Apr 1991 (SI 1991/1042)
17	*Not in force*
18	Repealed
19	1 Apr 1992 (SI 1992/266)
20	1 Apr 1991 (SI 1991/1042)
21	18 Feb 1993 (SI 1993/274)
22	1 Jan 1991 (so far as inserts Public Health (Control of Disease) Act 1984, s 7(4)(m)) (s 164(2))
	1 Apr 1991 (otherwise) (SI 1991/1042)
23	Repealed
24	1 Jan 1991 (s 164(2))
25–27	*Not in force*
28–30	Repealed
31(1)–(3)	31 May 1991 (SI 1991/1319)

Environmental Protection Act 1990 (c 43)—*cont*

Sch 15, para 31(4)(a)	31 May 1991 (SI 1991/1319)
(b)	1 Jan 1991 (s 164(2))
(c)	31 May 1991 (SI 1991/1319)
(5)(a)	1 Apr 1992 (SI 1991/2829)
(b), (c)	31 May 1991 (SI 1991/1319)
(6)	1 Apr 1992 (SI 1991/2829)
16, Pt I	*Not in force*
✗ II	31 May 1991 (repeals of or in Control of Pollution Act 1974, s 2; Control of Pollution (Amendment) Act 1989, ss 7(2), 9(1)) (SI 1991/1319)
	1 Apr 1992 (repeal of Control of Pollution (Amendment) Act 1989, s 9(2)) (SI 1991/2829)
	1 Apr 1992 (repeals of or in Control of Pollution Act 1974, ss 12, 13, 14(1)–(5), (7)–(11) (except so far as relate to industrial waste in England and Wales), 15; Civic Government (Scotland) Act 1982) (SI 1992/266)
	Not in force (otherwise)
III	1 Jan 1991 (s 164(2))
IV	1 Apr 1991 (SI 1991/1042)
V	1 Jan 1991 (SI 1990/2635)
VI	1 Apr 1991 (repeals of or in Countryside Act 1968; Wildlife and Countryside Act 1981) (SI 1991/685)
	1 Apr 1992 (repeals in Nature Conservancy Council Act 1973) (SI 1991/2829
	Not in force (otherwise)
VII	1 Jan 1992 (repeals in Planning (Hazardous Substances) Act 1990) (SI 1991/2829)
	18 Feb 1993 (repeals in Town and Country Planning (Scotland) Act 1972) (SI 1993/274)
	1 May 1993 (repeal in Housing and Planning Act 1986) (SI 1993/274)
	Not in force (otherwise)
VIII	*Not in force*
IX	1 Jan 1991 (repeal of Control of Pollution Act 1974, s 100) (s 164(2))
	1 Apr 1992 (repeals of or in Dogs Act 1906; Civic Government (Scotland) Act 1982; Local Government Act 1988) (SI 1992/266)
	18 Feb 1993 (repeals of Criminal Justice Act 1982, s 43; Criminal Justice Act 1988, s 58) (SI 1993/274)
	Not in force (otherwise)

Finance Act 1990 (c 29)

RA: 26 Jul 1990

See the note concerning Finance Acts at the front of this book

---

Food Safety Act 1990 (c 16)

RA: 29 Jun 1990

Commencement provisions: s 60(2)–(4); Food Safety Act 1990 (Commencement No 1) Order 1990, SI 1990/1383; Food Safety Act 1990 (Commencement No 2) Order

Food Safety Act 1990 (c 16)—*cont*
1990, SI 1990/2372; Food Safety Act 1990 (Commencement No 3) Order 1992,
SI 1992/57

s 1(1), (2)	3 Jul 1990 (for purposes of ss 13, 51) (SI 1990/1383)
	1 Dec 1990 (otherwise) (SI 1990/2372)
(3), (4)	3 Jul 1990 (for purposes of s 13) (SI 1990/1383)
	1 Dec 1990 (otherwise) (SI 1990/2372)
2, 3	3 Jul 1990 (for purposes of s 13) (SI 1990/1383)
	1 Dec 1990 (otherwise) (SI 1990/2372)
4(1)	1 Dec 1990 (SI 1990/2372)
(2)	3 Jul 1990 (for purposes of s 13) (SI 1990/1383)
	1 Dec 1990 (otherwise) (SI 1990/2372)
5, 6	3 Jul 1990 (for purposes of s 13) (SI 1990/1383)
	1 Dec 1990 (otherwise) (SI 1990/2372)
7(1), (2)	1 Jan 1991 (SI 1990/2372)
(3)	3 Jul 1990 (for purposes of s 13) (SI 1990/1383)
	1 Jan 1991 (otherwise) (SI 1990/2372)
8–12	1 Jan 1991 (SI 1990/2372)
13	29 Jun 1990 (s 60(2))
14, 15	1 Jan 1991 (SI 1990/2372)
16(1), (2)	1 Dec 1990 (SI 1990/2372)
(3)	See Sch 1 below
(4), (5)	1 Dec 1990 (SI 1990/2372)
17–19	1 Dec 1990 (SI 1990/2372)
20	3 Jul 1990 (for purposes of s 13) (SI 1990/1383)
	1 Jan 1991 (otherwise) (SI 1990/2372)
21(1)	3 Jul 1990 (for purposes of s 13) (SI 1990/1383)
	1 Jan 1991 (otherwise) (SI 1990/2372)
(2)–(4)	1 Jan 1991 (SI 1990/2372)
(5), (6)	3 Jul 1990 (for purposes of s 13) (SI 1990/1383)
	1 Jan 1991 (otherwise) (SI 1990/2372)
22	3 Jul 1990 (for purposes of s 13) (SI 1990/1383)
	1 Jan 1991 (otherwise) (SI 1990/2372)
23, 24	1 Jan 1991 (SI 1990/2372)
25, 26	1 Dec 1990 (SI 1990/2372)
27(1)	1 Jan 1991 (SI 1990/2372)
(2)	1 Dec 1990 (SI 1990/2372)
(3), (4)	1 Jan 1991 (SI 1990/2372)
(5)	1 Dec 1990 (SI 1990/2372)
28(1)	1 Jan 1991 (SI 1990/2372)
(2)	1 Dec 1990 (SI 1990/2372)
29	3 Jul 1990 (for purposes of s 13) (SI 1990/1383)
	1 Jan 1991 (otherwise) (SI 1990/2372)
30, 31	1 Dec 1990 (SI 1990/2372)
32–36	3 Jul 1990 (for purposes of s 13) (SI 1990/1383)
	1 Jan 1991 (otherwise) (SI 1990/2372)
37–39	1 Jan 1991 (SI 1990/2372)
40	1 Dec 1990 (SI 1990/2372)
41, 42	3 Jul 1990 (for purposes of s 13) (SI 1990/1383)
	1 Jan 1991 (otherwise) (SI 1990/2372)
43	1 Jan 1991 (SI 1990/2372)
44	3 Jul 1990 (for purposes of s 13) (SI 1990/1383)
	1 Jan 1991 (otherwise) (SI 1990/2372)
45	1 Dec 1990 (SI 1990/2372)
46	3 Jul 1990 (for purposes of s 13) (SI 1990/1383)
	1 Jan 1990 (otherwise) (SI 1990/2372)
47	1 Jan 1991 (SI 1990/2372)

Food Safety Act 1990 (c 16)—*cont*

s 48(1)–(3)	3 Jul 1990 (for purposes of s 13) (SI 1990/1383)
	1 Dec 1990 (otherwise) (SI 1990/2372)
(4), (5)	1 Dec 1990 (SI 1990/2372)
49(1)	3 Jul 1990 (for purposes of s 13) (SI 1990/1383)
	1 Jan 1991 (otherwise) (SI 1990/2372)
(2)	1 Dec 1990 (SI 1990/2372)
(3)–(5)	3 Jul 1990 (for purposes of s 13) (SI 1990/1383)
	1 Jan 1991 (otherwise) (SI 1990/2372)
50	3 Jul 1990 (for purposes of s 13) (SI 1990/1383)
	1 Jan 1991 (otherwise) (SI 1990/2372)
51	29 Jun 1990 (s 60(2))
52	See Sch 2 below
53(1)	3 Jul 1990 (for purposes of ss 13, 51) (SI 1990/1383)
	1 Dec 1990 (otherwise) (SI 1990/2372)
(2)–(4)	3 Jul 1990 (for purposes of s 13) (SI 1990/1383)
	1 Dec 1990 (otherwise) (SI 1990/2372)
(5)	1 Dec 1990 (SI 1990/2372)
54	1 Apr 1992 (SI 1990/2372)
55, 56	1 Jan 1991 (SI 1990/2372)
57(1)	3 Jul 1990 (for purposes of s 13) (SI 1990/1383)
	1 Dec 1990 (otherwise) (SI 1990/2372)
(2)	3 Jul 1990 (for purposes of s 13) (SI 1990/1383)
	1 Dec 1990 (otherwise) (SI 1990/2372)
58(1)	3 Jul 1990 (for purposes of s 13) (SI 1990/1383)
	1 Jan 1991 (otherwise) (SI 1990/2372)
(2)–(4)	1 Jan 1991 (SI 1990/2372)
59(1)	See Sch 3 below
(2)	1 Dec 1990 (SI 1990/2372)
(3)	See Sch 4 below
(4)	See Sch 5 below
60	1 Jan 1991 (SI 1990/2372)
Sch 1	1 Dec 1990 (SI 1990/2372)
2, para 1–11	1 Jan 1991 (SI 1990/2372)
12–15	29 Jun 1990 (s 60(2))
16	1 Jan 1991 (SI 1990/2372)
3, para 1–13	1 Jan 1991 (SI 1990/2372)
14	Repealed
15–28	1 Jan 1991 (SI 1990/2372)
29, 30	13 Jul 1990 (for purposes of s 51) (SI 1990/1383)
	1 Jan 1991 (otherwise) (SI 1990/2372)
31–38	1 Jan 1991 (SI 1990/2372)
4	1 Dec 1990 (SI 1990/2372)
5	1 Dec 1990 (so far as relates to Public Analysts (Scotland) Regulations 1956, SI 1956/1162 or Public Analysts Regulations 1957, SI 1957/237, repeals of or in Food and Drugs (Scotland) Act 1956, ss 27, 29, 56 and Food Act 1984, ss 76(2), 79(5)) (SI 1990/2372)
	1 Jan 1991 (all repeals so far as not already in force except those of or in Food Act 1984, s 13 so far as relating to regulations (see following notes), ss 16–20, 62–67, ss 92, 93 (so far as relate to ss 16 and 18), s 132(1) so far as relates to regulations (see following notes) (SI 1990/2372)

Food Safety Act 1990 (c 16)—*cont*

Sch 5—*cont*	1 Apr 1991 (repeals of Food Act 1984, ss 13, 132(1), so far as relate to Food Hygiene (Amendment) Regulations 1990, SI 1990/1431 (except reg 3(b), Sch 1 thereof)) (SI 1990/2372)
	1 Apr 1992 (repeals of Food Act 1984, ss 13, 132(1), so far as relate to Food Hygiene (Amendment) Regulations 1990, reg 3(b), Sch 1) (SI 1990/2372)
	3 Apr 1992 (repeals of or in Food Act 1984, ss 16– 20, Pt IV (ss 62–67), ss 92 (so far as relates to s 16(2)), 93 (so far as relates to s 18(4))) (SI 1992/ 57)

Gaming (Amendment) Act 1990 (c 26)

RA: 13 Jul 1990

Commencement provisions: s 2(2), (3); Gaming (Amendment) Act 1990 (Commencement) Order 1991, SI 1991/59

s 1	See Schedule below
2	13 Sep 1990 (s 2(2))
Sch	
para 1, 2	13 Sep 1990 (s 2(2))
3, 4	1 Apr 1991 (SI 1991/59)
5–10	13 Sep 1990 (s 2(2))

Government Trading Act 1990 (c 30)

RA: 26 Jul 1990

Commencement provisions: s 4(3); Government Trading Act 1990 (Appointed Day) Order 1991, SI 1991/132

s 1	26 Jul 1990 (RA)
2	See Sch 1 below
3	26 Jul 1990 (RA)
4	See Sch 2, Pt I below
5	See Sch 2, Pt II below
Sch 1	26 Jul 1990 (RA)
2, Pt I	11 Feb 1991 (SI 1991/132)
II	26 Jul 1990 (RA)

Greenwich Hospital Act 1990 (c 13)

RA: 29 Jun 1990

29 Jun 1990 (RA)

Horses (Protective Headgear for Young Riders) Act 1990 (c 25)

RA: 13 Jul 1990

Commencement provisions: s 5(2); Horses (Protective Headgear for Young Riders) Act 1990 (Commencement) Order 1992, SI 1992/1200

Horses (Protective Headgear for Young Riders) Act 1990 (c 25)—*cont*
s 1–3   30 Jun 1992 (SI 1992/1200)
 4, 5   13 Jul 1990 (s 5(2))

Human Fertilisation and Embryology Act 1990 (c 37)

RA: 1 Nov 1990

Commencement provisions: s 49(2); Human Fertilisation and Embryology Act 1990
  (Commencement No 1) Order 1990, SI 1990/2165; Human Fertilisation and
  Embryology Act 1990 (Commencement No 2 and Transitional Provision)
  Order 1991, SI 1991/480; Human Fertilisation and Embryology Act 1990
  (Commencement No 3 and Transitional Provisions) Order 1991, SI 1991/1400;
  Human Fertilisation and Embryology Act 1990 (Commencement No 4—
  Amendment of Transitional Provisions) Order 1991, SI 1991/1781

s 1   1 Aug 1991 (SI 1991/1400)★
  2(1)   7 Nov 1990 (so far as relates to the definition of 'the
                                           Authority') (SI 1990/2165)
                                        1 Aug 1991 (otherwise) (SI 1991/1400)★
  (2), (3)   1 Aug 1991 (SI 1991/1400)★
  3, 4   1 Aug 1991 (SI 1991/1400)★
  5(1), (2)   7 Nov 1990 (SI 1990/2165)
  (3)   See Sch 1 below
  6, 7   7 Nov 1990 (SI 1990/2165)
  8   1 Aug 1991 (SI 1991/1400)★
  9(1)–(4)   1 Aug 1991 (SI 1991/1400)★
  (5)   8 Jul 1991 (for purpose of making regulations) (SI
                                           1991/1400)
                                        1 Aug 1991 (otherwise) (SI 1991/1400)★
  (6)–(11)   1 Aug 1991 (SI 1991/1400)★
  10   8 Jul 1991 (for purpose of making regulations) (SI
                                           1991/1400)
                                        1 Aug 1991 (otherwise) (SI 1991/1400)★
  11–13   1 Aug 1991 (SI 1991/1400)★
  14(1)–(4)   1 Aug 1991 (SI 1991/1400)★
  (5)   8 Jul 1991 (for purpose of making regulations) (SI
                                           1991/1400)
                                        1 Aug 1991 (otherwise) (SI 1991/1400)★
  15   1 Aug 1991 (SI 1991/1400)★
  16(1)   8 Jul 1991 (for purpose of requiring that an
                                           application for a licence be made in an approved
                                           form and be accompanied by the initial fee) (SI
                                           1991/1400)
                                        1 Aug 1991 (otherwise) (SI 1991/1400)★
  (2)–(5)   1 Aug 1991 (SI 1991/1400)★
  (6)   8 Jul 1991 (for purpose of fixing the amount of the
                                           initial fee) (SI 1991/1400)
                                        1 Aug 1991 (otherwise) (SI 1991/1400)★
  (7)   1 Aug 1991 (SI 1991/1400)★
  17–25   1 Aug 1991 (SI 1991/1400)★
  26   7 Nov 1990 (SI 1990/2165)
  27–29   1 Aug 1991 (SI 1991/1400)★
  30   *Not in force*
  31, 32   1 Aug 1991 (SI 1991/1400)★
  33(1)   7 Nov 1990 (SI 1990/2165)

Human Fertilisation and Embryology Act 1990 (c 37)—*cont*

s 33(2)(a)	1 Aug 1991 (SI 1991/1400)★
(b)	7 Nov 1990 (SI 1990/2165)
(3)	1 Aug 1991 (SI 1991/1400)★
(4)	7 Nov 1990 (SI 1990/2165)
(5), (6)	1 Aug 1991 (SI 1991/1400)★
(6A)–(6G)	Inserted by Human Fertilisation and Embryology (Disclosure of Information) Act 1992, s 1(1), (3) (qv)
(7), (8)	1 Aug 1991 (SI 1991/1400)★
(9)	Added by Human Fertilisation and Embryology (Disclosure of Information) Act 1992, s 1(1), (4) (qv)
34, 35	1 Aug 1991 (SI 1991/1400)★
36	7 Nov 1990 (SI 1990/2165)
37	1 Apr 1991 (subject to transitional provisions) (SI 1991/480)
38, 39	1 Aug 1991 (SI 1991/1400)★
40	7 Nov 1990 (SI 1990/2165)
41(1), (2)	1 Aug 1991 (SI 1991/1400)★
(3)	8 Jul 1991 (SI 1991/1400)
(4)	8 Jul 1991 (so far as relates to s 41(3)) (SI 1991/1400) 1 Aug 1991 (otherwise) (SI 1991/1400)★
(5)	7 Nov 1990 (so far as relates to s 33(1), (2)(b), (4)) (SI 1990/2165) 1 Aug 1991 (otherwise) (SI 1991/1400)★
(6)	7 Nov 1990 (so far as relates to s 40) (SI 1990/2165) 1 Aug 1991 (otherwise) (SI 1991/1400)★
(7), (8)	1 Aug 1991 (SI 1991/1400)★
(9)	7 Nov 1990 (so far as relates to s 40) (SI 1990/2165) 1 Aug 1991 (otherwise) (SI 1991/1400)★
(10), (11)	1 Aug 1991 (SI 1991/1400)★
42	7 Nov 1990 (SI 1990/2165)
43(1)	8 Jul 1991 (for purpose of making regulations) (SI 1991/1400) 1 Aug 1991(otherwise) (SI 1991/1400)★
(2), (3)	1 Aug 1991 (SI 1991/1400)★
44	1 Aug 1991 (SI 1991/1400)★
45	8 Jul 1991 (SI 1991/1400)
46, 47	1 Aug 1991 (SI 1991/1400)★
48(1)	7 Nov 1990 (so far as relates to provisions brought into force by SI 1990/2165) (SI 1990/2165) 1 Apr 1991 (so far as relates to provisions brought into force by SI 1991/480) (SI 1991/480) 8 Jul 1991 (so far as relates to provisions brought into force by SI 1991/1400) (SI 1991/1400) 1 Aug 1991 (otherwise, except so far as relates to s 30) (SI 1991/1400)★ *Not in force* (exception noted above)
(2)	1 Aug 1991 (SI 1991/1400)★
49(1), (2)	7 Nov 1990 (SI 1990/2165)
(3), (4)	1 Aug 1991 (SI 1991/1400)★
(5)	See Sch 4 below
(6), (7)	7 Nov 1990 (SI 1990/2165)
Sch 1	7 Nov 1990 (SI 1990/2165)

Human Fertilisation and Embryology Act 1990 (c 37)—*cont*
Sch 2–4   1 Aug 1991 (SI 1991/1400)★

★ subject to transitional provisions set out in SI 1991/1400, arts 3, 4, as amended by
   SI 1991/1781, art 2

Import and Export Control Act 1990 (c 45)

RA: 6 Dec 1990

6 Dec 1990 (RA)

Landlord and Tenant (Licensed Premises) Act 1990 (c 39)

RA: 1 Nov 1990

Commencement provisions: s 2(3)

s 1(1)	1 Jan 1991 (s 2(3))
(2), (3)	1 Jan 1991 (subject to transitional provisions) (s 2(3))
(4)	1 Jan 1991 (s 2(3))
2	1 Jan 1991 (s 2(3))

Law Reform (Miscellaneous Provisions) (Scotland) Act 1990 (c 40)

RA: 1 Nov 1990

Commencement provisions: s 75(2)–(4); Law Reform (Miscellaneous Provisions)
   (Scotland) Act 1990 Commencement (No 1) Order 1990, SI 1990/2328; Law
   Reform (Miscellaneous Provisions) (Scotland) Act 1990 (Commencement No 2)
   Order 1990, SI 1990/2624); Law Reform (Miscellaneous Provisions) (Scotland)
   Act 1990 (Commencement No 3) Order 1991, SI 1991/330; Law Reform
   (Miscellaneous Provisions) (Scotland) Act 1990 (Commencement No 3) Order
   1991, SI 1991/330; Law Reform (Miscellaneous Provisions) (Scotland) Act 1990
   (Commencement No 4) Order 1991, SI 1991/822; Law Reform (Miscellaneous
   Provisions) (Scotland) Act 1990 (Commencement No 5) Order 1991, SI 1991/
   850; Law Reform (Miscellaneous Provisions) (Scotland) Act 1990
   (Commencement No 6) Order 1991, SI 1991/1252; Law Reform (Miscellaneous
   Provisions) (Scotland) Act 1990 (Commencement No 7) Order 1991, SI 1991/
   1903; Law Reform (Miscellaneous Provisions) (Scotland) Act 1990
   (Commencement No 8) Order 1991, SI 1991/2151; Law Reform (Miscellaneous
   Provisions) (Scotland) Act 1990 (Commencement No 9) Order 1991, SI 1991/
   2862; Law Reform (Miscellaneous Provisions) (Scotland) Act 1990
   (Commencement No 10) Order 1992, SI 1992/1599; Law Reform (Miscellaneous
   Provisions) (Scotland) Act 1990 (Commencement No 11) Order 1993, SI 1993/
   641; Law Reform (Miscellaneous Provisions) (Scotland) Act 1990
   (Commencement No 12) Order 1993, SI 1993/2253

s 1, 2	27 Jul 1992 (SI 1992/1599)
3(1)	4 Jul 1992 (for purpose of power to make order) (SI 1992/1599)
	27 Jul 1992 (otherwise) (SI 1992/1599)
(2)–(4)	27 Jul 1992 (SI 1992/1599)
4(1)–(3)	30 Sep 1992 (SI 1992/1599)
(4)	4 Jul 1992 (SI 1992/1599)
5(1), (2)	30 Sep 1992 (SI 1992/1599)

Law Reform (Miscellaneous Provisions) (Scotland) Act 1990 (c 40)—*cont*

s 34(1)	1 Apr 1991 (SI 1991/822)
(2)–(8)	3 Jun 1991 (SI 1991/1252)
(9)(a)–(c)	1 Apr 1991 (SI 1991/822)
(d)–(h)	*Not in force*
(10)	See Sch 3 below
35	1 Apr 1991 (SI 1991/822)
36(1)	20 Jul 1992 (SI 1992/1599)
(2)	4 Jul 1992 (for purpose of power to make act of sederunt) (SI 1992/1599)
	20 Jul 1992 (otherwise) (SI 1992/1599)
(3)	4 Jul 1992 (for purpose of power to make act of sederunt under Solicitors' (Scotland) Act 1980, s 61A) (SI 1992/1599)
	20 Jul 1992 (otherwise) (SI 1992/1599)
(4)	*Not in force*
37	20 Jul 1992 (SI 1992/1599)
38, 39	30 Sep 1991 (SI 1991/2151)
40–42	*Not in force*
43	3 Jun 1991 (SI 1991/1252)
44	1 Apr 1991 (SI 1991/822)
45–48	1 Jan 1991 (s 75(3)(a))
49(1)–(7)	1 Jan 1991 (s 75(3)(a))
(8)	See Sch 5 below
(9)–(11)	1 Jan 1991 (s 75(3)(a))
50–55	1 Jan 1991 (s 75(3)(a))
56	30 Sep 1991 (for purposes of proceedings in the High Court of Justiciary sitting at Edinburgh or Glasgow and any sheriff court in the sheriffdom of Glasgow and Strathkelvin or Lothian and Borders) (SI 1991/2151)
	Not in force (otherwise)
57–59	30 Sep 1991 (for purposes of proceedings in any sheriff court in the sheriffdom of Glasgow and Strathkelvin or Lothian and Borders) (SI 1991/2151)
	Not in force (otherwise)
60	30 Sep 1991 (SI 1991/2151)
61	1 Apr 1991 (SI 1991/850)
62(1)–(4)	1 Apr 1991 (SI 1991/850)
(5)	See Sch 6 below
(6)	1 Apr 1991 (SI 1991/850)
63	1 Dec 1990 (SI 1990/2328)
64, 65	1 Jan 1991 (SI 1990/2624)
66	See Sch 7 below
67	1 Jan 1991 (s 73(3)(b))
68	1 Apr 1991 (SI 1991/330)
69	1 Mar 1991 (SI 1991/330)
70, 71	1 Jan 1991 (s 75(3)(b))
72	1 Dec 1990 (SI 1990/2328)
73(1)(a)	17 Mar 1993 (SI 1993/641)
(b)–(e)	1 Apr 1991 (SI 1991/822)
(2)	17 Mar 1993 (SI 1993/641)
74(1)	See Sch 8 below
(2)	See Sch 9 below
75	1 Nov 1990 (RA)
Sch 1, Pt I	1 Apr 1991 (SI 1991/822)

Law Reform (Miscellaneous Provisions) (Scotland) Act 1990 (c 40)—*cont*

Sch 1, Pt II		*Not in force*
2		*Not in force*
3, 4		1 Apr 1991 (SI 1991/822)
5		1 Jan 1991 (s 75(3)(a))
6		1 Apr 1991 (SI 1991/850)
7		1 Jan 1991 (s 75(3)(a))
8, Pt I, para 1–18		31 Dec 1991 (SI 1991/2892)
II, para 19, 20		*Not in force*
21		1 Jan 1991 (s 75(3)(b))
22		*Not in force*
23		1 Apr 1991 (SI 1991/822)
24, 25		*Not in force*
26		1 Jan 1991 (SI 1990/2624)
27(1), (2)		3 Jun 1991 (SI 1991/1252)
(3)		1 Nov 1990 (s 75(4))
28		1 Apr 1991 (SI 1991/850)
29(1)–(4)		3 Jun 1991 (SI 1991/1252)
(5)(a), (b)		*Not in force*
(c)		17 Mar 1993 (SI 1993/641)
(d)		*Not in force*
(6)(a), (b)		1 Jan 1991 (SI 1990/2624)
(c)		*Not in force*
(7)		1 Jan 1991 (SI 1990/2624)
(8)–(14)		3 Jun 1991 (SI 1991/1252)
(15)(a)		3 Jun 1991 (SI 1991/1252)
(b)–(d)		17 Mar 1993 (SI 1993/641)
(e)		3 Jun 1991 (SI 1991/1252)
(f)		17 Mar 1993 (SI 1993/641)
(16), (17)		3 Jun 1991 (SI 1991/1252)
30		20 Jul 1992 (SI 1992/1599)
31, 32		1 Jan 1991 (SI 1990/2624)
33		1 Dec 1990 (SI 1990/2328)
34		1 Jan 1991 (s 75(3)(b))
35		1 Dec 1990 (SI 1990/2328)
36(1)		*Not in force*
(2)–(5)		30 Sep 1991 (SI 1991/2151)
(6)		26 Aug 1991 (SI 1991/1903)
(7)–(9)		*Not in force*
(10)–(15)		30 Sep 1991 (SI 1991/2151)
(16)		*Not in force*
37		1 Jan 1991 (SI 1990/2624)
38		3 Jun 1991 (SI 1991/1252)
39		1 Jan 1991 (SI 1990/2624)

9   1 Dec 1990 (repeals of or in Companies Act 1985, ss 38(1), 39(3), 186, 188(2), 462(2); Insolvency Act 1986, s 53(3); Companies Act 1989, s 130(3), Sch 17, paras 1(2), 2(4), 8, 10) (SI 1990/2328)

1 Jan 1991 (repeals of or in Matrimonial Homes (Family Protection) (Scotland) Act 1981, ss 6(3)(e), 8; Representation of the People Act 1983, s 42(3)(b)) (SI 1990/2624)

1 Apr 1991 (repeals of or in Unfair Contract Terms Act 1977, ss 15(1), 25(3)(d), (4)) (SI 1991/330)

3 Jun 1991 (repeals of or in Solicitors (Scotland) Act 1980, ss 20(1), 31(3), 63(1), Sch 4, paras 1, 17) (SI 1991/1252)

Law Reform (Miscellaneous Provisions) (Scotland) Act 1990 (c 40)—*cont*

Sch 9—*cont*   15 Aug 1991 (repeals of or in House of Commons
                                Disqualification Act 1975, Sch 1; Solicitors
                                (Scotland) Act 1980, ss 49, 65(1), Sch 5) (SI 1991/
                                1252)
                                30 Sep 1991 (repeals of or in Solicitors (Scotland)
                                Act 1980, s 29; Legal Aid (Scotland) Act 1986,
                                s 13(2)) (SI 1991/2151)
                                17 Mar 1993 (repeals of or in Licensing (Scotland)
                                Act 1976, ss 6, 18(1), 55, 61, 97(2), 131, 132,
                                133(4), Sch 4, paras 1, 12–17, 19–22; Solicitors
                                (Scotland) Act 1980, s 27; Family Law (Scotland)
                                Act 1985, s 8(1)(a); Law Reform (Miscellaneous
                                Provisions) (Scotland) Act 1985, Sch 1, Pt I, para
                                5) (SI 1993/641)
                                Not in force (otherwise)

Licensing (Low Alcohol Drinks) Act 1990 (c 21)

RA: 13 Jul 1990

Commencement provisions: s 3(2)

1 Jan 1994 (unless a day prior to that date is appointed by the Secretary of State)
   (s 3(2))

Marriage (Registration of Buildings) Act 1990 (c 33)

RA: 26 Jul 1990

Commencement provisions: s 2(2)

26 Sep 1990 (s 2(2))

National Health Service and Community Care Act 1990 (c 19)

RA: 29 Jun 1990

Commencement provisions: s 67(2); National Health Service and Community Care
   Act 1990 (Commencement No 1) Order 1990, SI 1990/1329 (as amended by SI
   1990/2511); National Health Service and Community Care Act 1990
   (Commencement No 2) (Scotland) Order 1990, SI 1990/1520; National Health
   Service and Community Care Act 1990 (Commencement No 3 and Transitional
   Provisions) (Scotland) Order 1990, SI 1990/1793 (as amended by SI 1990/2510,
   SI 1992/799); National Health Service and Community Care Act 1990
   (Commencement No 4 and Transitional Provision) Order 1990, SI 1990/2218;
   National Health Service and Community Care Act 1990 (Commencement No 5
   and Revocation) (Scotland) Order 1990, SI 1990/2510; National Health Service
   and Community Care Act 1990 (Commencement No 6–Amendment, and
   Transitional and Saving Provisions) Order 1990, SI 1990/2511; National Health
   Service and Community Care Act 1990 (Commencement No 7) Order 1991, SI
   1991/388; National Health Service and Community Care Act 1990
   (Commencement No 8 and Transitional Provisions) (Scotland) Order 1991, SI
   1991/607; National Health Service and Community Care Act 1990
   (Commencement No 9) Order 1992, SI 1992/567; National Health Service and

National Health Service and Community Care Act 1990 (c 19)—*cont*
Community Care Act 1990 (Commencement No 3 and Transitional Provisions)
(Scotland) (Amendment) Order 1992, SI 1992/799 (amending SI 1990/1793);
National Health Service and Community Care Act 1990 (Commencement No
10) Order 1992, SI 1992/2975

s 1(1)(a)	26 Jul 1990 (so far as has effect in relation to Regional Health Authorities) (SI 1990/1329)
	17 Sep 1990 (otherwise) (SI 1990/1329)
(b)	17 Sep 1990 (SI 1990/1329)
(c)	5 Jul 1990 (SI 1990/1329)
(2)	See Sch 1, Pt I below
(3)	See Sch 1, Pt III below
(4)(a)	25 Jul 1990 (so far as has effect in relation to Regional Health Authorities) (SI 1990/1329)
	16 Sep 1990 (otherwise) (SI 1990/1329)
(b)	16 Sep 1990 (SI 1990/1329)
(5)	25 Jul 1990 (so far as has effect in relation to Regional Health Authorities) (SI 1990/1329)
	16 Sep 1990 (otherwise) (SI 1990/1329)
2(1), (2)	17 Sep 1990 (SI 1990/1329)
(3)(a)	17 Sep 1990 (SI 1990/1329)
(b)	5 Jul 1990 (SI 1990/1329)
(4)	See Sch 1, Pt II below
(5)	16 Sep 1990 (SI 1990/1329)
(6), (7)	17 Sep 1990 (SI 1990/1329)
3(1), (2)	1 Apr 1991 (SI 1990/1329)
(3), (4)	17 Sep 1990 (SI 1990/1329)
(5), (6)	1 Apr 1991 (SI 1990/1329)
(6A)	Inserted by Health and Personal Social Services (Northern Ireland Consequential Amendments) Order 1991, SI 1991/195, art 7(1), (2), as from 1 Apr 1991
(7), (8)	1 Apr 1991 (SI 1990/1329)
4(1), (2)	6 Mar 1991 (so far as relate to a reference under s 4(4)) (SI 1991/388)
	1 Apr 1991 (otherwise) (SI 1990/1329)
(3)	1 Apr 1991 (SI 1990/1329)
(4)	6 Mar 1991 (SI 1991/388)
(5), (6)	6 Mar 1991 (so far as relate to a reference under s 4(4) (SI 1991/388)
	1 Apr 1991 (otherwise) (SI 1990/1329)
(7), (8)	1 Apr 1991 (SI 1990/1329)
(9)	6 Mar 1991 (so far as relates to a reference under s 4(4)) (SI 1991/388)
	1 Apr 1991 (otherwise) (SI 1990/1329)
(10)	Added by Health and Personal Social Services (Northern Ireland Consequential Amendments) Order 1991, SI 1991/195, art 7(1), (5), as from 1 Apr 1991
5	See Sch 2 below
6–8	5 Jul 1990 (SI 1990/1329)
9	See Sch 3 below
10, 11	5 Jul 1990 (SI 1990/1329)
12(1)–(3)	17 Sep 1990 (subject to transitional provisions) (SI 1990/1329)
(4)	1 Oct 1991 (subject to savings) (SI 1990/2511)
(5)	17 Sep 1990 (SI 1990/1329)

National Health Service and Community Care Act 1990 (c 19)—*cont*

s 13	1 Apr 1991 (SI 1990/1329)
14	17 Sep 1990 (SI 1990/1329)
15–19	1 Apr 1991 (SI 1990/1329)
20(1)	See Sch 4 below
(2), (3)	1 Oct 1990 (SI 1990/1329)
(4)–(7)	5 Jul 1990 (SI 1990/1329)
21	17 Sep 1990 (SI 1990/1329)
22	1 Jan 1991 (SI 1990/1329)
23(1)–(3)	1 Jan 1991 (subject to transitional provisions) (SI 1990/1329, as amended by SI 1990/2511)
(4)	1 Jan 1991 (except so far as repeals second paragraph of National Health Service Act 1977, s 33(5)) (subject to transitional provisions) (SI 1990/1329, as amended by SI 1990/2511)
	Not in force (exception noted above)
(5)–(8)	1 Jan 1991 (subject to transitional provisions) (SI 1990/1329)
24	17 Sep 1990 (SI 1990/1329)
25	1 Apr 1991 (SI 1990/1329)
26(1)	5 Jul 1990 (SI 1990/1329)
(2)(a)	5 Jul 1990 (SI 1990/1329)
(b)	17 Sep 1990 (SI 1990/1329)
(c)	5 Jul 1990 (SI 1990/1329)
(d)	5 Jul 1990 (so far as relates to definition of 'National Health Service trust') (SI 1990/1329)
	1 Apr 1991 (otherwise) (SI 1990/1329)
(e)	5 Jul 1990 (SI 1990/1329)
(f)	17 Sep 1990 (SI 1990/1329)
(g)	5 Jul 1990 (SI 1990/1329)
(h)	1 Apr 1991 (SI 1990/1329)
(i)	5 Jul 1990 (SI 1990/1329)
27(1), (2)	31 Mar 1991 (so far as have effect in relation to members of a Health Board or the management committee of the Common Services Agency for the Scottish Health Service) (SI 1990/1793)
	30 Jun 1992 (otherwise) (SI 1990/1793, as amended by SI 1992/799)
(3)	See Sch 5 below
28	17 Sep 1990 (SI 1990/1793)
29(1), (2)	17 Sep 1990 (SI 1990/1793)
(3)(a)	24 Jul 1990 (subject to a transitional provision and saving) (SI 1990/1520)
(b), (c)	24 Jul 1990 (SI 1990/1520)
(4)	24 Jul 1990 (SI 1990/1520)
30	1 Apr 1991 (SI 1990/1793)
31	24 Jul 1990 (SI 1990/1520)
32	See Sch 6 below
33	24 Jul 1990 (SI 1990/1520)
34	17 Sep 1990 (so far as relates to provisions of ss 87A, 87B(1) (so far as s 87B(1) provides for meaning of 'recognised fund–holding practice' and 'allotted sum'), to be inserted into the National Health Service (Scotland) Act 1978) (SI 1990/1793)
	1 Apr 1991 (otherwise) (SI 1990/1793)
35	1 Apr 1992 (SI 1990/1793)
36(1)	See Sch 7 below
(2)–(8)	17 Sep 1990 (SI 1990/1793)

National Health Service and Community Care Act 1990 (c 19)—*cont*

s 37	17 Sep 1990 (SI 1900/1793)
38	1 Apr 1991 (SI 1991/607)
39(1)–(3)	1 Apr 1991 (subject, in the case of s 39(2), to transitional provisions) (SI 1991/607)
(4)	1 Apr 1991 (except repeal in second paragraph of National Health Service (Scotland) Act 1978, s 23(5)) (SI 1991/607)
	Not in force (exception noted above)
(5)–(8)	1 Apr 1991 (SI 1991/607)
40, 41	17 Sep 1990 (SI 1990/1793)
42(1)	1 Apr 1993 (SI 1992/2975)
(2)	Repealed
(3)–(5)	1 Apr 1993 (SI 1992/2975)
(6), (7)	1 Apr 1991 (SI 1990/2218)
43, 44	1 Apr 1993 (SI 1992/2975)
45	12 Apr 1993 (SI 1992/2975)
46	1 Apr 1991 (SI 1990/2218)
47	1 Apr 1993 (SI 1992/2975)
48	1 Apr 1991 (SI 1990/2218)
49	10 Dec 1992 (SI 1992/2975)
50	1 Apr 1991 (SI 1990/2218)
51–54	1 Apr 1991 (SI 1990/2510)
55	1 Apr 1993 (SI 1992/2975)
56	1 Apr 1991 (so far as relates to insertion of Social Work (Scotland) Act 1968, s 13B) (SI 1990/2510)
	1 Apr 1993 (otherwise) (SI 1992/2975)
57	1 Apr 1993 (SI 1992/2975)
58	1 Apr 1991 (SI 1990/2510)
59(1)	26 Jul 1990 (so far as has effect in relation to Regional Health Authorities) (SI 1990/1329)
	17 Sep 1990 (otherwise) (SI 1990/1329)
(2)	5 Jul 1990 (SI 1990/1329)
(3)	1 Apr 1991 (SI 1991/607)
60	See Sch 8 below
61, 62	17 Sep 1990 (SI 1990/1329)
63	1 Apr 1991 (SI 1990/1329)
64, 65	5 Jul 1990 (SI 1990/1329)
66(1)	See Sch 9 below
(2)	See Sch 10 below
67	29 Jun 1990 (s 67(2))
Sch 1, Pt I, para 1	26 Jul 1990 (SI 1990/1329)
2, 3	17 Sep 1990 (SI 1990/1329)
II, para 4, 5	17 Sep 1990 (SI 1990/1329)
III, para 6	26 Jul 1990 (SI 1990/1329)
7	26 Jul 1990 (so far as has effect in relation to Regional Health Authorities) (SI 1990/1329)
	17 Sep 1990 (otherwise) (SI 1990/1329)
8, 9	26 Jul 1990 (SI 1990/1329)
10	26 Jul 1990 (so far as has effect in relation to Regional Health Authorities) (SI 1990/1329)
	17 Sep 1990 (otherwise) (SI 1990/1329)
2, 3	5 Jul 1990 (SI 1990/1329)
4, para 1–3	1 Oct 1990 (SI 1990/1329)
4	5 Jul 1990 (SI 1990/1329)
5–24	1 Oct 1990 (SI 1990/1329)
5	17 Sep 1990 (SI 1990/1793)

National Health Service and Community Care Act 1990 (c 19)—*cont*

Sch 6	24 Jul 1990 (SI 1990/1520)
7	*Not in force*
8	1 Apr 1991 (SI 1990/1329)
9, para 1	24 Jul 1990 (SI 1990/1520)
2	5 Jul 1990 (SI 1990/1329)
3, 4	24 Jul 1990 (SI 1990/1520)
5(1)–(3)	1 Apr 1993 (SI 1992/2975)
(4)	5 Jul 1990 (SI 1990/1329)
(5)	1 Apr 1993 (SI 1992/2975)
(6), (7)	1 Apr 1991 (SI 1990/2218)
(8)	1 Apr 1991 (SI 1990/2218; SI 1990/2510)
(9)(a)	1 Apr 1993 (SI 1992/2975)
(b)	1 Apr 1991 (SI 1990/2510)
6–9	5 Jul 1990 (SI 1990/1329)
10(1)	*Not in force*
(2)–(6)	1 Apr 1991 (SI 1990/2510)
(7), (8)	1 Apr 1993 (SI 1992/2975)
(9)–(11)	1 Apr 1991 (SI 1990/2510)
(12)	24 Jul 1990 (SI 1990/1520)
(13)	1 Apr 1991 (SI 1990/2510)
(14)(a)	1 Apr 1991 (SI 1990/2510)
(b)	24 Jul 1990 (SI 1990/1520)
11(a)	1 Apr 1993 (SI 1992/2975)
(b)	1 Apr 1991 (SI 1990/2218)
(c)	1 Apr 1991 (so far as relates to s 46) (SI 1990/2218)
	1 Apr 1993 (otherwise) (SI 1992/2975)
12	1 Apr 1991 (SI 1990/2218)
13	5 Jul 1990 (SI 1990/1329)
14	24 Jul 1990 (SI 1990/1520)
15	Repealed
16	10 Dec 1992 (SI 1992/2975)
17	5 Jul 1990 (SI 1990/1329)
18(1)(a)	17 Sep 1990 (SI 1990/1329)
(b)	5 Jul 1990 (SI 1990/1329)
(c)	17 Sep 1990 (SI 1990/1329)
(2)	17 Sep 1990 (SI 1990/1329)
(3)–(9)	5 Jul 1990 (SI 1990/1329)
(10), (11)	Repealed
(12), (13)	5 Jul 1990 (SI 1990/1329)
(14)	1 Apr 1993 (SI 1992/2975)
19(1)–(3)	17 Sep 1990 (SI 1990/1793)
(4), (5)	24 Jul 1990 (SI 1990/1520)
(6)	17 Sep 1990 (SI 1990/1793)
(7)(a)(i)	17 Sep 1990 (SI 1990/1793)
(ii)	24 Jul 1990 (SI 1990/1520)
(iii), (iv)	17 Sep 1990 (SI 1990/1793)
(b)–(d)	17 Sep 1990 (SI 1990/1793)
(8)	17 Sep 1990 (SI 1990/1793)
(9)–(14)	24 Jul 1990 (SI 1990/1520)
(15)	17 Sep 1990 (SI 1990/1793)
(16), (17)	24 Jul 1990 (SI 1990/1520)
(18)	Repealed
(19)	24 Jul 1990 (SI 1990/1520)
(20)	17 Sep 1990 (SI 1990/1793)
(21)	24 Jul 1990 (SI 1990/1520)
(22)	17 Sep 1990 (SI 1990/1793)
(b)	24 Jul 1990 (SI 1990/1520)

National Health Service and Community Care Act 1990 (c 19)—*cont*

Sch 9, para 19(22)(c)	24 Jul 1990 (so far as relates to definition 'National Health Service trust') (SI 1990/1520)
	1 Apr 1991 (otherwise) (SI 1990/1793)
(d)	24 Jul 1990 (SI 1990/1520)
(e)	17 Sep 1990 (SI 1990/1793)
(23)	1 Apr 1991 (SI 1990/1793)
(24)	24 Jul 1990 (SI 1990/1520)
20	5 Jul 1990 (SI 1990/1329)
21(a), (b)	5 Jul 1990 (SI 1990/1329)
(c)	24 Jul 1990 (SI 1990/1520)
22	5 Jul 1990 (SI 1990/1329); prospectively repealed by Education Act 1993, s 307(3), Sch 21 (qv)
23	5 Jul 1990 (SI 1990/1329)
24(1), (2)	5 Jul 1990 (SI 1990/1329)
(3)(a), (b)	5 Jul 1990 (SI 1990/1329)
(c)	17 Sep 1990 (SI 1990/1329)
(4), (5)	5 Jul 1990 (SI 1990/1329)
(6)	*Not in force*
(7)–(9)	5 Jul 1990 (SI 1990/1329)
25(1)	1 Apr 1993 (SI 1992/2975)
(2)	12 Apr 1993 (SI 1992/2975)
26, 27	5 Jul 1990 (SI 1990/1329)
28	24 Jul 1990 (SI 1990/1520)
29	5 Jul 1990 (SI 1990/1329)
30(1)(a)	5 Jul 1990 (SI 1990/1329)
(b), (c)	*Not in force*
(2)	5 Jul 1990 (SI 1990/1329)
31–33	5 Jul 1990 (SI 1990/1329)
34	17 Sep 1990 (SI 1990/1329)
35–37	5 Jul 1990 (SI 1990/1329)
10	5 Jul 1990 (repeals of or in National Health Service Act 1977, ss 8(5), 10(7)) (SI 1990/1329)
	17 Sep 1990 (repeals of or in National Health Service Act 1977, ss 8(1)–(3), 11(1), 12(a), 13(1), 14, 16, 18(3), 41(b), 55, 91(3)(b), 97(6), 99(1)(b), Sch 5, para 8; Health Services Act 1980, s 22, Sch 1; Public Health (Control of Disease) Act 1984) (SI 1990/1329)
	17 Sep 1990 (repeals of or in National Health Service (Scotland) Act 1978, ss 5, 6, 10(4), 85(1)(a), 108(1), Sch 3; Health and Medicines Act 1988, Sch 2, para 11) (SI 1990/1793)
	1 Oct 1990 (repeals of or in National Health Service Act 1977, s 98(1)(b), (3); Local Government and Housing Act 1989) (SI 1990/1329)
	1 Jan 1991 (repeals of or in National Health Service Act 1977, s 33(7)) (SI 1990/1329)
	1 Jan 1991 (repeals of National Health Service (Scotland) Act 1978, s 23(7)) (SI 1990/1793)
	1 Apr 1991 (repeals of or in Nursing Homes Registration (Scotland) Act 1938; Fire Precautions Act 1971; Health Services Act 1976; National Health Service Act 1977, Sch 5, para 15(2); National Health Service (Scotland) Act 1978; Employment Protection (Consolidation) Act

National Health Service and Community Care Act 1990 (c 19)—*cont*

Sch 10—*cont*   1978; Health Services Act 1980, ss 12–15, Schs 2–
                                            4; Registered Homes Act 1984; National Health
                                            Service (Amendment) Act 1986) (SI 1990/1329)
                                            1 Apr 1991 (repeals of or in National Health Service
                                            (Scotland) Act 1978, ss 7(2), 57(3)) (SI 1990/1793)
                                            1 Apr 1991 (repeals of or in National Assistance Act
                                            1948, ss 35(2), (3), 36, 54 (so far as s 54 relates to
                                            England and Wales, and subject to a transitional
                                            provision (see SI 1990/2218, art 3)); Health
                                            Services and Public Health Act 1968, s 45(5);
                                            Chronically Sick and Disabled Persons Act 1970,
                                            s 2(1) (so far as relates to England and Wales)) (SI
                                            1990/2218)
                                            1 Apr 1991 (so far as they apply to Scotland, repeals
                                            of or in National Assistance Act 1948, s 54; Social
                                            Work (Scotland) Act 1968, s 1(4); National Health
                                            Service (Scotland) Act 1978, ss 13A, 13B, Sch 15,
                                            para 15 ; Mental Health (Scotland) Act 1984,
                                            s 13(1)(c)) (S) (SI 1990/2510)
                                            6 Apr 1992 (repeal of National Assistance Act 1948,
                                            s 22(7)) (EW) (SI 1992/567)
                                            10 Dec 1992 (repeal in Children Act 1975, s 99(1)(b))
                                            (SI 1992/2975)
                                            1 Apr 1993 (repeals of or in National Assistance Act
                                            1948, ss 21(8), 26; National Health Service Act
                                            1977, Sch 8, para 2; Mental Health Act 1983,
                                            ss 124(3), 135(6); Social Security Act 1986, Sch 10,
                                            para 32(2); Local Government Act 1988, Sch 1,
                                            para 2(4)(b); Local Government Finance Act 1988,
                                            Sch 1, para 9(2)(b)) (SI 1992/2975)
                                            Not in force (otherwise)

Pakistan Act 1990 (c 14)

RA: 29 Jun 1990

Commencement provisions: s 2(3))

1 Oct 1989 (retrospective; s 2(3))

Pensions (Miscellaneous Provisions) Act 1990 (c 7)

RA: 24 May 1990

Commencement provisions: ss 1(8), 14(3)

s 1(1)	24 Jul 1990 (s 14(3))
(2)(a)	24 Jul 1990 (s 14(3))
(b)	1 Jan 1992 (s 1(8))
(3)	24 Jul 1990 (s 14(3))
(4)	1 Jan 1993 (s 1(8))
(5)–(8)	24 Jul 1990 (S 14(3))
2–11	24 Jul 1990 (s 14(3))
12	24 May 1990 (RA)
13	24 Jul 1990 (s 14(3))
14	24 May 1990 (RA)

Planning (Consequential Provisions) Act 1990 (c 11)

RA: 24 May 1990

Commencement provisions: s 7(2)

24 Aug 1990 (s 7(2))

Planning (Hazardous Substances) Act 1990 (c 10)

RA: 24 May 1990

Commencement provisions: s 41(2), (3); Planning (Hazardous Substances) Act 1990
  (Commencement and Transitional Provisions) Order 1992, SI 1992/725

11 Mar 1992 (so far as provisions of this Act confer on the Secretary of State a
  power, or impose upon him a duty, to make regulations, or make provision
  with respect to the exercise of any such power or duty, for the purpose only of
  enabling or requiring the Secretary of State to make regulations) (SI 1992/725)
1 Jun 1992 (otherwise) (SI 1992/725)

Planning (Listed Buildings and Conservation Areas) Act 1990 (c 9)

RA: 24 May 1990

Commencement provisions: s 94(2)

24 Aug 1990★ (s 94(2))

★ See, for transitory provisions, Planning (Consequential Provisions) Act 1990, s 6,
  Sch 4

Property Services Agency and Crown Suppliers Act 1990 (c 12)

RA: 29 Jun 1990

29 Jun 1990 (RA)

Representation of the People Act 1990 (c 32)

RA: 26 Jul 1990

Commencement provisions: s 2(2); Representation of the People Act 1990
  (Commencement No 1) Order 1991, SI 1991/1244; Representation of the People
  Act 1990 (Commencement No 2) Order 1991, SI 1991/1686

10 Jun 1991 (EW, S) (SI 1991/1244)
7 Aug 1991 (NI) (SI 1991/1686)

Rights of Way Act 1990 (c 24)

RA: 13 Jul 1990

Commencement provisions: s 6(2)

13 Aug 1990 (s 6(2))

Social Security Act 1990 (c 27)

RA: 13 Jul 1990

Commencement provisions: s 23(2), (3); Social Security Act 1990 (Commencement No 1) Order 1990, SI 1900/1446; Social Security Act 1990 (Commencement No 2) Order 1990, SI 1990/1942; Social Security Act 1990 (Commencement No 3) Order 1991, SI 1991/558; Social Security Act 1990 (Commencement No 4) Order 1992, SI 1992/632; Social Security Act 1990 (Commencement No 5) Order 1992, SI 1992/1532

s 1–5	Repealed
6(1)–(3)	Repealed
(4), (5)	13 Jul 1990 (s 23(2), (3))
7	See Sch 1 below
8–10	Repealed
(11	Prospectively repealed by Pension Schemes Act 1993, s 188(1), Sch 5 (qv))
11(1)	17 Aug 1990 (for purpose of giving effect to s 11(3)) (SI 1990/1446)
	Not in force (otherwise)
(2)	See Sch 2 below
(3)–(6)	17 Aug 1990 (SI 1990/1446)
12(1)	See Sch 3 below; prospectively repealed by Pension Schemes Act 1993, s 188(1), Sch 5 (qv)
(2)	Repealed
13	18 Jul 1990 (SI 1990/1446); prospectively repealed by Pension Schemes Act 1993, s 188(1), Sch 5 (qv)
14	See Sch 4 below; prospectively repealed by Pension Schemes Act 1993, s 188(1), Sch 5 (qv)
15(1)–(10)	13 Jul 1990 (s 23(2), (3))
(11)	*Not in force*
16	Repealed
17(1)–(9)	Repealed
(10)	6 Apr 1992 (SI 1992/632)
18–20	13 Jul 1990 (s 23(2), (3))
21(1)	See Sch 6 below
(2)	See Sch 7 below
(3)	13 Jul 1990 (s 23(2), (3))
22(1)	Repealed
(2), (3)	13 Jul 1990 (s 23(2), (3)); prospectively repealed by Pension Schemes Act 1993, s 188(1), Sch 5 (qv)
23	13 Jul 1990 (s 23(2), (3))
Sch 1, para 1–4	Repealed
5(1), (2)	Repealed
(3)	13 Jul 1990 (s 23(2), (3))
(4)	Repealed
6	Repealed
7	13 Jul 1990 (s 23(2), (3))
(2–4	Prospectively repealed by Pension Schemes Act 1993, s 188(1), Sch 5 (qv))
2	*Not in force*
3	18 Jul 1990 (for purpose of authorising the making of regulations under the Social Security Pensions Act 1975, s 59C(5), as inserted by Sch 3, which are expressed to come into force on or after 1 Oct 1990) (SI 1990/1446)
	1 Oct 1990 (otherwise) (SI 1990/1446)

Social Security Act 1990 (c 27)—*cont*

Sch 4, para 1		22 Oct 1990 (for purpose only of authorising the making of regulations) (SI 1990/1942)
		12 Nov 1990 (otherwise) (SI 1990/1942)
	2	29 Jun 1992 (SI 1992/1532)
	3	3 Dec 1990 (SI 1990/1942)
	4	1 Jan 1991 (SI 1990/1942)
	5	28 Feb 1991 (SI 1990/1942)
	6	13 Jul 1990 (s 23(2), (3))
	7	*Not in force*
	8, 9	13 Jul 1990 (s 23(2), (3))
	10	13 May 1991 (for purposes of regulations expressed to come into force on or after 4 Nov 1991) (SI 1991/558)
		4 Nov 1991 (otherwise) (SI 1991/558)
	11	1 Oct 1990 (SI 1990/1942)
	12–14	18 Jul 1990 (SI 1990/1446)
	15	13 Jul 1990 (s 23(2), (3))
5		Repealed
6, para 1		Repealed
	2	13 Jul 1990 (s 23(2), (3))
	3	Repealed
	4(1), (2)	Repealed
	(3)	13 Jul 1990 (s 23(2), (3))
	5–7	Repealed
	8(1)	Repealed
	(2)	Spent
	(3)	Repealed
	(4)	13 Jul 1990 (s 23(2), (3))
	(5)	Repealed
	(6)	Spent
	(7), (8)	Repealed
	(9), (10)	13 Jul 1990 (s 23(2), (3))
	(11)	Repealed
	(12)	13 Jul 1990 (s 23(2), (3))
	9–12	Repealed
	13	13 Jul 1990 (s 23(2), (3))
	14–26	Repealed
	27	13 Jul 1990 (s 23(2), (3))
	28	Repealed
	29	13 Jul 1990 (so far as consequential on any preceding provision brought into force on 13 Jul 1990) (s 23(2), (3))
		Not in force (otherwise)
	30	Repealed
	31	1 Oct 1990 (SI 1990/1942)
7		13 Jul 1990 (so far as consequential on any preceding provision brought into force on 13 Jul 1990) (s 23(2), (3))
		1 Oct 1990 (repeals of or in Social Security Act 1975, ss 59B(1), (3), (4), (7)(b), (8) and s 152(6); Social Security Pensions Act 1975, ss 33(2), 56B–56D, 56E(1)(c), 56F–56K, 56L(1)(a), (5)(b), (c), 56M, 56N; Social Security and Housing Benefits Act 1982, s 46(3); Social Security Act 1985, s 31(1), Sch 5, para 35; Social Security Act 1986, s 85(4)(a); Social Security Act 1988, s 2(8), (8A);

Social Security Act 1990 (c 27)—*cont*
Sch 7—*cont*   Social Security Act 1989, Sch 1, para 8(3), (4), (7),
                                                   Sch 2, Pt II, para 1(2), 4(b)) (SI 1990/1942)
                                                   21 Oct 1990 (repeals of or in Social Security Act
                                                       1986, s 79) (SI 1990/1942)
                                                   28 Feb 1991 (repeals in Social Security Pensions Act
                                                       1975, Sch 1A, paras 1, 2, 11, 12) (SI 1990/1942)
                                                   Not in force (otherwise)

Terms and Quarter Days (Scotland) Act 1990 (c 22)

RA: 13 Jul 1990

Commencement provisions: s 3(2)

s 1(1)–(4)	13 Jul 1991 (s 3(2))
(5), (6)	13 Jul 1990 (RA)
(7)	13 Jul 1991 (s 3(2))
2	13 Jul 1991 (s 3(2))
3	13 Jul 1990 (RA)

Town and Country Planning Act 1990 (c 8)

RA: 24 May 1990

Commencement provisions: s 337(2)

24 Aug 1990★ (s 337(2))

★ See, for transitory provisions, Planning (Consequential Provisions) Act 1990, s 6,
  Sch 4

1991

Age of Legal Capacity (Scotland) Act 1991 (c 50)

RA: 25 Jul 1991

Commencement provisions: s 11(2)

25 Sep 1991 (s 11(2))

Agricultural Holdings (Scotland) Act 1991 (c 55)

RA: 25 Jul 1991

Commencement provisions: s 89(2)

25 Sep 1991 (s 89(2))

Agriculture and Forestry (Financial Provisions) Act 1991 (c 33)

RA: 25 Jul 1991

Commencement provisions: ss 1(2)–(5), 5(2); Agricultural Mortgage Corporation (Specified Day for Repeals) Order 1991, SI 1991/1937; Scottish Agricultural Securities Corporation (Specified Day for Repeals) Order 1991, SI 1991/1978

s 1(1)	See Schedule below
(2)–(7)	25 Jul 1991 (RA)
2	25 Sep 1991 (s 5(2))
3–5	25 Jul 1991 (RA)
Schedule,	
Pt I	25 Sep 1991 (SI 1991/1937)
II	25 Sep 1991 (by virtue of s 1(3), SI 1991/1937)
III	25 Sep 1991 (SI 1991/1978)
IV	25 Sep 1991 (by virtue of s 1(5), SI 1991/1978)

Appropriation Act 1991 (c 32)

Whole Act repealed

Armed Forces Act 1991 (c 62)

RA: 25 Jul 1991

Commencement provisions: s 27(2)–(4); Armed Forces Act 1991 (Commencement No 1) Order 1991, SI 1991/2719

Armed Forces Act 1991 (c 62)—*cont*

s 1	25 Jul 1991 (RA)
2–5	1 Jan 1992 (SI 1991/2719)
6	1 Jan 1992 (with effect in relation to reception orders made after 31 Dec 1991) (SI 1991/2719)
7–16	1 Jan 1992 (SI 1991/2719)
17–23	*Not in force*
24(1), (2)	1 Jan 1992 (SI 1991/2719)
(3)	*Not in force*
(4), (5)	1 Jan 1992 (SI 1991/2719)
25	25 Jul 1991 (RA)
26(1)	See Sch 2 below
(2)	See Sch 3 below
27	25 Jul 1991 (RA)
Sch 1	1 Jan 1992 (SI 1991/2719)
2, para 1, 2	1 Jan 1992 (SI 1991/2719)
3	Repealed
4–6	1 Jan 1992 (SI 1991/2719)
7	1 Jan 1992 (with effect in relation to offences committed after 31 Dec 1991) (SI 1991/2719)
8	1 Jan 1992 (with effect in relation to appeals lodged after 31 Dec 1991) (SI 1991/2719)
9–11	1 Jan 1992 (SI 1991/2719)
3	1 Jan 1992 (repeal of Armed Forces Act 1986, s 1) (s 27(4))
	1 Jan 1992 (repeals of or in Naval and Marine Pay and Pensions Act 1865, ss 4, 5; Naval Forces (Enforcement of Maintenance Liabilities) Act 1947, ss 1(3), (5), 2; Army Act 1955, ss 71A(1B)(a), 71AA(1), (1A), (2), 93, 122(1), 127(2), 131(1), 145(1)(b), 150(1)(a), (5), 225(1), Sch 5A, paras 2, 6–9, 10(1A), 11(4), 15(3); Air Force Act 1955, ss 71A(1B)(a), 71AA(1), (1A), (2), 93, 122(1), 127(2), 131(1), 145(1)(b), 150(1)(a), (5), 223(1), Sch 5A, paras 2, 6–9, 10(1A), 11(4), 15(3); Naval Discipline Act 1957, ss, 43A(1B)(a), 43.AA, 60, 129(2), Sch 4A, paras 2, 6–9, 10(1A), 11(4), 15(3); Courts-Martial (Appeals) Act 1968; Rehabilitation of Offenders Act 1974; Rehabilitation of Offenders (Northern Ireland) Order 1978; Reserve Forces Act 1980; Reserve Forces Act 1982; Armed Forces Act 1986, Sch 1, para 12(3), (5); Children Act 1989) (SI 1991/2719)
	Not in force (otherwise)

Arms Control and Disarmament (Inspections) Act 1991 (c 41)

RA: 25 Jul 1991

Commencement provisions: s 6(2); Arms Control and Disarmament (Inspections) Act 1991 (Commencement) Order 1992, SI 1992/1750

s 1–5	17 Jul 1992 (SI 1992/1750)
6	25 Jul 1991 (RA)
Schedule	17 Jul 1992 (SI 1992/1750)

Atomic Weapons Establishment Act 1991 (c 46)

RA: 25 Jul 1991

Commencement provisions: s 6(2)

25 Sep 1991 (s 6(2))

Badgers Act 1991 (c 36)

Whole Act repealed

Badgers (Further Protection) Act 1991 (c 35)

Whole Act repealed

Breeding of Dogs Act 1991 (c 64)

RA: 25 Jul 1991

Commencement provisions: s 3(2)

25 Sep 1991 (s 3(2))

British Railways Board (Finance) Act 1991 (c 63)

RA: 25 Jul 1991

25 Jul 1991 (RA)

British Technology Group Act 1991 (c 66)

RA: 22 Oct 1991

Commencement provisions: ss 1(1), 11(2), 18(2)–(4); British Technology Group Act 1991 (Appointed Day) Order 1991, SI 1991/2721

s 1(1)–(5)	22 Oct 1991 (s 18(3))
(6)	See Sch 1 below
2	22 Oct 1991 (s 18(3))
3–6	6 Jan 1992 (ss 1(1), 18(2); SI 1991/2721)
7	22 Oct 1991 (s 18(3))
8–13	6 Jan 1992 (ss 1(1), 18(2); SI 1991/2721)
14	22 Oct 1991 (s 18(3))
15	6 Jan 1992 (ss 1(1), 18(2); SI 1991/2721)
16(1)	22 Oct 1991 (s 18(3))
(2)	6 Jan 1992 (ss 1(1), 18(2); SI 1991/2721)
17(1)	6 Jan 1992 (ss 1(1), 18(2); SI 1991/2721)
(2)	See Sch 2 below
(3)	See Sch 3 below
18	22 Oct 1991 (s 18(3))
Sch 1, para 1	22 Oct 1991 (s 18(3))
2–5	6 Jan 1992 (ss 1(1), 18(2); SI 1991/2721)

British Technology Group Act 1991 (c 66)—*cont*

Sch 2, Pt I	6 Jan 1992 (ss 1(1), 18(2); SI 1991/2721)
II, III	*Not in force*
3	6 Jan 1992 (ss 1(1), 18(2); SI 1991/2721)

Caravans (Standard Community Charge and Rating) Act 1991 (c 2)

RA: 12 Feb 1991

12 Feb 1991 (RA)

Care of Churches and Ecclesiastical Jurisdiction Measure 1991 (No 1)

RA: 25 Jul 1991

Commencement provisions: s 33(2)

31 Mar 1993 (the day appointed by the Archbishops of Canterbury and York under s 33(2))

Census (Confidentiality) Act 1991 (c 6)

RA: 7 Mar 1991

7 Mar 1991 (RA)

Child Support Act 1991 (c 48)

RA: 25 Jul 1991

Commencement provisions: s 58(2)–(7); Child Support Act 1991 (Commencement No 1) Order 1992, SI 1992/1431; Child Support Act 1991 (Commencement No 2) Order 1992, SI 1992/1938; Child Support Act 1991 (Commencement No 3 and Transitional Provisions) Order 1992, SI 1992/2644, as amended by SI 1993/966; Child Support Act 1991 (Commencement No 3 and Transitional Provisions) (Amendment) Order 1993, SI 1993/966 (amending SI 1992/2644, Schedule, which contains transitional provisions)

s 1, 2	5 Apr 1993 (SI 1992/2644)
3(1), (2)	5 Apr 1993 (SI 1992/2644)
(3)(a), (b)	5 Apr 1993 (SI 1992/2644)
(c)	17 Jun 1992 (SI 1992/1431)
(4)–(7)	5 Apr 1993 (SI 1992/2644)
4(1)–(3)	5 Apr 1993 (subject to transitional provisions) (SI 1992/2644, as amended by SI 1993/966)
(4)	17 Jun 1992 (SI 1992/1431)
(5), (6)	5 Apr 1993 (subject to transitional provisions) (SI 1992/2644, as amended by SI 1993/966)
(7), (8)	17 Jun 1992 (SI 1992/1431)
(9)	5 Apr 1993 (subject to transitional provisions) (SI 1992/2644, as amended by SI 1993/966)
5(1), (2)	5 Apr 1993 (SI 1992/2644)
(3)	17 Jun 1992 (SI 1992/1431)

Child Support Act 1991 (c 48)—*cont*

s 6(1)	17 Jun 1992 (so far as confers power to prescribe kinds of benefit for purposes of s 6(1)) (SI 1992/ 1431)
	5 Apr 1993 (otherwise) (SI 1992/2644)
(2)–(8)	5 Apr 1993 (SI 1992/2644)
(9), (10)	17 Jun 1992 (SI 1992/1431)
(11), (12)	5 Apr 1993 (SI 1992/2644)
(13)	17 Jun 1992 (SI 1992/1431)
(14)	5 Apr 1993 (SI 1992/2644)
7(1)–(4)	5 Apr 1993 (subject to transitional provisions) (SI 1992/2644, as amended by SI 1993/966)
(5)	17 Jun 1992 (SI 1992/1431)
(6), (7)	5 Apr 1993 (subject to transitional provisions) (SI 1992/2644, as amended by SI 1993/966)
(8), (9)	17 Jun 1992 (SI 1992/1431)
8(1)–(4)	5 Apr 1993 (subject to transitional provisions) (SI 1992/2644, as amended by SI 1993/966)
(5)	17 Jun 1992 (SI 1992/1431)
(6)–(8)	5 Apr 1993 (SI 1992/2644)
(9)	17 Jun 1992 (SI 1992/1431)
(10)	5 Apr 1993 (SI 1992/2644)
(11)(a)–(e)	5 Apr 1993 (SI 1992/2644)
(f)	17 Jun 1992 (SI 1992/1431)
9	5 Apr 1993 (subject to transitional provisions) (SI 1992/2644, as amended by SI 1993/966)
10	17 Jun 1992 (SI 1992/1431)
11(1)	5 Apr 1993 (SI 1992/2644)
(2), (3)	See Sch 1 below
12(1)	5 Apr 1993 (SI 1992/2644)
(2), (3)	17 Jun 1992 (SI 1992/1431)
(4)	5 Apr 1993 (SI 1992/2644)
(5)	17 Jun 1992 (SI 1992/1431)
13	1 Sep 1992 (SI 1992/1938)
14(1)	17 Jun 1992 (SI 1992/1431)
(2)	5 Apr 1993 (SI 1992/2644)
(3)	17 Jun 1992 (SI 1992/1431)
(4)	See Sch 2 below
15	5 Apr 1993 (SI 1992/2644)
16(1), (2)	17 Jun 1992 (SI 1992/1431)
(3), (4)	5 Apr 1993 (subject to transitional provisions) (SI 1992/2644)
(5), (6)	17 Jun 1992 (SI 1992/1431)
17(1)–(3)	5 Apr 1993 (subject to transitional provisions) (SI 1992/2644)
(4)	17 Jun 1992 (SI 1992/1431)
(5)	5 Apr 1993 (subject to transitional provisions) (SI 1992/2644)
(6)(a)	5 Apr 1993 (subject to transitional provisions) (SI 1992/2644)
(b)	17 Jun 1992 (SI 1992/1431)
18(1)–(7)	5 Apr 1993 (subject to transitional provisions) (SI 1992/2644)
(8)	17 Jun 1992 (SI 1992/1431)
(9), (10)	5 Apr 1993 (subject to transitional provisions) (SI 1992/2644)
(11)	17 Jun 1992 (SI 1992/1431)

Child Support Act 1991 (c 48)—*cont*

s 18(12)	5 Apr 1993 (subject to transitional provisions) (SI 1992/2644)
19(1), (2)	5 Apr 1993 (subject to transitional provisions) (SI 1992/2644)
(3)	*Not in force*
20	5 Apr 1993 (SI 1992/2644)
21(1)	1 Sep 1992 (SI 1992/1938)
(2), (3)	17 Jun 1992 (SI 1992/1431)
(4)	See Sch 3 below
22(1), (2)	1 Sep 1992 (SI 1992/1938)
(3), (4)	17 Jun 1992 (SI 1992/1431)
(5)	See Sch 4 below
23	1 Sep 1992 (SI 1992/1938)
24(1)–(5)	5 Apr 1993 (SI 1992/2644)
(6), (7)	17 Jun 1992 (SI 1992/1431)
(8)	5 Apr 1993 (SI 1992/2644)
(9)	1 Sep 1992 (SI 1992/1938)
25(1)	5 Apr 1993 (SI 1992/2644)
(2)(a)	17 Jun 1992 (SI 1992/1431)
(b)	5 Apr 1993 (SI 1992/2644)
(3)(a), (b)	5 Apr 1993 (SI 1992/2644)
(c)	17 Jun 1992 (SI 1992/1431)
(4)	5 Apr 1993 (SI 1992/2644)
(5), (6)	17 Jun 1992 (SI 1992/1431)
26–28	5 Apr 1993 (SI 1992/2644)
29(1)	5 Apr 1993 (SI 1992/2644)
(2), (3)	17 Jun 1992 (SI 1992/1431)
30(1)	17 Jun 1992 (SI 1992/1431)
(2)	*Not in force*
(3)	5 Apr 1993 (SI 1992/2644)
(4), (5)	17 Jun 1992 (SI 1992/1431)
31(1)–(7)	5 Apr 1993 (SI 1992/2644)
(8)	17 Jun 1992 (SI 1992/1431)
32(1)–(5)	17 Jun 1992 (SI 1992/1431)
(6)	5 Apr 1993 (SI 1992/2644)
(7)–(9)	17 Jun 1992 (SI 1992/1431)
(10)–(11)	5 Apr 1993 (SI 1992/2644)
33	5 Apr 1993 (SI 1992/2644)
34(1)	17 Jun 1992 (SI 1992/1431)
(2)	*Not in force*
35(1)	5 Apr 1993 (SI 1992/2644)
(2)(a)	5 Apr 1993 (SI 1992/2644)
(b)	17 Jun 1992 (SI 1992/1431)
(3)–(6)	5 Apr 1993 (SI 1992/2644)
(7), (8)	17 Jun 1992 (SI 1992/1431)
36	5 Apr 1993 (SI 1992/2644)
37(1)	5 Apr 1993 (SI 1992/2644)
(2), (3)	*Not in force*
38	5 Apr 1993 (SI 1992/2644)
39	17 Jun 1992 (SI 1992/1431)
40(1)–(3)	5 Apr 1993 (SI 1992/2644)
(4)(a)(i)	5 Apr 1993 (SI 1992/2644)
(ii)	17 Jun 1992 (SI 1992/1431)
(b)	5 Apr 1993 (SI 1992/2644)
(5)–(7)	5 Apr 1993 (SI 1992/2644)
(8)	17 Jun 1992 (SI 1992/1431)
(9), (10)	5 Apr 1993 (SI 1992/2644)

Child Support Act 1991 (c 48)—*cont*

s 40(11)	17 Jun 1992 (SI 1992/1431)
(12)–(14)	5 Apr 1993 (SI 1992/2644)
41(1)	5 Apr 1993 (SI 1992/2644)
(2)–(4)	17 Jun 1992 (SI 1992/1431)
(5), (6)	5 Apr 1993 (SI 1992/2644)
42	17 Jun 1992 (SI 1992/1431)
43(1)(a)	5 Apr 1993 (SI 1992/2644)
(b)	17 Jun 1992 (SI 1992/1431)
(2)(a)	17 Jun 1992 (SI 1992/1431)
(b)	5 Apr 1993 (SI 1992/2644)
44(1), (2)	5 Apr 1993 (SI 1992/2644)
(3)	17 Jun 1992 (SI 1992/1431)
45	17 Jun 1992 (SI 1992/1431)
46(1)–(10)	5 Apr 1993 (SI 1992/2644)
(11)	17 Jun 1992 (SI 1992/1431)
47	17 Jun 1992 (SI 1992/1431)
48	5 Apr 1993 (SI 1992/2644)
49	17 Jun 1992 (SI 1992/1431)
50(1)–(4)	5 Apr 1993 (SI 1992/2644)
(5)	17 Jun 1992 (SI 1992/1431)
(6)	5 Apr 1993 (SI 1992/2644)
(7)(a)–(c)	5 Apr 1993 (SI 1992/2644)
(d)	17 Jun 1992 (SI 1992/1431)
(8)	5 Apr 1993 (SI 1992/2644)
51, 52	17 Jun 1992 (SI 1992/1431)
53	5 Apr 1993 (SI 1992/2644)
54, 55	17 Jun 1992 (SI 1992/1431)
56(1)	25 Jul 1991 (s 58(2))
(2)–(4)	17 Jun 1992 (SI 1992/1431)
57	17 Jun 1992 (SI 1992/1431)
58(1)–(11)	25 Jul 1991 (s 58(2))
(12)	*Not in force*
(13)	See Sch 5 below
(14)	25 Jul 1991 (s 58(2))
Sch 1, para 1(1), (2)	5 Apr 1993 (SI 1992/2644)
(3)	17 Jun 1992 (SI 1992/1431)
(4)	5 Apr 1993 (SI 1992/2644)
(5)	17 Jun 1992 (SI 1992/1431)
2(1)	17 Jun 1992 (SI 1992/1431)
(2), (3)	5 Apr 1993 (SI 1992/2644)
3	5 Apr 1993 (SI 1992/2644)
4(1)	17 Jun 1992 (SI 1992/1431)
(2)	5 Apr 1993 (SI 1992/2644)
(3)	17 Jun 1992 (SI 1992/1431)
5(1), (2)	17 Jun 1992 (SI 1992/1431)
(3)	5 Apr 1993 (SI 1992/2644)
(4)	17 Jun 1992 (SI 1992/1431)
6(1)	5 Apr 1993 (SI 1992/2644)
(2)–(6)	17 Jun 1992 (SI 1992/1431)
(7)–(11)	5 Apr 1993 (SI 1992/2644)
7–9	17 Jun 1992 (SI 1992/1431)
10	5 Apr 1993 (SI 1992/2644)
11	17 Jun 1992 (SI 1992/1431)
12, 13	5 Apr 1993 (SI 1992/2644)
14	17 Jun 1992 (SI 1992/1431)
15	5 Apr 1993 (SI 1992/2644)

Child Support Act 1991 (c 48)—*cont*

Sch 1, para 16(1)–(4)	5 Apr 1993 (SI 1992/2644)	
(5)	17 Jun 1992 (SI 1992/1431)	
(6)–(9)	5 Apr 1993 (SI 1992/2644)	
(10), (11)	17 Jun 1992 (SI 1992/1431)	
2, para 1	5 Apr 1993 (SI 1992/2644)	
2(1)–(3)	5 Apr 1993 (SI 1992/2644)	
(4)	17 Jun 1992 (SI 1992/1431)	
3, para 1, 2	1 Sep 1992 (SI 1992/1938)	
3(1), (2)	1 Sep 1992 (SI 1992/1938)	
(3)	17 Jun 1992 (SI 1992/1431)	
4–8	1 Sep 1992 (SI 1992/1938)	
4	1 Sep 1992 (SI 1992/1938)	
5, para 1	Repealed	
2–4	1 Sep 1992 (SI 1992/1938)	
5–8	5 Apr 1993 (SI 1992/2644)	

Children and Young Persons (Protection from Tobacco) Act 1991 (c 23)

RA: 27 Jun 1991

Commencement provisions: s 8(2); Children and Young Persons (Protection from Tobacco) Act 1991 (Commencement No 1) Order 1991, SI 1991/2500; Children and Young Persons (Protection from Tobacco) Act 1991 (Commencement No 2) Order 1992, SI 1992/332; Children and Young Persons (Protection from Tobacco) Act 1991 (Commencement No 3) Order 1992, SI 1992/3227

s 1–3	1 Mar 1992 (SI 1992/332)
4(1), (2)	20 Feb 1993 (SI 1992/3227)
(3)	17 Dec 1992 (SI 1992/3227)
(4)–(8)	20 Feb 1993 (SI 1992/3227)
(9)	17 Dec 1992 (SI 1992/3227)
5–7	1 Mar 1992 (SI 1992/332)
8(1)	1 Mar 1992 (SI 1992/332)
(2)	27 Jun 1991 (RA)
(3)–(5)	1 Mar 1992 (SI 1992/332)
(6), (7)	11 Nov 1991 (NI) (SI 1992/2500)
	1 Mar 1992 (otherwise) (SI 1992/332)

Civil Jurisdiction and Judgments Act 1991 (c 12)

RA: 9 May 1991

Commencement provisions: s 5(3); Civil Jurisdiction and Judgments Act 1991 (Commencement) Order 1992, SI 1992/745

1 May 1992 (SI 1992/745)

Coal Mining Subsidence Act 1991 (c 45)

RA: 25 Jul 1991

Commencement provisions: s 54(2), (3); Coal Mining Subsidence Act 1991 (Commencement) Order 1991, SI 1991/2508

Coal Mining Subsidence Act 1991 (c 45)—*cont*
30 Nov 1991 (subject to transitional provision with respect to s 34(1)(a)) (SI 1991/
2508)

Community Charges (General Reduction) Act 1991 (c 9)

RA: 28 Mar 1991

28 Mar 1991 (RA)

Community Charges (Substitute Setting) Act 1991 (c 8)

Whole Act repealed

Consolidated Fund Act 1991 (c 7)

Whole Act repealed

Consolidated Fund (No 2) Act 1991 (c 10)

Whole Act repealed

Consolidated Fund (No 3) Act 1991 (c 68)

RA: 19 Dec 1991

19 Dec 1991 (RA)

Criminal Justice Act 1991 (c 53)

RA: 25 Jul 1991

Commencement provisions: s 102(2), (3); Criminal Justice Act 1991 (Commencement
No 1) Order 1991, SI 1991/2208; Criminal Justice Act 1991 (Commencement
No 2 and Transitional Provisions) Order 1991, SI 1991/2706; Criminal Justice
Act 1991 (Commencement No 3) Order 1992, SI 1992/333 (as amended by SI
1992/2118); Criminal Justice Act 1991 (Commencement No 3 (Amendment) and
Transitional Provisions and Savings) (Scotland) Order 1992, SI 1992/2118
(amending SI 1992/333)

s 1–7	1 Oct 1992 (SI 1992/333)
8(1), (2)	1 Oct 1992 (SI 1992/333)
(3)(a)	See Sch 1, Pt I below
(b)–(d)	1 Oct 1992 (SI 1992/333)
9(1)	1 Oct 1992 (SI 1992/333)
(2)	See Sch 1, Pt II below
10, 11	1 Oct 1992 (SI 1992/333)
12, 13	*Not in force*
14(1)	See Sch 2 below
(2)	1 Oct 1992 (SI 1992/333)
15, 16	1 Oct 1992 (SI 1992/333)

Criminal Justice Act 1991 (c 53)—*cont*

s 17	1 Oct 1992 (but does not apply in relation to any offence committed before 1 Oct 1992) (SI 1992/333, as amended by SI 1992/2118)
18	Substituted by Criminal Justice Act 1993, s 65(1) (qv)
19	Repealed
20	1 Oct 1992 (SI 1992/333)
21	Substituted by Criminal Justice Act 1993, s 65(3), Sch 3, para 3 (qv)
22	Repealed
23–25	1 Oct 1992 (SI 1992/333)
26(1), (2)	1 Oct 1992 (SI 1992/333)
(3)	Repealed
(4), (5)	31 Oct 1991 (SI 1991/2208)
27, 28	1 Oct 1992 (SI 1992/333)
29	Substituted by Criminal Justice Act 1993, s 66(6) (qv)
30, 31	1 Oct 1992 (SI 1992/333)
32(1)–(6)	1 Oct 1992 (SI 1992/333)
(7)	See Sch 5 below
33–52	1 Oct 1992 (SI 1992/333)
53(1)–(4)	1 Oct 1992 (SI 1992/333)
(5)	See Sch 6 below
(6), (7)	1 Oct 1992 (SI 1992/333)
54–59	1 Oct 1992 (SI 1992/333)
60(1)	1 Oct 1992 (SI 1992/333)
(2)(a)	1 Oct 1992 (SI 1992/333)
(b), (c)	*Not in force* (due to come into force on day appointed by order made by Secretary of State under s 62(1)) (SI 1992/333)
(3)	14 Oct 1991 (SI 1991/2208)
61–65	1 Oct 1992 (SI 1992/333)
66	See Sch 7 below
67	1 Oct 1992 (SI 1992/333)
68	See Sch 8 below
69, 70	1 Oct 1992 (SI 1992/333)
71	See Sch 9 below
72	1 Oct 1992 (SI 1992/333)
73–75	Repealed
76–79	1 Apr 1992 (SI 1992/333)
80–88	31 Oct 1991 (SI 1991/2208)
89(1)	31 Oct 1991 (SI 1991/2208)
(2)	See Sch 10 below
(3)	31 Oct 1991 (SI 1991/2208)
90, 91	31 Oct 1991 (SI 1991/2208)
92(1)	31 Oct 1991 (SI 1991/2208)
(2)	1 Apr 1992 (SI 1992/333)
(3)	*Not in force* (due to come into force on day appointed by order made by Secretary of State under s 62(1)) (SI 1992/333)
93	31 Oct 1991 (SI 1991/2208)
94	Repealed
95	31 Oct 1991 (SI 1991/2208)
96, 97	Repealed
98	31 Oct 1991 (SI 1991/2208)
99(1)	14 Oct 1991 (except definitions 'child' and 'young person') (SI 1991/2208)

Criminal Justice Act 1991 (c 53)—*cont*

s 99(1)—*cont*	1 Oct 1992 (exceptions noted above) (SI 1992/333)
(2)	1 Oct 1992 (SI 1992/333)
100	See Sch 11 below
101(1)	See Sch 12 below
(2)	See Sch 13 below
102	14 Oct 1991 (SI 1991/2208)
Sch 1–7	1 Oct 1992 (SI 1992/333)
8, para 1(1)	*Not in force*
(2)	1 Oct 1992 (SI 1992/333)
(3)	1 Oct 1992 (except to the extent that would otherwise apply to Children and Young Persons Act 1933, s 34) (SI 1992/333)
	Not in force (exception noted above)
2–6	1 Oct 1992 (SI 1992/333)
9	1 Oct 1992 (SI 1992/333)
10	31 Oct 1991 (SI 1991/2208)
11, para 1	1 Oct 1992 (SI 1992/333)
2(1)	1 Oct 1992 (SI 1992/333)
(2)(a)	1 Oct 1992 (SI 1992/333)
(b)	*Not in force* (comes into force on day appointed by order made by Secretary of State under s 62(1)) (SI 1992/333)
(3)	1 Oct 1992 (SI 1992/333)
(4)(a), (b)	1 Oct 1992 (SI 1992/333)
(c)	*Not in force* (due to come into force on day appointed by order made by Secretary of State under s 62(1)) (SI 1992/333)
3–16	1 Oct 1992 (SI 1992/333)
17	Repealed
18	1 Apr 1992 (SI 1992/333)
19–23	1 Oct 1992 (SI 1992/333)
24	Repealed
25–28	1 Oct 1992 (SI 1992/333)
29	1 Apr 1992 (SI 1992/333)
30–35	1 Oct 1992 (SI 1992/333)
36	14 Oct 1991 (SI 1991/2208)
37–41	1 Oct 1992 (SI 1992/333)
12, para 1–6	1 Oct 1992 (SI 1992/333)
7	25 Oct 1991 (SI 1991/2208)
8–14	1 Oct 1992 (SI 1992/333)
15(1), (2)	1 Oct 1992 (SI 1992/333)
(3)–(5)	*Not in force* (due to come into force on day appointed by order made by Secretary of State under s 62(1)) (SI 1992/333)
16(1)	1 Oct 1992 (SI 1992/333)
(2)–(4)	*Not in force* (due to come into force on day appointed by order made by Secretary of State under s 62(1)) (SI 1992/333)
17–22	1 Oct 1992 (SI 1992/333)
23	14 Oct 1991 (SI 1991/2208)
24	1 Oct 1992 (SI 1992/333)
13	31 Oct 1991 (repeal of Metropolitan Police Act 1839, s 11) (SI 1991/2208)
	1 Oct 1992 (otherwise, except repeal in Criminal Justice Act 1967, s 67(6)) (SI 1992/333)

Criminal Justice Act 1991 (c 53)—*cont*
Sch 13—*cont*   *Not in force* (exception noted above) (due to come
                                            into force on day appointed by order made by
                                            Secretary of State under s 62(1)) (SI 1992/333)

Criminal Procedure (Insanity and Unfitness to Plead) Act 1991 (c 25)

RA: 27 Jun 1991

Commencement provisions: s 9(2); Criminal Procedure (Insanity and Unfitness to
    Plead) Act 1991 (Commencement) Order 1991, SI 1991/2488

1 Jan 1992 (SI 1991/2488)

Crofter Forestry (Scotland) Act 1991 (c 18)

Whole Act repealed

Dangerous Dogs Act 1991 (c 65)

RA: 25 Jul 1991

Commencement provisions: s 10(4); Dangerous Dogs Act 1991 (Commencement and
    Appointed Day) Order 1991, SI 1991/1742

s 1–7	12 Aug 1991 (SI 1991/1742)
8	25 Jul 1991 (s 10(4))
9, 10	12 Aug 1991 (SI 1991/1742)

Deer Act 1991 (c 54)

RA: 25 Jul 1991

Commencement provisions: s 18(3)

25 Oct 1991 (s 18(3))

Development Board for Rural Wales Act 1991 (c 1)

RA: 12 Feb 1991

12 Feb 1991 (RA)

Diocesan Boards of Education Measure 1991 (No 2)

RA: 12 Jul 1991

Commencement provisions: s 13(3)

1 Aug 1991 (the day appointed by the Archbishops of Canterbury and York under
    s 13(3))

Disability Living Allowance and Disability Working Allowance Act 1991 (c 21)

RA: 27 Jun 1991

Commencement provisions: s 15(2), (3); Disability Living Allowance and Disability Working Allowance Act 1991 (Commencement No 1) Order 1991, SI 1991/1519; Disability Living Allowance and Disability Working Allowance Act 1991 (Commencement No 2) Order 1991, SI 1991/2617

s 1	Repealed
2(1)	Repealed
(2), (3)	6 Apr 1992 (SI 1991/2617)
3	Repealed
4(1)	Repealed
(2)	See Sch 2 below
5, 6	Repealed
7(1)	Repealed
(2)	See Sch 3 below
8, 9	Repealed
10	See Sch 4 below
11–14	Repealed
15	27 Jun 1991 (s 15(2), (3))
Sch 1	Repealed
2, para 1, 2	3 Feb 1992 (for purposes of making claims for, and determination of claims and questions relating to, disability living allowance, or for purposes of making by persons who will have attained the age of 65 on 6 Apr 1992 of claims for, and determination of claims and questions relating to, attendance allowance) (SI 1991/2617)
	6 Apr 1992 (otherwise) (SI 1991/2617)
3–5	Repealed
6, 7	3 Feb 1992 (for purposes noted to Sch 2, paras 1, 2 above) (SI 1991/2617)
	6 Apr 1992 (otherwise) (SI 1991/2617)
8–11	Repealed
12–14	3 Feb 1992 (for purposes noted to Sch 2, paras 1, 2 above) (SI 1991/2617)
	6 Apr 1992 (otherwise) (SI 1991/2617)
15–17	Repealed
18	3 Feb 1992 (for purposes noted to Sch 2, paras 1, 2 above) (SI 1991/2617)
	6 Apr 1992 (otherwise) (SI 1991/2617)
19	Repealed
20, 21	3 Feb 1992 (for purposes noted to Sch 2, paras 1, 2 above) (SI 1991/2617)
	6 Apr 1992 (otherwise) (SI 1991/2617)
22	3 Feb 1992 (for purposes noted to Sch 2, paras 1, 2 above) (SI 1991/2617)
	6 Apr 1992 (otherwise) (SI 1992/2617)
3, Pt I, paras 1–8	Repealed
II, paras 9–15	19 Nov 1991 (for purposes of making regulations expressed to come into force on or after 3 Feb 1992) (SI 1991/2617)
	10 Mar 1992 (for purposes of making claims for, and determination of claims and questions

**Disability Living Allowance and Disability Working Allowance Act 1991
(c 21)**—*cont*

Sch 3, Pt II, paras 9–15—*cont*	relation to, disability working allowance) (SI 1991/2617)
	6 Apr 1992 (otherwise) (SI 1991/2617)
4	6 Apr 1992 (SI 1991/2617)

Export and Investment Guarantees Act 1991 (c 67)

RA: 22 Oct 1991

Commencement provisions: s 15(6); Export and Investment Guarantees Act 1991
(Commencement) Order 1991, SI 1991/2430

23 Oct 1991 (SI 1991/2430)

Finance Act 1991 (c 31)

RA: 25 Jul 1991

See the note concerning Finance Acts at the front of this book

---

Football (Offences) Act 1991 (c 19)

RA: 27 Jun 1991

Commencement provisions: s 6(2); Football (Offences) Act 1991 (Commencement)
Order 1991, SI 1991/1564

10 Aug 1991 (SI 1991/1564)

Foreign Corporations Act 1991 (c 44)

RA: 25 Jul 1991

Commencement provisions: s 2(3)

25 Sep 1991 (s 2(3))

Forestry Act 1991 (c 43)

RA: 25 Jul 1991

Commencement provisions: s 2(2)

25 Sep 1991 (s 2(2))

Land Drainage Act 1991 (c 59)

RA: 25 Jul 1991

Commencement provisions: s 76(2)

1 Dec 1991 (s 76(2))

Local Government Finance and Valuation Act 1991 (c 51)

Whole Act repealed

Local Government Finance (Publicity for Auditors' Reports) Act 1991 (c 15)

RA: 27 Jun 1991

Commencement provisions: s 2(2)

27 Aug 1991 (s 2(2))

Maintenance Enforcement Act 1991 (c 17)

RA: 27 Jun 1991

Commencement provisions: s 12(2); Maintenance Enforcement Act 1991 (Commencement No 1) Order 1991, SI 1991/2042; Maintenance Enforcement Act 1991 (Commencement No 2) Order 1992, SI 1992/455

s 1–8	1 Apr 1992 (SI 1992/455)
9	Repealed
10	See Sch 1 below
11(1)	See Sch 2 below
(2)	See Sch 3 below
12	27 Jun 1991 (RA)
Sch 1, para 1–14	1 Apr 1992 (SI 1992/455)
15–17	*Not in force*; prospectively repealed by Maintenance Orders (Reciprocal Enforcement) Act 1992, s 2(2), Sch 3 (qv)
18, 19	1 Apr 1992 (SI 1992/455)
20	1 Apr 1992 (SI 1992/455); prospectively repealed by Maintenance Orders (Reciprocal Enforcement) Act 1992, s 2(2), Sch 3 (qv)
21	1 Apr 1992 (SI 1992/455)
2, para 1–10	1 Apr 1992 (SI 1992/455)
11	14 Oct 1991 (SI 1991/2042)
3	1 Apr 1992 (SI 1992/455)

Medical Qualifications (Amendment) Act 1991 (c 38)

RA: 25 Jul 1991

Commencement provisions: s 2(2); Medical Qualifications (Amendment) Act 1991 (Commencement) Order 1992, SI 1992/804

s 1	30 Mar 1992 (SI 1992/804)
2	25 Jul 1991 (RA)

Mental Health (Detention) (Scotland) Act 1991 (c 47)

RA: 25 Jul 1991

Commencement provisions: s 4(2); Mental Health (Detention) (Scotland) Act 1991
  (Commencement) Order 1992, SI 1992/357

9 Mar 1992 (SI 1992/357)

Ministerial and other Pensions and Salaries Act 1991 (c 5)

RA: 28 Feb 1991

28 Feb 1991 (RA)

Motor Vehicles (Safety Equipment for Children) Act 1991 (c 14)

RA: 27 Jun 1991

27 Jun 1991 (RA)

Namibia Act 1991 (c 4)

RA: 28 Feb 1991

Commencement provisions: s 2(2)

21 Mar 1990 (s 2(2))

Natural Heritage (Scotland) Act 1991 (c 28)

RA: 27 Jun 1991

Commencement provisions: s 28(2); Natural Heritage (Scotland) Act 1991
  (Commencement No 1) Order 1991, SI 1991/2187; Natural Heritage (Scotland)
  Act 1991 (Commencement No 2) Order 1991, SI 1991/2633

s 1	27 Nov 1991 (SI 1991/2633)
2(1)	27 Nov 1991 (SI 1991/2633)
(2)	1 Apr 1992 (SI 1991/2633)
3	27 Nov 1991 (SI 1991/2633)
4–7	1 Apr 1992 (SI 1991/2633)
8	27 Nov 1991 (SI 1991/2633)
9	1 Apr 1992 (SI 1991/2633)
10, 11	27 Nov 1991 (SI 1991/2633)
12, 13	1 Apr 1992 (SI 1991/2633)
14(1), (2)	27 Nov 1991 (SI 1991/2633)
(3), (4)	1 Apr 1992 (SI 1991/2633)
(5)	27 Nov 1991 (SI 1991/2633)
15–26	1 Oct 1991 (SI 1991/2187)
27(1)	See Sch 10 below
(2)	See Sch 11 below
28	27 Nov 1991 (SI 1991/2633)
Sch 1	27 Nov 1991 (SI 1991/2633)
2, 3	1 Apr 1992 (SI 1991/2633)

Natural Heritage (Scotland) Act 1991 (c 28)—*cont*

Sch 4	27 Nov 1991 (SI 1991/2633)
5–9	1 Oct 1991 (SI 1991/2187)
10, para 1	1 Oct 1991 (SI 1991/2187)
2	27 Nov 1991 (so far as inserts reference to Scottish Natural Heritage in Superannuation Act 1965, s 39(1), para 7) (SI 1991/2633)
	1 Apr 1992 (otherwise) (SI 1991/2633)
3	27 Nov 1991 (SI 1991/2633)
4	1 Apr 1992 (SI 1991/2633)
5–7	1 Oct 1991 (SI 1991/2187)
8	1 Apr 1992 (SI 1991/2633)
9	1 Oct 1991 (SI 1991/2187)
10	27 Nov 1991 (SI 1991/2633)
11–13	1 Apr 1992 (SI 1991/2633)
11	1 Oct 1991 (repeals of or in Spray Irrigation (Scotland) Act 1964; Water (Scotland) Act 1980, ss 77–79, Schs 5, 6) (SI 1991/2187)
	1 Apr 1992 (otherwise) (SI 1991/2633)

New Roads and Street Works Act 1991 (c 22)

RA: 27 Jun 1991

Commencement provisions: s 170(1); New Roads and Street Works Act 1991 (Commencement No 1) (Scotland) Order 1991, SI 1991/2286; New Roads and Street Works Act 1991 (Commencement No 1) Order 1991, SI 1991/2288; New Roads and Street Works Act 1991 (Commencement No 4) (Scotland) Order 1992, SI 1992/1671; New Roads and Street Works Act 1991 (Commencement No 3) Order 1992, SI 1992/1686; New Roads and Street Works Act 1991 (Commencement No 5 and Transitional Provisions and Savings) Order 1992, SI 1992/2984; New Roads and Street Works Act 1991 (Commencement No 6 and Transitional Provisions and Savings) (Scotland) Order 1992, SI 1992/2990

s 1–5	1 Nov 1991 (SI 1991/2288)
6(1), (2)	1 Nov 1991 (SI 1991/2288)
(3)	See Sch 2 below
(4)–(6)	1 Nov 1991 (SI 1991/2288)
7–26	1 Nov 1991 (SI 1991/2288)
27–42	21 Oct 1991 (SI 1991/2286)
43, 44	1 Nov 1991 (SI 1991/2288)
45–47	21 Oct 1991 (SI 1991/2286)
48, 49	14 Jul 1992 (SI 1992/1686)
50(1)–(3)	1 Jan 1993 (SI 1992/2984)
(4)	See Sch 3 below
(5)–(7)	1 Jan 1993 (SI 1992/2984)
51	1 Jan 1993 (SI 1992/2984)
52	14 Jul 1992 (SI 1992/1686)
53(1)–(3)	28 Nov 1992 (SI 1992/2984)
(4)–(6)	14 Jul 1992 (SI 1992/1686)
54	14 Jul 1992 (SI 1992/1686)
55	28 Nov 1992 (for purpose of making regulations) (SI 1992/2984)
	1 Jan 1993 (otherwise) (SI 1992/2984)
56	14 Jul 1992 (SI 1992/1686)
57, 58	28 Nov 1992 (SI 1992/2984)
59(1), (2)	1 Jan 1993 (SI 1992/2984)

New Roads and Street Works Act 1991 (c 22)—*cont*

s 59(3)	14 Jul 1992 (SI 1992/1686)
(4)–(6)	1 Jan 1993 (SI 1992/2984)
60(1)	1 Jan 1993 (SI 1992/2984)
(2)	14 Jul 1992 (SI 1992/1686)
(3)	1 Jan 1993 (SI 1992/2984)
61	1 Jan 1993 (SI 1992/2984)
62	14 Jul 1992 (SI 1992/1686)
63(1)	See Sch 4 below
(2)–(4)	14 Jul 1992 (SI 1992/1686)
64	14 Jul 1992 (SI 1992/1686)
65(1), (2)	1 Apr 1993 (SI 1992/2984)
(3)	14 Jul 1992 (SI 1992/1686)
(4)–(6)	1 Apr 1993 (SI 1992/2984)
66	1 Jan 1993 (SI 1992/2984)
67	14 Jul 1992 (SI 1992/1686)
68, 69	1 Jan 1993 (SI 1992/2984)
70(1)–(3)	1 Jan 1993 (SI 1992/2984)
(4)	14 Jul 1992 (SI 1992/1686)
(5)–(7)	1 Jan 1993 (SI 1992/2984)
71	14 Jul 1992 (SI 1992/1686)
72–74	1 Jan 1993 (SI 1992/2984)
75	14 Jul 1992 (SI 1992/1686)
76–78	1 Jan 1993 (SI 1992/2984)
79, 80	*Not in force*
81(1), (2)	1 Jan 1993 (SI 1992/2984)
(3), (4)	14 Jul 1992 (SI 1992/1686)
(5)–(7)	1 Jan 1993 (SI 1992/2984)
82, 83	1 Jan 1993 (SI 1992/2984)
84(1)	1 Jan 1993 (SI 1992/2984)
(2)	14 Jul 1992 (SI 1992/1686)
(3), (4)	1 Jan 1993 (SI 1992/2984)
85–87	14 Jul 1992 (SI 1992/1686)
88–96	1 Jan 1993 (SI 1992/2984)
97–99	14 Jul 1992 (SI 1992/1686)
100–103	1 Jan 1993 (SI 1992/2984)
104–106	14 Jul 1992 (SI 1992/1686)
107, 108	14 Jul 1992 (SI 1992/1671)
109, 110	1 Jan 1993 (SI 1992/2990)
111	14 Jul 1992 (SI 1992/1671)
112(1)–(3)	30 Nov 1992 (SI 1992/2990)
(4)–(6)	14 Jul 1992 (SI 1992/1671)
113	14 Jul 1992 (SI 1992/1671)
114	30 Nov 1992 (for purpose of making regulations) (SI 1992/2990)
	1 Jan 1993 (otherwise) (SI 1992/2990)
115	14 Jul 1992 (SI 1992/1671)
116, 117	30 Nov 1992 (SI 1992/2990)
118(1), (2)	1 Jan 1993 (SI 1992/2990)
(3)	14 Jul 1992 (SI 1992/1671)
(4)–(6)	1 Jan 1993 (SI 1992/2990)
119(1)	1 Jan 1993 (SI 1992/2990)
(2)	14 Jul 1992 (SI 1992/1671)
(3)	1 Jan 1993 (SI 1992/2990)
120	1 Jan 1993 (SI 1992/2990)
121	14 Jul 1992 (SI 1992/1671)
122(1)	See Sch 6 below
(2)–(5)	14 Jul 1992 (SI 1992/1671)

New Roads and Street Works Act 1991 (c 22)—*cont*

s 123	14 Jul 1992 (SI 1992/1671)
124(1), (2)	1 Apr 1993 (SI 1992/2990)
(3)	14 Jul 1992 (SI 1992/1671)
(4)–(6)	1 Apr 1993 (SI 1992/2990)
125	1 Jan 1993 (SI 1992/2990)
126	14 Jul 1992 (SI 1992/1671)
127, 128	1 Jan 1993 (SI 1992/2990)
129(1)–(3)	1 Jan 1993 (SI 1992/2990)
(4)	14 Jul 1992 (SI 1992/1671)
(5)–(7)	1 Jan 1993 (SI 1992/2990)
130	14 Jul 1992 (SI 1992/1671)
131–133	1 Jan 1993 (SI 1992/2990)
134	14 Jul 1992 (SI 1992/1671)
135–137	1 Jan 1993 (SI 1992/2990)
138, 139	*Not in force*
140(1), (2)	1 Jan 1993 (SI 1992/2990)
(3), (4)	14 Jul 1992 (SI 1992/1671)
(5)–(7)	1 Jan 1993 (SI 1992/2990)
141, 142	1 Jan 1993 (SI 1992/2990)
143(1)	1 Jan 1993 (SI 1992/2990)
(2)	14 Jul 1992 (SI 1992/1671)
(3), (4)	1 Jan 1993 (SI 1992/2990)
144–146	14 Jul 1992 (SI 1992/1671)
147–155	1 Jan 1993 (SI 1992/2990)
156–158	14 Jul 1992 (SI 1992/1671)
159–162	1 Jan 1993 (SI 1992/2990)
163–165	14 Jul 1992 (SI 1992/1671)
166(1)	21 Oct 1991 (so far as relates to offence committed under Pt II (ss 27–47)) (S) (SI 1991/2286)
	1 Nov 1991 (EW) (SI 1991/2288)
	1 Jan 1993 (otherwise) (S) (SI 1992/2990)
(2)	21 Oct 1991 (so far as relates to offence committed under Pt II (ss 27–47)) (SI 1991/2286)
	1 Jan 1993 (otherwise) (SI 1992/2990)
167(1)–(3)	21 Oct 1991 (so far as relate to Pt II (ss 27–47)) (S) (SI 1991/2286)
	1 Nov 1991 (EW) (SI 1991/2288)
	Not in force (otherwise) (S)
(4), (5)	14 Jul 1992 (S) (SI 1992/1671)
	14 Jul 1992 (EW) (SI 1992/1686)
(6)	21 Oct 1991 (so far as relates to Pt II (ss 27–47)) (S) (SI 1991/2286)
	1 Nov 1991 (EW) (SI 1991/2288)
	Not in force (otherwise) (S)
168(1)	See Sch 8 below
(2)	See Sch 9 below
169(1)	1 Nov 1991 (SI 1991/2288)
(2)	14 Jul 1992 (SI 1992/1671)
(3)	*Not in force*
170, 171	1 Nov 1991 (SI 1991/2288)
Sch 1, 2	1 Nov 1991 (SI 1991/2288)
3	1 Jan 1993 (SI 1992/2984)
4	14 Jul 1992 (SI 1992/1686)
5	1 Jan 1993 (SI 1992/2984)
6	14 Jul 1992 (SI 1992/1671)

New Roads and Street Works Act 1991 (c 22)—*cont*

Sch 7		1 Jan 1993 (SI 1992/2990)
8, Pt I, paras 1–16		1 Jan 1993 (SI 1992/2984)
II, paras 17–25		1 Nov 1991 (SI 1991/2286; SI 1991/2288)
	26	Repealed
	27–78	1 Nov 1991 (SI 1991/2286; SI 1991/2288)
	79	Repealed
	80	1 Nov 1991 (SI 1991/2286; SI 1991/2288)
III, paras 81–92		1 Jan 1993 (SI 1992/2990)
	93(a)	21 Oct 1991 (SI 1991/2286)
	(b)	1 Jan 1993 (SI 1992/2990)
	(c)	21 Oct 1991 (SI 1991/2286)
	94(a)	1 Jan 1993 (SI 1992/2990)
	(b)	21 Oct 1991 (SI 1991/2286)
	95	1 Jan 1993 (SI 1992/2990)
	96, 97	21 Oct 1991 (SI 1991/2286)
IV, para 98		Repealed
	99(1), (2)	1 Nov 1991 (SI 1991/2286; SI 1991/2288))
	(3)(a)	1 Nov 1991 (SI 1991/2288)
	(b)	1 Jan 1993 (SI 1992/2990)
	100, 101	1 Jan 1993 (SI 1992/2984; SI 1992/2990)
	102	1 Nov 1991 (SI 1991/2286)
	103	1 Jan 1993 (SI 1992/2990)
	104(a)	1 Nov 1991 (SI 1991/2286)
	(b)	1 Jan 1993 (SI 1992/2990)
	105	1 Jan 1993 (SI 1992/2990)
	106	1 Jan 1993 (SI 1992/2984)
	107	1 Nov 1991 (SI 1991/2288)
	108	1 Jan 1993 (SI 1992/2990)
	109	1 Jan 1993 (SI 1992/2984; SI 1992/2990)
	110	Repealed
	111	1 Jan 1993 (SI 1992/2984; SI 1992/2990)
	112	1 Nov 1991 (SI 1991/2288)
	113–115	1 Jan 1993 (SI 1992/2984; SI 1992/2990)
	116	1 Nov 1991 (SI 1991/2288)
	117	1 Nov 1991 (SI 1991/2286; SI 1991/2288)
	118(1), (2)	1 Nov 1991 (SI 1991/2286; SI 1991/2288)
	(3)	1 Jan 1993 (SI 1992/2984; SI 1992/2990)
	119(1)–(6)	1 Jan 1993 (SI 1992/2984; SI 1992/2990)
	(7)	1 Jan 1993 (SI 1992/2990)
	120(1), (2)	1 Jan 1993 (SI 1992/2984; SI 1992/2990)
	(3)	1 Jan 1993 (SI 1992/2990)
	121(1)	1 Nov 1991 (SI 1991/2286; SI 1991/2288)
	(2)	1 Jan 1993 (SI 1992/2984; SI 1992/2990)
	(3)	1 Nov 1991 (SI 1991/2286; SI 1991/2288)
	(4)	1 Nov 1991 (SI 1991/2288)
	122	Repealed
	123	1 Jan 1993 (SI 1992/2984; SI 1992/2990)
	124	1 Jan 1993 (SI 1992/2990)
	125	1 Jan 1993 (SI 1992/2984; SI 1992/2990)
	126(1), (2)	1 Nov 1991 (SI 1991/2288)
	(3)	1 Jan 1993 (SI 1992/2984)
	127	1 Jan 1993 (SI 1992/2990)
9		21 Oct 1991 (repeal in Roads (Scotland) Act 1984, s 143(2)(b)(ii)) (SI 1991/2286)
		1 Nov 1991 (repeals of or in Road Traffic Regulation Act 1984, ss 1(2), (4), (5), 3(1), 5(2),

New Roads and Street Works Act 1991 (c 22)—*cont*

Sch 9—*cont*	16(3), (4), 17(6), 19(3), 23(5), 34(1), 55(5), 68(1)(a), 86(4), 91, 106(8), 124(2), 132(6), 132A, Sch 9, paras 20(1), 21, 27(1); Roads (Scotland) Act 1984, s 127, Sch 7, paras 2, 3(a), (b), 4, Sch 9, paras 93(2)–(22), (23)(a), (24)–(38), (40), (42), (44)(a), (b), (d), (e), (45)(b); Transport Act 1985, s 137(1); Road Traffic Offenders Act 1988, Sch 3 (the entry relating to the Road Traffic Regulation Act 1984, s 29(3)); Environmental Protection Act 1990, Sch 8, para 7) (S) (SI 1991/2286)
	1 Nov 1991 (repeals of or in Road Traffic Regulation Act 1984; Transport Act 1985; Road Traffic Offenders Act 1988; Environmental Protection Act 1990) (EW) (SI 1991/2288)
	1 Nov 1991 (repeals in Local Government Act 1985, Sch 5) (SI 1991/2288)
	1 Jan 1993 (otherwise) (SI SI 1992/2984; 1992/2990)

Northern Ireland (Emergency Provisions) Act 1991 (c 24)

RA: 27 Jun 1991

Commencement provisions: s 69(1); Northern Ireland (Emergency Provisions) Act 1991 (Commencement) Order 1992, SI 1992/1181

Continuance orders: Northern Ireland (Emergency Provisions) Act 1991 (Continuance) Order 1992, SI 1992/1390; Northern Ireland (Emergency and Prevention of Terrorism Provisions) (Continuance) Order 1992, SI 1992/1413; Northern Ireland (Emergency and Prevention of Terrorism Provisions) (Continuance) Order 1993, SI 1993/1522

s 1–33	27 Aug 1991 (s 69(1))
34	See Sch 3 below
35–46	27 Aug 1991 (s 69(1))
47, 48	1 Jun 1992 (SI 1992/1181)
48A, 48B	Prospectively inserted by Criminal Justice Act 1993, s 37 (qv)
49–52	1 Jun 1992 (SI 1992/1181)
52A	Prospectively inserted by Criminal Justice Act 1993, s 39 (qv)
52B	Prospectively inserted by Criminal Justice Act 1993, s 42 (qv)
53, 54	1 Jun 1992 (SI 1992/1181)
54A	Prospectively inserted (UK) by Criminal Justice Act 1993, s 48 (qv)
55	See Sch 4 below
55A	Prospectively inserted (UK) by Criminal Justice Act 1993, s 77, Sch 4, para 6 (qv)
56	1 Jun 1992 (SI 1992/1181)
57–59	27 Aug 1991 (s 69(1))
60(1), (2)	27 Aug 1991 (s 69(1))
(3)	See Sch 6 below
(4)–(6)	27 Aug 1991 (s 69(1))
61–69	27 Aug 1991 (s 69(1))
70(1), (2)	27 Aug 1991 (s 69(1))
(3)	See Sch 7 below

Northern Ireland (Emergency Provisions) Act 1991 (c 24)—*cont*

s 70(4)   See Sch 8 below
71   27 Aug 1991 (s 69(1))

Sch 1, 2   27 Aug 1991 (s 69(1))
3   27 Aug 1991 (s 69(1), but note s 69(3), (4) which
                 provide that s 34 and Sch 3 are deemed to have
                 ceased to have effect immediately after coming
                 into force)
4   1 Jun 1992 (SI 1992/1181)
5–8   27 Aug 1991 (s 69(1))

S 34 and Sch 3 are brought into force again immediately before the end of 15 Jun
1992, continued in force from the beginning of 16 Jun 1992, and then cease to be
in force immediately after the coming into effect of their continuance (SI 1992/
1390)

Note that the temporary provisions of this Act (Pts I–VIII except ss 7, 63, 64,
Sch 1, Pt III, Sch 4, para 20, and, so far as they relate to offences which are
scheduled offences by virtue of Sch 1, Pt III, ss 3, 9, 10), except s 34 and Sch 3,
are continued in force for twelve months from 16 Jun 1993 (SI 1993/1522,
superseding SI 1992/1413)

Oversea Superannuation Act 1991 (c 16)

RA: 27 Jun 1991

Commencement provisions: s 3(2)

27 Aug 1991 (s 3(2))

Planning and Compensation Act 1991 (c 34)

RA: 25 Jul 1991

Commencement provisions: s 84(2)–(4); Planning and Compensation Act 1991
(Commencement No 1 and Transitional Provisions) Order 1991, SI 1991/2067;
Planning and Compensation Act 1991 (Commencement No 2 and Transitional
Provisions) (Scotland) Order 1991, SI 1991/2092; Planning and Compensation
Act 1991 (Commencement No 3) Order 1991, SI 1991/2272; Planning and
Compensation Act 1991 (Commencement No 4 and Transitional Provisions)
Order 1991, SI 1991/2728; Planning and Compensation Act 1991
(Commencement No 5 and Transitional Provisions) Order 1991, SI 1991/2905;
Planning and Compensation Act 1991 (Commencement No 6) (Scotland) Order
1992, SI 1992/71; Planning and Compensation Act 1991 (Commencement No 7
and Transitional Provisions) Order 1992, SI 1992/334; Planning and
Compensation Act 1991 (Commencement No 8) Order 1992, SI 1992/665;
Planning and Compensation Act 1991 (Commencement No 9 and Transitional
Provision) Order 1992, SI 1992/1279; Planning and Compensation Act 1991
(Commencement No 10 and Transitional Provision) Order 1992, SI 1992/1491;
Planning and Compensation Act 1991 (Commencement No 11 and Transitional
Provisions) Order 1992, SI 1992/1630; Planning and Compensation Act 1991
(Commencement No 12 and Transitional Provisions) (Scotland) Order 1992, SI
1992/1937; Planning and Compensation Act 1991 (Commencement No 13 and
Transitional Provision) Order 1992, SI 1992/2413; Planning and Compensation
Act 1991 (Commencement No 14 and Transitional Provision) Order 1992,

Planning and Compensation Act 1991 (c 34)—*cont*
SI 1992/2831; Planning and Compensation Act 1991 (Commencement No 15)
(Scotland) Order 1993, SI 1993/275

Abbreviation: "rules, etc" means "so much of the provision as enables provision to
be made by rules of court, confers on the Secretary of State a power or imposes
on him a duty to make or to make provision by development order or other
order or regulations or to give or revoke directions, or makes provision with
respect to the exercise of any such power or performance of any such duty, is
brought into force on the specified date"

s 1	2 Jan 1992 (SI 1991/2905)
2	27 Jul 1992 (SI 1992/1630)
3	25 Nov 1991 (rules, etc) (SI 1991/2728)
	2 Jan 1992 (otherwise) (SI 1991/2905)
4	2 Jan 1992 (except so far as relates to breach of condition notices) (SI 1991/2905)
	27 Jul 1992 (exception noted above) (SI 1992/1630)
5	25 Nov 1991 (rules, etc) (SI 1991/2728)
	2 Jan 1992 (otherwise) (SI 1991/2905)
6(1)–(4)	2 Jan 1992 (SI 1991/2905)
(5)	25 Nov 1991 (rules, etc) (SI 1991/2728)
	2 Jan 1992 (otherwise) (SI 1991/2905)
(6)	13 Oct 1991 (SI 1991/2272)
7–9	2 Jan 1992 (SI 1991/2905)
10	25 Nov 1991 (rules, etc) (SI 1991/2728)
	27 Jul 1992 (otherwise) (SI 1992/1630)
11	2 Jan 1992 (SI 1991/2905)
12(1)	25 Oct 1991 (so far as substitutes Town and Country Planning Act 1990, s 106) (SI 1991/2272)
	25 Nov 1991 (so far as substitutes of Town and Country Planning Act 1990, ss 106A, 106B) (rules, etc) (SI 1991/2728)
	9 Nov 1992 (otherwise) (SI 1992/2831)
(2), (3)	25 Oct 1991 (SI 1991/2272)
13(1)	27 Jul 1992 (SI 1992/1279)
(2)	25 Nov 1991 (rules, etc) (SI 1991/2728)
	27 Jul 1992 (otherwise) (SI 1992/1279)
(3)	27 Jul 1992 (SI 1992/1279)
14	2 Jan 1992 (SI 1991/2905)
15	25 Sep 1991 (SI 1991/2067)
16	25 Nov 1991 (rules, etc) (SI 1991/2728)
	17 Jul 1992 (otherwise) (SI 1992/1491)
17, 18	25 Sep 1991 (SI 1991/2067)
19	25 Nov 1991 (rules, etc) (SI 1991/2728)
	2 Jan 1992 (otherwise, except so far as relates to Town and Country Planning Act 1990, Sch 1, para 4(1), as it concerns applications for consent to the display of advertisements) (SI 1991/2905)
	6 Apr 1992 (exception noted above) (SI 1992/665)
20	25 Nov 1991 (rules, etc) (SI 1991/2728)
	17 Jul 1992 (otherwise) (SI 1992/1491)
21	See Sch 1 below
22	25 Sep 1991 (SI 1991/2067)
23(1)–(6)	2 Jan 1992 (SI 1991/2905)
(7)	25 Nov 1991 (so far as relates to Town and Country Planning Act 1990, s 214A(2)) (rules, etc) (SI 1991/2728)

Planning and Compensation Act 1991 (c 34)—*cont*

Planning and Compensation Act 1991 (c 34)—*cont*

60(7), (8)	25 Sep 1991 (SI 1991/2092)
61	See Sch 13 below
62–69	25 Sep 1991 (SI 1991/2067)
70	See Sch 15 below
71–78	25 Sep 1991 (SI 1991/2092)
79	See Sch 17 below
80	25 Sep 1991 (except in relation to entries noted to Sch 18 below) (EW) (SI 1991/2067)
	25 Sep 1991 (except in relation to entries noted to Sch 18 below) (S) (SI 1991/2092)
	2 Jan 1992 (otherwise) (EW) (SI 1991/2728)
	Not in force (otherwise) (S)
81	25 Sep 1991 (SI 1991/2067)
82	26 Mar 1992 (SI 1992/334)
83	25 Oct 1991 (SI 1991/2272)
84(1)–(5)	25 Jul 1991 (RA)
(6)	See Sch 19 below
(7)–(9)	25 Jul 1991 (RA)
Sch 1, 2	25 Sep 1991 (SI 1991/2067)
3, para 1	25 Sep 1991 (SI 1991/2067)
2–6	2 Jan 1992 (SI 1991/2905)
7	25 Nov 1991 (rules, etc) (SI 1991/2728)
	2 Jan 1992 (otherwise) (SI 1991/2905)
8–14	2 Jan 1992 (SI 1991/2905)
15	25 Nov 1991 (rules, etc) (SI 1991/2728)
	2 Jan 1992 (otherwise) (SI 1991/2905)
16–32	2 Jan 1992 (SI 1991/2905)
4, para 1, 2	25 Nov 1991 (rules, etc) (SI 1991/2728)
	10 Feb 1992 (otherwise) (SI 1991/2905)
3	10 Feb 1992 (SI 1991/2905)
4–25	25 Nov 1991 (rules, etc) (SI 1991/2728)
	10 Feb 1992 (otherwise) (SI 1991/2905)
26	10 Feb 1992 (SI 1991/2905)
27–51	25 Nov 1991 (rules, etc) (SI 1991/2728)
	10 Feb 1992 (otherwise) (SI 1991/2905)
5	25 Nov 1991 (rules, etc) (SI 1991/2728)
	9 Nov 1992 (otherwise; but note that amendments do not apply with respect to proposals which are or have been made available for inspection in accordance with Town and Country Planning Act 1990, Sch 7, para 5 or 6 before 12 Oct 1992 but simplified planning zone scheme had not yet come into operation on that date) (SI 1992/2413)
6, para 1	25 Jul 1991 (s 84(4))
2–4	25 Sep 1991 (SI 1991/2067)
5	25 Jul 1991 (s 84(4))
6–12	25 Sep 1991 (SI 1991/2067)
13	25 Jul 1991 (s 84(4))
14–49	25 Sep 1991 (SI 1991/2067)
7, para 1	27 Jul 1992 (SI 1992/1630)
2	2 Jan 1992 (SI 1991/2905)
3	27 Jul 1992 (SI 1992/1630)
4	2 Jan 1992 (SI 1991/2905)
5	2 Jan 1992 (except so far as relates to reference to s 187A) (SI 1991/2905)
	27 Jul 1992 (exception noted above) (SI 1992/1630)

Planning and Compensation Act 1991 (c 34)—*cont*

Sch 7, para 6	25 Oct 1991 (SI 1991/2272)
7	2 Jan 1992 (SI 1991/2905)
8	25 Sep 1991 (SI 1991/2067)
9(1)	2 Jan 1992 (SI 1991/2905)
(2)(a)	10 Feb 1992 (SI 1991/2905)
(b)	27 Jul 1992 (SI 1992/1630)
(c)	25 Sep 1991 (SI 1991/2067)
(d)	2 Jan 1992 (so far as relates to reference to s 171C) (SI 1991/2905)
	9 Nov 1992 (otherwise) (SI 1992/2831)
(e)	2 Jan 1992 (SI 1991/2905)
(f)	2 Jan 1992 (so far as relates to reference to s 187B) (SI 1991/2905)
	27 Jul 1992 (otherwise) (SI 1992/1630)
(g)	2 Jan 1992 (SI 1991/2905)
(h)	25 Oct 1991 (SI 1991/2272)
(i)	2 Jan 1992 (except so far as relates to substitution of reference to 'section 316(1) to (3)' by reference to 'section 316') (SI 1991/2905)
	17 Jul 1992 (exception noted above) (SI 1992/1491)
10(1)	25 Sep 1991 (SI 1991/2067)
(2)	27 Jul 1992 (SI 1992/1279)
11	2 Jan 1992 (SI 1991/2905)
12	27 Jul 1992 (SI 1992/1630)
13	2 Jan 1992 (SI 1991/2905)
14, 15	17 Jul 1992 (SI 1992/1491)
16	2 Jan 1992 (SI 1991/2905)
17	17 Jul 1992 (SI 1992/1491)
18, 19	2 Jan 1992 (so far as relate to inclusion in Town and Country Planning Act 1990, ss 77(4), 79(4), of reference to s 73A) (SI 1991/2905)
	17 Jul 1992 (otherwise) (SI 1992/1491)
20–23	2 Jan 1992 (SI 1991/2905)
24(1)(a)	2 Jan 1992 (SI 1991/2905)
(b)	27 Jul 1992 (SI 1992/1630)
(2), (3)	2 Jan 1992 (SI 1991/2905)
25	2 Jan 1992 (SI 1991/2905)
26	2 Jan 1992 (except so far as relates to breach of condition notices) (SI 1991/2905)
	27 Jul 1992 (exception noted above) (SI 1992/1630)
27–29	2 Jan 1992 (SI 1991/2905)
30	27 Jul 1992 (SI 1992/1630)
31	2 Jan 1992 (SI 1991/2905)
32, 33	27 Jul 1992 (SI 1992/1630)
34	17 Jul 1992 (SI 1992/1491)
35	2 Jan 1992 (SI 1991/2905)
36	25 Sep 1991 (SI 1991/2067)
37	17 Jul 1992 (SI 1992/1491)
38	6 Apr 1992 (SI 1992/665)
39–41	27 Jul 1992 (SI 1992/1630)
42	2 Jan 1992 (SI 1991/2905)
43, 44	27 Jul 1992 (SI 1992/1630)
45(1)	2 Jan 1992 (SI 1991/2905)
(2)	2 Jan 1992 (except so far as relates to reference to s 187A) (SI 1991/2905)
	27 Jul 1992 (exception noted above) (SI 1992/1630)
46	27 Jul 1992 (SI 1992/1630)

Planning and Compensation Act 1991 (c 34)—*cont*

Sch 7, para 47	2 Jan 1992 (SI 1991/2905)
48	25 Nov 1991 (rules, etc) (SI 1991/2728)
	17 Jul 1992 (otherwise) (SI 1992/1491)
49	25 Nov 1991 (rules, etc) (SI 1991/2728)
	27 Jul 1992 (otherwise) (SI 1992/1630)
50	2 Jan 1992 (SI 1991/2905)
51	25 Sep 1991 (SI 1991/2067)
52(1)	2 Jan 1992 (SI 1991/2905)
(2)(a)	2 Jan 1992 (except so far as relates to definition 'breach of condition notice') (SI 1991/2905)
	27 Jul 1992 (exception noted above) (SI 1992/1630)
(b)	2 Jan 1992 (SI 1991/2905)
(c)	27 Jul 1992 (but not relating to demolition of building on land where, before 27 Jul 1992, planning permission has been granted under Town and Country Planning Act 1990, Pt III, or has been deemed to have been granted under that Part of that Act, for the redevelopment of the land) (SI 1992/1279)
(d)	27 Jul 1992 (SI 1992/1630)
(e)	17 Jul 1992 (SI 1992/1491)
(f), (g)	2 Jan 1992 (SI 1991/2905)
(3)	17 Jul 1992 (SI 1992/1491)
(4)	2 Jan 1992 (SI 1991/2905)
53(1)	*Not in force*
(2)	27 Jul 1992 (SI 1992/1630)
(3)	2 Jan 1992 (except so far as relates to applications for consent to the display of advertisements) (SI 1991/2905)
	6 Apr 1992 (exception noted above) (SI 1992/665)
(4)	17 Jul 1992 (SI 1992/1491)
(5)	2 Jan 1992 (so far as confers on the Secretary of State a power to make provision by development order) (SI 1991/2905)
	9 Nov 1992 (otherwise; but note that does not apply to application for planning permission or application for approval of matter reserved under outline planning permission (within meaning of Town and Country Planning Act 1990, s 92, made before 6 Nov 1992 nor to any alteration to that application accepted by the authority) (SI 1992/2831)
(6)	2 Jan 1992 (so far as relates to insertion of the words 'planning contravention notices under s 171C or') (SI 1991/2905)
	27 Jul 1992 (otherwise) (SI 1992/1630)
(7), (8)	2 Jan 1992 (SI 1991/2905)
(9)	25 Oct 1991 (SI 1991/2272)
54(1)	25 Sep 1991 (SI 1991/2067)
(2)	9 Nov 1992 (SI 1992/2831)
(3)(a)	25 Sep 1991 (SI 1991/2067)
(b)	9 Nov 1992 (SI 1992/2831)
(c)	2 Jan 1992 (SI 1991/2905)
(d)	27 Jul 1992 (SI 1992/1630)
(e)	2 Jan 1992 (SI 1991/2905)
(f)	9 Nov 1992 (SI 1992/2831)
(g)	27 Jul 1992 (SI 1992/1630)

Planning and Compensation Act 1991 (c 34)—*cont*

Sch 7, para 54(4)	17 Jul 1992 (SI 1992/1491)
(5), (6)	*Not in force*
55	17 Jul 1992 (SI 1992/1491)
56	25 Sep 1991 (SI 1991/2067)
57(1)	25 Sep 1991 (SI 1991/2067)
(2)(a)	2 Jan 1992 (so far as relates to omission of reference to s 63) (SI 1991/2905)
	27 Jul 1992 (otherwise) (SI 1992/1630)
(b)	25 Sep 1991 (SI 1991/2067)
(c)	2 Jan 1992 (SI 1991/2905)
(d), (e)	17 Jul 1992 (SI 1992/1491)
(f)	9 Nov 1992 (SI 1992/2831)
(g)	2 Jan 1992 (so far as relates to references to ss 196A–196C) (SI 1991/2905)
	27 Jul 1992 (otherwise) (SI 1992/1630)
(h), (i)	2 Jan 1992 (SI 1991/2905)
(j), (k)	17 Jul 1992 (SI 1992/1491)
(3)(a)	17 Jul 1992 (SI 1992/1491)
(b)	25 Sep 1991 (SI 1991/2067)
(c)	2 Jan 1992 (SI 1991/2905)
(d)	2 Jan 1992 (except so far as relates to s 187A) (SI 1991/2905)
	27 Jul 1992 (exception noted above) (SI 1992/1630)
(4)	25 Sep 1991 (SI 1991/2067)
(5)	17 Jul 1992 (except so far as relates to omission of reference to Part IV) (SI 1992/1491)
	27 Jul 1992 (exception noted above) (SI 1992/1630)
(6)(a), (b)	17 Jul 1992 (SI 1992/1491)
(c)	27 Jul 1992 (SI 1992/1630)
(d)	17 Jul 1992 (SI 1992/1491)
58–61	2 Jan 1992 (SI 1991/2905)
8, 9	24 Jan 1992 (SI 1992/71)
10, para 1, 2	25 Sep 1991 (SI 1991/2092)
3	18 Feb 1993 (SI 1993/275)
4–8	26 Mar 1992 (SI 1992/334)
9	18 Feb 1993 (SI 1993/275)
10	26 Mar 1992 (SI 1992/334)
11	1 May 1993 (SI 1993/275)
12, 13	26 Mar 1992 (SI 1992/334)
11	*Not in force*
12	25 Sep 1991 (SI 1991/2092)
13, para 1	25 Sep 1992 (SI 1992/1937)
2	25 Sep 1991 (SI 1991/2092)
3, 4	*Not in force*
5, 6	25 Sep 1991 (SI 1991/2092)
7(a)(i)	*Not in force*
(ii), (iii)	25 Sep 1991 (SI 1991/2092)
(b)	25 Sep 1991 (SI 1991/2092)
8	26 Mar 1992 (SI 1992/334)
9	25 Sep 1991 (SI 1991/2092)
10(a)	26 Mar 1992 (so far as relates to substitution of reference to '27(1), 27A, 28A and 29') (SI 1992/334)
	Not in force (otherwise)
(b)	*Not in force*
11(a)	25 Sep 1991 (SI 1991/2092)
(b)(i), (ii)	*Not in force*

Planning and Compensation Act 1991 (c 34)—*cont*

Sch 13, para 11(b)(iii)	26 Mar 1992 (SI 1992/334)
(iv)	*Not in force*
(c)	25 Sep 1991 (SI 1991/2092)
12	25 Sep 1991 (SI 1991/2092)
13	26 Mar 1992 (SI 1992/334)
14	25 Sep 1991 (SI 1991/2092)
15	*Not in force*
16	26 Mar 1992 (SI 1992/334)
17, 18	25 Sep 1992 (SI 1992/1937)
19	26 Mar 1992 (SI 1992/334)
20(a), (b)	26 Mar 1992 (SI 1992/334)
(c)	26 Mar 1992 (except so far as para 20(c)(ii) relates to substitution of Town and Country Planning (Scotland) Act 1972, s 85(5)(d)) (SI 1992/334) 25 Sep 1992 (exception noted above) (SI 1992/1937)
(d)	25 Sep 1992 (SI 1992/1937)
(e)–(g)	26 Mar 1992 (SI 1992/334)
21	26 Mar 1992 (SI 1992/334)
22	10 Aug 1992 (SI 1992/1937)
23, 24	26 Mar 1992 (SI 1992/334)
25	26 Mar 1992 (except so far as substituted s 89A relates to breach of condition notice) (SI 1992/334) 25 Sep 1992 (exception noted above) (SI 1992/1937)
26	25 Sep 1992 (SI 1992/1937)
27	26 Mar 1992 (SI 1992/334)
28	25 Sep 1991 (SI 1991/2092)
29, 30	26 Mar 1992 (SI 1992/334)
31–34	25 Sep 1992 (SI 1992/1937)
35	26 Mar 1992 (SI 1992/334)
36	25 Sep 1991 (SI 1991/2092)
37	26 Mar 1992 (except insertion of reference to s 87AA) (SI 1992/334) 25 Sep 1992 (exception noted above) (SI 1992/1937)
38(a)–(d)	26 Mar 1992 (SI 1992/334)
(e)	25 Sep 1991 (SI 1991/2092)
(f)	26 Mar 1992 (SI 1992/334)
39	26 Mar 1992 (SI 1992/334)
40(1)(a)	26 Mar 1992 (so far as inserts definition 'breach of planning control') (SI 1992/334) 10 Aug 1992 (otherwise) (SI 1992/1937)
(b), (c)	*Not in force*
(d)	25 Sep 1992 (SI 1992/1937)
(e), (f)	26 Mar 1992 (SI 1992/334)
(2)	*Not in force*
41(1)	25 Sep 1991 (SI 1991/2092)
(2)	26 Mar 1992 (SI 1992/334)
(3), (4)	*Not in force*
42	*Not in force*
43(a)(i)	25 Sep 1991 (SI 1991/2092)
(ii)	25 Sep 1992 (SI 1992/1937)
(iii)	26 Mar 1992 (except insertion of reference to 'section 90A') (SI 1992/334) 25 Sep 1992 (exception noted above) (SI 1992/1937)
(iv)	26 Mar 1992 (SI 1992/334)
(b)(i)	25 Sep 1991 (SI 1991/2092)
(ii)	26 Mar 1992 (SI 1992/334)

Planning and Compensation Act 1991 (c 34)—*cont*

Sch 13, para 43(b)(iii)	25 Sep 1992 (SI 1992/1937)
(c)	26 Mar 1992 (SI 1992/334)
44	*Not in force*
45	13 Oct 1991 (SI 1991/2272; but note that SI 1992/334 also purports to bring this provision into force on 26 Mar 1992)
46	26 Mar 1992 (except insertion of reference to 'section 87AA') (SI 1992/334)
	25 Sep 1992 (exception noted above) (SI 1992/1937)
47	25 Sep 1992 (SI 1992/1937)
14	25 Sep 1991 (SI 1991/2067)
15, para 1–31	25 Sep 1991 (SI 1991/2067)
32	2 Jan 1992 (SI 1991/2728)
16, 17	25 Sep 1991 (SI 1991/2092)
18, Pt I	25 Sep 1991 (except entries relating to Planning (Hazardous Substances) Act 1990) (EW) (SI 1991/2067)
	25 Sep 1991 (except entries relating to Town and Country Planning (Scotland) Act 1972) (S) (SI 1991/2092)
	2 Jan 1992 (exception noted above) (EW) (SI 1991/2728
	Not in force (exception noted above) (S)
II	25 Sep 1991 (SI 1991/2067; SI 1991/2092))
19, Pt I	25 Sep 1991 (repeals of or in Town and Country Planning Act 1990, ss 55(6), 97(5), 219(6), 336(1) (definitions of 'development consisting of the winning and working of minerals', 'mineral compensation modifications', 'relevant order', 'restriction on the winning and working of minerals' and 'special consultations'), Sch 1, para 1(2), Sch 5, para 1(6), Sch 11, Sch 16, Pt III (entries relating to ss 312(2), 324(4)); Planning (Listed Buildings and Conservation Areas) Act 1990, s 9(5)) (SI 1991/2067)
	2 Jan 1992 (repeals of or in Town and Country Planning Act 1990, ss 63, 69(1), (3), 178(2), 186(1)(c), 190(4), 210(3), (5), 285(1), (2), (5), (6), 324(1)(b), (c), (2), 336(1) (definition of 'planning permission'), Sch 1, para 4(1) (except so far as concerns applications for consent to the display of advertisements), Sch 16 (entry relating to s 285); Planning (Listed Buildings and Conservation Areas) Act 1990, ss 38(2), 39(7), 42(7), 55(6), 88(6), 90(6)(b), 92(2)(b); Planning (Hazardous Substances) Act 1990, ss 25(1)(c), 36(5); Planning (Consequential Provisions) Act 1990, Sch 2, para 38) (SI 1991/2905)
	10 Feb 1992 (repeals of or in Town and Country Planning Act 1990, ss 12(4)(a), 14(3), 21(2), 22, 23(2)–(4), (9), (10), 49, 50, 51(1), 52(2), (3), 53(1), (2)(b), (g), (5), 284(1)(a), 287(1)–(3), (5), 306(2), Sch 2, Pt I, paras 3, 5, 6, Pt II, paras 3–16, 18, Sch 13; Planning (Consequential Provisions) Act 1990, Sch 4) (SI 1991/2905)
	6 Apr 1992 (repeal of Town and Country Planning

Planning and Compensation Act 1991 (c 34)—*cont*

Sch 19, Pt I—*cont*	Act 1990, Sch 1, para 4(1) (so far as not already in force)) (SI 1992/665)
	17 Jul 1992 (repeals of or in Town and Country Planning Act 1990, ss 74(2), 198(4)(a), 220(3)(a), 336(1), (9), Sch 16, Pt I, entries relating to ss 77, 78, 79, Pt V) (SI 1992/1491)
	27 Jul 1992 (repeals of or in Local Government (Miscellaneous Provisions) Act 1976, s 7(5)(a)(iii); Town and Country Planning Act 1990, ss 64, 188(1), 196, 250(2), 266(3), 284(3)(g), 286(1)(b), 290, 336(1), Sch 6, para 2(1)(c), (8), Sch 16, Pt IV; Planning (Consequential Provisions) Act 1990, Sch 2, paras 3(2), 35(1)(b)) (SI 1992/1630)
	9 Nov 1992 (repeals of or in Town and Country Planning Act 1990, Sch 1, para 9(2), (3), Sch 7, para 13(2)(e)) (SI 1992/2831)
II	25 Jul 1991 (repeals of Land Compensation Act 1961, s 15(4)(a), (b); Land Compensation Act 1973, s 5(3)(a), (b); Town and Country Planning Act 1990, s 114; Planning (Listed Buildings and Conservation Areas) Act 1990, s 27) (s 84(4))
	25 Sep 1991 (otherwise) (SI 1991/2067)
III	25 Sep 1991 (SI 1991/2067)
IV	25 Jul 1991 (repeals of Town and Country Planning (Scotland) Act 1972, ss 158, 160) (s 84(4))
	25 Sep 1991 (repeal in Land Compensation (Scotland) Act 1973, Sch 2, Pt II) (SI 1991/2067)
	25 Sep 1991 (repeals of or in Land Compensation (Scotland) Act 1963, ss 12, 23(4)(a), (b), 25(8), 30(3); Gas Act 1965, Sch 3, para 3; Public Expenditure and Receipts Act 1968, Sch 3, para 7(a); Town and Country Planning (Scotland) Act 1972, ss 19(5), 35, 36, 58(2)(a), 106, Pt VII (except s 145), 155(5), (6), 156, 157(1), (3), (4), 158, 160, 169(3), 231(3)(c), 244(2), 245, 246, 248, 249, 263, 264, 265, 275(1) (definitions of 'new development' and 'previous apportionment'), Sch 6, paras 3–9, 12, Sch 19, Pt I; Land Compensation (Scotland) Act 1973, ss 5(3)(a), (b), 27(1), (5), 31(6), 48(9)(b); Local Government, Planning and Land Act 1980, s 114(2); Civil Aviation Act 1982, s 53(1)(a); Airports Act 1986, s 61(1)(a)) (SI 1991/2092)
	26 Mar 1992 (repeals of or in Town and Country Planning (Scotland) Act 1972, ss 85(5), (11), 88(1), (2), 93(1)(k), (5), 98(1), (3), 166(2)(c), 265(1)(b), (2A)(a), (4), 275(1) (in definition 'planning permission', words from 'and in construing' to the end)) (SI 1992/334)
	25 Sep 1992 (repeals of or in Town and Country Planning (Scotland) Act 1972, ss 51, 91(3), (5), 201(5), 214(3), 234, 275(1)) (subject to transitional provisions) (SI 1992/1937)
	Not in force (otherwise)
V	25 Sep 1991 (SI 1991/2067)

Planning and Compensation Act 1991 (c 34)—*cont*
Note: the orders bringing this Act into force, as noted above, contain numerous
transitional and saving provisions which are too complex to set out in this work

Ports Act 1991 (c 52)

RA: 25 Jul 1991

Commencement provisions: ss 32(8), 42(2); Ports Act 1991 (Transfer of Local
Lighthouses: Appointed Day) Order 1992, SI 1992/2381

s 1–30	25 Jul 1991 (RA)
31	1 Apr 1993 (SI 1992/2381)
32	25 Jul 1991 (RA)
33	1 Apr 1993 (SI 1992/2381)
34	25 Jul 1991 (except so far as relates to ss 31, 33) (s 42(2))
	1 Apr 1993 (exception noted above) (SI 1992/2381)
35–42	25 Jul 1991 (RA)
Sch 1, 2	25 Jul 1991 (RA)

Property Misdescriptions Act 1991 (c 29)

RA: 27 Jun 1991

27 Jun 1991 (RA)

Radioactive Material (Road Transport) Act 1991 (c 27)

RA: 27 Jun 1991

Commencement provisions: s 9(3)

s 1–7	27 Aug 1991 (s 9(3))
8	27 Jun 1991 (RA)
9(1)	27 Aug 1991 (s 9(3))
(2)	See Schedule below
(3), (4)	27 Aug 1991 (s 9(3))
Schedule	27 Aug 1991 (s 9(3))

Registered Homes (Amendment) Act 1991 (c 20)

RA: 27 Jun 1991

Commencement provisions: s 2(2); Registered Homes (Amendment) Act 1991
(Commencement) Order 1992, SI 1992/2240

1 Apr 1993 (SI 1992/2240)

Representation of the People Act 1991 (c 11)

RA: 9 May 1991

Commencement provisions: s 3(2); Representation of the People Act 1991
(Commencement) Order 1991, SI 1991/1634

22 Jul 1991 (SI 1991/1634)

Road Traffic Act 1991 (c 40)

RA: 25 Jul 1991

Commencement provisions: s 84(1); Road Traffic Act 1991 (Commencement No 1)
Order 1991, SI 1991/2054; Road Traffic Act 1991 (Commencement No 2) Order
1992, SI 1992/199; Road Traffic Act 1991 (Commencement No 3) Order 1992,
SI 1992/421; Road Traffic Act 1991 (Commencement No 4 and Transitional
Provisions) Order 1992, SI 1992/1286 (as amended by SI 1992/1410); Road
Traffic Act 1991 (Commencement No 4 and Transitional Provisions)
(Amendment) Order 1992, SI 1992/1410 (amending SI 1992/1286); Road Traffic
Act 1991 (Commencement No 5 and Transitional Provisions) Order 1992, SI
1992/2010; Road Traffic Act 1991 (Commencement No 6) Order 1993, SI 1993/
975; Road Traffic Act 1991 (Commencement No 6 and Transitional Provisions)
Order 1993, SI 1993/1461, as amended by SI 1993/1686, SI 1993/2229; Road
Traffic Act 1991 (Commencement No 6 and Transitional Provisions)
(Amendment) Order 1993, SI 1993/1686; Road Traffic Act 1991
(Commencement No 7 and Transitional Provisions) Order 1993, SI 1993/2229;
Road Traffic Act 1991 (Commencement No 8 and Transitional Provisions)
Order 1993, SI 1993/2803; Road Traffic Act 1991 (Commencement No 9 and
Transitional Provisions) Order 1993, SI 1993/3238

s 1–21	1 Jul 1992 (SI 1992/1286)
22	See Sch 1 below
23–25	1 Jul 1992 (SI 1992/1286)
26	See Sch 2 below
27–34	1 Jul 1992 (SI 1992/1286)
35(1)	1 Oct 1991 (so far as relates to s 35(2), (5)) (SI 1991/ 2054)
	2 Mar 1992 (otherwise) (SI 1992/199)
(2)	1 Oct 1991 (SI 1991/2054)
(3), (4)	2 Mar 1992 (SI 1992/199)
(5)	1 Oct 1991 (SI 1991/2054)
(6)	2 Mar 1992 (SI 1992/199)
36–40	1 Jul 1992 (SI 1992/1286)
41, 42	5 Jul 1993 (EW) (SI 1993/1461, as amended by SI 1993/1686)
	Not in force (S)
43	1 Oct 1991 (EW) (SI 1991/2054)
	Not in force (S)
44	1 Oct 1991 (SI 1991/2054)
45, 46	1 Jul 1992 (SI 1992/1286)
47	1 Apr 1992 (SI 1992/421)
48	See Sch 4 below
49	1 Jul 1992 (SI 1992/1286)
50, 51	1 Oct 1991 (SI 1991/2054)
52(1)	1 Oct 1991 (SI 1991/2054)
(2)	See Sch 5 below
(3)–(9)	1 Oct 1991 (SI 1991/2054)

Road Traffic Act 1991 (c 40)—*cont*

s 53–63	1 Oct 1991 (SI 1991/2054)
64(1)	5 Jul 1993 (only in London borough of Wandsworth) (subject to transitional provisions) (SI 1993/1461)
	4 Oct 1993 (only in London boroughs of Bromley, Hammersmith and Fulham and Lewisham) (SI 1993/2229)
	6 Dec 1993 (only in London boroughs of Camden, Hackney and Hounslow) (SI 1993/2803)
	31 Jan 1994 (only in London boroughs of Richmond upon Thames and Southwark) (SI 1993/3238)
	Not in force (otherwise)
(2)	1 Oct 1991 (SI 1991/2054)
65	5 Jul 1993 (only in London borough of Wandsworth) (SI 1993/1461)
	4 Oct 1993 (only in London boroughs of Bromley, Hammersmith and Fulham and Lewisham) (SI 1993/2229)
	6 Dec 1993 (only in London boroughs of Camden, Hackney and Hounslow) (SI 1993/2803)
	31 Jan 1994 (only in London boroughs of Richmond upon Thames and Southwark) (SI 1993/3238)
	Not in force (otherwise)
66(1)–(6)	5 Jul 1993 (only in London borough of Wandsworth) (subject to transitional provisions) (SI 1993/1461)
	4 Oct 1993 (only in London boroughs of Bromley, Hammersmith and Fulham and Lewisham) (subject to transitional provisions) (SI 1993/2229)
	6 Dec 1993 (only in London boroughs of Camden, Hackney and Hounslow) (subject to transitional provisions) (SI 1993/2803)
	31 Jan 1994 (only in London boroughs of Richmond upon Thames and Southwark) (subject to transitional provisions) (SI 1993/3238)
	Not in force (otherwise)
(7)	See Sch 6 below
67(1)–(3)	5 Jul 1993 (subject to transitional provisions) (SI 1993/1461)
(4)	5 Jul 1993 (only in relation to vehicles found in London borough of Wandsworth) (subject to transitional provisions) (SI 1993/1461)
	4 Oct 1993 (only in relation to vehicles found in London boroughs of Bromley, Hammersmith and Fulham and Lewisham) (subject to transitional provisions) (SI 1993/2229)
	6 Dec 1993 (only in relation to vehicles found in London boroughs of Camden, Hackney and Hounslow) (subject to transitional provisions) (SI 1993/2803)
	31 Jan 1994 (only in relation to vehicles found in London boroughs of Richmond upon Thames and Southwark) (subject to transitional provisions) (SI 1993/3238)
	Not in force (otherwise)
(5)	5 Jul 1993 (subject to transitional provisions) (SI 1993/1461)

Road Traffic Act 1991 (c 40)—*cont*

s 67(6)	5 Jul 1993 (only in relation to vehicles found in London borough of Wandsworth) (subject to transitional provisions) (SI 1993/1461) 4 Oct 1993 (only in relation to vehicles found in London boroughs of Bromley, Hammersmith and Fulham and Lewisham) (subject to transitional provisions) (SI 1993/2229) 6 Dec 1993 (only in relation to vehicles found in London boroughs of Camden, Hackney and Hounslow) (subject to transitional provisions) (SI 1993/2803) 31 Jan 1994 (only in relation to vehicles found in London boroughs of Richmond upon Thames and Southwark) (subject to transitional provisions) (SI 1993/3238) *Not in force* (otherwise)
(7)	5 Jul 1993 (subject to transitional provisions) (SI 1993/1461)
68(1)	5 Jul 1993 (subject to transitional provisions) (SI 1993/1461)
(2)(a)	5 Jul 1993 (subject to transitional provisions) (SI 1993/1461)
(b)	5 Jul 1993 (only in relation to council of London borough of Wandsworth) (subject to transitional provisions) (SI 1993/1461) 4 Oct 1993 (only in relation to councils of London boroughs of Bromley, Hammersmith and Fulham and Lewisham) (subject to transitional provisions) (SI 1993/2229) 6 Dec 1993 (only in relation to councils of London boroughs of Camden, Hackney and Hounslow) (subject to transitional provisions) (SI 1993/2803) 31 Jan 1994 (only in relation to councils of London boroughs of Richmond upon Thames and Southwark) (subject to transitional provisions) (SI 1993/3238) *Not in force* (otherwise)
(3), (4)	5 Jul 1993 (subject to transitional provisions) (SI 1993/1461)
69	5 Jul 1993 (only in London borough of Wandsworth) (SI 1993/1461) 4 Oct 1993 (only in London boroughs of Bromley, Hammersmith and Fulham and Lewisham) (SI 1993/2229) 6 Dec 1993 (only in London boroughs of Camden, Hackney and Hounslow) (SI 1993/2803) 31 Jan 1994 (only in London boroughs of Richmond upon Thames and Southwark) (SI 1993/3238) *Not in force* (otherwise)
70–72	5 Jul 1993 (SI 1993/1461)
73–78	1 Oct 1991 (SI 1991/2054) 5 Jul 1993 (SI 1993/1461)
80	1 Oct 1991 (SI 1991/2054)
81	See Sch 7 below
82	1 Oct 1991 (SI 1991/2054)
83	See Sch 8 below
84–87	25 Jul 1991 (RA)

Road Traffic Act 1991 (c 40)—*cont*

Sch 1, 2	1 Jul 1992 (SI 1992/1286)
3	1 Oct 1991 (SI 1991/2054)
4, para 1–26	1 Jul 1992 (SI 1992/1286)
27, 28	1 Oct 1991 (SI 1991/2054)
29, 30	1 Jul 1992 (SI 1992/1286)
31–35	1 Oct 1991 (SI 1991/2054)
36	1 Apr 1992 (SI 1992/421)
37–49	1 Jul 1992 (SI 1992/1286)
50	1 Apr 1992 (SI 1992/421)
51–72	1 Jul 1992 (SI 1992/1286)
73(1)	1 Apr 1992 (so far as relates to para 73(2), (3)) (SI 1992/421)
	1 Jul 1992 (otherwise) (SI 1992/1286)
(2), (3)	1 Apr 1992 (SI 1992/421)
(4)–(6)	1 Jul 1992 (SI 1992/1286)
74	1 Jul 1992 (SI 1992/1286)
75	1 Apr 1992 (SI 1992/421)
76–78	1 Jul 1992 (SI 1992/1286)
79	Repealed
80–84	1 Jul 1992 (SI 1992/1286)
85	1 Apr 1993 (for purposes of summary criminal proceedings in Scotland commenced on or after that date) (SI 1993/975)
	Not in force (otherwise)
86–101	1 Jul 1992 (SI 1992/1286)
102	1 Apr 1992 (but does not apply to offence alleged to have been committed before 1 Apr 1992) (SI 1992/199)
103–105	1 Jul 1992 (SI 1992/1286)
106	1 Oct 1991 (SI 1991/2054)
107–114	1 Jul 1992 (SI 1992/1286)
5	1 Oct 1991 (SI 1991/2054)
6	5 Jul 1993 (SI 1993/1461)
7, para 1	Repealed
2	1 Jul 1992 (SI 1992/1286)
3, 4	1 Oct 1991 (SI 1991/2054)
5(1)	1 Oct 1991 (SI 1991/2054)
(2), (3)	5 Jul 1993 (only in London borough of Wandsworth) (SI 1993/1461)
	4 Oct 1993 (only in London boroughs of Bromley, Hammersmith and Fulham and Lewisham) (SI 1993/2229)
	6 Dec 1993 (only in London boroughs of Camden, Hackney and Hounslow) (SI 1993/2803)
	31 Jan 1994 (only in London boroughs of Richmond upon Thames and Southwark) (SI 1993/3238)
	Not in force (otherwise)
(4)	1 Oct 1991 (SI 1991/2054)
6	*Not in force*
7	1 Oct 1991 (SI 1991/2054)
8	1 Sep 1992 (subject to transitional provisions with respect to a notice of a proposal to exercise a power to which the Local Government Act 1985, Sch 5, para 5(2), applies, given before 1 Sep 1992) (SI 1992/2010)
9–11	1 Oct 1991 (SI 1991/2054)
12	*Not in force*

Road Traffic Act 1991 (c 40)—*cont*

Sch 8	1 Oct 1991 (repeals of or in Chronically Sick and Disabled Persons Act 1970, s 21(5); Road Traffic Regulation Act 1984, ss 35(9), 51(5), 55(4)(c), 99(2), 104(10), 105(3)(b), 106(2)–(6), (9), (10), 117(3)) (SI 1991/2054)
	1 Apr 1992 (repeal of Road Traffic Act 1988, s 41(3)(b), (c)) (SI 1992/421)
	1 Jul 1992 (otherwise, except repeals in Public Passenger Vehicles Act 1981, s 66A; Road Traffic Regulation Act 1984, s 102) (SI 1992/1286)
	5 Jul 1993 (repeals in Road Traffic Regulation Act 1984, s 102) (SI 1993/1461)
	Not in force (repeal in Public Passenger Vehicles Act 1981, s 66A)

Road Traffic (Temporary Restrictions) Act 1991 (c 26)

RA: 27 Jun 1991

Commencement provisions: s 2(7); Road Traffic (Temporary Restrictions) Act 1991 (Commencement) Order 1992, SI 1992/1218

1 Jul 1992 (SI 1992/1218)

School Teachers' Pay and Conditions Act 1991 (c 49)

RA: 25 Jul 1991

Commencement provisions: s 6(5); School Teachers' Pay and Conditions Act 1991 (Commencement No 1) Order 1991, SI 1991/1874; School Teachers' Pay and Conditions Act 1991 (Commencement No 2 and Transitional Provision) Order 1992, SI 1992/532; School Teachers' Pay and Conditions Act 1991 (Commencement No 3) Order 1992, SI 1992/988; School Teachers' Pay and Conditions Act 1991 (Commencement No 4) Order 1992, SI 1992/3070

s 1, 2	22 Aug 1991 (SI 1991/1874)
2(1)–(6)	6 Mar 1992 SI 1992/532)
(7)	4 Dec 1992 (SI 1992/3070)
(8)	6 Mar 1992 SI 1992/532)
(9)	30 Mar 1992 (SI 1992/988)
3	6 Mar 1992 (SI 1992/532)
3A	Prospectively inserted by Education Act 1993, s 289 (qv)
4, 5	22 Aug 1991 (SI 1991/1874)
6(1), (2)	22 Aug 1991 (SI 1991/1874)
(3)	See Sch 2 below
(4), (5)	22 Aug 1991 (SI 1991/1874)
Sch 1	22 Aug 1991 (SI 1991/1874)
2	6 Mar 1992 (SI 1992/532)

Smoke Detectors Act 1991 (c 37)

RA: 25 Jul 1991

Commencement provisions: s 7(3)

Not in force

Social Security (Contributions) Act 1991 (c 42)

Whole Act repealed

Statute Law Revision (Isle of Man) Act 1991 (c 61)

RA: 25 Jul 1991

25 Jul 1991 (RA)

Statutory Sick Pay Act 1991 (c 3)

RA: 12 Feb 1991

Commencement provisions: s 4(2); Statutory Sick Pay Act 1991 (Commencement) Order 1991, SI 1991/260

s 1	Repealed
3(1)	12 Feb 1991 (s 4(2))
(2)	See Schedule below
(3)–(5)	Repealed
(6)	12 Feb 1991 (s 4(2))
4	12 Feb 1991 (s 4(2))
Schedule	6 Apr 1991 (SI 1991/260

Statutory Water Companies Act 1991 (c 58)

RA: 25 Jul 1991

Commencement provisions: s 17(2)

1 Dec 1991 (s 17(2))

War Crimes Act 1991 (c 13)

RA: 9 May 1991

Commencement provisions: s 3(4)

s 1(1)–(3)	9 May 1991 (s 3(4))
(4)	See Schedule below
2, 3	9 May 1991 (s 3(4))
Schedule	*Not in force*

Water Consolidation (Consequential Provisions) Act 1991 (c 60)

RA: 25 Jul 1991

Commencement provisions: s 4(2)

1 Dec 1991 (s 4(2))

Water Industry Act 1991 (c 56)

RA: 25 Jul 1991

Commencement provisions: s 223(2)

1 Dec 1991 (s 223(2))

Water Resources Act 1991 (c 57)

RA: 25 Jul 1991

Commencement provisions: s 225(2)

1 Dec 1991 (s 225(2))

Welfare of Animals at Slaughter Act 1991 (c 30)

RA: 27 Jun 1991

Commencement provisions: s 7(2)

27 Aug 1991 (s 7(2))

Welsh Development Agency Act 1991 (c 69)

RA: 19 Dec 1991

19 Dec 1991 (RA)

Wildlife and Countryside (Amendment) Act 1991 (c 39)

RA: 25 Jul 1991

Commencement provisions: s 3(3)

25 Sep 1991 (s 3(3))

1992

Access to Neighbouring Land Act 1992 (c 23)

RA: 16 Mar 1992

Commencement provisions: s 9(2); Access to Neighbouring Land Act 1992 (Commencement) Order 1992, SI 1992/3349

31 Jan 1993 (SI 1992/3349)

Aggravated Vehicle-Taking Act 1992 (c 11)

RA: 6 Mar 1992

Commencement provisions: s 4(2); Aggravated Vehicle-Taking Act 1992 (Commencement) Order 1992, SI 1992/764

1 Apr 1992 (SI 1992/764)

Appropriation Act 1992 (c 22)

RA: 16 Mar 1992

16 Mar 1992 (RA)

Appropriation (No 2) Act 1992 (c 47)

RA: 16 Jul 1992

16 Jul 1992 (RA)

Army Act 1992 (c 39)

RA: 16 Mar 1992

Commencement provision: s 5

1 Jul 1992 (s 5)

Bingo Act 1992 (c 10)

RA: 6 Mar 1992

Commencement provision: s 2(2)

6 May 1992 (s 2(2))

Boundary Commissions Act 1992 (c 55)

RA: 12 Nov 1992

12 Nov 1992 (RA)

Car Tax (Abolition) Act 1992 (c 58)

RA: 3 Dec 1992

Commencement provision: s 5

13 Nov 1992 (s 5)

Carriage of Goods by Sea Act 1992 (c 50)

RA: 16 Jul 1992

Commencement provision: s 6(3)

16 Sep 1992 (s 6(3))

Charities Act 1992 (c 41)

RA: 16 Mar 1992

Commencement provisions: s 79(2); Charities Act 1992 (Commencement No 1 and Transitional Provisions) Order 1992, SI 1992/1900

s 1	1 Sep 1992 (except definitions 'financial year', 'independent examiner' and 'special trust' in sub-ss (1), (3)) (SI 1992/1900)
	Not in force (exception noted above)
2–28	Repealed
29	1 Sep 1992 (SI 1992/1900)
30–35	Repealed
36	1 Jan 1993 (SI 1992/1900)
37–48	Repealed
49, 50	1 Sep 1992 (SI 1992/1900)
51–57	Repealed
58–74	*Not in force*
75–79	1 Sep 1992 (SI 1992/1900)
Sch 1–4	Repealed
5	1 Sep 1992 (SI 1992/1900)
6, para 1	1 Jan 1993 (SI 1992/1900)
2	1 Sep 1992 (SI 1992/1900)
3–5	1 Jan 1993 (SI 1992/1900)
6–12	Repealed
13(1)	1 Jan 1993 (SI 1992/1900)
(2)	*Not in force*
(3)	1 Jan 1993 (SI 1992/1900)
14–17	1 Sep 1992 (SI 1992/1900)
7	1 Sep 1992 (repeals of or in War Charities Act 1940; National Assistance Act 1948, s 41; Trading Representations (Disabled Persons) Act 1958,

Charities Act 1992 (c 41)—*cont*

Sch 7—*cont*
s 1(2)(b); Mental Health Act 1959, s 8(3); Charities Act 1960, ss 4(6), 6(6), (9) (subject to transitional provisions), 7(4), 16(2), 19(6), 22(6), (9), 30C(1)(c), 31, 45(3), 46, Sch 1, para 1(3), Sch 6; Local Government Act 1966, Sch 3, Pt II, column 1, para 20; Local Authority Social Services Act 1970, Sch 1; Local Government Act 1972, s 210(8); Health and Social Services and Social Security Adjudications Act 1983, s 30(3); National Heritage Act 1983, Sch 4, paras 13, 14; Companies Consolidation (Consequential Provisions) Act 1985, Sch 2; Charities Act 1985 (except s 1) (subject to transitional provisions); Finance Act 1986, s 33) (SI 1992/1900)

1 Jan 1993 (repeals of or in Charitable Trustees Incorporation Act 1872, ss 2, 4, 5, 7, Schedule; Charities Act 1960, ss 27 (subject to transitional provisions), 29, 44) (SI 1992/1900)

Not in force (otherwise)

Cheques Act 1992 (c 32)

RA: 16 Mar 1992

Commencement provision: s 4(2)

16 Jun 1992 (s 4(2))

Church of England (Miscellaneous Provisions) Measure 1992 (No 1)

RA: 6 Mar 1992

Commencement provision: s 19(2)

The provisions of this measure are brought into force on the following dates by appointed day notices signed by the Archbishops of Canterbury and York, and dated 27 May 1992 and 11 Jul 1992 (made under s 19(2))

s 1	1 Jun 1992
2, 3	11 Jul 1992
4	*Not in force*
5–14	1 Jun 1992
15	11 Jul 1992
16–19	1 Jun 1992
Sch 1	*Not in force*
2	1 Jun 1992
3, para 1	11 Jul 1992
2–4	1 Jun 1992
5	11 Jul 1992
6–11	1 Jun 1992
12	11 Jul 1992
13–27	1 Jun 1992
4, Pt I	1 Jun 1992

Church of England (Miscellaneous Provisions) Measure 1992 (No 1)—*cont*
Sch 4, Pt II   1 Jun 1992 (except entry relating to Cremation Act
                                         1902, s 11)
                                      11 Jul 1992 (exception noted above)

Civil Service (Management Functions) Act 1992 (c 61)

RA: 17 Dec 1992

17 Dec 1992 (RA)

Coal Industry Act 1992 (c 17)

RA: 6 Mar 1992

Commencement provisions: s 3(4); Coal Industry Act 1992 (Commencement) Order
  1993, SI 1993/2514

s 1	6 Mar 1992 (RA)
2	20 Nov 1993 (SI 1993/2514)
3(1), (2)	6 Mar 1992 (RA)
(3)	See Schedule below
(4), (5)	6 Mar 1992 (RA)
Schedule,	
Pt I	6 Mar 1992 (RA)
II	20 Nov 1993 (SI 1993/2514)

Community Care (Residential Accommodation) Act 1992 (c 49)

RA: 16 Jul 1992

Commencement provisions: s 2(2); Community Care (Residential Accommodation)
  Act 1992 (Commencement) Order 1992, SI 1992/2976

s 1	1 Apr 1993 (SI 1992/2976)
2	16 Jul 1992 (RA)

Competition and Service (Utilities) Act 1992 (c 43)

RA: 16 Mar 1992

Commencement provisions: s 56(2); Competition and Service (Utilities) Act 1992
  (Commencement No 1) Order 1992, dated 29 May 1992 (note that, due to a
  drafting error, commencement orders under this Act are not made by statutory
  instrument)

Abbreviation: 'No 1' means the Competition and Service (Utilities) Act 1992
  (Commencement No 1) Order 1992

s 1–4	1 Jul 1992 (No 1)
5	1 Sep 1992 (No 1)
6(1)	1 Jul 1992 (except so far as inserts
	Telecommunications Act 1984, s 27G(8)) (No 1)
	Not in force (exception noted above)
(2)	1 Jul 1992 (No 1)

Competition and Service (Utilities) Act 1992 (c 43)—*cont*

s 7	1 Jul 1992 (except so far as inserts
	Telecommunications Act 1984, s 27H(4)) (No 1)
	Not in force (exception noted above)
8–15	1 Jul 1992 (No 1)
16	1 Sep 1992 (No 1)
17	*Not in force*
18–22	1 Jul 1992 (No 1)
23	*Not in force*
24–33	1 Jul 1992 (No 1)
34, 35	1 Sep 1992 (No 1)
36	*Not in force*
37	30 May 1992 (No 1)
38–50	1 Jul 1992 (No 1)
51	1 Sep 1992 (No 1)
52, 53	1 Jul 1992 (No 1)
54	16 Mar 1992 (s 56(2))
55	30 May 1992 (No 1)
56(1)–(5)	16 Mar 1992 (s 56(2))
(6)	See Sch 1 below
(7)	See Sch 2 below
Sch 1, para 1–30	1 Jul 1992 (No 1)
31	1 Sep 1992 (No 1)
2	1 Jul 1992 (No 1)

Consolidated Fund Act 1992 (c 1)

RA: 13 Feb 1992

13 Feb 1992 (RA)

Consolidated Fund (No 2) Act 1992 (c 21)

RA: 16 Mar 1992

16 Mar 1992 (RA)

Consolidated Fund (No 3) Act 1992 (c 59)

RA: 17 Dec 1992

17 Dec 1992 (RA)

Education (Schools) Act 1992 (c 38)

RA: 16 Mar 1992

Commencement provisions: s 21(3); Education (Schools) Act 1992 (Commencement No 1) Order 1992, SI 1992/1157; Education (Schools) Act 1992 (Commencement No 2 and Transitional Provision) Order 1993, SI 1993/1190; Education (Schools) Act 1992 (Commencement No 3) Order 1993, SI 1993/1491

s 1(1)–(4)	16 May 1992 (SI 1992/1157)
(5), (6)	31 Aug 1992 (SI 1992/1157)
2(1), (2)	31 Aug 1992 (SI 1992/1157)

Education (Schools) Act 1992 (c 38)—*cont*

s 2(3)(a), (b)	31 Aug 1992 (SI 1992/1157)
(c), (d)	*Not in force*
(e)	31 Aug 1992 (SI 1992/1157)
(4)–(6)	31 Aug 1992 (SI 1992/1157)
3(1)	31 Aug 1992 (SI 1992/1157)
(2)	*Not in force*
(3)–(5)	31 Aug 1992 (SI 1992/1157)
4	31 Aug 1992 (SI 1992/1157)
5(1)–(4)	16 May 1992 (SI 1992/1157)
(5), (6)	31 Aug 1992 (SI 1992/1157)
6(1), (2)	31 Aug 1992 (SI 1992/1157)
(3)(a), (b)	31 Aug 1992 (SI 1992/1157)
(c), (d)	*Not in force*
(e)	31 Aug 1992 (SI 1992/1157)
(4)–(6)	31 Aug 1992 (SI 1992/1157)
7(1)	31 Aug 1992 (SI 1992/1157)
(2)	*Not in force*
(3)–(5)	31 Aug 1992 (SI 1992/1157)
8	31 Aug 1992 (SI 1992/1157)
9(1)–(6)	12 Jun 1993 (SI 1993/1491)
(7)	See Sch 2 below
10(1)–(3)	31 Aug 1992 (SI 1992/1157)
(4)(a)	31 Aug 1992 (SI 1992/1157)
(b)	16 May 1992 (SI 1992/1157)
(5)–(9)	31 Aug 1992 (SI 1992/1157)
11, 12	31 Aug 1992 (SI 1992/1157)
13	12 Jun 1993 (SI 1993/1491)
14	1 May 1993 (SI 1993/1190) (and note that SI 1993/1491 purports to bring this section into force on 12 Jun 1993)
15	1 Sep 1993 (in relation to secondary schools) (SI 1993/1491)
	1 Sep 1994 (in relation to other schools) (SI 1993/1491)
16	16 May 1992 (SI 1992/1157)
17	1 May 1993 (SI 1993/1190)
18(1)	16 May 1992 (SI 1992/1157)
(2), (3)	31 Aug 1992 (SI 1992/1157)
(4)	16 May 1992 (SI 1992/1157)
19, 20	16 May 1992 (SI 1992/1157)
21(1)–(6)	16 Mar 1992 (s 21(3))
(7)	See Sch 4 below
(8)	See Sch 5 below
Sch 1, para 1–6	31 Aug 1992 (SI 1992/1157)
7–9	31 Aug 1992 (EW) (SI 1992/1157)
	1 May 1993 (S) (SI 1993/1190)
2, para 1–3	1 May 1993 (SI 1993/1190)
4, 5	31 Aug 1992 (SI 1992/1157)
6–8	12 Jun 1993 (SI 1993/1491)
9–9C	Substituted for original para 9 by Education Act 1993, s 307(1), Sch 19, para 173(5) (qv)
10–12	Substituted by Education Act 1993, s 307(1), Sch 19, para 173(6), (7) (qv)
13–15	31 Aug 1992 (SI 1992/1157)
3	31 Aug 1992 (SI 1992/1157)
4, para 1	*Not in force*

Education (Schools) Act 1992 (c 38)—*cont*

Sch 4, para 2, 3	Repealed
4	1 May 1993 (subject to a transitional provision) (SI 1993/1190)
5, 6	16 May 1992 (SI 1992/1157)
7	31 Aug 1992 (SI 1992/1157)
5	16 May 1992 (repeals in Education Reform Act 1988, s 22) (SI 1992/1157)
	12 Jun 1993 (repeal of Education Act 1944, s 77(6)) (SI 1993/1491)
	1 Sep 1993 (in relation to secondary schools, repeals of or in Education Act 1944, s 77(1), (5)) (SI 1993/1491)
	1 Sep 1994 (in relation to schools other than secondary schools, repeals of or in Education Act 1944, s 77(1), (5)) (SI 1993/1491)
	Not in force (otherwise)

Finance Act 1992 (c 20)

RA: 16 Mar 1992

See the note concerning Finance Acts at the front of this book

---

Finance (No 2) Act 1992 (c 48)

RA: 16 Jul 1992

See the note concerning Finance Acts at the front of this book

---

Firearms (Amendment) Act 1992 (c 31)

RA: 16 Mar 1992

16 Mar 1992 (RA)

Friendly Societies Act 1992 (c 40)

RA: 16 Mar 1992

Commencement provisions: s 126(2); Friendly Societies Act 1992 (Commencement No 1) Order 1992, SI 1992/1325; Friendly Societies Act 1992 (Commencement No 2) Order 1992, SI 1992/3117; Friendly Societies Act 1992 (Commencement No 3 and Transitional Provisions) Order 1993, SI 1993/16; Friendly Societies Act 1992 (Commencement No 4) Order 1993, SI 1993/197; Friendly Societies Act 1992 (Commencement No 5 and Savings) Order 1993, SI 1993/1186; Friendly Societies Act 1992 (Commencement No 6 and Transitional Provisions) Order 1993, SI 1993/2213; Friendly Societies Act 1992 (Commencement No 7 and Transitional Provisions and Savings) Order 1993, SI 1993/3226

s 1–4	8 Jun 1992 (SI 1992/1325)
5(1)–(5)	1 Feb 1993 (SI 1993/16)
(6)	See Sch 3 below
(7)	1 Feb 1993 (SI 1993/16)
6–26	1 Feb 1993 (SI 1993/16)

Friendly Societies Act 1992 (c 40)—*cont*

s 27(1)–(4)
13 Jan 1993 (for purpose of management and administration of incorporated friendly societies) (SI 1993/16)
1 Jan 1994 (otherwise) (SI 1993/2213)

(5)
See Sch 11 below

28, 29
13 Jan 1993 (for purpose of management and administration of incorporated friendly societies) (SI 1993/16)
1 Jan 1994 (otherwise) (subject to transitional provisions) (SI 1993/2213)

30
See Sch 12 below

31
13 Jan 1993 (for purpose of carrying on business by incorporated friendly societies) (SI 1993/16)
1 Jan 1994 (in relation to registered friendly societies the value of whose specified income for the relevant year exceeded £3,000 and which do not apply for authorisation before 1 Jan 1994) (SI 1993/2213)
1 Jan 1994 (for purpose of carrying on by a registered friendly society of insurance business in respect of which the society is deemed to be granted authorisation under s 32(7)) (SI 1993/2213)
1 Jul 1994 (in relation to registered friendly societies the value of whose specified income for the relevant year exceeded £3,000 and which apply for authorisation before 1 Jan 1994) (SI 1993/2213)
1 Jan 1995 (in relation to carrying on of any insurance or non-insurance business by a friendly society to which s 96(2) of this Act applies) (SI 1993/3226)

32(1)–(5)
13 Jan 1993 (for purpose of authorisation of incorporated friendly societies following application from such societies and from registered friendly societies seeking to be incorporated under this Act) (SI 1993/16)
13 Sep 1993 (otherwise) (SI 1993/2213)

(6)
See Sch 13 below

(7)
13 Jan 1993 (for purpose of authorisation of incorporated friendly societies following application from such societies and from registered friendly societies seeking to be incorporated under this Act) (SI 1993/16)
1 Jan 1994 (otherwise) (SI 1993/2213)

(8), (9)
13 Jan 1993 (for purpose of authorisation of incorporated friendly societies following application from such societies and from registered friendly societies seeking to be incorporated under this Act) (SI 1993/16)
13 Sep 1993 (otherwise) (SI 1993/2213)

33
13 Jan 1993 (for purpose of applications from registered friendly societies seeking to be incorporated under this Act and from incorporated friendly societies for authorisation to carry on existing business as incorporated friendly societies) (SI 1993/16)

Friendly Societies Act 1992 (c 40)—*cont*

s 33—*cont*	13 Sep 1993 (otherwise) (SI 1993/2213)
34, 35	13 Jan 1993 (for purpose of grant and extension of authorisation of incorporated friendly societies following applications from incorporated friendly societies and from registered friendly societies seeking to be incorporated under Friendly Societies Act 1992) (SI 1993/16)
	13 Sep 1993 (otherwise) (SI 1993/2213)
36	13 Jan 1993 (for purpose of control of conduct of business by incorporated friendly societies) (SI 1993/16)
	13 Sep 1993 (otherwise) (SI 1993/2213)
36A	Inserted by Friendly Societies (Amendment) Regulations 1993, SI 1993/2519, reg 2(1)
37–43	13 Jan 1993 (for purpose of control of conduct of business by incorporated friendly societies) (SI 1993/16)
	13 Sep 1993 (otherwise) (SI 1993/2213)
44(1)–(7)	13 Jan 1993 (for purpose of regulation of business of incorporated friendly societies) (SI 1993/16)
	1 Jan 1994 (otherwise) (SI 1993/2213)
(8)	13 Jan 1993 (for purpose of regulation of business of incorporated friendly societies) (SI 1993/16)
45	13 Sep 1993 (otherwise) (SI 1993/2213)
	13 Jan 1993 (for purpose of regulation of business of incorporated friendly societies) (SI 1993/16)
	13 Sep 1993 (otherwise) (SI 1993/2213)
46(1)	13 Jan 1993 (for purpose of regulation of business of incorporated friendly societies) (SI 1993/16)
	13 Sep 1993 (otherwise) (SI 1993/2213)
(2)	13 Jan 1993 (for purpose of regulation of business of incorporated friendly societies) (SI 1993/16)
	1 Jan 1994 (otherwise) (SI 1993/2213)
(3)	13 Jan 1993 (for purpose of regulation of business of incorporated friendly societies) (SI 1993/16)
	13 Sep 1993 (otherwise) (SI 1993/2213)
(4)–(7)	3 Jan 1993 (for purpose of regulation of business of incorporated friendly societies) (SI 1993/16)
	1 Jan 1994 (otherwise) (SI 1993/2213)
(8)	13 Jan 1993 (for purpose of regulation of business of incorporated friendly societies) (SI 1993/16)
	13 Sep 1993 (otherwise) (SI 1993/2213)
47	13 Jan 1993 (for purpose of regulation of business of incorporated friendly societies) (SI 1993/16)[1]
	1 Jan 1994 (otherwise) (SI 1993/2213)
48(1), (2)	13 Jan 1993 (for purpose of regulation of business of incorporated friendly societies) (SI 1993/16)
	13 Sep 1993 (so far as confers powers to make regulations for purposes of section) (SI 1993/2213)
	1 Jan 1994 (otherwise) (SI 1993/2213)
(3)–(5)	13 Jan 1993 (for purpose of regulation of business of incorporated friendly societies) (SI 1993/16)
	1 Jan 1994 (otherwise) (SI 1993/2213)
(6), (7)	13 Jan 1993 (for purpose of regulation of business of incorporated friendly societies) (SI 1993/16)

Friendly Societies Act 1992 (c 40)—*cont*

s 48(6), (7)—*cont*	13 Sep 1993 (so far as confers powers to make regulations for purposes of section) (SI 1993/2213)
	1 Jan 1994 (otherwise) (SI 1993/2213)
49(1)	13 Jan 1993 (for purpose of regulation of business of incorporated friendly societies) (SI 1993/16)
	13 Sep 1993 (otherwise) (SI 1993/2213)
(2), (3)	13 Jan 1993 (for purpose of regulation of business of incorporated friendly societies) (SI 1993/16)
	1 Jan 1994 (otherwise) (SI 1993/2213)
50	13 Jan 1993 (for purpose of regulation of business of incorporated friendly societies) (SI 1993/16)
	13 Sep 1993 (otherwise) (SI 1993/2213)
51–54	13 Jan 1993 (for purpose of regulation of business of incorporated friendly societies) (SI 1993/16)
	28 Apr 1993 (otherwise) (SI 1993/1186)
55	13 Jan 1993 (for purpose of regulation of business of incorporated friendly societies) (SI 1993/16)
	1 Jan 1994 (otherwise) (SI 1993/2213)
56, 57	13 Jan 1993 (for purpose of regulation of business of incorporated friendly societies) (SI 1993/16)
	28 Apr 1993 (otherwise) (SI 1993/1186)
57A	Inserted by Friendly Societies (Amendment No. 2) Regulations 1993, SI 1993/2521, reg 4(2)
58–61	13 Jan 1993 (SI 1993/16)
62–67	13 Jan 1993 (for purpose of regulation of business of incorporated friendly societies) (SI 1993/16)
	28 Apr 1993 (otherwise) (SI 1993/1186)
68, 69	13 Jan 1993 (for purpose of accounts and audit of incorporated friendly societies) (SI 1993/16)
	1 Jan 1994 (otherwise) (SI 1993/2213)
70(1)–(4)	13 Jan 1993 (for purpose of accounts and audit of incorporated friendly societies) (SI 1993/16)
	1 Jan 1994 (otherwise) (SI 1993/2213)
(5)–(7)	13 Jan 1993 (for purpose of accounts and audit of incorporated friendly societies) (SI 1993/16)
	13 Sep 1993 (otherwise) (SI 1993/2213)
(8)–(11)	13 Jan 1993 (for purpose of accounts and audit of incorporated friendly societies) (SI 1993/16)
	1 Jan 1994 (otherwise) (SI 1993/2213)
71(1), (2)	13 Jan 1993 (for purpose of accounts and audit of incorporated friendly societies) (SI 1993/16)
	13 Sep 1993 (so far as confers powers to make regulations for purposes of section) (SI 1993/2213)
	1 Jan 1994 (otherwise) (SI 1993/2213)
(3)	13 Jan 1993 (for purpose of accounts and audit of incorporated friendly societies) (SI 1993/16)
	1 Jan 1994 (otherwise) (SI 1993/2213)
72(1)	13 Jan 1993 (for purpose of accounts and audit of incorporated friendly societies) (SI 1993/16)
	1 Jan 1994 (otherwise) (SI 1993/2213)
(2)	See Sch 14 below
73–79	13 Jan 1993 (for purpose of accounts and audit of incorporated friendly societies) (SI 1993/16)
	1 Jan 1994 (otherwise) (SI 1993/2213)

Friendly Societies Act 1992 (c 40)—*cont*

Sch 13	13 Jan 1993 (for purpose of authorisation of incorporated friendly societies and applications for authorisation from registered friendly societies to carry on business as incorporated friendly societies) (SI 1993/16)
	13 Sep 1993 (otherwise) (SI 1993/2213)
14, para 1–6	13 Jan 1993 (for purpose of auditors of incorporated friendly societies) (SI 1993/16)
	1 Jan 1994 (otherwise) (SI 1993/2213)
7(1)–(3)	1 Jan 1994 (SI 1993/2213)
(4)	13 Sep 1993 (SI 1993/2213)
(5)–(7)	1 Jan 1994 (SI 1993/2213)
8–16	13 Jan 1993 (for purpose of auditors of incorporated friendly societies) (SI 1993/16)
	1 Jan 1994 (otherwise) (SI 1993/2213)
17	13 Jan 1993 (for purpose of auditors of incorporated friendly societies) (SI 1993/16)
	13 Sep 1993 (otherwise) (SI 1993/2213)
15	13 Sep 1993 (SI 1993/2213)
16, para 1	See paras 2–52 below
2(1)(a)	13 Jan 1993 (SI 1993/16)
(b)	1 Jan 1994 (SI 1993/3226)
(2)	1 Jan 1994 (SI 1993/3226)
(3)	13 Jan 1993 (SI 1993/16)
3	28 Apr 1993 (SI 1993/1186)
4(a)	1 Feb 1993 (SI 1993/16)
(b)	1 Jan 1994 (subject to transitional provisions) (SI 1993/2213)
(c)	1 Feb 1993 (SI 1993/16)
5–7	1 Feb 1993 (SI 1993/16)
8, 9	1 Jan 1994 (SI 1993/2213)
10	1 Feb 1993 (SI 1993/16)
11, 12	1 Jan 1994 (subject to transitional provisions) (SI 1993/2213)
13, 14	1 Jan 1994 (SI 1993/3226)
15	1 Jan 1994 (SI 1993/2213)
16	1 Feb 1993 (SI 1993/16)
17	1 Jan 1994 (SI 1993/2213)
18(1)(a)	1 Jan 1994 (SI 1993/2213)
(b)	1 Jan 1994 (SI 1993/3226)
19	1 Feb 1993 (SI 1993/16)
20, 21	1 Jan 1994 (SI 1993/3226)
22, 23	1 Jan 1994 (subject to transitional provisions) (SI 1993/2213)
24	1 Feb 1993 (so far as repeals Friendly Societies Act 1974, ss 70–73, 75) (subject to transitional provisions) (SI 1993/16)
	Not in force (otherwise)
25, 26	13 Jan 1993 (subject to transitional provisions) (SI 1993/16)
27	1 Jan 1994 (SI 1993/3226)
28	13 Jan 1993 (SI 1993/16)
29	13 Sep 1993 (subject to transitional provisions) (SI 1993/2213)
30	1 Jan 1994 (SI 1993/3226)
31	13 Sep 1993 (SI 1993/2213)

Friendly Societies Act 1992 (c 40)—*cont*

Sch 16, para 32	1 Feb 1993 (insertion of Friendly Societies Act 1974, s 84A(1)–(7)) (SI 1993/16)[2]
	1 Jan 1994 (insertion of Friendly Societies Act 1974, s 84A(8)) (SI 1993/3226)
33	13 Sep 1993 (subject to transitional provisions) (SI 1993/2213)
34–36	28 Apr 1993 (SI 1993/1186)
37	1 Feb 1993 (SI 1993/16)
38(a)	1 Feb 1993 (subject to transitional provisions) (SI 1993/16)
(b)	28 Apr 1993 (SI 1993/1186)
(c)	28 Apr 1993 (so far as relates to Friendly Societies Act 1974, s 93(3)(a), (b)) (SI 1993/1186)
	1 Jan 1994 (so far as relates to Friendly Societies Act 1974, s 93(3)(c)) (SI 1993/3226)
39–41	28 Apr 1993 (SI 1993/1186)
42(a)	1 Feb 1993 (SI 1993/16)
(b), (c)	1 Jan 1994 (SI 1993/3226)
43	1 Jan 1994 (SI 1993/2213)
44	1 Jan 1994 (SI 1993/3226)
45	1 Feb 1993 (SI 1993/16)
46	1 Jan 1994 (SI 1993/3226)
47	1 Feb 1993 (SI 1993/16)
48(a)	1 Jan 1994 (SI 1993/3226)
(b)	1 Feb 1993 (SI 1993/16)
(c), (d)	1 Jan 1994 (SI 1993/3226)
(e)	1 Feb 1993 (SI 1993/16)
49, 50	1 Jan 1994 (SI 1993/3226)
51	1 Jan 1994 (SI 1993/2213)
52	1 Feb 1993 (SI 1993/16)
17	*Not in force*
18, Pt I, para 1, 2	1 Feb 1993 (for purpose of application of Financial Services Act 1986 to incorporated friendly societies) (SI 1993/16)
	1 Jan 1994 (otherwise) (SI 1993/2213)
3	1 Feb 1993 (for purpose of application of Financial Services Act 1986 to incorporated friendly societies) (SI 1993/16)
	28 Apr 1993 (otherwise) (SI 1993/1186)
4–9	1 Feb 1993 (for purpose of application of Financial Services Act 1986 to incorporated friendly societies) (SI 1993/16)
	1 Jan 1994 (otherwise) (SI 1993/2213)
II, para 10–12	1 Feb 1993 (for purpose of application of Financial Services Act 1986 to incorporated friendly societies) (SI 1993/16)
	1 Jan 1994 (otherwise) (SI 1993/2213)
13	1 Feb 1993 (for purpose of application of Financial Services Act 1986 to incorporated friendly societies) (SI 1993/16)
	1 Jan 1994 (otherwise) (SI 1993/3226)
14–22	1 Feb 1993 (for purpose of application of Financial Services Act 1986 to incorporated friendly societies) (SI 1993/16)
	1 Jan 1994 (otherwise) (SI 1993/2213)
19, Pt I, para 1	See paras 2–16 below
2(1)	1 Feb 1993 (SI 1993/16)

Friendly Societies Act 1992 (c 40)—*cont*

Sch 19, Pt I, para 2(2)	1 Feb 1993 (in relation to incorporated friendly societies and industrial assurance companies) (SI 1993/16)
	28 Apr 1993 (otherwise) (SI 1993/1186)
3	1 Feb 1993 (in relation to incorporated friendly societies and industrial assurance companies) (SI 1993/16)[3]
	28 Apr 1993 (otherwise) (SI 1993/1186)
4	1 Feb 1993 (in relation to incorporated friendly societies and industrial assurance companies) (SI 1993/16)
	28 Apr 1993 (otherwise) (SI 1993/1186)
5(1)(a), (b)	1 Feb 1993 (in relation to incorporated friendly societies and industrial assurance companies) (SI 1993/16)
	28 Apr 1993 (otherwise) (SI 1993/1186)
(c)	1 Jan 1994 (SI 1993/2213)
(d), (e)	1 Feb 1993 (in relation to incorporated friendly societies and industrial assurance companies) (SI 1993/16)
	28 Apr 1993 (otherwise) (SI 1993/1186)
(2)(a)	1 Feb 1993 (in relation to incorporated friendly societies and industrial assurance companies) (SI 1993/16)
	28 Apr 1993 (otherwise) (SI 1993/1186)
(b)	1 Jan 1994 (SI 1993/2213)
6	1 Feb 1993 (SI 1993/16)
7	1 Jan 1994 (SI 1993/2213)
8	*Not in force*
9	13 Jan 1993 (SI 1993/16)
10	*Not in forc*
11	1 Feb 1993 (in relation to incorporated friendly societies and industrial assurance companies) (SI 1993/16)
	28 Apr 1993 (otherwise, subject to a saving) (SI 1993/1186)
12	1 Feb 1993 (SI 1993/16)
13	1 Feb 1993 (in relation to incorporated friendly societies and industrial assurance companies) (SI 1993/16)
	28 Apr 1993 (otherwise) (SI 1993/1186)
14	1 Feb 1993 (in relation to incorporated friendly societies and industrial assurance companies) (subject to transitional provisions) (SI 1993/16)
	13 Sep 1993 (otherwise) (subject to transitional provisions) (SI 1993/2213)
15, 16	1 Feb 1993 (in relation to incorporated friendly societies and industrial assurance companies) (SI 1993/16)
	28 Apr 1993 (otherwise) (SI 1993/1186)
II, para 17	See paras 18–32 below
18–25	1 Jan 1994 (subject to savings) (SI 1993/3226)
26	*Not in force*
27	1 Jan 1994 (SI 1993/3226)
28	*Not in force*
29–32	1 Jan 1994 (SI 1993/3226)
20, Pt I	1 Feb 1993 (SI 1993/16)

Friendly Societies Act 1992 (c 40)—*cont*

Sch 20, Pt II	Added (and original Sch 20 renumbered as Sch 20, Pt I) by Friendly Societies (Amendment) Regulations 1993, SI 1993/2519, reg 6(3)(a), (4)
21, Pt I, para 1	1 Feb 1993 (SI 1993/16)
2–4	1 Jan 1993 (SI 1992/3117)
5–11	1 Feb 1993 (SI 1993/16)
12–17	*Not in force*
18, 19	1 Jan 1994 (SI 1993/3226)
II	1 Jan 1994 (SI 1993/3226)
22, Pt I	13 Jan 1993 (repeals of or in Friendly Societies Act 1974, ss 76(1)(c), (d), (e), (5), 77, 78(1), (2), (3), 79(1), 80(1)) (subject to transitional provisions) (SI 1993/16)

1 Feb 1993 (repeals of or in Industrial Assurance Act 1923, ss 2(1) (words "and anything which under" to the end), 4, 7, 8(3), Sch 1; Industrial Assurance and Friendly Societies Act 1948, ss 6, 7, 10(1)(b), (c) (and words from "and shall, on demand" to the end of sub-s (1)), (2), (3), 11, Sch 1; Friendly Societies Act 1974, ss 8, 11(1), 13(2), 15 (words "society or", in each place they appear[4]),17, 70–73, 75) (subject to transitional provisions) (SI 1993/16)

1 Feb 1993 (in relation to incorporated friendly societies which are collecting societies, repeals of or in: Industrial Assurance Act 1923, ss 8(2), (4), 15, 16, 18, 19(1)–(3), 35; Industrial Assurance and Friendly Societies Act 1948, s 13(3)) (SI 1993/16)

5 Feb 1993 (repeals of Industrial Assurance Act 1923, s 8(1)(b), in relation to collecting societies (as defined by s 1(1A) thereof) to which the criteria of prudent management described in Friendly Societies Act 1992, s 50(3) apply; Friendly Societies Act 1974, Sch 5) (SI 1993/197)

28 Apr 1993 (in relation to incorporated friendly societies, repeals of or in Financial Services Act 1986, ss 139(3)–(5), 207(1), Sch 11, paras 1, 26(1), (3), 27, 38(1)(a), 43, Sch 15, para 14(1), (3)) (SI 1993/1186)

28 Apr 1993 (repeals of or in Friendly Societies Act 1974, ss 6(2), 16, 88, 89, 106; Industrial Assurance Act 1948, s 17A(2)) (SI 1993/1186)

13 Sep 1993 (repeals of or in Industrial Assurance Act 1923, ss 36, 38; Friendly Societies Act 1974, s 82, Sch 9, para 5) (subject to transitional provisions) (SI 1993/2213)

1 Jan 1994 (so far as not already in force) (repeals of or in Industrial Assurance Act 1923, ss 8(2), (4), 15, 16, 18, 19(1)–(3), 35; Industrial Assurance and Friendly Societies Act 1948, s 13(3); Financial Services Act 1986, ss 139(3)–(5), 207(1), Sch 11, paras 1, 26(1), (3), 27, 38(1)(a), 43, Sch 15, para 14(1), (3) (SI 1993/2213)

1 Jan 1994 (repeals of or in Loan Societies Act 1840; Friendly Societies Act 1896; Industrial Assurance Act 1923, ss 20(1)(b), 31, 44, 45(2); Industrial Assurance and Friendly Societies Act 1929;

Friendly Societies Act 1992 (c 40)—*cont*

Sch 22, Pt I—*cont*

Industrial Assurance and Friendly Societies Act 1948, ss 1, 4, 23(1), Schs 2, 3; Friendly Societies Act 1955, s 3(2); Industrial Assurance Act 1948 (Amendment) Act 1958; Friendly Societies Act 1974, ss 9(2), (3), 27, 28, 30(5), 46, 53(3), 107(1), Schs 1, 2, 3, Sch 9, paras 2, 6, 8, 10(1); Banking Act 1987, s 84(1); Income and Corporation Taxes Act 1988; Companies Act 1989) (subject to transitional provisions) (SI 1993/2213)

1 Jan 1994 (repeals of or in Industrial Assurance and Friendly Societies Act 1948, ss 2, 10(1)(a) (words "signed by two of the committee of management and by the secretary" only); Consumer Credit Act 1974, s 189(1); Friendly Societies Act 1974, ss 98, 111(6), 115, 117(3), Sch 3; Finance Act 1984; Friendly Societies Act 1984, s 3; Companies Act 1985, s 449; Building Societies Act 1986, s 7; Banking Act 1987, s 96, Sch 2) (SI 1993/3226)

Not in force (otherwise)

II

1 Jan 1994 (except so far as repeals Industrial Assurance (Northern Ireland) Order 1979, arts 4(1) (other than words "and in the exercise and performance of his powers and duties as Registrar under the Friendly Societies Act in relation to collecting societies" which are repealed), (3), 5, 9(1)(a) (other than words "signed by two of the committee of management and by the secretary" which are repealed)) (subject to transitional provisions) (SI 1993/3226)

Not in force (exceptions noted above)

[1] For transitional provisions (in respect of ss 46(2)(a)(ii), (2)(c), 47(1)(a), (b)), see the Friendly Societies Act 1992 (Transitional and Consequential Provisions and Savings) Regulations 1993, SI 1993/932, regs 3–5

[2] Note that SI 1993/16 purports to bring into force Sch 16, para 32 (except sub-para (8)). As para 32 contains no sub-paragraphs, it is thought that it was intended to bring into force s 84A(1)–(7) of the 1974 Act, but not sub-s (8) thereof. Note also that SI 1993/2213 purports to bring Sch 16, para 32 (except s 84A(8)) into force for all remaining purposes on 13 Sep 1993

[3] For a saving in respect of the amendment made by Sch 19, Pt I, para 3, see the Friendly Societies Act 1992 (Transitional and Consequential Provisions and Savings) Regulations 1993, SI 1993/932, reg 10

[4] Note that the repeal of those words by the Friendly Societies Act 1992, s 120(2), Sch 22, Pt I, is made to the Friendly Societies Act 1974, s 16, and not to s 15 thereof

---

Further and Higher Education Act 1992 (c 13)

RA: 6 Mar 1992

Commencement provisions: s 94(3); Further and Higher Education Act 1992 (Commencement No 1 and Transitional Provisions) Order 1992, SI 1992/831 (as amended by SI 1992/2041); Further and Higher Education Act 1992 (Commencement No 1 and Transitional Provisions) (Amendment) Order 1992, SI 1992/2041 (amending SI 1992/831); Further and Higher Education Act 1992 (Commencement No 2) Order 1992, SI 1992/2377; Further and Higher Education Act 1992 (Commencement No 2) Order 1992, SI 1992/3057

Further and Higher Education Act 1992 (c 13)—*cont*

s 1	6 May 1992 (SI 1992/831)
2–4	1 Apr 1993 (SI 1992/831)
5(1), (2)	1 Apr 1993 (SI 1992/831)
(3)	30 Sep 1992 (SI 1992/831)
(4)	1 Apr 1993 (SI 1992/831)
(5)–(8)	6 May 1992 (SI 1992/831)
6(1)	1 Apr 1993 (SI 1992/831)
(2)–(4)	6 May 1992 (SI 1992/831)
(5), (6)	30 Sep 1992 (SI 1992/831)
7, 8	6 May 1992 (SI 1992/831)
9(1)–(3)	1 Apr 1993 (SI 1992/831)
(4)	1 Apr 1993 (SI 1992/2377)
(5)	1 Apr 1993 (SI 1992/831)
10, 11	1 Apr 1993 (SI 1992/831)
12	1 Aug 1993 (SI 1992/831)
13	1 Aug 1993 (SI 1992/831); prospectively repealed by Education Act 1993, s 307(1), (3), Sch 19, para 168, Sch 21, Pt I (qv)
14(1)–(4)	6 May 1992 (for purposes of provisions brought into force on 6 May 1992 by SI 1992/831, art 2, Sch 1) (SI 1992/831)
	30 Sep 1992 (for purposes of provisions brought into force on 30 Sep 1992 by SI 1992/831, art 2, Sch 2) (SI 1992/831)
	1 Apr 1993 (otherwise) (SI 1992/831)
(5)	1 Apr 1993 (SI 1992/831)
(6)	1 Aug 1993 (SI 1992/831)
15(1)–(3)	6 May 1992 (SI 1992/831)
(4)	30 Sep 1992 (SI 1992/831)
(5)–(7)	6 May 1992 (SI 1992/831)
16	30 Sep 1992 (SI 1992/831)
17	6 May 1992 (SI 1992/831)
18–25	30 Sep 1992 (SI 1992/831)
26	30 Sep 1992 (except in respect of persons employed by a local authority to work solely at the institution the corporation is established to conduct and who are so employed in connection with an arrangement for the supply by that local authority of goods or services for the purposes of that institution in pursuance of a bid prepared under Local Government Act 1988, s 7) (SI 1992/ 831, as amended by SI 1992/2041)
	Not in force (exception noted above)
27	30 Sep 1992 (SI 1992/831)
28–33	6 May 1992 (SI 1992/831)
34, 35	1 Apr 1993 (SI 1992/831)
36	30 Sep 1992 (SI 1992/831)
37, 38	1 Apr 1993 (SI 1992/831)
39–43	6 May 1992 (SI 1992/831)
44	1 Apr 1993 (in respect of institutions which, before they became institutions within the further education sector, were schools maintained by a local education authority or grant-maintained schools) (SI 1992/831)
	Not in force (otherwise)
45	1 Apr 1993 (in respect of institutions which, before they became institutions within the further

Further and Higher Education Act 1992 (c 13)—*cont*

s 45—*cont*	education sector, were schools maintained by a local education authority or grant-maintained schools) (SI 1992/831)
	Not in force (otherwise)
46–50	1 Apr 1993 (SI 1992/831)
51	30 Sep 1992 (SI 1992/831)
52	1 Apr 1993 (SI 1992/831)
53	30 Sep 1992 (SI 1992/831)
54(1)	6 May 1992 (SI 1992/831)
(2)	1 Apr 1993 (SI 1992/831)
55(1)–(3)	1 Apr 1993 (E) (SI 1992/831)
	Not in force (W)
(4)–(6)	1 Apr 1993 (SI 1992/831)
(7)(a)	1 Apr 1993 (SI 1992/831)
(b)	*Not in force*
(c)	1 Apr 1993 (SI 1992/831)
56	6 May 1992 (SI 1992/831)
57(1), (2)	1 Apr 1993 (SI 1992/831)
(3)–(6)	6 May 1992 (so far as apply to the Further Education Funding Councils) (SI 1992/831)
	1 Apr 1993 (otherwise) (SI 1992/831)
58	30 Sep 1992 (SI 1992/831)
59(1), (2)	30 Sep 1992 (SI 1992/831)
(3), (4)	6 May 1992 (SI 1992/831)
(5)	6 May 1992 (SI 1992/831); prospectively repealed by Education Act 1993, s 307(1), (3), Sch 19, para 169, Sch 21, Pt I (qv)
60	1 Apr 1993 (SI 1992/831)
61, 62	6 May 1992 (SI 1992/831)
63	1 Apr 1993 (SI 1992/831)
64	6 May 1992 (SI 1992/831)
65, 66	1 Apr 1993 (SI 1992/831)
67(1)	1 Apr 1993 (SI 1992/831)
(2)–(5)	6 May 1992 (SI 1992/831)
68–73	6 May 1992 (SI 1992/831)
74	1 Apr 1993 (SI 1992/831)
75–84	6 May 1992 (SI 1992/831)
85	1 Apr 1993 (SI 1992/831)
86	6 May 1992 (SI 1992/831)
87	30 Sep 1992 (SI 1992/831)
88–92	6 May 1992 (SI 1992/831)
93(1)	See Sch 8 below
(2)	See Sch 9 below
94	6 May 1992 (SI 1992/831)
Sch 1	6 May 1992 (SI 1992/831)
2	30 Sep 1992 (SI 1992/831)
3	6 May 1992 (SI 1992/831)
4, 5	30 Sep 1992 (SI 1992/831)
6	6 May 1992 (SI 1992/831)
7	30 Sep 1992 (SI 1992/831)
8, para 1	6 May 1992 (SI 1992/831)
2–5	1 Apr 1993 (SI 1992/831)
6	1 Apr 1993 (SI 1992/831); prospectively repealed by Education Act 1993, s 307(3), Sch 21, Pt I (qv)
7, 8	1 Apr 1993 (SI 1992/831)

Further and Higher Education Act 1992 (c 13)—*cont*

Sch 8, para 9	6 May 1992 (SI 1992/831)
10	1 Sep 1992 (so far as relates to institutions within the PCFC funding sector) (E) (SI 1992/831)
	1 Sep 1992 (so far as relates to institutions within the PCFC funding sector) (W) (SI 1992/2377)
	7 Dec 1992 (otherwise) (E) (SI 1992/3057)
	1 Apr 1993 (otherwise) (W) (SI 1992/2377)
11, 12	1 Apr 1993 (SI 1992/831)
13(1)	6 May 1992 (SI 1992/831)
(2)(a)	6 May 1992 (in relation to references to 'further education' in provisions of this Act as they are brought into force) (SI 1992/831)
	1 Apr 1993 (otherwise) (SI 1992/831)
(b), (c)	1 Apr 1993 (SI 1992/831)
(d)	1 Aug 1993 (SI 1992/831)
(e)–(g)	1 Apr 1993 (SI 1992/831)
(3), (4)	1 Apr 1993 (SI 1992/831)
14–16	1 Apr 1993 (SI 1992/831)
17	1 Aug 1993 (SI 1992/831)
18	6 May 1992 (SI 1992/831); prospectively repealed by Education Act 1993, s 307(1), (3), Sch 19, para 171(a), Sch 21, Pt I (qv)
19, 20	1 Apr 1993 (SI 1992/831)
21	30 Sep 1992 (SI 1992/831)
22, 23	1 Apr 1993 (SI 1992/831)
24	1 Apr 1993 (note that amendments made by para 24(a) do not have effect in relation to provision for further education made by a local education authority before 1 Apr 1993) (SI 1992/831)
25, 26	1 Apr 1993 (SI 1992/831)
27	6 May 1992 (SI 1992/831)
28	1 Apr 1993 (SI 1992/831)
29	1 Aug 1993 (SI 1992/831); prospectively repealed by Education Act 1993, s 307(1), (3), Sch 19, para 171(a), Sch 21, Pt I (qv)
30	1 Apr 1993 (SI 1992/831)
31	6 May 1992 (SI 1992/831)
32(a)	1 Apr 1993 (SI 1992/831)
(b)	6 May 1992 (SI 1992/831)
33	1 Apr 1993 (SI 1992/831)
34	6 May 1992 (SI 1992/831)
35	1 Apr 1993 (SI 1992/831)
36(a)	6 May 1992 (SI 1992/831)
(b)	1 Apr 1993 (SI 1992/831)
37(a)	1 Apr 1993 (SI 1992/831)
(b)	6 May 1992 (SI 1992/831)
38	6 May 1992 (SI 1992/831)
39–42	1 Apr 1993 (SI 1992/831)
43	6 May 1992 (SI 1992/831)
44–47	1 Apr 1993 (SI 1992/831)
48	6 May 1992 (SI 1992/831)
49	1 Apr 1993 (SI 1992/831)
50	6 May 1992 (so far as relates to Education Reform Act 1988, s 219(2)(e)) (SI 1992/831)
	1 Apr 1993 (otherwise) (SI 1992/831)
51	6 May 1992 (SI 1992/831)
52, 53	1 Apr 1993 (SI 1992/831)

Further and Higher Education Act 1992 (c 13)—*cont*

Sch 8, para 54	6 May 1992 (SI 1992/831)
55	1 Apr 1993 (SI 1992/831)
56(a)	1 Apr 1993 (SI 1992/831)
(b), (c)	6 May 1992 (SI 1992/831)
57, 58	1 Apr 1993 (SI 1992/831)
59	6 May 1992 (SI 1992/831)
60	1 Apr 1993 (SI 1992/831)
61–65	6 May 1992 (subject to saving in relation to any matter notified to the Secretary of State by the Education Assets Board pursuant to Education Reform Act 1988, Sch 10, para 3, before 6 May 1992) (SI 1992/831)
66, 67	1 Apr 1993 (SI 1992/831)
68	6 May 1992 (SI 1992/831)
69	Repealed
70–74	1 Apr 1993 (SI 1992/831)
75, 76	6 May 1992 (SI 1992/831)
77	1 Aug 1993 (SI 1992/831)
78, 79	6 May 1992 (SI 1992/831)
80	1 Aug 1993 (SI 1992/831)
81–83	1 Apr 1993 (SI 1992/831)
84, 85	6 May 1992 (SI 1992/831)
86	1 Aug 1993 (SI 1992/831)
87, 88	6 May 1992 (SI 1992/831)
89	30 Sep 1992 (SI 1992/831)
90–92	1 Apr 1993 (SI 1992/831)
93(a)	1 Apr 1993 (SI 1992/831)
(b)	6 May 1992 (SI 1992/831)
94, 95	1 Apr 1993 (SI 1992/831)
9	6 May 1992 (repeals of or in Education Reform Act 1988, ss 122(2)–(5), 129(3), (4), 136(3)–(7), 137(2) (expression 'or 129(3)'), 156 (so far as relates to institutions designated under Education Reform Act 1988, s 129), 219(2)(e), 227(2)–(4), 232(3) (expression 'or 227'), 232(4)(b) (expression '227'), Sch 7, para 19) (SI 1992/831)
	1 Apr 1993 (repeals of or in Education Act 1944, ss 8(3), 67(4A), 85(2), (3), 114(1), (1A), (1B), (1C); Education (Miscellaneous Provisions) Act 1948, s 3(3); Superannuation Act 1972, Sch 1; House of Commons Disqualification Act 1975, Sch 1, Pt III; Education (No 2) Act 1986, ss 43(5)(c), (7), 49(3)(d), (da), 51(2)(b), (5), (6), 58(3), (4), (5)(a), (ab); Education Reform Act 1988, ss 120, 124(4), 131, 132, 134, Pt II, Chapter III (ss 139–155), s 156 (so far as still in force), ss 157, 158(2), 159(2)(b), 161(1)(c), 205(6), 211(c), 218(10)(b), 219, 221(1)(c), (3), 222(2)(b), (3)(c), 230(1), (3)(c)(ii), 232(2), 234(2)(b), 235(2)(a), (h), Sch 12, paras 68, 69(2), 70, 100(2), 101(4); Environmental Protection Act 1990, s 98(2)(a)) (SI 1992/831)
	1 Aug 1993 (repeal in Education Reform Act 1988, s 105(2)(b)) (SI 1992/831)

Further and Higher Education (Scotland) Act 1992 (c 37)

RA: 16 Mar 1992

Commencement provisions: s 63(2); Further and Higher Education (Scotland) Act
  1992 (Commencement No 1 and Saving Provisions) Order 1992, SI 1992/817

s 1(1), (2)	1 Apr 1993 (SI 1992/817)
(3)–(5)	16 May 1992 (SI 1992/817)
(6)	1 Apr 1993 (SI 1992/817)
2	1 Apr 1993 (SI 1992/817)
3(1)–(4)	1 Apr 1993 (SI 1992/817)
(5)	16 May 1992 (SI 1992/817)
(6)	1 Apr 1993 (SI 1992/817)
4, 5	1 Apr 1993 (SI 1992/817)
6	16 May 1992 (SI 1992/817)
7–10	*Not in force*
11, 12	16 May 1992 (SI 1992/817)
13, 14	1 Apr 1993 (SI 1992/817)
15	16 May 1992 (SI 1992/817)
16	1 Sep 1992 (SI 1992/817)
17	1 Apr 1993 (SI 1992/817)
18	16 May 1992 (SI 1992/817)
19–25	1 Apr 1993 (SI 1992/817)
26–36	16 May 1992 (SI 1992/817)
37	1 Jun 1992 (SI 1992/817)
38	16 May 1992 (SI 1992/817)
39	1 Jun 1992 (so far as relates to institutions for whose activities the Council are considering providing financial support) (SI 1992/817)
	1 Apr 1993 (otherwise) (SI 1992/817)
40, 41	1 Apr 1993 (SI 1992/817)
42(1)	1 Jun 1992 (SI 1992/817)
(2), (3)	1 Apr 1993 (SI 1992/817)
(4)	1 Jun 1992 (SI 1992/817)
43(1)	1 Jun 1992 (SI 1992/817)
(2)	1 Apr 1993 (SI 1992/817)
(3)–(8)	1 Jun 1992 (SI 1992/817)
44	25 Apr 1992 (for purpose of authorising the making under s 44 of an Order which is expressed to come into force on or after 16 May 1992) (SI 1992/817)
	16 May 1992 (otherwise) (SI 1992/817)
45–49	16 May 1992 (SI 1992/817)
50, 51	1 Jun 1992 (SI 1992/817)
52	16 May 1992 (SI 1992/817)
53	1 Apr 1993 (SI 1992/817)
54(1), (2)	1 Jun 1992 (SI 1992/817)
(3)	1 Apr 1993 (SI 1992/817)
55–61	16 May 1992 (SI 1992/817)
62(1)	See Sch 8 below
(2)	See Sch 9 below
(3)	See Sch 10 below
63	25 Apr 1992 (SI 1992/817)
Sch 1	*Not in force*
2	16 May 1992 (SI 1992/817)
3, 4	1 Sep 1992 (SI 1992/817)

Further and Higher Education (Scotland) Act 1992 (c 37)—*cont*

Sch 5, 6	16 May 1992 (SI 1992/817)
7	1 Jun 1992 (SI 1992/817)
8	16 May 1992 (SI 1992/817)
9, para 1	16 May 1992 (SI 1992/817)
2(a)	1 Apr 1993 (SI 1992/817)
(b), (c)	16 May 1992 (SI 1992/817)
3	16 May 1992 (SI 1992/817)
4(1), (2)	16 May 1992 (SI 1992/817)
(3)	1 Jun 1992 (so far as relates to the Scottish Higher Education Funding Council) (SI 1992/817)
	Not in force (otherwise)
(4)–(6)	16 May 1992 (SI 1992/817)
(1), (2)	16 May 1992 (SI 1992/817)
(3)	1 Jun 1992 (so far as relates to the Scottish Higher Education Funding Council) (SI 1992/817)
	Not in force (otherwise)
(4), (5)	16 May 1992 (SI 1992/817)
6	16 May 1992 (SI 1992/817)
7(1)	16 May 1992 (SI 1992/817)
(2)–(6)	1 Apr 1993 (SI 1992/817)
(7)	16 May 1992 (SI 1992/817)
8(1), (2)	16 May 1992 (SI 1992/817)
(3)	1 Apr 1993 (SI 1992/817)
9	1 Apr 1993 (SI 1992/817)
10	1 Jun 1992 (SI 1992/817)
11	1 Apr 1993 (SI 1992/817)
12(1), (2)	16 May 1992 (SI 1992/817)
(3)	1 Apr 1993 (SI 1992/817)
13(a)	1 Apr 1993 (SI 1992/817)
(b), (c)	16 May 1992 (SI 1992/817)
10	16 May 1992 (repeals of or in Employment Protection (Consolidation) Act 1978, s 29; Education (Scotland) Act 1980, ss 3, 7, 77, 135(1)) (SI 1992/817)
	1 Apr 1993 (repeals of or in School Boards (Scotland) Act 1988, ss 8, 22; Self-Governing Schools etc (Scotland) Act 1989, ss 54–66, 80) (SI 1992/817)

Human Fertilisation and Embryology (Disclosure of Information) Act 1992 (c 54)

RA: 16 Jul 1992

16 Jul 1992 (RA)

Licensing (Amendment) (Scotland) Act 1992 (c 18)

RA: 6 Mar 1992

Commencement provisions: s 2(2); Licensing (Amendment) (Scotland) Act 1992 (Commencement and Savings) Order 1992, SI 1992/819

s 1	15 Apr 1992 (subject to savings with respect to any licence temporarily transferred under the

Licensing (Amendment) (Scotland) Act 1992 (c 18)—*cont*
s 1—*cont*	Licensing (Scotland) Act 1976, s 25(1), before 15 Apr 1992) (SI 1992/819)
2	6 Mar 1992 (RA)

Local Government Act 1992 (c 19)

RA: 6 Mar 1992

Commencement provisions: s 30(2), (3); Local Government Act 1992 (Commencement No 1) Order 1992, SI 1992/2371; Local Government Act 1992 (Commencement No 2) Order 1992, SI 1992/3241; Local Government Act 1992 (Commencement No 3) Order 1993, SI 1993/3169

s 1–7	6 May 1992 (s 30(2))
8	*Not in force*
9	4 Jan 1993 (SI 1992/3241)
10	14 Feb 1993 (SI 1992/3241)
11	See Sch 1 below
12–23	6 Mar 1992 (RA)
24	31 Oct 1992 (SI 1992/2371)
25–30	6 Mar 1992 (RA)

Sch 1, para 1	14 Feb 1993 (SI 1992/3241)
2(1)	*Not in force*
(2), (3)	14 Mar 1994 (SI 1992/3241)
3–5	*Not in force*
6, 7	4 Jan 1993 (SI 1992/3241)
8	14 Mar 1994 (SI 1992/3241)
9, 10	*Not in force*
11	14 Feb 1993 (SI 1992/3241)
12	6 Jan 1994 (SI 1993/3169)
13, 14	4 Jan 1993 (SI 1992/3241)
2	6 Mar 1992 (RA)
3	31 Oct 1992 (SI 1992/2371)
4, Pt I	6 May 1992 (repeal in Local Government Finance Act 1982, s 15(1)) (s 30(2))
	Not in force (otherwise)
II	31 Oct 1992 (SI 1992/2371)

Local Government Finance Act 1992 (c 14)

RA: 6 Mar 1992

Commencement provisions: s 119(2); Local Government Finance Act 1992 (Commencement No 1) Order 1992, SI 1992/473; Local Government Finance Act 1992 (Commencement No 2) Order 1992, SI 1992/818; Local Government Finance Act 1992 (Commencement No 3) Order 1992, SI 1992/1460; Local Government Finance Act 1992 (Commencement No 4) Order 1992, SI 1992/1755; Local Government Finance Act 1992 (Commencement No 5 and Transitional Provisions) Order 1992, SI 1992/2183; Local Government Finance Act 1992 (Commencement No 6 and Transitional Provisions) Order 1992, SI 1992/2454; Local Government Finance Act 1992 (Commencement No 7 and Amendment) Order 1993, SI 1993/194 (amending SI 1992/2454); Local Government Finance Act 1992 (Commencement No 8 and Transitional Provisions) Order 1993, SI 1993/575

Local Government Finance Act 1992 (c 14)—*cont*

s 1–98	6 Mar 1992 (RA)
99(1)	6 Mar 1992 (RA)
(2)	1 Apr 1993 (SI 1993/575)
(3)	6 Mar 1992 (RA)
100–103	6 Mar 1992 (RA)
104	See Sch 10 below
105, 106	6 Mar 1992 (RA)
107	See Sch 11 below
108, 109	6 Mar 1992 (RA)
110(1)	1 Oct 1992 (subject to transitional provisions in relation to any financial year beginning before 1 Apr 1993) (SI 1992/2183)
(2), (3)	*Not in force*
(4)	1 Oct 1992 (subject to transitional provisions in relation to any financial year beginning before 1 Apr 1993) (SI 1992/2183)
111	1 Apr 1993 (SI 1993/575)
112–116	6 Mar 1992 (RA)
117(1)	See Sch 13 below
(2)	See Sch 14 below
118, 119	6 Mar 1992 (RA)
Sch 1–9	6 Mar 1992 (RA)
10, para 1	18 Jun 1992 (SI 1992/1460)
2	7 Mar 1992 (SI 1992/473)
3	1 Apr 1992 (SI 1992/473)
4	7 Mar 1992 (so far as enables provision to be made by regulations) (SI 1992/473) 1 Apr 1992 (otherwise) (SI 1992/473)
5–24	6 Mar 1992 (RA)
11, para 1–28	6 Mar 1992 (RA)
29(a)	1 Apr 1993 (SI 1993/575)
(b)	6 Mar 1992 (RA)
30	1 Apr 1993 (SI 1993/575)
31(a)	6 Mar 1992 (RA)
(b)	1 Oct 1992 (subject to transitional provisions in relation to any financial year beginning before 1 Apr 1993) (SI 1992/2183)
32–36	1 Apr 1993 (SI 1993/575)
37	1 Oct 1992 (subject to transitional provisions in relation to any financial year beginning before 1 Apr 1993) (SI 1992/2183)
38(a)	1 Oct 1992 (subject to transitional provisions in relation to any financial year beginning before 1 Apr 1993) (SI 1992/2183)
(b)	1 Apr 1993 (SI 1993/575)
(c)	1 Oct 1992 (subject to transitional provisions in relation to any financial year beginning before 1 Apr 1993) (SI 1992/2183)
(d)	6 Mar 1992 (RA)
(e)	1 Apr 1993 (SI 1993/575)
(f)	6 Mar 1992 (RA)
12	6 Mar 1992 (RA)
13, para 1	1 Apr 1993 (SI 1993/194)
2	1 Apr 1993 (SI 1993/575)
3–5	1 Apr 1993 (SI 1992/2454)

Local Government Finance Act 1992 (c 14)—*cont*

Sch 13, para 6–8	2 Nov 1992 (SI 1992/2454)
9	1 Apr 1993 (SI 1993/575)
10, 11	1 Apr 1992 (SI 1992/818)
12–14	2 Nov 1992 (SI 1992/2454)
15–25	6 Mar 1992 (RA)
26	2 Nov 1992 (SI 1992/2454)
27, 28	1 Apr 1993 (SI 1993/194)
29, 30	2 Nov 1992 (SI 1992/2454)
31	Repealed
32	1 Feb 1993 (SI 1993/194, amending SI 1992/2454)
33	*Not in force*
34	1 Apr 1993 (SI 1992/2454)
35	1 Apr 1993 (SI 1993/575)
36	1 Oct 1992 (subject to transitional provisions in relation to any financial year beginning before 1 Apr 1993) (SI 1992/2183)
37(1)	*Not in force*
(2)	1 Apr 1993 (SI 1993/575)
38	1 Oct 1992 (so far as relates to Local Government (Scotland) Act 1973, s 110A) (subject to transitional provisions in relation to any financial year beginning before 1 Apr 1993) (SI 1992/2183) 1 Apr 1993 (otherwise) (SI 1993/575)
39	*Not in force*
40	1 Apr 1993 (SI 1993/575)
41	1 Apr 1992 (SI 1992/818)
42	6 Mar 1992 (RA)
43	1 Oct 1992 (subject to transitional provisions in relation to any financial year beginning before 1 Apr 1993) (SI 1992/2183)
44(a), (b)	1 Apr 1993 (SI 1993/575)
(c)	6 Mar 1992 (RA)
(d)	1 Apr 1993 (SI 1993/575)
45–47	6 Mar 1992 (RA)
48	2 Nov 1992 (SI 1992/2454)
49	1 Oct 1992 (subject to transitional provisions in relation to any financial year beginning before 1 Apr 1993) (SI 1992/2183)
50–52	2 Nov 1992 (SI 1992/2454)
53–56	1 Apr 1993 (SI 1993/575)
57	1 Apr 1993 (SI 1992/2454)
58	1 Apr 1993 (SI 1992/2454); prospectively repealed by Education Act 1993, s 307(3), Sch 21, Pt I (qv)
59–74	6 Mar 1992 (RA)
75	1 Oct 1992 (subject to transitional provisions in relation to any financial year beginning before 1 Apr 1993) (SI 1992/2183)
76–88	6 Mar 1992 (RA)
89	1 Apr 1992 (SI 1992/818)
90, 91	2 Nov 1992 (SI 1992/2454)
92	6 Mar 1992 (RA)
93	1 Apr 1993 (SI 1993/575)
94	1 Apr 1993 (SI 1993/194)
95–98	1 Aug 1992 (subject to transitional provisions in relation to any financial year beginning before 1 Apr 1993) (SI 1992/1755)
99, 100	6 Mar 1992 (RA)

Local Government Finance Act 1992 (c 14)—*cont*

Sch 14[1]

6 Mar 1992 (repeals of or in Local Government Finance Act 1988 (except Sch 12); Social Security Contributions and Benefits Act 1992; Social Security Administration Act 1992) (RA)

1 Apr 1992 (repeals of or in Local Government (Financial Provisions) (Scotland) Act 1963, s 10; Local Government (Scotland) Act 1975, s 37(1); Local Government, Planning and Land Act 1980, s 46; Abolition of Domestic Rates etc (Scotland) Act 1987, Sch 1, para 19; Local Government Finance Act 1988, Sch 12, para 5; Local Government and Housing Act 1989, Sch 6, para 8) (SI 1992/818)

1 Aug 1992 (repeals of or in Local Government and Housing Act 1989, Sch 5, para 30(4); Water Resources Act 1991, ss 11, 135, 136 (subject to transitional provisions)) (SI 1992/1755)

1 Oct 1992 (repeals of or in Local Government (Scotland) Act 1973, s 110A; Abolition of Domestic Rates Etc (Scotland) Act 1987, ss 3A, 9, 10(7A), 11B, 28, Sch 2, paras 1(2), 2(1), Sch 5, paras 2–5, 9, 10, 14, 15, 17–19, 21, 25; Local Government Finance Act 1988, Sch 12, paras 10, 13) (subject to transitional provisions in relation to any financial year beginning before 1 Apr 1993) (SI 1992/2183)

1 Apr 1993 (repeals of or in Education Reform Act 1988, s 81(8A); Local Government and Housing Act 1989, s 146 (subject to transitional provisions), Sch 5, paras 2–18, 43, 49–54, 55(3), 56, 58, 59, 61, 63–65, 70, 71, 73, 74, 76(3), 77, 78, Sch 11, para 98; Community Charges (Substitute Setting) Act 1991) (SI 1992/2454)

1 Apr 1993 (repeal of Local Government Finance and Valuation Act 1991) (SI 1993/194)

1 Apr 1993 (repeals of or in Registration of Births, Deaths and Marriages (Scotland) Act 1965, s 28B; Local Government (Scotland) Act 1966, Sch 1, Pt I, para 2A; Local Government (Scotland) Act 1973, ss 110, 118(1)(b); Local Government (Scotland) Act 1975, Sch 3, para 31; Water (Scotland) Act 1980, ss 41(2), (2A), 54(3)(b), 109(1); Debtors (Scotland) Act 1987, s 106; Abolition of Domestic Rates Etc (Scotland) Act 1987, ss 1–7, 14, 18(2A), 20(10), 25(1), (3), 26(1), (2), 27, 33, Sch 1, Sch 3, paras 1–4, 5(1), 7, Sch 5, paras 1, 6, 12, 13, 16, 19A, 20, 22–24, 26–49; Local Government Finance Act 1988, Sch 12, paras 8, 15, 17, 23, 27; Local Government and Housing Act 1989, ss 140, 141, Sch 6, paras 20, 21; Environmental Protection Act 1990, Sch 15, para 1; Caravans (Standard Community Charge and Rating) Act 1991, s 2) (subject to transitional provisions) (SI 1993/575)

Not in force (otherwise)

[1] For savings in relation to the repeals of the Abolition of Domestic Rates

Local Government Finance Act 1992 (c 14)—*cont*
(Scotland) Act 1987, Sch 2, para 7A, and the Local Government Finance Act
1988, Sch 4, para 6, see the Local Government Finance Act 1992 (Recovery of
Community Charge) Saving Order 1993, SI 1993/1780

Maintenance Orders (Reciprocal Enforcement) Act 1992 (c 56)

RA: 12 Nov 1992

Commencement provisions: s 3; Maintenance Orders (Reciprocal Enforcement) Act
1992 (Commencement) Order 1993, SI 1993/618

5 Apr 1993 (Whole Act) (SI 1993/618)

Mauritius Republic Act 1992 (c 45)

RA: 18 Jun 1992

18 Jun 1992 (RA; but note that s 1 deemed to have come into force on 12 Mar 1992
(s 1(4))

Medicinal Products: Prescription by Nurses etc Act 1992 (c 28)

RA: 16 Mar 1992

Commencement provision: s 6(2)

s 1–3	*Not in force*
4–6	16 Mar 1992 (RA)

Museums and Galleries Act 1992 (c 44)

RA: 16 Mar 1992

Commencement provisions: s 11(4); Museums and Galleries Act 1992
(Commencement) Order 1992, SI 1992/1874

s 1–8	1 Sep 1992 (SI 1992/1874)
9	1 Apr 1993 (SI 1992/1874)
10, 11	1 Sep 1992 (SI 1992/1874)
Sch 1–7	1 Sep 1992 (SI 1992/1874)
8, para 1(1)–(6)	1 Sep 1992 (SI 1992/1874)
(7)	Repealed
(8), (9)	1 Sep 1992 (SI 1992/1874)
2	Repealed
3	1 Sep 1992 (SI 1992/1874)
4	Repealed
5–9	1 Sep 1992 (SI 1992/1874)
10	Repealed
11–14	1 Sep 1992 (SI 1992/1874)
9	1 Sep 1992 (SI 1992/1874)

Non-Domestic Rating Act 1992 (c 46)

RA: 18 Jun 1992

Commencement provisions: s 10(2); Non-Domestic Rating Act 1992 (Commencement
No 1) Order 1992, SI 1992/1486; Non-Domestic Rating Act 1992
(Commencement No 2) Order 1992, SI 1992/1642

s 1–4	16 Jul 1992 (SI 1992/1642)
5(1)	16 Jul 1992 (SI 1992/1642)
(2)	23 Jun 1992 (SI 1992/1486)
6	16 Jul 1992 (SI 1992/1642)
7	23 Jun 1992 (SI 1992/1486)
8	16 Jul 1992 (SI 1992/1642)
9	23 Jun 1992 (SI 1992/1486)
10	18 Jun 1992 (RA)

Nurses, Midwives and Health Visitors Act 1992 (c 16)

RA: 6 Mar 1992

Commencement provisions: s 17(3); Nurses, Midwives and Health Visitors Act 1992
(Commencement No 1) Order 1993, SI 1993/588

s 1(1)	1 Apr 1993 (SI 1993/588)
(2)	See Sch 1 below
2	6 Mar 1992 (RA)
3	1 Apr 1993 (SI 1993/588)
4	1 Apr 1993 (except so far as substitutes Nurses, Midwives and Health Visitors Act 1979, s 5(8)(e) and s 5(9) (so far as that substitution consists of removal of that provision in its application to Sch 2, para 7 to the 1979 Act)) (SI 1993/588)
	Not in force (exceptions noted above)
5(1)	1 Apr 1993 (SI 1993/588)
(2)	1 Apr 1993 (except in Northern Ireland) (SI 1993/588)
	Not in force (exception noted above)
(3)–(5)	1 Apr 1993 (SI 1993/588)
6–14	1 Apr 1993 (SI 1993/588)
15	6 Mar 1992 (RA)
16(1)	See Sch 2 below
(2)	See Sch 3 below
17(1), (2)	1 Apr 1993 (SI 1993/588)
(3)	6 Mar 1992 (RA)
(4)	1 Apr 1993 (except so far as applies to s 5(2)) (SI 1993/588)
	Not in force (exception noted above)
Sch 1, 2	1 Apr 1993 (SI 1993/588)
3	1 Apr 1993 (except repeal of Nurses, Midwives and Health Visitors Act 1979, Sch 2, para 7) (SI 1993/588)
	Not in force (exception noted above)

Offshore Safety Act 1992 (c 15)

RA: 6 Mar 1992

Commencement provisions: s 7(3); Offshore Safety Act 1992 (Commencement No 1)
  Order 1993, SI 1993/2406

s 1	6 Mar 1992 (RA)
2(1), (2)	6 Mar 1992 (RA)
(3)(a)	6 Mar 1992 (RA)
(b), (c)	*Not in force*
(4)	6 Mar 1992 (RA)
3(1)(a)	30 Nov 1993 (SI 1993/2406)
(b)–(d)	6 Mar 1992 (RA)
(e)	30 Nov 1993 (SI 1993/2406)
(2)	30 Nov 1993 (SI 1993/2406)
(3)(a)	6 Mar 1992 (RA)
(b)	*Not in force*
(c), (d)	6 Mar 1992 (RA)
(4)	6 Mar 1992 (RA)
4–6	6 Mar 1992 (RA)
7(1)	6 Mar 1992 (RA)
(2)	See Sch 2 below
(3), (4)	6 Mar 1992 (RA)
Sch 1	30 Nov 1993 (SI 1993/2406)
2	6 Mar 1992 (except repeals in Continental Shelf Act 1964; Gas Act 1986, s 47(5)) (RA)
	30 Nov 1993 (repeal in Continental Shelf Act 1964) (SI 1993/2406)
	Not in force (repeal, for certain purposes, of Gas Act 1986, s 47(5))

Offshore Safety (Protection Against Victimisation) Act 1992 (c 24)

Whole Act repealed

Parliamentary Corporate Bodies Act 1992 (c 27)

RA: 16 Mar 1992

16 Mar 1992 (RA)

Prison Security Act 1992 (c 25)

RA: 16 Mar 1992

Commencement provision: s 3(2)

16 May 1992 (s 3(2))

Protection of Badgers Act 1992 (c 51)

RA: 16 Jul 1992

Commencement provision: s 15(3)

16 Oct 1992 (s 15(3))

Sea Fish (Conservation) Act 1992 (c 60)

RA: 17 Dec 1992

Commencement provision: s 11(1), (2)

s 1(1)	17 Dec 1992 (RA)
(2)	17 Jan 1993 (except in relation to vessels of an overall length of 10 metres or less until such day as may be appointed) (s 11(1), (2))
	Not in force (exception noted above)
(3)	17 Dec 1992 (RA)
(4), (5)	17 Jan 1993 (s 11(1))
2	17 Dec 1992 (RA)
3	17 Jan 1993 (s 11(1))
4	17 Dec 1992 (RA)
5	17 Jan 1993 (s 11(1))
6–13	17 Dec 1992 (RA)

Sea Fisheries (Wildlife Conservation) Act 1992 (c 36)

RA: 16 Mar 1992

Commencement provision: s 2(2)

16 May 1992 (s 2(2))

Severn Bridges Act 1992 (c 3)

RA: 13 Feb 1992

Commencement provisions: ss 39(1), 42(1); Severn Bridges Act 1992 (Appointed Day) Order 1992, SI 1992/578

s 1–15	13 Feb 1992 (RA)
16	26 Apr 1992 (SI 1992/578)
17–21	13 Feb 1992 (RA)
22(1), (2)	26 Apr 1992 (SI 1992/578)
(3)	13 Feb 1992 (RA)
23–33	13 Feb 1992 (RA)
34	26 Apr 1992 (SI 1992/578)
35–39	13 Feb 1992 (RA)
40	See Sch 5 below
41, 42	13 Feb 1992 (RA)
Sch 1–4	13 Feb 1992 (RA)
5	26 Apr 1992 (SI 1992/578)

Sexual Offences (Amendment) Act 1992 (c 34)

RA: 16 Mar 1992

Commencement provisions: s 8(3)–(5); Sexual Offences (Amendment) Act 1992 (Commencement) Order 1992, SI 1992/1336

s 1–7	1 Aug 1992 (SI 1992/1336)
8	16 Mar 1992 (s 8(3))

Social Security Administration Act 1992 (c 5)

RA: 13 Feb 1992

Commencement provision: s 192(4)

1 Jul 1992 (s 192(4); but note transitory modifications in Social Security (Consequential Provisions) Act 1992, Sch 4)

Social Security Administration (Northern Ireland) Act 1992 (c 8)

RA: 13 Feb 1992

Commencement provision: s 168(4)

1 Jul 1992 (s 168(4); but note transitory modifications in Social Security (Consequential Provisions) (Northern Ireland) Act 1992, Sch 4)

Social Security (Consequential Provisions) Act 1992 (c 6)

RA: 13 Feb 1992

Commencement provision: s 7(2)

1 Jul 1992 (s 7(2))

Social Security (Consequential Provisions) (Northern Ireland) Act 1992 (c 9)

RA: 13 Feb 1992

Commencement provision: s 7(2)

1 Jul 1992 (s 7(2))

Social Security Contributions and Benefits Act 1992 (c 4)

RA: 13 Feb 1992

Commencement provision: s 177(4)

1 Jul 1992 (s 177(4); but note transitory modifications in Social Security (Consequential Provisions) Act 1992, Sch 4)

Social Security Contributions and Benefits (Northern Ireland) Act 1992 (c 7)

RA: 13 Feb 1992

Commencement provision: s 173(4)

1 Jul 1992 (s 173(4); but note transitory modifications in Social Security (Consequential Provisions) (Northern Ireland) Act 1992, Sch 4)

Social Security (Mortgage Interest Payments) Act 1992 (c 33)

RA: 16 Mar 1992

16 Mar 1992 (RA; but note that s 1(1) ceased to have effect on 1 Jul 1992, by virtue of s 1(2))

Sporting Events (Control of Alcohol etc) (Amendment) Act 1992 (c 57)

RA: 3 Dec 1992

3 Dec 1992 (RA)

Stamp Duty (Temporary Provisions) Act 1992 (c 2)

RA: 13 Feb 1992

Commencement provision: s 1(4)

s 1	16 Jan 1992 (s 1(4))
2, 3	13 Feb 1992 (RA)

Still-Birth (Definition) Act 1992 (c 29)

RA: 16 Mar 1992

Commencement provision: s 4(2)

s 1, 2	1 Oct 1992 (s 4(2))
3	16 Mar 1992 (RA)
4	1 Oct 1992 (s 4(2))

Taxation of Chargeable Gains Act 1992 (c 12)

RA: 6 Mar 1992

Commencement provision: s 289

So much of any provision of this Act as authorises the making of any order or other instrument, and, except where the tax concerned is all tax for chargeable periods to which this Act does not apply, so much of any provision of this Act as confers any duty the exercise or performance of which operates or may

Taxation of Chargeable Gains Act 1992 (c 12)—*cont*
operate in relation to tax for more than one chargeable period, comes into force
for all purposes on 6 Apr 1992 to the exclusion of corresponding enactments
repealed by this Act; otherwise this Act has effect in relation to tax for the year
1992–93 and subsequent years of assessment (s 289)

Timeshare Act 1992 (c 35)

RA: 16 Mar 1992

Commencement provisions: s 13(2); Timeshare Act 1992 (Commencement) Order
1992, SI 1992/1941

12 Oct 1992 (SI 1992/1941)

Tourism (Overseas Promotion) (Wales) Act 1992 (c 26)

RA: 16 Mar 1992

Commencement provision: s 3

16 May 1992 (s 3)

Trade Union and Labour Relations (Consolidation) Act 1992 (c 52)

RA: 16 Jul 1992

Commencement provision: s 302

16 Oct 1992 (s 302)

Traffic Calming Act 1992 (c 30)

RA: 16 Mar 1992

Commencement provision: s 3

16 May 1992 (s 3)

Transport and Works Act 1992 (c 42)

RA: 16 Mar 1992

Commencement provisions: s 70; Transport and Works Act 1992 (Commencement
No 1) Order 1992, SI 1992/1347; Transport and Works Act 1992
(Commencement No 2) Order 1992, SI 1992/2043; Transport and Works Act
1992 (Commencement No 3 and Transitional Provisions) Order 1992, SI 1992/
2784; Transport and Works Act 1992 (Commencement No 4) Order 1992, SI
1992/3144

s 1–25	1 Jan 1993 (SI 1992/2784)
26–40	7 Dec 1992 (SI 1992/2043)
41, 42	31 Jan 1993 (SI 1992/3144)
43, 44	*Not in force*
45, 46	15 Jul 1992 (SI 1992/1347)

Transport and Works Act 1992 (c 42)—*cont*

s 47(1)	See Sch 2 below
(2)	31 Jan 1993 (SI 1992/3144)
48	31 Jan 1993 (SI 1992/3144)
49	15 Jul 1992 (SI 1992/1347)
50	*Not in force*
51	31 Jan 1993 (SI 1992/3144)
52–56	*Not in force*
57–60	15 Jul 1992 (SI 1992/1347)
61	31 Jan 1993 (SI 1992/3144)
62	*Not in force*
63	15 Jul 1992 (subject to transitional provisions with respect to certain Harbour Revision Orders and Harbour Empowerment Orders) (SI 1992/1347)
64	31 Jan 1993 (SI 1992/3144)
65(1)(a)	15 Jul 1992 (SI 1992/1347)
(b)	1 Jan 1993 (except words 'in section 25, the words 'and shall not be opened' onwards,'; and 'section 48.'') (SI 1992/2784)
(c), (d)	1 Jan 1993 (SI 1992/2784)
(e)	15 Jul 1992 (SI 1992/1347)
(f)	1 Jan 1993 (SI 1992/2784)
(2)	15 Jul 1992 (SI 1992/1347)
66, 67	15 Jul 1992 (SI 1992/1347)
68(1)	See Sch 4 below
(2)	*Not in force*
69	15 Jul 1992 (SI 1992/1347)
70–72	16 Mar 1992 (s 70)
Sch 1	1 Jan 1993 (SI 1992/2784)
2	22 Dec 1992 (for purpose of conferring on Secretary of State power to make regulation in relation to rail crossing extinguishment orders or rail crossing diversion orders) (SI 1992/3144)
	31 Jan 1993 (otherwise) (SI 1992/3144)
3	15 Jul 1992 (subject to transitional provisions with respect to certain Harbour Revision Orders and Harbour Empowerment Orders) (SI 1992/1347)
4, Pt I	15 Jul 1992 (repeals of or in British Railways Act 1965; London Transport Act 1965; Criminal Justice Act 1967; London Transport Act 1977; British Railways Act 1977) (subject to transitional provisions with respect to certain Harbour Revision Orders and Harbour Empowerment Orders) (SI 1992/1347)
	7 Dec 1992 (repeal in Railway Regulation Act 1842) (SI 1992/2043)
	1 Jan 1993 (repeals of or in Tramways Act 1870 (except words 'and shall not be opened' onwards in s 25, and s 48); Municipal Corporations Act 1882; Military Tramways Act 1887; Light Railways Act 1896; Railways (Electrical Power) Act 1903; Light Railways Act 1912; Railways Act 1921; Transport Act 1962; Administration of Justice Act 1965; Transport Act 1968 (expect ss 124, 125(4)); Local Government Act 1972; Supply Powers Act 1975; Administration of Justice Act 1982; Telecommunications Act 1984;

Transport and Works Act 1992 (c 42)—*cont*

Sch 4, Pt I—*cont*   Roads (Scotland) Act 1984; Insolvency Act 1986)
(subject to transitional provisions) (SI 1992/2784)
31 Jan 1993 (repeals of or in Regulation of Railways
Act 1871, s 3; Highways Act 1980) (SI 1992/3144)
Not in force (otherwise)

II   15 Jul 1992 (subject to transitional provisions with
respect to certain Harbour Revision Orders and
Harbour Empowerment Orders) (SI 1992/1347)

Tribunals and Inquiries Act 1992 (c 53)

RA: 16 Jul 1992

Commencement provision: s 19(2)

1 Oct 1992 (s 19(2))

1993

Agriculture Act 1993 (c 37)

RA: 27 Jul 1993

Commencement provisions: ss 1(2)–(4), 21(2), (3), 26(2)–(4), 54(2), 55(3), 65(2), (3); Agriculture Act 1993 (Commencement No 1) Order 1993, SI 1993/2038

s 1(1)(a)	1 Oct 1994 (s 1(2)(b); but note that the appropriate authority may by order provide that s 1(2)(b) shall have effect with the substitution for that date of such later date before 1 Jan 1996 as may be specified in the order (s 1(3), and note also s 1(4), (5)))
(b)–(d)	1 Apr 1994 (s 1(2)(a); but note that the appropriate authority may by order provide that s 1(2)(a) shall have effect with the substitution for that date of such later date before 1 Jan 1996 as may be specified in the order (s 1(3), and note also s 1(4), (5))
(2)–(5)	27 Jul 1993 (RA)
2–11	27 Jul 1993 (RA)
12	See Sch 2 below
13–20	27 Jul 1993 (RA)
21(1)	Day on which s 1(1) comes into force completely (s 21(2), (3))
(2), (3)	27 Jul 1993 (RA)
22–25	27 Jul 1993 (RA)
26(1)	*Not in force*
(2)–(5)	27 Jul 1993 (RA)
27–35	27 Jul 1993 (RA)
36	See Sch 4 below
37–49	27 Jul 1993 (RA)
50–53	27 Sep 1993 (s 65(2))
54	27 Jul 1993 (RA)
55	4 Aug 1993 (SI 1993/2038)
56–58	27 Jul 1993 (RA)
59	4 Aug 1993 (SI 1993/2038)
60–65	27 Jul 1993 (RA)
Sch 1–4	27 Jul 1993 (RA)
5	27 Jul 1993 (except so far as repeals relate to potatoes and revocation of Potato Marketing Scheme, para 67) (RA)
	4 Aug 1993 (exceptions noted above) (SI 1993/2038)

Appropriation Act 1993 (c 33)

RA: 27 Jul 1993

27 Jul 1993 (RA)

Asylum and Immigration Appeals Act 1993 (c 23)

RA: 1 Jul 1993

Commencement provisions: s 14; Asylum and Immigration Appeals Act 1993
(Commencement and Transitional Provisions) Order 1993, SI 1993/1655

s 1	1 Jul 1993 (except so far as relates to ss 4–11) (RA)
	26 Jul 1993 (exception noted above) (SI 1993/1655)
2, 3	1 Jul 1993 (RA)
4–7	26 Jul 1993 (SI 1993/1655)
8–11	26 Jul 1993 (subject to savings) (SI 1993/1655)
12–16	1 Jul 1993 (RA)
Sch 1, 2	26 Jul 1993 (SI 1993/1655)

Bail (Amendment) Act 1993 (c 26)

RA: 20 Jul 1993

Commencement provision: s 2(2)

s 1	*Not in force*
2	20 Jul 1993 (s 2(2))

Bankruptcy (Scotland) Act 1993 (c 6)

RA: 18 Feb 1993

Commencement provisions: s 12(3)–(6); Bankruptcy (Scotland) Act 1993
Commencement and Savings Order 1993, SI 1993/438

s 1–7	1 Apr 1993 (SI 1993/438)
8, 9	18 Feb 1993 (s 12(3))
10	1 Apr 1993 (SI 1993/438)
11(1), (2)	1 Apr 1993 (SI 1993/438)
(3)	See Sch 1 below
(4)	See Sch 2 below
12	18 Feb 1993 (s 12(3))
Sch 1, para 1–21	1 Apr 1993 (SI 1993/438)
22(1)–(4)	1 Apr 1993 (SI 1993/438)
(5)	18 Feb 1993 (s 12(3))
23	18 Feb 1993 (s 12(3))
24–30	1 Apr 1993 (SI 1993/438)
31(1)–(3)	1 Apr 1993 (SI 1993/438)
(4), (5)	18 Feb 1993 (s 12(3))
32	1 Apr 1993 (SI 1993/438)
2	1 Apr 1993 (SI 1993/438)

British Coal and British Rail (Transfer Proposals) Act 1993 (c 2)

RA: 19 Jan 1993

19 Jan 1993 (RA); prospectively repealed in relation to the British Railways Board by Railways Act 1993, s 152, Sch 12, para 32 (qv)

Cardiff Bay Barrage Act 1993 (c 42)

RA: 5 Nov 1993

5 Nov 1993 (RA)

Carrying of Knives etc (Scotland) Act 1993 (c 13)

RA: 27 May 1993

27 May 1993 (RA)

Charities Act 1993 (c 10)

RA: 27 May 1993

Commencement provision: s 99

s 1–4	1 Aug 1993 (s 99(1))
5(1)	1 Aug 1993 (subject to transitional provisions) (s 99(1), (4))
(2)	1 Aug 1993 (s 99(1))
(2A)	Inserted by Welsh Language Act 1993, s 32(3) (qv)
(3)–(6)	1 Aug 1993 (s 99(1))
6–40	1 Aug 1993 (s 99(1))
41–49	*Not in force*
50–68	1 Aug 1993 (s 99(1))
69	*Not in force*
70–73	1 Aug 1993 (s 99(1))
74(1)(a)	1 Aug 1993 (subject to transitional provisions) (s 99(1), (4))
(b)	1 Aug 1993 (s 99(1))
(2)–(12)	1 Aug 1993 (s 99(1))
75(1)(a)	1 Aug 1993 (s 99(1))
(b)	1 Aug 1993 (subject to transitional provisions) (s 99(1), (4))
(2)–(10)	1 Aug 1993 (s 99(1))
76–97	1 Aug 1993 (s 99(1))
98(1)	See Sch 6 below
(2)	See Sch 7 below
99, 100	1 Aug 1993 (s 99(1))
Sch 1–5	1 Aug 1993 (s 99(1))
6, para 1–20	1 Aug 1993 (s 99(1))
21(1), (2)	1 Aug 1993 (s 99(1))
(3)	*Not in force*
(4), (5)	1 Aug 1993 (s 99(1))
22–30	1 Aug 1993 (s 99(1))

Charities Act 1993 (c 10)—*cont*
Sch 7   1 Aug 1993 (subject to transitional provisions)
         (s 99(1)–(3))
   8   1 Aug 1993 (s 99(1))

Clean Air Act 1993 (c 11)

RA: 27 May 1993

Commencement provision: s 68(2)

27 Aug 1993 (s 68(2))

Consolidated Fund Act 1993 (c 4)

RA: 18 Feb 1993

18 Feb 1993 (RA)

Consolidated Fund (No 2) Act 1993 (c 7)

RA: 29 Mar 1993

29 Mar 1993 (RA)

Consolidated Fund (No 3) Act 1993 (c 52)

RA: 17 Dec 1993

17 Dec 1993 (RA)

Criminal Justice Act 1993 (c 36)

RA: 27 Jul 1993

Commencement provisions: s 78; Criminal Justice Act 1993 (Commencement No 1) Order 1993, SI 1993/1968; Criminal Justice Act 1993 (Commencement No 2 Transitional Provisions and Savings) (Scotland) Order 1993, SI 1993/2035; Criminal Justice Act 1993 (Commencement No 3) Order 1993, SI 1993/2734; Criminal Justice Act 1993 (Commencement No 4) Order 1994, SI 1994/71

s 1–15	*Not in force*
16, 17	15 Feb 1994 (SI 1994/71)
18, 19	*Not in force*
20–23	1 Dec 1993 (SI 1993/2734)
24–28	*Not in force*
29–31	15 Feb 1994 (SI 1994/71)
32	*Not in force*
33	15 Feb 1994 (SI 1994/71)
34, 35	1 Dec 1993 (SI 1993/2734)
36–43	*Not in force*
44–46	1 Dec 1993 (SI 1993/2734)
47	15 Feb 1994 (SI 1994/71)
48	*Not in force*
49	15 Feb 1994 (SI 1994/71)

Criminal Justice Act 1993 (c 36)—*cont*

s 50–64	*Not in force*
65	20 Sep 1993 (SI 1993/1968)
66	16 Aug 1993 (SI 1993/1968)
67(1)	16 Aug 1993 (EW) (SI 1993/1968)
	16 Aug 1993 (S) (subject to savings) (SI 1993/2035)
(2)	16 Aug 1993 (SI 1993/1968)
68, 69	27 Jul 1993 (s 78(2))
70, 71	27 Sep 1993 (s 78(1))
72	*Not in force*
73	1 Dec 1993 (SI 1993/2734)
74	15 Feb 1994 (SI 1994/71)
75, 76	27 Jul 1993 (s 78(2))
77	*Not in force*
78	27 Jul 1993 (partly) (RA)
	15 Feb 1994 (otherwise) (SI 1994/71)
79(1)–(12)	27 Jul 1993 (s 78(2))
(13)	See Sch 5 below
(14)	See Sch 6 below
Sch 1, 2	*Not in force*
3	20 Sep 1993 (SI 1993/1968)
4	*Not in force*
5, para 1	*Not in force*
2	27 Jul 1993 (s 78(2))
3–13	*Not in force*
14	15 Feb 1994 (SI 1994/71)
15–22	*Not in force*
6, Pt I	27 Jul 1993 (repeals in Criminal Procedure (Scotland) Act 1975; Prisoners and Criminal Proceedings (Scotland) Act 1993) (s 78(2))
	20 Sep 1993 (repeals in Magistrates' Courts Act 1980; Criminal Justice Act 1991) (SI 1993/1968)
	15 Feb 1994 (repeals of or in Drug Trafficking Offences Act 1986, ss 1(5)(b)(iii), 27(5); Criminal Justice Act 1988, ss 48 (EW only), 98; Prevention of Terrorism (Temporary Provisions) Act 1989; Criminal Justice (International Co-operation) Act 1990; Northern Ireland (Emergency Provisions) Act 1991, ss 50(2), 67(6)) (SI 1994/71)
	Not in force (otherwise)
II	*Not in force*

Crofters (Scotland) Act 1993 (c 44)

RA: 5 Nov 1993

Commencement provisions: ss 28(17), 64(2)

s 1–27	5 Jan 1994 (s 64(2))
28	*Not in force*
29–64	5 Jan 1994 (s 64(2))
Sch 1–7	5 Jan 1994 (s 64(2))

Damages (Scotland) Act 1993 (c 5)

RA: 18 Feb 1993

Commencement provision: s 8(3)

18 Apr 1993 (s 8(3))

Disability (Grants) Act 1993 (c 14)

RA: 27 May 1993

27 May 1993 (RA)

Education Act 1993 (c 35)

RA: 27 Jul 1993

Commencement provisions: s 308(3); Education Act 1993 (Commencement No 1 and Transitional Provisions) Order 1993, SI 1993/1975; Education Act 1993 (Commencement No 2 and Transitional Provisions) Order 1993, SI 1993/3106

s 1, 2	1 Oct 1993 (SI 1993/1975)
3, 4	*Not in force*
5	1 Sep 1993 (SI 1993/1975)
6–21	*Not in force*
22(1)	1 Jan 1994 (SI 1993/3106)
(2)(a)	1 Jan 1994 (SI 1993/3106)
(b)	1 Jan 1994 (for purpose of defining expression "proposals for the establishment of a new grant-maintained school") (SI 1993/3106)
	Not in force (otherwise)
(c)	*Not in force*
(3)	1 Jan 1994 (SI 1993/3106)
(4)	*Not in force*
23	1 Jan 1994 (subject to transitional provisions) (SI 1993/3106)
24	9 Dec 1993 (SI 1993/3106)
25–35	1 Jan 1994 (subject to transitional provisions) (SI 1993/3106)
36(1), (2)	1 Jan 1994 (subject to transitional provisions) (SI 1993/3106)
(3)–(5)	*Not in force*
37–46	1 Jan 1994 (subject to transitional provisions) (SI 1993/3106)
47(1)–(4)	*Not in force*
(5)–(9)	1 Jan 1994 (subject to transitional provisions) (SI 1993/3106)
48–54	*Not in force*
55–58	1 Jan 1994 (SI 1993/3106)
59–67	1 Jan 1994 (subject to transitional provisions) (SI 1993/3106)
68–70	*Not in force*
71–77	1 Jan 1994 (subject to transitional provisions) (SI 1993/3106)
78	*Not in force*
79, 80	1 Jan 1994 (SI 1993/3106)

Education Act 1993 (c 35)—*cont*

s 81–91	*Not in force*
92	1 Jan 1994 (SI 1993/3106)
93–135	*Not in force*
136(1)	1 Jan 1994 (SI 1993/3106)
(2)	*Not in force*
(3)	1 Jan 1994 (SI 1993/3106)
137	1 Jan 1994 (SI 1993/3106)
138–151	*Not in force*
152	1 Jan 1994 (SI 1993/3106)
153(1), (2)	1 Jan 1994 (SI 1993/3106)
(3)	*Not in force*
(4)	1 Jan 1994 (SI 1993/3106)
(5)	*Not in force*
154	*Not in force*
155–158	1 Jan 1994 (SI 1993/3106)
159, 160	*Not in force*
161(1)–(4)	*Not in force*
(5)	1 Jan 1994 (SI 1993/3106)
162–176	*Not in force*
177(1)	*Not in force*
(2)–(6)	1 Jan 1994 (SI 1993/3106)
178, 179	1 Jan 1994 (SI 1993/3106)
180(1), (2)	1 Jan 1994 (SI 1993/3106)
(3)–(6)	*Not in force*
181	1 Jan 1994 (SI 1993/3106)
182(1)–(3)	*Not in force*
(4)	See Sch 11 below
183–191	*Not in force*
192(1)–(5)	1 Oct 1993 (SI 1993/1975)
(6), (7)	1 Oct 1993 (for purposes of school attendance orders with respect to children other than those for whom a statement is maintained under the Education Act 1981, s 7) (SI 1993/1975)
	Not in force (otherwise)
(8)	1 Oct 1993 (SI 1993/1975)
193(1)	1 Oct 1993 (subject to transitional provisions) (SI 1993/1975)
(2)–(6)	1 Oct 1993 (SI 1993/1975)
194(1)	1 Oct 1993 (SI 1993/1975)
(2)	1 Oct 1993 (subject to transitional provisions) (SI 1993/1975)
(3)–(8)	1 Oct 1993 (SI 1993/1975)
195(1)	1 Oct 1993 (subject to transitional provisions) (SI 1993/1975)
(2)–(4)	1 Oct 1993 (SI 1993/1975)
196	*Not in force*
197(1)–(4)	1 Oct 1993 (SI 1993/1975)
(5)	*Not in force*
(6)	1 Oct 1993 (SI 1993/1975)
198–203	1 Oct 1993 (SI 1993/1975)
204–212	1 Sep 1993 (subject to transitional provisions) (SI 1993/1975)
213–216	1 Jan 1994 (SI 1993/3106)
217(1)	1 Jan 1994 (SI 1993/3106)
(2)	*Not in force*
218–223	1 Jan 1994 (subject to transitional provisions) (SI 1993/3106)

Education Act 1993 (c 35)—*cont*

s 224–226	*Not in force*
227	1 Jan 1994 (SI 1993/3106)
228(1)–(3)	1 Jan 1994 (SI 1993/3106)
(4)	*Not in force*
229(1)	1 Oct 1993 (so far as amends Education Act 1980, s 12(1)(d) (insertion of words "or to transfer a county school to a new site in the area")) (SI 1993/1975)
	Not in force (otherwise)
(2), (3)	*Not in force*
230(1)	1 Oct 1993 (so far as amends the Education Act 1980, s 13(1)(b) (insertion of words "or to transfer the school to a new site")) (SI 1993/1975)
	Not in force (otherwise)
(2)	*Not in force*
(3)–(5)	1 Oct 1993 (SI 1993/1975)
(6)	*Not in force*
231–237	*Not in force*
238, 239	1 Jan 1994 (SI 1993/3106)
240	27 Jul 1993 (RA)
241	*Not in force*
242–245	1 Oct 1993 (SI 1993/1975)
246	1 Jan 1994 (SI 1993/3106)
247–251	1 Oct 1993 (SI 1993/1975)
252–258	*Not in force*
259(1)	1 Oct 1993 (SI 1993/1975)
(2)	1 Oct 1993 (subject to transitional provisions) (SI 1993/1975)
(3)	1 Oct 1993 (SI 1993/1975)
260	1 Oct 1993 (SI 1993/1975)
261, 262	*Not in force*
263–265	1 Oct 1993 (SI 1993/1975)
266–268	1 Jan 1994 (subject to transitional provisions) (SI 1993/3106)
269	1 Oct 1993 (subject to transitional provisions) (SI 1993/1975)
270	1 Oct 1993 (SI 1993/1975)
271	1 Jan 1994 (SI 1993/3106)
272, 273	*Not in force*
274–276	1 Jan 1994 (subject to transitional provisions) (SI 1993/3106)
277–279	*Not in force*
280	1 Oct 1993 (SI 1993/1975)
281	1 Jan 1994 (SI 1993/3106)
282–286	1 Oct 1993 (SI 1993/1975)
287, 288	1 Jan 1994 (SI 1993/3106)
289	*Not in force*
290–292	1 Jan 1994 (SI 1993/3106)
293, 294	1 Oct 1993 (SI 1993/1975)
295–298	*Not in force*
299, 300	1 Jan 1994 (SI 1993/3106)
301–303	27 Jul 1993 (RA)
304	*Not in force*
305, 306	27 Jul 1993 (RA)
307(1)	See Sch 19 below
(2)	See Sch 20 below
(3)	See Sch 21 below

Education Act 1993 (c 35)—*cont*

s 308	27 Jul 1993 (RA)
Sch 1, 2	*Not in force*
3, Pt I	1 Jan 1994 (subject to transitional provisions) (SI 1993/3106)
II	*Not in force*
4–7	1 Jan 1994 (subject to transitional provisions) (SI 1993/3106)
8–10	*Not in force*
11, para 1–13	*Not in force*
14	1 Jan 1994 (SI 1993/3106)
12	1 Jan 1994 (SI 1993/3106)
13	1 Jan 1994 (subject to transitional provisions) (SI 1993/3106)
14	1 Oct 1993 (SI 1993/1975)
15	*Not in force*
16, 17	1 Jan 1994 (SI 1993/3106)
18	*Not in force*
19, para 1	1 Oct 1993 (SI 1993/1975)
2	*Not in force*
3–5	1 Oct 1993 (SI 1993/1975)
6	*Not in force*
7	1 Jan 1994 (SI 1993/3106)
8	1 Oct 1993 (SI 1993/1975)
9, 10	*Not in force*
11	1 Oct 1993 (SI 1993/1975)
12, 13	*Not in force*
14, 15	1 Oct 1993 (SI 1993/1975)
16–19	*Not in force*
20(a)	1 Oct 1993 (SI 1993/1975)
(b)	*Not in force*
21	*Not in force*
22	1 Jan 1994 (SI 1993/3106
23(a)(i)	1 Oct 1993 (so far as amends the Education Act 1944, s 105(2)(c)(i) (insertion of words "or on a transfer of the school to a new site")) (SI 1993/1975)
	1 Jan 1994 (otherwise) (SI 1993/3106)
(ii)–(iv)	1 Jan 1994 (SI 1993/3106)
(b)	*Not in force*
24(a)(i)	*Not in force*
(ii), (iii)	1 Oct 1993 (SI 1993/1975)
(iv)	1 Jan 1994 (SI 1993/3106)
(b)	1 Jan 1994 (subject to transitional provisions) (SI 1993/3106)
25	1 Oct 1993 (SI 1993/1975)
26, 27	*Not in force*
28	1 Oct 1993 (SI 1993/1975)
29	1 Jan 1994 (SI 1993/3106)
30	1 Oct 1993 (SI 1993/1975)
31	*Not in force*
32	1 Oct 1993 (SI 1993/1975)
33	*Not in force*
34	1 Oct 1993 (so far as relates to the Curriculum Council for Wales and the School Curriculum and Assessment Authority) (SI 1993/1975)
	Not in force (otherwise)

Education Act 1993 (c 35)—*cont*

Sch 19, para 35	1 Oct 1993 (SI 1993/1975)
36–38	*Not in force*
39	1 Jan 1994 (SI 1993/3106)
40–43	1 Oct 1993 (SI 1993/1975)
44–54	*Not in force*
55(a)	*Not in force*
(b)	1 Jan 1994 (SI 1993/3106)
56	1 Oct 1993 (SI 1993/1975)
57–63	*Not in force*
64	1 Oct 1993 (SI 1993/1975)
65–67	*Not in force*
68, 69	1 Oct 1993 (SI 1993/1975)
70, 71	*Not in force*
72	1 Oct 1993 (SI 1993/1975)
73, 74	*Not in force*
75	1 Oct 1993 (SI 1993/1975)
76	*Not in force*
77(a)	1 Oct 1993 (SI 1993/1975)
(b)	*Not in force*
78	1 Oct 1993 (SI 1993/1975)
79	*Not in force*
80	1 Oct 1993 (SI 1993/1975)
81	*Not in force*
82	1 Jan 1994 (so far as repeals Education Act 1981, s 1) (SI 1993/3106)
	Not in force (otherwise)
83	1 Jan 1994 (SI 1993/3106)
84	1 Oct 1993 (SI 1993/1975)
85–89	*Not in force*
90	1 Jan 1994 (so far as provides for the Education (No 2) Act 1986, s 9(5), to have effect as if the transfer of a school to a new site in pursuance of the Education Act 1980, s 16(1A)(c) were an alteration of the kind mentioned in sub-s (5) of that section) (SI 1993/3106)
	Not in force (otherwise)
91–108	*Not in force*
109(a)	1 Jan 1994 (SI 1993/3106)
(b)(i)	1 Jan 1994 (SI 1993/3106)
(ii)	*Not in force*
(c), (d)	*Not in force*
(e)	1 Jan 1994 (SI 1993/3106)
110, 111	*Not in force*
112	1 Oct 1993 (SI 1993/1975)
113–117	*Not in force*
118(a)	1 Jan 1994 (SI 1993/3106)
(b)–(d)	1 Oct 1993 (subject to transitional provisions) (SI 1993/1975)
(e)	1 Jan 1994 (SI 1993/3106)
119	1 Oct 1993 (SI 1993/1975)
120, 121	*Not in force*
122	1 Oct 1993 (SI 1993/1975)
123	1 Jan 1994 (SI 1993/3106)
124	1 Oct 1993 (SI 1993/1975)
125	*Not in force*
126	1 Jan 1994 (so far as repeals Education Reform Act 1988, ss 52(3)–(9), 53–56, 58–72, 74–78, 104(1)(a),

Education Act 1993 (c 35)—*cont*

Sch 19, para 126—*cont*	(b), (f)–(h), (2), (3) (definition "incorporation date" only)) (subject to transitional provisions) (SI 1993/3106)
	Not in force (otherwise)
127–129	*Not in force*
130	1 Jan 1994 (so far as repeals reference to "52(4)" in Education Reform Act 1988, s 119(2)) (subject to transitional provisions) (SI 1993/3106)
	Not in force (otherwise)
131, 132	1 Oct 1993 (SI 1993/1975)
133–135	1 Jan 1994 (subject to transitional provisions) (SI 1993/3106)
136	*Not in force*
137	1 Jan 1994 (so far as repeals words "section 74 (taken with Schedule 10)" in Education Reform Act 1988, s 230(1)) (subject to transitional provisions) (SI 1993/3106)
	Not in force (otherwise)
138(a)	1 Jan 1994 (SI 1993/3106)
(b)(i)	1 Jan 1994 (so far as repeals references to "58(2), 59(1)" and "102" in Education Reform Act 1988, s 232(2)) (SI 1993/3106)
	Not in force (otherwise)
(ii)	1 Jan 1994 (SI 1993/3106)
139(a)(i)	*Not in force*
(ii)	1 Jan 1994 (subject to transitional provisions) (SI 1993/3106)
(b), (c)	1 Jan 1994 (subject to transitional provisions) (SI 1993/3106)
140	*Not in force*
141	1 Oct 1993 (SI 1993/1975)
142	*Not in force*
143, 144	1 Jan 1994 (subject to transitional provisions) (SI 1993/3106)
145–148	*Not in force*
149	1 Oct 1993 (SI 1993/1975)
150	1 Jan 1994 (SI 1993/3106)
151	*Not in force*
152	1 Oct 1993 (SI 1993/1975)
153	1 Jan 1994 (SI 1993/3106)
154	1 Oct 1993 (so far as relates to Children Act 1989, Sch 12, para 4) (SI 1993/1975)
	Not in force (otherwise)
155	1 Oct 1993 (SI 1993/1975)
156–161	*Not in force*
162	1 Jan 1994 (SI 1993/3106)
163(a)	1 Jan 1994 (subject to transitional provisions) (SI 1993/3106)
(b)	*Not in force*
(c)	1 Jan 1994 (subject to transitional provisions) (SI 1993/3106)
164	1 Jan 1994 (subject to transitional provisions) (SI 1993/3106)
165, 166	1 Jan 1994 (SI 1993/3106)
167(a)	*Not in force*
(b)	1 Jan 1994 (SI 1993/3106)
168, 169	*Not in force*

Education Act 1993 (c 35)—*cont*

Sch 19, para 170	1 Oct 1993 (SI 1993/1975)
171, 172	*Not in force*
173(1)(a)	*Not in force*
(b)	1 Oct 1993 (SI 1993/1975)
(c)	1 Sep 1993 (SI 1993/1975)
(2)	1 Aug 1993 (for purpose of prescribing matters which fall to be prescribed under Education (Schools) Act 1992, Sch 2) (SI 1993/1975) 1 Sep 1993 (otherwise) (SI 1993/1975)
(3)	1 Aug 1993 (for purpose of prescribing matters which fall to be prescribed under Education (Schools) Act 1992, Sch 2) (SI 1993/1975) 1 Sep 1993 (otherwise) (SI 1993/1975)
(4)	1 Sep 1993 (SI 1993/1975)
(5)	1 Aug 1993 (for purpose of prescribing matters which fall to be prescribed under Education (Schools) Act 1992, Sch 2) (subject to transitional provisions) (SI 1993/1975) 1 Sep 1993 (otherwise) (subject to transitional provisions) (SI 1993/1975)
(6)	1 Aug 1993 (for purpose of prescribing matters which fall to be prescribed under Education (Schools) Act 1992, Sch 2) (subject to transitional provisions) (SI 1993/1975) 1 Sep 1993 (otherwise) (subject to transitional provisions) (SI 1993/1975)
(7)	1 Sep 1993 (SI 1993/1975)
(8)(a)	1 Aug 1993 (for purpose of prescribing matters which fall to be prescribed under Education (Schools) Act 1992, Sch 2) (SI 1993/1975) 1 Oct 1993 (otherwise) (SI 1993/1975)
(b)	1 Oct 1993 (SI 1993/1975)
(9)(a)	1 Aug 1993 (for purpose of prescribing matters which fall to be prescribed under Education (Schools) Act 1992, Sch 2) (SI 1993/1975) 1 Oct 1993 (otherwise) (SI 1993/1975)
(b)	1 Oct 1993 (SI 1993/1975)
174	1 Jan 1994 (SI 1993/3106)
175	1 Oct 1993 (SI 1993/1975)
20, para 1	1 Jan 1994 (SI 1993/3106)
2	*Not in force*
3	1 Jan 1994 (SI 1993/3106)
4	*Not in force*
5–7	1 Jan 1994 (SI 1993/3106)
21	1 Oct 1993 (repeals of or in Children and Young Persons Act 1933, s 10; Education Act 1944, ss 1, 6, 16, 37, 39, 40, 114, Sch 8; Education (Miscellaneous Provisions) Act 1948, s 9; Education (Miscellaneous Provisions) Act 1953, s 10; Criminal Justice Act 1967; Education Act 1968, s 3, Sch 1, para 1; Children and Young Persons Act 1969; Criminal Law Act 1977; Education Act 1980, ss 10, 11, Sch 1, para 10; Education Reform Act 1988, ss 14(4), (5), 25, Sch 2, para 18; Children Act 1989, s 36, Sch 13) (SI 1993/1975)

Education Act 1993 (c 35)—*cont*

Sch 21—*cont*   1 Jan 1994 (repeals of or in Education Act 1944,
                               ss 102, 103, 105(2); Education Act 1967, s 1;
                               Superannuation Act 1972, Sch 1; House of
                               Commons Disqualification Act 1975, Sch 1;
                               Education Act 1981, s 1; Education Reform Act
                               1988, ss 14(1), 42, 52(3)–(9), 53–56, 58–72, 74–78,
                               102, 103, 104(1)(a), (b), (f)–(h), (2), (3) (definition
                               "incorporation date" only), 119(2) (reference to
                               "52(4)" only), 198(1), 200, 230(1) (words "section
                               74 (taken with Schedule 10)" only), 232(2)
                               (references to "58(2), 59(1)" and "102" only),
                               (4)(b), 235 (except definition "the 1981 Act" in
                               sub-s (1)), Sch 2, paras 1, 9 (entries relating to
                               membership of the National Curriculum Council
                               and the School Examinations and Assessment
                               Council only), 10(5) (entries relating to National
                               Curriculum Council and the School
                               Examinations and Assessment Council only),
                               Sch 4, para 2, Sch 5; Children Act 1989, Sch 12,
                               para 4; Diocesian Boards of Education Measure
                               1991, s 3(6)) (subject to transitional provisions) (SI
                               1993/3106)
                               Not in force (otherwise)

European Communities (Amendment) Act 1993 (c 32)

RA: 20 Jul 1993

Commencement provision: s 7

23 Jul 1993 (s 7)

European Economic Area Act 1993 (c 51)

RA: 5 Nov 1993

5 Nov 1993 (RA)

European Parliamentary Elections Act 1993 (c 41)

RA: 5 Nov 1993

Commencement provision: s 3(3)

s 1   *Not in force*
  2, 3   5 Nov 1993 (RA)

Schedule   5 Nov 1993 (RA)

Finance Act 1993 (c 34)

RA: 27 Jul 1993

See the note concerning Finance Acts at the front of this book

Foreign Compensation (Amendment) Act 1993 (c 16)

RA: 27 May 1993

Commencement provision: s 3(1)

27 Jul 1993 (s 3(1))

Gas (Exempt Supplies) Act 1993 (c 1)

RA: 19 Jan 1993

Commencement provision: s 4(2)

Not in force

Health Service Commissioners Act 1993 (c 46)

RA: 5 Nov 1993

Commencement provision: s 22(4)

5 Feb 1994 (s 22(4))

Incumbents (Vacation of Benefices) (Amendment) Measure 1993 (No 1)

RA: 27 Jul 1993

Commencement provision: s 16(2)

Not in force

Judicial Pensions and Retirement Act 1993 (c 8)

RA: 29 Mar 1993

Commencement provision: s 31(2)

Not in force

Leasehold Reform, Housing and Urban Development Act 1993 (c 28)

RA: 20 Jul 1993

Commencement provisions: ss 138(2), 188(2), (3); Leasehold Reform, Housing and
  Urban Development Act 1993 (Commencement and Transitional Provisions No
  1) Order 1993, SI 1993/2134; Leasehold Reform, Housing and Urban
  Development Act 1993 (Commencement No 2) (Scotland) Order 1993, SI 1993/
  2163; Leasehold Reform, Housing and Urban Development Act 1993
  (Commencement and Transitional Provisions No 3) Order 1993, SI 1993/2762

s 1–25	1 Nov 1993 (SI 1993/2134)
26(1)–(8)	1 Nov 1993 (SI 1993/2134)
(9)	2 Sep 1993 (SI 1993/2134)

Leasehold Reform, Housing and Urban Development Act 1993 (c 28)—*cont*

s 27–66	1 Nov 1993 (SI 1993/2134)
67, 68	1 Nov 1993 (subject to savings) (SI 1993/2134)
69–74	1 Nov 1993 (SI 1993/2134)
75	2 Sep 1993 (so far as confers on Secretary of State a power to make orders, regulations or declarations) (SI 1993/2134)
	1 Nov 1993 (otherwise) (SI 1993/2134)
76–84	1 Nov 1993 (SI 1993/2134)
85, 86	1 Nov 1993 (subject to savings) (SI 1993/2134)
87	1 Nov 1993 (SI 1993/2134)
88	2 Sep 1993 (so far as confers on Secretary of State a power to make orders, regulations or declarations) (SI 1993/2134)
	1 Nov 1993 (otherwise) (SI 1993/2134)
89, 90	1 Nov 1993 (SI 1993/2134)
91	2 Sep 1993 (so far as confers on Secretary of State a power to make orders, regulations or declarations) (SI 1993/2134)
	1 Nov 1993 (otherwise) (SI 1993/2134)
92–97	1 Nov 1993 (SI 1993/2134)
98	2 Sep 1993 (SI 1993/2134)
99	2 Sep 1993 (so far as confers on Secretary of State a power to make orders, regulations or declarations) (SI 1993/2134)
	1 Nov 1993 (otherwise) (SI 1993/2134)
100	2 Sep 1993 (SI 1993/2134)
101–103	1 Nov 1993 (SI 1993/2134)
104–107	11 Oct 1993 (subject to savings) (SI 1993/2134)
108	2 Sep 1993 (so far as confers on Secretary of State a power to make orders, regulations or declarations) (SI 1993/2134)
	11 Oct 1993 (otherwise) (subject to savings) (SI 1993/2134)
109–120	11 Oct 1993 (subject to savings) (SI 1993/2134)
121	1 Dec 1993 (subject to transitional provisions) (SI 1993/2762)
122	1 Feb 1994 (subject to transitional provisions) (SI 1993/2762)
123	11 Oct 1993 (SI 1993/2134)
124, 125	11 Oct 1993 (subject to savings) (SI 1993/2134)
126, 127	20 Jul 1993 (RA)
128, 129	11 Oct 1993 (SI 1993/2134)
130	11 Oct 1993 (subject to savings) (SI 1993/2134)
131	11 Oct 1993 (SI 1993/2134)
132	10 Nov 1993 (so far as confers on the Secretary of State a power to make regulations) (SI 1993/2762)
	Not in force (otherwise)
133, 134	11 Oct 1993 (subject to savings) (SI 1993/2134)
135–137	20 Jul 1993 (RA)
138	1 Jan 1993 (s 138(2))
139, 140	20 Jul 1993 (RA)
141–145	27 Sep 1993 (SI 1993/2163)
146, 147	1 Apr 1994 (SI 1993/2163)
148	27 Sep 1993 (SI 1993/2163)
149–151	20 Jul 1993 (RA)
152, 153	1 Apr 1994 (SI 1993/2163)
154–157	27 Sep 1993 (SI 1993/2163)

Leasehold Reform, Housing and Urban Development Act 1993 (c 28)—*cont*

s 158–173	10 Nov 1993 (SI 1993/2762)
174	11 Oct 1993 (SI 1993/2134)
175	10 Nov 1993 (SI 1993/2762)
176	11 Oct 1993 (SI 1993/2134)
177	10 Nov 1993 (SI 1993/2762)
178	11 Oct 1993 (subject to savings) (SI 1993/2134)
179	11 Oct 1993 (SI 1993/2134)
180	11 Oct 1993 (except so far as relates to insertion of s 165A(2) of the 1980 Act) (SI 1993/2134)
	10 Nov 1993 (otherwise) (SI 1993/2762)
181(1), (2)	20 Jul 1993 (RA)
(3)	10 Nov 1993 (SI 1993/2762)
(4)	20 Jul 1993 (RA)
182	11 Oct 1993 (SI 1993/2134)
183	10 Nov 1993 (SI 1993/2762)
184	*Not in force*
185	10 Nov 1993 (SI 1993/2762)
186	20 Jul 1993 (RA)
187(1)	See Sch 21 below
(2)	See Sch 22 below
188	20 Jul 1993 (RA)
Sch 1–15	1 Nov 1993 (SI 1993/2134)
16	11 Oct 1993 (subject to savings) (SI 1993/2134)
17–20	10 Nov 1993 (SI 1993/2762)
21, para 1	1 Nov 1993 (SI 1993/2134)
2	*Not in force*
3	10 Nov 1993 (SI 1993/2762)
4	2 Sep 1993 (SI 1993/2134)
5	1 Nov 1993 (subject to savings) (SI 1993/2134)
6	10 Nov 1993 (SI 1993/2762)
7	2 Sep 1993 (SI 1993/2134)
8	10 Nov 1993 (SI 1993/2762)
9	1 Nov 1993 (SI 1993/2134)
10	11 Oct 1993 (SI 1993/2134)
11–25	11 Oct 1993 (subject to savings) (SI 1993/2134)
26	1 Nov 1993 (SI 1993/2134)
27	2 Sep 1993 (SI 1993/2134)
28, 29	10 Nov 1993 (SI 1993/2762)
30	1 Nov 1993 (SI 1993/2134)
31, 32	10 Nov 1993 (SI 1993/2762)
22	20 Jul 1993 (repeal in Local Government and Housing Act 1989, s 80(1)) (RA)
	2 Sep 1993 (repeals of Housing Act 1988, s 41(1); Local Government and Housing Act 1989, Sch 11, para 51) (SI 1993/2134)
	27 Sep 1993 (repeals in Housing Scotland Act 1987) (SI 1993/2163)
	11 Oct 1993 (repeals in Local Government, Planning and Land Act 1980; Housing Act 1988, s 69(2)) (SI 1993/2134)
	11 Oct 1993 (repeals of or in Housing Act 1985, ss 124(3), 128(6), 132–135, 137, 138(1), 139(3), 140(5), 142, 153A(1), 153B(1), 164(6), 166(6), 169(3), 171C(2), 171H, 177, 180, 181(1), 182(1), 187, 188, Schs 6, 7–9; Housing and Planning Act 1986, Sch 5, para 5; Housing Act 1988, s 79; Local

Leasehold Reform, Housing and Urban Development Act 1993 (c 28)—*cont*

Sch 22—*cont*
Government and Housing Act 1989, s 164) (subject to savings) (SI 1993/2134)

1 Nov 1993 (repeals in Housing Act 1980; Housing (Consequential Provisions) Act 1985) (SI 1993/2134)

1 Nov 1993 (repeals in Landlord and Tenant Act 1987) (subject to savings) (SI 1993/2134)

10 Nov 1993 (repeal in Land Compensation Act 1961) (SI 1993/2762)

Not in force (otherwise)

Licensing (Amendment) (Scotland) Act 1993 (c 20)

RA: 1 Jul 1993

1 Jul 1993 (RA)

Local Government (Amendment) Act 1993 (c 27)

RA: 20 Jul 1993

Commencement provision: s 3(2)

20 Sep 1993 (s 3(2))

Local Government (Overseas Assistance) Act 1993 (c 25)

RA: 20 Jul 1993

Commencement provision: s 2(2)

20 Sep 1993 (s 2(2))

Merchant Shipping (Registration, etc) Act 1993 (c 22)

RA: 1 Jul 1993

Commencement provisions: s 10(2), (3); Merchant Shipping (Registration, etc) Act 1993 (Commencement No 1 and Transitional Provisions) Order 1993, SI 1993/3137

s 1–7	21 Mar 1994 (SI 1993/3137)
8(1)	See Sch 2 below
(2)	See Sch 3 below
(3)	See Sch 4 below
(4)	See Sch 5 below
9, 10	21 Mar 1994 (SI 1993/3137)
Sch 1–3	21 Mar 1994 (SI 1993/3137)
4, para 1–17	1 May 1994 (SI 1993/3137)
18	*Not in force*
19–35	1 May 1994 (SI 1993/3137)
36	*Not in force*
37–51	1 May 1994 (SI 1993/3137)
52	*Not in force*

Merchant Shipping (Registration, etc) Act 1993 (c 22)—*cont*

Sch 4, para 53	1 May 1994 (SI 1993/3137)
54	1 May 1994 (except so far as repeals Merchant Shipping (Mercantile Marine Fund) Act 1898, s 2(3), so far as that provision applies to the lighthouse at Sombrero in the Leeward Islands) (SI 1993/3137)
	Not in force (exception noted above)
55–79	1 May 1994 (SI 1993/3137)
5, Pt I	21 Mar 1994 (SI 1993/3137)[1]
II	1 May 1994 (except repeals of or in Merchant Shipping Act 1894, ss 634, 669; Merchant Shipping (Mercantile Marine Fund) Act 1898, s 2(3), so far as that provision applies to the lighthouse at Sombrero in the Leeward Islands); Merchant Shipping (Safety Convention) Act 1949, ss 28(1), 33(2)) (SI 1993/3137)[1]
	Not in force (exceptions noted above, and see also the note below)

[1] For savings relating to registration under, and instruments made under, certain provisions repealed by this Act, see SI 1993/3137, arts 4, 5, 7, Sch 3. Note also that by SI 1993/3137, art 3(2), Sch 2, Appendix, the Merchant Shipping (Safety Convention) Act 1949, s 28(1), remains in force for the sole purpose of enabling exemptions to be made from the requirements of rules made under the Merchant Shipping Act 1894, s 427, and rules made under s 3 of the 1949 Act, and that s 33(2) of the 1949 Act remains in force for the sole purpose of enabling regulations to be made prescribing maximum fees for measurement of a ship's tonnage.

National Lottery etc Act 1993 (c 39)

RA: 21 Oct 1993

Commencement provisions: s 65; National Lottery etc Act 1993 (Commencement No 1 and Transitional Provisions) Order 1993, SI 1993/2632

s 1–15	25 Oct 1993 (SI 1993/2632)
16	21 Dec 1993 (SI 1993/2632)
17	25 Oct 1993 (SI 1993/2632)
18	21 Dec 1993 (subject to transitional provisions) (SI 1993/2632)
19, 20	25 Oct 1993 (SI 1993/2632)
21–25	21 Dec 1993 (SI 1993/2632)
26(1)	25 Oct 1993 (SI 1993/2632)
(2)	21 Dec 1993 (SI 1993/2632)
(3)–(5)	25 Oct 1993 (SI 1993/2632)
27–39	21 Dec 1993 (SI 1993/2632)
40–44	25 Oct 1993 (SI 1993/2632)
45–47	21 Dec 1993 (SI 1993/2632)
48–59	*Not in force*
60–63	25 Oct 1993 (SI 1993/2632)
64	See Sch 10 below
65, 66	25 Oct 1993 (SI 1993/2632)
Sch 1–3	25 Oct 1993 (SI 1993/2632)
4, 5	21 Dec 1993 (SI 1993/2632)

National Lottery etc Act 1993 (c 39)—*cont*

Sch 6	25 Oct 1993 (SI 1993/2632)
7–9	*Not in force*
10	21 Dec 1993 (repeals in Revenue Act 1898; National Heritage Act 1980) (SI 1993/2632)
	Not in force (repeals in Lotteries and Amusements Act 1976)

Noise and Statutory Nuisance Act 1993 (c 40)

RA: 5 Nov 1993

Commencement provision: s 12

s 1–8	5 Jan 1994 (s 12(1))
9	*Not in force*
10–14	5 Jan 1994 (s 12(1))
Sch 1, 2	5 Jan 1994 (s 12(1))
3	*Not in force*

Non-Domestic Rating Act 1993 (c 17)

RA: 27 May 1993

Commencement provisions: s 6(2); Non-Domestic Rating Act 1993 (Commencement No 1) Order 1993, SI 1993/1418; Non-Domestic Rating Act 1993 (Commencement No 2) Order 1993, SI 1993/1512

s 1(1)	6 Jul 1993 (SI 1993/1512)
(2)	4 Jun 1993 (SI 1993/1418)
(3)–(5)	6 Jul 1993 (SI 1993/1512)
2, 3	6 Jul 1993 (SI 1993/1512)
4	4 Jun 1993 (SI 1993/1418)
5, 6	6 Jul 1993 (SI 1993/1512)

Ordination of Women (Financial Provisions) Measure 1993 (No 3)

RA: 5 Nov 1993

5 Nov 1993 (RA)

Osteopaths Act 1993 (c 21)

RA: 1 Jul 1993

Commencement provision: s 42(2)–(5)

Not in force

Pension Schemes Act 1993 (c 48)

RA: 5 Nov 1993

Commencement provisions: s 193(2), (3)

Not in force

Pension Schemes (Northern Ireland) Act 1993 (c 49)

RA: 5 Nov 1993

Commencement provisions: s 186(2), (3)

Not in force

Priests (Ordination of Women) Measure 1993 (No 2)

RA: 5 Nov 1993

Commencement provision: s 12(2)

Not in force

Prisoners and Criminal Proceedings (Scotland) Act 1993 (c 9)

RA: 29 Mar 1993

Commencement provisions: s 48(2)–(4); Prisoners and Criminal Proceedings (Scotland) Act 1993 Commencement, Transitional Provisions and Savings Order 1993, SI 1993/2050

s 1–5	1 Oct 1993 (SI 1993/2050)
6(1), (2)	1 Oct 1993 (SI 1993/2050)
(3)	18 Aug 1993 (for purpose of enabling orders to be made so as to come into force on or after 1 Oct 1993) (SI 1993/2050)
	1 Oct 1993 (otherwise) (SI 1993/2050)
7(1)–(5)	1 Oct 1993 (SI 1993/2050)
(6)	18 Aug 1993 (for purpose of enabling orders to be made so as to come into force on or after 1 Oct 1993) (SI 1993/2050)
	1 Oct 1993 (otherwise) (SI 1993/2050)
(7)	1 Oct 1993 (SI 1993/2050)
8–19	1 Oct 1993 (SI 1993/2050)
20(1), (2)	1 Oct 1993 (SI 1993/2050)
(3)	18 Aug 1993 (for purpose of enabling orders to be made so as to come into force on or after 1 Oct 1993) (SI 1993/2050)
	1 Oct 1993 (otherwise) (SI 1993/2050)
(4), (5)	18 Aug 1993 (for purpose of enabling rules to be made, and directions to be given, so as to come into force on or after 1 Oct 1993) (SI 1993/2050)
	1 Oct 1993 (otherwise) (SI 1993/2050)
(6)	1 Oct 1993 (SI 1993/2050)
21–23	1 Oct 1993 (SI 1993/2050)
24, 25	18 Aug 1993 (SI 1993/2050)
26	1 Oct 1993 (SI 1993/2050)
27(1)–(3)	18 Aug 1993 (for purpose of enabling an order to be made so as to come into force on or after 1 Oct 1993) (SI 1993/2050)
	1 Oct 1993 (otherwise) (SI 1993/2050)
(4)–(7)	1 Oct 1993 (SI 1993/2050)
28, 29	1 Oct 1993 (subject to a saving) (SI 1993/2050)
30	1 Jan 1994 (subject to a saving) (SI 1993/2050)

Prisoners and Criminal Proceedings (Scotland) Act 1993 (c 9)—*cont*

s 31	18 Sep 1993 (subject to a saving) (SI 1993/2050)
32	1 Oct 1993 (subject to a saving) (SI 1993/2050)
33–35	1 Jan 1994 (subject to a saving) (SI 1993/2050)
36	18 Sep 1993 (subject to a saving) (SI 1993/2050)
37	1 Oct 1993 (subject to a saving) (SI 1993/2050)
38–41	18 Sep 1993 (subject to savings) (SI 1993/2050)
42	1 Oct 1993 (subject to savings) (SI 1993/2050)
43	18 Sep 1993 (subject to a saving) (SI 1993/2050)
44	1 Oct 1993 (SI 1993/2050)
45, 46	18 Aug 1993 (SI 1993/2050)
47(1)	See Sch 5 below
(2)	See Sch 6 below
(3)	See Sch 7 below
48	29 Mar 1993 (s 48(4))
Sch 1–3	1 Oct 1993 (subject to a saving) (SI 1993/2050)
4	1 Oct 1993 (subject to a saving) (SI 1993/2050); prospectively repealed by Criminal Justice Act 1993, s 77 (qv)
5, para 1(1), (2)	1 Oct 1993 (subject to a saving) (SI 1993/2050)
(3)–(6)	18 Sep 1993 (subject to savings) (SI 1993/2050)
(7)–(26)	1 Oct 1993 (subject to savings) (SI 1993/2050)
(27)	18 Aug 1993 (for purpose of enabling an order to be made under s 275(3) of the 1975 Act so as to come into force on or after 1 Oct 1993) (subject to a saving) (SI 1993/2050)
	1 Oct 1993 (otherwise) (subject to a saving) (SI 1993/2050)
(28)	18 Sep 1993 (SI 1993/2050)
(29)	1 Oct 1993 (subject to a saving) (SI 1993/2050)
(30), (31)	18 Sep 1993 (subject to a saving) (SI 1993/2050)
(32)–(38)	1 Oct 1993 (subject to savings) (SI 1993/2050)
2–4	1 Oct 1993 (SI 1993/2050)
5	29 Mar 1993 (s 48(4))
6(1)–(4)	18 Aug 1993 (SI 1993/2050)
(5)	1 Oct 1993 (SI 1993/2050)
(6)	18 Aug 1993 (SI 1993/2050)
(7)	1 Oct 1993 (SI 1993/2050)
(8)	18 Aug 1993 (SI 1993/2050)
(9)	1 Oct 1993 (SI 1993/2050)
6	1 Oct 1993 (SI 1993/2050)
7	18 Sep 1993 (repeals of or in Criminal Procedure (Scotland) Act 1975, ss 108, 289D, 328; Criminal Justice (Scotland) Act 1980, Sch 3; Criminal Justice (Scotland) Act 1987, s 62) (subject to savings) (SI 1993/2050)
	1 Oct 1993 (otherwise) (subject to savings) (SI 1993/2050)

Probation Service Act 1993 (c 47)

RA: 5 Nov 1993

Commencement provision: s 33(2)

5 Feb 1994 (s 33(2))

Protection of Animals (Scotland) Act 1993 (c 15)

RA: 27 May 1993

Commencement provision: s 2(2)

27 Jul 1993 (s 2(2))

Radioactive Substances Act 1993 (c 12)

RA: 27 May 1993

Commencement provision: s 51(2)

27 Aug 1993 (s 51(2))

Railways Act 1993 (c 43)

RA: 5 Nov 1993

Commencement provisions: s 154(2); Railways Act 1993 (Commencement No 1) Order 1993, SI 1993/3237

s 1	5 Nov 1993 (s 154(2))
2, 3	*Not in force*
4(1)	24 Dec 1993 (for purposes of functions of Secretary of State under s 33) (SI 1993/3237)
	Not in force (otherwise)
(2)	*Not in force*
(3)	24 Dec 1993 (for purposes of functions of Secretary of State under s 33) (SI 1993/3237)
	Not in force (otherwise)
(4)–(6)	*Not in force*
(7)	24 Dec 1993 (for purposes of functions of Secretary of State under s 33) (SI 1993/3237)
	Not in force (otherwise)
(8)	*Not in force*
(9)	24 Dec 1993 (for purposes of definitions "environment" and "through ticket") (SI 1993/3237)
	Not in force (otherwise)
5	*Not in force*
6(1)	*Not in force*
(2)	6 Jan 1994 (SI 1993/3237)
(3), (4)	*Not in force*
7–22	*Not in force*
23(1), (2)	*Not in force*
(3), (4)	6 Jan 1994 (SI 1993/3237)
24	*Not in force*
25(1), (2)	6 Jan 1994 (for purpose of providing definition "public sector operator" (SI 1993/3237)
	Not in force (otherwise)
(3)–(9)	*Not in force*
26–28	*Not in force*
29(1)–(7)	*Not in force*
(8)	6 Jan 1994 (SI 1993/3237)
30, 31	*Not in force*

Railways Act 1993 (c 43)—*cont*

s 32, 33	24 Dec 1993 (SI 1993/3237)
34–80	*Not in force*
81, 82	24 Dec 1993 (SI 1993/3237)
83(1)	24 Dec 1993 (for purposes of definitions "goods", "light maintenance services", "locomotive", "network", "network services", "premises", "passenger service operator", "railway", "railway services", "railway vehicle", "rolling stock", "station", "station services", "track", "train" and "vehicle" (SI 1993/3237)
	6 Jan 1994 (for purposes of definitions "additional railway asset", "the Director", "franchise agreement", "franchise operator", "franchise term", "franchised services", "franchisee", "information", "licence" and "licence holder", "light maintenance depot", "operator", "passenger licence", "private sector operator", "public sector operator", "railway asset", "railway passenger service", "records" and "station licence") (SI 1993/3237)
	Not in force (otherwise)
(2)	24 Dec 1993 (SI 1993/3237)
84, 85	6 Jan 1994 (SI 1993/3237)
86	*Not in force*
87(1)	6 Jan 1994 (for purpose of enabling Secretary of State to transfer functions to himself) (SI 1993/3237)
	Not in force (otherwise)
(2)	6 Jan 1994 (SI 1993/3237)
(3), (4)	*Not in force*
(5)	6 Jan 1994 (SI 1993/3237)
88–92	6 Jan 1994 (SI 1993/3237)
93(1), (2)	6 Jan 1994 (SI 1993/3237)
(3)(a)	6 Jan 1994 (SI 1993/3237)
(b)	*Not in force*
(4)–(13)	6 Jan 1994 (SI 1993/3237)
94–116	6 Jan 1994 (SI 1993/3237)
117–125	*Not in force*
126–128	6 Jan 1994 (SI 1993/3237)
129	*Not in force*
130, 131	6 Jan 1994 (SI 1993/3237)
132, 133	*Not in force*
134(1)	See Sch 11 below
(2), (3)	6 Jan 1994 (SI 1993/3237)
135–140	*Not in force*
141(1)	6 Jan 1994 (except para (a)) (SI 1993/3237)
	Not in force (para (a))
(2)–(5)	6 Jan 1994 (SI 1993/3237)
142–144	24 Dec 1993 (SI 1993/3237)
145(1)–(6)	24 Dec 1993 (except for purposes of sub-s (5)(a), (b)(i)) (SI 1993/3237)
	Not in force (exceptions noted above)
(7)	*Not in force*
146–149	24 Dec 1993 (SI 1993/3237)
150(1)–(3)	24 Dec 1993 (SI 1993/3237)
(4)	*Not in force*

Railways Act 1993 (c 43)—*cont*

s 151(1)	24 Dec 1993 (for purposes of definitions "the Board", "body corporate", "company", "contravention", "the Franchising Director", "functions", "local authority", "the Monopolies Commission", "notice", "the Regulator", "subsidiary" and "wholly owned subsidiary") (SI 1993/3237)
	6 Jan 1994 (otherwise) (SI 1993/3237)
(2)–(4)	6 Jan 1994 (SI 1993/3237)
(5)	24 Dec 1993 (SI 1993/3237)
(6)–(9)	6 Jan 1994 (SI 1993/3237)
152(1)	See Sch 12 below
(2)	See Sch 13 below
(3)	See Sch 14 below
153	6 Jan 1994 (SI 1993/3237)
154	24 Dec 1993 (SI 1993/3237)
Sch 1	5 Nov 1993 (s 154(2))
2–7	*Not in force*
8, 9	6 Jan 1994 (SI 1993/3237)
10	*Not in force*
11, para 1–8	6 Jan 1994 (SI 1993/3237)
9(1), (2)	6 Jan 1994 (SI 1993/3237)
(3)	6 Jan 1994 (for purpose of inserting Transport Act 1980, s 52D(6)–(8)) (SI 1993/3237)
	Not in force (otherwise)
(4)	6 Jan 1994 (SI 1993/3237)
10	6 Jan 1994 (SI 1993/3237)
11	*Not in force*
12–14	6 Jan 1994 (SI 1993/3237)
12, para 1–3	*Not in force*
4, 5	6 Jan 1994 (SI 1993/3237)
6(1)–(5)	6 Jan 1994 (SI 1993/3237)
(6)	*Not in force*
(7)	6 Jan 1994 (SI 1993/3237)
7, 8	6 Jan 1994 (SI 1993/3237)
9	*Not in force*
10–13	6 Jan 1994 (SI 1993/3237)
14(1)–(3)	6 Jan 1994 (SI 1993/3237)
(4)–(6)	*Not in force*
15–22	*Not in force*
23, 24	6 Jan 1994 (SI 1993/3237)
25	*Not in force*
26	6 Jan 1994 (SI 1993/3237)
27	*Not in force*
28	6 Jan 1994 (SI 1993/3237)
29	*Not in force*
30, 31	6 Jan 1994 (SI 1993/3237)
32	*Not in force*
13	*Not in force*
14	6 Jan 1994 (repeals of or in British Transport Commission Act 1950, s 43; Transport Act 1962, ss 4, 5, 13, 53; Transport Act 1968, ss 42, 45, 50, 137) (SI 1993/3237)
	Not in force (otherwise)

Reinsurance (Acts of Terrorism) Act 1993 (c 18)

RA: 27 May 1993

27 May 1993 (RA)

Representation of the People Act 1993 (c 29)

RA: 20 Jul 1993

20 Jul 1993 (RA)

Road Traffic (Driving Instruction by Disabled Persons) Act 1993 (c 31)

RA: 20 Jul 1993

Commencement provision: s 7(2)

Not in force

Scottish Land Court Act 1993 (c 45)

RA: 5 Nov 1993

Commencement provision: s 2(3)

5 Jan 1994 (s 2(3))

Sexual Offences Act 1993 (c 30)

RA: 20 Jul 1993

Commencement provision: s 2(2)

20 Sep 1993 (s 2(2))

Social Security Act 1993 (c 3)

RA: 29 Jan 1993

29 Jan 1993 (RA; but note s 5(2), (3))

Statute Law (Repeals) Act 1993 (c 50)

RA: 5 Nov 1993

Commencement provision: s 4(2), (3)

s 1(1)	See Sch 1 below
(2)	See Sch 2 below
2–4	5 Nov 1993 (RA)

Statute Law (Repeals) Act 1993 (c 50)—*cont*
Sch 1   5 Nov 1993[1] (except so far as repeals Shipbuilding
                                     (Redundancy Payments) Act 1978, Shipbuilding
                                     Act 1985, s 1) (RA)
                                     Not in force (exceptions noted above)
2   5 Nov 1993 (RA)

[1] By s 4(2), repeals of National Loans Act 1939, Sch 2, para 5, Bank of England
Act 1946, Sch 1, para 10, Coal Industry Nationalisation Act 1946, s 33(8) have
effect, so far as relating to stock registered in the National Savings Stock
Register, on the coming into force of the first regulations made by virtue of the
National Debt Act 1972, s 3(1)(bb)

Trade Union Reform and Employment Rights Act 1993 (c 19)

RA: 1 Jul 1993

Commencement provisions: ss 7(4), 52; Trade Union Reform and Employment Rights
    Act 1993 (Commencement No 1 and Transitional Provisions) Order 1993, SI
    1993/1908; Trade Union Reform and Employment Rights Act 1993
    (Commencement No 2 and Transitional Provisions) Order 1993, SI 1993/2503

s 1, 2   30 Aug 1993 (subject to transitional provisions) (SI
                                     1993/1908)
3   See Sch 1 below
4–6   30 Aug 1993 (subject to transitional provisions) (SI
                                     1993/1908)
7(1)   1 Apr 1996 (s 7(4))
  (2)–(4)   1 Apr 1996 (SI 1993/1908)
8, 9   1 Jan 1994 (SI 1993/1908)
10–12   30 Aug 1993 (SI 1993/1908)
13   30 Aug 1993 (subject to transitional provisions) (SI
                                     1993/1908)
14   30 Nov 1993 (SI 1993/1908)
15, 16   30 Aug 1993 (SI 1993/1908)
17   30 Aug 1993 (subject to transitional provisions) (SI
                                     1993/1908)
18(1)   30 Aug 1993 (SI 1993/1908)
  (2)   30 Aug 1993 (subject to transitional provisions) (SI
                                     1993/1908)
19–21   30 Aug 1993 (subject to transitional provisions) (SI
                                     1993/1908)
22   30 Aug 1993 (SI 1993/1908)
23   *Not in force*
24(1)   *Not in force*
  (2), (3)   30 Aug 1993 (except for purpose of giving effect to
                                     s 60(a)–(f) of the 1978 Act) (subject to transitional
                                     provisions) (SI 1993/1908)
                                     Not in force (exception noted above)
  (4)   *Not in force*
25   *Not in force*
26, 27   30 Nov 1993 (SI 1993/2503)
28   See Sch 5 below
29, 30   30 Aug 1993 (subject to transitional provisions) (SI
                                     1993/1908)
31   *Not in force*
32   30 Nov 1993 (SI 1993/2503)

Trade Union Reform and Employment Rights Act 1993 (c 19)—*cont*

s 33	30 Aug 1993 (SI 1993/1908)
34	30 Aug 1993 (subject to transitional provisions) (SI 1993/1908)
35	30 Aug 1993 (SI 1993/1908)
36(1), (2)	30 Nov 1993 (subject to transitional provisions) (SI 1993/2503)
(3)	30 Aug 1993 (for purpose of inserting s 128(5) of the 1978 Act) (SI 1993/1908)
	30 Nov 1993 (otherwise) (subject to transitional provisions) (SI 1993/2503)
37	30 Nov 1993 (SI 1993/2503)
38	30 Aug 1993 (SI 1993/1908)
39(1)	30 Aug 1993 (SI 1993/1908)
(2)	See Sch 6 below
40, 41	30 Aug 1993 (SI 1993/1908)
42	30 Nov 1993 (SI 1993/2503)
43, 44	30 Aug 1993 (SI 1993/1908)
45	30 Nov 1993 (so far as substitutes s 10(7) of the 1973 Act) (SI 1993/2503)
	1 Apr 1994 (otherwise) (ES) (SI 1993/2503)
	1 Apr 1995 (otherwise) (SI 1993/2503)
46	1 Apr 1994 (ES) (SI 1993/2503)
	1 Apr 1995 (otherwise) (SI 1993/2503)
47, 48	30 Aug 1993 (SI 1993/1908)
49(1)	See Sch 7 below
(2)	See Sch 8 below
50	See Sch 9 below
51	See Sch 10 below
52–55	1 Jul 1993 (RA)
Sch 1	30 Aug 1993 (subject to transitional provisions) (SI 1993/1908)
2, 3	*Not in force*
4	30 Nov 1993 (SI 1993/2503)
5	30 Aug 1993 (subject to transitional provisions) (SI 1993/1908)
6	30 Aug 1993 (SI 1993/1908)
7, para 1, 2	30 Aug 1993 (SI 1993/1908)
3(a)	30 Nov 1993 (SI 1993/2503)
(b)	30 Nov 1993 (except so far as relates to s 60 of the 1978 Act) (SI 1993/2503)
	Not in force (exception noted above)
4	30 Nov 1993 (SI 1993/2503)
5	30 Nov 1993 (except so far as relates to s 60 of the 1978 Act) (SI 1993/2503)
	Not in force (exception noted above)
6(a)	30 Nov 1993 (SI 1993/2503)
(b)	30 Nov 1993 (except so far as relates to s 60 of the 1978 Act) (SI 1993/2503)
	Not in force (exception noted above)
7	15 Oct 1993 (SI 1993/2503)
8–12	30 Nov 1993 (SI 1993/2503)
13–27	30 Aug 1993 (SI 1993/1908)
8, para 1	1 Apr 1994 (ES) (SI 1993/2503)
	1 Apr 1995 (otherwise) (SI 1993/2503)
2	30 Aug 1993 (SI 1993/1908)

Trade Union Reform and Employment Rights Act 1993 (c 19)—*cont*

Sch 8, para 3–5	1 Apr 1994 (ES) (SI 1993/2503)
	1 Apr 1995 (otherwise) (SI 1993/2503)
6, 7	30 Aug 1993 (SI 1993/1908)
8, 9	1 Apr 1994 (ES) (SI 1993/2503)
	1 Apr 1995 (otherwise) (SI 1993/2503)
10	30 Nov 1993 (SI 1993/2503)
11	30 Aug 1993 (SI 1993/1908)
12, 13	*Not in force*
14	30 Aug 1993 (SI 1993/1908)
15	*Not in force*
16	30 Aug 1993 (so far as relates to s 60A(1) of the 1978 Act) (SI 1993/1908)
	Not in force (otherwise)
17–19	*Not in force*
20(a)	30 Aug 1993 (SI 1993/1908)
(b)	*Not in force*
21	30 Aug 1993 (SI 1993/1908)
22, 23	30 Nov 1993 (SI 1993/2503)
24	30 Aug 1993 (SI 1993/1908)
25(a)	*Not in force*
(b)	30 Nov 1993 (SI 1993/2503)
26(a)(i)	30 Aug 1993 (SI 1993/1908)
(ii), (iii)	*Not in force*
(b)–(e)	*Not in force*
27	*Not in force*
28(a)	*Not in force*
(b), (c)	15 Oct 1993 (SI 1993/2503)
29	30 Aug 1993 (SI 1993/1908)
30	15 Oct 1993 (SI 1993/2503)
31	*Not in force*
32(a)	*Not in force*
(b)	30 Aug 1993 (SI 1993/1908)
33, 34	1 Apr 1994 (ES) (SI 1993/2503)
	1 Apr 1995 (otherwise) (SI 1993/2503)
35	*Not in force*
36–41	30 Aug 1993 (SI 1993/1908)
42	1 Jan 1994 (SI 1993/1908)
43(a)	1 Jan 1994 (SI 1993/1908)
(b)	30 Aug 1993 (SI 1993/1908)
44, 45	1 Jan 1994 (SI 1993/1908)
46, 47	30 Aug 1993 (SI 1993/1908)
48	30 Nov 1993 (SI 1993/1908)
49	30 Aug 1993 (SI 1993/1908)
50, 51	30 Nov 1993 (SI 1993/1908)
52–61	30 Aug 1993 (SI 1993/1908)
62(a)	1 Jan 1994 (SI 1993/1908)
(b)	30 Aug 1993 (SI 1993/1908)
63	30 Aug 1993 (SI 1993/1908)
64(a)	1 Jan 1994 (SI 1993/1908)
(b), (c)	30 Aug 1993 (SI 1993/1908)
65	30 Aug 1993 (SI 1993/1908)
66(a)	1 Jan 1994 (SI 1993/1908)
(b)	30 Aug 1993 (SI 1993/1908)
67–75	30 Aug 1993 (SI 1993/1908)
76, 77	30 Aug 1993 (so far as relate to s 57A of the 1978 Act) (SI 1993/1908)
	Not in force (otherwise)

Trade Union Reform and Employment Rights Act 1993 (c 19)—*cont*
Sch 8, para 78–84   30 Aug 1993 (SI 1993/1908)
    85   30 Nov 1993 (SI 1993/2503)
    86–89   30 Aug 1993 (SI 1993/1908)
 9, para 1   30 Aug 1993 (SI 1993/1908)
    2   30 Aug 1993 (subject to transitional provisions) (SI 1993/1908)
    3   30 Nov 1993 (SI 1993/2503)
    4, 5   30 Aug 1993 (SI 1993/1908)
  10   30 Aug 1993 (repeals of or in Factories Act 1961; Contracts of Employment and Redundancy Payments Act (Northern Ireland) 1965; Transport Act 1968; House of Commons Disqualification Act 1975; Northern Ireland Assembly Disqualification Act 1975; Industrial Relations (Northern Ireland) Order 1976; Employment Protection (Consolidation) Act 1978, ss 18, 53, 55, 64A, 93, 94, 95, 100, 123, 149, Schs 12, 13; Employment Act 1980, s 8, Sch 1; Transfer of Undertakings (Protection of Employment) Regulations 1981; Wages Act 1986; Income and Corporation Taxes Act 1988; Enterprise and New Towns (Scotland) Act 1990; Offshore Safety (Protection Against Victimisation) Act 1992; Trade Union and Labour Relations (Consolidation) Act 1992, ss 24, 34, 43, 52, 65, 74, 78, 118, 135, 154, 188, 190, 209, 246, 249, 256, 273, 283, 299, Sch 2, paras 15, 34) (SI 1993/1908)
15 Oct 1993 (repeal in Employment Protection (Consolidation) Act 1978, Sch 9, para 1A) (SI 1993/2503)
30 Nov 1993 (repeals in Trade Union and Labour Relations (Consolidation) Act 1992, ss 67, 288, 290, 291) (SI 1993/1908)
30 Nov 1993 (repeals of or in Employment Protection (Consolidation) Act 1978, ss 11(3), (7), 128(4), 133(1), 138(1), (2) (so far as words repealed relate to sub-ss (4), (5)), 139(1), 146(4), Sch 9, para 8; Employment Act 1982; Dock Work Act 1989; Employment Act 1989; Trade Union and Labour Relations (Consolidation) Act 1992, s 277(2), Sch 2, para 24(3)) (SI 1993/2503)
1 Jan 1994 (repeal in Trade Union and Labour Relations (Consolidation) Act 1992, s 32) (SI 1993/1908)
1 Apr 1994 (ES) (repeals in Finance Act 1969; Chronically Sick and Disabled Persons Act 1970; Employment and Training Act 1973; Education (Scotland) Act 1980; Agricultural Training Board Act 1982; Industrial Training Act 1982) (SI 1993/2503)
1 Apr 1995 (in so far as not already in force) (repeals in Finance Act 1969; Chronically Sick and Disabled Persons Act 1970; Employment and Training Act 1973; Education (Scotland) Act 1980; Agricultural Training Board Act 1982; Industrial Training Act 1982) (SI 1993/2503)

Trade Union Reform and Employment Rights Act 1993 (c 19)—*cont*

Sch 10—*cont*   1 Apr 1996 (repeals of Trade Union and Labour
                                   Relations (Consolidation) Act 1992, ss 115, 116)
                                   (SI 1993/1908)
                                   Not in force (otherwise)

Video Recordings Act 1993 (c 24)

RA: 20 Jul 1993

Commencement provision: s 6(2)

20 Sep 1993 (s 6(2))

Welsh Language Act 1993 (c 38)

RA: 21 Oct 1993

Commencement provision: s 36

s 1–29	21 Dec 1993 (s 36(1))
30, 31	*Not in force*
32–34	21 Dec 1993 (s 36(1))
35(1)	See Sch 2 below
(2)	*Not in force*
(3)–(5)	21 Dec 1993 (s 36(1))
36, 37	21 Dec 1993 (s 36(1))
Sch 1	21 Dec 1993 (s 36(1))
2	21 Dec 1993 (except repeals in Companies Act 1985) (s 36(1), (2))
	Not in force (exception noted above)